ROUTLEDGE HANDBOOK OF THE CHINESE ECONOMY

T0360919

China's rapid rise to become the world's second largest economy has resulted in an unprecedented impact on the global system and an urgent need to understand more about the newest economic superpower.

The *Routledge Handbook of the Chinese Economy* is an advanced-level reference guide which surveys the current economic situation in China and its integration into the global economy. An internationally renowned line-up of scholars contribute chapters on the key components of the contemporary economy and its historical foundations.

Topics covered include:

- the history of the Chinese economy from ancient times onwards;
- economic growth and development;
- population, the labor market, income distribution, and poverty;
- legal, political, and financial institutions; and
- foreign trade and investments.

Offering a cutting-edge overview of the Chinese economy, the *Handbook* is an invaluable resource for academics, researchers, economists, graduate, and undergraduate students studying this ever-evolving field.

Gregory C. Chow is Professor of Economics and Class of 1913 Professor of Political Economy, emeritus, at Princeton University, USA and has been on the Princeton faculty since 1970.

Dwight H. Perkins is the Harold Hitchings Burbank Professor of Political Economy, emeritus, at Harvard University, USA and has been on the Harvard faculty since 1963.

In this volume, Gregory Chow and Dwight Perkins assemble a global array of authors to provide a comprehensive account of China's economic development both before and after the reform initiatives of the late 1970s. While many of the contributors focus on institutions, policies and outcomes at the national level, detailed accounts by reform participants Wu Jinglian and Yi Gang along with an iconoclastic essay by Lynn White provide readers with unusual insight into the operational mechanisms of China's political economy.

Thomas G. Rawski, *Professor of Economics and History, University of Pittsburgh, USA*

The *Routledge Handbook of the Chinese Economy* excels in the breadth of its contributors and topics. Professors Chow and Perkins have assembled an all-star group of authors ranging from international academic leaders to those with relevant experience within the Chinese government. Topics range from historical perspectives to current economic issues on the road to reform. Anyone interested in the Chinese economy will find this *Handbook* must reading.

Burton G. Malkiel, *Professor of Economics, Princeton University, USA*

Gregory Chow and Dwight Perkins, two giants in economic science, were major figures in helping to start the process of training Chinese students in modern economics in 1986 through their chairmen-ship of the US–China Committee on Economics Education and Research at the U.S. National Academy of Sciences. We must thank them again now for sharing with us some of the significant fruits of that transformational training program. The many excellent articles in this *Handbook* on a broad range of topics make it indispensable to the library of a China scholar.

Wing Thye Woo, *Professor of Economics, University of California, Davis, USA*

ROUTLEDGE HANDBOOK OF THE CHINESE ECONOMY

Edited by Gregory C. Chow and Dwight H. Perkins

LONDON AND NEW YORK

First published 2015
by Routledge

2 Park Square, Milton Park, Abingdon, Oxfordshire OX14 4RN
52 Vanderbilt Avenue, New York, NY 10017

Routledge is an imprint of the Taylor & Francis Group, an informa business

First issued in paperback 2019

British Library Cataloguing in Publication Data
A catalogue record for this book is available from the British Library

Library of Congress Cataloging-in-Publication Data
Routledge handbook of the Chinese economy / edited by Gregory C. Chow and Dwight H. Perkins.
pages cm
Includes bibliographical references and index.
1. China–Economic conditions. 2. China–Economic policy. 3. Economic development. I. Chow, Gregory C. II. Perkins, Dwight H. (Dwight Heald)
HC427.R667 2014
330.951–dc23
2014000039

ISBN: 978-0-415-64344-3 (hbk)
ISBN: 978-0-367-86766-9 (pbk)

Typeset in Bembo
by Cenveo Publisher Services

CONTENTS

FIGURES

TABLES

CONTRIBUTORS

Kenneth S. Chan, Professor emeritus, McMaster University. He was the Head and Professor at the Department of Economics and Finance, City University of Hong Kong. His research is in the area of international economics, with numerous publications in leading journals. He is the Editor of the *Pacific Economic Review*, and sits on many journal editorial boards.

Gregory C. Chow is the 1913 Professor of Political Economy, emeritus, at Princeton. He was Director of the Economic Research Program at Princeton, now named the Gregory C. Chow Econometric Research Program. He advised top leaders of Taiwan and China and introduced economics education in China. Author of 16 books and over 200 articles, he is a columnist for three major newspapers in China, one in Hong Kong and one in Taiwan. A recipient of honorary degrees from Zhongshan University, Lingnan University, and the Hong Kong University of Science and Technology, he is a member of the American Philosophical Society and of Academia Sinica, a Distinguished Fellow of the American Economic Association, and a Fellow of the Econometric Society and the American Statistical Association.

Jacques deLisle is Stephen A. Cozen Professor of Law, Professor of Political Science, Director of the Center for East Asian Studies, and Deputy Director of the Center for the Study of Contemporary China at the University of Pennsylvania. His scholarship focuses on domestic legal reform in China, the roles of law in addressing crises in China, and China's engagement with the international legal order.

Fan Shitao is a Lecturer at Beijing Normal University. He primarily researches the history of the Chinese economy. His recent papers include "Inclusive Institutions, Extractive Institutions and Sustainability of Prosperity" and "How Had the Cultural Revolution been Started?".

Richard B. Freeman holds the Ascherman Chair in Economics at Harvard University and is Faculty Co-Director of the Labor and Worklife Program at the Harvard Law School. He directs the Science and Engineering Workforce Project at the National Bureau of Economic Research, and is a Fellow of the American Academy of Arts and Science.

K. C. Fung is Professor of Economics at the University of California, Santa Cruz. His research interests include international economics and Asian economies. He was a senior economist in the Clinton Administration White House Council of Economic Advisers. His most recent book is *Sino-Latin American Economic Relations* (2012).

Kai Guo is Director at the People's Bank of China. He has a Ph.D. in economics from Harvard University and an MA in economics from Peking University. His area of research includes international finance, macroeconomics, development economics (with an emphasis on the Chinese economy), and economic growth.

Jikun Huang is the Founder and Director of the Center for Chinese Agricultural Policy of the Chinese Academy of Sciences, Professor of the Institute of Geographic Sciences and Natural Resources Research. He is also Vice President of the Chinese Association of Agricultural Economics and the Chinese Association of Agro-Technology Economics. He has served as a board member for the International Food & Agricultural Trade Policy Council, the International Service for the Acquisition of Agri-biotech Applications, and African Agricultural Technology Foundation. Dr. Huang has a BS from Nanjing Agricultural University and a Ph.D. in economics from the University of the Philippines at Los Banos. His research covers a wide range of issues on China's agricultural and rural development, including work on agricultural R&D policy, water resource economics, price and marketing, food consumption, poverty, trade policy, and climate change.

Yasheng Huang is a Professor of International Management and an Associate Dean at MIT Sloan School of Management. His research focuses on political economy and international business as related to China. Professor Huang has published in all the relative leading academic journals. Professor Huang has also published *Inflation and Investment Controls in China* (1996), *FDI in China* (1998), *Selling China* (2003, Chinese edition in 2005), *Financial Reform in China* (2005, co-edited with Tony Saich and Edward Steinfeld), and *Capitalism with Chinese Characteristics* (2008). He has also published in Chinese, including, *The Transformation of Chinese Private Sector* (2012), *What Exactly Is the China Model?* (winner of Blue Lion Prize for best book in 2011), and *The Path of Big Enterprises* (2010).

Jean-Pierre Laffargue has been Professor of Economics at the University of Paris since 1983 and is also a Research Fellow at CEPREMAP. His areas of research include macroeconomics, economic development, and computational economics. He holds a Ph.D. in statistics from the Faculté des sciences de Paris as well as a Ph.D. in economics from the University of Paris (Pantheon-Sorbonne). He has published articles in a wide variety of publications.

David Daokui Li is the Mansfield Freeman Chair Professor of Economics and the founding Dean of the Schwarzman Scholars Program at Tsinghua University, which is a fellowship program with a master's degree curriculum. The program's objective is to bring future global leaders to Tsinghua as a way to bridge the gap between China and the rest of the world. As a leading Chinese economist, Professor Li is active in policy advising and discussions. He served on China's Monetary Policy Committee and was an external adviser to the IMF. He is a member of the CPPCC and a member of the Global Agenda Council of the World Economic Forum based in Switzerland. Professor Li holds a BS and Ph.D. in economics from Tsinghua University and Harvard University, respectively.

Justin Yifu Lin is Professor and Honorary Dean, National School of Development at Peking University. He was the Chief Economist of the World Bank (2008–2012) and Founding Director of the China Centre for Economic Research at Peking University. His research areas are economic development and transition. He is a Corresponding Fellow of the British Academy and a Fellow of the Academy of Sciences for Developing World.

Man-houng Lin, a Research Fellow at the Institute of Modern History, Academia Sinica, is working on a book titled "'Pacificbound: Taiwanese Merchants" Overseas Economic Activities, 1895–1945'. Her book, *China Upside Down: Currency, Society and Ideologies, 1808–1856* (2006) links China's change from the center of the East Asian order to its modern tragedy with the Latin American Independence Movement.

Dwight H. Perkins is the Harold Hitchings Burbank Professor of Political Economy, emeritus, at Harvard University and has been on the Harvard faculty since 1963. He is the author, co-author, or editor of 21 books and over 100 articles, many on China and other East Asian developing economies.

Carl Riskin is Distinguished Professor of Economics at Queens College, CUNY and Senior Research Scholar at the Weatherhead East Asian Institute of Columbia University. The author of *China's Political Economy and Inequality* and *Poverty in China in the Age of Globalization* (with A. R. Khan), he works on social and human development issues.

Scott Rozelle holds the Helen Farnsworth Endowed Professorship at Stanford University and is Senior Fellow in the Food Security and Environment Program and the Shorenstein Asia-Pacific Research Center, Freeman Spogli Institute for International Studies. He is the Director of the Rural Education Action Project. Dr. Rozelle's research focuses almost exclusively on China and is concerned with three general themes: (a) agricultural policy, including the supply, demand, and trade in agricultural projects; (b) issues involving rural resources, especially the management of water, the forests, and cultivated land; (c) the economics of poverty – with an emphasis on the economics of education and health.

Ligang Song is Associate Professor at Crawford School of Public Policy, Australian National University. His research focuses on international economics, development economics, and the Chinese economy. His publications include a monograph *Changing Global Comparative Advantage* (1996), and two co-authored books: *Private Enterprise in China* (2001); *China's Ownership Transformation: Process, Outcomes, Prospects* (2005).

Sarah Y. Tong is Senior Research Fellow at the East Asian Institute. She obtained her Ph.D. in economics from the University of California at San Diego and held an academic position in the University of Hong Kong before joining NUS. Her research interests include international trade, foreign direct investment, economic reforms, and industrial restructuring. Her publications have appeared in international journals such as *China: An International Journal, China and the World Economy, China Economic Review, Global Economic Review, Journal of International Economics,* and *Review of Development Economics*.

Lynn T. White is Professor emeritus and Senior Research Scholar in the Woodrow Wilson School, Politics Department, and East Asian Studies Program at Princeton. His books include *Political Booms, Unstately Power, Policies of Chaos,* and *Careers in Shanghai.* He has published in the

Journal of Asian Studies, American Political Science Review, Asian Survey, China Information, and elsewhere. He is currently writing about local politics in China and in the Philippines.

Peng Xizhe received his Ph.D. in population studies from London School of Economics and Political Sciences. He is a Professor of Population and Development Studies at Fudan University in China. Dr. Peng's research activities cover a wide range of population-related issues. He is the author (or editor) of more than 18 books and 150 journal articles.

Gang Yi is the Administrator of the State Administration of Foreign Exchange (SAFE) and a Deputy Governor of the People's Bank of China. He is also a Professor at the China Center for Economic Research (Peking University), which he co-founded in 1994. His research interests include money, banking, and the Chinese economy and his most recent book is *On the Financial Reform of China* (2009).

Yu Yongding is an academician and Senior Fellow in the Chinese Academy of Social Sciences (CASS). He was Director-General of the Institute of World Economics and Politics at CASS (1998–2009) and President of the China Society of World Economics (2003–2011). He holds a Ph.D. in economics from the University of Oxford.

Eden S. H. Yu is Dean of the Faculty of Business and Chair Professor of Economics, Chu Hai College of Higher Education in Hong Kong. He was Distinguished Professor of Business Administration, Louisiana State University, (Chair) Professor of Managerial Economics, Chinese University of Hong Kong, and Chair Professor of Economics, City University of Hong Kong. He has been a Visiting Professor at Renmin University, Shanghai Jiaotong University, Fudan University, Zhejiang University, and National Taiwan University. He has published over 100 journal articles. A Founding Editor of the *Pacific Economic Review* (1995–2004) he is Editor of *Asian Issues* and Associate Editor of the *World Economy*. He received his Ph.D. in economics from Washington University at St Louis, USA.

Wu Jinglian is Senior Research Fellow at the Development Research Centre of the State Council of the PRC, and Bao Steel Chair Professor of Economics at CEIBS. His main research interests are comparative institutional analysis, and theory and policy of the economic reform of China. His books include *Voice of Reform in China* (2013), *The Resumption of the Reform Agenda* (2013), and *Understanding and Interpreting Chinese Economic Reform* (2005).

ZhongXiang Zhang is a university Distinguished Professor at the School of Economics, Fudan University, China. He is Co-Editor of both *Environmental Economics and Policy Studies* and *International Journal of Ecological Economics & Statistics*, and serves on the editorial boards of ten other international journals. He has authored over 200 publications, and authored/edited 20 books and special issues of international journals. He is a Fellow of the Asia and the Pacific Policy Society.

PREFACE

There are many books and essays about the Chinese economy but there are very few dealing with this subject that are both comprehensive and up to date. This volume is designed to fill both of these gaps. The focus of the book is on the Chinese economy, not politics or culture, but there are a great many topics that need to be covered if a book is to provide a comprehensive view of that economy. The book must cover subjects ranging from the many different sectors of the economy such as agriculture, labor, foreign trade, and finance. It must also cover the many policy changes particularly those occurring after the reform period began in 1978 such as state enterprise reform, macroeconomic policies, and the general nature of reform. To really understand the policy changes after 1978, however, one must have some understanding of the way the economy was organized prior to the beginning of the reform period. And for some issues, it is desirable to go further back to the nature of the institutions governing the Chinese economy during the centuries before the contemporary era that began in 1949. At the other end of the spectrum, it is helpful for understanding the present to speculate on how the current system is likely to evolve and shape China's economic and political future and the author of one of the chapters does just that.

To understand the nature of economic reform in China (and elsewhere) a reader must know something about the political context in which these reforms occurred and that requires discussion of the politics of reform in some of the chapters and, in addition, a separate chapter on politics and corruption that shaped economic policies and performance. Closely related to the political context of economic reform is the legal context in which reform occurs and therefore there is a chapter on the development of the Chinese legal system as it affects economic activity.

Altogether there are 19 separate chapters in this volume covering these and additional topics written by 22 individual authors. The authors are all among the most distinguished observers of the Chinese economy and related political and legal institutions. They are based in universities and research institutes in China, the United States, France, and Australia. Their essays are written first of all for university students around the world who have some background in economics, but, for the most part, the chapters should also be accessible to well-educated people interested in these topics regardless of whether or not they have studied formal economic analysis.

The editors of this volume are grateful to the various individual authors for contributing to this effort, to Leila Adu for ably editing and formatting the 19 chapters, and to the editors of Routledge for seeing this effort through to publication. The first editor acknowledges with thanks the financial support for his work from the Gregory C. Chow Econometric Research Program of Princeton University.

Gregory C. Chow
Princeton University

Dwight H. Perkins
Harvard University

ABBREVIATIONS

ABC	Agricultural Bank of China
ACFTU	All-China Federation of Trade Unions
AMC	Asset Management Company
ASEAN	Association of Southeast Asian Nations
BOC	Bank of China
BoComm	Bank of Communications
CAEP	Chinese Academy for Environmental Planning
CAR	Capital Adequacy Ratio
CBRC	China Banking Regulatory Commission
CCB	China Construction Bank
CCCPC	Communist Party of China Central Committee
CCP	Chinese Communist Party
CCS	carbon capture and storage
CEC	China Electricity Council
CEMS	continuous emission monitoring systems
CHIP	China Household Income Project
CIRC	China Insurance Regulatory Commission
CNBS	China National Bureau of Statistics
CNOOC	China National Offshore Oil Corporation
COD	chemical oxygen demand
COMTRADE	UN COMTRADE Database
CPC	Communist Party of China
CPPCC	Chinese People's Political Consultative Conference
CSRC	China Security Regulatory Commission
CV	coefficient of variation
ECEs	ethnically Chinese economies
EMC	energy management companies
EPBs	environmental protection bureaus
EU	European Union
FBI	Foreign Broadcast Information Service
FDI	foreign direct investment

FGD	flue gas desulphurization
FIEs	foreign-invested enterprises
FPA	Farmer's Professional Association
FSAP	Financial Sector Assessment Program
FT	*Financial Times*
FYP	Five-Year Plan
GDP	gross domestic product
GE	general entropy
GVAO	gross value of agricultural output
GW	gigawatt
HDR	Human Development Report
HDXXB	*Huadong xinxi bao* (East China News)
HRS	household responsibility system
ICAC	Independent Commission Against Corruption
ICBC	Industrial and Commercial Bank of China
IEA	International Energy Agency
IFDI	inward foreign direct investment
IFO	international financial organization
IMF	International Monetary Fund
IPO	Initial Public Offering
JFRB	*Jiefang ribao* (Liberation Daily)
KMT	Kuomintang Party [Nationalist Party that ruled in the period of the Republic of China]
kWh	kilowatt-hour
MEP	Ministry of Environmental Protection of China
MOHURD	Ministry of Housing and Urban–Rural Development of China
Mtec	million ton of coal equivalent
MW	megawatt
NAFTA	North American Free Trade Agreement
NBS	National Bureau of Statistics of China
NBSC	National Bureau of Statistics, China
NCMS	New Cooperative Medical Scheme
NDRC	National Development and Reform Commission
NEER	nominal effective exchange rate
NGO	non-governmental organization
NMRB	*Nongmin Ribao* (Farmer's Daily)
NO$_x$	nitrogen oxides
NPC	National People's Congress
NPL	non-performing loan
NTB	non-tariff barrier
NYT	*New York Times*
OECD	Organization of Economic Co-operation and Development
ODI	overseas direct investment
OFDI	outbound foreign direct investment
PBOC	People's Bank of China
PLA	People's Liberation Army
PPP	purchasing power parity
PRC	People's Republic of China

PRD	performance ratings and disclosure
PROPER	Program for Pollution Control, Evaluation and Rating
PWT	Penn World Table
QDII	Qualified Domestic Institutional Investor
QFII	Qualified Foreign Institutional Investor
R&D	research and development
RCC	Rural Credit Cooperative
RCMS	Rural Cooperative Medical System
REER	real effective exchange rate
RLCL	Rural Land Contract Law
RMB	renminbi [China's currency]
RMRB	*Renmin Ribao* (People's Daily)
RQFII	RMB Qualified Foreign Institutional Investor
SASAC	State-Owned Asset Supervision and Administration Commission
SC	supercritical
SCMP	*South China Morning Post*
SCRES	State Commission for Restructuring the Economic System
SEZ	Special Economic Zone
SDPC	State Development and Planning Commission
SEPA	State Environmental Protection Agency of China
SHIBOR	Shanghai Interbank Offer Rate
SHJJNJ	*Shanghai jingji nianjian* (Shanghai Statistical Yearbook)
SITC	Standard International Trade Classification
SME	small and medium enterprise
SO$_2$	sulfur dioxide
SOE	state-owned enterprise
SPC	State Planning Commission
SPDs	Special Purpose Designations
SSB	State Statistical Bureau
tce	tons of coal equivalent
TFP	total factor productivity
TVE	township and village enterprise
UEBHI	Urban Employee Basic Health Insurance
UCC	Urban Credit Cooperative
UN BEC	United Nations Broad Economic Category Classifications
UNDP	United Nations Development Programme
URBHI	Urban Residents Basic Health Insurance
USC	ultra-supercritical
USD	US dollar
VOCs	volatile organic compounds
VS	vertical specialization
WDI	Word Development Indicators (database)
WHO	World Health Organization
WTO	World Trade Organization

1

THE CHARACTERISTICS OF CHINA'S TRADITIONAL ECONOMY

Man-houng Lin

This chapter depicts the characteristics of China's traditional economy developed in the seven thousand years before China encountered the impact of the West in the mid-nineteenth century. The concept of cultural complex has been applied and it emphasizes the interrelations among the geographical basis, mode of production, ideologies, economic institutions, and the change of time. International comparisons are made to highlight Chinese characteristics. The purpose of this description is to provide a background for understanding the economic development of present-day China.

The findings include the following: the unique beginning of the Chinese civilization which was in a loess highland, rather than in the alluvial plains of other civilizations; this led to the development of a more labor-intensive economy and an industrious population in China. The traditional Chinese economy that was developed more by the people than by the government, in contrast with the economy after 1949. The historical shift of the economic center since the eleventh century, from the northwest to the coastal area in the southeast, which has enabled the latter area to develop international cooperation in modern times. The intimate rural–urban relation in the Chinese tradition was jeopardized as some of the Chinese coastal cities were more integrated with the international market than the domestic market. Finally, China's traditional economy, which was not stagnant but experienced long-term economic growth although it is interrupted by natural and political disasters.

In the view of some economists, a traditional economy is one developed without the influence of modern science, which was developed in the seventeenth-century European Scientific Revolution (Kuznets 1966: ch.1). China's adoption of such a modern economy began in the mid-nineteenth century, but some elements of China's traditional economy have lasted up to the present.

Some scholars see China's traditional economy as having been precocious and only later stagnating. This view was debated among Chinese scholars in the 1930s and after 1949 (Schwartz 1954; Feuerwerker 1968), including a book related to the Tiananmen Incident (Jin Guantao and Liu Qingfong 1987). This chapter will point out that China's traditional agriculture and commerce did continue to develop, although economic downturns and the political and natural disasters created some fluctuations around the upward trend.

Karl A. Wittfogel's *Oriental Despotism* and other Marxian scholars tended to view China's traditional economy through a totalitarian lens (Wittfogel 1957: 372–411). This chapter argues that despite the large state bureaucracy, small-scale private economic institutions dominated China's traditional economy. In the early imperial period, the relationship between the government and merchants was characteristically one of dominance and subordination, but by the late imperial period, this relationship had become one of mutual dependence. An official statement of 1844 to allow commoners to open new mines declared: "Natural resources on Earth are provided for the use of millions and millions of people," "It is also one way of hiding economic wealth among the people" (*cangfu yumin*), and "Neither can the officials repress or manipulate all affairs" (Lin 2006: 191). This chapter aims to reveal this tradition of popular wealth dispersal, a concept originating in ancient China and described in *Hanshu, the Han Record* (Zhu 1999: 132).

In ancient China, there were two prominent schools of egalitarian thought with regard to the distribution of wealth: the Mozi school advocated the equal distribution of wealth without status differentiation, while the Confucian school argued in favor of an egalitarian distribution with status differentiation. Historically, most Chinese scholars who addressed egalitarianism elaborated their ideas along the lines of the Confucian school (Li Quanshi 1928: 18–19). This chapter will demonstrate how this mainstream school of economic thought was manifested in China's economy in the dominance of small-scale production and exchange activities, and long-lasting economic institutions capable of bolstering economic incentives and facilitating greater social mobility compared with contemporaneous societies.

China is a vast country, integrating various cultures, each of which developed in a particular manner and at a particular pace. Small-scale production started in Northwest China around 5,000 BC. Although China's civilization originated in this inland northwestern region, its economic center shifted to the southeastern littoral region in the eleventh century (Chi 1936: 78, 89). The reasons for this shift include the following: frequent wars between the Han and the non-Han people on the northern frontier, the devastation of the irrigation works in the north, the threat of floods along the Yellow River valley, more suitable geographical conditions for the development of agriculture and commerce in the south, and the development of international commerce in the east. Furthermore, China's geographical shift of economic power from northwest to southeast differs from the shift of Europe's economic center from the southeast, along the shores of the Mediterranean, to the North Atlantic area in the northwest. This chapter will relate the change of China's economic center to changes in its traditional economy over a period of approximately seven thousand years.

The chapter will be divided into six sections: section 1 will depict China's broad social basis constituted of small-scale production and exchange activities. The existence of technological progress in China's traditional economy will be discussed in section 2. Section 3 will point out the compatibility of the landlord and tenancy system, capital accumulation system, trade and ideologies with the rise of merchants. The close rural–urban relation in China with its rather broad rural basis, which was strengthened in the late imperial period, will be discussed in section 4. Section 5 will deal with the role of the government. Section 6 will describe China's economic cycles in the process of its long-term growth, particularly the final economic downturn which caused China to drop from its dominant position in the East Asian order in the mid-nineteenth century when China encountered the West. Finally, an epilogue will be provided to summarize the characteristics of the traditional economy relevant for the development of modern China.

1 Economic institutions of small-scale production and exchange

1.1 The initiation of small-scale farming

Earlier studies of cultural diffusion stated that agriculture first originated in the alluvial deltas of Egypt and Mesopotamia and featured large-scale irrigation works and production units. They also stated that Chinese agriculture followed a similar pattern, beginning in the alluvial delta of the lower stream of the Yellow River in northern China. In fact, Chinese agriculture made its independent start in the loess of the northwest, which shaped the small farming as key aspect of the Chinese mode of production and other cultural traits.

1.2 *The labor-intensive bent in the loess*

Chinese civilization emerged in the upstream loess highland area of the Yellow River. Standing an average 50–150 meters above sea level, with an average rainfall of 250–500 millimeters, and possessing an irregular and vertically cut loess geology, large-scale irrigation of wheat crops, as practiced in ancient Egyptian and Mesopotamian civilizations, was impossible. Chinese agriculture instead practiced small-scale millet cultivation, which required less water and could better draw the water and mineral content of the loess. The irregularly cut loess was similarly unable to sustain large-scale animal husbandry, meaning that China could not rely upon animal energy to scale up agricultural production. The resultant labor-intensive technological bent encouraged population growth and an industrious spirit. This focus on population growth also bolstered ancestor worship, which underscores the extension of the bloodline (Ho 1975).

1.3 *Less animal input*

Such a mode of labor-intensive agricultural production without significant animal input was much extended in the later historical period. While large-scale farms using the multiple-hitch oxen ploughs were developed and practiced in the former Han period (206 BC–AD 220), this practice was replaced by a single-hitch plough in the later Han period due to the lack of oxen (Wang Zhirui 1964: 100; Li Jiannong 1981a: 155). In the later Han period (AD 25–220), a smaller farm size of 667 square meters replaced a bigger farm size of 831 square meters (60×60 *chi* – one *chi* of Han dynasty equals 23.09 cm) prevalent in the Former Han period (Li Jiannong 1981a: 156–158). The tendency to rely on labor-intensive technologies was reinforced after the Song period (960–1279), when China's economic center shifted from the north to the south, where animal husbandry was even more difficult to develop due to the region's higher population density (Wang Zhirui 1964: 99–100). In addition, high population density could hasten the spread of contagious diseases.

Considering that an acre of land used to produce wheat could, in a good harvest year, provide 2,988,000 calories of nutrition; if that piece of land were used instead to raise lamb, it would provide only 318,750 calories of nutrition. To offer a simple comparison, if a section of land sown in wheat yielded 100 calories, raising pigs would yield 7, sheep 11, dairy production 43, rice 131, beans 129, potatoes 260, and sweet potatoes 482. As cropland produced ten to seventy times more calories to feed the growing population than could pasture land, large-scale animal husbandry was discouraged (Majia 1930: 202–204).

As a result, human-hauled ploughs or hoes were more often used than ox-hauled ploughs after the Song period (Majia 1930: 209; Sudo 1962: 73–138). In the 1910s, animal husbandry made up only around 1 percent of China's agricultural production (Perkins 1969: 30).

1.4 *Bloodline concept*

The tendency towards labor-intensive technology affected China's emphasis on extending familial bloodlines. The Chinese concept of lineage extension differs from that of the Japanese, which underscored the expansion of family properties or prestige. The Japanese inheritance system had featured primogeniture since the seventeenth century due to the more competitive life challenge in the Warring States period. The Japanese system tended to promote one capable son, or lead to the adoption of a capable son from another family, in order to extend a well-established family's property or prestige.

By contrast, China had employed equal distribution since the Han dynasty (206 BC–AD 220) and there are many interpretations for such practice. In the feudal period or semi-feudal period before the unification of the Chinese empire in the Qin dynasty, inheritance included the feudal ranks. As a rank could not be divided in the same manner as economic resources, both the rank together with the economic resources were inherited by only one heir. After the feudal or semi-feudal system was replaced by the imperial administration, each registered household had to pay taxes to the government; the equal division inheritance system secured the basis for tax payment. Furthermore, Confucian persuasion for equal wealth, Chinese emphasis on the bloodline extension, and the small-scale mode of production of traditional China had also facilitated this practice (Liu Xinning: 1, 132–136).

This inheritance system is significant in that the Chinese system made possible a higher marriage ratio of males than did the Japanese as Chinese males had a better economic basis to get married. China also had the baby-daughter-in-law system, which saw girls adopted as daughters and married to an elder son of the step-parents when they became of age. This system enabled poor males with no chance of inheritance to marry. The concubine system, on the other hand, enabled rich men to have more offspring.

China's marriage ratios for men and women were both higher than those in Europe, and China's male marriage ratio was higher than that of Japan. Marital age in China was younger than that of Europe, and remarriage encouraged. The family dynamics in China effectively implemented the Confucian maxims that "a boy or a girl should be married," and "an ideal society should be one in which there are no unmarried men or women" (Lin 1991).

With some use of birth control, family sizes in traditional China were about the same as those in early modern Europe or Japan. However, China's higher marriage ratio or lower marriage age, together with other exogenous factors, resulted in China's more vivid population growth.

1.5 Population growth

During the Northern Song dynasty (960–1126), the Chinese population increased to 100 million (in 1086) as compared with the 70 million reached during the Western Han era (206 BC–AD 25). In the early Qing period (around 1760) it reached 200 million, around 1790, the population rose to 300 million, and by 1850, topped 430 million (Durand 1960; Liu and Hwang 1979: 88). Dwight Perkins has estimated the average annual population growth rate of China from 1400 to 1957 as 0.39 percent (Perkins 1969: 81). Hanley and Yamamura estimated that the average annual growth rate for Japan's population was 0.03 percent from 1721 to 1846 (1977: 63). Thus the overall annual population growth rate of Japan's entire late Tokugawa period was significantly lower than that of China from 1400 to 1957.

1.6 Small farming

Typically, a Chinese peasant household would average 5.5 people (Durand 1960) and cultivate one or two hectares of land (Wu 1947: 49). Even though China had a landlord system, land holdings were usually scattered, and each individual farm plot was small. The reason was that these lands might be purchased at different times, distributed among several sons, or tilled by several tenants (Wu 1947: 55–56). Although earlier scholars describe the distribution of land during the Northern dynasties (386–581) through to the Tang dynasty (618–907) as befitting a manorial economy, the average farm size was actually about 22.5 *mou* (one hectare was about 15 *mou*), and there were about five or six tillers per farm (Watanabe 1974).

In China, the tendency towards smaller units of production went hand in hand with a tendency towards smaller units of exchange.

1.7 Small-scale commercial activities

China's long-term copper coinage by the governments reflects China's prevalence of small-scale exchange in the traditional period. During the Western Zhou dynasty (?1027–771 BC), Chinese people started to use copper-cast shell money. In the late Warring States period, the coins in the shape of the spinning wheel were transformed into circular copper coins with square holes in the center (Peng 1954: 78). For the next two thousand years, in China, copper coins were the standard currency of retail exchange (Peng 1954: 67–92, 179).

China's widespread use of copper coinage differs from the practices of other countries. In the seventeenth century, about three-quarters of Japan's money was coined from gold or silver. In the eighteenth century, this share dropped to approximately one-half before increasing again to about 90 percent in the nineteenth century (Takehiko Ohkura and Hiroshi Shimbo 1978: 118–119). In early modern France, the coins cast by the king's mint were mainly gold and silver, and only when these metals became scarce and Japanese copper was imported into France in the seventeenth century did France begin casting copper coins for the use of the poor (Miskimin 1984: 127–260).

China minted copper coins whose value was only about one-hundredth that of silver around 1800. It would be too bulky to use copper coins in large-scale and long-distance transactions (Lin 2006: 4). Silver's value in relation to gold was maintained at between 1 (gold):14.5 (silver) and 1:15.1 in the period between Columbus' arrival in America and the widespread adoption of the gold standard in the 1870s (Peng 1954: 611). Silver used in China was obtained by the market, but not coined by the state. In a Chinese traditional period without a central bank to manage the monetary system, metal money was used mostly as a real currency which reflected its actual intrinsic value, except at times when it was turned into fiat money to inflate its face value to some extent. The long-term and prevalent use of copper coins cast by the Chinese imperial state illustrates the particular dominance of small-scale exchanges in traditional China.

The medium- and small-scale merchants were the chief members of *huiguan*, the interprovincial native-place association, more shaped in the Ming–Qing period for China's interregional trade. Medium- and small-scale merchants were sometimes involved in international trade. Taiyi Hao, a merchant family from the Jinmen archipelago (Quemoy) in Fujian province, settled in Nagasaki in 1850 to conduct trade between Japan, Taiwan, and China, yet only employed around ten employees (Lin 1998: 28).

Although Chinese production and exchange were mostly engaged and earned by small peasants or traders, which facilitated a more equal distribution of wealth, China also experienced technological progress and had institutions for social mobility.

2 The existence of technology progress

In the 1920s, R. H. Tawney observed that China's peasants "ploughed with iron when Europe used wood, and continued to plough with it when Europe used steel" (Tawney 1996: 11). This anecdote is often taken to imply early Chinese technological sophistication and later stagnation. In fact, China witnessed other technological progress, aside from the iron plough.

2.1 Technology transfer from abroad

Wheat, barley, oxen, sheep, and the cart wheel were introduced from the West into China via Siberia around 1300 BC; glaze, glass, cucumbers, and grapes were introduced to the Han dynasty (206–220 BC) from the West; and tea and silk cotton (*bombax malabaricum*) were introduced from Southeast Asia to Han dynasty China (Ho 1978: ch. 2; Liu Boji 1951: ch. 4).

2.2 Irrigation

Dykes were invented in the Former Han dynasty and artificial ponds were started during the Later Han dynasty (Huang Yaoneng 1978). Waterwheels to pump water from low land to high appeared at the end of the Han dynasty (Li Jiannong 1981a: 45). Water dams were created during the Ming dynasty (1368–1644) (Needham 1971–1973: 44). The number of irrigation works was 56 in the Han dynasty, 254 in the Tang dynasty, 1,116 in the Song dynasty, 2,270 in the Ming dynasty, and 3,234 in the Qing dynasty (Chi 1970: 36).

2.3 Changes in the cropping system

Initial modifications in the cropping system included the elimination of fallow land during the Han dynasty (Li Jiannong 1981a: 155) and in the latter Han dynasty the change from broadcasting the seed to confining it to a particular area to facilitate frequent mowing, watering and fertilizing, double cropping, or multiple cropping, on the same piece of land (Perkins 1969: 41; Majia 1930: 204). In the second and third centuries AD, Chinese people began learning how to improve seed varieties to adjust to natural disasters (Majia 1930: 176–177). The practice of growing wheat in winter, after the autumn harvest of the spring-planted rice, began at the end of Han dynasty – following the introduction of the waterwheel for milling wheat. Mulberry trees, hemp, tea, and wheat were introduced into southern China from the north during the Tang–Song period. After the Tang–Song transition, in the eleventh century, early-ripening rice from Annam was introduced; in the fifteenth and sixteenth centuries, sweet potatoes, maize, peanuts, and potatoes were introduced from America (Ho 1956: 200–218). When much of the wood from slow-growing forests was consumed by the huge population, fast-growing bamboo was grown as a substitute for housing material and fuel (Majia 1930: 139–140, 170).

2.4 Keeping the fertility of the land

One reason for the decline of Mesopotamian civilization was the loss of soil fertility (Fairsewis 1967: 42). Maintaining the fertility of agricultural lands in China for approximately seven thousand years to feed a large population is a demanding task, particularly since a portion of the land was also used for producing fibrous materials.

In Western Europe, lambswool replaced hemp and flax as the main inputs in cloth production in the fifteenth and sixteenth centuries, and cotton replaced wool in the eighteenth and nineteenth centuries. Except in some northern areas, China did not pass through a period of wool production. Cotton, which came to China in the fifth century, had become the most important material for cloth production during the twelfth to fourteenth centuries. Production of cotton, hemp, and silk (the secrets of silk had been discovered several thousand years earlier) all require arable land (Majia 1930: 90, 139).

The Chinese maintained land fertility in the following ways:

1   Growing bean or other plants: from the Han period onward, Chinese farmers realized that beans increased nitrogen levels in the soil, and began planting beans before sowing grain. Simultaneously growing a variety of plants, or seasonally changing the crops grown on the same piece of land, were other means of improving soil fertility.
2   Chaff burning and drainage: in the fourth century, Chinese farmers learned to burn the chaff of the previous crop to maintain the soil fertility. Also, Chinese advances in irrigation technology were accompanied by the employment of drainage technology so as to protect the land against salinization.
3   Growing plants that demanded less fertilizer: China grew increasingly more rice, corn, and millet, which needed less fertilizer than wheat, barley, or oatmeal.
4   The use of fertilizer: heavy use of fertilizer has long been a salient feature of Chinese agricultural technology. During the Zhou dynasty (1134–256 BC), people started to make fertilizer from manure, bone soup, and grass ash. In the Spring and Autumn period and the Warring States period, people also started to make green manure (Majia 1930: 135–179, 218). From the Song period onward, China had large-scale enterprises involved in collecting human waste (Hucker 1975: 343). Around 1500, soybean cake was invented for use as a fertilizer (Perkins 1969: 70).

As a whole, the pre-Song period produced more labor-saving agricultural technological inventions – such as the plough, hoe, waterwheel, dyke – than the post-Song period, but the post-Song period produced more labor-intensive or land-intensive agricultural technologies, such as early-ripening rice, Latin American crops, bean cake, and dams among others. Once China's growing population was being adequately nourished by the expanding economy after the Song dynasty, greater attention was paid to human relations. This emphasis distracted some energy that was invested in science, technology, and economic production, to great effect, in the West (Tang Qingzeng 1975: 6). However, in comparison with the West, traditional China realized some outstanding achievements in terms of general technological advancements before and after the Song dynasty.

2.5 Advancement of China's technology

Agriculture: not until the seventeenth century did Western Europe dispense with the fallow field system of land use that China left behind during the Han dynasty (Majia 1930: 175–176). It was not until the agricultural revolution in Europe that green manure was produced, while China started making use of it in the Warring States period (403–221 BC) (Majia 1930: 139, 142).

   Industry and mining: the Chinese discovered iron later than the West, but the Chinese were able to cast iron earlier than the West. In 1050, the Chinese started to replace charcoal with coal as an energy source, whereas Europe made the same shift on the eve of its Industrial Revolution (Hartwell 1962).

   Science and technology: the sciences and technologies introduced to the West from Asia, in which China played the most important role, include: the breast-strap harness (between the fourth and sixth centuries), foot-stirrup (eighth century); equine collar harness and the simple trebuchet in the field of artillery (tenth century); the magnetic compass, the stern-post rudder, paper making, the concept of the windmill, wheelbarrow, counter-weighted trebuchet (the twelfth century); gunpowder, silk machinery, the mechanical clock, and the segmental arch bridge, blast furnace for making cast iron, block printing, movable-type printing (the thirteenth to fourteenth century); the spit vane wheel, the helicopter top, the horizontal windmill, the ball-and-chain flywheel, the lock-gates in canals (the fifteenth century); the kite, the equatorial mounting, and equatorial coordinates, the doctrine of infinite empty space, the iron-chain suspension bridge, the sailing carriage (the sixteenth century); and porcelain technology, the rotary-fan winnowing-machine and watertight compartments at sea (eighteenth century) (Needham 1964: 299–300).

With these advances and other reasons, China's arable land increased from 370 million *shih mou* in 1400 to 950 million *shih mou* in 1770, to 1.2 billion *shih mou* in 1850. Agricultural output per *shih mou* had been 139 catty (one catty is 0.681 kilogram) in 1400, and increased to 203 catty in 1770, and 243 catty in 1850 (Perkins 1969: 16–17).

China's territory is vast, and technological diffusion takes time. Thus, old technology continues to be applied in some areas, while new technologies are adopted elsewhere (Li Jiannong 1981b: 45).

3 Economic systems compatible with development

3.1 Landownership

The concept of ownership in China can be traced to the Neolithic era. Before the emergence of this concept, a gathering economy also signified public ownership, as the possibility of gathering was decided less by human effort than by luck. After married couples settled down to till the land in this period, the concept of ownership emerged as it provided useful incentives (Deng 1942: 45–46). Ancient China has been, to a great extent, deemed as a feudal society by scholars from the People's Republic of China (PRC). This feudal concept was based upon Karl Marx's perception of the European Middle Ages, in which peasants were serfs of the feudal lord and could not purchase or own land. In China, in contrast, the privatization of land was started in the Spring and Autumn era (722–481 BC).

The term "*dizhu*" (for landlord) was coined in the Weijin period (220–420) (Shu 1963: 33–64). Even under the redistribution system for the land holdings from the Weijin to the Tang period, private land was maintained. Only public land won in war was distributed equally among the war-stricken people – some portion of this land could be inherited by sons and maintained as private land (Shu 1963: 46).

Private landownership could be secured by written contract from the Song dynasty (960–1279) onward (Wang Zhirui 1964: 118–119). The dynasties established by foreign conquerors, such as the Liao (907–1125), Jurchen Jin (1125–1234), Yuan (1279–1368), and Qing (1644–1911), as well as the Ming dynasty (1368–1644) established by the Han Chinese, saw land taken by the imperial families and held privately.

In 1865, private land accounted for 92.2 percent of the total for the whole country; public land, including the lands used for schools, lineages, worship, and soldiers, accounted for 4.1 percent of the total, with the remainder maintained as government land. In 1947, private land accounted for 93.3 percent of the total, while public land, including lands for schools, lineages, temples, soldiers, and welfare purposes accounted for 5.7 percent, and government land accounted for 1.0 percent (Wu 1947: 108–109). This land privatization allows for the differentiation of social status.

3.2 Tenancy

In the early Republican period, the tenancy ratio of China was lower than that of Australia, England, Japan, New Zealand, and about the same as those of Belgium and the US, and higher than those of Germany, Holland, France, Austria, Hungary, and Denmark. Therefore, the tenancy ratio in China was not particularly high. Was a high tenancy ratio unfavorable to agricultural productivity? In Japan, the tenancy ratio was high and farms small and fragmentary, yet the country enjoyed agricultural growth in the modern period (Ohkawa and Rosovsky 1960: 56–68).

In China, the tenancy ratio was higher in the south than in the north. In the south, tenancy was further divided between a subsoil landlord with landownership and a topsoil landlord with usage rights over the land. Tenants rented the land to till from the topsoil landlord, and topsoil landlords rented land from subsoil landlords. But agricultural productivity was higher in the south than in the north (Wu 1947: 139, 142; Perkins 1969: 102). Hence, the greater tenancy ratio did not necessarily lead to lower rates of agricultural productivity.

In principle, self-cultivation should enhance the farmer's motivation for increasing production activity, but a reasonable tenancy contract would still promote agricultural development. In the case of England, the tenancy ratio was high, but the rent low, and agricultural productivity continued to increase.

In China, under the well-field system of the Zhou dynasty, the peasants were in some way, tenants of the government as they tilled the lands of feudal lords, but more like serfs as their lives were at the disposition of the lords. From the Qin dynasty (248–206 BC) onward, the landlords had only economic relations with their tenants. In the period between the Han and Tang dynasties, though some tenants had tried to evade the heavy taxes charged by the government by becoming the subordinates of powerful landlords, and thereby lost their freedom, they could leave their landlords and return to being subjects of the government. Since the Tang dynasty (618–907), thanks to more advanced commercial developments, peasants' non-agricultural income increased, and tenants' labor obligations to their landlords mostly disappeared. Before, and in the Tang period, rents were mostly fixed at a fifty-fifty split of the harvest between the landlords and tenants; after the Song period, the rental contract tended to set a fixed rent, regardless of the harvest.

For those tenants under fixed ratio rents, landlords would provide more capital and technology instruction. Those tenants under contract to pay a fixed rent had stronger incentives to increase productivity as they could retain more of the increase. In recently developed areas, where harvests would be less consistent, fixed ratio rents were the norm (Wu 1947: 167).

Before the Northern Song dynasty (960–1126), there were more fixed, absolute rents in northern China, and more fixed ratio rents in southern China. After the Northern Song period, this situation was reversed (Shu 1963). In the 1930s, according to an investigation by the Central Agricultural Experiment Institute across twenty-two provinces, fixed ratio rents prevailed in the less-developed northwest, north, and southwest areas. In general, from the Song through to the Republican period, the percentage of fixed amount contracts had increased for the whole of China. In the 1930s, during the Republican period, the percentage of fixed amount rental contracts had risen to 78 percent, and the percentage of fixed ratio rents had fallen to 22 percent (Wu 1947: 211). The coerced labor system could only be found in Tibet, Sikang, the southern section of Yunnan, and western Section of Sichuan. The tenancy situation in China therefore had changed greatly from the coerced labor system, to the fixed ratio system, and then to the fixed amount system.

3.3 Institutions and ideologies for the rise of merchants

When barter trade started in the Shang period (?1523–?1027 BC), China did not have merchants, and trade was conducted by the producers themselves. It was not until the Western Zhou period (1027–771 BC) that professional merchants emerged, mainly to serve feudal aristocrats by supplying them with the desired commodities. Only in the Spring and Autumn (770–403 BC) and the Warring States period (403–221 BC), when agricultural technology was much improved, did households retain sufficient surpluses that professional merchants found it profitable to serve the ordinary people (Sa 1966: 29).

During the Zhou dynasty (1134–256 BC) onward, merchants' guilds based on family relationships came into being (Chuan 1978). Before the Sui (589–618) and Tang (618–907) dynasties, merchants could open stores only in restricted locations, and merchant guilds were localized. After the Sui and Tang dynasties, the restrictions on store locations were lifted. From the Ming and Qing period onward, long-distance traders started to organize guilds on the basis of their native places, which gives some indication of more interregional trade being developed (Kato 1978: 68–69).

Some long-distance trade extended to become international trade. Historically, China engaged in continental trade with Manchuria, Mongolia, Central Asia, and neighboring countries to the southwest, and maritime trade with Southeast Asia, Japan, Africa, and America. The continental trade was most prosperous during the early Tang and Yuan dynasties; it was developed, and yet not as prosperous in the Han and Six Dynasties and declined in the Song period because other political powers were hindering the contact in between, and again developed to some extent in the Ming and Qing periods. By contrast, the maritime trade in general prospered from the Tang period until the maritime ban of the Ming and the early Qing periods (Kato 1978: 80–88). Hence, various trades gave rise to various types of merchants.

Partnerships began to appear in the Song period and prevailed in China in the late nineteenth and twentieth centuries which also helped with capital accumulation (Lin 1998: 70–72). And contrary to what Max Weber wrote, this method of capital accumulation was not limited to family members (Weber 1951: 95).

By contrast with the lower-intrinsic-value coinage, higher-intrinsic-value currency was also available in China for more convenient capital accumulation. China used gold or bronze of higher quality for the storage of greater wealth and larger-scale exchanges from the Warring States period to the Han period. Silver and deerskins began to be used for value storage sometime in the Han period. During the Six Dynasties and the Tang dynasty, because of the invasion of northern intruders, trust in the convertibility of money into goods waned and a barter economy based upon woven products prevailed. From the Song through to the early Ming dynasty, convertible paper exchange notes were mainly used for large-scale exchange. From the mid Ming dynasty until 1933, silver replaced paper exchange notes for this purpose (Peng 1954: 257–290; 370–392; 429–460; 521–565). As silver was obtained mainly by merchants through international trade, and silver had been regulated by the government for taxation and long-distance trade, the late imperial Chinese economy was very different from that of a modern state with a central bank. Merchants held the dominant currency, silver, while the government controlled the auxiliary currency, copper coins (Lin 2006: introduction and ch.1). This monetary arrangement greatly facilitated merchants' capital accumulation.

The secularization of knowledge developed from the mid-Tang by the Zen Buddhists, in the Ming period by the Wang Yangming school Confucian scholars and by the Daoists, facilitated the printing of commercial handbooks in the Ming and Qing dynasties. These books promoted diligence, honesty, and charitable works as mercantile ethics. It also encouraged merchants to gain religious merit and to command social respect by performing beneficent works (Yu 1987).

4 Close rural–urban relations

With a rather broad social basis and quite flexible social mobility, China had a particularly close rural–urban relation in its traditional economy.

Though a city commanded more resources than a rural area, as a whole, cities accounted for fewer resources than the countryside. In the Republican period, only 7–8 percent of rural products were sold to regions 30 miles away from where they were produced. During the Qing dynasty, cities accounted for only 5–6 percent of the total population (Skinner 1977: table 4).

Government taxation amounted to a kind of resource forwarded from the countryside to cities. In Qing times, land taxation accounted for only around 2 percent of the total national income (Wang Yeh-chien 1973: 133). Albert Feuerwerker calculated the percentage of state revenue as a proportion of national income at 13 percent for the Northern Song dynasty around 1080, 6–8 percent for the Ming dynasty around 1550, 4–8 percent for the Qing dynasty around 1750, 7.5 percent for the Qing dynasty in the 1880s, and 5–10 percent for the Qing dynasty around 1908 (1984: 297–326).

Government loans existed from the time of the Zhou dynasty onward (Peng 1954: 62). In general, the share of government loans that went to the peasantry was very small. In 1933, a census of peasant families in 850 districts of 22 provinces showed that 56 percent of peasant families found it necessary to borrow money. For their source of loan, modern cooperatives shared 1.3 percent, relatives shared 8.3 percent, landlords shared 9 percent, rich farmers shared 45.1 percent, merchants shared 17.3 percent, pawnshops shared 8.7 percent, and granaries or churches shared 10.1 percent (Amano Motonosuke 1936).

For Chinese traditional economy, there is a metaphor: man tills the land; woman weaves the clothes. The rural industries for making silk, bamboo, and wood products began in the Zhou dynasty and continued ever afterward (Moritani 1936: 47–52). However, in L. Buck's rural investigation in the early Republican period, only 20 percent of the rural families were involved in rural industries, and the income derived from rural industry products accounted for only 3 percent of the total agricultural income (Potter 1968: 174–212). Hence, the rural villages themselves could not constitute a self-sufficient economic unit.

According to Skinner's study, in an open, flat area, about 18 villages would periodically hold a standard market to facilitate exchanges with each other. The area encompassed by a standard market also constituted an area sharing the same measures, dialect, and folk religion. Such markets also facilitated the work of runners and clerks who issued taxation notices and accepted copper or silver in payment of those same taxes. Local elders would also take the opportunity to read imperial edicts or Confucian teachings to the country folk (Skinner 1964–1965).

The urban upper class comprised the gentry and merchants. As no strict class restrictions were in place for sitting the imperial examination, those from the countryside comprised a large number of the gentry. In 1947, Pan Guangdan and Fei Xiaotong analyzed the metropolitan degree holders of 1862–1908, and found that 52.5 percent of the metropolitan degree holders in Beijing came from great cities, 6.3 percent from market towns, and 41.2 percent from the countryside. Of metropolitan degree holders in Shandong, Anhui, Henan, and Shanxi, 36.6 percent came from the great cities, 7.6 percent came from market towns, and 55.9 percent from the countryside (Skinner 1977: 266–267).

Chinese tenants were not tied to the land they tilled; they could go out and open their own business. As doing business was risky and legal protections in traditional China were insecure, merchants tended to form partnerships through kinship groups or native-place groups. Native-place chiefly referred to the standard market area, from which merchants in the cities took apprentices and were responsible to their parents at home with whom these bosses were acquainted. That is why Chinese merchants formed into groups by territory, for example: Shanxi, Shaanxi, Anhui, Fujian, and Guangdong. Traditional commercial organizations, such as native banks and pawnshops, as well as the Hong merchants of Canton and the new comprador merchants who emerged after the mid-nineteenth century, were mostly based upon blood ties and native-place relationships built in the rural area (Murphey 1977: 180–196).

A survey conducted in 1941 in the 12 provinces under the rule of the Chongqing government led by Guomingdang revealed that 72.6 percent of landlords lived in the countryside (Wu 1947: 116). Members of the gentry and the merchants, who went to the cities, sometimes left their families in the countryside. Money they earned in the cities could be remitted back home to relieve their relatives or for investment in property. In China, the relationship between the countryside and cities was much closer than that found in the West (Mote 1970).

Qing China's social structure appears to have been more broadly based than that of Tokugawa Japan. Despite a population less than one-tenth that of Qing China, Tokugawa Japan had Edo as large as Beijing. In the more than two hundred years of the Tokugawa era, Japan's urban population increased two and half times, and its society became more centralized around its capital. In contrast, when the Qing population increased two or three times over, the local market towns of China were more the focus of the increase than the administrative centers (Rozman 1973: xv, 60, 281, 282, 285, 298). At the same time, a Chinese landlord might own plots totaling as much as fifteen thousand *mou* (Wu 1947: 118–119), such estates were rather modest in comparison with the several tens of thousands of hectares often attached to European manors (Tawney 1966: 31–32). This evidence shows China's tendency to have more equal income distribution.

5 The government, merchants, and the economy

With China's broad social basis and intimate rural–urban relation, how could a despotic government as depicted by Wittfogel be possible? What was the exact relation between the government and merchants, or between the government and the economy in traditional China?

5.1 Government and the economy

The imperial government maintained relatively steady revenues with light taxation. Given its vast territory, when one jurisdiction experienced a fiscal deficit, the surplus of another could ease the resulting difficulty. The imperial state did not need to tax merchants heavily, instead it mostly let merchants run their businesses without interference. With that steady revenue, the state maintained granaries to help relieve famine (Wong 1997: 132–139). Through the issuance of copper coins and maintenance of the granaries, the government could adjust the prices to some extent. Additionally, due to the building irrigation works, the encouragement of the cultivation of new crops, and the development of transportation routes, the government greatly facilitated economic growth.

The Grand Canal to connect southern and northern China was started in the Spring and Autumn period (770–403 BC), completed in the Sui dynasty (581–618), and improved in the Yuan dynasty (1279–1367). In the Tang (618–907) and Song periods (960–1279), the Three Gorges were opened to connect the upper stream of the Yangtze River and its lower streams (Bai 1937: 101–102).

The postal system was launched in the Zhou dynasty (1134–256 BC) and reached a climax during the Yuan dynasty (1279–1367). The imperial horse road opened in the Chin dynasty was barely used by the monarch. The postal route could serve for civilian use and was much longer. During the Qing dynasty, there were 1,956 stations in total, and the route stretched 80,000 *li*. Each province had between several hundred and a thousand substations. Each station had hotels, used mainly for official or military purposes. Commoners' communications had to pass through friends, messengers, sedan carriers, or travelers, who could also cover these routes (Cheng 1970: 37).

12

5.2 Government and merchants

Records of the Grand Historian or *Han Record* recorded that in the early Han dynasty, the government imposed several limitations on the merchants: merchants could not serve as officials, purchase land, ride horses or carts, wear luxurious or gorgeous clothing, and were subject to heavy taxes. This has often been cited as the Chinese government's policy towards merchants in each dynasty. In fact, these policies were not really implemented, even in the early Han period. It has been noted that officials in each dynasty were privately involved with commerce (Wang Xiaotong, 1965).

Yang Lien-sheng and Etienne Balazs argue that each dynasty tried both to control and utilize the merchants. To control the merchants, the government tended to ask that the merchants serve as guarantors for each other, and the merchants had their own particular household registrations. But, from the Tang dynasty (618–907) onward, control was much relaxed. The government no longer relied upon guilds to keep an eye on the merchants. Merchants could contribute money to win official positions, and official money could be deposited at merchants' shops to earn interest. Some governmental monopolies were farmed out to merchants for profit. During the Sui (581–18), Tang (618–907), and Liao (907–1125) dynasties, merchants and their offspring could not serve as officials. During the Song dynasty (960–1279), merchants themselves could not join the officialdom. During the Ming and Qing dynasties (1368–1911), the offspring of salt merchants had a special quota permitting some to attend the imperial examination, commercial taxes were lowered, and the merchants' position improved (Yang 1970; Balazs 1970: ch. 4).

The symbiotic relationship between the Qing bureaucracy and merchants differentiates China's traditional merchants from Henri Pirenne's autonomous city merchants, who arose in the course of European expansion. Among the top guild were merchants doing business across the Taiwan Strait, who came from Fujian during the Qing period, some were of Fujian bureaucratic families and had family members serving in such high posts as governor-general of Sichuan and governor-general of Guangdong and Guangxi (Lin 2001: 131–132). The rise of the Shanxi merchants was related to military provisioning for the Qing state during its conquest of China and during the Ten Campaigns in the Qianlong period. From the initial years of the Taiping Rebellion onward, remittance banks started to distribute state revenue among the provinces (Lin 1998: 68–70).

5.3 Government and the market

As for the relationship between the government and the market, China's monetary crisis, which occurred in the 1820–1850 period, reveals much divergence from stereotypical views of China's despotic intra-governmental structure or government–market relationship. In such a crisis, the copper coin – the government-issued currency, depreciated by about half against silver – was the currency supplied by the international market through merchants. In the intra-governmental discussion between the emperor and officials in the province, the proposal to use more copper coins to replace silver was dropped because of objections from provincial governments.

The government-issued copper coins were not national coins in a modern sense: they were issued by various provinces, mainly for use in that province. The weight of copper coins would be about 240 times that of silver coins of the same value in the early nineteenth century. Thus, copper coins could hardly replace silver for long-distance trade. Provincial mints circulated the copper coins they cast in order to pay the salaries of soldiers in copper. In addition, the provincial mints also paid for some governmental purchase of civil goods or services in copper coins, and so passed the coins into circulation. A fixed official rate of 1 *liang* of silver for 1,000 *wen* of copper coins was used. Nevertheless, the market exchange rate between silver and copper coins rose from 1:1,000 to 1:2,500 in this period. More and more, the soldiers and the commoners refused to accept their pay in copper coins.

The government needed to spend silver to mint copper coins, to acquire copper from far-away southwest China, or Japan. With demand for additional copper coins and their value falling, the value of the silver needed for copper coinage developed to be four times the value of the silver with which the cast copper coin could be exchanged. The Qing state could not replace the 1:1,000 official rates with the market rate as it lacked the capacity to gather information and respond to a floating exchange rate. As a result, the Qing dynasty – deemed the most despotic period in Chinese imperial history – had most of its provincial mints closed, or issued fewer coins.

The Discourse of Salt and Iron of Han dynasty (206 BC–AD 220) has been taken as symbolic of China's traditionally interventionist political–economic ideologies. In the monetary crisis of 1820–1850, the perceptions of, and arguments over, the dominance of markets over the government gained more and more social support as people saw vividly the uncontrollability of the market by the state. Wei Yuan (1794–1856) – who was a metropolitan degree holder, private secretary, magistrate, and prefect – made a proposal to allow the common people to open silver mines; the proposal also mentioned that private mining had coexisted with government-run mining as far back as 1133. Wei's historical retrospect revealed to some extent the government–merchant relation for strategic resources as mines in imperial China (1967: juan 14, 36a–b).

Copper coins for retail trade were mostly used in the standard market areas. As copper coins were issued by the government, the lowest reach of the imperial power was not the district level, as many previous studies have stated. The supply of copper coins still affected people's daily lives at the lowest level. On the other hand, silver was used more in the cities. The silver–copper coin exchange rates set by the bank shops in the cities would affect the number of coins that those living in rural areas paid for their taxes set in silver, or for products purchased from far-away places set in silver. Thereby, both the state and society were under the sway of the silver-holding merchants (Lin 2006: introduction, chs.1, 3, 4, 8).

6 Economic cycles in long-term growth

Over several thousand years of China's traditional economy, despite ups and downs in agriculture or commerce, there was long-term growth in general. Within this trend, aside from external invasions, there was a dynastic cycle with intervals of roughly 250 years.

The dynastic cycle proceeded with the following pattern: the monarch who established a new dynasty would work to rebuild the economy and undertake infrastructure projects, such as irrigation works, transportation, the opening of new land, and granaries, which would nourish more people. Their dynastic successors might not prove as capable or prudent, and might not invest in the maintenance or upgrading of the infrastructure. This would result in a period in which population growth outstripped economic growth. It would stimulate the migration of rural people to urban areas and, for a time, contribute to the prosperity of urban areas. The enriched merchants would use their capital to purchase rural land, thereby widening the social gap between the rich and the poor. Soon, landless vagrants would become a source of discontent, increasing the chances of large-scale rebellion. The associated expense would result in an increase in taxes imposed by various governments and damage the rural economy. Without favorable rural markets, the urban economy declined. Such social instability often invited external invasion. The result would be the collapse of the old dynasty, significant population loss, and the founding of a new dynasty. Such a 250-year interval is far longer than modern economic cycles, which occur in periods of fifty, ten, or three to four years (Fei 1935: 1–13; Feuerwerker 1968).

The economies of China's urban and rural areas were closely tied together. When the rural economy was strong, the countryside provided markets, capital, and labor for the urban areas; when the urban economy was weak, in the absence of other factors, the rural economy would be ruined. The main source of economic crises in rural areas was population pressure, while those in urban areas were due to market contractions (Lin 2004; Lin 2006: 126).

Some crises were caused by both sources. For example, many scholars argue that eighteenth-century Qing China's economy fell from prosperity into poverty. An early indicator of prosperity was the doubling of arable land, greater interregional trade, the cultivation of new crops, and development of handicraft industries, which fed a population that doubled or tripled in size in half a century, outpacing the population growth of previous periods. But, around 1748, starvation became an issue.

This was not only the result of population growth; it was also a result of falling supply of money available to each person. From the sixteenth century onward, China's money supply relied more and more on silver imports from abroad. From 1550 to 1700, Japan provided China with more silver than Latin America, while from 1700 onward, Latin America became a more important source of silver. In 1748 the population increased, while silver did not increase at the same pace, as Japanese silver decreased in supply and the Latin American silver did not increase as fast as the population. In twenty years (1775–1795), the rate of population increase slowed, the supply of Latin American silver increased, and per capita income improved. Consequently, the 1748 starvation issue was eased (Lin 2004).

In the 1820–1850 period, the rate of population increase remained slow, but the supply of silver on international markets fell drastically with the advent of the Latin American independence movement; thus, the livelihoods of the Chinese people deteriorated and social tensions were exacerbated – providing a background for the outbreak of the Taiping Rebellion and the civil wars that followed. These wars took the lives of between one in twenty and one in nine people out of a population of approximately 430 million. The result of this late imperial economic crisis was a reversal of the relative positions of China and Japan in the Asian geopolitical order. The silver-owning Japan, which escaped the silver supply crisis initiated from Latin America, went on to prominence under the Meiji Restoration (Lin 2006: chs. 1–3).

7 Epilogue

The characteristics of China's traditional economy described in this chapter provide background and contrast for China in the modern times, which could be discussed in the following four aspects.

7.1 Deep cultural bases for a large industrious population

The conditions of the unique start of the Chinese traditional economy in the Northwest loess highland, with small land plots cut here and there, resulted in a decrease in the supply of animal energy. The fertility of the loess and the small supply of rainfall dictate industrious human effort. This Chinese propensity for industriousness and need for population growth was reinforced when China's center of economy was moved from the north to the south in the Song dynasty, as population–land ratio was increased with a more mountainous geographical basis. This deep Chinese tradition has prepared the larger Chinese population bases for contemporary China, which shares about one-fifth of the world population.

7.2 Limited role of the government

The Wittfogel despotic perception of China's tradition was based upon the centralized hydraulic system built early in the Chinese imperial period when control of water conveyed power: the so-called Asiatic mode of production (Wittfogel 1957: ch. 9: 369–411). And yet, as described in this chapter, although imperial governments provided infrastructure and macroeconomic schemes for economic improvement, the traditional Chinese economy was largely built by the people. Technological progress and institutional incentives in the landlord–tenancy system, and the monetary and capital formation systems were increasingly reinforced as the empire evolved. The dominance of small-scale production and exchange units, the existence of private owner-ship and the freedom to move and choose one's job contributed to making the nation wealthy, and to distributing the wealth more equally among the people. Even during the Qing dynasty – described as the most despotic by Naito Konan – most resources, including the key currency, were controlled by the people (Lin 2006: ch. 1).

The Chinese empire had economic cycles of about 250 years. The outbreak of the Taiping Rebellion, when China was just starting to enter into contact with the West in modern times, did much damage to China, particularly in light of Japan's Meiji Restoration. With the Taiping Rebellion and ongoing internal and external wars, China witnessed the reinforcement of state power (Lin 2006: ch. 8). But private property and the market economy were, for the most part, maintained until 1949. The centralization of the economy after 1949 was a great rupture from Chinese traditional economy.

7.3 Unequal spatial distribution of economic development

With the long-term shift of China's economic center from northwest to the southeast, when Western countries came to China in the mid-nineteenth century, they preferred to cooperate with the pros-perous southeast coastal China. This coastal China gained much in terms of technology and markets, and the regional gap between the coastal area and the interior area was generally widened. Jeffrey G. Williamson observed that this kind of dual economy issue tends to be more serious if the area open to modern international trade is also the center of food and industrial materials production (1965: 3–45). China happened to possess such an economy due to its long-term historical development.

Rhoads Murphey used the dual economy model to describe the relationship between the treaty ports and China's hinterland after 1840, arguing that imported foreign goods were, by and large, used only in the treaty port areas, and that the treaty ports constituted a kind of enclave economy. Unlike China's traditional cities, the treaty ports had little connection with rural China (Murphey 1970: 52–57).

Lin (2005) has offered modifications to this theory. Between the late 1870s and 1906, inte-rior products which satisfied the following conditions were still sold to the international market: (1) products whose profits were sufficient to cover transportation costs from inland China to the coast, such as native opium, bristle, or cotton cloth; (2) products whose production demanded less capital and whose production technology was easy to learn such as matches; (3) products whose raw materials were found in the countryside, such as pottery. In the wartime period (1937–1945), the Guomindang-led Republic of China (ROC) moved to Chongqing, which also developed interior China. For the rest of the period between 1850 and 1949, China's coastal region was more integrated with the international economy than the economy of the interior and there was an excessive concentration of economic resources in coastal China. In spite of enormous efforts after 1949, the gaps between prosperous coastal China and poor inte-rior China still exist today (Lin 2005: 179–197).

7.4 *Dependence of development on historical tradition*

After studying many less developed countries, Gerschenkhron pointed out that in the process of transformation from a traditional to a modern economy, only by frankly recognizing the strengths of the existing tradition, and attempting to develop fully, rather than to stifle that tradition, can modernity be more smoothly achieved (1962: 30). After China contacted the West in the mid-nineteenth century, traditional native banks rivaled foreign banks for providing credit to the import and export trade. A major reason for this was that Chinese society was still based on blood relationships or native-place relationships, and native banks could maneuver through these traditional ties better than foreign banks. The earliest modern industries in China, including textiles, silk filature, and coal mining were started mostly where the traditional industries were already in place (Hubei daxue 1958: 234–235).

In the land collectivization process, in one single year, even though family farms occupied just 6.4 percent of the total agricultural land in the nation, they accounted for 30 percent of the production value. Meanwhile, because the output of communal land was taken by the government, even though it accounted for 88.8 percent of total cultivation, its output contributed just 66 percent of national agricultural value (Gao 1973: 321–322). By contrast, the family farm system in Taiwan was maintained after the land reform process of the ROC, which has ruled Taiwan since 1945. Before this, when Taiwan was ruled by Japan during the 1895–1945 period, the subsoil landlords' landownership was exchanged for stock in modern companies. In the Republican period, topsoil landownership was also exchanged for stock in modern companies. Mainly through the use of fertilizer and new plant varieties, as with China's traditional economy, modern agriculture developed quickly in Taiwan and with it the ability to nurture a modern economy and democratic politics (Lin 1979). In the decade between 1979 and 1989 of the PRC, the collective sector, consisting mainly of rural community enterprises grew at a rate of more than 20 percent per year. It was this sector, more than any other, which accounted for the impressive 9.5 percent growth per annum in the economy as a whole during that decade (Huang 1993: 238–239).

Although many previous studies have stated that China's traditional economy was stagnant; in fact it witnessed long-term economic growth interrupted by natural and political disasters as described in this chapter. In Taiwan and in some cases in mainland China in the modern period, development has been more based upon Chinese tradition. The relation between China's historical tradition and its economic development is a topic worthy of attention.

Bibliography

Amano Motonosuke (1936) *Shina ni okeru tendo ni tsuite* (The pawnshops of China), *Mantetsu chōsa getsupō* (Manchuria railway investigation society monthly), Mantetsu chōsakai, 16–9, 1936 (Showa 11), 9/15, pp. 69–90.

Bai Shouyi (1937) *Zhongguo jiaotongshi* (Chinese transportation history), Shanghai: Commercial Press.

Balazs, E. (1970) trans. H. M. Wright, *Chinese Civilization and Bureaucracy,* New Haven, CT: Yale University Press.

Cheng, Y. (1970) *Postal Communication in China and Its Modernization, 1860–1896*, Cambridge, MA: East Asian Research Center, Harvard University.

Chi, C. (Ji Chaoding) (1936) *Key Economic Areas in Chinese History: As Revealed in the Development of Public Works for Water-Control*, London: Allen & Unwin.

Deng Chumin (1942) *Zhongguo shehuishi jiaochen* (A textbook for Chinese social history), Guilin: Cultural Press.

Durand, J. D. (1960) 'The Population Statistics of China, AD 2–1953', *Population Statistics*, 13: 209–56.

Fairsewis, W. A. (1967) 'The Origin, Character, and Decline of an Early Civilization', *American Museum Novitates*, 2303.

Fei Ssu (1935) 'Zhongguo shehuisi fenqi zhi shangque' (A critique of the periodization of Chinese social history), *Shihuo Bimonthly*, 2(11): 1–13.

Feuerwerker, A. (1968) *History in Communist China*, Cambridge, MA and London: MIT Press.

Feuerwerker, A. (1984) 'The State and the Economy in Late Imperial China', *Theory and Society*, 13(3): 297–326.

Gao Xianggao (1973) *Gongfei jingji wenti lunji* (Anthology on the Chinese Communists' economic problems), Taipei: Institute for International Relations.

Gerschenkron, A. (1962) *Economic Backwardness in Historical Perspective*, Cambridge, MA: Harvard University Press.

Hanley, S.B. and Kozo Yamamura (1977) *Economic and Demographic Change in Pre-industrial Japan, 1600–1868*, Princeton, NJ: Princeton University Press.

Hartwell, R. (1962) 'A Revolution in the Chinese Iron and Coal Industries during the Northern Sung, 960–1126', *Journal of Asian Studies*, 21(2): 153–162.

Ho, P. (He Bingdi) (1956) 'Early-ripening Rice in Chinese History', *Economic History Review*, 9.

Ho, P. (1959) *Studies on the Population of China, 1368–1953*, Cambridge, MA: Harvard University Press.

Ho, P. (1975) *The Cradle of the East: An Inquiry into the Indigenous Origins of Techniques and Ideas of Neolithic and Early Historic China, 5000–1000 BC*, Chicago, IL: University of Chicago Press.

Huang, P. (1993) '"Public Sphere"/"Civil Society" in China? The Third Realm between State and Society', *Modern China*, 19(2): 216–240.

Huang Yaoneng (1978) *Zhongguo gudai nongye shuilishi yanjiu* (A study of agricultural irrigation in ancient China), Taipei: Liuguo Press.

Hubei daxue zhengzhi jingjixue jiaoyanzu (1958) *Zhongguo jindai guomin jingjishi* (National economic history of modern China), Hubei: gaodeng jiaoyu.

Hucker, C. O. (1975) *China's Imperial Past: An Introduction to Chinese History and Culture*, Stanford, CA: Stanford University Press.

Jin Guantao and Liu Qingfeng (1987) *Xingsheng yu weiji–lun Zhongguo shehui de chao wending jiegou* (Prosperity and crisis: the super-stability structure of China's society), Taipei: Gufeng Press.

Kato Shigeru (1978) *Zhongguo shehui jingjishi gaishuo*, trans. Z. Du, Taipei: Huashi.

Kuznets, S. (1966) *Modern Economic Growth: Rate, Structure, and Speed*, New York: Feffer & Simons.

Li Jiannong (1981a) *Xianqing Lianghan jingji shigao* (A draft for the history of the ancient China and the Han dynasty), Taipei: Huashi Press.

Li Jiannong (1981b) *Weijin Nanbeichao Tang chao jingji shigao* (A draft for the history of the Six dynasties and the Tang dynasty), Taipei: Huashi Press.

Li Quanshi (1928) *Zhongguo jingji sixiang xiaoshi* (A short history of Chinese economic thought), Shanghai: shijie shuju.

Lin, M. (Lin Man-houng) (1979) 'Riju shidai Taiwan jingjishi yanjiu zhi zonghe pingjie' (Studies on the economic history of Taiwan under Japanese rule, 1895–1945: A survey), *Shixue pinglun* (Historical review) 1(Jul.): 161–210.

Lin, M. (1991) 'The Perpetuation of Bloodline versus Family Property: A Crucial Factor for the Different Demographic Dynamics of Pre-industrial China and Japan', *Zhongguo xiandaihua lunwenji* (The modernization of China conference proceedings), pp. 165–208. ed. and pub, Taipei: Zhongyang yanjiuyuan jindaishi yanjiusuo (Institute of Modern History, Academia Sinica).

Lin, M. (1998) 'Interpretive Trends in Taiwan Scholarship on Chinese Business History', *Chinese Studies in History*, 31(3–4): 65–94; and also in R. Gardella, A. McElderry and J. Leonard (eds.), *Chinese Business History, Interpretive Trends and Priorities for the Future*, New York: M.E. Sharpe, ch. 4.

Lin, M. (2001) 'Decline or Prosperity? Guild Merchants Trading Across the Taiwan Straits, 1820s–1895.' In *Commercial Networks in Modern Asia*, ed. Sinya Sugiyama and Linda Grove, London: Curzon Press, pp. 116–139.

Lin, M. (2004) 'The Shift from East Asia to the World: The Role of Maritime Silver in China's Economy in the Seventeenth to Late Eighteenth Centuries.' In Wang Gungwu and Ng Chin-keong (eds.), *Maritime China in Transition 1750–1850*. Wiesbaden, Germany: Harrassowitz, pp. 77–96.

Lin, M. (2005) 'The Development of "Dual Economy" in China's Fluctuating International Trade Relations, 1842–1949.' In Kaoru Sugihara (ed.), *Japan, China, and the Growth of the Asian International Economy, 1850–1949*, Oxford: Oxford University Press, pt 3, ch. 8, pp. 179–197.

Lin, M. (2006) *China Upside Down: Currency, Society, and Ideologies, 1808–1856*, Cambridge, MA: Harvard University Asia Center.

Liu Boji (1951) *Zhongxi wenhua jiaotong xiaoshi* (A history of cultural exchange between China and the West), Taipei: Zhengzhong.

Liu, P. K. C. and Kuo-shu Huang (1979) 'Population Change and Economic Development in Main land China since 1400.' In C. Hou and T. Yu (eds.), *Modern Chinese Economic History*, pp. 61–94.

Liu Xinning (2007) *Yiu Zhangjiashan Hanjian (Ernianluling) lun Hanchu de jichengzhidu* (Inheritance during the early Han based on the legal texts of the year Two from the bamboo slips of Zhang Jia Shan), Taipei: National Taiwan University.

Majia (1930) trans. Z. Hua, *Zhongguo nongcun jingji zhi texing* (Characteristics of modern agricultural economics), *Zhongyang yanjiuyuan shehui kexue yanjiusuo nongcun jingji cankao ziliao*, No. 3, Shanghai: Beixin Book Co.

Miskimin, H. A. (1984) *Money and Power in Fifteenth-Century France*, New Haven, CT: Yale University Press.

Moritani Katsuni (1936) trans. Chen Qangwei, *Zhongguo she hui jingji shi* (Chinese socio-economic history), Shanghai: Commercial.

Mote, F. W. (1970) 'The City in Traditional Chinese Civilization.' In J. T. C. Liu and W. Tu (eds.), *Traditional China*, Englewood Cliffs, NJ: Prentice-Hall, pp. 42–49.

Murphey, R. (1970) *The Treaty Ports and China's Modernization: What Went Wrong?* Ann Arbor, MI: University of Michigan, Center for Chinese Studies, No. 7.

Murphey, R. (1977) *The Outsiders – The Western Experience in India and China*, Ann Arbor, MI: University of Michigan Press.

Needham, J. (1964) 'Science and China's Influence on the World.' In R. Dawsons (ed.), *The Legacy of China*, Oxford: Oxford University Press.

Needham, J. (1971–1973) Chen Lifu trans. *Zhongguo zhi kexue yu wenming* (Chinese science and civilization), Taipei: Commercial Press.

Ohkawa, K. and Rosovsky, H. (1960) 'The Role of Agriculture in Modern Japanese Economic Development', in *Economic Development and Cultural Change*, vol. IX, pt 2.

Peng Xinwei (1954) *Zhongguo huobishi* (Chinese monetary history), Shanghai: Qunlian Press.

Perkins, D. H. (1969) *Agricultural Development in China, 1368–1968*, Chicago, IL: Aldine.

Potter, J. M. (1968) *Capitalism and the Chinese Peasant, Social and Economic Change in a Hong Kong Village*, Berkeley, CA: University of California Press.

Quan Hansheng (1935 orig. prt.; 1978 reprinted) *Zhongguo hanghui zhidushi* (A history of guilds in China), Taipei: Shihuo Press; first printed in Shanghai, reprinted in Taiwan.

Rozman, G. (1973) *Urban Networks in Ch'ing China and Tokugawa Japan*, Princeton, NJ: Princeton University Press.

Sa Mengwu (1966) *Zhongguo shehui zhengzhishi* (Chinese socio-political history), vol. I, Taipei: Sanming book store.

Schwartz, B. I. (1954) 'A Marxist Controversy on China', *Far East Quarterly*, 13(2): 143–153.

Shu Shicheng (1963) 'HanSong jian de diannong diwei (The status of tenants in the period between the Han and Song dynasties)', *Zhonghua wenshi luncong* (Anthologies for Chinese literature and history), Taipei: Zhonghua book store, pp. 33–64.

Skinner, G. W. (1964; 1965a; 1965b) 'Marketing and Social Structure in Rural China', *Journal of Asian Studies*, 24(1): 3–44; 24(2): 195–228; 24(3): 363–399.

Skinner, G. W. (1977) *The City in Late Imperial China*, Stanford, CA: Stanford University Press.

Spooner, F. C. (1972) *The International Economy and Monetary Movements in France, 1493–1725*, Cambridge, MA: Harvard University Press.

Sudo, Y. (1962) *Sodai keizaishi kenkyu* (An economic history of Song period), pp. 73–138.

Takehiko Ohkura and Hiroshi Shimbo (1978) 'The Tokugawa Monetary Policy in the Eighteenth and Nineteenth Centuries', *Explorations in Economic History*, 15: 101–124.

Tang Qingzeng (1975) *Zhongguo Shanggu jingji sixiangshi* (A history of Ancient Chinese economic thought), Guting bookstore.

Tawney, R. H. (1966) *Land and Labour in China*, Boston, MA: Beacon Press.

Wang Xiaotong (1965) *Zhongguo shangyeshi* (Chinese business history), Taipei: Commercial Press.

Wang, Yeh-chien (1973) *Land Taxation in Imperial China, 1750–1911*, Cambridge, MA: Harvard University Press.

Wang Zhirui (1964) *Song Yuan jingji shi* (A history of the Song and Yuan periods), Taipei: Commercial Press.

Watanabe Xinichiro (1974) *Han Rokucho ki ni okeru dai tochi soyiu to keie* (The great land ownership in Han and Six dynasties), *Toyoshi kenkyu*, 33(1); 33(2).

Weber, M. (1951) *The Religion of China*, New York: Free Press.

Wei Yuan (1967) *Shengwu ji* (Chinese military history), reprint, Taipei: Wenhai Publisher.

Williamson, J. G. (1965) 'Regional Inequality and the Process of National Development: A Description of the Patterns', *Economic Development and Cultural Change*, 13: 3–45.

Wittfogel, K. A. (1957) *Oriental Despotism: A Comparative Study of Total Power*, New Haven, CT: Yale University Press.

Wong, R. B. (1997) *China Transformed: Historical Change and Limits of European Experience*, Ithaca, NY: Cornell University Press.

Wu Wenhui (1947) *Zhongguo tudi wenti jiqi duice* (China's land problem and its solutions), Shanghai: Commercial Press.

Yang, L. (1970) 'The Chinese Imperial Government's Rule over Urban Merchant', *Ch'inghua hsuehpao* (Tsing Hua Journal), 8(1–2): 186–209.

Yu Yingshi (1987) *Zhongguo jinshi zhongjiao lunli yu shangren jingshen* (Religious ethic and the merchant spirit of Modern China), Taipei: Lianjing.

Zhu Zuyan (1999) *Hanyu chengyu cihai* (Chinese idioms), Wuhan: Wuhan Press.

2

THE LATE QING DYNASTY TO THE EARLY REPUBLIC OF CHINA

A period of great institutional transformation[1]

Kenneth S. Chan

In the period from the late Qing dynasty until the Republic of China, a far-reaching transformation in the social institutions of China took place. The traditional institutions and social values in the late Qing dynasty were unable to bring China out from the Malthusian trap into modern economic growth. Above all, it was the wars with – and defeats from – the imperialist nations that had brought China to this great institutional transformation. This chapter summarizes China's response to the changing external environment in the Qing dynasty (the Republic of China) which was then under highly rigid and centralized (highly *de*centralized) institutions. Economic progress was observed in the early period of the Republic although, as the nation was fragmented, it never reached its full potential.

Introduction

During the transition from the Tang to the Song dynasty in China, a major transformation of the social institution had taken place, in which China moved from a highly aristocratic society to a more populist society.[2] The social values, such as cultural norms, social customs, and beliefs, also went through a sea change. However, an even more significant institutional transformation in China occurred in the period from late Qing to the Republic of China. This transformation had much more far-reaching implications than the one during the Tang–Song transition. The economic and social impact of the Qing–Republic institutional transformation will be the main focus of this chapter.

This chapter is organized as follows. Section 1 summarizes some relevant theoretical economic models from the literature together with their predictions. By and large, these predictions receive support from the historical events. Section 2 describes the changing external environment and the economy in the Qing dynasty, governed under a highly centralized institution. Section 3 describes those in the Republic of China period when China was under a highly decentralized institution. Economic progress was observed in the period of the Republic, although it never reached its full potential, as the nation was fragmented (Rawski 1989). Section 4 sketches a version of the Malthusian and modern growth model that is relevant for the Chinese economy in this period. Section 5 concludes that it took major wars and defeats to undermine China from the traditional institutions which would have stalled China's modern development.

1 Statement of hypothesis from the literature

The following topics from the literature are relevant for later discussions.

1.1 Institution

North argued that institutions are the rules of the game that provide incentives and constraints for human interactions in a society. This is why institutions are so important for economic development. North also noted that institutions are persistent or slow to change. To explain the importance of institutions for development and their persistency, Acemoglu and Robinson (2012) made a distinction between economic and political institutions. Economic institutions are where economic policies are made, while political institutions are where political power is distributed. They argue that the political institution chooses and upholds economic institutions based not only on their efficiency and ideology, but also on their distributional consequences for the powerful interests or elites, who are at the core of the political institution and stand to reap benefits. The interplay between economic gains and political power helps to safeguard the persistency of the institution. Therefore an institution can only be changed by unanticipated shocks (such as wars and natural calamities) which redistribute the political power of the interest groups or elites. Hence, their theory predicts that:

> *Prediction 1:* It takes unanticipated shocks, such as wars and natural calamities, to disrupt the structure of the interest groups and eventually bring changes to the institutions.

1.2 The distinction between formal and informal institutions

A formal institution governs through a well-structured organization and is usually impersonal and rule based. An informal institution governs through relations/network within the community, based on shared social values and norms (Williamson 2000).[3] China's informal institution, based on the Confucian communitarian ethos, was vital in governing China because of its huge land mass and population.[4] Similar to the formal institutions, the informal institutions are also persistent. There are also interest groups that benefit from the existing informal institutions. Hence, *Prediction 1* also applies to the case of informal institutions.

1.3 Centralized versus decentralized formal institutions

Decentralization is defined as the devolution of political power to the local level.[5] There are both merits and demerits of decentralization for industrialization in developing economies. Local governments are better managers and more accountable to local needs because they are better informed about local conditions. Decentralization also introduces more intergovernmental competition and provides institutional checks and balances. A strong central government, on the other hand, can better exploit the economies of scale in enforcing law and order, in protecting property rights, and in providing national public goods than can local governments. It can coordinate different jurisdictions more effectively than letting local governments do so among them. More importantly, decentralized local governments can be easily captured by local powerful elites and local services tend to favor them at the expense of non-elites. On the other hand, provision from a centralized authority can prevent elites from hijacking local services.

The meritorious impact on the per-capita GDP, whether it is from a decentralized or centralized system, must eventually face diminishing returns. Hence, there should be a middle ground which offers the optimal merits from both systems. A centralized authority that provides law and order can break up the initial state of Hobbesian anarchy, foster the development of the economy and raise the per-capita GDP. But this can be short-lived. An overly centralized and rigid institution will strangle the economy, causing a fall in the per-capita GDP. In Figure 2.1, moving rightwards along the horizontal axis indicates an increase in the centralization of authority.[6] Point M on the inverted U-shaped curve illustrates the optimal degree of centralization which offers the highest per-capita GDP. The above discussion predicts the following:

> *Prediction 2:* A highly centralized or a highly decentralized institution will eventually lower the level of per-capita GDP of the economy.

1.4 Taste for dominance

North (1984: 260) raised the question: why dictators, with all their authority, did not adopt economic policies that were conducive to economic growth of their subjects from which they could increase their appropriation? North suggested that dictators may not adopt productive economic policies because they do not want their dominance to be threatened by those policies. Since a highly centralized economy is less threatening, dictators face a trade-off between their own dominance/authority and the output of the economy from which they can appropriate (the trade-off frontier MCB in Figure 2.1).

Note that the emperor's utility is driven by more than economic motives. Chinese emperors, bureaucrats, and political elites obtain satisfaction from being on the top of the strong hierarchical structure of the society and from the submissive behavior of their subjects. In terms of Maslow's hierarchy of needs, higher order needs are self-esteem and status. And, for the emperor, it is power, authority, and glory. For simplicity, we will call this "the preference for dominance." The Confucian hierarchical system required each level to develop submissive behavior toward the level above. The emperor and elites derived much pleasure and satisfaction from dominating the inferior and the supreme social status as a result of the dominance.[7]

Commercial and innovative activities erode the stability of the society and hence threaten the dominance of the emperor. The creative destruction of innovative activities, as Schumpeter put it, would face much opposition from the entrenched elites who stand to lose from those activities

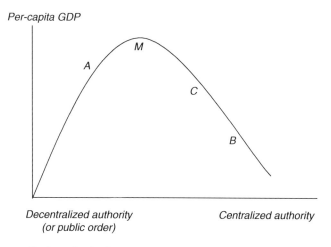

Figure 2.1 The centralization of authority

(Parente and Prescott 2002). It also threatens the dominance of the emperor. Commercial activities, with their ups and downs, would have the same effects as innovative activities. Therefore, during peace time, the emperor prefers to maintain his dominance rather than more appropriable income from his subject. The emperor may pick a point such as point B in Figure 2.1. When faced with an unstable environment, such as the threat of war from other nations or domestic unrest, a more prosperous economy would help the emperor to guard his country. The emperor would also be more conciliatory with domestic groups to win their support. He would choose higher income and subdue his dominance (Chan 2008), Chan and Laffargue (2012a, b), such as point C or M in Figure 2.1. The above discussion narrows down *Prediction 1* to a more specific prediction:

> *Prediction 3:* An unstable environment, such as war or domestic unrests, provides an important impetus for economic reform, promoting technological innovations and commercial activities.

Centralized institutions are prone to rigidity, which makes them incapable of adapting to the ever-changing environment. By mid-Qing, many rules and regulations in the Qing government were outdated and unable to match the modern needs of society. With this mismatch, corruption crept in and undermined the effectiveness of the institution. Many scholars believe it was the institutional rigidity, as a result of the centralized authority, that had led to the deterioration of the Qing institution.[8] This deterioration would also loosen the grip of centralized authority.

Table 2.1 presents the chronological events from Qing dynasty to the period of the Republic of China. Sections below will follow the chronological order in Table 2.1.

2 The Qing dynasty (1644–1911)

In the Qing dynasty, China, with a majority of Han nationality, was ruled by an alien nationality, the Manchus. Among all the Qing emperors, the first four, Shunzhi, Kangxi, Yongzheng, and Qianlong were extremely capable rulers. Under their rule, the empire acquired a huge land mass and won most of the battles against the nomads from the north and northwest regions of present day China.

The Qing court under Emperor Kangxi stopped the Russians from advancing into western Mongolia and reached a settlement with them in the Treaty of Nerchinsk in 1689. Emperors Kangxi and Qianlong both fought hard-won battles with Dzungar, a powerful empire in the northwestern part of China and eventually eliminated them. In the south, battles were fought with the Burmese, the Yao and Miao ethnic groups in the southwest, the Nepalese, and the Qing army made incursions into Tibet, Vietnam, and Taiwan. The victories won the Qing dynasty an extended period of peace – although this was both good and bad for the country. It allowed the country to prosper under a firmly centralized institution. However, the peace, stability, and autonomy enjoyed at the county level had allowed the interest groups to grow unabated. It also made the Qing government complacent and the economy stagnated, facing few external challenges until the late Qing period when the country woke up to European and Japanese aggression. Ironically, the extended period of peace laid the seed for the empire's own destruction.

The Qing government, similar to the Ming government before, was highly centralized and inward-looking. Without outside threats from early to mid-Qing, the emperor looked inwards and increased his domination at home.[9] The Qing court strengthened its rule by sidelining the Censorate, a traditional agency in Chinese imperial polity that spoke out against abuses of

Table 2.1 Chronological events from Qing dynasty to the period of the Republic of China

Year	Important events	Comments
1644	Fall of the Ming empire and the beginning of the Qing dynasty	Under Emperor Shunzhi
1662		Succeeded by Emperor Kangxi
1673–1681	Revolt of three feudatories in southern China	
1683	Annexed Taiwan	
1684	Lifting of the sea ban; but maintained the control of foreign trade	
1689	Treaty of Nerchinsk with Russia	
1720	Occupied Lhasa, Tibet	
1723		Succeeded by Emperor Yongzheng
1736		Succeeded by Emperor Qianlong The period from Kangxi to Qianlong was the height of the Qing dynasty
1750–1760	Won major battle war with Dzungar, an empire in the present-day Xinjiang area	
1757	Restricted foreign trade with European nations to the city of Canton	
1793	Lord Macartney asked Qianlong to ease restrictions on trade with Britain, but was refused	
1796–1804	White Lotus Rebellion	Under Emperor Jiaqing
1800–1820	Successive floods in Northern China	
1821		Under Emperor Daoguang
1839–1842	First Opium War with Britain	Treaty of Nanking; 27 million taels of silver for the indemnity; ceded Hong Kong to Britain; opened five seaports to trade
1850–1864	Taiping Rebellion; 20 million people died. Qing government decentralized its power, de facto	Under Emperor Xianfeng
1856–1860	Second Opium War with Britain, France, and Russia	Treaty of Tianjin and Treaty of Peking; Opened 11 more ports, ceded Kowloon to Britain
1861–1895	Self-Strengthening Movement (*Yangmu*) sought end after the disastrous defeat of China's modern Beiyang fleets by the Japanese	Under the short-lived Emperor Tongzhi, followed by Emperor Guangxu and Empress Dowager Cixi
1871–1897	War with Japan, Russia, France, and Britain	Indemnity of 5 million taels to Russia; 200 million taels to Japan; ceded Ryukyu Islands and Taiwan to Japan
1898	The Hundred Days' Reform was initiated by the young Emperor Guangxu, which were ended by conservative opponents led by Empress Dowager Cixi. Many reformers left the country	
1898	The Boxer Rebellion highlighted hostility to foreigners and domestic political frustration. The movement targeted foreign concessions and missionaries in China	
1900	European powers and Japan (the Eight-Nation Alliance) jointly declared war on China	450 million taels indemnity

(Continued)

Table 2.1 (Continued)

Year	Important events	Comments
1908	After the defeat, Cixi and Guangxu initiated a more comprehensive reform, which ended with their death in 1908	
1911	The Chinese (Xinhai) Revolution: Guangzhou Uprising followed by the Wuchang Uprising	The Qing dynasty was overthrown in less than a year
1912	Birth of the Republic of China under the leadership of Sun Yat-sen on January 1; the last Qing emperor, Puyi, abdicated. Soon after, Yuan Shikai was elected provisional president of the Republic of China	
1914–1918	World War I, followed by a postwar recession from 1921–1922	
1915–1916	Yuan Shikai abolished the national and provincial assemblies, and declared himself to be the emperor in 1915. He died in 1916	
1917	General Zhang Xun attempted another restoration of the monarchy with Puyi as the emperor, but failed shortly after a brief war with the nationalist government	
1919	The May Fourth Movement started as a response to the terms imposed on China by the Treaty of Versailles at the end of World War I	
1920	The warlord era: Sun Yat-sen led a northern expedition to unite the fragmented country until his death in 1925. Chiang Kai-shek took control over the Nationalist Party (the Kuomintang) and the Chinese government. The nationalist government under Chiang Kai-shek carried on with the northern expedition against the warlords	
1927	The Communist Party of China was founded in 1921. Chiang Kai-shek began his campaign against the Communists. The Communists led by Mao started the long march to Yan'an in 1927 and established a guerrilla base	
1931–1937	Skirmish with the Japanese intensified	
July 1937	Sino-Japanese war started	
1945	Japan surrenders. World War II ended. The civil war between Communist Party under Mao and the nationalist party under Chiang restarted	
1949	The People's Republic of China was founded after the defeat of the nationalist government	

imperial power. The office of the Prime Minster was dispensed (as in the Ming Dynasty), the collection of tax revenue was centralized (Myers and Wang 2002: 604). Literary inquisition was imposed to intimidate the Han intellectuals from speaking their minds. Qianlong even installed a community-based system of law enforcement and civil control known as the *Baojia* system of punishment to control his subjects.[10]

Despite its small government size, the Qing court had an elaborate system of indirect checks and balances installed to ensure effective control over officials in the field. This included duplicated efforts by local officers as a means of monitoring one another's compliance to central directives; supervision of military officials over their civil counterparts; regular rotation of officials; the avoidance of posting field officers in their home districts; supervision of Han officials by Manchu or Mongol officials and vice versa (Rowe 2009). By and large, this indirect control method was effective in early Qing.

2.1 Preference for dominance

The preference for dominance over economic benefits (see section 1.4) was clearly observed from the behavior of the earlier emperors. Mote (1999: 906) wrote that Yongzheng was more concerned with retaining and enhancing his authority than anything else. As for Qianlong, he did not care about efficiency as much as encroachments on his imperial dignity.[11] Even after the defeat of the first Opium War in 1839, the emperor Daoguang was more concerned with his own dignity than the unequal terms and war indemnities in the treaty. He wanted the English officials kneeling down in front of him, instead of sitting down at the table.

2.2 Excessive control over merchants activities in early Qing

During the height of the authority of the Qing dynasty and in the absence of any external threats, merchants' activities were carefully controlled; evidence that supports *Prediction 3* in section 1. Unlike farmers, who were tied to their land, merchants traveled around. And monitoring the activities of the traveling merchants was costly. Farmers' outputs and activities were easy to monitor and hence easier to control. Kangxi refused the merchants' requests to open new mines which hired a huge labor force (Myers and Wang 2002: 609).

Emperor Yongzheng was worried that the merchants could pose a threat of disorder to the stable agrarian economy. He reckoned that local officials could conspire with the merchants, strengthen their power and threaten the emperor's dominance. To control the growth of the merchants, he imposed a quota of licenses for merchants to operate in the marketplace and prevented their excessive growth in 1733. Only the upright and law-abiding merchants were eligible for the licenses. This was done at the expense of the tax revenue that the Qing court received from commercial activities. In the year 1737, the government collected from merchants 1.9 million tael of silver of tax. This amount was about 5.4 percent of the total tax revenue of the central government. And in 1954, the government collected from merchants 5.6 million tael of silver. This was about 13.1 percent of the total government tax revenue (Myers and Wang 2002: 606). The tax revenue from commercial activities was not insignificant. Yet the Qing government continued to shun commercial activities, in spite of the lucrative tax revenue they generated for the Qing court. Emperor Qianlong went even further by introducing a sliding scale of licensing fees to discourage commercial activities in 1758.

After the defeat in the first Opium War, the Qing court was forced to open up to trade with foreign powers.[12] This led to an accelerated growth of the merchant class and commerce in the coastal areas in late Qing.

2.3 The First Opium War (1839–1842)

The first Opium War was partly triggered by trade control in early Qing. To maintain the emperor's dominance at home, strict control of foreign influences brought about by trade was deemed necessary. Emperor Kangxi restricted trade to a few easily controlled coastal ports. In 1682, he established the *Shanghang*, a semi-private monopoly, to handle foreign trade.

In 1757, under Qianlong, only Guangdong, tucked in the far south away from Beijing's control, was allowed to trade with foreigners. Foreigners were only allowed to settle in designated quarters, for fear that their lifestyles and ideas could contaminate and threaten the dominance of the emperor. Guangdong stayed far from the mainstream of Chinese polity.

To ban the consumption of opium, the government could have put up a high consumption tax as the first-best solution. That was difficult, as the court was losing control of its front-line officers to enforce its orders in mid and late Qing. Moreover, front-line officers and local gentry were often actively involved in the lucrative opium trade and the consumption of opium. The second-best solution was to ban the import of opium. But banning imports encouraged smuggling, illegal domestic production of opium and might invite war with Great Britain to reopen trade, which was what eventually happened.

After China's defeat in the first Opium War, the treaty of Nanjing was signed. As a result, five ports were forced to open to foreign trade and Hong Kong was ceded to Great Britain, among other indemnities.

2.4 The Taiping Rebellion (1850–1864)

The Taiping Rebellion grew out of the uprisings from the landless peasants under the worsening famine in Guangxi and Guangdong provinces. The cult leader Hong Xiuquan led the rebellion under the banner of Christianity. Motivated by the Christian ideology of peace and brotherhood, the Taiping army fought hard. General Zheng Guofan was appointed to suppress the rebellion. Zheng trained a traditional army from Hunan and Hubei. It was not until 1864 that the Qing army successfully crushed the revolt with a death count of twenty to thirty million.

The causes of the rebellion

The population in the Qing dynasty doubled by mid-Qing (see Table 2.3, Maddison's data). The sharp rise in population was the result of many factors. First, peace and prosperity in the beginning of the Qing dynasty led to a rise in the fertility of the population. The farm taxes were low. Emperor Kangxi's tax policy, that there would be no head tax for the new born, favored fertility. Second, the American sweet potato, first introduced in 1570s, is particularly rich in nutritional value. Its use spread quickly throughout China between 1700 and 1800, becoming the third most important source of food in the entire country after rice and wheat.

Due to the rapid growth of population, there was insufficient farmland for everyone. A large pool of landless peasants was amassed. Instead of developing farm land reclamation or the commercial sector to absorb the excess population, the Qing government did very little. The rigidity of the Qing institution could be blamed for this. Worse still, since it was difficult to locate the landless peasants and to control their activities, they were dismissed by the Qing court as landless rebels (Zhang 2012: 65–69).

To fund the army against the rebels, the Qing government had to raise tax revenue from the commercial sectors. Out of necessity, the longstanding, rigid, outdated anti-commerce policy was finally broken up.

After the Taiping Rebellion was put down, the social status of the Han people rose. Oppression of the Han by the Manchus was loosened up. The political power of the regional governments also grew at the expense of the central government. This led to the expansion of the commercial sector and prosperity in the late Qing.

2.5 The Second Opium War (1856–1860) and the Boxer Rebellion (1898)

The rise of colonialism had led more European powers to follow the British footsteps and to share the spoils. After the renegotiation of the Treaty of Nanjing failed to bear fruit, the Second Opium War lasted from 1856–1860, with China against Britain, France, and Russia. The crushing defeat of the Qing army led to the Treaties of Tianjin and Beijing. China faced another invasion from the European powers and Japan in 1871–1897, conceding even more territories (including the Ryukyu Islands and Taiwan to Japan, China's northeastern territories to Russia, and coastal ports to other Imperial Powers) and war indemnities.

The Boxer Rebellion in 1898 was a backlash of hostility to foreigners and domestic political frustration. The movement targeted foreigners and missionaries in China. The German ambassador was murdered by the Boxer rebels. The year after the event, the Eight-Nation Alliance declared war on China. With another humiliating defeat and the burning-down of the Summer Palace in Beijing, Empress Dowager Cixi finally accepted the peace terms with scores of concessional demands and indemnities. About 30 percent of the Qing government's spending went into paying the indemnities during the entire period of the 1890s (see Li 2003: 9).

2.6 Reforms in the late Qing

As previously discussed in *Prediction 3* in section 1, wars, together with a series of humiliating defeats, give impetus for reforms. There were three modernization reforms in the late Qing. The first one was the Self-Strengthening Reform Movement (*Yangmu yundong*) from 1861–1895. This reform movement was initiated by the leading governing officer, Zheng Guofan and his colleague and former student Li Hongzhang. They set out to modernize the institution, the army and the navy, and sent students abroad to learn Western sciences and technologies. The reform worked within the fundamental imperial institutional framework of the time. But the modernized yet inexperienced Beiyang fleets were completely annihilated by the Japanese in the first Sino-Japanese War. This defeat gave the opposition of the Self-Strengthening Movement plenty of reasons to stall the reform.

The second reform movement, called the Hundred Days' Reform, was initiated by Emperor Guangxu and his cabinet in 1898. The emperor initiated a more comprehensive reform than the preceding Self-Strengthening Movement in which new laws were put in place and some old rules were abolished; selection of bureaucrats by examination only from old Confucian classics was downplayed; the education curriculum was modernized; private enterprises were encouraged, and so on. However, due to opposition from entrenched interests, the reform movement only lasted a hundred days. Empress dowager Cixi, who controlled the Qing court, called off the emperor's reform and put the emperor under house arrest.

The third reform movement came after China's humiliating defeat by the Eight-Nation Alliance in 1900. Massive public discontent forced Cixi and Guangxu to initiate the dynasty's "New Policy," which included a blueprint for a constitutional monarchy and were, by far, the most progressive reform agenda. But the reform ended with their deaths in 1908.[13]

In spite of the failed reforms, the top-down control from the Qing court was loosened up by the reform attempts. They had made a small step towards decentralization in the late Qing. More importantly, the failed reforms nonetheless inspired the Chinese people to move towards modernization and a new set of social values. The economy also benefited from the loosened controls.

After years of stagnation, the Chinese economy began to pick up pace in the late Qing (Rosenthal and Wong 2011). From the data in Table 2.3, the per-capita GDP in international dollars rose from the bottom at $530 in 1870 (around the time of the Self-Strengthening Movement) to $545 in 1900, near the end of the Qing dynasty. The rebound in real wage away from the subsistence level in Figure 2.3 also confirms this turning point.[14] Lin (1983) documented the burgeoning commercial activities in late Qing. Businesses were organized and conducted in the traditional relationship-based manner, while the embryonic industrial sectors were headed by the bureaucrats. Lin (1983) argued that the slow change in the formal and informal institutions in late Qing had held back further industrial development. Corruption weakened the government-led industrialization. Moreover, the traditional relationship-based economy was upheld by local interests and the traditional Confucian values of the people, making it impossible for a modern rule-based market economy to take shape.[15]

2.7 Institutional rigidity and the fiscal revenue in the Qing dynasty

As mentioned in section 1, the highly centralized political institution became too rigid to cope with the changing economic environment. When the political institution and its policies were not in line with economic reality, corruption grew and eventually undermined that institution. In the literature, Rankin *et al.* (1986: 53) commented on the highly centralized institution in the Qing dynasty, "The Qing government structure was riddled with flaws, but collapse came not so much from internal bureaucratic inadequacy or court degeneracy as from failure to adjust to societal developments." Perkins (1967: 478) commented, "The government can play an important role in both areas [technologies and investments]…The failures of the Qing government of the nineteenth-century China were in these areas. China's retarded industrialization was more a result of sins of omission than of commission."

The deterioration of the Qing institution had started around the mid-Qing, under Emperor Qianlong. Corruption scandals became a regular occurrence. There was the famous guardsman Heshen's corruption case during Qianlong – he had accumulated wealth equivalent to several years' expenses of the Qing government. Ni and Van (2006) estimated corruption to be about 22 percent of the agricultural output in 1873.

The most important impact of institutional rigidity in the Qing dynasty is the declining revenue from state tax over time (see Sng 2010; Li 2003). The fiscal position in the early Qing was very healthy (Li 2003) but gradually deteriorated around mid-Qing long before the arrival of European colonialism. Most of the tax revenue was from land taxes. Sng (2010) shows that the increase in population and migration had led to an increase in agency cost (monitoring cost) in tax collection which had also led to rising corruption. The decline in state revenue, in sharp contrast with that of Britain during the same period, as shown by Sng, is reproduced in Figure 2.2. Sng's study also demonstrates that the rigid Qing institution could not cope with the changing economic environment, in particular, with the massive expansion in population and migration.

The Qing government did not adjust the rigid tax system on a regular basis. At the beginning of the nineteenth century, as the institution was loosening its grip, China's economy was fueled by the commercialization of agricultural production and limited expansions in foreign trade. But the rigid institution did not allow room for the reform of commercial tax, which could have become a major financial source for the Qing government. The reform was only taken seriously and carried out in the late Qing when the fiscal position had deteriorated substantially. The Qing court could have financed its fiscal shortfalls and modernized its economy and the army much sooner, by taxing the commercial sector and setting tariffs to international trade activities. The decline in state revenue is evidence of institutional rigidity.

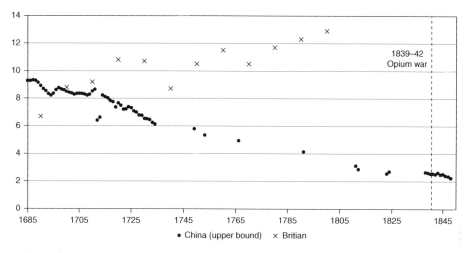

Figure 2.2 The tax-to-GDP ratio: China and Britain (%)

Source: Sng (2010, figure 7)

3 The Republic of China (1911–1949)

Inspired by Sun Yat-sen's ideal of a democratic republic and frustrated by the Qing court's endless defeats and inability to reform, the Chinese people plotted to overthrow the Qing imperial government. The Wuchang Uprising, followed spontaneously by other uprisings, began on October 10, 1911. The Qing government was brought down quickly.[16] The Republic of China was formed on March 12, 1912 with Sun Yat-sen, the founder of the Republic of China, as president.

Soon after, Sun was forced to turn the government over to Yuan Shikai, commander of the mighty Beiyang army. Yuan eventually proceeded to abolish the national and provincial assemblies. In 1915, he declared himself emperor of China. Faced with fierce opposition from the public and possible mutiny from his army, Yuan abdicated in 1916, and died shortly after. There was another futile attempt by Zhang Xun, Yuan's former officer, to restore the monarchy. The failed restoration marked the beginning of the warlord era.

In 1919, the May Fourth Movement began as a response to the terms imposed on China by the Treaty of Versailles at the end of World War I, but quickly became a social movement targeting the domestic situation in China. The neo-Confucian values were questioned, many of which were overhauled by intellectuals. Foreign liberal ideas and Marxism were accepted into the mainstream.

In the 1920s, Sun Yat-sen built a military base with a well-trained army in Guangdong Province in the south. He set out to reunite the fragmented nation with his army. At the first general meeting of the Nationalist party in 1925, the Communist Party was invited to join. After Sun's death in 1925, one of his commanders, Chiang Kai-shek, seized control of the Kuomintang (the Nationalist Party, or KMT). Chiang started a northern military campaign and succeeded in bringing most of the warlords in the southern and central part of China under his rule. Chiang began to make peace with the warlords in the North and turned his attention to the Chinese Communist Party. He relentlessly fought and chased the Communist armies and its leaders from their bases. The Communists led by Mao Zedong embarked on the famous Long March across China in 1934 to establish a guerrilla base in Yanan, in the northwestern part of China.

In 1937, the Sino-Japanese war broke out. For fear of mutiny among his army officers, Chiang agreed to join forces with the communists under Mao, to fight the Japanese. For eight years, the Chinese people fought against Japanese aggression. Then in 1939, World War II started and Japan eventually surrendered after the US dropped the two atomic bombs on Japan, which ended World War II.

3.1 Economic performance under the Republic of China up to the Sino-Japanese War (1911–1937)

Some historians portrayed the Republic of China as stagnated, chaotic, semi-feudal, and semi-colonial. The lack of data for in-depth research may be the reason for this view. In fact, the opposite is true. The economy under the Republic of China was very dynamic, despite political and social chaos.

There are a few estimates of the performance of the economy during the early period of the Republic of China. They all range from small positive per-capita GDP growth to modest growth of about 1.2 percent per annum. Chang's calculation (1969) was broken down into different periods for a more accurate picture. The period of 1920–1922 was omitted because of the post-World War I worldwide recession. Table 2.2 summarizes the statistics from key studies.

From the summary in Table 2.2, the economy had performed reasonably well. In what follows, I will summarize from the literature the substantial qualitative changes that occurred in the Chinese economy.

The agricultural sector: growth in this sector was small compared to others, but nonetheless sufficient to feed the population growth during that period, which is close to 1 percent per annum. Estimates by Liu and Yeh (1965) and Rawski (1989) are about 0.8 percent and 1.4–1.7 percent respectively. There was evidence of increase in productivity as farm wages rose slightly in this period.

The industrial and transportation sectors: despite their small sizes, they were the fastest growing sectors in the Chinese economy, at 2 percent per year (Perkins 1975: 117). The most successful cotton and textile industries had benefited from the adoption of Western technologies. A modern form of transportation by railways and steamships began to take shape.

The financial sector: commercial banking and a modern financial market began to flourish in Shanghai and in other coastal cities, replacing the old traditional financial system (the *qian-zhuang*). A modern monetary system, based on the banking system of credits, checks, and banknotes, replaced the traditional silver and copper currencies.

Modern industries appeared side by side with the traditional industries. Both the modern and the traditional industries competed vigorously, specializing in a variety of products. As distinct from the Qing dynasty, the transfer of foreign technologies in the period under the Republic of China was unabated. Business transactions were done both in the traditional method of relationship-based transactions (*guanxi*) and legal contracts. The fusion of foreign technologies and indigenous methods was widely observed. These economic activities were remarkably similar to that in the Meiji period in Japan (Rawski 1989). They were evidence of a robust embryonic capitalist economy.

3.2 Institutional changes in the period of the Republic of China

The overthrow of the Qing dynasty was relatively quick and spontaneous. Surprisingly, the 1911 revolution was completed in half a year. Sun's under-trained militias came mainly from the intellectuals, some military officials and soldiers, bandits, and underground rebels of all factions. It was a revolution supported neither by the peasants nor the workers. The Qing government essentially crumbled from inside, from loss of legitimacy to govern.

Table 2.2 Summary of key statistics in the Chinese economy (1911–1936)

Authors	Key findings				
Chang (1969)	Average annual industrial growth rates in sub-periods (%)				
	1912–1949	1912–1936	1912–1920	1923–1936	1936–1942
	5.6	9.4	13.4	8.7	4.5
Feuerwerker (1977)	Survey of empirical findings				
	Output grew only slowly; negligible increase in GDP per capita; sporadic rapid industrial growth				
	Impact of foreign colonialism and social instability were also taken into consideration				
Perkins (1969, 1975); Liu and Yeh (1965)	From World War I to 1937: 1.4% average annual GDP growth				
	Output per capita rose by less than 10% during interwar decades				
	Using 1914 as base year, GDP (GDP per capita) in 1936 increased by 20–26% (3–14%)				
Rawski (1989)	A comprehensive study on all sectors				
	From 1914/18 to 1931/36:				
	1.8–2.0% average annual real GDP growth rate				
	1.2% average annual real GDP per-capita growth rate				
	Coastal regions grow much faster				
	1914/18=100	1931/36	1946	1949	1952
	Total real output	140	132	119	166
	Real output per capita	122.8	110.6	97.4	145.3
Ma (2008)	Per-capita net-domestic-product growth rate between 1914–1918 and 1931–1936 (%):				
			Jiang–Zhe Provinces	Lower Yangzi Macro-Region	Japan
	China				
	0.53		1.0	1.1	1.4

Many local interests left behind from the overthrown Qing dynasty continued to survive. Warlords sprang up all over China to take over the spoils from the Qing dynasty. The formal institution during this period was weak and decentralized.

It is noteworthy that, once consolidated, these warlords behaved more like the stationary bandits than the revolving bandits, a distinction made by Olson (2000). Stationary bandits, as opposed to the revolving bandits who had very short-sighted goals, would not over-appropriate the commoners who might either out-migrate, which would produce less prosperity, or become political insurgents. Unlike the short-sighted revolving bandits, stationary bandits might even invest in more long-term public goods, to improve the economic well-being of their subjects, so as to improve their optimal appropriation. Warlords competed with each another. To strengthen their own position against other warlords, they promoted economic development. In fact, the prosperity of the northeastern coastal region and trade had supported the Beiyang army held by Yuan Shikai. The sound economic foundation of Guangdong province and foreign trade helped to fund the northern expedition by Sun Yat-sen against the warlords.

The national government initiated industries, but the building of infrastructure was limited by lack of revenue from taxation. The national government revenue and expenditure was small, around 2–3 percent of GDP from 1932 to 1936 (Rawski 1989: 15). Out of the national expenditure, around 40 percent went to the military with little left over for economic development. Most of the development was accomplished by the private sectors and foreign firms. Fragmentation of the country also blocked the mobility of trade and people across different regions. The territorial instability of a fragmented China raised the cost of investment. Consequently, the Chinese economy had not reached its full potential.

Compared with the highly centralized institution in the early Qing dynasty, the formal institution in the period of the Republic of China was highly decentralized, as represented by point A in Figure 2.1.[17]

3.3 The May Fourth Movement

While China's formal institutions had lost their grip, the revolution in the informal institutions forged on. The change in social values continued to gain momentum, as exemplified by the May Fourth Movement in 1919. Two facts are noteworthy. First, similar to the case of the formal institutions, the change in China's social values was a response to external threats, as predicted. Second, the change in social values was quite substantial. Major changes in social values include: a free, practical style of writing replaced the classical literary style; the liberation of women and freedom to marry; individual freedoms and rights were upheld; a rise in the social status of merchants; a positive attitude towards science and technology; an open mind towards foreign ideologies such as democracy and communism. Some old Confucian rituals, the imperial hierarchical structure of the society, as well as the loyalty between employers and employees, were downplayed, if not outright discarded. However, the collectivist ethics, relationship to family, respect to elders and friends, basic civic ethics, the value of education, work ethics, and frugality had remained intact. China was moving towards liberalism and away from social conformity. It was more of a streamlining process than complete destruction of the neo-Confucian value system. It is perhaps safe to conclude over half of the old values has been either eliminated or modified to fit the modern society. There is no denying that reform in the informal institutions was earth-shaking.[18]

The tug between the new and the old values continued throughout the entire period of the Republic. The periodic revival of the old values can be seen in the debates at that time over whether China should be governed by a constitutional monarchy, a democratic president, or the Communist Party. But the wave of new social values got the upper hand. It was the strong public opposition to government by monarchy that had led to the failure of Yuan Shikai to reestablish a monarchy.

3.4 The Communist Revolution (1945–1949)

Chiang Kai-shek had transformed Sun Yat-sen's revolutionary movement and the democratic ideals of the Three People's Principles into a military–authoritarian regime. The movement's early revolutionary commitments were eroded by factionalism and corruption. After the surrender of the Japanese in 1945, the war between the KMT under Chiang and the Communists under Mao, resumed. The handover process of Chinese territories and assets from the Japanese to the KMT government led to a scramble among KMT officials and the military to lay claim to enemy properties. Carpetbagging KMT officials were seen everywhere. The KMT government was riddled with incompetence and corruption. Worse still, the incapable postwar government and war with the Communists brought in huge fiscal deficits. The KMT government had to resort to inflationary finance. Inflation rose two thousand times between 1937 and 1949 (Pepper 1986: 741). After four years of war, the Communists finally defeated the KMT. The People's Republic of China was born in 1949.

4 Relevant growth models

The Industrial Revolution in Europe occurred around the time of the mid-Qing. Why didn't a similar industrial revolution occur in China? To address that question is beyond the remit of this chapter. But there are a few noteworthy points related to this question. First, the difference in institutions between China and Europe is important. The Industrial Revolution in Britain was an outgrowth of the institutional changes brought about by the Civil War in England and the Glorious Revolution of 1688. Second, China's internal markets were reasonably competitive and sophisticated (Myers and Wang 2002). But this is insufficient for industrial development, which requires an appropriate set of institutions (Acemoglu and Robinson 2012). As noted by Perkins (1967: 478), "the Qing officers not only understood commerce, but were deeply involved in it themselves ... The more significant question, however, is whether a reasonably sophisticated commercial system leads readily into industrialization. The answer, of course, is that it does not... For the late-developing countries – that is every nation except England – the government can play an important role in both areas [technologies and investments]." Market growth in Qing was therefore an "extensive" type of growth with little technological progress. And, third, Great Britain could expand exceptionally fast from the availability of a cheap source of coal near its manufacturing centers, and raw materials from its colonies, in ways that China and others could not (Pomeranz 2000).

The data series compiled by Maddison in Table 2.3 illustrates the great divergence between China and Europe.[19] The divergence between China and Europe occurred around the late 1700s to early 1800s. But the per-capita GDP in China reached its height in the Song dynasty, stayed flat in the Ming and early Qing dynasties, and started its decline from Mid-Qing until fifty years before the end of the Qing dynasty. It rose steadily again into the dawn of the Republic, though it never saw the same income level as that in the Song dynasty. Recent important studies on real wage trends in China and Europe by Allen *et al.* (2011: figure 5) and Baten *et al.* (2010: figure 1) also find a declining trend in real wage, which remains close to the subsistence level. The real wage in China fell below subsistence between the years from 1819 to 1880. Using a welfare ratio that would be suitable for cross-country comparison, Beijing also trended much lower than other European cities (London, Amsterdam, Leipzig), except for Milan. The main concern is the dip in per-capita income or real wage. And this is what Pomeranz (2000) could not explain. At the same time, the population rose rapidly, doubling suddenly in the mid-Qing in 1820, before the Taiping Rebellion.[20] The data suggests that a variance of the Malthusian model could help.[21]

Elvin (1973) argued in a Malthusian framework that China with a large surplus labor could be locked in a high-level equilibrium trap in agriculture in which the pre-modern technology was efficient enough to prevent the use of modern technology that required high initial capital.

As shown in the model by Galor and Weil (2000) and many others, Malthusian stagnation cannot move into modern economic growth without technological progress. Although a large growing population could lead to Malthusian population stagnation, at the same time, a large population provides the market and demand for technological innovations. Since technological innovation is a public good, a large population generates a larger supply and demand for innovation, as well as more rapid diffusion of new ideas. To escape the Malthusian population trap in the Galor–Weil model, technological progress must move beyond a certain threshold, after which per-capita income grows above subsistence level. With higher income, parents would then switch out of quantity into the quality of children. Moreover, as was argued forcefully by Galor and Weil (2000), technological progress raises the rate of return to human capital. And, a larger stock of human capital further raises the speed of technical progress, forming a virtuous circle.

By the mid-Qing, the size of the Chinese population was conducive to technological progress. The "creative destruction" of innovation, as Schumpeter called it, would hurt the interest of the incumbent ruling elites (Mokyr 1990; Parente and Prescott 2002) and undermine the dominance of the emperor. Moreover, active government developmental policies are needed initially to provide the proper conditions for the Galor–Weil technological threshold. The Qing government's

Table 2.3 Comparison of China and Western Europe

	China			Western Europe	
Year	*Population (in millions)*	*GDP (billion 1990 int. $)*	*Per-capita GDP (1990 int. $)*	*Population (in millions)*	*Per-capita GDP (1990 int. $)*
1	59.6	26.82	450	24.7	450
1000	59.0	27.49	466	25.4	400
1300	100.0	60.0	600	58.4	593
1400	72.9	43.2	600	41.5	676
1500	103.0	61.8	600	57.3	771
1600	160.0	96.0	600		
1700	138.0	82.8	600		
1820	381.0	228.6	600	133.0	1,204
1830	409.0				
1840	412.0				
1850	412.0	247.2	600		
1860	377.0				
1870	358.0	189.74	530		
1880	368.0				
1890	380.0	205.38	540.47		
1900	400.0	218.15	545.39		
1910	423.0				
1911	427.66				
1913	437.14	241.43	552.30	261.0	3,458
1920	472.00				
1929	487.27	274.09	562.50		
1930	489.00	277.57	567.62		
1931	492.64	280.39	569.16		
1932	496.31	289.30	582.91		
1933	500.00	289.30	578.61		
1934	502.64	264.09	525.41		
1935	505.29	285.40	564.83		
1936	507.96	303.43	597.36		
1937	510.64	296.04	579.75		
1938	513.34	288.65	562.31		
1950	546.82	244.99	448.02	304.9	4,579

Source: Data taken from Maddison (1998)

developmental policy was inadequate and inactive (Perkins 1967). It was the interests, the over-centralization, and the rigidity of the Qing institutions that stalled technological progress.[22]

5 Concluding remarks

The period of peace from early to mid-Qing had nurtured centralized and rigid institutions. The emperor was more interested in consolidating his power and position of dominance rather than the economy. The highly centralized institutions could not cope with the ever-changing environment. Consequently, per-capita GDP went down in the mid-Qing. Faced with challenges and defeats from European and Japanese colonialism in the late Qing, the highly centralized institutions began to open up. Prosperity returned, but was too little too late for the dynasty to survive.

The above conclusion is derived from the traditional view that the government was highly centralized in early Qing (Qian 2002 and Fairbank 1957: 204–231). The revisionist view (Rosenthal and Wong 2011; Pomeranz 2000; Deng 2012) on the other hand, argues that the small size of the Qing state and the low taxes, which under-provided sufficient resources to govern China, were the main culprit.[23] Apart from following the Confucian ideal of benevolent governance by "hoarding wealth in the people," the Qing authority chose to share power with locals also as a means to pacify and rule the Han people. The Qing state voluntarily stopped at the county level, leaving much freedom to the Han locals. The gentry and village officials were responsible for the local governance and fiscal conditions, which explained how the Qing government could stay small with low taxes. To control the locals, it was more cost-effective for the court to ally with agents of order than by direct government involvement.[24] Although this freedom at the local level stimulated commercial activities, it had allowed local interests to grow unabated, in the way Olson (2000) had described. A new hybrid gentry-merchant class began to emerge by mid-Qing (Rowe 2009). By the mid-seventeenth century, with less than 1 percent of the population, the gentry owned 25 percent of the farmland (Crossley 2010: 28). Corruption became widespread. These growing vested interests soon became part of the political institution, contributing to its rigidity (Acemoglu and Robinson 2012). Economic development was impossible without compromising the entrenched interests. Consequently, the Qing institutions were increasingly rigid and ineffective (Rowe 2009). In a way, the traditional and revisionist views could be complementary.

The Republic's complete break from monarchy had transformed China's institutions from a highly centralized imperial institution into (highly) decentralized democratic institutions, fragmented by warlords. Although the Chinese economy had not reached its full potential, economic progress, both quantitatively and qualitatively, had been observed in the period of the Republic.

The most important change in the period of the Republic was in the social norms and values among the common people. That change had liberalized all of the informal institutions.[25] Many scholars think that the embrace of communism and other foreign ideas were the result of the May Fourth Movement in 1919. That change in social values had laid an important foundation for the birth of the People's Republic of China in 1949.[26]

To conclude, it was the wars with the imperialist nations that brought China to this great institutional transformation.

Notes

1 Comments from Dwight Perkins, Gregory Chow, Tuan-Hwee Sng, J. P. Laffargue, Patrick Leung, Kent Deng, Man-houng Lin, and C. Chen are gratefully acknowledged.
2 This is the Naito hypothesis, see Miyakawa (1955).
3 Some authors prefer the term "social capital" to "informal institution" (see Nannicini *et al.* 2010).
4 That could explain why the Qing rulers ruled effectively with a small government (Myers and Wang 2002: 576); see also n. 24.
5 This is not the same as administrative delegation of functions from the center to the locals, at which no power devolution takes place. The material in this section is taken from Bardhan (2002) and Xu (2011).
6 An identical diagram, modeling on Hobbes' Leviathan, is provided by Eggertsson (1990: 317–326). Eggertsson used "Public Order" instead of "centralized authority" on the horizontal axis.
7 These points are well developed by Jones, that is that the observed conspicuous consumption of the emperor was also a means for him to exert his dominance: "Emperors were surrounded by sycophants. They possessed multiple wives, concubines and harems of young women, a phenomenon that may have been less the prerequisite of wealth and power than the assertion of dominance relationships, the propensity to use people as objects. The amassing of households full of slaves for display purpose rather than work may have had a similar ethological significance. Great attention was paid to submission symbols, kneeling, prostration, the kowtow, in recognition of the emperor's personal dominance" (2003: 109).

8　See, for example, Qian (2002); Perkins (1967); Rankin *et al.* (1986: 53).

9　See Fairbank (1957); Qian (2002); Mote (1999).

10　The *Baojia* system is a surveillance mechanism in which neighboring families were divided into groups of ten and within each group all the member families were held responsible for the crimes or improper deeds committed by other members (see Mote 1999: 918–922).

11　For Qianlong, Mote noted that "as his long reign wore on, however, imperial pomp came more obviously to serve his voracious need for personal gratification" (1999: 920).

12　This institutional change supports *Prediction 1*.

13　These reforms, induced by wars, support *Prediction 3*.

14　This rebound supports *Prediction 2*.

15　Nonetheless, the political uncertainties of the time would seem to be the most important factor for holding back industrialization. I am indebted to Professor Perkins for pointing this out.

16　This abrupt collapse of the imperial institution supports *Prediction 1*.

17　This supports *Prediction 2*.

18　The overhaul of the informal institution induced by wars supports *Prediction 1*.

19　Maddison's data was chosen because it is a comprehensive study, based on a consistent methodology, over time and over different parts of the world.

20　Europe also doubled its population around that time.

21　Two centuries ago, Thomas Malthus's theory of population predicted that the power of population growth would ultimately outpace agricultural production and force the human population to return to a perpetual subsistence-level condition.

22　Wars broke up the domestic interests and brought big changes in the institutions (*Prediction 1*), paving the way for the adoption of new technologies in the period of the Republic. Mokyr (1990) observes that historically major technological innovations were more likely to occur during war time.

23　The query here is why the Qing court could not fix this problem. In fact, the tax–GDP ratio in early Qing was not small. It was almost identical to that in Britain (see Figure 2.2). The decline of the tax–GDP ratio later on came from institutional rigidity and decay as explained in section 2.7.

24　The Qing government also promoted orthodox Confucian social norms at the grassroots for tighter controls of the people through the informal institution. The control is vividly described in Lu Xun short stories (2003), on the life of Chinese people under the oppressive Confucian norms in late Qing. Cities, including towns and market settlements, in imperial China, according to Rozman (see Chan 2008), can be classified into administrative cites and economic cities. The location of the former was based on strategic defense and cosmology while the latter had market and locational comparative advantage. Because of this distinction, the share of population of administrative cities (levels 1 and 2 in Rozman's data) can be used as evidence for the emperor's power to appropriate, directly and indirectly, while the population share from the economic cities (levels 4, 5, 6) can be used as evidence of the prosperity of the economy, or the well-being of the commoners. The population share of administrative cities at Mid-Tang (AD 762), Mid-Song (AD 1120), Mid-Ming (1506), early Qing (1650), and mid-Qing (1820, after the huge jump in population) were 0.015, 0.008, 0.014, 0.016, and 0.015 respectively. The population ratios of administrative cities to economic cities were 0.484, 0.238, 0.318, 0.348, and 0.414 respectively. From these numbers, the Qing institutions were highly appropriative and centralized on a par with the Tang and the Ming dynasties.

25　Williamson (2000) thinks that the informal institution poses a stronger resistance against changes than the formal institution.

26　See the short stories by Lu (2003). Mao Zedong is known to have been inspired by the May Fourth Movement.

References

Acemoglu, D. and Robinson, J. A. (2012) *Why Nations Fail: The Origins of Power, Prosperity, and Poverty*, New York: Crown Business.

Allen, R., Bassino, J., Ma, D., Moll-Murata, C., and van Zanden, J. (2011) 'Wages, Prices, and Living Standards in China, 1738–1925: in Comparison with Europe, Japan and India,' *Economic History Review*, 8–38.

Bardhan, P. (2002) 'Decentralization of Governance and Development,' *Journal of Economic Perspectives*, 185–205.

Baten, J., Ma, D., Morgan, S., and Wang, Q. (2010) 'Evolution of Living Standards and Human Capital in China in the 18–20th Centuries: Evidences from Real Wages, Age-Heaping, and Anthropometrics,' *Explorations in Economic History*, 374–359.

Chan, K. S. (2008) 'Foreign Trade, Commercial Policies and the Political Economy of the Song and Ming Dynasties of China,' *Australian Economic History Review*, 48(1), 68–90.

Chan, K. S. and Laffargue, J. P. (2012a) 'Foreign Threats, Technological Progress and the Rise and Decline of Imperial China,' *Pacific Economic Review*, 280–303.

Chan, K. S. and Laffargue, J. P. (2012b) 'The Growth and Decline of the Modern Sector and the Merchant Class in Imperial China,' forthcoming, *Review of Development Economics*.

Chang, J. K. (1969) *Industrial Development in Pre-communist China: A Quantitative Analysis*, Edinburgh, UK: Edinburgh University Press.

Crossley, P. K. (2010) *The Wobbling Pivot: China since 1800*, Oxford: Wiley-Blackwell.

Deng, K. (2012) *China's Political Economy in Modern Times: Changes and Economic Consequences, 1800–2000*, Abingdon, UK: Routledge.

Eggertsson, T. (1990) *Economic Behavior and Institutions*, Cambridge, UK: Cambridge University Press.

Elvin, M. (1973) *The Pattern of the Chinese Past: A Social and Economic Interpretation*, Stanford, CA: Stanford University Press.

Fairbank, J. K. (ed.) (1957) *Chinese Thought and Institutions*, Chicago, IL: University of Chicago Press.

Feuerwerker, A. (1977) 'Economic Trends in the Republic of China 1912–49,' *Michigan Papers in Chinese Studies*, 31.

Galor, O. and Weil, D. N. (2000) 'Population, Technology and Growth: From Malthusian Stagnation to the Demographic Transition and Beyond,' *American Economics Review*, 806–828.

Jones, E. (2003) *The European Miracle. Environment, Economics and Geopolitics in the History of Europe and Asia*, 3rd edn, Cambridge, UK: Cambridge University Press.

Li, M. (2003) 'Essays on public finance and economic development in a historical institutional perspective: China 1840–1911,' Ph.D. thesis, Stanford, CA: Stanford University.

Lin, Man-houng (1983) 林满红 : "现代经济的起步 – 清季的经济发展 (1840–1911)" in 中华民国经济发展史; 秦孝仪主编(台北 : 近代中国出版社).

Liu, T. and Yeh, K. C. (1965) *The Economy of the Chinese Mainland: National Income and Economic Development 1933–1959*, Princeton, NJ: Princeton University Press.

Lu Xun (2003) 鲁迅, 鲁迅选集 (中国: 山东文艺出版社).

Ma, D. (2008) 'Economic Growth in the Lower Yangzi Region of China in 1911–1937: A Quantitative and Historical Perspective,' *Journal of Economic History*, 385–392.

Maddison, A. (1998) *Chinese Economic Development in the Long Run*, Paris: OECD.

Miyakawa, H. (1955) 'An Outline of the Naito Hypothesis and Its Effects on Japanese Studies of China,' *Far Eastern Quarterly*, 533–552.

Mokyr, J. (1990) *The Lever of Riches: Technological Creativity and Economic Progress*, New York: Oxford University Press.

Mote, F. W. (1999) *Imperial China, 900–1900*, Cambridge, MA: Harvard University Press.

Myers, R. and Wang, Y. (2002) 'Economic Development 1644–1800,' in J. K. Fairbank and D. Twitchett (eds.), *Cambridge History of China*, Cambridge, UK: Cambridge University Press, vol. IX, ch.10, pp. 563–641.

Nannicini, T., Stella, A., Tabellini, G., and Troiano, U. (2010) 'Social Capital and Political Accountability,' Milan: Bocconi University, Department of Economics.

Ni, S. and van, P. H. (2006) 'High Corruption Income in Ming and Qing China,' *Journal of Development Economics*, 316–336.

North, D. C. (1984) 'Government and the Cost of Exchange in History,' *Journal of Economic History*, 255–264.

Olson, M. (2000) *Power and Prosperity: Outgrowing Communist and Capitalist Dictatorship*, New York: Basic Books.

Parente, S. L. and Prescott, E.C. (2002) *Barriers to Riches*, Cambridge, MA: MIT Press.

Pepper, S. (1986) 'The KMT–CCP Conflict 1945–1949,' in J. K. Fairbank and D. Twitchett (eds.), *Cambridge History of China*, Cambridge, UK: Cambridge University Press, vol. XIII, pp. 723–782.

Perkins, D. H. (1967) 'Government as an Obstacle to Industrialization: The Case of Nineteenth-Century China,' *Journal of Economic History*, 478–92.

Perkins, D. H. (1969) *Agricultural Development in China 1368–1968*, Chicago, IL: Aldine.

Perkins, D. H. (ed.) (1975) *China's Modern Economy in Historical Perspective*, Stanford, CA: Stanford University Press.

Pomeranz, K. (2000) *The Great Divergence: China, Europe and the Making of the Modern World Economy*, Princeton, NJ: Princeton University Press.

Qian, Mu (2002) 钱穆：中 国 政 治 得 失, Hong Kong: Joint Publishing.

Rankin, M. B., Fairbank, J. K., and Feuerwerker, A. (1986) 'Introduction on Modern China's History,' in J. K. Fairbank and D. Twitchett (eds.), *Cambridge History of China*, Cambridge, UK: Cambridge University Press, vol. XIII, pp. 1–49.

Rawski, T. G. (1989) *Economic Growth in Prewar China*, Berkeley, CA: University of California Press.

Rosenthal, J. L. and Bin Wong, R. (2011) *Before and Beyond Divergence: The Politics of Economic Change in China and Europe*, Cambridge, MA: Harvard University Press.

Rowe, W. T. (2009) *China's Last Empire: The Great Qing*, Cambridge, MA: Harvard University Press.

Sng, Tuan-Hwee (2010) 'Size and Dynastic Decline: The Principal–Agent Problem in Late Imperial China 1700–1850,' working paper, Northwestern University, IL.

Williamson, O.E. (2000) 'The New Institutional Economics: Taking Stock, Looking Ahead,' *Journal of Economic Literature*, 595–613.

Xu, C. (2011) 'The Fundamental Institutions of China's Reforms and Development,' *Journal of Economic Literature*, 49(4): 1076–1151.

Zhang, M. (2012) 张鸣：从说中国近代史, Hong Kong: Open Page Publishing.

3

THE CENTRALLY PLANNED COMMAND ECONOMY (1949–84)

Dwight H. Perkins

Introduction

When the Chinese Communist Party took over the government of China in 1949, it set out to fundamentally change the way the economy was organized. Initially the main task was to control the hyperinflation of the pre-1949 years and this was followed by the state takeover of ownership of most of industry and commerce. This in turn was followed by the replacement of household agriculture with agricultural producer cooperatives, a process largely accomplished in the winter of 1955–6. With the state takeover of industry and commerce, the government then moved to replace the production and distribution system, which up to that point had largely been governed by market forces, with a system of central planning where the government decided what would be produced, who would produce it, and from whom enterprises would receive the inputs required for this production.

This system of government control of the production and allocation of industrial products was patterned on the system then in place in the Soviet Union. The decisions as to what to produce with what inputs was made by a central planning agency that in China was called the State Planning Commission (SPC). The SPC drew up output targets for each industry together with targets indicating which inputs in what quantity would be used to produce those products. These output and input targets were then broken down into comparable targets for individual enterprises. The managers of these enterprises were then expected to carry out their part of the plan as spelled out by these SPC targets. There were a variety of implementation measures designed to ensure that the managers would do precisely that and these will be described below. Industrial inputs and output were not bought and sold on the market – they were allocated administratively by a government agency that completely replaced the market in most cases.

The decision to adopt this system is difficult to understand from the perspective of the twenty-first century, given that the system failed in the Soviet Union and Eastern Europe, and was largely abandoned by China (beginning in 1984) and the Soviet Union, Eastern Europe, and Vietnam (beginning in 1989). The Chinese decision to adopt this system, however, was not as irrational as it now seems. There were three major reasons why China went ahead with this transformation in the management of its economy.

1   Markets in the 1940s were seen, by many in the developing world, as associated with capital-
    ism, imperialism, and colonialism; they were seen as vehicles for repressing the citizens of
    the countries in the developing world. This view was reinforced in China and in the ruling
    Chinese Communist Party whose ideology was based on Marx's labor theory of value that
    implied that markets were irrational rather than forces for the efficient allocation of goods.

2   The economic growth model used by the Soviet Union beginning in the 1930s and by China
    in the 1950s assumed that international trade would play only a very minor role in these
    economies. The development strategy would be based on a "closed economy." In a closed
    economy a country must produce all of the goods that it needs or wants. Importing the goods
    from elsewhere is for the most part not an option. Domestic producers therefore must manu-
    facture not only garments, shoes, and foodstuffs, as is the case in the early stages of develop-
    ment of most countries, but they must also produce the steel, machinery, and other heavy
    industry products required for development of the country's infrastructure and production
    capacity. China in the early 1950s had few heavy industries of this type and thus had to build
    most of them from scratch. The centrally planned system implemented through government
    commands was a more rapid way to create these new industries than reliance on market forces
    alone would have been. Heavy industries were also needed to produce weapons and China,
    like the Soviet Union, saw itself as surrounded by enemies and in 1953 had just completed a
    war with the United States in South Korea. During and after that war most of the world's
    market economies imposed an embargo on trade with China that lasted for nearly two
    decades. A closed economy strategy makes little sense in the world of the twenty-first century,
    but it was not irrational in a country at war, or contemplating being at war. The Soviet Union
    itself adopted this system in the 1930s when it faced possible war with the greatest military
    power at that time, Nazi Germany. The model that most influenced the Soviet Union was the
    economic system used by Germany during the First World War in 1914–18.

3   The economic system of the Soviet Union in the 1950s was also seen by most people in the
    world as being successful at achieving a relatively high rate of economic growth and a mod-
    ernizing economy capable of defeating Germany and holding its own, at least in military
    competition, with the United States. China's leaders for nearly a century had been trying to
    make the country "wealthy and powerful" without much success, and the Soviet economic
    model seemed to make both goals possible. By the 1980s after years of near economic stag-
    nation in the Soviet Union and Eastern Europe and slow growth in China, the image of this
    Soviet system was mostly negative but that was much later.

1 The nature of the centrally planned command system

What was the nature of this closed economy planned system that China adopted from the Soviet
Union? To begin with the full Soviet-type centrally planned command system applied mainly
to the industrial sector. Agricultural production did not lend itself well to central planning.
There were hundreds of thousands of farm production units after the formation of producer
cooperatives and Communes each facing production situations dictated by weather, different
soils, different topography, and much else. Efforts to centrally plan agriculture were quickly
abandoned and replaced by government-set procurement quotas for grain and other major
products. These procurement quotas effectively set minimum targets for the output of key farm
products that were reinforced by government efforts to ensure that each producing unit devoted
a certain amount of its land to grain and other key farm products. Many farm products ranging
from vegetables to hogs were not planned at all and farm producers could usually sell those
products on local markets.

The industrial planning system started with the drawing up of a central plan that produced targets for the output of each industry as well as targets for the inputs that would be used in producing that output. The leading plan was the five-year plan and each five-year plan, at least in principle, was broken down into five annual plans. Data needed to draw up these plans was for the most part collected from the enterprises that were designated to produce particular products. The data were collected by the SPC which was responsible for producing the five-year and annual plans. The main task was to ensure that all of the plan targets were coordinated with each other so that each enterprise and each industry would receive the inputs it needed to generate the required outputs.

In all economies there must be a mechanism for coordinating inputs and outputs, so that enterprises can obtain the right amount of each input needed to manufacture the products that consumers, other producers, or the government demand. In a market economy this coordination problem is solved by market forces that raise the prices (and profits) of products in short supply and lowers the prices and profits of products that have a large surplus. In a centrally planned command economy, this problem is solved by planners (who were the SPC in China's case). The process is called "material balances planning" and the specific ways that the staff of the planning commission decide whether to increase or decrease a target for a given industry, involve bureaucratic procedures that are difficult to describe, even in an essay considerably longer than this one.[1] In essence the process was an ad hoc one where planners in one sector, such as steel, attempted to match their output goals and input needs with the output goals and input needs of other closely related sectors. What these planners were trying to do can be best understood using input–output analysis even though the central planners in China (and in other centrally planned economies) did not formally use the input–output technique.[2] Their ad hoc methods, however, did have to approximate the results of formal input–output analysis if the plans were to provide a reasonably efficient set of coordinated inputs and outputs. Thus the use of input–output analysis, to describe the nature of what relatively efficient planning required, is a succinct way of illustrating the enormous information requirements of a centrally planned command system. It also illustrates well the reasons that China had great difficulty implementing this system efficiently.

The core of input–output analysis is a matrix that is full of coefficients that tell one the amount of a given product, steel for example, that is needed to produce a unit of another product, as in machinery. A certain amount of this machinery is needed to produce an automobile, as is a certain amount of steel. These coefficients can then be arrayed in a matrix where the vertical axis of the matrix lists the output of the products being planned and the horizontal axis lists all of the inputs that go into these various outputs. Thus going down one column in the matrix, from top to bottom, are the coefficients of the inputs required to produce a particular product (each column in effect listed the inputs for one product, such as the amount of cotton in clothing, or the amount of steel and machinery in a truck). Going from left to right along a single row gives the coefficients of a particular input, steel for example, used by a unit of every product in the table.[3]

The first job of the central planners is to estimate the coefficients in this entire matrix. In the case of China, the SPC in 1957 was responsible for planning 729 products although probably only around 235 involved systematically coordinating inputs and outputs. If this coordination had been handled through formal input–output techniques, a matrix with the dimensions 235 x 235 would be required, or over 55,000 separate entries although many of the elements of the matrix would be zero (a given input was not used in that particular product). In practice, as already indicated, China used a less formal coordination mechanism but the number of coefficients for which estimates had to be made was still very large. These coefficients, it should be noted, are estimates of what the input–output relationship would be in the coming year or the next five years, not the actual relationship in the year just past.

Together with estimating these input–output coefficients or, in the case of China, their ad hoc equivalent, the planners have also to decide how much of each product to produce. The broad guidelines come from the political leaders of the country, but these have to be translated into what in input–output analysis is called "final demand" although the term was not used in the Chinese planning process. Final demand is the total amount of each product that is available for consumption by consumers, is exported, or is invested in new production capacity. The planners then see if the desired list of final demand products is feasible – will there be enough inputs to supply the desired output left over for final demand, after much of the output is used up as intermediate products during the production process? If that is not the case, the planners then have to adjust their final demand targets so that there are sufficient inputs to meet those targets. If mistakes are made in estimating the input–output coefficients, and mistakes in this complex of a system are inevitable, some of the final demand products fall short of their targets while others may have a surplus of one input, or another that is of no immediate use in production. In China as in the Soviet Union, when inputs did fall short and the production of some products had to be cut back, it was typically the producer goods sector or the military that had priority for whatever product was available. Consumers typically got a lower priority and simply had to do without. In addition to the production plan, there was then a plan for investment in new capacity. This investment plan is the one aspect of this formal planning process that was still operational after China abandoned most central planning in favor of reliance on markets in the late 1980s and 1990s.

The determination of output and input targets, however, was only the beginning of the process. The planners then had to draw up a variety of related targets that had to be broken down to a degree whereby each industrial enterprise of any size received specific targets designed for that enterprise.[4] Altogether each enterprise each year through 1957 received 14 separate targets, seven expressed in terms of physical quantities and seven in terms of money values. The targets were as follows:

- Output of major products
- Total number of employees
- Trial manufacture of new products
- Total employees at year's end
- Consumption of raw materials
- Level of mechanization
- Rate of equipment utilization
- Gross value of output
- Cost reduction rate
- Cost reduction quota
- Total wage bill
- The average wage
- Labor productivity
- Profits

Formally each of these targets had the force of law behind them through 1957 but after 1957 formally only four were "compulsory" and the rest were "advisory." In reality it was impossible to draw up so many targets for so many industries and firms that large errors in setting these targets were inevitable. The managers of enterprises both before and after 1957 thus had to choose which of these targets were most important including choosing between where maximum effort should be mainly placed among the four compulsory targets.[5] The answer generally was the physical output targets because failure to meet these, particularly for producers of intermediate targets, meant that users down the line did not get the inputs they needed and thus they also would fail to meet their output targets. Profits in this system were not very important because most profits simply had to be turned over to the government and could not be retained by the enterprise.

The fact that these targets had the force of law was only the beginning of how enterprise obedience to these targets was enforced and not a very important beginning since so many of them had to be ignored as impractical. The real enforcement mechanisms for the annual and five-year plans were elsewhere. Probably the most important single mechanism was that China's government was responsible for allocating most industrial inputs to the individual enterprises that needed them and this allocation was based on the plan targets for that enterprise. If the plan called for a given enterprise to receive 50 tons of steel plate of specific dimensions, the government allocation agency delivered that amount, no more and no less.

Further backing up this administrative allocation of inputs in accordance with the plan was the Chinese banking system. The Chinese banking system was basically one single bank, a mono-bank, which combined the functions of both the central bank and the commercial banks. It had two principal duties:

1   The enterprises were required to keep most of their surplus funds in the bank and it was the task of the bank to monitor the use of those funds to ensure that they were used in accordance with the plan. In principle and sometimes in practice they could refuse an enterprise withdrawal of its funds if the use was not in accordance with the plan.
2   The bank would lend money to firms that needed additional mostly short-term funds to meet their plan targets.

The bank did not lend long term for investment to these producing enterprises. Investment was handled separately by enterprises set up to build increased capacity in all industries and much of it was paid for out of the government budget. A principal source of the funds for that investment was the enterprise profits that had to be turned over to the government. When the construction of the new capacity was completed, the new plant then would be turned over to the producing enterprise to operate. Enterprises producing industrial products, therefore, did not have the authority to decide on whether to expand their production capacity, nor did they have access to the funding necessary to pay for such an expansion. Control was firmly in the hands of the SPC. In the 1960s and 1970s, this system of control over investment was modified from time to time, and enterprises were allowed to retain a small portion of their profits and to use those funds to invest in improvements to their enterprise, typically improvements designed to upgrade key equipment. Nevertheless, major investment projects designed to expand capacity in major ways continued to be controlled by the SPC or its provincial equivalents throughout the period of central planning and the command economy.

Marketing in this kind of system plays little role. When business professors went to China in the early 1980s to teach classes on marketing, many in their audience found the idea that you could teach marketing – or that a firm should even be concerned with marketing – an alien concept. Enterprise managers did not have to market their products. They simply turned what they produced over to the state allocation agency and that agency delivered the products to where the central plan directed. This writer has visited factories in China where the product of the factory was simply placed outside the factory gate in rain and shine waiting for the government allocation agency to pick it up. These products, as the managers made clear, were no longer their responsibility.

Finally this system had to devise a method for incorporating foreign trade – because no country can practice complete autarchy that eliminates all imports and exports and hope to achieve sustained economic growth. The central plan determined where production of particular products was likely to fall short of demand, thus making imports of that item necessary. Similarly the plan would estimate where industries were likely to generate a surplus above domestic needs and thus could be exported. Most of China's foreign trade in the 1950s was with countries in Eastern Europe and the Soviet Union and trade between these countries and China was determined by bilateral and multilateral negotiations between these countries. Implementation of the plan was carried out by special foreign trade corporations set up to handle the trade in particular industrial and agricultural sectors. Industrial enterprises themselves were not allowed to negotiate directly for imports or to sell exports. The foreign trade corporations would get their instructions from the planners and the imports would be delivered to the ultimate user in accordance with the plan. This system had to change somewhat when China broke with the Soviet Union and its allies in 1960 due to the fact that China was selling to and buying most imports from market economies. However, the monopoly foreign trade corporations still handled all of China's foreign trade meeting with potential suppliers of imports and purchasers of Chinese exports in various venues, notably the annual trade fare in Guangzhou. Foreign suppliers and purchasers had no direct contact with the enterprises that used their products, or from whom their purchases came.

2 The centrally planned economy in practice

The discussion to this point has focused on how the formal planning and plan implementation process was designed to work both in China and elsewhere in Soviet-type economies. The reality was often different.

To begin with, the planning process produced five-year plans and it has continued to do so in the twenty-first century. However, the first Five-Year Plan nominally covered the years 1953–7 but it was not really fully drawn up until 1955. The second Five-Year Plan was supposed to cover the years 1958–62 but the Great Leap Forward also began in 1958 and all planning was effectively thrown out the window. Furthermore, during the Great Leap Forward enterprises came under great political pressure to compete with each other by steadily increasing their plan targets, without respect to whether they would ever get the inputs or increased capacity to meet those higher targets. By 1960, the result of this politically inspired but unplanned expansion was chaos in industry because there was no real coordination of inputs and outputs of any kind. In 1960, this problem was exacerbated by the break between China and the Soviet Union, over foreign policy issues for the most part, that led to an end to Soviet technical assistance and an end to many Soviet deliveries of key inputs into industry. Industrial output fell sharply in 1960 and 1961 even in high priority areas such as the production of military weapons. This crisis in industry was combined with a famine, caused by massive dislocation in the countryside due to the first phase of the People's Communes, that led to tens of millions dying from malnutrition and related causes.

After an interregnum during 1962 through 1965, order and coordination were restored in industry although much of this coordination now occurred at the provincial level, at least in theory. The ownership of many of the industrial enterprises was turned over to the provinces and the major cities on the grounds that they were closer to the industries in their jurisdictions and thus could do a better job of identifying and correcting problems. The third Five-Year Plan subsequently began with the intention of guiding the economy during 1966–70. Mao Zedong by that time, however, had regained control of the political system and, together with certain of his political allies, launched what was called the Great Proletarian Cultural Revolution. The Cultural Revolution unleashed millions of students and other activists on the society and economy causing considerable chaos particularly in 1967–8. This chaos was combined with a decision to force most of the government bureaucracy along with many others to spend time, often several years, in the countryside being "reeducated." These "sent down" cadres included many from the SPC making it impossible to do very much planning. Industrial value added fell by 15.1 percent in 1967 and another 8.2 percent in 1968. Somewhat surprisingly industry recovered rapidly in 1969 and 1970 and by the latter year was 40 percent above the level of 1966. Some kind of planning must have been going on during these years because there was no alternative coordinating mechanism in place.

The fourth and fifth Five-Year Plans (1971–5, 1976–80) took place during the last years of the life of Mao Zedong and Zhou Enlai while there was considerable political infighting at the top, including over economic policy, so systematic planning would have been difficult but annual plans still had to be drawn up to guide production and input allocation. The year 1976 saw the death of first Zhou Enlai, followed by the purge for the second time of Deng Xiaoping, the death of Mao Zedong, and then the arrest of the radical leftists knows as the "gang of four." That year was followed by the restoration of order; however, the most dramatic change in terms of economic policy was when Deng Xiaoping returned to power and in late 1978 launched the process that over the next two decades was to transform China's economy into one dominated by market forces, rather than central plans and government commands. The fifth Five-Year Plan thus was dead long before its five years ended.

That is the macro picture but there was much going on at the micro level during good years and bad that was driven by the nature of the centrally planned command economic system. There were three basic problems with this system at the micro level:

1   The data requirements of this system were very large and introducing these requirements into a large developing country with little experience with modern accounting practices or any other data collection procedures was problematic. The fact that industrial enterprises in China varied enormously in size and sophistication from each other (and in some cases within an industry itself) and had widely varying cost structures made the task of collecting data needed for planning much more difficult.
2   A system that emphasizes physical targets for output and inputs inevitably generates enterprise management behavior that leads to quality problems and cost overruns.
3   The difficulty in getting the right inputs to the proper places caused (in part but only in part) by poor data leads to other forms of behavior that raise costs. Inventories, for example, build up because producers who receive more of an item than they need do not return it to the planners. They put it in their warehouses in case they need it next year or they keep it to trade with another enterprise for something they do need, a practice that was common although not really legal under the command system.

The lack of good data effectively meant that it was impossible to set targets that were anywhere close to what actual performance was likely to be. Data for the first Five-Year Plan are presented in Table 3.1.

Table 3.1 supports two conclusions. First, Chinese plan targets in the first Five-Year Plan period had little relationship to actual industry performance. Second, with the exception of the production of petroleum, the industries that did not meet their plan targets were in the consumer

Table 3.1 The first Five-Year Plan

| | First Five-Year Plan completion record | | | | |
| | Realized output/planned output = Index | | | | |
	1953	*1954*	*1955***	*1956*	*1957*
Steel	143.2	164.9		96.9	169.5
Electricity	112.9	134.2		161.4	121.1
Cement	210.8	208.7		105	112.7
Coal	*	197.8		108.1	284.2
Petroleum	103.9	163.7		83.8	87.5
Cotton yarn	148.1	193.5		113.3	97.6
Paper	785.7	185.7		135.3	na
Sugar	na	38.8		32.3	na
Cigarettes	na	30.1		36.2	na

Source: This table is a modified version of a table in Perkins (1968: 611)

Notes: Na indicates data were not available to the author in constructing this table

*The plan called for little or no increase in coal output but in fact output grew by 3 million tons

**Data on plan completion were not available to the author for this year

goods sector which throughout the centrally planned command economy period received a lower priority for inputs than producer goods industries. The consumer goods in the table were also dependent on the vagaries of the harvest for cotton, sugarcane, and tobacco. Plan targets that missed by 50 or 100 percent or more could not have had much influence on enterprise decision making.

The problems with obtaining high product quality and low cost were inherent in this kind of system. The job of an enterprise manager was to meet the company's plan targets and the physical output target and the gross value output targets were the most important. It was difficult to impossible for central planners to define and enforce these targets in sufficient detail to ensure that the products met high-quality standards, such as a failure rate of only 1 percent. No one would know whether they had met that target until the product was in use and even then it would not be clear why a particular item failed. In a market economy a regular high failure rate would become widely known and users would stop buying the product, but that was not the case in China where the user was typically dealing with a supplier who had a monopoly of the local market; a supplier determined by the planners not the purchasing enterprise. You accepted what was delivered to you and hoped for the best. The producer of this intermediate product would focus mainly on making sure he made enough machines or steel to meet his target. In a market economy the production of a low-quality product might also lead to the fall in its price, but the state set these prices and did not usually change them based on market conditions. In any case, a monopolist does not have to lower prices to sell an essential intermediate product.

Cost overruns were the result of similar problems with the nature of plan targets. Given the importance of the output targets, it was more important for an enterprise manager to meet that target even if it meant using more of a given input than was called for in the plan thus raising costs per unit of output. The central planners set targets for the use of these inputs that were designed to prevent the manager from using too much of a given input but there were several problems with these input plans.

First, given that meeting the output plan was more important, the enterprise manager would simply ignore the input plan. More commonly the enterprise manager would try to negotiate with the central planners to receive a higher allocation of critical inputs. The central planners depended to some degree on the enterprise to provide them with the data to set these input plan targets and the enterprises regularly tried to convince the planners that their input coefficients per unit of output were larger than was actually the case. The planning process more generally was a negotiation between the planners and the enterprises with the latter trying to get as low an output target as possible (so as to be sure to be able to surpass that target) and as high an input target as possible. The planners, knowing that that was what the enterprises were trying to do, would push back. In the Soviet Union the planners introduced taught planning where input plans and output plans were set in a way that made it difficult to achieve the output target with the planned input targets. In China, however, taught planning did not work as well, in part because it was so difficult for the planners to come up with accurate estimates of input and output requirements, as evidenced by the previously described undershooting and overshooting of plan targets by large margins.

Second, the problems with the allocation system, getting the right inputs to the correct users, were also an important source of cost overruns. Enterprises could not go on the market and purchase what the planners failed to deliver to them. There were no regular markets for intermediate industrial products. Given the inaccurate nature of many of the plan targets, it was common for an enterprise to receive both more and less of given inputs than it needed. In principle the enterprise should have given the unneeded item back to the government allocations bureau and ask the allocation bureau for more of an item where it was short. In practice one had great difficulty getting more of a needed item if it was not already in the plan and getting the plan changed was a formidable bureaucratic undertaking. Enterprises dealt with the problem by holding on to all the surplus inputs that they received whether they needed them or not. The result was that enterprises in China as in all Soviet-type economies typically accumulated large inventories of inputs.

In a market economy producers often keep inventories of what they produce in order to meet possible increases in consumer demand for their product. Soviet-type producers do not keep inventories of their final product because they are not responsible for marketing it. They do keep large, often huge, inventories of inputs because they can do one of two things with these inventories. They can use them the next year to produce more and thus surpass their output target or they can trade the items in their inventory that they do not need with another enterprise in exchange for something that they do need. The Hungarian economist, Janos Kornai, used this situation to develop an index of the ratio in a country of total input inventories to total output inventories.[6] The higher the ratio, the more the economy was dominated by centrally planned commands while market economies typically had a low ratio.

It should be noted that in the Soviet Union, trading between enterprises of surplus items in their inventories was technically not supposed to occur and there could be stiff penalties for such practices. Even with stiff penalties, however, most enterprises were actively involved in exchanges of this kind because there was no way to meet plan output targets without doing so. In contrast, in China there was never much effort to enforce prohibitions on exchanges of this kind and occasionally open formal exchanges to facilitate the process were allowed.

Finally the problems with this approach to planning also created problems for the banking system. As already indicated, the most important targets were the output targets and anything that interfered with obtaining or surpassing those output targets was opposed at the highest levels of the government. Thus the bank's authority to ensure that all money in enterprise accounts was spent according to the plan in practice meant that they would allow most expenditure that had anything to do with meeting the plan output targets. Similarly, if a firm needed a short-term loan to meet a need, the bank would supply it if it met a plan need. In practice the definition of what constituted a legitimate use was not determined by the bank but by higher up political authorities, both in the localities and at the central level. Similarly investment funds for the separate investment enterprises could also bring pressure on the bank through the political authorities for loans to cover investment project needs that were above what was supplied from the government budget.

In this context the People's Bank of China, the only bank, was much weaker than its monopoly of banking might make it appear. In market economies independence of the central bank is often seen as critical for keeping politics out of lending and in ensuring that inflation is kept under control. In China during the centrally planned command period, inflationary pressures were controlled by the SPC and not the People's Bank. It was the SPC and higher government authorities that set the labor employment targets and set all urban wages. Enterprises were expected to hire individuals through government labor bureaus and those bureaus would enforce the plan targets. Wages set by the state, for the most part, had no relationship to labor market forces. There was no labor market. Inflation on the consumer market was controlled by making sure that the total wage bill (the average wage times the total number of employed) together with the money income of farmers (obtained from selling goods at state-set prices to government purchasing agencies) was not larger than the availability of marketed consumer goods and that was the job of the planning agency, not the People's Bank. The resulting weakness of the banking system in the sense of not being able to resist political pressures persisted well into the post-1978 reform period.

For all of the problems of this system, it did produce economic growth but at a very slow rate. The official estimated GDP growth rate for 1953–78 was 6.1 percent per year and for 1958–78 it was 5.4 percent a year but these rates are overstated by the use of high state-set relative prices for industrial products that exaggerate the contribution of industrial growth to GDP growth. Revaluing GDP in Chinese market prices of the year 2000 lowers the GDP growth rate in these two periods to 4.4 and 3.9 percent per year respectively (Perkins and Rawski, 2008: 859). Given that population growth during these years averaged 2.0 percent per year and a rising share of GDP went to investment, the rise in consumption of the average Chinese family was not much over 1 percent per year after 1957 through 1978.

3 Efforts to modify and then abandon the centrally planned command system

The Chinese leadership from almost the beginning was not very satisfied with the rigidity of this centralized system for managing the economy. In 1957 shortly after the centrally planned system was first set up the government experimented with the use of market forces in areas where central planning and government commands could not readily function well. That effort was short-lived because it gave way to the Great Leap Forward where Mao Zedong used his formidable political mobilization skills in an attempt to accelerate growth and catch up with the West.

As explained above, the Great Leap Forward did decentralize industrial decision making to the enterprise but failed to provide any mechanism for coordination of inputs and outputs. Instead, enterprises in the spirit of the times simply raised their output targets by large amounts, whether or not there was any realistic prospect of getting the necessary intermediate inputs and investment goods to carry out these expanded plans. One of the more extreme elements of what went on was the practice of using backyard iron and steel furnaces to melt down perfectly useful steel farm implements and the like, and turning them into low-quality steel. By 1959–60 the industrial economy had collapsed even in high priority sectors such as those serving the military.

Restoration of order in industrial planning in the early 1960s did not return to the highly centralized system of the Soviet Union that informed China's first efforts in the 1950s to introduce the centrally planned command economy. Instead, as mentioned above, a large proportion of the industrial enterprises were decentralized to ownership and control (including planning) at the provincial and large city level. Smaller scale firms, notably what in the 1970s were called rural small-scale industries, were turned over to counties, Communes and Commune brigades to manage. Decentralization of this sort simplified the planning process at the center because most of these smaller firms decentralized and got many of their inputs from within the political units that owned them. Thus considerable coordination could be done without much involvement of outside provinces or even outside counties. Strategic industries of national scope mostly remained under the control of the central government and the SPC, even if some of them may have been formally owned by provinces and cities.

In the aftermath of the collapse of the Great Leap Forward there were also periodic attempts to improve the performance of enterprise management. These included everything from providing bonuses or other material incentives to managers and workers to allowing enterprises to keep a portion of their profits. Few of the changes in the way profits were handled had more than a marginal impact on enterprise efficiency, however, largely because the emphasis on achieving and surpassing output targets still dominated.

During the height of the Great Leap Forward material incentives of all kinds had come under attack, they were to come under attack again during the Great Proletarian Cultural Revolution and were effectively abolished for a time only to be restored later. Hiring remained tightly controlled and the urban workforce was sharply reduced from 61 million to 45 million between 1960 and 1962 before being allowed to expand again reaching 95 million in 1978 (National Statistical Office, 2009: 609). Few rural workers were allowed to migrate to the cities so most of this increase in urban employment occurred within the population already registered as urban residents and their children. One positive result of these restrictions on rural migration to the cities was that enterprises hired more women who were already registered as urban residents to make up for the shortage of men, but in order to make up for the shortage of registered urban workers, enterprises also used more capital intensive techniques in production than otherwise would have been necessary.

Highly skilled workers, notably university graduates, were assigned to jobs where the planners determined they were most needed, even when that sometimes meant sending husbands and wives to separate cities. This system of job assignment for skilled workers, together with tightly restricted migration to the cities of rural unskilled workers, did not disappear overnight with the reforms that began with the Third Plenum of Eleventh National Party Congress in December 1978. Some of the restrictions on rural migrants, notably their lack of access to urban health care and other urban welfare benefits, persisted into the twenty-first century.

The initial reforms in the early 1980s involved mainly agriculture – notably the return to household farming and the abolition of the Commune system – and the opening up of the economy to expanding foreign trade. The expansion of foreign trade, however, continued for a time to be handled in much the same way as during the earlier part of the 1970s. Foreign trade corporations continued their monopoly of imports and exports in their particular sectors and many trade deals were negotiated at the Guangzhou Fair. This changed gradually over the next two decades first by expanding the number of trading corporations and eventually making it possible for enterprises sometimes to deal directly with their suppliers and their export markets (Lardy, 1992). By the 1990s and particularly during the first decade of the twenty-first century, China's most important controls over foreign trade were mostly through use of macroeconomic measures found in all market economies, including the management of the foreign exchange rate.

The change in the way industry was planned and managed came mostly after reforms that were initiated in October 1984. There were further efforts before then which were similar to earlier efforts to increase the role of profits, or give enterprise management somewhat more autonomy in decision making. However, the change that made a real difference was in 1984 when the government decided to open up markets for intermediate industrial products and to allow these markets to set the prices for these products. The state enterprises would have resisted this change because they were used to receiving these inputs at state-set prices that were often much lower than the new market-determined prices. To deal with this political problem the government introduced a dual price system with the state enterprises still able to get their government-supplied intermediate inputs at low state-set prices (but only in limited quantities while these state enterprises purchased the rest of inputs at higher market prices). Meanwhile everyone else purchased these inputs on the market at market prices.

"Everyone else" in this case means the majority of the rural small-scale industries that came to be known as "township and village enterprises," as well as their counterparts in urban areas, the "urban collective enterprises." In the 1970s, rural small-scale industries operated as a part of the centrally planned command economy, except that most of the planning was done at the county level or below.[7] If the rural industry could get the inputs it needed locally, or could manufacture these inputs themselves, it did not have to deal with higher level planning offices. But many of these industries required steel and equipment from outside the county and for those inputs they had to apply to higher planning authorities who generally gave priority to the larger enterprises under provincial or national direction.[8] Thus making these key inputs after 1984 available on the market often made it possible for these enterprises to obtain what they needed simply by going to the market. Far from resenting the higher market prices, the rural and urban enterprises that bought their inputs on these markets welcomed the ability to get whatever they needed. This ability resulted in the now well-known boom in township and village enterprises that accounted for much of China's high GDP growth from the middle of the 1980s to the middle of the 1990s.

The dual price system also had two other impacts – one positive and one negative. The positive impact was that as market prices became more and more the dominant prices at which goods were sold, the inefficiencies of the state-owned enterprises that were in effect subsidized by the low state-set prices became more and more apparent and many began to make losses.[9] Second, on the negative side dual prices created an opportunity for politically influential people to corruptly obtain goods at state-set prices and quickly resell at large profits at market prices. The dual price system gradually came to an end in the 1990s not so much by government decree, but because enterprises producing these intermediate inputs clearly preferred to sell them at market prices. The enterprises selling the products had many ways around government rules that in effect made it difficult for the purchasing enterprises to get the inputs they needed at state-set prices and so they went to the market as well.

By the 1990s the inefficiency of many of the state-owned enterprises was seen as an increasing problem both in being a drag on GDP growth and also a source of inflationary pressures during boom times (such as 1988–9 and 1993–5). Most of the dynamism in industry was coming from the rapidly expanding foreign direct investment sector together with the township and village enterprises both of which responded mainly to market forces, not state plans. The biggest problem in the state sector, despite all the efforts at reform, was that the state sector still faced relatively little competition or other pressures to perform at a level comparable to the other enterprises. China's leaders, notably Premier Zhu Rongji, increasingly used foreign competitive pressures by joining the World Trade Organization in 2001 in order to force a higher level of performance on the state sector. By this date, however, there was little left of the centrally planned command economy. The five-year plans continued to be drawn up but they mainly set the general direction of government policy and the government investment program. The State

Planning Commission's name was changed to the National Development and Reform Commission (NDRC) and it continued to be the most powerful government economics organization largely because large-scale investment projects, public and private, still had to be approved by the Commission. The setting of plan targets for enterprises was largely a thing of the past. China was a market economy and government influence over that economy, as in all market economies, was largely through the government's infrastructure investment program and its use of macroeconomic controls.

At the end of the first decade of the twenty-first century, the NDRC continued to draw up five-year plans but the operative targets of these plans, as represented by the twelfth Five-Year Plan (2011–15), were macroeconomic – setting the overall target rate for GDP growth, for the growth of urban employment, for the share of research and development in GDP, for various environmental and energy use goals, and a variety of economic reform and restructuring efforts. The authority to approve these targets remained with the Politburo of the Chinese Communist Party and its Standing Committee, but the NDRC was the primary implementing agency (in large part through its authority mentioned above) to approve or deny major investment projects. The NDRC was also directly responsible for major special programs such as the Western Region Development Program and the development of the energy sector (as well as the management of the national oil reserves).

Notes

1   For a description of parts of the way this system worked, see Chow (2007: 36–41).
2   Hungary attempted, under the leadership of Janos Kornai, to formally use input–output analysis in drawing up a Five-Year Plan during its command economy period, although in the end the planning agency reverted to its more ad hoc procedures. Many countries and analysts today, including in China, use input–output analysis to understand how various development strategies affect growth of individual sectors of the economy, but these plans and this analysis are not used to derive targets that industries are expected to obey. Plans of this sort are called "indicative plans" in that they indicate where the planners think the economy is going and thus can act as a voluntary guide to enterprise managers as to how the demand for their product is likely to evolve.
3   Formally input–output analysis can be expressed as $X = AX + D$ where X is the vector of the total output of each product being planned, A is the input–output matrix that contains all of the inputs used in producing a unit of the various products, and D is the vector of final demand which is the amount of each product that is left over and can be consumed by consumers, invested by investors in new plant and equipment, or exported. AX is the amount of each product that is used up in the production of other products and is not available for consumption, investment, or export. This can be converted to $(I - A)^{-1}D = X$. In practice in China much of the planning done by the SPC involved finding the appropriate coefficients for the matrix A even though these coefficients were not actually put into a formal matrix. The other key planning decisions involved making sure that industry produced enough of the high priority items in the vector D of final demand. These high priority products were typically products needed for the investment program and for the military. Consumer products in D were typically derived as a residual in China and in other command economies whereas in a market economy with consumer sovereignty the consumer products in D would have priority. In practice, as stated above, the SPC did not use formal input–output analysis in their production planning but in effect they still had to know the amount of inputs required for each item of output (the coefficients in A) even though they did not put those coefficients into a formal matrix. Realistic plan targets for output (the vector X) thus had to be large enough but not too large so that there would be enough left over (the vector D) to provide for the needs of investment and consumption. In practice planners in China could simplify the process because many of the inputs were unique to particular products (cotton was mainly used to make yarn that was used to make cloth for example and had limited other uses). It was also the case that many inputs for certain products could be obtained locally within a province and in that case the coordination problem could be handled at the provincial level rather than having everything centralized in Beijing.

4   This discussion of the planning process as it actually worked in the 1950s and 1960s is based mainly on Perkins (1968: 597–636; and 1966: chs. V–VII).

5   For a more detailed discussion of the steps involved in meeting plan requirements in a particular industry, the production of lathes, see Chow (2007: 271–5).

6   The logic behind why a shortage economy leads to the build-up of input inventories is discussed in Kornai (1992: 249–50).

7   For a more in-depth discussion of how these enterprises operated in the 1970s under the centrally planned command system, see the American Rural Small-scale Industry Delegation (1977).

8   In one rural small-scale enterprise that the author visited in 1975, the enterprise was actually producing a crude truck using materials that for the most part it possessed locally or could be taken from other used equipment (the engine for example). Trucks in the 1970s were in short supply and were generally not available to these enterprises through the plan allocation process.

9   Under the dual price system the state enterprises did receive a fixed subsidy because the amount of inputs they could purchase at the lower prices was limited. Receiving a fixed subsidy, to the degree that it was really fixed and was not subject to negotiation, did not affect their efficient decision making. For a discussion of the dual price system and how and why it was introduced written by participants in the 1980s reforms see Hua *et al.* (1993).

Bibliography

American Rural Small-scale Industry Delegation (1977) *Rural Small-scale Industry in the People's Republic of China*, Berkeley, CA: University of California Press.

Chow, Gregory (2007) *China's Economic Transformation*, 2nd edition, Malden, MA and Oxford: Blackwell.

Hua, Sheng, Xuejun Zhang, and Xiaopeng Luo (1993) *China: From Reform to Revolution*, Cambridge: Cambridge University Press.

Kornai, Janos (1992) *The Socialist System: The Political Economy of Communism*, Princeton, NJ: Princeton University Press.

Lardy, Nicholas (1992) *Foreign Trade and Economic Reform in China, 1978–1990*, Cambridge: Cambridge University Press.

National Statistical Office (2009) *Xin zhongguo 60 nian* [New China's 60 years], Beijing: China Statistics Press.

Perkins, Dwight H. (1966) *Market Control and Planning in Communist China*, Cambridge, MA: Harvard University Press.

Perkins, Dwight H. (1968) 'Industrial Planning and Management', in Alexander Eckstein, Walter Galenson, and Ta-chung Liu (eds.), *Economic Trends in Communist China*, Chicago, IL: Aldine Press.

Perkins, Dwight H. and Thomas G. Rawski (2008) 'Forecasting China's Economic Growth to 2025', in Loren Brandt and Thomas G. Rawski (eds.), *China's Great Economic Transformation*, Cambridge: Cambridge University Press.

4

CHINA'S ECONOMIC REFORM

Processes, issues, and prospects (1978–2012)

Wu Jinglian and Fan Shitao[1]

This chapter analyzes China's economic reform processes, achievements, and shortcomings over the past thirty-plus years.

In the early stages of reform, China adopted a limited set of measures to expand the decision-making powers of SOEs (state-owned enterprises). But when these measures met with setbacks, the non-state-owned economy was allowed to mature by means of "crossing the river by feeling the stones." In the mid-1980s, China tried to go beyond the strategy of partial reform and explored ways to carry out comprehensive change. But inflation due to expansionary macro-economic policies and the spread of corruption under the dual-pricing system in the late 1980s aroused great public dissatisfaction, which led to the political turmoil of 1989. In the aftermath, the reform was reversed.

In order to prevent economic or political crises in the early 1990s, the Chinese leadership decided to resume economic reforms. In 1992, China declared that a market economy was the goal of reform. Comprehensive reform was undertaken, achieving breakthroughs in key areas after 1993 and making extensive adjustments to the ownership structure after 1997. By the end of the twentieth century, China had established a basic framework for a market economy.

However, China's reforms were not entirely successful. The state sector still held a dominant position in the national economy. In reality, what existed in China was a "semi-command, semi-market" system. Under this type of system, economic and social problems increased and China once again faced a historical choice regarding its future direction.

Introduction

In 1953, as China's economy was just recovering from the trauma of a long period of war, its leader Mao Zedong abandoned his promise to build a "new-democratic society" and launched the "transition from capitalism to socialism." In 1956, the "socialist transformation of agriculture, handicrafts, and capitalist industry and commerce" was completed, thus establishing a command economy modeled after the Stalinist system. In 1958, the agricultural producers' cooperatives were further transformed into people's communes that merged "workers, peasants, soldiers, students, and merchants." On the basis of this fully nationalized system, the Great Leap Forward campaign was promoted in order to overtake Britain and catch up with the United States within a few years. This led directly to the Great Famine of 1959–1961 in which tens of millions of people lost their lives. In 1966, Mao launched the Great Proletarian Cultural Revolution with the stated aim of "removing bourgeois influences from inside and outside the Communist Party." The Cultural Revolution lasted for ten years, and caused the deaths of 20 million people, brought suffering to 100 million officials and civilians, or one-ninth of the entire population, and wasted 3.8 trillion yuan (Ye Jianying, 1996: 494). These extreme practices brought the Chinese society to the brink of collapse.

Following the death of Mao Zedong in September 1976, Mao's successors moved quickly to arrest several of his radical followers. Thereafter, an enlightenment movement to emancipate the mind swept across the country. In December 1978, the Third Plenary Session of the Eleventh Central Committee of the Communist Party of China (CPC) formally repudiated the party line of the Mao era and announced that the focus of future work would shift to economic development and reform of the economic management system. Since then, China has gradually carried out this reform.

This chapter analyzes China's economic reform processes, achievements, and shortcomings over the past thirty-plus years. The first section discusses the partial reforms of 1978–1983 when the command economy was still dominant and the fate of the overall reform during the period from 1984–1988. The second section discusses the comprehensive advance of the market-economy reforms between 1992 and 2002. The third section discusses the problems with the semi-command and semi-market economic structure of the last ten years. The final section briefly analyzes future prospects for reform in China.

1 Partial reforms in the early 1980s and the fate of the overall reform in the latter half of the 1980s

In the early stages of reform, China adopted limited reform measures to expand the decision-making power of enterprises. But when these measures met with setbacks, the non-state-owned economy was allowed to mature using the strategy of "crossing the river by feeling the stones." In the mid-1980s, China tried to go beyond the limited reforms and explored ways to carry out comprehensive change.

1.1 Strategy of "crossing the river by feeling the stones"

By the late 1970s, after China had extricated itself from the turmoil of the Cultural Revolution, people eagerly longed to pursue economic recovery through reforms. However, there were no clear ideas about how to achieve such reforms. For this reason, the Chinese government dispatched delegations around the globe to learn from the experiences of other countries. In 1978 alone, China dispatched twelve leaders at or above the level of vice premier or vice chairman of the National People's Congress on twenty trips to visit more than fifty countries. During his visit to North Korea, Deng Xiaoping told Kim Il Sung: "Our comrades have been traveling to other countries to have a look, and the more they see, the more they feel that we have fallen behind. What is modernization? It was one thing in the 1950s, another thing in the 1960s, and a completely different thing in the 1970s" (CCCPC Party Literature Research Office 1998: 76–77).

The first countries to which Chinese reformers turned their attention were the socialist countries of Eastern Europe, which earlier had been in a similar situation but by the mid-twentieth century had already begun enacting reforms. The main idea was to implement market socialism (Brus 1987: 337),[2] which mainly referred to expanding the operational autonomy of the SOEs.

In the late 1970s, in accordance with this idea, Sichuan province selected six SOEs for a pilot project to expand enterprise autonomy. Thereafter, the State Council decided to expand this pilot reform nationwide. By 1980, more than 6,600 SOEs were carrying out the pilot reform, with output value accounting for 60 percent of industrial output of the national budget and 70 percent of the profits of the country's industrial enterprises.

The reform to expand enterprise autonomy was similar to Soviet Premier Alexei Kosygin's "full economic accounting system" reform introduced in 1965: first, the objective was to simplify planning targets and ease planning controls; second, the goal was to increase funding and strengthen material incentives for enterprises and workers.

During the first several months, the expansion of enterprise autonomy significantly expanded the enthusiasm of enterprise employees to increase output and revenue. Nevertheless, problems soon arose: the soft budget constraints resulted in an escalation of enterprise spending, fiscal deficits, and inflationary pressures, leaving the reform in dire straits and causing a resurgence of planning controls. Thereafter, market socialism was no longer regarded as the objective of China's reform.

Under these circumstances, Chinese leaders proposed the partial reform strategy known as "crossing the river by feeling the stones"[3] and carried out various pilot reforms. The focus of these pilots was to make some modifications to the institutional arrangements in order to mobilize the enthusiasm of the people and to allow the beleaguered economy to recover and develop, while at the same time maintaining the dominant position of the command economy. The following are the most important institutional arrangements:

First, where rural land still belonged to the collectives, a household-based contract system was adopted to restore family farms. In 1980, after assuming actual leadership of the CPC Central Committee, Deng Xiaoping allowed farmers throughout the country to implement the household responsibility contract system on a voluntary basis. Within a mere two years, the household responsibility contract system had replaced the people's commune system in most areas of the country, as farmers established their own private farms on rented collective land. As a result, China's rural economy underwent a dramatic transformation. Between 1980 and 1985, the value of agricultural output increased 61 percent[4] and per capita disposable annual income of rural residents rose from 191 yuan to 398 yuan.[5]

Second, allowing the development of non-state-owned enterprises, while at the same time maintaining control over the state-owned economy. At the beginning of reform, with tens of millions of urban residents unemployed, it was necessary to stimulate employment. Based on suggestions by a number of economists, in 1980 the Chinese government began to allow self-employed workers to set up private enterprises. In 1981, government policy supported private enterprises that did not employ more than eight people. The July 1981 "State Council Policy Provisions on the Urban Non-Agricultural Private Economy" states that self-employed households may, when necessary, "seek the assistance of one or two helpers; technology-based businesses or businesses requiring special skills may take on two or three and no more than five apprentices." But by the beginning of 1983, the number of employees in private enterprises in many places greatly exceeded eight people, thereby refueling debate about the private economy. Some politicians and theorists argued that capitalism was springing up across the country. However, Deng Xiaoping responded, "Don't argue ... that problem can be set aside for a couple of years." In this way, the private sector was allowed to develop under the aegis of Deng Xiaoping's phrase "Don't argue."[6] It was not until the Thirteenth CPC National Congress in 1987 that the legal existence of the private economy was formally recognized.

At the same time, on the basis of rural land reform, township and village enterprises (TVEs) also began to flourish. According to official Chinese statistics, these enterprises are considered part of the collective sector, but in fact some TVEs were private enterprises masquerading as collective enterprises in order to insure political protection. There were also some community-owned enterprises with vague property rights.

Third, in the absence of an integrated market, local economic "ecosytems" in the form of Special Economic Zones (SEZs) were created to link up with the global market. Following the formal announcement of the policy of "opening up" in December 1978, the Chinese government selected Guangdong and Fujian provinces to implement "special policies and flexible measures." In 1980, the government established four SEZs, and in 1984, fourteen port cities were opened up, gradually creating a system of open zones along China's coast, rivers, and borders.

Under these flexible institutional arrangements, the government sought to give the market-oriented non-state sector space to survive and grow. This was China's earliest attempt at "incremental reform." From then on, China differed from most of the Eastern European countries in terms of its strategy to reform the SOEs.

1.2 Market development under the dual system

The most important achievement of the incremental reform strategy was the growth of the non-state sector, which includes collective as well as private firms. By the mid-1980s, the non-state sector, accounting for one-third of industrial output, not only held a large share of industrial production but also of the national economy (see Table 4.1). Meanwhile, its share of retail business grew at an even faster rate (see Table 4.2). Thus, a situation was created whereby the command and market economies coexisted.

1.3 Determining that the reform objective was to establish a "commodity economy"

After the flexible reform policies achieved a measure of success, Chinese leaders, led by Deng Xiaoping, discovered that it was necessary to define a clearer institutional objective.

The Third Plenary Session of the Twelfth Central Committee of the CPC in October 1984 announced that the objective of China's reforms was to "establish a planned commodity economy based on public ownership,"[7] indicating that reforms would be based on market-oriented principles. However, Chinese leaders did not establish a clear basic framework or an operational mode for the "planned commodity economy."[8] The objective and basic path of reform were further clarified in 1985 when four important events took place.

First, a comprehensive investigation by a joint Chinese-foreign team was carried out for the first time. In 1984, based on a suggestion by Deng Xiaoping, the World Bank assembled a large team of international experts, with the support of a Chinese working group, to carry out a comprehensive investigation of the Chinese economy. In 1985 the team published its final report, entitled *China: Long-Term Development Issues and Options* (World Bank 1985). This report not only comprehensively analyzed the main problems facing the Chinese economy, but also presented options for solving them based on a comparative study of the experiences of other countries.

Table 4.1 Proportion of total industrial output value for each sector of the economy (1978–1985)

	1978	1980	1985
SOEs	77.6	76.0	64.9
Collectively owned enterprises	22.4	23.5	32.1
Other*	0.0	0.5	3.0

Source: National Bureau of Statistics, *China Statistical Yearbook 1978, 1980, 1985*

Note: *"Other" refers to private enterprises and foreign-invested enterprises

Table 4.2 Proportion of total sales of retail businesses in each sector of the economy (1978–1985)

	1978	1980	1985
SOEs	54.6	51.4	40.4
Collectively owned enterprises	43.3	44.6	37.2
Other*	2.1	4.0	22.4

Source: National Bureau of Statistics, *China Statistical Yearbook 1978, 1980, 1985*
Note: *"Other" refers to private enterprises and foreign-invested enterprises

Second, the first "Overall Plan for Reform of the Economic System" was formulated. In May 1985, Guo Shuqing and two other graduate students at the Graduate School of the Chinese Academy of Social Sciences wrote a letter to Premier Zhao Ziyang of the State Council requesting that an overall plan be drawn up for a comprehensive reform. With the support of Zhao, the State Commission for Restructuring the Economic System (SCRES) formed a small research team consisting of nine young economists, including Lou Jiwei, Guo Shuqing, Xu Meizheng, Wang Qin, Liu Jirui, Li Hong, Qiu Shufang, Gong Zhuming, and Jia Heting. The team wrote "Ideas for an Overall Plan for Reform of the Economic System (Draft)" which suggested that the reforms should be carried out in two stages. The first would center on price reforms in commodity markets, accompanied by reforms of enterprises, the fiscal and taxation systems, and the financial system, and the establishment of a central bank. The second would establish a sound market for factors, eliminate mandatory planning, and complete the transition from a planned economy to a "commodity economy."

Third, in September 1985, the SCRES, the Chinese Academy of Social Sciences, and the World Bank jointly held the International Seminar on Macroeconomic Management (the "*Bashan* Steamboat Conference"), which represented a major milestone in China's reform. The well-known international experts attending this meeting included James Tobin, Sir Alexander Cairncross, Janos Kornai, Wlodzimierz Brus, and Otmer Emminger. The Chinese participants included economic officials Xue Muqiao, An Zhiwen, Ma Hong, Liao Jili, Xiang Huaicheng, Gao Shangquan, and Yang Qixian, and also economists Liu Guoguang, Dai Yuanchen, Zhou Shulian, Wu Jinglian, Zhang Zhuoyuan, Zhao Renwei, Chen Jiyuan, Lou Jiwei, Guo Shuqing, and Tian Yuan.

To begin, the conference participants engaged in heated discussions about what institutional objectives were most desirable for China's reforms based on ideas formulated by Hungarian economist Janos Kornai. Kornai classifies state macroeconomic management systems into two main types: those with administrative control (I) and those with market coordination (II). The former can be divided into those with direct administrative control (IA) and those with indirect administrative control (IB). The latter can be divided into those in which market coordination is completely free (IIA) and those in which market coordination is subject to macro controls (IIB). Kornai proposed that economic reform in a socialist country should choose indirect administrative control (IB) or market coordination with macro control (IIB), and he argued that the main reason that Hungary's reforms did not achieve the expected results was that for a long time it languished at the stage of indirect administrative control (IB), which kept enterprises under soft budget constraints, whereby they received administrative protection from the government. Kornai was of the opinion that IIB economic systems had clear advantages (Research Department of the Institute of Economics of the Chinese Academy of Social Sciences (ed.) 1987: 1–4). Foreign economists expanded upon Kornai's analysis of the advantages of a market economy with macro controls, and those Chinese economists with a firm grasp of modern economics agreed with Kornai's analysis and recognized that market coordination with macro controls (IIB) was the best choice for China's reforms.

Following this, the conference participants also held heated discussions about what kind of macroeconomic policies should be adopted during the transition period. The early 1980s had been a period of intense debates in China about the value of expansionary policies, and it was widely believed that Western economics tended to be supportive of such expansionary policies. The *Bashan* Steamboat Conference helped to resolve these debates (and correct Chinese understandings of related mainstream Western economic ideas), as both the majority of Chinese scholars attending the conference and the foreign participants agreed that during the transition period China should adopt contractionary fiscal, monetary, and income policies to counteract inflation and economic overheating.

On the basis of the consensus arrived at by the economists and economic officials, in 1985 a sound macroeconomic policy for the initial stage of economic reform was incorporated into the Seventh Five-Year Plan (1986–1990) so as to create a favorable environment to carry out a smooth economic reform.

Fourth, in late September 1985, a plenary session of the CPC Central Committee accepted the economists' research results and drew up the Guidelines for Formulating the Seventh Five-Year Plan (1986–1990), setting forth the following objectives: (1) to transform the SOEs into commodity producers that are responsible for their own profits and losses; (2) to develop a market system consisting of a commodities market, capital market, and labor market; and (3) to gradually move from mainly direct state regulation to mainly indirect state regulation of the economy. The guidelines also proposed accompanying reforms of the entire economic system in order to lay the foundation for a new economic system.

1.4 Debate regarding the reform roadmap and policy changes

After the reform objective was determined, there were differing opinions about how to achieve it and what policies should be adopted. The focus of the debates was on how to deal with the dual-track system and the dual-pricing system.

During the planned economy era, raw materials, equipment, and other production materials were allocated according to plans and their prices were determined by state planning guidelines. Following implementation of the reform and opening policy at the end of the 1970s, some SOEs were granted autonomy to sell through their own channels output that exceeded their designated quotas, and the new non-state-owned enterprises were required to buy their production materials from the market, thus creating a dual-pricing system.[9]

The dual-pricing system had both positive and negative impacts on the Chinese economy (Wu Jinglian and Zhao Renwei 1987: 309–318). On the one hand, a whole new world dictated by the market was opened up, imbuing economic life with a new vitality. On the other hand, the existence of the dual-pricing system led to rent-seeking and the spread of corruption, making it difficult to create a level playing field for competition among enterprises. Those who were well connected were able make a fortune by using their powers to resell supplies earmarked for allocation by the state, ultimately leading to public outcries (Editorial Department of Comparative Economic and Social Systems (ed.) 1989). Thus, in the middle and late 1980s, an important topic of debate was how to further guide the reform of the dual-pricing system.

In general, two distinct strategies emerged. The first emphasized liberalizing prices and creating a competitive market, as well as slowing down the pace of short-term economic growth, in order to promote market-oriented reforms and to create a stable macroeconomic environment. The second emphasized reform of SOEs and implementation of expansionary macroeconomic policies to support the rapid growth of the economy in order to create a profitable business environment for enterprises (Wu Jinglian 2005: 75–82). In the mid-1980s, Chinese leaders adopted the former strategy.

In March 1986, Premier Zhao Ziyang stated that all the problems the country was facing at that time were due to "the stalemate between the old and new systems that causes friction and gives rise to conflicts." He maintained:

> This situation should not be allowed to drag on … We should make even greater progress regarding the economic system and implement indirect macroeconomic management so that enterprises will be genuinely responsible for their own profits and losses. We should also create conditions under which enterprises can compete on a roughly equal basis … In particular, the design and research on the reform to be implemented in the next year should focus on the following three areas: (i) prices; (ii) taxation; and (iii) the fiscal system … The key element is the reform of the pricing mechanism; all the other reforms are related to this.
>
> *(Zhao Ziyang 1986)*

On the basis of a decision by the State Council and the CPC Central Committee's Financial Work Leading Group, the Chinese government announced that in 1986 work would be devoted to making preparations for taking decisive reform steps in 1987. At the same time, the Economic Reform Program Discussion Group was established, led by Tian Jiyun, vice premier of the State Council. Under this group, a planning team was put together consisting of economists and officials. Its task was to formulate an economic reform plan on the basis of Zhao Ziyang's March speech. In August, the Economic Reform Planning Office submitted its plan for overall reforms in the areas of prices, taxation, the fiscal system, banking, and trade to the State Council and the Central Committee's Financial Work Leading Group. This plan was approved by the Chinese government and was supported by Deng Xiaoping.

However, as a result of changes in the economic situation and government personnel changes, the plan's implementation was suspended in the fall of 1986. Beginning in 1987 the government substituted a contract system for the SOEs, while at the same time adopting expansionary macroeconomic policies to maintain rapid economic growth.

At that time, the second view held sway. As a great innovation in the reform of China's economic system, the dual-track system was said to allow a series of price reforms with Chinese characteristics, and even a whole new path of reform (Hua Sheng *et al.* 1985). It would increase supply and bring into play its positive role in invigorating the market, so there was no need to introduce reforms too early (Hua Sheng *et al.* 1986).

Other economists advocated slowing down the growth rate to create a relatively favorable macroeconomic environment and to quickly carry out price reforms to create a competitive market. Scholars holding this view included Xue Muqiao, a senior Chinese economist, Qian Jiaju, a member of the Chinese People's Political Consultative Conference (CPPCC) Standing Committee, and Milton Friedman.

At the plenary session of the CPPCC National Committee in 1988, Qian Jiaju had criticized the dual-pricing system, stating that the system "does not reflect supply and demand relations in the market" and it gives rise to "widespread bribery." He thus suggested reforming the dual-pricing system and decontrolling prices. Since capital investment was too high, which had led to treasury deficits and an excessive issuance of currency, he pointed out that "Greatly reducing capital investment … will avoid inflation" (Qian Jiaju 1988).

When Milton Friedman visited China in September 1988, he candidly told Chinese leaders that "The present dual-pricing system for many products in China is an open invitation to corruption and waste." He suggested curbing inflation by controlling the rate of increase in the money supply and by quickly decontrolling prices and wages and reforming the dual-pricing system. He also suggested ending exchange controls and replacing centralized government controls of the economy and state enterprises by decentralization and private control (Friedman 1998: 607–609).

Unfortunately, these suggestions were not accepted by Chinese leaders. When the reforms were slowed down and excessive quantities of currency were issued in the late 1980s, China faced two serious problems.

First, the expansionary policy maintained the rapid growth, but the inevitable result was a sharp increase in the issuance of currency and inflationary pressures. In the summer of 1988, when it was discovered that it was impossible to circumvent price reforms, an attempt was made to reinstitute them at a time when sporadic panic buying had already begun, with the result that as soon as the new round of price and wage reforms was announced in August, a wave of panic buying spread throughout the country. In 1988 and 1989 the CPI rose 18.8 percent and 18 percent respectively. Serious inflation and widespread panic buying ruined the reputation of the reform.

Second, the coexistence of a powerful command economy and a subordinate market economy, and dual prices for the means of production and dual interest rates and exchange rates, provided an institutional basis for rent-seeking activities. One economist estimates that between 1987 and 1988 such rent accounted for as much as 20–30 percent of GDP (Hu Heli 1989). This huge quantity of rent led to a rapid spread of corrupt behavior by using administrative power over resource allocations for personal gain.

Inflation and corruption aroused a great deal of public dissatisfaction and led to the political turmoil in 1989. In the aftermath, the reform and opening policy were reversed.

2 Comprehensively advancing economic reform

After the economic disturbances in 1988 and the political disturbances in 1989, China's reforms came to a complete halt. The economic debates over a planned economy versus a commodity economy became political debates about socialism versus capitalism. A number of "politicians" and "theoreticians"[10] holding important positions in the government declared that "marketization [is] the peaceful evolution to capitalism." They argued, "In the final analysis, the reforms of the economic system [put forth by] those who support bourgeois liberalization will first supplant public ownership with private ownership, and second supplant the planned economy with a market economy" (Wang Renzhi 1989). Therefore, concrete policy measures to stifle the privately run economy, including the development of TVEs, and the strengthening of the dominant position of the SOEs were implemented.

These policy measures had inevitable serious consequences, the most prominent of which was that the economic growth rate fell sharply and employment difficulties began to appear. In 1989 and 1990, GDP growth was only 4.1 percent and 3.8 percent, respectively. In order to prevent the outbreak of any new economic or political crises, Chinese leaders, led by Deng Xiaoping, made the decision to resume economic reforms.

2.1 Reestablishing the goal of implementing a market-economy system

In 1990 and 1991, Deng Xiaoping made two important speeches concerning the market economy. The first was on December 24, 1990, on the eve of the Seventh Plenary Session of the Thirteenth Central Committee. In a discussion with Jiang Zemin and other leaders of the Central Committee, he said, "You must not think that if we have some market economy we shall be taking the capitalist road … If we did not have a market economy, we would have no access to information from other countries and we would have to reconcile ourselves to lagging behind." In early 1991, Deng also stressed, "Don't think that any planned economy is socialist and any market economy is capitalist. That's not the way things are. In fact, planning and regulation by the market are both means of controlling economic activity, and the market can also serve socialism" (Deng Xiaoping 1994: 3: 51, 2354).

At the same time, a number of CPC leaders who supported reform began to consider how to reinstitute the market reforms. Between October and December 1991, CPC General Secretary Jiang Zemin chaired eleven meetings, during which leaders and economists discussed major international and domestic issues including how to establish "socialism with Chinese characteristics."[11] All of the economists opposed a return to the command economy and advocated the market-oriented reforms.

In January and February 1992 Deng Xiaoping went on an inspection tour of a number of cities in south China. Speaking directly to grassroots-level leaders, he reiterated, "There are markets under socialism too," and he emphasized "We should be bolder than before in conducting reform and opening to the outside" and we should "try bold experiments and blaze new trails" (Deng Xiaoping 1994: 3: 360–362). Deng's speeches were warmly received by both the cadres and the public alike.

Thereafter, on June 9, 1992, Jiang Zemin presented a speech at the Central Party School in which he proposed a "socialist market economic system." Jiang criticized a number of individuals who "rarely consider the positive role markets play in encouraging competition among enterprises and promoting economic development." Jiang also noted, "[M]arkets are an effective way to allocate resources and provide incentives" (Jiang Zemin 2010: 1–190). Jiang's speech was well received by the high-level cadres attending the meeting.

In October 1992, the CPC's Fourteenth National Party Congress formally decided that: "The objective of China's economic restructuring is to establish a socialist market economy." The congress report stated: "Let market forces, subject to macro-management by the state, serve as the basic means of regulating the allocation of resources" (Jiang Zemin 2010: 1: 188–194).

2.2 Implementing a new reform strategy: comprehensive advances with breakthroughs in key areas

When the CPC's Fourteenth National Party Congress established that the objective was the establishment of a market economy, the reforms were still not in full swing. Governments at all levels were more enthusiastic about increasing investment and launching investment projects. In 1992, non-governmental fixed investment increased 40 percent over 1991, and in 1993 it increased 50 percent over 1992. At the same time, in 1993 the CPI increased by 14.7 percent.

Against this backdrop, the Chinese government adopted a set of measures to put the brakes on economic overheating and directed its energies to design an overall plan for carrying out the market-economy reforms.

In late June 1993, the CPC Central Committee and the State Council issued the "Guidelines on the Present Economic Situation and Strengthening Macro Controls." On this basis, the banking sector was put in order, macroeconomic controls were strengthened, and the overheated economy was cooled down, thereby creating a suitable macroeconomic environment to introduce comprehensive reforms in 1994.

In order to draw up plans for comprehensive reform, in May 1993 a document-drafting group, established directly under the CPC Central Committee, was given responsibility to draft a plan for a comprehensive market reform. The office of the CPC Central Committee's Financial Work Leading Group formed sixteen investigative teams, involving more than 300 people, to carry out thorough investigations in all localities and sectors and to write up background materials for the drafting group to use as reference.

In mid-June, the State Commission for Economic Restructuring, the Chinese Ministry of Finance, and the World Bank hosted an International Conference on China's Macroeconomic Management in Dalian. The participants included Franco Modigliani, a recipient of the Nobel Prize for Economics; Nicholas Stern, professor at the London School of Economics; K. T. Lee, the "driving force behind Taiwan's economic miracle"; and a number of other famous Chinese and foreign scholars. This conference discussed the reforms that the central government was in the process of formulating, which included raising real interest rates on savings deposits to a level above 0 percent, putting a cap on credit, unifying the two renminbi exchange rates, and implementing price reforms.

After 150 days of hard work and eight revisions, the drafting group submitted the draft of a general plan called "The Decision of the CPC Central Committee on a Number of Questions Concerning Establishing a Market Economy" to the CPC Central Committee.

In November 1993, the Third Plenary Session of the Fourteenth CPC Central Committee passed the above "Decision." The decision set forth a reform strategy for integrating overall reform with breakthroughs in key areas; called for carrying out systematic reforms in the market system, the nature of enterprises, the public finance and taxation systems, the banking system, the social security system, and macroeconomic management; and established the goal of putting in place a basic market-economy system by the end of the twentieth century.

Comprehensive reforms were rapidly launched on the basis of the roadmap that had just been laid down. The progress and actual results of the reform of the exchange rate system are most noteworthy.

On December 1, 1993, the People's Bank of China announced that beginning on January 1, 1994, the dual exchange rate system would be abolished and a managed floating exchange rate based on market supply and demand would be implemented. The renminbi exchange rate would be determined by the market, and the Central Bank would only enter the market to buy and sell foreign exchange when exchange rate fluctuations exceeded a certain level (in order to maintain the stability of the renminbi exchange rate). On January 1, 1994, the exchange rate was 1 US dollar:8.72 renminbi. This was lower than the lowest exchange rate in the swap centers prior to the exchange rate reform, and it represented a 51 percent depreciation of the highest official exchange rate of 1 US dollar:5.76 renminbi. From that time until the outbreak of the Asian financial crisis in October 1997, the exchange rate of the renminbi relative to the US dollar rose to 1 US dollar:8.28 renminbi. After the Asian financial crisis, China kept this exchange rate unchanged in light of the role the renminbi played in maintaining stability in the neighboring Asian countries. However, the exchange rate mechanism thereafter became pegged to the US dollar and remained at about 1 US dollar:8.27 renminbi until July 21, 2005, when a new round of reform of the exchange rate was carried out and the value of the renminbi slowly began to rise.

After the exchange rate reform was successfully carried out, beginning in 1994 China's export and import trade maintained rapid growth, and the balance of payments shifted from a pattern of deficits occurring more often than surpluses to a pattern of constant surpluses (see Figure 4.1), especially after November 2001, when China formally became a member of the WTO. Over the course of fifteen years of negotiations, China had greatly reduced trade barriers, eliminated import quotas, and lowered the level of trade protectionism. After becoming a member of the WTO, beginning on January 1, 2002, China lowered tariffs on more than 5,300 items, with the average tariff rate dropping from 15.3 percent to 11.3 percent, and it fully joined the global market. The policies guiding exports were hugely successful.

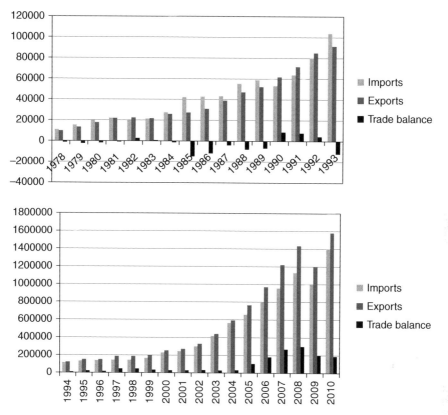

Figure 4.1   China's export and import trade (1978–2010) (US$m.)

Source: CEIC Databank

In addition to the exchange rate reform, other reforms also made progress and the basics of integrated commodities, credit, and foreign exchange markets began to appear.

2.3 Changes in the ownership structure at the turn of the century

Another breakthrough in the overall reform was made at the CPC's Fifteenth National Party Congress in 1997 by realigning the ownership basis for a market economy.

As the reforms of the 1990s progressed, privately run enterprises came to occupy an ever-more important position in the national economy and the share of the state-owned economy declined. This greatly displeased those politicians and theorists who were committed to the old system and who claimed that "scientific socialism takes the system of ownership by the whole people (state ownership) as the highest form of ownership and the goal that must be pursued" (Contributing Commentator 1996).

The supporters of the market-oriented reforms responded by arguing that the essence of socialism is the achievement of common prosperity and not that the state sector is in the dominant position. In addition, they argued that there are many forms of public ownership, and thus there is no reason to take state ownership as "the highest form of ownership." Moreover, looking at the issue from the perspective of the contemporary situation, they noted that "limited state capital is incapable of supporting the huge state sector." Therefore, "the state sector needs to contract in scope … shifting out of ordinary competitive sectors and concentrating in strategic sectors that the state must control" (Wu Jinglian *et al.* 1997).

In September 1997, the CPC National Party Congress issued its verdict when it announced a contraction in the scope of the state-owned economy. The congress designated the "non-public sector" as "an important component of the socialist market economy," and called for an adjustment to the pattern of ownership on the basis of the criterion of the "three favorables,"[12] with state capital gradually being confined to "important industries and key areas affecting the lifelines of the national economy" (Jiang Zemin 2010: 2: 19). In 1999, the Fourth Plenary Session of the Fifteenth Party Central Committee redefined the "important industries and key areas affecting the lifelines of the national economy" as "industries affecting national security, industries engaged in natural monopolies, industries that provide important public goods and services, and important key enterprises in pillar and hi-tech industries,"[13] thus further limiting its scope.

The above decisions by the CPC National Party Congress were written into the Revised Constitution of the People's Republic of China in 1998: "During the primary stage of socialism, the state adheres to the basic economic system with public ownership remaining dominant and diverse sectors of the economy developing side by side … Non-public economies, including the individual and private economies, are an important component of our socialist market economy … The state protects the legitimate rights and interests of the individual and private economy."

On the basis of the above provisions, China carried out extensive adjustments to the ownership structure. In addition to a reorganization of a number of large and medium-sized SOEs, the vast majority of the millions of TVEs controlled by local governments were turned into privately owned enterprises. In this way, the pattern in the Chinese economy changed from one where the state-owned sector dwarfed all other sectors to one where enterprises of all forms of ownership developed together (see Table 4.3). Except for a small number of key industries, the private economy (including the private sector plus the collective sector) was generally in the dominant position, and it was the private enterprises that contributed to employment growth.

The basic establishment of a market economy open to the global market liberated the productive forces that had long been constrained by the ossified command economy.

First, it became possible for ordinary people to start businesses. As the reforms progressed, the people's entrepreneurial spirit and enthusiasm to start businesses burst forth. By the end of the twentieth century, there were already more than 30 million private enterprises, and they were the most basic driving force behind China's economic growth.

Table 4.3 Proportion of GDP generated by different sectors of the economy

	State sector	*Collective sector*	*Private sector**
1990	47.7	18.5	33.8
1995	42.1	20.2	37.7
1996	40.4	21.3	38.3
1997	38.4	22.1	39.5
1998	38.9	19.3	41.9
1999	37.4	18.4	44.2
2000	37.3	16.5	46.2
2001	37.9	14.6	47.5

Source: *China Statistical Yearbook* (for the relevant years); CEIC Databank
Note: *Private sector includes all rural–urban economic entities that are not part of the state or collective sectors

Second, large quantities of underutilized human and material resources were put to more effective use. As people started setting up new businesses, production factors flowed from industries with lower productivity to industries with higher productivity. During the period following the onset of reform, about 250 million surplus rural workers migrated to the cities to work in industry and commerce. At the same time, about 70,000 sq. km of agricultural land, roughly equivalent to the size of Ireland, was transformed into urban land.

Third, in the 1990s, as the strategy of export-oriented industrialization was successfully implemented, China made use of the opportunity presented by the low savings rate in the developed countries to expand exports and to use net export demand to compensate for weak domestic demand and to sustain rapid economic growth.

Fourth, the introduction of advanced equipment and technology rapidly closed the technological gap between China and the developed countries that had accumulated over the course of 200 years.

Due to the impetus from the above forces, in the latter half of the 1990s China's economy embarked on a sound pattern of high growth and low inflation (see Figure 4.2).

3 China's economy at the fork in the road

At the end of the twentieth century, China announced that it had established a basic framework for a market economy. However, the reforms had not been entirely successful and the state sector still held a dominant position in the national economy. In reality, China had a "semi-command, semi-market" system. Under this type of system, economic and social problems increased and China again faced a historical choice regarding its future direction.

3.1 The semi-command, semi-market economy and the two possible development paths

In the mid-1980s, Chinese officials, heads of industry, and scholars decided that China's medium-term reform objective should be to establish the type of so-called "government-led" market economy that Japan and the other East Asian countries had established after World War II. In

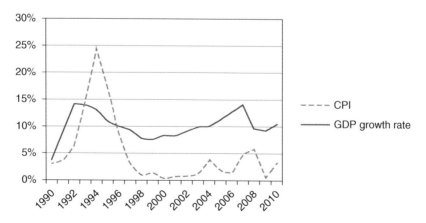

Figure 4.2 China's economic growth (1990–2010)

Source: CEIC Databank

such an economy the government assumed a more important role than that in the free market economies. By the turn of the century, China had largely achieved this objective.

However, unlike the other East Asian countries, China's market economy evolved from a "State Syndicate," or the "Party-State Inc.," as discussed by Lenin and the Eastern European scholars. The "commanding heights" of the national economy were always controlled by the state sector under the dictatorship of the proletariat, which was represented by the party. Accordingly, the Chinese government's interference in and control over the economy was much greater than that of governments under authoritarian developmentalism, such as Japan, Korea, and Singapore during their phases of rapid growth.

First, although by the start of the twenty-first century most small and medium-sized state-owned and rural enterprises had been restructured and the state sector no longer accounted for the majority of GDP, key areas of the national economy were still controlled by the state, including most strategic industries such as electricity, oil, telecommunications, railways, and finance, and the governance structures of these enterprises retained their basic characteristics from the command economy era.

Second, every level of government held significant power to control the flows of land, funds, and other important economic resources, and they used the substantial resources at their disposal to create short-term rapid GDP growth by supporting the SOEs and private enterprises of their choosing.

Third, the rule of law necessary for a modern market economy had not yet been established and there was a lack of effective constraints on the use of power. Thus government officials at every level frequently directly intervened in the micro-economic activities of enterprises by approving investment projects, controlling access to markets through administrative licensing, and controlling prices.

This semi-command, semi-market economy faced two possible development paths: first, the government would gradually reduce its intervention in micro-economic activities, strengthen its functions in areas such as macroeconomic management and the provision of public goods in cases of market failure, and the system would gradually evolve into a rule-based market economy; second, the government's control of and intervention in the market would constantly increase, the power of the state sector oligopolies would continue to expand, and the economy would be transformed into a state-capitalist economy. In China's case, it would be difficult to avoid state capitalism from further evolving into crony capitalism.

China's reformers were well aware of the system's shortcomings. Indeed, in 2003 the Third Plenary Session of the Sixteenth Central Committee of the CPC pointed out that there still existed "numerous institutional obstacles" to economic and social development. In order to overcome these obstacles, the plenary session passed a resolution that called for further promoting reforms in order to improve the market economy.[14]

Nevertheless, as the economy seemed to be prospering, people in power became increasingly unwilling to give up their power by resolutely implementing reform. Therefore, the CPC Central Committee's 2003 resolution was not earnestly implemented.

The other reason for the slower pace of reform was ideological. Anti-market left-wing thinking had always been highly influential in Chinese society, and toward the end of the twentieth century the spread of corruption and the widening gap between the rich and poor caused an "ultra-leftist" ideology, which had long been abandoned by the majority of Chinese people, to undergo a resurgence. Some supporters of the old system claimed that many of the current social problems were the result of the market-oriented reforms and they sought to use extreme methods, similar to those common during the Cultural Revolution, to resolve the problems in Chinese society.[15]

As a result, the economic system established at the turn of the century not only did not make any improvements, but instead degenerated into state capitalism. This was prominently demonstrated in the role given to "strong government" as the main feature of the so-called "China model" during China's rise.

3.2 *"Strong government" as the main feature of the "China model"*

The rise of statism and the increased urbanization at the beginning of the new century were directly related. Under Chinese law, rural land belongs to the collectives and urban land belongs to the state, which means governments can procure land at extremely low prices. Using this system, governments at all levels obtained assets worth trillions of yuan, greatly enhancing their power and the strength of the state sector.

Moreover, because the legal framework for restructuring the SOEs at the turn of the century was opaque and was dominated by administrative power, some people with powerful backgrounds were provided with opportunities to acquire huge amounts of public assets. This situation was an important impetus to establish the rule of law, but due to erroneous propaganda and general dissatisfaction with the privatization of public assets by influential officials, many people opposed further reforms, which only served to strengthen the state sector.

In December 2006, the State-owned Assets Supervision and Administration Commission of the State Council announced new measures to strengthen control over the economy and society, including the requirement that the state sector "maintain absolute control over important industries and key fields related to national security and the lifeblood of the national economy," such as the military, electricity, petroleum and petrochemicals, telecommunications, coal, and the civil aviation and shipping industries. Furthermore, the state sector was to "maintain relatively strong control over important backbone enterprises in fundamental and pillar industries and fields," including the nine major industries of equipment manufacturing, automobiles, electronics, construction, iron and steel, nonferrous metals, chemical engineering, surveying and design, and science and technology.[16] Thereafter, the power of the state sector in some industries and regions grew, whereas that of the private sector declined and state-holding and state-owned enterprises either bought or merged with small and medium-sized private enterprises, thus further strengthening the state sector.

As the state sector was strengthened and state intervention increased, an alternative proposal, known as the "China model," that was opposed to legal, democratic, and market-oriented reforms began to gain momentum. Its main characteristics are that the market is "driven" by a strong government, and the state sector guides the national economy. It is said to be capable of "concentrating resources to accomplish large undertakings," including the "miracles" of the Beijing Olympics in 2008, the opening of the high-speed railway in 2010, and continuous GDP growth of around 15 percent in Chongqing, and it had allowed China to weather the storm created by the global financial crisis and to serve as an example for other countries. In essence, it is state capitalism or authoritarian developmentalism with strong government intervention.

Between 2009 and 2011, the notion of the "China model" grew in influence, thus placing the question of "Where should China go from here?" squarely in front of China's leaders and people.

In reality, despite achieving some short-term economic results, state capitalism and authoritarian developmentalism did not improve the economic and social situations in China.

In term of economics, the most prominent issue is the ever-increasing disastrous micro- and macroeconomic consequences of authoritarian developmentalism's reliance on strong government, giant SOEs, and massive investments.

After 2003, every locality invested heavily in capital-intensive industries and demanded movement in the direction of heavy industries in the hopes of supporting rapid GDP growth. It is certainly possible to maintain rapid growth in the short term, but in the long term such growth will be unsustainable. In recent years, this mode of growth has created increasingly serious problems of resource depletion, energy shortages, and environmental degradation.

At the same time, the rate of investment in the national economy has remained at nearly 50 percent (see Figure 4.3), while workers' wages have risen slowly and consumer spending as a proportion of GDP has fallen significantly (see Figure 4.4). In order to create greater external demand, prior to 2005 the government adopted policies to prevent the renminbi from appreciating against other currencies, and starting in July 2005 it implemented a policy of creeping appreciation. To control the pace of renminbi appreciation, the Central Bank bought up large amounts of foreign exchange, while releasing large amounts of liquidity into the system, which led to a rapid rise in M2/GDP (see Figure 4.5) and created asset bubbles, most notably in real estate.

Moreover, as the supply of surplus rural labor gradually runs out and the technological levels of China's manufacturing industry catch up with those of the developed countries, in order to maintain its high growth rate China must increasingly rely on innovation to handle the transition from an investment-driven to an efficiency-driven growth model. If it is unable to quickly overcome the institutional obstacles and transform its economic growth mode, it will be impossible to prevent a sharp slowing down of the Chinese economy.

In terms of society, growth promoted by strong government has given rise to two main problems.

First, a significant rent-seeking culture has led to the rapid spread of corruption, and in some regions and departments the buying and selling of official positions has even become the norm. According to estimates by one economist, "grey income" in China almost doubled between 2005 and 2008, reaching almost 15 percent of GDP.[17] This grey income mostly came from the corruption associated with the allocation of public funds and public resources, rent-seeking, and the seizure of public funds and the income of others.

Second, given that investment as a proportion of GDP is increasing, there has been a long-term decline in workers' wages as a proportion of national income, and increases in the income

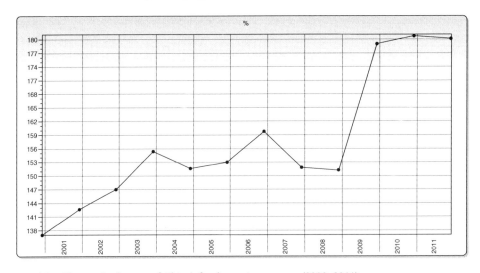

Figure 4.3   Changes in the rate of China's fixed-asset investments (2000–2011)

Source: CEIC Databank

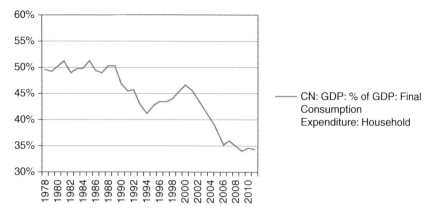

Figure 4.4 Falling consumption as a proportion of GDP (1978–2010)

Source: CEIC Databank

of all types of workers have slowed. This has further widened the gap between the rich and poor. According to estimates by Li Shi, between 2003 and 2007 China's Gini coefficient increased from 0.45 to 0.48; after allowing for sampling errors (mainly among high-income groups), the number reached 0.52 (Li Shi and Luo Chuliang 2011). Even though the Gini coefficient of personal incomes in China has been higher than 0.47 since 2003, as announced by the National Bureau of Statistics in 2013, it is still widely believed to be even higher (see Table 4.4).

Intervention by the government aimed at stimulating growth has led to serious economic and social dislocations and to an intensification of conflicts between officials (or government) and citizens, and it has even exacerbated social unrest. Without fast-paced legal, democratic, and market-oriented reforms to prevent these problems from becoming worse, China may become stuck on a path leading from state capitalism to crony capitalism.

4 Will we see a new round of reform in China in the future?

After 2011, China's political and social situation underwent some subtle changes. On the one hand, as the debates about where China should go from here intensified, many people realized

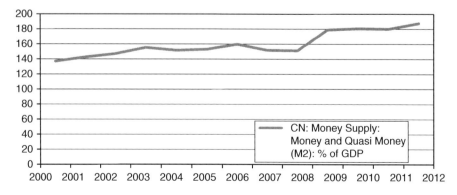

Figure 4.5 Changes in China's M2/GDP (2000–2012)

Source: CEIC Databank

Table 4.4 Personal distribution of incomes (1988–2012)

Year	1988	1995	2003	2004	2005	2006	2007	2008	2009	2010	2011	2012
Gini coefficient	0.39	0.44	0.479	0.473	0.485	0.487	0.484	0.491	0.490	0.481	0.477	0.474

Sources: Gini coefficients for 1988 and 1995 are from Li Shi (2003); Gini coefficients for 2003–12 are from NBS data (January 18, 2013) (http://www.scio.gov.cn/xwfbh/xwbfbh/wqfbh/2013/0118/index.htm)

that there was no turning back. On the other hand, problems that had remained concealed for several years gradually emerged, for example, the staggering corruption and waste involved in major projects under the authoritarian–developmentalist system, like the construction of the high-speed rail network. The 2012 events in Chongqing also served as a warning of the dangers of unchecked political power.

Since the spring of 2012, China's reform climate has begun to warm, and the possibility of creating a new consensus on reform has emerged. An increasing number of people are arguing that the reform agenda should be restored, and many people believe that the next round of reform should include implementation of both market-oriented economic reforms and also political reforms aimed at strengthening the legal system and democracy.

At the same time, experimental reforms have been introduced at the central and local levels. For example, the People's Bank of China has adopted flexible measures to gradually make deposit and lending rates more market based. The China Securities Regulatory Commission is taking steps to change its regulatory approach from the current model dependent on substantive approvals to compliance-based supervision with mandatory information disclosures. The city of Shanghai is in the process of implementing a plan to withdraw state capital from dozens of non-strategic industries. Several institutional innovations in Guangdong province are also worthy of note: first, the reform to allow the establishment of civil organizations that are not government affiliated, which began in Shenzhen, has already been rolled out across the province. Second, with the permission of the State Administration for Industry and Commerce, a pilot project to streamline the business registration system in Guangdong has been implemented. These measures may lead to non-public organizations being granted freedom to enter previously restricted economic and social areas.

The Eighteenth Party Congress held in November 2012 noted, "We should, with greater political courage and vision, lose no time in deepening reform in key sectors." In the area of economic reform it is necessary to "continue to improve the socialist market economy … strike a balance between the role of the government and that of the market … leverage to a greater extent and in a wider scope the basic role of the market in allocating resources." In the area of political reform, it was suggested that the party "work harder to enhance socialist democracy in a systemic way … [and to] ensure that all governance functions are performed in accordance with the law." This represents a possible first step in restoring reform in China. In December 2012, the Central Economic Work Conference also called for "explicitly establishing an overall plan, roadmap, and schedule for comprehensively deepening reform."

At present, people from all walks of life are engaged in lively discussions about overall plans and ideas regarding a new round of reform. Due to the traditional "leftist" ideology and the wealth that has accrued in recent years to special interest groups by virtue of their power, the next step of reform will not be without obstacles or barriers. But a new stage of reform, with the prospect of moving closer to a prosperous, democratic, civilized, and harmonious modern country, is something to look forward to.

Notes

1 The authors would like to thank Gregory Chow, Nancy Hearst, Nicholas Martin, and Chenggang Xu for their patience, comments, and suggestions.

2 Market socialism, originating in the socialist countries of Eastern Europe, was a highly influential school of thought in the reforms of the Soviet Union and the Eastern European countries. According to a definition by one of its main advocates, market socialism is a theoretical model of an economic system, in which the means of production are owned by a state or collective and the allocation of resources follows the rules of the market (Brus 1987).

3 At a Central Work Conference on December 16, 1980, in his report, "The Economic Situation and Our Experience and Lessons," CPC leader Chen Yun proposed the reform guideline for "crossing the river by feeling the stones" (1995: 2:152). At the closing ceremony of the conference, Deng Xiaoping expressed his full agreement with Chen Yun's speech.

4 National Bureau of Statistics (1989: 228).

5 Calculations based on National Bureau of Statistics (1981, 1985).

6 In October 1984, Deng Xiaoping recalled, "A few years ago, the employment issue caused quite a stir and everybody was incredibly worried. My advice was to put it aside for a couple of years" (1994: 3: 91). During his 1992 southern talks, Deng Xiaoping said, "It was my idea to discourage contention so as to have more time for action. Once disputes begin, they complicate matters and waste a lot of time. As a result, nothing is accomplished" (1994: 3: 374).

7 A "commodity economy" is a Russian term for a "market economy." However, for ideological reasons the term "market economy" was seldom used in China in the 1980s.

8 The Third Plenary Session of the Twelfth Central Committee of the CPC proposed two basic points regarding the establishment of the "planned commodity economy." First, SOEs would be allowed more autonomy so as to make them "relatively independent socialist commodity producers and operators" and to "enhance enterprise vitality as a central link in the reform of the economic system." Second, the scope of state intervention would be gradually reduced and the scope of price fluctuations and free prices would be expanded appropriately because achieving "reform of the pricing system is the key to the success or the failure of the reform of the entire economic system."

9 In May 1984, the State Council stipulated that the prices of the means of production sold by the SOEs in excess of the plan could not be more than 20 percent higher or lower than the state-set prices. However, in reality, the 20 percent limit was not strictly adhered to. On January 1, 1985, the government abolished this restriction.

10 This is a reference to comments by Deng Xiaoping during his southern tour to "certain leaders" who still supported the old system and the Mao-era ideas (1994: 3: 266).

11 "Socialism with Chinese characteristics" was first used by Deng Xiaoping as a special term to mean that China would follow a path different from that of the Soviet Union.

12 During his southern inspection tour in 1992, Deng Xiaoping proposed that the criterion for deciding what is right and what is wrong should be based on whether it is favorable to promote growth of the productive forces in a socialist society, to increase the overall strength of the socialist state, and to raise living standards (1994: 3: 360).

13 Decision of the CPC Central Committee on Some Major Questions Concerning the Reform and Development of SOEs.

14 Resolution on Several Issues Concerning Improving the Socialist Market Economy, October 14, 2003.

15 Between 2003 and 2010, "www.wyzxsx.com" and other "left-wing" websites published numerous articles that criticized the market-based reforms and that called for a return to "Mao Zedong's revolutionary line." Such writings attracted the attention of some people.

16 See "Guidelines for Promoting the Regulation of State Capital and Reorganization of the SOEs" by the State-owned Assets Supervision and Administration Commission, released by the General Office of the State Council, December 5, 2006.

17 "Grey income" refers to two types of income: the first is income that is not clearly defined as legal or illegal under existing laws and regulations; the second is income gained through illegal means but without clear evidence to prove that it is illegal. See Wang Xiaolu (2010).

Bibliography

Acemoglu, D. and Robinson, J. (2012) *Why Nations Fail: The Origins of Power, Prosperity, and Poverty*, New York: Crown Business.

Bai Chong-En and Zhenjie Qian (2010) 'The Factor Income Distribution in China: 1978–2007', *China Economic Review* 21(4) (December), 650–670.

Brus, W. (1987) 'Market Socialism', in Eatwell, J. *et al.* (eds.) *The New Palgrave Dictionary of Economics*, London: Macmillan, pp. 3, 337.

CCCPC Party Literature Research Office (1998) *Deng Xiaoping Sixiang Nianpu (1975–97)* (Chronicle of Deng Xiaoping's Thought [1975–97]), Beijing: Central Party Literature Publishing House.

Chen Jun and Hong Nan (eds.) (2012) *Jiang Zemin yu Shehuizhuyi Shichang Jingji de Tichu* (Jiang Zemin and the Proposal for a Socialist Market Economy: Looking Back at 20 Years of the Socialist Market Economy), Beijing: Central Party Literature Publishing House.

Chen Yun (1995) *Chen Yun Wenxuan* (Selected Works of Chen Yun), Beijing: People's Publishing House.

Chow, G. (2007) *China's Economic Transformation*, Oxford: Blackwell.

Coase, R. and Ning Wang (2012) *How China Became Capitalist*, Basingstoke, UK: Palgrave Macmillan.

Contributing Commentator (1996) 'Yi Gongyouzhi Wei Zhuti de Jiben Biaozhi ji Zenyang Caineng Jianchi Gongyouzhi de Zhuti Diwei' (Basic Designation of the Primacy of the System of Public Ownership and How to Maintain Its Position of Prominence), *Contemporary Ideological Trends*, no. 4, 2–17.

Deng Xiaoping (1994) *Selected Works of Deng Xiaoping*, Beijing: Foreign Languages Press.

Editorial Department of Comparative Economic and Social Systems (ed.) (1989) *Fubai: Huobi yu Quanli de Jiaohuan* (Corruption: Currency and Power Exchange), Beijing: China Prospect Press.

Friedman, M. (1998) 'Memorandum from Milton Friedman to Zhao Ziyang', reprinted in Milton and Rose D. Friedman, *Two Lucky People*, Chicago, IL: University of Chicago Press, pp. 607–609.

Hu Heli (1989) 'Lianzheng San Ce' (Three Recommendations on Anti-Corruption), *Comparative Economic and Social Systems*, no. 2, 19–23.

Hua Sheng, He Jiacheng, Jiang Yue, Gao Liang and Zhang Shaojie (1985) 'Lun Juyou Zhongguo Tese de Jiage Gaige Daolu' (The Path of Price Reform with Chinese Characteristics), *Economic Research*, no. 2, 27–32.

Hua Sheng, He Jiacheng, Zhang Xuejun, Lao Xiaopeng and Bian Yongzhuang (1986) 'Jingji Yunxing Moshi de Zhuanhuan: Shilun Zhongguo Jinyibu Gaige de Wenti he Silu' (Transformation of the Mode of Economic Operations: Questions and Thoughts on Further Reform in China), *Economic Research*, no. 2, 3–11.

Jiang Zemin (2006) *Jiang Zemin Lun Shehuizhuyi Shichang Jingji* (On the Socialist Market Economy), Beijing: Central Party Literature Publishing House.

Jiang Zemin (2010) *Selected Works of Jiang Zemin*, Beijing: Foreign Languages Press.

Kornai, J. (1992) *The Socialist System: The Political Economy of Communism*, Princeton, NJ: Princeton University Press.

Li Shi (2003) 'Zhongguo geren shouru fenpei yanjiu huigu yu zhanwang' (Review and Prospects of Personal Income Distribution in China), *Jingjixue Jikan* (China Economic Quarterly), no. 2, 379–404.

Li Shi and Luo Chuliang (2011) 'Zhongguo shouru chajujiujing you duoda?' (How Big is China's Income Gap?), *Economic Research*, no. 4, 68–79.

Li Shi and Yue Ximing (2004) 'Zhongguo Chengxiang Shouru Chaju Diaocha' (Investigating the Urban/Rural Income Gap), *Caijing*, nos. 3–4.

Naughton, B. (2007) *The Chinese Economy: Transitions and Growth*, Cambridge, MA: MIT Press.

Qian Jiaju (1988) 'Guanyu Wujia, Jiaoyu, Shehui Fengqi de Jidian Yijian' (Some Suggestions Regarding Prices, Education, and the Social Atmosphere), April 2, reprinted in *Haiwai Youzi Sheng* (The Voice of Overseas Chinese), Hong Kong: Cosmos Books, 1992.

Qian Yingyi and Chenggang Xu (1993) 'Why China's Economic Reforms Differ: The M-form Hierarchy and Entry/Expansion of the Non-state Sector', *Economics of Transition* 1(2), 135–170.

Research Department of the Institute of Economics of the Chinese Academy of Social Sciences (ed.) (1987) *Zhongguo de Jingji Tizhi Gaige: Bashanlun Hongguan Jingji Guanli Guoji Taolunhui Wenji* (China Economic Reform: Collected Works from the International Seminar on Macroeconomic Management), Beijing: China Economic Publishing House.

Vogel, E. F. (2011) *Deng Xiaoping and the Transformation of China*, Cambridge, MA: Harvard University Press.

Wang Renzhi (1989) 'Guanyu Fandui Zichanjieji Ziyouhua' (Opposing Bourgeois Liberalization), speech presented to the Party Building Theory Research Class at the CPC Central Party School on December 15, 1989; reprinted in *Renmin Ribao* (People's Daily), February 22, 1990, p.1, and *Qiushi*, no. 4 (1996), pp. 2–13.

Wang Xiaolu (2010) 'Huise Shouru yu Guomin Shouru Fenpei' (Distribution of Grey Income and National Income), *Comparative Studies*, no. 3, 1–29.

World Bank (1985) *China: Long-Term Development Issues and Options*, Baltimore, MD: Johns Hopkins University Press.

Wu Jinglian (2005) *Understanding and Interpreting Chinese Economic Reform*, Mason, OH: Thomson/South-Western.

Wu Jinglian (2012) 'Economics and China's Economic Rise', in Aoki, M. and Wu, J. (eds.) *The Chinese Economy: A New Transition*, Basingstoke, UK: Palgrave Macmillan, pp. 13–31.

Wu Jinglian, Zhang Junkuang, Lü Wei, Long Guoqiang, and Zhang Chunlin (1997) 'Shixian Guoyou Jingji de Zhanluexing Gaizu: Guoyou Qiye Gaige de Yizhong Silu' (Achieving a Strategic Restructuring of the State-owned Economy: Reflections on the Reform of SOEs), *Management World*, no. 5, 13–22.

Wu Jinglian and Zhao Renwei (1987) 'The Dual Pricing System Problem in Chinese Industry', *Journal of Comparative Economics* 11(3), 309–318.

Xu Chenggang (2011) 'The Fundamental Institutions of China's Reforms and Development', *Journal of Economic Literature* 49(4), 1076–1151.

Ye Jianying (1996) 'Speech at the Closing of Ceremony of the Central Work Conference of the CPC Central Committee', December 13, 1978, *Ye Jianying Xuanji* (Selected Works of Ye Jianying), Beijing: People's Publishing House, pp. 493–502.

Zhang Weiwei (2012) *The China Wave: Rise of a Civilisational State*, Hackensack, NJ: World Century.

Zhao Ziyang (1986) Speeches at the March 13 Meeting of the CPC Central Committee's Financial Work Leading Group and at the March 15 Executive Meeting of the State Council, unpublished report.

5

ECONOMIC GROWTH AND DEVELOPMENT

Justin Yifu Lin

China's economic development has been miraculous, with an average annual GDP growth rate of 9.9 percent and trade growth rate of 16.3 percent, since the transition from a planned economy to a market economy in 1979. This chapter attempts to provide answers to five related questions: why was it possible for China to achieve such extraordinary growth performance during its transition? Why was China unable to attain similar success before its transition started? Why did most other transition economies, both socialist and nonsocialist, fail to achieve a similar performance? What costs does China pay for its extraordinary success? Can China maintain dynamic growth in the coming decades? The chapter argues that China's extraordinary development performance in the transition was a result of developing its economy according to its comparative advantages which allowed China to tap into the "latecomer advantage." The poor performance before the transition was due to China's attempt to develop comparative advantage–defying capital-intensive heavy industries while China was a capital-scarce agrarian economy. Other transition economies failed to achieve a similar performance because they adopted a shock therapy causing the collapse of their economies; whereas China adopted a gradual dual-track approach, which achieves stability and dynamic growth simultaneously. The costs of this transition approach are widening income disparities and other social economic issues – China, however, has the potential to maintain dynamic growth in the coming decades if the remaining distortions as a legacy of dual-track transition are eliminated.

China was one of the most advanced and powerful countries in the world for more than a thousand years before the modern era. Even in the nineteenth century it dominated the world economic landscape. According to Angus Maddison, the famous economic historian, China accounted for a third of global GDP in purchasing power parity in 1820 (Figure 5.1). But with the Industrial Revolution in the eighteenth century, the West quickly rose, and China slid. And, with a weaker economy, it was defeated repeatedly by the Western powers, becoming a quasi-colony, ceding extraterritorial rights in treaty ports to twenty foreign countries. Its customs revenues were controlled by foreigners, and it surrendered territory to Britain, Japan, and Russia.

Since China's defeat in the Opium War in 1840, the country's elites, like those in other parts of the developing world, strived to make their motherland a powerful and respected nation again. But their efforts produced little success. China's share of global GDP shrank to about 5 percent and stayed low until 1979 (Figure 5.1).

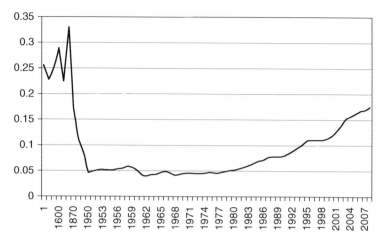

Figure 5.1 China's share in global GDP

Source: Maddison (2010)

China's economic fate then changed dramatically at the end of the 1970s when it started to implement the reform and opening strategy. Since then, its economic performance has been miraculous. Between 1979 and 1990, China's average annual growth rate was 9.0 percent.[1] At the end of that period and even up to the early 2000s, many scholars still believed that China could not continue that growth rate much longer due to the lack of fundamental reforms.[2] But China's annual growth rate during the period 1991–2011 increased to 10.4 percent. On the global economic scene, China's growth over the last three decades has been unprecedented. This was a dramatic contrast with the depressing performance of other transitional economies in Eastern Europe and the former Soviet Union.

As a result of the extraordinary performance, there has been a dramatic change in China's status in the global economy. In 1979, China barely registered on the global economic scale, commanding a mere 0.98 percent of global GDP in current US dollars. Today, it is the world's second largest economy and produces 8.4 percent of global GDP (in 2011).

In 1979, China was a low-income country; its income per capita of US$82, as at the current US dollar value, was less than one-third of the average in sub-Saharan countries. It is now an upper middle-income country. In 2011 its income per capita reached US$5,444 over three times the level of sub-Saharan Africa. As a result of this extraordinary performance, more than 600 million people have got out of poverty in China.

At the start of this transition, China was also an inward-oriented economy with a trade dependence (trade-to-GDP) ratio of 17.9 percent, less than one half of the world average. China's average annual trade growth rate measured in current US dollars between 1979 and 2011 was an astonishing 16.3 percent. Now China is the largest exporter of goods in the world. Its imports and exports contributed to 8.4 percent of the global trade in 2011.

Behind this growth and trade expansion, there has been a dramatic structural transformation – in particular, rapid urbanization and industrialization. At the start of economic reforms in 1979, China was primarily an agrarian economy; 81 percent of its population lived in rural areas, and primary products comprised 31.3 percent of GDP. The shares declined to 48.7 percent and

10.1 percent respectively in 2011. A similar change also occurred in the composition of China's exports. In 1980 primary products comprised 50.3 percent of merchandise exports. Now, 80.6 percent of China's exports are manufactures.

Accompanying the change in the composition of China's exports is the accumulation of foreign reserves. Even up to 1990, China's foreign reserves were US$11.1 billion, barely enough to cover 2.5 months of imports, and its reserves today are over US$3 trillion – the largest in the world.

China's dynamic growth made significant contributions to the world as well. China withstood the shocks and maintained dynamic growth in the East Asian financial crisis in 1998 and the global crisis in 2008. China's decision to maintain the renminbi's stability helped other East Asian economies avoid a competitive devaluation, which contributed tremendously to quick recovery of the crisis-affected countries. China's dynamic growth in the current global crisis was a driving force for the global recovery.

The spectacular performance over the past three decades far exceeded the expectations of anyone at the outset of the transition, including Deng Xiaoping, the architect of China's reform and opening-up strategy.[3]

Can China maintain dynamic growth in the coming decades? The chapter will conclude with a few lessons from the experiences of China's development for other countries.

1 The reason for China's extraordinary performance in transition

Rapid, sustained increase in per capita income is a modern phenomenon. Studies by economic historians, such as Angus Maddison (2001), show that average annual per capita income growth in the West was only 0.05 percent before the eighteenth century, jumping to about 1 percent in the nineteenth century and reaching about 2 percent in the twentieth century. That means that per capita income in Europe took 1,400 years to double before the eighteenth century, about 70 years in the nineteenth century, and 35 years thereafter.

A continuous stream of technological innovation and industrial upgrading is the basis for sustained growth in any economy in any time (Lin 2012b). The dramatic surge in growth in modern times in the West is a result of a paradigm shift in technological innovation. Before the Industrial Revolution in the eighteenth century, technological innovations were generated mostly by the experiences of craftsmen and farmers in their daily production. After the Industrial Revolution, experience-based innovation was increasingly replaced by field experimentation and, later, by science-based experiments conducted in scientific laboratories (Lin 1995; Landes 1998). This shift accelerated the rate of technological innovation, marking the coming of modern economic growth and contributing to the dramatic acceleration of income growth in the nineteenth and twentieth centuries (Kuznets 1966).

The Industrial Revolution not only accelerated the rate of technological innovation but also transformed industrial, economic, and social structures. Before the eighteenth century every economy was agrarian; 85 percent or more of the labor force worked in agriculture, mostly in self-sufficient production for the family. The acceleration of growth was accompanied by a move of labor from agriculture to manufacturing and services. The manufacturing sector gradually moved from very labor-intensive industries at the beginning to more capital-intensive heavy and high-tech industries. Finally, the service sector came to dominate the economy. Accompanying the change in industrial structure was an increase in the scale of production, the required capital and skill, the market scope, and the risks. To exploit the potential unleashed by new technology and industry, and to reduce the transaction costs and share risks requires innovations as well as improvements in an economy's hard infrastructure, such as power and road networks, and its soft infrastructure. Soft infrastructure consists of such elements as belief, the legal framework, financial institutions, and the education system (Lewis 1954; Kuznets 1966; North 1981; Lin 2011).

A developing country such as China, which started its modernization drive in 1949, potentially has the advantage of backwardness in its pursuit of technological innovation and structural transformation (Gerschenkron 1962; World Bank 2008). In advanced high-income countries technological innovation and industrial upgrading require costly and risky investments in research and development, because their technologies and industries are located on the global frontier. Moreover, the institutional innovation, which is required for realizing the potential of new technology and industry, often proceeds in a costly trial-and-error, path-dependent, evolutionary process (Fei and Ranis 1997). By contrast, a latecomer country in the catching-up process can borrow technology, industry, and institutions from the advanced countries at low risk and costs. So if a developing country knows how to tap the advantage of backwardness in technology, industry, and social and economic institutions, it can grow at an annual rate several times that of high-income countries for decades before closing its income gap with those countries.

In the post-World War II period, 13 of the world's economies achieved average annual growth of 7 percent or above for 25 years or more. The Commission on Growth and Development, headed by Nobel Laureate Michael Spence, finds that the first of five common features of these thirteen economies is their ability to tap the potential of the advantage of backwardness. In the commission's language, the 13 economies: "imported what the rest of the world knew and exported what it wanted" (World Bank 2008: 22).[4]

After the transition was initiated by Deng Xiaoping in 1979, China became one of those 13 successful economies by adopting an opening-up strategy and starting to tap this potential (of importing what the rest of the world knows and exporting what the world wants). This is demonstrated by the large inflows of foreign direct investment and the rapid growth in its international trade, the dramatic increase in its trade dependence ratio. While in 1979 primary and processed primary goods accounted for more than 75 percent of China's exports, the share of manufactured goods had increased to 95 percent by 2010. Moreover, China's manufactured exports upgraded from simple toys, textiles, and other cheap products in the 1980s and 1990s to high-value and technologically sophisticated machinery and information and communication technology products in the 2000s. The exploitation of the advantage of backwardness has allowed China to emerge as the world's workshop and to achieve extraordinary economic growth by reducing the costs of innovation, industrial upgrading, and social and economic transformation (Lin 2012a).

2 Why did China fail to achieve rapid growth before 1979?

China possessed the advantage of backwardness long before the transition began in 1979. The socialist government won the revolution in 1949 and started modernizing in earnest in 1953. Why had China failed to tap the potential of the advantage of backwardness and achieve dynamic growth before 1979? This failure came about because China adopted a wrong development strategy at that time.

China was the largest economy and among the most advanced, powerful countries in the world before pre-modern times (Maddison 2007). Mao Zedong, Zhou Enlai, and other first-generation revolutionary leaders in China, like many other Chinese social and political elites, were inspired by the dream of achieving rapid modernization.

The lack of industrialization – especially the lack of large heavy industries that were the basis of military strength and economic power – was perceived as the root cause of the country's backwardness. Thus it was natural for the social and political elites in China to start nation building by prioritizing the development of large, heavy, advanced industries after the Revolution.[5] In the nineteenth century the political leaders of France, Germany, the United States, and other Western countries pursued effectively the same strategy, motivated by the contrast between Britain's rising industrial power and the backwardness of their own industry (Gerschenkron 1962; Chang 2003).

Starting in 1953, China adopted a series of ambitious Five-Year Plans to accelerate the building of modern advanced industries with the goal of overtaking Britain in ten years and catching up to the United States in fifteen. But China was a low-income agrarian economy at that time. In 1953, 83.5 percent of its labor force was employed in the primary sector, and its per capita income (measured in purchasing power parity terms) was only 4.8 percent of that of the United States (Maddison 2001). Given China's employment structure and income level, the country did not possess a comparative advantage in the modern advanced capital-intensive industries of high-income countries; furthermore, Chinese firms in those industries were not viable in an open competitive market.[6]

To achieve its strategic goal, the Chinese government needed to protect the priority industries by giving firms in those industries a monopoly and subsidizing them through various price distortions, including suppressed interest rates, an overvalued exchange rate, and lower prices for inputs. The price distortions created shortages, and the government was obliged to use administrative measures to mobilize and allocate resources directly to nonviable firms (Lin 2009; Lin and Li 2009).

These interventions enabled China to quickly establish modern advanced industries, test nuclear bombs in the 1960s, and launch satellites in the 1970s. But the resources were misallocated, the incentives were distorted, and the development of labor-intensive sectors in which China had a comparative advantage was repressed. As a result, economic efficiency was low, and the growth before 1979 was driven mainly by an increase in inputs.[7] Despite a very respectable average annual GDP growth rate of 6.1 percent in 1952–1978 and the possession of a wide range of large modern industries, China was still a poor agrarian economy in terms of employment structure before the transition started in 1979, with 71.3 percent of its labor force in traditional agriculture. In 1952–1978 household consumption grew by only 2.3 percent a year, in sharp contrast to the 7.1 percent average growth after 1979.

3 Why didn't other transition economies perform equally well?

All other socialist countries and many developing countries after World War II adopted a development strategy similar to that of China. Most colonies gained political independence after the 1950s. Compared with developed countries, these newly independent developing countries had extremely low per capita income, high birth and death rates, low average educational attainment, and very little infrastructure – and were heavily specialized in the production and export of primary commodities while importing most manufactured goods. The development of modern advanced industries was perceived as the only way to achieve rapid economic takeoff, avoid dependence on the Western industrial powers, and eliminate poverty (Prebisch 1950).

It became a fad after the 1950s for developing countries in both the socialist and the non-socialist camps to adopt an import substitution strategy to accelerate the development of capital-intensive modern advanced industry in their countries (Lal and Mynt 1996; Lin 2012c). But the capital-intensive modern industries on their priority lists defied the comparative advantages determined by the endowment structure of their low-income agrarian economies. To implement their development strategy, both socialist and nonsocialist developing countries introduced distortions and government interventions similar to those in China.[8] This strategy made it possible to establish some modern industries and achieve investment-led growth for one or two decades in the 1950s to the 1970s. Nevertheless, the distortions led to pervasive soft budget constraints, rent-seeking, and misallocation of resources (Lin and Tan 1999). Economic efficiency was unavoidably low. Stagnation and frequent social and economic crises began to beset most socialist and nonsocialist developing countries by the 1970s and 1980s. Liberalization from excessive state intervention became a trend in the 1980s and 1990s.

The symptoms of poor economic performance and social and economic crises, and their root cause in distortions and government interventions, were common to China and other socialist transition economies as well as other developing countries. But the academic and policy communities in the 1980s did not realize that those distortions were second-best institutional arrangements, endogenous to the needs of protecting nonviable firms in the priority sectors. As a result, they recommended that socialist and other developing countries immediately remove all distortions by implementing simultaneous programs of liberalization, privatization, and marketization with the aim of quickly achieving efficient, first-best outcomes (Lin 2009).

But if those distortions were eliminated immediately, many nonviable firms in the priority sectors would collapse, causing a contraction of GDP, a surge in unemployment, and acute social disorders. To avoid those dreadful consequences, many governments continued to subsidize the nonviable firms through other, disguised, less efficient subsidies and protections (Lin and Tan 1999). Transition and developing countries thus had even poorer growth performance and stability in the 1980s and 1990s than in the 1960s and 1970s (Easterly 2001).

During the transition process China adopted a pragmatic, gradual, dual-track approach. The government first improved the incentives and productivity by allowing the workers in the collective farms and state-owned firms to be residual claimants and to set the prices for selling at the market after delivering the quota obligations to the state at fixed prices (Lin 1992, 2012a). At the same time, the government continued to provide necessary protections to nonviable firms in the priority sectors and simultaneously, liberalized the entry of private enterprises, joint ventures, and foreign direct investment in labor-intensive sectors in which China had a comparative advantage but that were repressed before the transition. This transition strategy allowed China both to maintain stability by avoiding the collapse of old priority industries and to achieve dynamic growth by simultaneously pursuing its comparative advantage and tapping the advantage of backwardness in the industrial upgrading process. In addition, the dynamic growth in the newly liberalized sectors created the conditions for reforming the old priority sectors. Through this gradual, dual-track approach China achieved "reform without losers" (Naughton 1995; Lau *et al.* 2000; Lin *et al.* 2003) and moved gradually but steadily to a well-functioning market economy.

A few other socialist economies – such as Poland,[9] Slovenia, and Vietnam, which achieved outstanding performance during their transitions – adopted a similar gradual, dual-track approach (Lin 2009). Mauritius adopted a similar approach in the 1970s to reform distortions caused by the import-substitution strategy to become Africa's success story (Subramanian and Roy 2003).[10]

4 What costs does China pay for its success?

The gradual, dual-track approach to transition is a double-edged sword. While it enables China to achieve enviable stability and growth in the transition process, it also brings with it a number of structural problems, particularly the disparities in income distribution, consumption and savings, and external account.[11] When the transition started in 1979, China was a relatively egalitarian society. With the rapid growth, the income distribution has become increasingly unequal. The Gini coefficient, a measurement of income inequality, increased from .31 in 1981 to .47 in 2008 (Ravallion and Chen 2007). Meanwhile, household consumption as a percentage of GDP dropped from about 50 percent down to about 35 percent, whereas the fixed asset investment increased from around 30 percent to more than 45 percent of GDP (see top panel of Figure 5.2), and the net exports increased from almost nothing to a high of 8.8 percentage of GDP in 2007 (see bottom panel of Figure 5.2). As I will elaborate below, such disparities are the by-products of remaining distortions in the dual-track approach to transition, which favor the large corporations and the rich.

During the transition process, the Chinese government retained some distortions as a way to provide continuous support to nonviable firms in the previous strategy's priority industries (see section 3). Major remaining distortions include the concentration of financial services in the four large state-owned banks and equity market, the almost zero royalty on natural resources, and the monopoly of major service industries, including telecommunication, power, and banking.[12]

Those distortions contribute to the stability in China's transition process. They also contribute to the rising income disparity and other imbalances in the economy. This is because only big

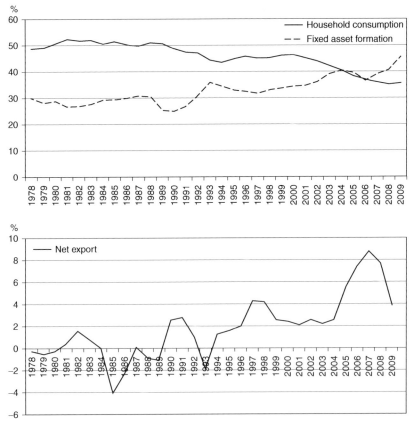

Figure 5.2 Contributions of household consumption, fixed asset formation, and net exports to GDP

Source: National Statistical Bureau (2010: 36)

companies and rich people have access to credit services provided by the big banks and equity market and the interest rates are artificially repressed. As a result, big companies and rich people are receiving subsidies from the depositors who have no access to banks' credit services and are relatively poor. The story is similar for the equity market. The concentration of profits and wealth in large companies and widening of income disparities are unavoidable. The low royalty levies of natural resources and the monopoly in the service sector have similar effects.

In general, the higher-income households have a lower marginal propensity to consume than the lower-income households. Therefore, if wealth is disproportionately concentrated in the higher-income group, the nation's consumption-to-GDP ratio will be lower and saving's ratio will be higher. The concentration of wealth in the large firms has a similar effect. A consequence of such an income distribution pattern is the relative high household savings and extraordinarily high corporate savings in China as shown in Figure 5.3.

The high household and corporate savings in turn lead to a high rate of investment and quick building up of production capacity. A large trade surplus is a natural consequence of limited domestic absorption capacity due to low consumption ratio. Therefore, it is imperative for China to address the structural imbalances, by removing the remaining distortions in the finance, natural resources, and service sectors so as to complete the transition to a well-functioning market economy. The necessary reforms include: first, removing the financial repression and allowing the development of small and local financing institutions, including local banks, so as to increase financial services, especially access to credit, to household farms as well as small- and medium-size enterprises in manufacturing and service sectors; second, reforming the pension system, removing the old retired workers' pension burden from the state-owned mining companies and levying appropriate royalty taxes on natural resources; and, third, encouraging entry and competition in the telecommunication, power, and financial sectors.

5 Can China maintain dynamic growth in the coming decades?

No country other than China has maintained annual growth of 9 percent for more than three decades. Can China keep growing that fast for another two decades or even longer? The answer,

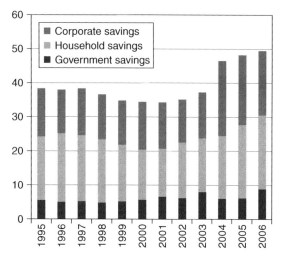

Figure 5.3 China's corporate, household, and government savings as percentage of GDP

Source: China Statistical Yearbook (1998–2009)

based not on some optimistic estimate but on the potential advantages of backwardness, is yes. In 2008 China's per capita income was 21 percent of that of the US, measured in purchasing power parity by Maddison's estimates.[13] The income gap between China and the US indicates that there is still a large technological gap between China and the industrialized countries. China can thus continue to enjoy the advantages of backwardness before closing the gap.

Maddison's estimates show that China's current status relative to the US is similar to that of Japan in 1951, Singapore in 1967, Taiwan, China in 1975, and Korea in 1977. GDP grew 9.2 percent in Japan between 1951 and1971, 8.6 percent in Singapore between 1967 and 1987, 8.3 percent in Taiwan, China between 1975 and 1995, and 7.6 percent in Korea between 1977 and 1997. China's development strategy after the reform in 1979 is similar to that of Japan, Singapore, Korea, and Taiwan, China. Therefore, from the point of advantage of backwardness, China has the potential to achieve another 20 years of 8 percent growth.

Japan's income per capita measured in purchasing power parity was 65.6 percent of that of the US in 1971, Singapore's was 53.8 percent in 1987, Taiwan's was 54.2 percent in 1995, and Korea's was 50.2 percent in 1997. If China can realize the potential, 20 years from now, China's per capita income measured in purchasing power parity may reach about 50 percent of the US per capita income. Measured by purchasing power parity, China's economy may be twice as large as that of the US in 2030; measured by market exchange rates, depending on how fast China revalues its currency, Chinese economy may be at least about the same size as that of the US.

Many economic and noneconomic factors will decide whether China can realize its full potential. Along with its rapid growth, China, as a developing country in transition, has encountered problems never seen before – problems that need to be addressed.

5.1 Ever-widening income disparity and urban–rural gap

In the very early stages of the reform and opening, the gaps between the urban and rural areas and those between the eastern, central, and western parts of the country were narrowing. But after 1985 they widened. The Gini coefficient (a measure of income equality, with a coefficient of 0 as perfect equality, and 1 as perfect inequality) increased from 0.31 in 1981 to 0.42 in 2005, approaching the level of Latin American countries (World Bank 2010). As Confucius once said: "Inequity is worse than scarcity." Indeed, a widening income disparity would cause bitter resentment among the low-income group. In addition, the educational, medical, and public health systems are underdeveloped. So the income gap could cause tensions, undermining social harmony and stability.

5.2 Inefficient use of resources and environmental imbalances

China's rapid growth has consumed massive energy and resources. In 2006, with 5.5 percent of the world's GDP, it consumed 9 percent of the world's oil, 23 percent of alumina, 28 percent of steel, 38 percent of coal, and 48 percent of cement. Natural resources are limited. So, if China doesn't change its growth pattern or reduce its resource consumption, the fallout will inflict harm on other countries for generations to come. In addition, rising resource prices will increase the cost of overconsumption, which runs counter to the scientific development strategy promoted by the Communist Party.

The environmental problems caused by breakneck development are also serious. The mining disasters and natural calamities in recent years are testimony to environmental deterioration.

Natural disasters can deliver fatal blows, so protecting the environment to prevent disasters is important in China as well.

5.3 *External imbalances and currency appreciation*

China has had both current account surpluses and capital account surpluses since 1994. Before 2005 the current account surplus was relatively small, but it reached 7.6 percent of GDP in 2007. As a result of the large trade surplus, China accumulated foreign reserves rapidly, with more than US$3 trillion – the largest in the world.

Accompanying the rising trade surpluses was the rising trade deficit in the United States. The imbalances received much attention before the current global financial crisis in 2008. In a testimony before the United States Congress, C. Fred Bergsten of the Peterson Institute stated in 2007: "The global imbalances probably represent the single largest current threat to the continued growth and stability of the United States and world economies" (Bergsten 2007). Throughout the crisis, there have been claims that the most severe global recession since the Great Depression was caused in part or wholly, by global imbalances, especially the imbalances between the United States and China. Some economists, such as Nobel Laureate Paul Krugman, argued that the undervaluation of the renminbi caused the large US trade deficit and that the consequent Chinese purchases of US Treasury bonds lowered interest rates and caused the US equity and real estate bubbles, leading to the financial crisis (Krugman 2009, 2010). Others argued that a revaluation of the renminbi to rebalance US and China trade was a prerequisite for a sustained global recovery (Goldstein 2010).

5.4 *Corruption*

Before the reform, when people from different social circles had but a single income source, corruption was visible and easy to prevent. But in the post-reform era, when material incentives became major tools to enhance efficiency, income sources became more diversified, and various gray and dark incomes harder to spot. Widespread official corruption has further widened the income gap, increasing resentment among the groups whose interests have been undermined and impairing the credibility of the government. Once that happens, it's hard to maintain social cohesion in a major crisis, and economic and social stability can be undermined.

5.5 *Education*

China's education policies focus more on quantity than quality, which is detrimental to training workers and to long-term social progress. No matter what form technological innovation takes, borrowing from abroad or conducting domestic R&D, China has to rely on talent, and without good education, innovation is impossible.

The above hurdles are not the only ones. Others include underdeveloped social security systems, low levels of technology, rampant local protectionism, mounting challenges from globalization, inadequate legal systems, and many other political, economic, social, and even external problems, each of which needs to be identified and addressed. If they cannot be addressed promptly, any one of them could produce social and economic havoc, even political instability. Without a stable political and economic climate, China will not achieve its goal of rapid growth and fulfill its economic potential. To realize the potential, China needs to remove the remaining distortions as legacies of the dual-track approach to reform, complete the transition to a well-functioning market economy, and overcome other social, political, and geopolitical hurdles in its modernization process.

6 Concluding remarks: lessons of China's development for other developing countries

Are there useful lessons that can be drawn from China's development experiences over the past six decades? The answer is clearly yes. Every developing country has the opportunity to accelerate its growth if it knows how to develop its industries according to its comparative advantage at each level of development and to tap the advantage of backwardness in its technological innovation and structural transformation. A well-functioning market is a precondition for developing an economy's industries according to its comparative advantages, because only with such a market can relative prices reflect the relative scarcities of factors of production in the economy. Such a well-functioning market naturally propels firms to enter industries consistent with the country's comparative advantages. If a developing country follows its comparative advantage in technological and industrial development, it will be competitive in domestic and international markets. In other words, it will grow fast, accumulate capital rapidly, and upgrade its endowment structure quickly. When the endowment structure is upgraded, the economy's comparative advantage changes and its industrial structure as well as hard and soft infrastructure need to be upgraded accordingly. In the process it is desirable for the state to play a proactive, facilitating role in compensating for externalities created by pioneer firms in the industrial upgrading and coordinating the desirable investments and improvements in soft and hard infrastructure, for which individual firms cannot internalize in their decisions. Through the appropriate functions of competitive markets and a proactive, facilitating state, a developing country can tap the potential of the advantage of backwardness and achieve dynamic growth (Lin 2011).

Many developing countries, as a result of their governments' previous development strategies, have various kinds of distortions and many existing firms are nonviable in an open competitive market. In this respect, China's experience in the transition process in the past 30 years also provides useful lessons. In the reform process it is desirable for a developing country to remove various distortions of incentives to improve productivity and at the same time adopt a dual-track approach, providing some transitory protections to nonviable firms to maintain stability but liberalizing entry into sectors in which the country has comparative advantages so as to improve the resource allocation and to tap the advantage of backwardness. If they can do this, other developing countries can also achieve stability and dynamic growth in their economic liberalization process.

Thirty years ago no one would have imagined that China would be among the 13 economies that tapped the potential of the advantage of backwardness and realized average annual growth of 7 percent or above for 25 or more years. For developing countries now fighting to eradicate poverty and close the gap with high-income countries, the lessons from China's transition and development will help them join the list of those realizing growth of 7 percent or more for 25 or more years in the coming decades.

Notes

1 Unless indicated otherwise, statistics on the Chinese economy reported in this chapter are taken from World Bank (2012), National Statistical Bureau (2009, 2012), and various editions of the *China Statistical Yearbook*.

2 *The Coming Collapse of China* by Gordon H. Chang, published in 2001 by Random House, was one representation of such views.

3 Deng's goal at that time was to quadruple the size of China's economy in 20 years, which would have meant an average annual growth of 7.2 percent. Most people in the 1980s, and even as late as the early 1990s, thought that achieving that goal was an impossible mission.

4 The remaining features are, respectively, macroeconomic stability, high rates of saving and investment, market system, and committed, credible, and capable governments. Lin and Monga (2010) show that the first three features are the result of following the economy's comparative advantages in developing industries at each stage of its development, and the last two features are the preconditions for the economy to follow its comparative advantages in developing industries.

5 The desire to develop heavy industries existed before the socialist elites obtained political power. Dr. Sun Yat-sen, the father of modern China, proposed the development of "key and basic industries" as a priority in his plan for China's industrialization in 1919 (Sun 1929).

6 While the policy goals of France, Germany, and the United States in the late nineteenth century were similar to that of China in the mid-1950s, the per capita incomes of the three countries were about 60–75 percent of Britain's at the time. The small gap in per capita incomes indicated that the industries on the governments' priority lists were the latent comparative advantages of the three countries (Lin and Monga 2011).

7 Estimates by Perkins and Rawski (2008) suggest that the average annual growth of total factor productivity was 0.5 percent in 1952–1978 and 3.8 percent in 1978–2005.

8 There are different explanations for the pervasive distortions in developing countries. Acemoglu *et al.* (2005), Engerman and Sokoloff (1997), and Grossman and Helpman (1996) proposed that these distortions were caused by the capture of government by powerful vested interests. Lin (2012a, 2009, and 2003) and Lin and Li (2009) propose that the distortions were a result of conflicts between the comparative advantages of the economies and the priority industries that political elites, influenced by the dominant social thinking of the time, targeted for the modernization of their nations.

9 In spite of its attempt to implement a shock therapy at the beginning, Poland did not privatize its large state-owned enterprises until very late in the transition.

10 In the 1980s, the former Soviet Union, Hungary, and Poland adopted a gradual reform approach. However, unlike the case in China, their state-owned firms were not allowed to set the prices for selling at markets after fulfilling their quota obligations and the private firms' entry to the repressed sectors was subject to severe restrictions, but the wages were liberalized (while in China the wage increase was subject to state regulation). These reforms led to wage inflations and exacerbated shortages. See the discussions about the differences in the gradual approach in China and the former Soviet Union and Eastern Europe in Lin (2009: 88–9).

11 Many of China's problems today including environment degradation and the lack of social protections are generic to developing countries. In this section, I will only focus on a few prominent issues that arose specifically from China's dual-track approach to transition. The collective volume edited by Brandt and Rawski (2008) provides excellent discussions of other development and transition issues in China.

12 Before the transition, the state-owned enterprises (SOEs) obtained their investment and operation funds directly from the government's budgets at no cost. The government established four large state banks in the early 1980s, when the fiscal appropriation system was replaced by bank lending, and later the equity market. The interest rates have been kept artificially low in order to subsidize the SOEs. Prices of natural resources were kept at an extremely low level so as to reduce the input costs of heavy industries. In return the mining firms' royalty payments were waived. After the transition, the natural resources' prices were liberalized in the early 1990s but royalties remained nominal to compensate for the transfer of pension provision for retired workers from the state to the state-owned mining companies. However, the private and joint-ventured mining companies, which did not enter until the 1980s and thereafter, did not have any pension burdens. The low royalty payment was equivalent to a direct transfer of natural resource rents from the state to these companies, which made them highly profitable. The rationale for giving firms in the telecommunication and power sectors a monopoly position before the transition was that they provided public services and made payments on large capital investment. Due to rapid development and fast capital accumulation after the transition, capital is less of a constraint now but the Chinese government continues to allow the service sector to enjoy monopoly rents (Lin *et al.* 2003; Lin 2012a).

13 The national statistics used in this and the next paragraphs are taken from Maddison (2010).

Bibliography

Acemoglu, D., Johnson, S., and Robinson, J. A. (2005) 'Institutions as the Fundamental Cause of Long-Run Growth', in *Handbook of Economic Growth*, vol. 1A (eds.) P. Aghion and S. N. Durlauf, 385–472. Amsterdam: Elsevier.

Bergsten, C. F. (2007) 'Currency Misalignments and the U.S. Economy', statement before the US Congress, May 9 <http://www.sasft.org/Content/ContentGroups/PublicPolicy2/ChinaFocus/pp_china_bergsten_tstmny.pdf>.

Brandt, L. and Rawski, T. G. (eds.) (2008) *China's Great Economic Transformation*, Cambridge: Cambridge University Press.

Chang, G. H. (2001) *The Coming Collapse of China*, New York: Random House.

Chang, H. (2003) *Kicking away the Ladder: Development Strategy in Historical Perspective*, London: Anthem Press.

Easterly, W. (2001) *The Elusive Quest for Growth: Economists' Adventures and Misadventures in the Tropics*, Cambridge, MA: MIT Press.

Engerman, S. L. and Sokoloff, K. L. (1997) 'Factor Endowments, Institutions, and Differential Paths of Growth among New World Economies: A View from Economic Historians of the United States', in *How Latin America Fell Behind* (ed.) S. Haber, 260–304. Stanford, CA: Stanford University Press.

Fei, J. and Ranis, G. (1997) *Growth and Development from an Evolutionary Perspective*, Malden, MA: Blackwell.

Gerschenkron, A. (1962) *Economic Backwardness in Historical Perspective: A Book of Essays*, Cambridge, MA: Belknap Press of Harvard University Press.

Goldstein, M. (2010) 'Confronting Asset Bubbles, Too Big to Fail, and Beggar-thy-Neighbor Exchange Rate Policies', paper based on remarks delivered on December 15, 2009, at the workshop 'The International Monetary System: Looking to the Future, Lessons from the Past' sponsored by the International Monetary Fund and the UK Economic and Research Council, Peterson Institute of International Economics, 2010.

Grossman, G. M. and Helpman, E. (1996) 'Electoral Competition and Special Interest Politics', *Review of Economic Studies*, 63(2): 265–286.

Krugman, P. (2009) 'World Out of Balance', *New York Times*, November 15.

—— (2010) 'Chinese New Year', *New York Times*, January 1.

Kuznets, S. (1966) *Modern Economic Growth: Rate, Structure and Spread*, New Haven, CT: Yale University Press.

Lal, D. and Mynt, H. (1996) *The Political Economy of Poverty, Equity, and Growth: A Comparative Study*, Oxford: Clarendon Press.

Landes, D. (1998) *The Wealth and Poverty of Nations: Why Some Are So Rich and Some So Poor*, New York: Norton.

Lau, L. J., Qian, Y., and Roland, G. (2000) 'Reform without Losers: An Interpretation of China's Dual-Track Approach to Transition', *Journal of Political Economy* 108(1): 120–143.

Lewis, W. A. (1954) 'Economic Development with Unlimited Supply of Labour', *Manchester School of Economic and Social Studies* 22(2): 139–191.

Lin, J. Y. (1992) 'Rural Reforms and Agricultural Growth in China', *American Economic Review* 82(1): 34–51.

—— (1995) 'The Needham Puzzle: Why the Industrial Revolution Did Not Originate in China', *Economic Development and Cultural Change* 43(2): 269–292.

—— (2003) 'Development Strategy, Viability and Economic Convergence', *Economic Development and Cultural Change* 53(2): 277–308.

—— (2009) *Economic Development and Transition: Thought, Strategy, and Viability*, Cambridge: Cambridge University Press.

—— (2011) 'New Structural Economics: A Framework for Rethinking Development', *The World Bank Research Observer* 26(2): 193–221 (included in Lin 2012b).

—— (2012a) *Demystifying the Chinese Economy*, Cambridge: Cambridge University Press.

—— (2012b) *New Structural Economics: A Framework for Rethinking Development and Policy*, Washington, DC: World Bank.

—— (2012c) *The Quest for Prosperity: How Developing Countries Can Take off*, Princeton, NJ: Princeton University Press.

Lin, J. Y. and Li, F. (2009) 'Development Strategy, Viability, and Economic Distortions in Developing Countries', Policy Research Working Paper 4906, World Bank, Washington, DC.

Lin, J. Y. and Monga, C. (2010) 'The Growth Report and New Structural Economics', Policy Research Working Paper 5336, World Bank, Washington, DC (included in Lin 2012b).

—— (2011) 'Growth Identification and Facilitation: The Role of the State in the Dynamics of Structural Change', *Development Policy Review* 29(3) (included in Lin 2012b: 264–290).

Lin, J.Y. and Tan, G. (1999) 'Policy Burdens, Accountability, and Soft Budget Constraints', *American Economic Review* 89(2): 426–431.

Lin, J. Y., Cai, F., and Li, Z. (2003) *The China Miracle: Development Strategy and Economic Reform*, Hong Kong SAR, China: Chinese University Press.

Maddison, A. (2001) *The World Economy: A Millennial Perspective*, Paris: OECD Development Centre.

—— (2007) *Chinese Economic Performance in the Long Run – Second Edition, Revised and Updated: 960–2030 AD*, Paris: OECD Development Centre.

—— (2010) *Historical Statistics of the World Economy: 1–2008 AD*. <www.ggdc.net/maddison/>

National Statistical Bureau (1991) *China Statistical Yearbook, 1991*, Beijing: China Statistical Press.

—— (2009) *China Compendium of Statistics 1949–2008*, Beijing: China Statistical Press.

—— (2012) *The China Statistical Abstract 2012*, Beijing: China Statistical Press.

Naughton, B. (1995) *Growing out of the Plan: Chinese Economic Reform, 1978–1993*, New York: Cambridge University Press.

North, D. (1981) *Structure and Change in Economic History*, New York: Norton.

Perkins, D. H. and Rawski, T. G. (2008) 'Forecasting China's Economic Growth to 2025', in *China's Great Economic Transformation* (eds.) L. Brandt and T. G. Rawski, 829–885. Cambridge: Cambridge University Press.

Prebisch, R. (1950) 'The Economic Development of Latin America and Its Principal Problems, New York: United Nations', reprinted in *Economic Bulletin for Latin America* 7, no. 1 (1962): 1–22.

Ravallion, M. and Chen, S. (2007) 'China's (Uneven) Progress against Poverty', *Journal of Development Economics*, 82(1): 1–42.

Subramanian, A. and Roy, D. (2003) 'Who Can Explain the Mauritian Miracle? Mede, Romer, Sachs, or Rodrik?', in *In Search of Prosperity: Analytic Narratives on Economic Growth* (ed.) D. Rodrik, 205–243. Princeton, NJ: Princeton University Press.

Sun, Y. S. (1929) *The International Development of China* (Shih yeh chi hua). 2nd ed. New York: G.P. Putnam's Sons.

World Bank (on behalf Commission on Growth and Development) (2008) *The Growth Report: Strategies for Sustained Growth and Inclusive Development*, Washington, DC: World Bank.

—— (2010) *World Development Indicators, 2010*, Washington, DC: World Bank.

—— (2012) *World Development Indicators, 2012*, Washington, DC: World Bank.

6

POPULATION IN CHINA

Changes and future perspectives

Peng Xizhe[1]

China has experienced a fundamental social and demographic transition, particularly over the past three decades. While the total fertility rate has maintained at below replacement level since the middle 1990s, life expectancy has been rising continuously. Government-sponsored programs, including family planning and the public health care, played crucial roles in these demographic changes, in addition to socioeconomic development. Huge migration flow reshapes population distribution and the urbanization process has accelerated in recent years. Population aging is underway and changes in total labor supply will be more dramatic in the coming decades. The past imbalance in sex ratio at birth will result in a marriage squeeze. Such demographic changes have already been important factors contributing to China's past economic miracle, and the trends will continue in the future and inevitably affect China's future economic growth.

1 A brief review

Over the last half century, China has witnessed a profound demographic transition. Both mortality and fertility have declined substantively in a relatively short time period: life expectancy in China rose from 43 to around 74 years during the 1950–2010 period, while the fertility level dropped from more than six to fewer than two children per woman. China has approached the end of a demographic transition (see Figure 6.1).

China experienced an impressive decline in death rates, and a high, even rising birth rate in the early part of the 1950s due mainly to a great improvement in people's living conditions and social stability after continuous wars during the 1930s and 1940s. As a result, population growth in China speeded up to an alarming level. The 1953 population census, the first nationwide modern census in China, estimated that the total population of China amounted to 600 million which is a figure larger than the common view at that time.

Such a trend was stopped by a demographic crisis characterized by excessive mortality and a sharp decline in the birth rate during the period of 1959–1961. This was caused mainly by the Great Famine and institutional failure. While accurate official information of the casualties is not available yet, academic researchers estimated that the number of excess deaths ranged from thirteen to thirty million and that there could have been twenty million deficient births due to postponement of childbearing (Peng 1987). China recovered from the crisis in the following few years. While the death rate returned to its long-term trend in 1962, the birth rate surged to a

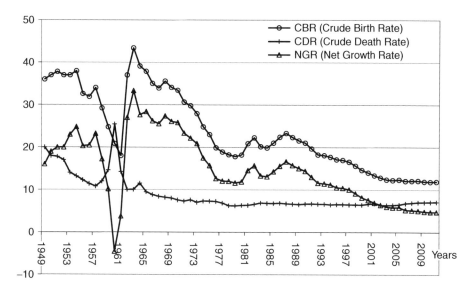

Figure 6.1 Population dynamics in China (1949–2011)

peak in 1963, and was maintained at a high level for the rest of 1960s. Overall, during the eleven-year period of 1953–1964, China's population increased from 594.4 million to 694.6 million, an average annual net growth rate of 1.31 percent or more than nine million each year.

The "Cultural Revolution" that burst onto the scene in 1966 dominated China's socioeconomic development for more than one decade. Despite nationwide disturbances, the demographic indicators did not show serious changes and the population growth rate remained very high. It was in the early 1970s that rapid fertility decline began. Although signs of early fertility decline emerged in China's urban areas in the mid-1960s, China's nationwide fertility transition started in the early 1970s. The total fertility rate for China as a whole declined sharply from 5.8 in 1970 to 2.8 in 1979, a more than 50 percent decrease. This is one of the most rapid fertility declines ever recorded in the world. The death rate continued to decrease even during the turmoil of the "Cultural Revolution" period (1966–1976). Consequently, China experienced a very rapid population growth in the 1960s and 1970s with a total increase of 313 million people, or an annual net growth of 17.4 million. The annual population growth rate for the period of 1964–1982 was 2.09 percent.

China entered the era of economic reform in late 1978. With the introduction of the "One Child Policy," the fertility level decreased further to below replacement level in the 1990s, while the mortality level continued its gradual decline. However, the 1980s witnessed another "baby boom" owing mainly to the childbearing impact of the large baby boomer cohorts who were born in 1950–1960s despite the implementation of a more rigid birth control program. The annual population growth rate amounted to 1.48 percent for that decade. Thereafter, China's population continued its growth, but the speed slowed further from the early 1990s. The annual growth rate declined from 1.11 percent in the 1990s to 0.57 percent in the first decade of the twenty-first century. Nevertheless, due mainly to the large population base, the number of annual births in China remained as high as around sixteen million, and the annual net increment in population amounted to seven million in this period.

Overall, the demographic pattern of China has transformed from one characterized as high birth, high death, and low growth before the 1950s, to high birth, low death, and high growth in the 1960s and 1970s, and to one characterized by low birth, low death and low growth in sub-sequent decades.

The quality of Chinese population statistics is a highly debated topic (Zhang and Zhao 2006).[2] This is a result partly of the shortcomings of China's statistical reporting and collection system, and partly of the complexity of relevant issues. Although there are disagreements about the accuracy of the data, there is little doubt about the general trend of China's demographic dynamics.

It is certain that China's population will continue to grow in the near future. Various population projections have been made based on different assumptions regarding future trends in fertility and mortality (Qiao 2006, Zeng 2007, Zhai 2010, UNPD 2011, Wang 2011). There are big differences in these projections. China's total population, according to the lowest projection, will only increase to 1.4 billion before growth finally stops around 2025. The medium-growth scenario projected by the United Nations, based on the assumption of some relaxation in the current population policy, anticipates that in the next half century the population of China will reach 1.5 billion – a net increase of 160 million from the present figure. About two-thirds of the growth is anticipated to occur within the next decade. India will finally overtake China as the country with the largest population in the world around 2030 (see Figure 6.2).

2 Age structure of Chinese population

Along with marked changes in both fertility and mortality patterns, China's population age structure also changed significantly over the years. Information from Figure 6.3 shows that population under age 15 accounted for 40 percent of the total Chinese population in 1970, but the proportion was reduced to only slightly above 16 percent in 2010. On the other hand, the elderly population increased sharply both in absolute numbers and in proportion. In 1953, only 7.32 percent of Chinese, or 42.64 million, were older than 60 years. The number of the over 60 elderly increased to 177.65 million, accounting for 13.26 percent of the total population, in 2010. Based on international criteria, China entered the aging society in 2000 when more than 10 percent of the Chinese population was 60 years and older. The growth rate of the elderly population is much

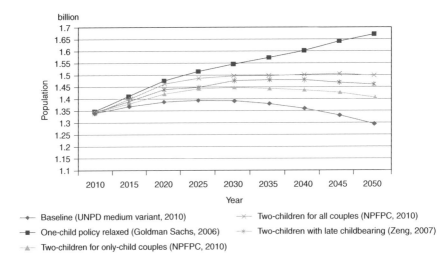

Figure 6.2 Population projections

Source: Peng (2011)

higher compared to the growth of the national population. Meanwhile, the number and proportion of working-age population (people aged 15–69 years) has increased steadily from the 1980s, and reached a peak in 2012. Both the proportion and the absolute number of the working-age population have begun to decline in China since then. These data show us that while China benefitted greatly from the abundant supply of young labor force in the past several decades, population aging is on the way and will accelerate in the coming years. (See Figure 6.3.)

Changes in age structure can also be seen from the age pyramid of the Chinese population. There are peaks and troughs in the age pyramid, which are mainly determined by differences in birth cohorts. The population size of the large birth cohort in the 1980s resulted from the larger baby-boom cohort in the 1950s and the 1960s. The smaller age group aged in their fifties in 2010 reflects the demographic crisis of the Great Famine period, and the following two troughs are the results of changes in fertility behavior in the corresponding time periods. Such an unsmooth age structure created fluctuating changes in the demand for and supply of various social services and economic situations including labor force and pension provisions. (See Figure 6.4.)

3 Fertility decline and government family planning program

Universal marriage and early childbearing prevailed in traditional China. This pattern persisted in the 1950s. Changes in reproductive behavior emerged among China's urban residents as early as in the mid-1960s, which is indicated by the very short period of compensational childbearing[3] in China's urban areas immediately after the Great Famine. It is worth noting that the total fertility rate in urban China had already dropped to around three in the mid-1960s while the number in China's countryside was maintained at a level higher than six. This was attributed partially to the availability of contraceptive services provided to urban residents.

China's nationwide fertility transition started in the early 1970s with the implementation of a government-sponsored family planning program, known as "later marriage, later childbearing, longer birth interval, fewer but healthier children" (also called "later, longer, and fewer" in abbreviation).

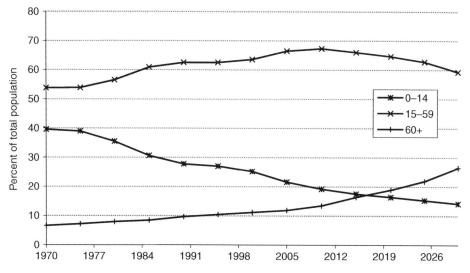

Figure 6.3 Changes of age structure in China (1970–2030)

Source: World Population Prospects (2010 rev., medium variants UNPD)

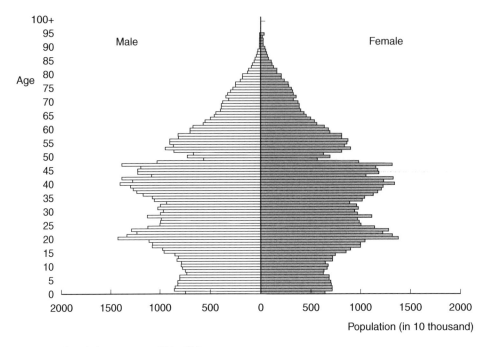

Figure 6.4 Population age pyramid in China

Source: Population Census Office of National Bureau of Statistics of China (2012)

This program had achieved great success in slowing down China's rapid population growth without heavy government intervention but in the heavily politicized socioeconomic context of the Cultural Revolution period. For instance, the so-called "later age at marriage" had been set up locally; usually 28 for men and 25 for women in cities and lower in the villages, despite the fact that the legal age at marriage stipulated by the marriage law at that time was 20 and 18 for men and women respectively. These regulations were able to be carried out because marriage needed to be first approved by both the working units of the bride and the bridegroom before it could be legally recognized in that time period.

The "One Child Policy" proposal was first put forward in 1979 and became fully operational in the early 1980s. The current national family planning policy took its original form in the mid-1980s, and after 1991 the political commitment to population control was reaffirmed.

One of the notable features of China's family planning program is its decentralized policy formation and program implementation with central guidance. China's current local family planning regulations can be grouped into several major categories. In general, the "One Child Policy" has been implemented more rigidly in urban areas among urban residents and government employees, while the majority of rural families are permitted 1.5 to two children depending on the local situation. The rationale for this is that farm families depend on strong labor for agricultural production and family support (primarily provided by married son(s) in their parents' old age, as there was almost no well-functioning government-sponsored pension system operating for Chinese farmers until very recently). Families belonging to minorities are entitled to have even more children. In this sense, the "One Child Policy" is an overly simplified term. If all Chinese couples followed local family planning regulations, the total fertility rate in China would be 1.62 for the 1990s, declining to around 1.5 in the 2000s, as more people became urban residents and thus changed their birth control categories[4] (Guo *et al.* 2003). (See Figure 6.5.)

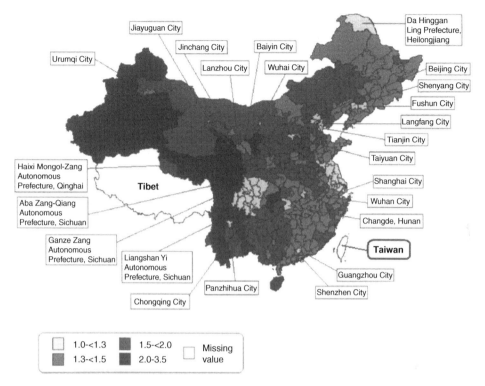

Figure 6.5 Geographic distribution of policy fertility at the prefecture level, China (late 1990s)

Source: Gu *et al.* (2007)

Both incentive and disincentive measures have been used to operate and manage the program. Levying fines on those parents who gave birth outside the birth control quota was treated as one of the most effective ways of the program implementation, an approach that has been increasingly criticized in recent years.

China's total fertility rate dropped to below replacement level in the mid-1990s and has remained there since. However, there are disagreements on the exact level of China's fertility. It's the author's view that the total fertility rate is around 1.5 at present.

This fertility transition is characterized by its rapidity and has had a profound impact on China's socioeconomic development. Moreover, there are marked regional and rural–urban variations in the path and timing of the fertility transition. By the late 1990s, the total fertility rate ranged from below 1 in big metropolitan cities like Shanghai and Beijing, to 3.11 in the Tibet autonomous region. Such regional diversity can be observed with respect to many other aspects of China's demographics.

There are debates about the impact of government's role and the efficiency of the birth control policy in China's fertility decline. Socioeconomic development is certainly a decisive factor facilitating demographic transition. To a large extent, lower birth and death rates are by-products of socioeconomic development. Dr. Wang Feng and Cai Yong argued that China's total fertility rate would have reduced to the current level even if there had been no government policy intervention (Wang *et al.* 2012). They reached their conclusion by applying the set of models developed by the UN's Population Division and statisticians from the University of Washington based on fertility change history and fertility trends in other countries (Wang and Cai 2010). On the other hand, official statements from government agencies intended to overstate the importance and achievement of government policies and programs.[5]

However, government intervention should be treated as one of the crucial factors that brought down China's fertility level and its impact is remarkably significant at least in the early period of the policy's implementation (Peng 2013). To a large extent, China's demographic transition was initialized by strong and effective government-sponsored public health and family planning programs. Some of these interventions were carried out in a coercive manner, which should be understood in the context of China's authoritarian governance system, and should be entirely forbidden. On the whole, government polices related to fertility behavior have played a profound role in bringing about the demographic transition in China, and shaping the regional pattern of China's demographic dynamics.

As the objective of the current family planning policy to reduce the growth rate of Chinese population has been reached, and the negative impacts and risk of continued implementation of the policy have grown, it is time for the Chinese government to change, and ultimately abandon, the policy. Furthermore, as the costs of childbearing and childrearing are rising remarkably – which has mainly resulted from the rapid improvement in people's living conditions and education level – the reproductive desire and behavior of young Chinese couples have changed saliently. Low fertility will prevail in China in the near future.

4 Mortality change and public health care system

Over the past several decades the standard of living of the vast majority of the Chinese population has remarkably improved, owing to the rapid development of China's economy which was brought about by its economic reform, and improvement s in the public health care system. An extraordinary mortality decline has been recorded in China in the last sixty years except for the famine period. Life expectancy in China has doubled from below forty years before 1950 to around seventy-five years by around 2011.

During the last fifty or more years, causes of death have changed enormously in China. The five major killers were respiratory disease, infectious disease, pulmonary tuberculosis, digestive disease, and heart disease in 1957. These diseases caused about 50 percent of deaths. In 2010, however, the five leading causes of death were malignant tumors, cerebrovascular disease, heart disease, respiratory disease, and injury and toxicosis, which accounted for 85 percent of deaths (Ministry of Health 2011).

Deaths caused by infectious disease, pulmonary tuberculosis, and digestive disease have fallen markedly. In urban areas, for instance, deaths from infectious disease dropped from 60/100,000 to 1.06/100,000 people between 1974 and 2010. Pulmonary tuberculosis deaths fell from about 40/100,000 to about 0.22/100,000.

During the same period, however, deaths from cerebrovascular disease, malignant tumors, circulatory system disease, and diabetes have been on the rise. Malignant tumors' death rate doubled in urban areas from 70/100,000 to about 162.93/100,000. Cerebrovascular disease deaths increased from 65/100,000 to 132.09/100,000. Circulatory system disease deaths showed a noticeable rise from 115.34/100,000 to more than 250/100,000 in 1990. Deaths linked to diabetes increased by sevenfold from about 2/100,000 to 18.89/100,000.

The major causes of death in the Chinese population have increasingly become similar to those observed in many developed countries, but some noticeable differences between them are also notable. For example, deaths caused by liver cancer were very high in China in comparison with those in many European populations.

China introduced the barefoot doctor system, or rural cooperative medical system (RCMS), in the 1970s. Barefoot doctors had dramatically improved access to health care in China's rural communities. Their work effectively reduced health care costs by focusing on prevention rather than cures through providing mostly primary health care services, including immunization, delivery for pregnant women, and improvements in sanitation. Barefoot doctors were usually farmers with limited medical training combining western and traditional medicines. The WHO regarded RCMS as a successful example of solving shortages of medical services in rural areas (WHO, 2008). Such a system ceased functioning in 1981 with the end of the people's commune system as part of the rural reform (Zhang and Unschuld 2008)

At present, China's health care system consists of three tiers of hospitals or clinics. In urban areas, there are community health care centers, specialized hospitals, and the comprehensive hospitals. In rural areas, the village clinics provide primary care for villagers. On the whole, state-owned hospitals provide most of the services (more than 70 percent). China's current health insurance systems are fragmental, including at least three main systems: the Urban Employee Basic Health Insurance (UEBHI) covering all formal employees and urban pension-ers, Urban Residents Basic Health Insurance (URBHI) covering urban unemployed, students, children, and housewives, and the rural New Cooperative Medical Scheme (NCMS) providing all health insurance for rural residents.

Health financing in China was relatively low (Whyte and Sun 2010) and the health expenditure per capita per year was less than US$150, while out-of-pocket was the main source for health financ-ing but the proportion of self-payment goes down. Furthermore, the health financing gap between rural and urban is increasing. "Too difficult to see a doctor, and too expensive to see a doctor" become one of the major public complaints. Other complaints include increasing health financing inequity and poor accessibility to health care. Some people have suggested that the encouragement of establishing private hospitals will increase the supply and reduce the cost of health care.

While China has had great success in reducing mortality, it also faces the daunting task of further improving the health status of the population. Air pollution and smoking (China's 300 million smokers consume five billion cigarettes daily) have become major killers (Yang and Wang *et al.* 2013; Jha and Peto 2014). The aging population will also lead to a great burden of prevent-ing and curing illnesses linked to the biological aging process. Furthermore, as shown in recent demographic data, further reduction in mortality seems to have become more difficult than twenty years ago.

5 China's labor force and the demographic dividend

The working-age population (ages 15 to 59) can be treated as the potential labor force supply. The baby boom in the 1950s and the 1960s provided an abundant labor force since the early 1980s. At the moment, more than 68 percent of the Chinese population is of working age, and the proportion will remain above 65 percent at least for the next decade and above 60 percent until the early 2030s. The current proportion of the labor force in China as a percentage of its population is much higher than that in most other countries. (See Figure 6.6.)

The increased supply in labor force, both in terms of absolute numbers and with respect to the proportion of the total population resulted from high fertility in the 1950s and the 1960s, with fertility declining for the next three decades. The huge labor force that was matched by the greater employment opportunities created by the openness and economic reform initiated in the later 1970s by Deng Xiaoping is one of the decisive factors of China's economic miracle over the past thirty and more years. China has been harvesting a demographic dividend from the increase in investment and saving that resulted (Cai 2004; Bloom and Finlay 2009).

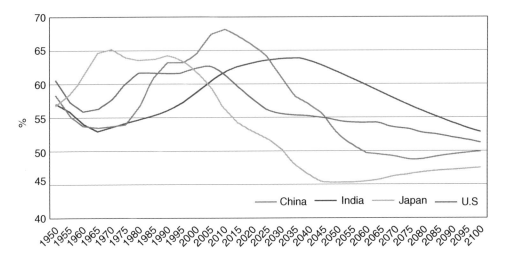

Figure 6.6 Percentage of working age (15–59) in total population

Source: Population Division, United Nations Department of Economic and Social Affairs (2010) (rev., medium variants)

The turning point was 2012 when the total number of the working-age population (those aged 15–59 years old) began to shrink for the first time in five decades. The decline will continue in the future and China's total labor force will never return to its peak in 2012. This trend mainly resulted from the continuous decline in China's fertility level over the past thirty years. The speed and depth of the labor force decline will be largely determined by the future fertility behavior of China's current young people, and government policy on family planning as well.

Nevertheless, this trend does not indicate a major shortage of labor supply in China at present or for the near future. As a matter of fact, the labor force in China is still sufficient, and unemployment, rather than the labor shortage, remains a great challenge. Furthermore, changes in the quality of the labor force have occurred mainly through the rapid expansion in China's higher education system. The numbers in annual enrollment in Chinese universities increased from one million in 1997 up to around seven million at the end of the first decade of the twenty-first century (Ministry of Education 2010). This creates a sound basis on which China can improve future labor productivity, and to rebalance labor supply and demand.

In other words, the window for harvesting the demographic dividend is still open but will gradually close in about fifteen years. There is also regional variation in terms of timing of the demographic window of opportunity.

6 Migration and urbanization

China was for a long time a dual society. There was rural–urban separation, both economic and social, and migration was strictly controlled, particularly before the 1980s. For the three decades between 1950s–1970s, less than 20 percent of the Chinese population were classified as urban residents. The fundamental changes have occurred since the early 1980s. By the end of 2010, 670 million mainland Chinese are classified as urban residents, accounting for about 50 percent of the total population. They live in more than 660 cities and over 20,000 towns. The urbanization process accelerated especially in the past decade as urban development was treated by the Chinese government as a strategic measure for poverty reduction and social development. The urban population increased by 1.3 percentage points over the last ten years, and the process will continue (see Figure 6.7).

Chinese cities are divided. Of 700 million urban residents, about 500 million are with permanent (local) urban status, while 200 million are migrants. The Household Registration System (*hukou*) was the core institutional arrangement for the rural–urban segregation. *Hukou* was first implemented in the late 1950s primarily for social control and population registration. This system had gradually become the basis for all social rights and social welfare. Although there has been great relaxation of the controls on migration and a reduction in the function of the system, *hukou* remains an institutional barrier for social integration of those migrants into mainstream urban society (Zhang 2012). In some locations, tensions between the local and migrant population over public resources are rising.

It was the introduction of the Rural Household Responsibility System in the late 1970s that provided freedom for peasant households to allocate family labor to various economic activities. Rural surplus laborers in the early 1980s began to migrate to coastal regions, especially the Pearl River Delta area where a great inflow of foreign and Hong Kong/Macao capital created huge demand for manual labor.

Different from "permanent" or "formal" migrants, they were called "Floating Population" with certain special features. First, they usually kept rural household registration status, so that they were not recognized as new urban permanent residents no matter how long they stayed in the cities; second, they were primarily engaged in temporary jobs that were determined mainly by their own level of education and skill, and partly caused by existing household registration systems which provide employment protection for urban residents while setting up discriminative treatments for migrant laborers; and, third, they were basically not covered by the social security system available for urban residents. These basic features in general have been maintained even though changes have occurred gradually over the past three decades.

Based on China's 2010 national population census, there were more than 260 million Chinese who were classified as migrants living in places not their hometown for more than half a year. Among them were 220 million rural–urban migrants. However, due mainly to their special migration features, it is very difficult to get really accurate estimates of the real volume of the migration.

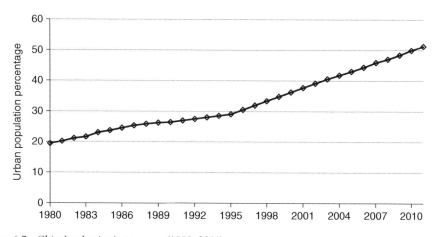

Figure 6.7   China's urbanization process (1980–2011)

Source: National Bureau of Statistics of China (2013)

Trans-regional migration existed everywhere in China. The main destinations of the migration were three major industrial and also urban clusters: the Pearl River Delta region, the Yangtze River Delta Region, and the area around the Bo-Hai Sea, including Beijing and Tianjin. The direction of migration reflected the diversification of economic development and the market allocation of human resources. This trend has changed recently as rapid inland development, including the development programs in western and northeast China has attracted many migrants to return to their hometowns. (See Figure 6.8.)

Such a large-scale rural–urban (temporary) migration is certainly an unprecedented new phenomenon in modern China. Demographically speaking, rural–urban migration changes China's population spatial distribution, affects patterns and the path of urbanization, and slows down the population aging process in urban areas. Its contribution to economic growth is also remarkable. Large rural–urban, and west–east, migration plays a very important role in balancing the supply and demand on the labor market in China.

7 Abnormal sex ratio at birth and potential marriage squeeze

The imbalance in China's sex ratio at birth first appeared in the 1980s, with the ratio of 111.42:100 reported by 1990 population census, and has been deteriorating since then. The 2010 population census reported a sex ratio at birth at 118:100, which is slightly lower than the figure of 119:100 that was released in 2005. There are marked regional differences in this regard. In general, the sex

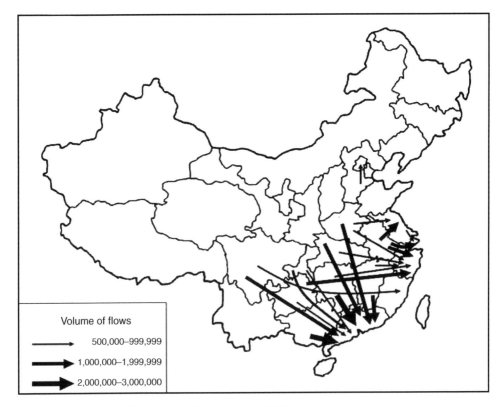

Figure 6.8 Main flows of inter-provincial migration of China

Source: Population Census Office of National Bureau of Statistics of China (2012)

ratio at birth in western provinces and autonomous regions is more or less within the normal range, while serious abnormalities of this ratio are reported for the central and southern parts of China.

It is now clear that the direct cause of the imbalance is the pre-birth sex identification and selective abortion of female fetuses. The Chinese government has introduced tough regulations to crack down on such illegal activities. However, as technologies, such as ultrasound examination as part of the maternal health care and also known as one of the most efficient ways for sex identification of the fetuses, are widely available at affordable cost to Chinese pregnant couples, these regulations achieved limited success, and the problem remains serious. Furthermore, the traditional idea of son preference persists partially due to the lack of old-age security for the elderly in China's countryside. The promotion of the rural pension system will create a fundamental social environment to reduce the son preference and return the sex ratio at birth to normal.

One of the accumulated consequences of the abnormality over the last twenty and more years is the imbalance of men and women in the marriage market in China. This is called marriage squeeze. It is estimated that there will be more than twenty million more men than women in the 20–40-year age group in the next two decades (Li 2007). A huge number of young men will not be able to get married because of the shortage of young women. This may become a serious social problem in the near future in China, and may also result in salient changes in patterns and practice of marriage and childbearing, even consumption and economic development (Wei and Zhang 2009).

8 Conclusion

China has experienced a fundamental social and demographic transition, particularly over the past three decades. While the total fertility rate has maintained at below replacement level since the mid-1990s, life expectancy has been rising continuously. Government-sponsored programs, including family planning and public health care, played crucial roles in these demographic changes, in addition to socioeconomic development. Massive migration flow reshapes population distribution and the urbanization process accelerated in recent years. Population aging is underway and changes in total labor supply will be more dramatic in the coming decades. The past imbalance in sex ratio at birth will result in marriage squeeze. Such demographic changes have already been important factors, contributing to China's past economic miracle, and the trends will continue in the future and inevitably affect China's future economic growth.

Notes

1 Editorial assistance given by Miss Le Xin, and encouragement and help from Dr. Chow are highly appreciated.
2 It is my opinion that government statistics remain one of the best data sources at present even though they suffer from misreporting. This is particularly true concerning the national data.
3 A larger than normal number of people got married and gave birth to children in the years after the famine was over. These marriages and births were postponed because of famine. The phenomenon is called the compensational fertility in this chapter.
4 This is viewed as the "policy fertility," a weighted average assuming the reproductive behavior of all couples of different nationalities in different locations conforms to the local government family planning regulations.
5 For example, the commissioner of the State Population and Family Planning Commission, Ms. Li Bin, claimed on September 10, 2009 that 400 million births had been prevented due to the implementation of the family planning policy over the last thirty years (from the late 1970s). See: http://www.gov.cn/jrzg/2009-09/17/content_1419703.htm.

Bibliography

Bloom, D. and Finlay, J. (2009) 'Demographic Change and Economic Growth in Asia', *Asian Economic Policy Review*, 4(1): 45–64.

Cai, F. (2004) 'Population Transition, Population Dividend and Sustainability of Economic Growth – Discussion on How Full Employment Promotes Economic Growth', Population Research (in Chinese), 28(2): 2–9.

Gu, B., Wang, F., and Guo, Z. (2007) 'China's Local and National Fertility Policies at the End of the Twentieth Century', *Population and Development Review*, 33(1): 129–147.

Guo, Z., Zhang, E., Gu, B., and Wang, F. (2003) 'Diversity of China's Fertility Policy by Policy Fertility', Population Research (in Chinese), 27(5): 1–10.

Jha, Prabhat and Richard Peto (2014) 'Global Effects of Smoking, of Quitting, and of Taxing Tobacco', *New England Journal of Medicine* 370: 60–8 (DOI: 10.1056/NEJMra1308383).

Li, S. (2007) 'Imbalanced Sex Ratio at Birth and Comprehensive Intervention in China', UNFPA publication, <www.unfpa.org/gender/docs/studies/china.pdf>.

Ministry of Education, People's Republic of China (2010) 'Statistical Communiqué on National Educational Development in 2009', <www.moe.edu.cn/publicfiles/business/htmlfiles/moe/moe_633/201008/93763.html>.

Ministry of Health, People's Republic of China (2011) 'China Health Statistical Yearbook', <http://www.moh.gov.cn/htmlfiles/zwgkzt/ptjnj/year2011/index2011.html>.

National Bureau of Statistics of China (2013) *China Statistical Yearbook 2012*, Beijing: China Statistics Press.

Peng, X. (1987) 'Demographic Consequences of the Great Leap Forward in China's Provinces', *Population and Development Review*, 13(4): 639–670.

Peng, X. (2011) 'China's Demographic History and Future Challenges', *Science*, 333(6042): 581–587.

Peng, X. (2013) 'China's Demographic Challenge Requires an Integrated Coping Strategy', *Journal of Policy Analysis and Management*, 32(2): 399–406.

Population Census Office of National Bureau of Statistics of China (2012) *Tabulation in the 2010 Population Census*, Beijing: China Statistics Press.

Population Division, United Nations Department of Economics and Social Affairs (2010) 'World Population Prospects: The 2010 Revision'.

Qiao, H. (2006) 'Will China Grow Old Before Getting Rich', *Global Economics Paper 138*, New York: Goldman Sachs.

Wang, F. (2011) 'The Future of a Demographic Overachiever: Long-term Implications of the Demographic Transition in China', *Population and Development Review*, 37(supplement 1): 173–190.

Wang, F. and Cai, Y. (2010) 'Were There 400 Million Less Births in China?', China Reform (in Chinese), 7: 85–88.

Wang, F., Cai, Y., and Gu, B. (2012) 'Population, Policy, and Politics: How Will History Judge China's One-Child Policy?', *Population and Development Review*, 38(supplement): 115–129.

Wei, S. and Zhang, X. (2009) 'The Competitive Saving Motives: Evidence from the Rising Sex Ratio and Saving Rates in China', NBER Working paper 15093, Cambridge.

WHO (2008) 'China's Village Doctors Take Great Strides', *Bulletin of the World Health Organization*, 86: 909–988.

Whyte, M.K. and Sun, Z. (2010) 'The Impact of China's Market Reforms on the Health of Chinese Citizens: Examining Two Puzzles', *China: An International Journal*, 8(1): 1–32.

Yang, Gonghuan and Yu Wang et al. (2013) 'Rapid Health Transition in China, 1990–2010: Findings from the Global Burden of Disease Study 2010', *The Lancet*, 381(9882), 8–14 June.

Zeng, Y. (2007) 'Options for Fertility Policy Transition in China', *Population and Development Review*, 33(2): 215–246.

Zhai, Z. (2010) 'China's Demographic Trends under Different Fertility Policy Scenarios' (in Chinese), National Population and Family Planning Commission, Beijing.

Zhang, D. and Unschuld, P. U. (2008) 'China's Barefoot Doctor: Past, Present, and Future', *The Lancet*, 372(9653): 1865–1867.

Zhang, G. and Zhao, Z. (2006) 'Reexamining China's Fertility Puzzle: Data Collection and Quality over the Last Two Decades', *Population and Development Review*, 32(2): 293–321.

Zhang, L. (2012) 'Economic Migration and Urban Citizenship in China: The Role of Points Systems', *Population and Development Review*, 38(3): 503–533.

7

A LABOR MARKET WITH CHINESE CHARACTERISTICS

Richard B. Freeman

Prior to its economic reforms, China did not have an operating labor market. The government assigned workers to firms rather than allowing them to choose their own place of work and used *hukou* residency policies to keep rural people from migrating to cities. Firms hired the workers assigned by the labor bureaus regardless of economic need and paid them according to a national wage grid from a payroll budget set by the government.

Bureaucratic allocation of labor and determination of pay may work well in a single firm or government agency but is inconsistent with a market economy where hundreds of millions of workers and consumers and millions of firms interact in multiple economic transactions. As China reformed its urban economy from the 1980s through the 2000s, the government relaxed its control of workers and firms. It gave greater leeway to supply and demand to set employment, wages, and working conditions, producing the labor market with the Chinese characteristics that this the chapter elaborates on.

The chapter tells how China moved from state determination of labor outcomes to a genuine labor market and how the new labor market has operated. It then examines three big labor problems that face the country on its path of continued economic growth: labor–management conflict; absorbing millions of university graduates into fruitful jobs; and bringing rural persons and informal-sector workers fully into the modern economy.

1 Starting point: state determination of labor outcomes?

Before its economic reforms, China relied on administrative ruling to set employment, wages, and conditions of work. State-owned enterprises (SOEs) were the predominant business organization. Government labor bureaus decided how many workers the SOEs hired. Managers did not have the authority to lay off workers, nor to alter wages in ways they thought would benefit the firm. Workers could not move from their assigned firm without government approval. Workers were viewed as cadres whose function was to follow orders to attain national goals (much as an army views conscripts). Labor bureaus assigned workers to jobs to further the government's Five-Year Plan.[1]

In this administered labor system, firms set wages according to a government wage grid. The grid had eight grades for blue-collar workers and twenty-four grades for white-collar workers, including professional, technical, and managerial employees. To keep inequality low, the grid

allowed for only small differences across enterprises, industries, and regions. Seniority dominated the wage distribution within industrial enterprises. Along with pay, SOEs were responsible for housing, retirement, and medical care of employees.

Work units known as *danwei* were the critical institution controlling urban labor. The government assigned every worker to a *danwei*, which regulated aspects of their lives from travel to
marriage to provision of food in centralized canteens to access to entertainment. The Communist
Party kept dossiers on the activities of workers (*dangan*)[2] and penalized workers who broke
administrative rules with loss of pay or allocation to less desirable housing or work assignments.[3]
For their part, workers relied on personal connections (*guanxi*) with decision-makers to influence the government decisions that affected their lives. Perhaps an uncle working for the city
could help a nephew get a job in a workplace near his home rather than in Mongolia. Perhaps
a family could do a favor for the party official who determined work assignments, who would
reciprocate by assigning someone the type of work they wanted. Personal connections substituted for market freedom in matching workers with jobs.[4]

Workers who sought to change their job relied on *guanxi* help from family connections, former
classmates, or relatives. Persons with party membership or other official status did best in moving to
more desirable jobs but most workers remained with the firm to which the state had initially
assigned them. In a 1999 survey 79 percent of urban workers reported that they had only a single
employer in their working life.[5] As reforms proceeded the government recognized the legitimacy of
individuals applying for jobs on their own and of employers screening applicants and choosing their
hires but reforming the assignment system came late in the process of modernizing the economy.[6]

Exemplifying the way the job assignment process worked, in the 1970s when urban areas
faced potential high levels of youth unemployment, the government ordered SOEs to promise
older workers who retired early that the firm would give their job to their son or daughter. In
1979 about 90 per cent of the 8,000 new workers for Chongqing Iron and Steel Company were
the children of employees, of whom over 3,000 directly replaced retiring parents.[7] Some SOEs
formed new collective factories or other companies to create jobs for their employees' children.
The goal was to assure that urban China had full employment.

To control the rural workforce the government used the *hukou* household registration
system. This system required citizens to register their permanent place of residence with the
government. Persons with urban *hukou* were entitled to jobs in SOEs and to education, housing,
and health care. From the mid-1950s through the 1970s urban residents received ration cards
for buying grain and other necessities. Individuals who had rural *hukou* but who were residing
in urban areas received none of these benefits.

The government prohibited urban units from recruiting rural workers and required rural
persons to obtain a temporary certificate to visit an urban area for more than three days.[8]
Without the urban *hukou*, unauthorized rural migrants would have problems finding a place to
sleep and buying food in a city. The few rural workers who gained urban *hukou* did so by joining the People's Army or the Communist Party or getting a university degree and shifting their
hukou to the university.

Assigning workers to a *danwei* and keeping rural persons from migrating to urban areas gave
the government control over the allocation of labor. Setting industry wages and agriculture
prices low enabled the government to accumulate capital to invest in its goal of capital-intensive
industrialization. The administered labor system produced an "iron rice bowl" of lifetime job
security, income, and benefits for urban workers.[9] It prevented the massive rural-to-urban
migration found in most developing countries. But the system failed to match workers and jobs
efficiently or to motivate workers fully in the workplace. It created an apartheid-like society that
made second-class citizens of the 80 percent or so of the Chinese population in rural areas.

The column "Before Reforms" of Table 7.1 summarizes the labor system in this period of time.

2 Reforms toward labor market

China started its economic reforms in the late 1970s in agriculture. The government contracted land to individual farmers and allowed the farmers to sell their produce on open markets once they had met the quota the government set to provide food for urban workers. This *household responsibility system* induced farmers to raise agricultural productivity. The increase in productivity freed many agricultural workers to seek work off the farm in the rural area where they had their *hukou* residency. The increase in productivity coupled with increased prices for rural goods raised rural incomes relative to urban incomes. Local governments responded to the increased supply of rural labor and greater demand for goods and services from farmers by forming or encouraging individuals to form township and village enterprises (TVEs) to produce non-agricultural goods and services in rural China.

The government next turned to reforming the industrial sector. Much as it had allowed farmers to profit from exceeding agricultural quotas the government allowed SOEs to keep the revenues from production that exceeded the levels dictated by the Five Year Plans. The government gave SOEs leeway to determine employment and pay though it maintained control over their total payroll.[10] Seeking to increase effort and productivity, SOE managers introduced piecework-type wages, point systems for bonuses, and linked hiring and promotion to performance and skills.[11] The government also allowed management to fire employees who did not perform adequately and to select employees by examinations that tested them for technical skill and work performance.

In the 1990s the Ministry of Labor began to relieve enterprises from providing housing, medical service, and pension benefits to their employees. The goal was to develop portable national pension, health, and unemployment insurance programs comparable to social security systems in most other countries. To protect older workers in the transition, the state differentiated between workers who retired or who started work before 1997 and were still working then and those who started after 1997. The older cohorts received a housing subsidy when their firm did

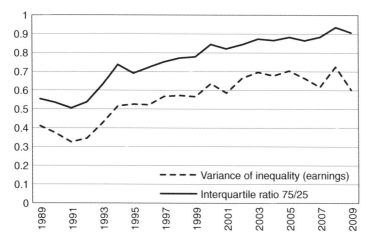

Figure 7.1 Measures of inequality

Source: Chi et al. (2012)

not provide them apartments while newer cohorts did not receive a subsidy. The government described this policy as "New People new rule, old people old rule."

Another step in non-agricultural reforms was to allow non-SOEs – TVEs in rural areas; private firms; foreign-owned multinationals – to enter or expand in the market. The percentage of workers in TVEs increased from 9 percent in 1980 to 26 percent in 1995 and the TVEs became more privately controlled.[12] In the urban sector, employment in SOEs (run by the central government) or in urban collective enterprises (run by cities or other lower jurisdictions) dropped from about 90 percent of urban workers in the 1970s to 50 percent in the 1990s and kept falling through the 2000s. By 2010 just 30 percent of urban workers worked in state-owned or collective enterprises; about 60 percent were self-employed or worked in privately owned firms, including 10 percent in foreign-owned and Hong Kong, Macao, or Taiwanese firms; while the rest were in cooperatives, or joint or limited liability firms over which government had some control.[13]

Freeing SOE management to operate by market principles and allowing private enterprise to employ a majority of the workforce sounded the death knell for the system of labor bureaus assigning workers to jobs. Young workers increasingly found jobs on their own. By 2001 the state assigned only 5 percent of college graduates to jobs and shortly thereafter it ended the job assignment system.

China's economic reforms set off one of the greatest economic expansions in history. Firms desperately sought workers to produce goods for export and for building infrastructure and domestic consumption. With rural people able to rent housing and buy food, and other consumption items on the open market and to set up their own businesses in the informal sector, some 150–160 million rural persons migrated to work in cities between 1980 and 2010.[14] Benefiting from this "floating population" of migrants, cities encouraged rural residents to migrate to work but cities withheld from migrants the benefits of urban amenities such as health care and the right to enroll their children in regular urban schools, the right to buy housing. As an example of the discrimination against migrants, pregnant women were told to go back to hospitals in their rural area to bear children rather than use the urban medical facilities. Cities sold urban *hukou* at prices that varied depending on the size and attractiveness of the city.[15]

At the turn of the millennium parts of the administered labor system remained but market forces had replaced administrative orders as the driving force for employment, wages, and working conditions in China. How did the new labor market change wage and employment outcomes from those set by the government administrative rule?

3 The new labor market: wages and income

Market determination of pay increased wage and income differentials along a variety of dimensions (see Table 7.2). Urban incomes increased more rapidly than rural incomes, which produced the highest urban–rural income gap on record: urban incomes 3.13 times rural incomes in 2011 (Table 7.2, column 1). The earnings premium of junior college or bachelors graduates over high-school graduates of the same age increased from the 1990s through 2009 (Table 7.2, column 2). The earnings advantages of workers in the highest paying industries relative to workers in the lowest paying industries increased substantially over the period (Table 7.2, column 3). Incomes in the more industrialized and thus high-income coastal regions pulled further ahead of incomes in the lower-income provinces in the interior of the country and in the north and west, so that even though geographic disparity in earnings declined in the 2000s it remained far higher than in the 1980s and 1990s (Table 7.2, column 4). The last column (in

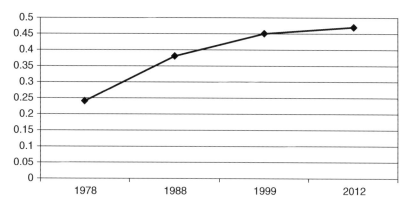

Figure 7.2   Gini coefficients for total income

Source: China Statistical Yearbooks (1990–2011), based on official statistics; 1980 unofficial estimate

Table 7.2) compares the incomes of college graduates aged 25 to the incomes of migrant work-ers. It shows an increase in the ratio of young college to migrant workers in the 1990s but a drop in the 2000s as migrant incomes increased greatly, generating claims that China had entered a new phase of labor market development (the Lewis turning point) that I discuss shortly.

3.1 Why did market forces raise earnings differentials so greatly?

One reason is that when the government controlled the economy it set wage differentials far below market-clearing levels. It did not have to pay people more to acquire skills or move to particular sectors. It assigned people to those activities. Once workers could move among jobs and firms could alter pay to attract the workers they wanted, supply and demand raised pay more in higher skilled/paid activities than in lower skilled/paid activities.

A second reason is that as the economy grew supply and demand changed in favor of more skilled and higher-paid work activities. Growth of GDP, for example, shifted demand for labor to higher skill occupations and industries, which raised the earnings of college graduates.[16]

The increase in wage differentials raised inequality in earnings. Figure 7.1 shows two mea-sures of inequality in labor earnings: the variance of the log earnings of workers and the ratio of the earnings of workers at the 75th percentile of the earnings distribution to the earnings of workers at the 25th percentile. Both statistics show a trend increase in inequality with a modest dip in 2009, possibly because of the global economic recession.

Figure 7.2 displays inequality in total income, as measured by Gini coefficients for total income. Inequality of total income depends on the distribution of national income between labor and capital, which shifted toward capital in China as in most other countries, and on the level of inequality in capital income, which far exceeds inequality in labor income in all coun-tries. The Gini coefficients increased greatly over the period. Chinese officials pay close attention to the Gini coefficient in the belief that values above 0.40–0.45 foment social unrest. The esti-mated Gini coefficient of 0.47 in 2012 was in the danger range but estimates from other sources suggest that the Gini could be much higher.[17] Statistical measures aside, opinion polls show that China's citizens view inequality as a huge problem, and place it and corruption at the top of their list of concerns.[18]

Table 7.1 Supply, demand, and labor institutions before and after labor market reforms

	Before labor market reforms, 1970s–early 1980s	After reforms – 1990s through 2013	Policies to regulate new labor market
Firm employment	Determined by the state employment quotas; only formal employment in SOEs	Shift of employment to private sector	Labor contract law policy to move short-term workers to permanent contracts
Wage determination	Set by national wage grid with little variation among sectors, employ- ers, or skills; minimal inequality	Market-determined with large increase in dispersion of earnings	City minimum wages increase rapidly; college to migrant earnings gap falls with huge graduating classes; possible Lewis turning point
Provision of housing, medical insurance, retirement pay, other social amenities	Mandated benefits part of compensation package for firms; ration cards for consumer commodities for workers with urban *hukou*	Eliminate the requirement that firms provide benefits; require contributions to portable national benefit system	Portable benefit system still work-in-progress
Migration from initial location	*Hukou* restrictions; rural workers	Huge "floating popula- tion" without urban amenities	Contract labor law to assure workers of legal rights with individual contracts
Worker choice of employer	State assigns workers to firm; almost all urban workers employed by state-owned or collective enterprises	Workers choose own job; employers hire who they want; graduates favor safe jobs in government but biggest growth is informal sector work	Firms favor applicants with city *hukou* and from elite institution
Freedom to quit and find new employer	Cannot leave job without *danwei* approval; most workers stay with single firm their entire life	High worker mobility	Firms complain about excessive mobility
Union activity	ACFTU operates as Leninist transmission belt	ACFTU lobbies for worker interests within some branches of government	

4 Turnover, mobility, and productivity

China's economic reforms opened the door for firms to hire and fire workers freely and for workers to change jobs as they saw fit. Lifetime security for workers disappeared. Holding work- ers in a single firm for their working lives disappeared. SOEs laid workers off when they deemed it necessary and hired temporary workers when they deemed it profitable. Urban workers, par- ticularly young educated persons, changed jobs frequently in pursuit of higher-paying and better work. Rural workers poured into cities, moving from employer to employer.

Table 7.2 Market-driven widening of wage and income differentials (1980–2011)

Year	Urban–rural	Junior college or BA degree/high school (aged 35)	Top-paying industries/ lowest-paying industries	Top-paying provinces/lowest paying provinces	Junior college or BA aged 25/rural migrant
1980	2.50		1.42	1.37	
1990	2.20	1.18★	1.61	1.84	1.30★
2000	2.79	1.24	1.87	2.84	2.30
2011	3.13	1.43★★	3.03	2.35	1.43★★

Source: China Statistical Yearbook; Junior college or BA to high school based on annual income from micro China Urban Household Survey data with ★1992; ★★2009. Top and bottom industries and top and bottom provinces change over time, so this measures spread of distribution. For industries, unweighted average of top three and bottom three; for provinces unweighted average of top five and bottom five. The data cover fewer industry groups than province groups. College aged 21 from China Urban Household Survey micro-data. Rural migrant wage per month from Feng Lu (2012). College income of persons aged 25 divided by 12 to provide monthly basis

The most striking shift in employer behavior occurred in the late 1990s when SOEs and urban collectives undertook the biggest layoff of workers in history. Seeing these enterprises as an inefficient drag on the economy and burdens on governmental budgets, the central government announced the goal of restructuring, privatizing, or closing thousands of SOEs and reducing employment in the state-owned sector by 30 percent. Under the slogan "Grasp the Large, Release the Small" the government closed many large firms and privatized smaller firms. From 1995 to 2000, employment in SOEs fell by 36 million persons while employment in urban collective enterprises fell by 21 million persons. Many workers who lost their jobs had few skills beyond those used at their workplace. None had experience of searching for work in the labor market.[19] The result was that the official rate of joblessness, which had been near zero in the pre-reform period, reached 4.3 percent in 2002. But this underestimated the extent of job loss because many enterprises kept workers on the books as *xiagang* – off-post – workers, paying them modest benefits without work.[20] Counting these persons as unemployed, the rate of joblessness exceeded 10 percent or so.

The late 1990s retrenchment of the state-owned and collective enterprise sector[21] was China's version of the "big bang" shift from a planned economy to a market economy that the former Soviet Union and Eastern Europe undertook following the fall of communism. But in contrast to the 10–15 percent declines in GDP associated with the transition to markets in most European transition economies, GDP continued to grow during big-bang retrenchment of the state sector. But few of the laid-off once-privileged SOE and urban collective workers enjoyed the fruits of higher GDP. The government provided some unemployment compensation and training programs to the displaced workers but nothing that could ameliorate the loss of the iron rice bowl. The biggest beneficiaries of privatizing state-owned businesses were factory managers or relatives or friends of party officials with *guanxi* who bought the profitable parts of firms at bargain prices and left the unprofitable parts and commitments to pension and medical costs of workers in government hands. In some provinces, such as Liaoning in the North, tens of thousands of *xiagang* workers protested the loss of jobs and corrupt privatization – the first massive protest against the communist state in modern times, but to no avail.

Continued economic growth shifted the locus of turnover from firms to workers. With firms no longer providing social benefits, workers were less tied to their employer than in the past. Young urban workers moved from firm to firm in search of better job matches and higher pay.

Turnover rates in major firms rose to 20 percent or so per year[22] – a proportion of voluntary leaving similar to the yearly quit rate for US workers,[23] and far above turnover in many other advanced countries. The huge flow of migrants added millions more persons who shifted jobs frequently, some working self-employed in the informal sector and some working on short-term stints at construction sites and for firms. A substantial proportion of migrants would return to their village at the spring holiday and then find other work instead of going back to the same employer.

When the economic reforms kicked in China had relatively few college graduates. Mao's Cultural Revolution had wrecked China's higher education system so that fewer than 100,000 students were enrolled at university in 1970.[24] From 1978 through 1988 China averaged fewer than 300,000 graduates per year. It expanded enrollments moderately in the 1980s and 1990s; added hundreds of new institutions of higher education in the 2000s, and produced a massive increase in enrollments and graduates in the 2000s.[25] The number of bachelors graduates increased to 600,000 in 1990, doubled to 1.2 million in 2002, and then jumped by over fivefold to 7 million in 2013. In three decades China had transformed a train-wreck higher education system into a system that educated the "best and brightest" top scorers on the national entrance and then into a system of mass higher education.

Businesses complain about the costs of voluntary labor turnover and seek ways to reduce it. When workers quit their jobs, it is costly to find and train new workers to replace them. For some period of time, the productivity of new employees is often lower than that of the experienced worker who has left. Thus, high turnover is associated with higher costs of production and lower profits for an individual firm. But from the standpoint of the economy writ large, turnover often improves economic performance. Workers who move to higher-paying more productive jobs not only raise their own incomes but increase national output. As China reformed its economy, workers moved from lower-paying rural jobs to higher-paying jobs in rural township and village enterprises to the coastal province factories that led its export boom and construction and service sector jobs in cities. Within manufacturing, employment shifted from light export industries to high value-added high-tech industries. It is difficult to imagine that China could have increased productivity as rapidly and reallocated workers among sectors as successfully as it did without a market-driven labor system with high labor turnover.

5 The "Lewis turning point" debate and informal urban sector

In the 1950s Arthur Lewis developed a model of economic development that captures some of the problems faced by China half a century later. Lewis divided developing economies into two sectors: a low productivity agricultural sector with an "unlimited" supply of labor and a high productivity modern industrial sector that expands by drawing labor from agriculture. With an unlimited (infinitely elastic) supply of labor from agriculture, urban firms are able to increase employment without raising wages. This allows them to earn considerable profits which they can then invest in expanding their business or other businesses to produce a self-sustaining drive to modernization. As more and more rural workers obtain jobs in the urban economy, the supply of labor changes from infinitely elastic to an upward sloping curve. This is the Lewis turning point, where development has advanced sufficiently that firms must raise wages to attract more low-skilled workers.

Lewis based his model on the experience of Caribbean economies but the model offers insights into any economy where migration from a lower productivity sector to higher productivity sector is an important component of development. In the 2000s migrant wages began rising in China's cities, suggesting to some economists that China had reached the Lewis turning point. Other economists disagreed, arguing that rural China still harbored millions of "surplus workers" who would move to cities without wage increases. Differences in the ratio of urban to rural incomes in various data sources and disagreement over the key indicators that identified the turning point fueled the debate.[26] Over the same period, urban China experienced a huge increase in the proportion of persons in *informal employment*, by which I mean working as self-employed, for family-owned or small enterprises that faced no pressure to follow the labor laws, or by working without formal status in large firms. The informalization of the workforce added a new twist to the relation between economic growth and employment. In advanced economies most workers work for *formal sector* firms that offer permanent jobs, standard hours, and social security benefits as set by employment laws, collective bargaining, and firm-based human resource policies. In developing countries, by contrast, most work in jobs that are temporary, irregular, and without legal benefits or protection. With the exception of some self-employed persons who run successful businesses, informal-sector workers invariably earn less and work under worse conditions than workers in the formal sector. Until the 1990s and 2000s the prevailing view among development experts was that economic growth would shrink the informal sector in the same way that it shrinks the agriculture sector in the Lewis model. Some warned governments against improving protections and benefits for urban workers for fear that the increased labor costs would slow movement of jobs from the informal to the formal sector.

But economic growth in the 1990s and 2000s did not reduce the informal-sector share of employment irrespective of labor and social policies, which led the OECD to conclude that the informal had become normal.[27] Productivity increases in manufacturing and the introduction of new capital-intensive technologies in the modern sector of developing economies kept formal sector jobs from increasing rapidly as they had done in advanced countries decades earlier. The informal or irregular share of urban employment in Korea, arguably the most successful of all developing countries, expanded as the country grew. In China even as the country became the manufacturing center of the world economy, the share of workers in manufacturing fell from 16 percent in 1990 to 13 percent in 2009 while the urban share of manufacturing employment fell even more, due in large part to the 1990s retrenchment of state-owned manufacturing enterprises.

While China's statistical agencies do not provide official estimates of informal-sector work, analyses of employment data tell a clear story about the expansion of the informal sector to over half of the urban workforce in the 2000s.[28] Rural migrants constitute a large proportion of the sector, working long hours for low pay. In the 1990s rural migrants in the informal sector worked 72 hours per week compared to 42 hours per week for persons with an urban *hukou* in formal-sector jobs; earned 30 percent lower monthly income; 2 percent of the informal-sector workers had pension coverage compared to 82 percent of the workers with an urban *hukou*.[29] Many large firms in export and construction employed migrant workers without giving them the individual employment contracts and legally required fringe benefits. Lacking legal documentation of their work status that they could take to labor arbitration committees responsible for dealing with the rights of workers, workers increasingly undertook protests against the way management treated them, ranging from wildcat strikes to civil disobedience – blocking roads, surrounding work sites in large numbers, etc. – which the government viewed as threatening social stability (Lee, 2007).

To strengthen the ability of workers to defend their rights through legal channels, in 2007 the Chinese government enacted a new Labor Contract Law. This law required that employers give workers written contracts and that employees who accumulate tenure on their job obtain permanent rather than temporary contracts. The law was enacted after a remarkably wide-ranging open debate. Pro-worker rights forces in China, led by the government-run All China Federation of Trade Unions (ACFTU), favored the new initiative. Labor and human rights groups in the US and other advanced countries endorsed it. Business groups in China and the US opposed the law on the grounds that it would bring back the iron rice bowl and reduce employment by raising labor costs.

Despite China's generally weak implementation of labor laws, the new law improved conditions for migrant workers. After the law took effect in January 2008, there was a jump in the proportion of migrants who obtained individual contracts and in the proportion who received legally mandated social insurances and a drop in the proportion whose wage payments were delayed or reduced by the employer.[30] Because the great recession-induced decline in export demand hit China shortly after the law was implemented, it is not possible to determine whether the law adversely affected employment as its opponents feared. Employer and employee responses to the recession and recovery dominated employment in the late 2000s.

6 The great recession test

The 2007–8 global economic decline tested the resilience of labor markets around the world. When Chinese exports to advanced countries dropped sharply in winter 2008–9, many worried how the country's new labor market would respond. The immediate impact was a huge decline in jobs.[31] World Bank researchers estimate that between October 2008 and April 2009 49 million rural migrants lost their off-the-farm jobs – 6.8 percent of the rural workforce – and that the wages of migrant workers fell by 10.5 percent.[32] Some advanced countries, such as the US, also experienced large job losses while others, such as Germany, introduced various forms of work-sharing to preserve employment.

Many labor analysts, who had heralded the US as the advanced world's great jobs machine for its performance in the 1990s, expected the US to have a robust job recovery. It did not. The US had an extraordinarily weak job recovery, with employment lower four years after the recession officially ended than it had been before the recession. Many other advanced countries also had weak recoveries. Unemployment in advanced European countries was in double digits in 2013, with Germany being the exception with a rate of unemployment lower after the recession than before.

The new labor market with Chinese characteristics did remarkably well in recovering the huge recession-related losses. Chinese workers found jobs rapidly. Nearly half of the displaced workers were re-employed by April 2009. One year after the crisis most workers had obtained new work. Some found employment in the informal sector. Some returned to their family's land but returned to off-farm work as China's aggressive stimulus package[33] spurred employment in the non-traded goods parts of the economy. The fall in wages may have also induced some firms to increase employment quickly. The difference between China's recovery of jobs after it lost millions of jobs in the 2008–9 global recession and its sluggish job creation after the late 1990s layoffs is in part a story of workers and firms learning how to navigate a market-driven economy. With some amazement, the World Bank team remarked on "the speed of the labor force adjustment in the crisis"[34] in China compared to sluggish adjustments in the US and Europe.

7 Labor challenges

The creation of a functioning labor market notwithstanding, China faces major labor problems to continue to bring the benefits of modern economic development to its nearly 1.4 billion people. The most important challenges are (1) to develop an effective labor relations system to resolve the labor and management conflicts that invariably arise in a market economy; (2) to absorb the huge supply of university graduates and; (3) to extend social benefits and opportunity to rural citizens and informal-sector workers. Resolving these problems will ameliorate the inequalities that accompanied its growth spurt and that potentially threaten future social stability.

Historically, trade unions have been the key institution through which workers defend their economic interests and collective bargaining has been the mechanism by which unions and management resolve workplace disagreements over pay, benefits, and working conditions. On paper China has the largest trade union movement in the world. In 2010, the government-sponsored ACFTU claimed membership of 239 million workers, including 89 million migrants.[35] Unlike independent unions formed by workers, however, the ACFTU has traditionally sought to defuse worker discontent and encourage "harmonious labor relations" rather than fighting for workers.[36] Per the worker in the *New York Times* interview summarized below, many workers saw the union as an extension of authority over them rather than their voice in the economy:

> (Worker) "Trade union? … What's that?"
> (Reporter) "Was there no state-sponsored union in their factories, as required in principle?"
> (Worker) "Oh, yeah, I guess maybe we do have one of those … when management has some new demand or request, they call us together for a meeting."[37]

The shift to a labor market dominated by private employers fundamentally changed the nature of China's labor relations. Workers could protest conditions at work and seek redress from their employers without challenging government authority. The number of labor disputes brought to the Labor Dispute Arbitration Committees (the legal entity set up to resolve disputes) skyrocketed from 8,150 in 1992 to 135,206 in 2000 to 1,280,000 or so in 2010.[38] Acting on their own with no help from the official unions, workers began striking in large numbers for better conditions in different parts of the country.[39] In summer 2010 a strike by Honda workers in Guangdong made headlines around the world when it produced a collective agreement with improved pay and benefits.[40]

China's labor laws require firms to accept unions and give the ACFTU exclusive right to represent workers, which explains its huge membership. The usual ACFTU mode of organizing a union has been to remind management of its legal responsibilities and to ask it to set up a union and appoint a company official to be union head, with the promise that "unlike western unions, which always stand against the employer, Chinese unions are obliged to boost the corporation's development and maintain sound labour relations."[41] Even operating in this fashion, AFCTU unions are associated with higher wages and greater worker benefits in China,[42] perhaps because the firms that agreed to set up a union viewed this as part of a positive labor relations policy to prevent worker activism. But putting the interests of the employer or government above those of workers did not fit the reality of the new labor market. Both the government and the ACFTU sought ways for the official unions to operate differently and represent workers in ways that would help China develop a new effective labor relations system. In some parts of the country, such as Shenzhen or Guangzhou, the ACFTU has broken new ground by establishing procedures for workers to elect union leaders. The head of the Guangdong ACFTU committed his organization to put workers' interests first in all of its activities. But it is unclear how far the ACFTU can reform itself. Local and provincial party organizations appoint union leaders, and they often favor business development above all else. Still in 2011, after reviewing the changing labor scene on the Mainland, Han Dongfang, the Hong Kong-based advocate of independent unionism, called on the international union movement to engage the ACFTU to help it morph into a genuine representative of workers.[43]

The explosive increase in the supply of college graduates from the 1990s through the 2010s poses a different challenge to China's labor market. The following headlines (obtained by Googling the words, "China university graduate employment" in July 2013) give the magnitude of the challenge:

College Grads Are Jobless in China's "High-Growth" Economy
(Forbes, *May 26, 2013*)

China's Graduates Face Glut
(Wall Street Journal, *August 22, 2011*)

Dearth of Work for China's College Grads
(Businessweek, *September 1, 2010*)

China's Ant Tribe: Millions of Unemployed College Grads
(Christian Science Monitor, *December 21, 2009*)

Two facts lie behind the headlines. The first is that many graduates from the huge bachelor's degree classes in the late 1990s–early 2010s failed to obtain regular jobs upon graduation, with some remaining without work months or even one to two years later.[44] A national survey found that 16.4 percent of college graduates aged 21 to 25 years were unemployed in 2011 compared to 8.2 percent of similarly aged high-school graduates,[45] while by contrast older college graduates had much lower unemployment rates than older less educated workers. The second is that the huge graduating classes of the period reduced the college earnings premium for new graduates relative to less educated workers to such an extent that starting graduates' pay was barely greater than that of migrants.[46] The critical issue for the labor market is whether the higher unemployment and lower pay at the outset of their work lives will permanently lower the lifetime income trajectory of graduates, as it has in the US,[47] or whether it will be a temporary blip from which graduates will catch up as they gain experience.

The labor market has additional ways to adjust to the huge increase in graduate supply that should ameliorate the headline-making problems. On the demand side, with more graduates available at lower wages, industries that rely most extensively on graduate workers have an incentive to expand their share of output and employment. In the global market, these sectors should increase their exports and compete better with imports from similar industries in other countries. On the supply side, with jobs hard to find and pay depressed, some graduates will choose to invest in higher-level degrees and delay entry into the job market. Their improved skills should help them gain better jobs in the future. Geographic mobility of graduates will also help the market equilibrate. Graduates who seek work outside the major coastal cities and provinces which have employed most of China's highly educated workers in years past will find a better supply–demand balance than in the urban hotspots. More graduates working in China's second- and third-tier cities rather than Beijing, Shanghai, Guangzhou, etc. will give the graduates new opportunities and boost economic growth in those areas while reducing the surplus of graduates in the largest cities.

The experience of the US and Korea in responding to large influxes of university graduates suggests that the most important market adjustment is through graduates using their education working in occupations that traditionally relied on less educated workers. This requires that employers offer these jobs to graduates and that graduates accept them and that both find ways for the graduates to use their skills in raising productivity in those jobs. News stories report that, although graduates earn more than non-graduates and presumably get promoted more quickly in non-traditional graduate occupations in China as in other countries, many Chinese graduates reject such career paths. Under the headline "Chinese Graduates Say No Thanks to Factory Jobs,"[48] the *New York Times* reported on the unwillingness of Chinese graduates to accept jobs that required manual labor. But a period of joblessness or of temporary work may change those views. Upgrading the education levels of occupations and industries across the board will ultimately benefit the overall economy as graduates bring their skills to these areas and it is likely to offer career paths into management and other high-paying jobs for graduates as they build work experience.

Because disgruntled young graduates can be the cutting edge of social disorder, the Chinese government has developed special programs to help them overcome their job problems. In response to the reduction in employment opportunities in the global recession the government encouraged graduates to accept employment outside the major cities, with higher wages and other benefits. In 2013 it ordered schools, government agencies, and SOEs to hire more graduates to help relieve joblessness. In the troubled Xinjiang Uygur autonomous region, the state government set aside posts in government departments and institutions, and, in SOEs, for students to work a one-year on-the-job training program.[49] Government programs can help improve the matching of graduates with jobs and can encourage universities to develop more job-oriented educational programs but the bulk of the adjustment to mass higher education rests with graduates and employers.

The third big problem facing China's labor market is to move from a dualistic labor market in which earnings and social benefits are markedly higher for workers in the formal urban sector than for workers with rural *hukou* and workers in the informal sector to a market that provides similar social benefits and opportunity to all workers. Virtually everyone in China appreciates the unfair nature of the *hukou* system that restricts the opportunities and benefits for persons with rural *hukou* when they reside and work in a city. Top leaders and government bodies advocate *hukou* reforms. Public opinion favors reforms.[50] And various cities and provinces have experimented with ways to weaken the disadvantage of the rural *hukou*. But cities have been sluggish instituting changes to help migrants when the changes reduce the well-being of city residents – for instance by expanding city schools to accept the children of migrants or opening urban medical facilities to migrant workers. With limited city budgets and ways to raise money, and local opposition, it is difficult to make radical changes in the system. The most success in reforming the *hukou* system has come in small- and medium-sized cities where urban amenities are limited. Some large cities have offered point systems through which rural persons can gain urban *hukou*. Some cities privilege persons with rural *hukou* in the same province. Still, the issue is not whether China will ultimately scrap a system that disadvantages so many people but how quickly it will do so.

Because a disproportionate share of informal-sector workers are migrants with rural *hukou*, extending social benefits and rights to persons with rural *hukou* will benefit many informal-sector workers. But the problem of the informal sector goes beyond the *hukou* issue. The problem of low wages, high working hours, and lack of pensions and other job-related social insurances for informal-sector workers is universal among developing countries. Increasing the proportion of workers with individual contracts, as the 2007 Labor Contract Law did, was a significant step toward helping informal workers employed by large formal enterprises. But it had no direct effect on the self-employed, or persons in small family or other businesses. All developing countries are struggling to find ways to extend benefits and protections to informal-sector workers. Thus far none has come up with a "magic bullet" solution. Benefits given to persons through citizenship regardless of employment status – such as national health insurance – offers one solution, but require an effective tax system and the willingness of workers and firms in the formal sector to fund benefits for those in the informal sector.

8 Conclusion

China's transformation from a society dominated by an administered labor system to one with a functioning labor market is a remarkable achievement. The before/after contrasts summarized in Table 7.1 and described in the text reflect a unique "natural experiment" of the difference between having a labor market determine employment and compensation and determining those outcomes without a market. Resolving the three big labor challenges that currently face the country: creating a modern labor relations system; absorbing huge numbers of college graduates; and extending social benefits and equal opportunity to persons with rural *hukou* and those working in the informal sector – will require strong institutions and policies responsive to the needs and concerns of the participants in China's new labor market with Chinese characteristics.

Notes

1 Bian (1994: 971).
2 <http://en.wikipedia.org/wiki/Public_records_in_China>.
3 Walder (1986) is the classic account of this system.
4 Bian (1994).
5 Knight and Yueh (2003: 10). Consistent with this a 1995 survey found that 75 percent of urban workers worked at a state-assigned job. See Bian (1994: table 5).
6 Bian (1994: 273, table 5).
7 Shirk (1981).
8 Walder (1986).
9 <http://en.wikipedia.org/wiki/Iron_rice_bowl>.
10 As reported in Xia, Q. *et al.* (2013).
11 Shirk (1981).
12 Sabin (1994).
13 Rush (2011: graph 4).
14 Different studies report different numbers of migrant workers. The 160 million number comes from Li Shi (2008). Li Bin (2011), head of the National Population and Family Planning Commission, also estimated that the floating population numbered 160 million but put the total floating population at 221 million. Li Jing (2008: 1083) reports 200 million on the basis of a report from the Research Office of the State Council. The 2011 Migrant Worker Report from National Bureau of Statistics of China puts the total amount of migrant workers at 250 million.
15 Zhang [n.d., table 3].
16 Chi *et al.* (2012).
17 The annual Household Finance Survey of Chengdu's Southwestern University of Finance and Economics China gives an estimated Gini coefficient of 0.61, which would make China one of the most unequal countries in the world <http://english.caixin.com/print/print_en.jsp>. Estimates of the number of billionaires in China also suggest an extremely high level of inequality. On Forbes' 2012 billionaires list Mainland China was number 2 in billionaires with 122 compared to the US's 442 while Hong Kong had 39 more. The Shanghai-based Hurun Rich List, which estimates the hidden wealth of China's richest citizens, reports that China had 317 billionaires compared to 408 US billionaires <www.hurun.net/usen/NewsShow.aspx?nid=418>.
18 A February 2012 poll reported that income inequality and soaring house prices were top concerns. A March 2012 poll put corruption and income distribution as top concerns; a November 2012 poll rated the wealth gap, corruption, and the power of vested interests as top issues <www.economist.com/news/briefing/21583245-china-worlds-worst-polluter-largest-investor-green-energy-its-rise-will-have>.
19 Of the 8.9 million *xiagang* workers in 1996, about 3.6 million had found jobs. Another 2.3 million were not looking for jobs and were thus out of the labor market. The remaining 3 million were looking for jobs. For a description of the problem SOE employees had in finding jobs in this period, see Song (1997).

20 These are defined as the workers "who went home from enterprises due to poor performance of enterprise but still maintained some nominal relationship with their enterprises" (Song (1997)).

21 The division between private and state-owned and collectively owned enterprises is not as sharp as in other countries, as government agencies hold some shares <www.mansfieldfdn.org/backup/programs/program_pdfs/ent_china.pdf>.

22 <http://www.globaloutsourcinginfo.com/chinese-employees-average-salary-jumps-9-1-turnover-rate-up-18-9-in-2012/> reported a 19 percent turnover rate in 2012.

23 <www.bls.gov/news.release/pdf/jolts.pdf>.

24 The Cultural Revolution began in 1966 and continued for some years afterwards. From 1967 through 1976 the government cancelled university entrance exams, restoring them in 1977 under Deng Xiaoping. But the country lost many intellectuals who spent years in rural labor camps, and some of whom left China when the Revolution ended. <http://en.wikipedia.org/wiki/Cultural_Revolution>.

25 Li (2010).

26 The main articles in this debate are Cai (2010), Cai and Wang (2007, 2011), Chan (2010), Golley and Meng (2011), Huang and Cai (2013), Knight *et al.* (2011), Zhang *et al.* (2011).

27 See for example, OECD (2009); Freeman (2009).

28 Huang (2009) estimates that the informal-sector share of urban jobs doubled between the 1990s and the early 2000s and had 1.5 times as many workers as the formal sector. Kuruvilla *et al.* (2011) estimated that Chinese enterprises shifted 39 percent of China's urban workforce from permanent employment to the "informal" sector; Park and Cai (2011) estimate that in 2005 over half of urban workers were informal, with about 10 percent self-employed and another 36 percent undocumented in government statistics on employer ownership types with many employed in the service sector.

29 The article provides finer comparisons with data on migrants in the formal sector and of persons with *hukou* in the informal sector, who fit between the two groups in the text (Park and Cai (2011)).

30 Freeman and Li (2013).

31 There are diverse estimates of job loss in the crisis. The National Bureau of Statistics (2009) estimated that 23 million migrant workers were displaced in the crisis. Other analysts reported that 20 million migrant workers lost their employment and returned to their villages, but others gave lower estimates (Chen, D. (2010); Giles *et al.* (2012) review several studies of job loss). The press gave considerable play to 20 million that Che Xiwen estimated lost their jobs from a survey of 150 villages (Tan, Y. and Xin, D. (2009)).

32 Huang *et al.* (2010).

33 In November 2008 China declared that it would spend 4 trillion (US$ 586 billion) for infrastructure <http://en.wikipedia.org/wiki/Chinese_economic_stimulus_program>. The IMF estimated that the combined 2009 and 2010 amount was 5.8 percent of GDP, which exceeded the US stimulus and was third to Russia and Saudi Arabia in its relative size of their stimulus <www.treasury.gov.au/PublicationsAndMedia/Publications/2011/Chinese-Macroeconomic-Management-Through-the-Crisis-and-Beyond/working-paper-2011-01/Chinas-stimulus-package>. While the official estimates included spending that would have occurred in any case, such as relief for the earthquake in Setchuan and while some may have been wasted, China acted aggressively to fill in the lost demand for exports.

34 Huang *et al.* (2010: 23).

35 <http://english.acftu.org/template/10002/file.jsp?cid=63&aid=622>.

36 In the communist tradition, this makes it a Leninist transmission belt organization <www.marxists.org/archive/lenin/works/1921/dec/30.htm>.

37 August 22, 2001.

38 China Labour Statistical Yearbooks published figures regularly until recent years. For 2007–9 the statistics are reported in Cai, F. and Wang, M. (2012).

39 <http://en.wikipedia.org/wiki/2010_Chinese_labour_unrest>.

40 As evidence that the Honda strike was not unique, the Chinastrikes website, which maps over time by area of the country on the basis of news articles and reports, shows increased strike activity over time concentrated in major urban areas <www.chinastrikes.crowdmap.com/main>.

41 Senior AFCTU official Guo Chen cited in Han Dongfang, 'China's main union has yet to earn a job', *Guardian*, June 26, 2011 <www.theguardian.com/commentisfree/2011/jun/26/china-trade-union-global-movement>.

42 Ge, Y. (2014); Yao, Y. and Zhong, N. (2013); Fang, T. and Ge, Y. (2013).

43 <www.theguardian.com/commentisfree/2011/jun/26/china-trade-union-global-movement>.

44 In the class of 2008, for instance, 27 percent did not have jobs by year's end. In March 2012 Prime Minister Wen Jiabao reported that 22 percent of the 2011 class of graduates were still jobless (reported in *New York Times*, January 24, 2013, 'Chinese graduates say no thanks to factory jobs'). The Beijing Municipal Commission of Education reported that through summer 2013 just 33.6 percent of college graduates in the city had signed employment contracts while the China Development Research Foundation found fewer than half of 2013 graduates found jobs. Summarizing the reports from several cities under the headline 'Chinese college graduates cannot secure jobs: 28% of Beijing's 2013 graduates and 44% of Shanghai's have found a job', an *International Business Times* article on May 17, 2013 shows the problem to be endemic <www.ibtimes.com/chinese-college-graduates-cannot-secure-jobs-28-beijings-2013-graduates-44-shanghais-have-found-job>.

45 China Household Finance Survey at Southwestern University of Finance and Economics in Chengdu data reported in <http://english.caixin.com/print/print_en.jsp>.

46 Statistics for 2003, 2005, and 2008 showed that the average starting salary of college graduates stayed around 1,500 yuan per month, but monthly wages for migrant workers rose from 700 yuan to 1,200 yuan ('University graduates earn little more than migrant workers', *Willingbird Sunday*, February 13, 2011). A 2011 survey of more than 6,000 new graduates conducted in Beijing said that entry-level salaries of 69 percent of college graduates are lower than those of the migrant workers who come from the countryside to service Chinese factories. Graduates from lower-level universities make an average of 1,903 yuan a month, with 2,200 yuan (US$345) a month for migrants (*Wall Street Journal*, 2012).

47 Kahn (2010).

48 August 15, 2013, 'As graduates rise in China, office jobs fail to keep up' <www.nytimes.com/2013/01/25/business/as-graduates-rise-in-china-office-jobs-fail-to-keep-up.html?pagewanted=all&pagewanted=print 1/7>; January 24, 2013 'Chinese graduates say no thanks to factory jobs', by Keith Bradsher (NYTimes.com).

49 See Shao Wei and Mao Weihua 'Training program to boost employment in Xinjiang', *China Daily*, 26 March, 2011.

50 China.org reports in an article 'Hukou – obstacle to market economy' that 92 percent of respondents agreed that the *hukou* system was in need of reform; 53 percent said the government should eliminate restrictive policies attached to the system, such as limits on access to education, health care, employment, and social insurance and 38 percent called for the system to be ended entirely.

Bibliography

Bao, S., Bodvarsson, O. B., Hou, J. W., and Zhao, Y. (2009) 'The Regulation of Migration in a Transition Economy: China's *Hukou* System', IIZA Discussion Paper No. 4493.

Bian, Y. (1994) 'Guanxi and the Allocation of Urban Jobs in China', *China Quarterly* 140 (December): 971–99.

Bian, Y., Zhang, W., and Cheng, C. (2012) 'A Social Network Model of the Job-Search Process: Testing a Relational Effect Hypothesis', *Chinese Journal of Sociology* 32(3): 24–7.

Cai, Fang (2010) 'Demographic Transition, Demographic Dividend, and the Lewis Turning Point in China', *China Economic Journal* 3(2): 107–19.

Cai, Fang and Wang, Meiyan (2007) 'Re-assessment of Rural Surplus Labor and Some Correlated Facts', *Chinese Rural Economy* 10: 4–12.

Cai, Fang and Wang, Meiyan (2011) 'Chinese Wages and the Turning Point in the Chinese Economy', *EastAsiaForum*, January 29 <www.eastasiaforum.org/2011/01/29/chinese-wages-and-the-turning-point-in-the-chinese-economy>.

Cai, Fang and Wang, Meiyan (2012) 'Labour Market Changes, Labour Disputes and Social Cohesion in China', OECD Development Centre Working Paper No. 307 (January).

Cao, Y., Qian, Y., and Weingast, B. R. (1999) 'From Federalism, Chinese Style, to Privatization, Chinese Style', *Economics of Transition* 7(1) (March): 103–31.

Chan, K. and Zhang, L. 'The *Hukou* System and Rural–Urban Migration', *China Quarterly* 160 (December): 818–55.

Chan, Kam Wing (2010) 'A China Paradox: Migrant Labor Shortage amidst Rural Labor Supply Abundance', *Eurasian Geography and Economics* 51(4): 513–30.

Chen, Dahong (2010) 'Trend of Migration Employment and Demand for Migrant Workers in 2010: Analysis Based on MOHRSS Survey', in Cai Fang (ed.), *Population and Labor Report in 2010*, Beijing: Social Sciences Academic Press, pp. 23–34.

Chi, W., Freeman, R. B., and Li, H. (2012) 'Adjusting to Really Big Changes: The Labor Market in China, 1989–2009', NBER Working Paper 17721 January.

Fang, C., Yang, D., and Meiyan, W. (2009) 'Employment and Inequality Outcomes in China', OECD, <http://www.oecd.org/els/emp/42546043.pdf>.

Fang, T. and Ge, Y. (2013) 'Chinese Unions and Enterprises Performance', IZA Discussion Paper No. 7870 (December).

Freeman, R. B. (2009) 'Labor Regulations, Unions, and Social Protection in Developing Countries: Market Distortion or Efficient Institutions', in Dani Rodrik and Mark R. Rosenzweig (eds), *Handbook of Development Economics*, vol. 5, Amsterdam: Elsevier, ch. 70, pp. 4657–702.

Freeman, R. B. and Li, X. (2013) 'How Does China's New Labor Contract Law Affect Floating Workers?', NBER Working Paper No. 19254 (July).

Ge, Y. (2007) 'What Do Unions Do in China?' <http://ssrn.com/abstract=1031084 or http://dx.doi.org/10.2139/ssrn.1031084>.

Ge, Y. (2014) 'Do Chinese Unions Have "Real" Effects on Employee Compensation', *Contemporary Economic Policy* 32(1) (January): 187–202.

Giles, John, Park, Albert, Cai, Fang, and Du, Yang (2012) 'Weathering a Storm: Survey-based Perspectives on Employment in China in the Aftermath of the Global Financial Crisis', Policy Research Working Paper No. 5984 (March) Washington, DC: World Bank.

Golley, Jane and Meng, Xin (2011) 'Has China Run out of Surplus Labour?', *China Economic Review* 22(4) (December): 555–72.

Huang, J., Zhi, J., Huang, Z., Rozell. S., and Giles, J. (2010) 'The Impact of the Global Financial Crisis on Off-farm Employment and Earnings in Rural China', World Bank Policy Research Working Paper No. 5439, October.

Huang, P. C. C. (2009) 'China's Neglected Informal Economy: Reality and Theory', *Modern China* 35(4): 405–38.

Huang, Yiping and Cai, Fang (eds) (2013) *Debating the Lewis Turning Point in China*, New York: Routledge.

Kahn, Lisa (2010) 'The Long-Term Labor Market Consequences of Graduating College in a Bad Economy', *Labour Economics* 17(2): 303–16.

Knight, J. and Yueh, L. (2003) 'Job Mobility of Residents and Migrants in Urban China', Oxford Working Paper No. 163.

Knight, John, Deng, Quheng, and Li, Shi (2011) 'The Puzzle of Migrant Labour Shortage and Rural Labour Surplus in China', *China Economic Review* 22(4) (December): 585–600.

Kuruvilla, S., Gallagher, M., and Lee, C. (eds.) (2011) *From Iron Rice Bowl to Informalization: Markets, State and Workers in a Changing China*, Ithaca, NY: Cornell University Press.

Li, Bin (2011) quoted at China.org.cn, 'China's "floating population" exceeds 221 mln', March 1 <www.china.org.cn/china/2011-03/01/content_22025827.htm>.

Li, H. (2010) 'Higher Education in China: Complement or Competition to US Universities?', in Charles T. Clotfelter (ed.), *American University in a Global Market*, University of Chicago Press for NBER, ch. 8, pp. 269–305.

Li, H. and Zax, J. (2002) 'Economic transition and the labor market in China', unpublished ms <www.researchgate.net>.

Li, Jing (2008) 'China's New Labor Contract Law and Protection of Workers', *Fordham International Law Journal* 32(3): 1083–131.

Li, Shi (2008) 'Rural Migrant Workers in China: Scenario, Challenges and Public Policy', Working Paper No. 89, International Labour Office, Geneva, June.

Li, W. and Putterman, L. (2008) 'Reforming China's SOEs: An Overview', *Comparative Economic Studies* 50: 353–80.

Lu, F. (2012) 'Wage Trends among Chinese Migrant Workers, 1979–2010', *China Social Science* 7: 47–67.

Lu, X. and Perry, E. J. (eds) (1997) *Danwei: The Changing Chinese Workplace in Historical and Comparative Perspective*, New York: M.E. Sharpe.

Lu, Y., Tao, Z., and Wang, Y. (2009) 'Union effects on performance and employment relations: evidence from China', unpublished ms, August.

Maurer-Fazio, M. (1995) 'Labor Reform in China: Crossing the River by Feeling the Stones', *Comparative Economic Studies* 37(4): 111–23.

Meng, X. (2000) *Labour Market Reform and Outcomes*, Cambridge: Cambridge University Press.

National Bureau of Statistics (2009) 'There Are 225.42 Million Migrant Workers at the End of 2008', March 25.

OECD (2009) *Is Informal Normal? Towards More and Better Jobs in Developing Countries*, Johannes P. Jütting, and Juan R. de Laiglesia (eds), March 31 <www.stats.gov.cn/tjfx/fxbg/t20090325_402547406.htm>.

Park, A. F. and Cai, F. (2011) 'The Informalization of the Chinese Labor Market', in Sarosh Kuruvilla, Mary Gallagher, and Ching-kwan Lee (eds), *From Iron Rice Bowl to Informalization: Markets, State and Workers in a Changing China*, Ithaca, NY: Cornell University Press, pp. 17–35.

Rush, A. (2011) 'China's Labour Market', Reserve Bank of Australia, bulletin (September quarter), 29–38 <www.rba.gov.au/publications/bulletin/2011/sep/pdf/bu-0911-4.pdf>.

Sabin, L. (1994) 'New Bosses in the Workers' State: The Growth of Non-State Sector Employment in China', *China Quarterly* 140 (December): 944–70.

Shirk, Susan L. (1981) 'Recent Chinese Labour Policies and the Transformation of Industrial Organization in China', *China Quarterly* 88 (December): 575–93.

Smyth, R., Tam, O. K., Warner, M., and Zhu, C. J. (eds) (2004) *China's Business Reforms: Institutional Challenges in a Globalised Economy*, Abingdon, Oxon.: Routledge-Curzon.

Song, Changqing (1997) 'Reemployment: A Difficult Issue', *Qiye Guanli* (Enterprise Management), May.

Tan, Yingzi and Xin, Dingding (2009) '20 Million Migrants Lost Jobs: Survey', *China Daily* <www.chinadaily.com.cn/china/2009-02/03/content_7440106.htm>.

Walder, A. G. (1986) *Communist Neo-Traditionalism: Work and Authority in Chinese Industry*, Berkeley, CA: University of California Press.

Wall Street Journal (2012) 'China's Graduates Face Glut', August 22 <http://online.wsj.com/news/articles/SB10000872396390443545504577566752847208984>.

Xia, Q., Song, L., Li, S., and Appleton, S. (2013) 'The Effects of the State Sector on Wage Inequality in Urban China: 1988–2007', IZA Discussion Paper No. 7142 (January), p. 3.

Xie, Y. and Wu, X. (2008) 'Danwei Profitability and Earnings Inequality in Urban China', *China Quarterly* 195: 558–81.

Yao, Y. and Zhong, N. (2013) 'Unions and Workers' Welfare in Chinese Firms', *Journal of Labor Economics* 31(3): 633–67.

Zhang, L. [n.d.] 'Reform of the *hukou* system and rural–urban migration in China: the challenges ahead', unpublished manuscript.

Zhang, W. and Cheng, C. (2012) 'A Social Network Model of Job-Search Processes: Testing the Guanxi Effect Hypothesis', *Chinese Journal of Sociology* 3: 24–7.

Zhang, Xiaobo, Yang, Jin, and Wang, Shenglin (2011) 'China Has Reached the Lewis Turning Point', *China Economic Review* 22(4) (December): 542–54.

8

THE CHINESE SAVINGS PUZZLES[1]

Jean-Pierre Laffargue and Eden S. H. Yu

The Chinese savings puzzle is defined by its increasing national savings rate since the early 1990s and reaching an unusually high level in recent years. There are two main causes for this puzzle. The first one is the high and increasing share of Chinese firms and financial institutions in the national disposable income (these agents have no final consumption and so save their whole disposable income). This can be partly explained by an uneven sharing of value added, which favors profits to the detriment of wages, due to the high and increasing supply of labor in urban areas. The high corporate saving also results from the low distribution of firms' income. State-owned enterprises (SOEs) generally have little incentive to distribute dividends, and those that are distributed, are usually reinvested; private firms face rationing in the credit market and need to finance a bulk of investments with their own retained earnings.

The second cause of China's savings puzzle relates to the increasing and high household savings rate. This can be explained by the life-cycle hypothesis while taking into account of a set of pertinent Chinese factors, such as the one-child policy, which induces parents to save more in the absence of sufficient children to support their post-retirement life, and the necessity for households to accumulate enough savings in order to buy a house when the mortgage market is still quite limited. A complementary explanation is the higher precautionary savings accumulated by households to prepare for contingencies, e.g. unemployment and health risks.

Introduction

In this chapter, we delineate several puzzles in the Chinese saving behaviors. China's national savings rate, that is the ratio of its savings to its national disposable income, has increased from 36.3 percent in 1992 to 50.6 percent in 2009. For the same year, the savings rate of Korea, Japan and France were respectively equal to 30.2 percent, 21.6 percent and 17.2 percent. China's exceptional saving behavior is usually called the *Chinese savings puzzle*.

If we break down China's savings rate among the contributions of its households, business, and government sectors, we can see that households in China save much more than the counterparts in other countries, although their share in China's national disposable income is low and has steadily decreased from 1997 to 2008. This results from their high and increasing savings rate – the ratio between their savings and their disposable income – that is called the *household saving puzzle*. The savings of China's firms and financial institutions have shown an increasing share of the national disposable income from 1997 to 2008 – a share that was higher than in any other country in 2009. This is usually called the *corporate savings puzzle*. Finally, the Chinese government saves a share of its disposable income, which was high in the early 1990s and the late 2000s.

Section 1 presents the two savings puzzles. Section 2 investigates the corporate savings puzzle. It is found that the increasing and high savings of firms results from the low and decreasing share in the national disposable income of their distributed properties income (dividends and interest). The puzzle is also related to a low and decreasing share of firms' value-added going to wages for the firms' workers while the share of profits (and other returns to capital) is high and rising. This section also proposes several detailed explanations of these empirical results.

Section 3 reviews the explanations for the puzzle concerning household savings. There are basically two kinds of explanations. The first explanation is based on the life-cycle hypothesis by focusing on the dynamics of household savings. Namely, how do households allocate their savings over their lifetime, and how does the national savings rate increase with the relative number and income of people in the high savings period of their life? This approach allows a partial but correct understanding of the puzzle, if some specific and important features of the Chinese economy and society are taken into account. For instance, the opening up of the housing market and/or the reforms of the public pension system in the second half of the 1990s are pertinent.

The second kind of explanation of the household savings puzzle focuses on the level and changes in the following types of uncertainty: the risk of having to pay large medical bills or of losing one's job, in the face of poor publicly provided insurance and safety nets. This uncertainty induces households to accumulate significant savings for precautionary purpose. Section 4 offers some concluding remarks.

1 The China savings puzzles

The best statistical source available for analyzing the macroeconomic trends of China is the flow-of-funds tables, which show a matrix of institutional sectors by transaction items. We use them to compute the ratios of the national savings as well as sectoral savings of China to the country's national disposable income.[2] We plot the ratios covering the period of the early 1990s to 2009 in Figure 8.1.

The national accounts of the OECD use a nomenclature similar to that of the flow-of-funds tables of China. We use the data to compute the ratios of the national gross savings as well as sector-based savings to the gross disposable income for the United States, France, Japan, Korea, and Mexico in 2009. The results are presented in Table 8.1.

We observe from the graph in Figure 8.1 that China's national savings rate fluctuated around 38 percent from 1992 to 2000, and then steadily increased to the value of 50.6 percent in 2009. Table 8.1 shows that these values are unusually high. The second and third highest savings ratios in 2009 occurred in Korea and Japan, respectively equal to 30.2 percent and 21.6 percent.

Many countries have gone through long periods of high levels of savings, investment, and economic growth, accompanied by rapid industrialization. During the developmental process, labor was induced to migrate from rural areas and/or foreign countries to the industrial urban sector. This happened in both continental Western Europe and Japan after the Second World War and South Korea two decades later. The increasing labor supply in the urban areas led to somewhat moderate labor wages and thus high business profits and corporate savings. As banks were compelled by governments to favor producers over consumers in their allocation of credits, households had to save a great deal in order to buy a real estate unit or durable goods.

The high levels of household and business-sector savings provided financing to support a high level of investment sustaining and spurring economic growth – depicted by the standard economic

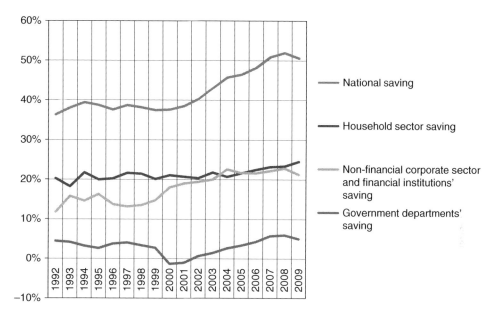

Figure 8.1 Ratios of sectoral savings to Chinese national disposable income

development model. However, what has been happening in China in the recent decades is far more than what this standard model can capture. Kuijs (2006) estimates a savings equation, based partly on the theoretical insight of this development model, on a panel of 134 countries over the period of 1960–2004. He obtains a good fit for most countries, but China is an outlier. The equation predicts a savings ratio of only 32 percent of GDP for China for the final period of the estimation. In contrast, the observed value actually was 44 percent. Kraay (2000) and Hung and Qian (2010) conduct similar estimations using different data sets, and reach the same conclusion.

China's savings puzzles have also been investigated by using dynamic general equilibrium models. Such general equilibrium frameworks are useful for studying a variety of economic issues while taking into account the interactions among several markets or sectors in an economy. Simple static general equilibrium models have been deployed to examine the various effects during a single period, whereas dynamic general equilibrium models capture the effects over multiple periods. Generally, the latter starts with some objective functions, such as social welfare, which are maximized by agents subject to a set of pertinent constraints over a finite, or infinite span of time.

The optimizing conditions and results are often revealing and shed light on understanding the behavior of economic agents. The main results obtained using the dynamic general equilibrium

Table 8.1 Gross saving: comparison between China and five OECD countries (2009)

Ratio to national disposable income	China	United States	France	Japan	Korea	Mexico
Total domestic economy	50.6%	10.9%	17.2%	21.6%	30.2%	22.5%
Household sector	24.4%	7.8%	11.1%	5.9%	5.3%	7.9%
Non-financial corporate sector and financial institutions	21.2%	11%	9.5%	21.4%	18.1%	14%
Government departments	4.9%	−7.9%	−3.4%	−5.7%	6.8%	0.6%

frameworks are either that Chinese households exhibit a very high preference for the future (Fehr, Jokisch, and Kotlikoff, 2005), or that they face a very high level of uncertainty, inducing them to build up a significant amount of precautionary savings (Yu and Ng 2010), or that China simply saves too much (Lu and McDonald, 2006).

We plot on Figure 8.1 the ratios of the savings of China's household sector, its non-financial corporate sector and financial institutions, and its sector of government departments to China's national disposable income. For the household sector, the savings ratio has been fluctuating a bit above 20 percent and increasing since 2002. However, the saving ratio has been increasing for the business sector since 1997 and for the government sector since 2000. It is noteworthy that the savings rates of the household sector and of the business sector have been about the same since 2001 at about 21 percent of the national disposable income, whereas savings of government sector were much lower (peaked at 5.9 percent of the national disposable income in 2008).

For purpose of comparison, we use the National Accounts of the OECD countries to compute the savings ratios of the same three sectors in 2009 for five OECD countries and the results are presented in Table 8.1. We observe that regarding the savings ratio of households, the outlier is China, which has the highest ratio among the six nations. France comes next with a household savings ratio of only 11.1 percent, against 24.4 percent in China. On the other hand, the savings ratio of 21.2 percent scored by the Chinese business sector in 2009 is not so different from the ratio of 21.4 percent in Japan and 18.1 percent in Korea. However, it is notable that the Chinese government sector has a relatively high savings ratio of 4.9 percent, higher than the other countries in the sample, except Korea (with 6.8 percent).

The ratio of the savings of each of the three sectors (household, business, and government) to national disposable income is the product of its savings rate – the ratio of its savings to its disposable income – by the share of its income in national income. Thus, the savings ratio of a sector can increase either because of a rise in its savings rate or because its disposable income increases faster than national income.

Figure 8.2 shows that the savings rate of the household sector increased sharply since 1999 while the rate of the government departments dropped significantly from 1997 to 2000 and bounced back dramatically since then. Both types of savings rates reached very high values (respectively 40.4 percent and 27 percent) in 2009. As there is no final consumption by the business sector, its savings rate is always equal to 100 percent.

Turning to Figure 8.3, in which we plot the shares in the national disposable income of the three sectors, a notable feature is the sharp increase in the share of the business sector beginning 1997, while the share of government departments has been on the rise since 2000. On the other hand, the share of the household sector has steadily decreased since 1997. The respective shares of the household sector, the business sector, and government sector in 2009 were 60.5 percent, 21.2 percent and 18.3 percent respectively.

Table 8.2 presents the shares in the national disposable income and gross savings rates of the three sectors in China as compared to the same selected five OECD nations. The data are derived from the National Accounts of the OECD countries. We observe from Table 8.2 that the household savings rate in China is extremely high in comparison to other nations. The savings rate of the government sector is also high, but about the same as in Korea. The share of the household sector in the national disposable income is low (and about the same as in Korea), whereas the share of the business sector is high (but only slightly higher than that in Japan). Furthermore, the share of the Chinese government sector is also high (but less than the counterparts in Korea and France).

In short, the high and increasing Chinese national savings rate since 2000 mainly results from the following two savings puzzles (see He and Cao, 2007, for similar conclusions):

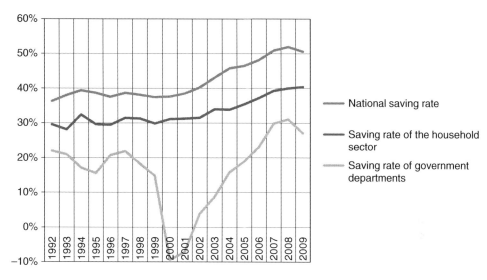

Figure 8.2 National and disaggregated savings rates

- The increasingly high share of the business sector savings – which is the same as its disposable income – in the national disposable income since 1997. This is the corporate savings puzzle.
- The high and increasing household sector savings rate since 1999, referred to as the household savings puzzle.

Moreover, we note that the savings rate of the Chinese government departments has sharply increased since 2000 and its value peaked at the end of the decade. Several studies on the economic conditions in China attempted to explain this observation (see for instance the

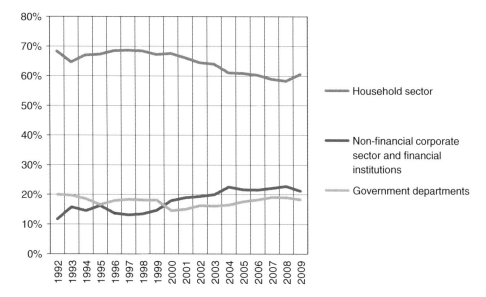

Figure 8.3 Shares of the three domestic agents in national disposable income

Table 8.2 Shares in national disposable income and gross saving rates of the three sectors: comparison between China and five OECD countries (2009)

	China	United States	France	Japan	Korea	Mexico
Household sector						
Share in national disposable income	60.5%	79.2%	69.2%	65.1%	59%	71.3%
Gross savings rate	40.4%	9.8%	16.1%	9%	9%	11.1%
Non-financial corporate sector and financial institutions						
Share in national disposable income	21.2%	11%	9.5%	21%	18.1%	16.2%
Government departments						
Share in national disposable income	18.3%	9.7%	21.3%	13.9%	22.7%	12.5%
Gross savings rate	27%	−81.1%	−16%	−40.8%	29.9%	4.6%

publications of OECD, 2010 and 2012). The flow-of-funds tables reveal that the government savings have been utilized in the 2000s to finance either capital transfers or capital formation, especially in building up infrastructure and financial investment. It was concluded by the OECD studies that the policies of the Chinese government have differed from those of most other countries in the recent decade of 2000s in that China stresses on social capital accumulation rather than public consumption.

We will examine further in the following sections the corporate savings puzzle and the household savings puzzle.

2 The corporate savings puzzle

We have just observed that the share of the business sector in national disposable income has been on the rise since 1997 and it reached the high rate of 21.2 percent in 2009. We use the flow-of-funds tables to decompose the trend into three parts: the contributions of the current transfers paid by the business sector; second, of the income from properties distributed by the sector; and third, of the sharing of its value added. We will also provide some explanations for the changes in the levels of each of the three contributions.

2.1 The role of the current transfers

We state the following accounting identity:

Disposable income = income from primary distribution + current transfers

Here, current transfers include income taxes, payments to social securities, social allowances, and other current transfers.

Figure 8.4 depicts the share in national disposable income of the net current transfers *paid by* the business sector. The share values decreased from 1992 to 2000, and then climbed up again. The share in national disposable income of the business sector income from primary distribution is almost parallel to the share of business disposable income. Hence, current transfers do not explain much of the corporate savings puzzle.

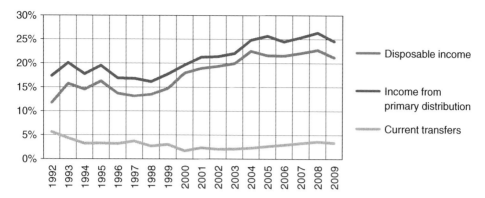

Figure 8.4 Business sector shares in national disposable income

2.2 *The role of the income from properties*

We state the following accounting identity:

Income from primary distribution = gross operating surplus + income from properties

Income from properties includes interest payments, dividends and land rent. We divide the two sides of this identity by the national disposable income and plot its components in Figure 8.5. We note that the income of properties *distributed* by the business sector is low and that its share in the national disposable income has been decreasing from 1996 to 2005 before increasing again by a small amount.

Some explanations for the above observations are proposed by Ferri and Liu (2010) and Yang, Zhang and Zhou (2011) in terms of policy reforms, which had been implemented since the early 1990s. It is pointed out that the government delayed requiring SOEs to pay dividends until 2008,[3] even though they had enjoyed handsome profits since the state-sector restructuring in the late 1990s. Furthermore, SOEs generally paid low interest, whereas private firms had encountered difficulty in borrowing from banks. As a result, private firms need to resort to informal and private financing channels or relying on their own funds – i.e. their retained earnings or savings – to finance investment. Bayoumi, Tong, and Wei (2010) examine the micro data of a large sample of listed firms over the period of 2002 to 2007. In contrast to the previous studies, they find that

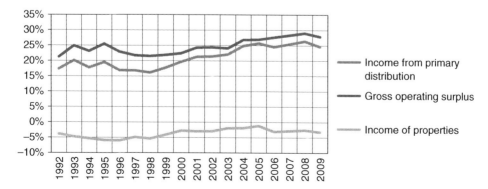

Figure 8.5 Business sector shares in national disposable income

Chinese corporate savings rates and dividends distribution are not that different from other economies. Further, there is within China no significant difference between the majority SOEs and majority privately owned firms so far as savings rates and dividends distribution are concerned.

2.3 The sharing of the value added

Finally, we state the following accounting identity:

> Value-added = gross operating surplus + remuneration of employees + net taxes on production

Dividing the two sides of this identity by the national disposable income, we plot its components in Figure 8.6. We observe from the graph that the share of the gross operating surplus of this sector has increased since 1998, while the share of the remuneration of employees has decreased since 1997. It is somewhat surprising that these two components are of the same order of magnitude, in contrast to most countries where the remuneration of employees is twice as large as the operating surplus. Furthermore, the ratio of net taxes on production to the national disposable income has slightly increased since 2000.

Aziz and Cui (2007) develop a model to explain the low and decreasing share of labor income in China's national disposable income, based on the observation that it is easier for Chinese firms to finance fixed than it is for them to finance working capital. This imperfection of the capital market has the effect of suppressing the demand for labor, hence lowering wages and urban employment. More generally, the low share of labor income is probably related to abundant young workers and a large surplus of rural labor (Ma and Yi, 2010).

Recently, questions have been raised as to how long this situation will last (for instance Miles, 2011, OECD, 2010 and 2012, Yang, Zhang, and Zhou, 2010). It is notable that there are strong indications of an increase in labor wages, which could lead to a redistribution of income from profit seekers to wage earners. Moreover, this could lead to an increase in consumption and a decrease in savings. There are also reports of increasing labor unrest in China and sentiments favoring the protection of the rights of workers. By July 2010, eighteen provinces had announced increases in minimum wages by an average of 20 percent. In 2011 labor incomes rose strongly, especially for rural migrant workers. Furthermore, one may also wonder whether China has reached the point at which industrial wages will start to rise rapidly as a consequence of the

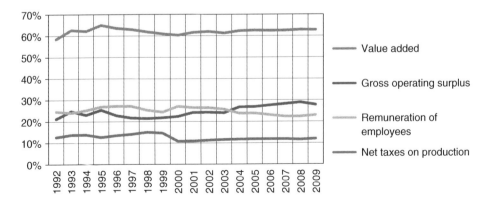

Figure 8.6 Business sector shares in national disposable income

disappearance of the rural labor surplus. Is China's large supply of labor beginning to vanish as a consequence of the one-child policy?

There is still a large surplus of labor in rural areas at this point, and policies are being introduced or are being discussed by Chinese officials and scholars to help release rural labor to support urban manufacturing, as follows: liberalizing the household registration – *hukou* – system, reforming rural land ownership, or development of mechanization and consolidation of land plots.[4] The demographic consequences of the one-child policy will not be fully manifested perhaps until 2020 or even later, if the retirement age (presently very low in China) were to be raised. Thus, there are good reasons for us to expect that it will take years for income distribution to evolve and become more favorable to labor.

3 The household savings puzzle

The ratio of household savings to the national disposable income has fluctuated around 20 percent since 1992 for about a decade and then steadily increased from 2002 to 2008. This upward movement results from the combination of a decreasing share of household income in the national disposable income, by 10 percentage points from 1992 to 2008, and concomitantly an increasing and high savings rate.

The reasons for the decreasing share of households in the national disposable income are symmetric to the causes underlying the increasing share of the business sector. The shares of both the net current transfers and the income from properties *received by* the household sector have steadily decreased. This is a consequence of the rise in the social welfare contributions of the sector and of the fall in bank deposit interest rates (see Yang, Zhang, and You, 2010). The ratio of the net remuneration of employees to the national disposable income has also decreased.

We begin our investigation of the household savings puzzle, in subsection 3.1, by presenting another data source in which urban households are separated from rural households. The data allows us to compute the Chinese household savings rates over a longer span of time. We also use the computed rates to trace the path and compare it to the paths in Japan and Korea obtained for the periods of fast growth of these two countries, i.e. after the Second World War and the Korean War, respectively.

There are two complementary strands of the literature in explaining the puzzle. The first set of explanations, presented in subsection 3.2, focuses on the dynamics of household behavior by attempting to answer the following: how do households allocate their savings over their lifetime and how does the national savings rate rise when the relative number and income of the people in the high saving period of their life increases? The second set of explanations rests on the level and changes in uncertainty (for instance the probability of becoming unemployed, or having to face expensive medical bills). This will be presented in subsection 3.3.[5]

3.1 More facts

Using the surveys on urban households and rural households, provided by the Office of Household Survey of the National Bureau of Statistics,[6] we compute another set of the savings rates of urban and rural households for each year from 1993 to 2011, and for a few years before 1993. These savings rates are shown in Figure 8.7.

We recall that according to the flow-of-funds tables, the household savings rate fluctuated around 30 percent from 1992 to 1999, and sharply increased from 1999 to 2009 reaching the high rate of 40.4 percent. The household surveys, however, show lower savings rates. Specifically, the urban household savings rate steadily increased from 8.9 percent in 1985 to 30.5 percent in

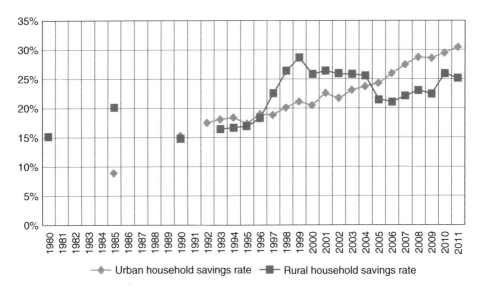

Figure 8.7 Household savings rate (household surveys data)

2011, whereas the rural household savings rate fluctuated quite a bit, but along an upward trend. The observed divergence of the rates estimated using the surveys versus the flow-of-funds tables can be explained by the fact that the surveys tend to underestimate income, while they provide a more accurate estimate of consumption figures. Thus, the surveys underestimate savings and the savings rate.

Eastern Asia provides a series of cases of countries that were severely war-torn or very poor in the 1950s, but recovered and bounced back three decades later; some even reached a record-high income level and caught up with the world's most advanced industrialized nations. We observe in Figures 8.8 and 8.9 that two such Asian countries achieved high levels and growth of household savings during the process of rapid development. The household savings rate in Japan and Korea[7] started at low values, and then steadily increased. After reaching the high values of 21.8 percent and 25.9 percent for Japan and Korea, respectively, the savings rates steadily decreased. The rates decrease became significant in Japan after 1978 and also in Korea but 20 years later.

According to the Penn World Table, 7.1 (see Heston, Summers, and Aten, 2012) the per capita GDP of Japan in 1978 and Korea in 1998, converted by purchasing power parity (PPP) at 2005 constant prices, was US$17,600 and US$15,500 respectively. In comparison, the per capita GDP of China was US$7,400 in 2010 (an average of the two measures given by PWT 7.1), when its urban and rural savings rates stood respectively at 29.5 percent and 26 percent. It is notable that this per capita GDP level was achieved by Japan in 1962, when its household savings rate was equal only to 13.9 percent and by Korea in 1985 with a savings rate of 15.4 percent.

Figures 8.8 and 8.9 seem to suggest the existence of a savings cycle as follows: the household savings rate would initially increase, when per capita GDP rises, and then the rate decreases, when per capita GDP passes over a threshold amount of about US$16,000–US$18,000 (at 2005 US$). Assuming that this cycle exists, China at its current stage of development would support a much higher rate of household savings than expected, and this higher savings rate would continue to increase for many years to come. In any event, we argue that the savings behavior of Chinese households is exceptional.

Figure 8.8   Household savings rate (Japan)

3.2 Explanations resting upon the life-cycle hypothesis

The life-cycle hypothesis is related to explaining consumer behavior in a model developed in the 1950s by Franco Modigliani and his collaborators, Albert Ando and Richard Brumberg. The basic idea of the hypothesis is that income varies over a person's life span and saving allows moving income from the times in one's life when income is high to those times when it is low. More specifically, to smooth out consumption over one's life time, a typical person saves little in

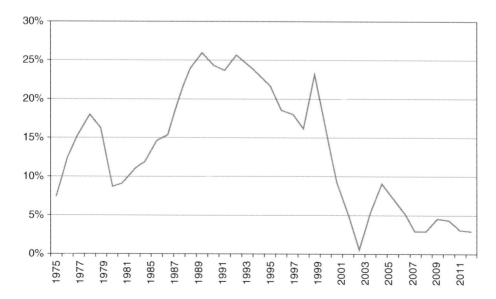

Figure 8.9   Household savings rate (Korea)

early adult life when income is still low. This person saves a great deal in the middle and toward the end of his or her work life. After retirement, when income is low again because pensions are in general lower than wages, the person dis-saves to maintain his or her living standard.

The total savings of an economy in a given year is the difference between the savings of the active households and the dis-savings of the retired people. If the economy grows fast, the savings of active households generally draw from a higher income pool than the income of retired people, saved earlier during their active years. This inter-temporal gap in earned income increases the savings rate computed based on the whole set of households. Similarly, the household savings rate rises if the proportion of "big savers," that is, people in their forties or fifties, in the population increases.

Modigliani and Cao (2004) offer an explanation of China's high household savings rate based on the life-cycle hypothesis (see also Horioka and Wan, 2007). They come up with a more complete story by noting that the one-child policy has lowered the cost of rearing children for the young active adults, resulting in an increased net income available for saving. They add that this policy also has the effect of reducing financial support for retired parents from their children; a working couple after marriage may need to support four parents, and this is quite a heavy burden on their grown-up children. To alleviate this burden, there is a strong inducement for some active households to save more especially in a country where the public pension system is still weak.

Modigliani and Cao run a series of econometric regressions to explain the aggregate household savings rate in China over the 1953–2000 period. They find that the long-term growth rate, computed as an average on the past 14 years, and the inverse of the young dependency ratio, defined as the number of persons employed divided by the number of persons 14 years or younger, are the two most important explanatory variables; both show strong positive effects on the savings rate.

The econometric results of Modigliani and Cao are supportive of the life-cycle hypothesis. However, other studies on testing the hypothesis have yielded different findings. For instance, Chamon and Prasad (2010) investigate the saving behavior of Chinese households by using household data from 16 consecutive Urban Household Surveys from 1990 to 2005. This pseudo panel data allows the use of a method developed by Deaton and Paxson (1993) so as to separate the effects of changes in the income and the savings of a household based on age, or life cycle, from the effect of increasing wages over time, a result from the development of the Chinese economy. The authors obtain an unusual age profile of savings covering the period of mid-1990s through the 2000s, in which the younger and older households exhibit relatively high savings rates. This is contrary to the "hump shaped" profile of savings assumed by the life cycle hypothesis. The age cohorts most affected by the one-child policy are not among the highest savers. Moreover, the overall savings rates have increased across all demographic groups.

Chamon and Prasad argue that their results can be better explained by the rising burden of private spending on housing and education for the young cohort and on health care for the elderly. It is notable that only 17 percent of urban households owned their home in 1990; however, a new policy of massive sale of public housing to their tenants occurred around 1998 and this continued afterward. The new owners purchased their housing at good bargain prices that were well below the market rates. Since then, the private housing market became active in China. By 2005, 86 percent of urban households owned their home. In that year, only 5 percent of households used mortgage financing and repaid a home loan, implying that access of Chinese households in the credit markets was much constrained. Young adults need to save a lot to buy a housing unit before they get married, and this alone, according to the authors, could explain a 3 percentage points increase in the urban savings rate from the early 1990s to 2005.

Wei and Zhang (2011) observe that parents in China typically pay for the housing for adult sons to facilitate their marriage. To help their sons to get married in a country where the girl–boy ratio has been decreasing quickly and where the competition for finding a spouse has become tougher, parents want to be able to provide their sons with a better home. This leads to a greater demand for housing and hence higher housing prices, which in turn induces even the households without a son to save more in order to afford decent housing. This chain, spiral effect on housing demand and prices, coupled with the increasing disequilibrium of the marriage market between men and women provide a good explanation for the rise of household savings in China, about half of the actual increase in the household savings rate during 1990–2007.[8]

A lack of availability of credit leads to a higher household savings rate. In China, credit to households has been strictly rationed in the past. A recent study of the Chinese economy (OECD, 2010) notes that China's consumer credit market is still relatively small compared to the credit market for enterprises. But the former is developing quickly; banks have rapidly expanded mortgage lending with an increase of over 20 percent annually since 2006, though mortgage lending represented only 10 percent of total bank lending in mid-2009. However, farmers are still not allowed to use their land as collateral to borrow. Furthermore, the assets which can be used by small and medium private firms as collateral are still limited, thereby inducing higher savings of the self-employed and small businesses, shown in the Household Surveys of the National Bureau of Statistics.

Modigliani and Cao's analysis is based on the econometric estimation of a reduced form equation consistent with the life-cycle hypothesis. Chao, Laffargue and Yu (2011) opt to estimate a structural model, which includes all the ingredients of the life-cycle hypothesis, and to check if this model can reproduce the rise of the urban Chinese household savings rate for the period of 1975 to 2005 (see also Chamon and Prasad, 2008, and Curtis, Lugauer, and Mark, 2011). They find that wage growth and demographic changes can explain no more than one third of the surge in the household savings rate. However, when housing investment is incorporated into the model, similar to the results of Chamon and Prasad, and Wei and Zhang, the model can reproduce the increase in the household savings rate, from the mid-1990s to 2005.

Several micro-econometric studies have attempted to explain why after 1995 there was a large increase in the savings rates among the youngest households living in urban areas. Feng, He, and Sato (2011) base their explanation on the public pension reforms of 1995–97. The reforms significantly reduced the amount of pensions for public workers, when they retire. However, the eldest workers were wholly or partly exempted from this effect. According to the life-cycle hypothesis, the younger workers should react to these reforms by saving more in order to compensate for their lowered pensions and accumulating more wealth for their retirement. Meanwhile, the eldest workers with pensions minimally affected by the reforms should also raise their savings, but by a smaller amount. The empirical results of Feng, He, and Sato are consistent with the life-cycle hypothesis. Their estimations show that due to the pension reforms, the household savings rate increased by 2–3 percentage points for the cohort aged 50–59 and by 6–9 percentage points for the cohort aged 25–29 in 1999.

Song and Yang (2010) find that much of annual wage growth is realized as upward shifts in the level of life-cycle earnings profiles for successive cohorts of young workers. On the other hand, earnings profiles have actually become flattened cohort by cohort. These results are confirmed by estimating the Mincer's equations[9] for each of the successive years of their sample, suggesting a drop in the rate of return to workers' experience, but an increase in the return to education. The flattening of the earnings profile together with the assumption of an interest rate larger than the household discount rate, lead to a positive and increasing savings rate of young households.

Other micro-econometric studies focus on specific aspects of the household savings behavior. For example, Banerjee, Meng, and Qian (2010) verify the conjecture that parents save more when they have fewer children. Cai, Giles, and Meng (2006) find that children transfer money to support their retired and poor parents. These transfers rise along with the decrease in the income of the parents, but are insufficient to fully compensate for the loss in parents' income. The amount of transfer to parents also increases with the number and educational attainment of their children. Ding and Zhang (2011) conclude that the arrival of a son in a rural family induces the family to increase its investment, in order to raise their son's life-long earning so as to enhance his ability to take care of his aging parents in the future.

3.3 The precautionary savings motive

There is a very different set of explanations for the Chinese household savings puzzle, which rests on the effects of increasing uncertainty. Uncertainty, which characterizes all the economies in transition, especially China, has induced households to build up high precautionary savings (Blanchard and Giavazzi, 2006). To test the validity of this explanation, it is essential to develop good indicators of risk. Wei and Zhang (2011) perform a panel regression using data from 31 provinces in China for the period of 1980 to 2007. In the analysis, the proportion of the local labor force that works for state-owned firms or government agencies is used as a proxy for the degree of job security. The share of local labor force enrolled in social security is included as a proxy for the extent of the local social safety net. Coefficients for both variables are negative and statistically significant, lending support to the precautionary savings motive.

China has implemented a household registration system, known as *hukou*, which acts as a kind of domestic passport for Chinese and limits the access of rural migrants to public services in the cities where they work and live. Moreover, the migrants are discriminated against within the urban labor market. How would *hukou* affect the saving rates? Chen, Lu, and Zhong (2012) run a series of regressions on a sample of urban and migrant households and find that migrants without an urban *hukou* spend 31 percent less than otherwise similar urban residents. These differential consumption gaps suggest that rural migrants save more for precautionary purposes due to higher income risks and the lack of social security coverage. Further, the authors estimate that removal of the *hukou* system would lead to a rise of 4.2 percent in aggregate household consumption and 1.8 percent in GDP.

Empirical analyses of various types of risks also point to the strong precautionary motive for savings by Chinese households (for example, see Chamon and Prasad, 2010, on health risk; Meng, 2003, on unemployment risk; Chamon, Liu, and Prasad, 2010, on income risk; Giles and Yoo, 2007, on agricultural activities risk measured by rainfall variability – see also Jalan and Ravaillon, 2001).

4 Conclusion

The national savings of China has been increasing at faster rates than its national disposable income, especially since the early 1990s, and the savings rate has reached an extremely high level in recent years. We have shown that this puzzle of China's remarkable savings growth can be attributable to two main causes: An increasing and high share of firms' and financial institutions' disposable income in the national disposable income and a rising and high household savings rate.

The corporate savings puzzle can be explained by the low and decreasing share in the national disposable income of firms' distributed properties income (dividends and interest), and a distribution of value-added, increasingly in favor of the firm owners possibly at the expense of workers. The household savings puzzle can be partly resolved by the life-cycle hypothesis. People generally save a great deal in the second half of their working life, when their income is the highest, and they dis-save to support their living standard after retirement. In the event that wages increase at high rate as a result of rapid economic growth, or there is a high proportion of middle-age workers in the population, the income of middle-age workers is higher than the income retired people earned when they were themselves active. Thus, savings by the former workers are higher than dis-saving by retired people and high national savings rate ensues. However, the life-cycle hypothesis needs to be extended in several directions to better explain the savings puzzle for China. Household savings have been encouraged by a mix of social and financial developments in China: reductions in pension benefits due to economic reform, decreased support for retired parents by their children because of the one-child policy, and limited access of households to credit forcing them to save more to buy a home. The level and changes in uncertainty can also play a role in the saving behavior of households. The risks of incurring large medical costs, or of losing one's job in the presence of insufficient coverage of public insurance, induce households to accumulate savings for precautionary purpose.

Notes

1 We owe special thanks to Gregory Chow and Dwight Perkins for their very useful criticisms and advice. We are indebted to Mi Lin for excellent research assistance. This research was done when Jean-Pierre Laffargue was visiting City University of Hong Kong in July and August 2012. We gratefully acknowledge the financial support of the Research Center for International Economics of City University of Hong Kong.

2 The China Statistical database, available on the website of the National Bureau of Statistics of China (www.stats.gov.cn/english), includes the most recent version of the flow-of-funds accounts from 1992 to 2009 (the latter year being the most recent one available in January 2013 when we finished writing this chapter). The definitions of the indicators used in this chapter can be found on the website: http://www.stats.gov.cn/tjsj/ndsj/2012/indexeh.htm, in 'National accounts', at 'Brief introduction' and, 'Explanatory notes on main statistical indicators'. The national disposable income is equal to GDP plus the net factor income from abroad and the net current transfers from the rest of the world. We can deduce from the flow-of-funds tables that the national disposable income was less than GDP until 2002, and has increased faster than GDP since 1995. This evolution resulted from favorable trends in the net current transfers (for instance higher tourism receipts) and the net factor incomes of China from abroad (for instance the higher interest income of the large official reserves).

3 Cox (2012) notes that since the 2007 reform, SOEs' dividends have increased to the modest value of 5–15 percent of profits, depending on the industry. However, these dividends are not handed over to the finance ministry to spend as it sees fit but paid into a special budget reserved for financing state enterprises. SOEs dividends, in other words, are divided among SOEs.

4 The current system of collective property of land, with its periodical reallocation to farmers who can work it, induces many young men to stay in rural areas to prevent their families from losing their land rights. However, much of the surplus labor in the countryside is over the age of 40 and people of this age seldom migrate to urban areas. It is noteworthy that migration from agriculture was important and had a significant positive effect on the growth of Germany, Italy, and Spain over the 1950–90 period, even though the share of employment in agriculture in these three countries in 1950 was less than in China nowadays (see van Ark, 1996).

5 There exist a few other explanations for the household savings puzzle. For instance, Lin (2012) and Li (2013) assume that the *marginal* propensity to consume decreases with income. Then, if we consider two households earning each the household average income, and if we transfer 1,000 yuans from the first to the second household, income inequality increases and total household consumption decreases. Then, the two authors conclude that the rising income disparity that we observe in China has contributed to the rise in the household savings rate. Nabar (2011) develops a model where a household targets a level of wealth, for instance the down payment necessary to obtain a mortgage and buy a home. When the real interest rate decreases, *a fortiori* if it becomes negative, the building of this wealth requires a higher

level of savings. Nabar concludes that, over the period 1996–2009, the decrease in the real interest rate in China can explain a part of the rise in the urban household savings rate (see also Wang and Wen, 2012). Mankiw (2012) has an excellent chapter surveying the different theories of consumption and savings, including those used here.

6   These data are available in the National accounts of 2012 and before, under the denomination *People's living conditions.* Table 10.2 gives the per capita annual disposable income of urban households and the per capita annual net income of rural households. Table 10.5 gives the per capita annual consumption expenditure of urban households. Table 10.18 gives the per capita expenses on household consumption of rural households.

7   Each graph plots the household and non-profit institutions serving households net savings ratio and was built out of the *OECD Economic Outlook* No. 91.

8   The sex ratio at birth in China was close to being normal in 1980 with 106 boys per 100 girls, but climbed steadily since the mid-1980s to over 120 boys for each 100 girls in 2005 and is estimated to be 123 boys per 100 girls in 2008 and 119 boys per 100 girls in 2011.

9   The Mincer's equation explains the wage rate by several factors, the most important of which are the number of years of education and the number of years of work. Thus, this equation, which is estimated on a sample of workers, gives an estimate of the returns on education and on experience.

Bibliography

Aziz, J. and Cui, L. (2007) 'Explaining China's low consumption: The neglected role of household income', IMF Working Paper WP/07/181, December.

Banerjee, A., Meng, X., and Qian, N. (2010) 'The life cycle model and household saving: Micro evidence from urban China', <http://afd.pku.edu.cn/files/09.pdf>.

Bayoumi, T., Tong, H., and Wei, S.J. (2010) 'The Chinese corporate saving puzzle: A firm-level cross-country perspective', NBER Working Paper 16432.

Blanchard, O. J. and Giavazzi, F. (2006) 'Rebalancing growth in China: A three-handed approach', *China and World Economy*, 14(4): 1–20.

Cai, F., Giles, J., and Meng, X. (2006) 'How well do children insure parents against low retirement income? An analysis using survey data from urban China', *Journal of Public Economics*, 90: 2229–55.

Chamon, M. and Prasad, E. (2008) 'Why are saving rates of urban households in China rising?', IMF Working Paper WP/08/145.

Chamon, M. and Prasad, E. (2010) 'Why are saving rates of urban households in China rising?', *American Economic Journal: Macroeconomics*, 2(1): 93–130.

Chamon, M., Liu, K., and Prasad, E. (2010) 'Income uncertainty and household savings in China', NBER Working Paper 16565.

Chao, C.C., Laffargue, J.P., and Yu, E. (2011) 'The Chinese saving puzzle and the life-cycle hypothesis: A revaluation', *China Economic Review*, 22: 108–20.

Chen, B., Lu, M., and Zhong, N. (2012) '*Hukou* and consumption heterogeneity: Migrants' expenditure is depressed by institutional constraints in urban China', Global COE Hi-Stat Discussion Paper Series 221, Hitotsubashi University.

Cox, S. (2012) 'Peddling prosperity. Special report. China's economy', *The Economist*, May 26.

Curtis, C.C., Lugauer, S., and Mark, N.C. (2011) 'Demographic patterns and household saving in China', NBER Working Paper 16828.

Deaton, A.S. and Paxson, C.H. (1993) 'Saving, growth, and aging in Taiwan', NBER Working Paper 4330.

Ding, W. and Zhang, Y. (2011) 'When a son is born: The impact of fertility patterns in family finance in rural China', Queen's University, Kingston, Ontario, <http://post.queensu.ca/~dingw/sons_and_loans.pdf>.

Fehr, H., Jokisch, S., and Kotlikoff, L. J. (2005) 'Will China eat our lunch or take us out to dinner? Simulating the transition paths for the US, EU, Japan and China', NBER Working Paper 11688.

Feng, J., He, L., and Sato, H. (2011) 'Public pension and household saving: Evidence from urban China', *Journal of Comparative Economics*, 39: 470–85.

Ferri, G. and Liu, L.G. (2010) 'Honor thy creditors before thy shareholders: Are the profits of Chinese state-owned enterprises real?', *Asian Economic Papers*, 9(3): 50–71.

Giles, J. and Yoo, K. (2007) 'Precautionary behavior, migrant networks, and household consumption decisions: an empirical analysis using household panel data from rural China', *Review of Economics and Statistics*, 89(3): 534–51.

He, X. and Cao, Y. (2007) 'Understanding high saving rate in China', *China & World Economy*, 15(1): 1–13.

Heston, A., Summers, R., and Aten, B. (2012) 'Penn World Table Version 7.1', Center for International Comparisons of Production, Income and Prices at the University of Pennsylvania, November <http://pwt.econ.upenn.edu/php_site/pwt_index.php>.

Horioka, C.Y. and Wan, J. (2007) 'The determinants of household saving in China: A dynamic panel analysis of provincial data', *Journal of Money, Credit and Banking*, 39(8): 2077–96.

Hung, J. and Qian, R. (2010) 'Why is China's saving rate so high? A comparative study of cross-country panel data', paper presented at Cesifo Venice Summer institute, The Evolving Role of China in the Global Economy, 23–24 July.

Jalan, J. and Ravaillon, M. (2001) 'Behavioral responses to risk in rural China', *Journal of Development Economics*, 66(1): 23–49.

Kraay, A. (2000) 'Household saving in China', *World Bank Economic Review*, 14(3): 545–70.

Kuijs, L. (2006) 'How will China's saving-investment balance evolve?', World Bank Policy Research Working Paper 3958.

Li, G. (2013) 'Charting China's family value', *Wall Street Journal*, <http://blogs.wsj.com/chinarealtime/2012/12/10/perception-vs-reality-charting-chinas-family-value/> January 8.

Lin, J.Y. (2012) *Demystifying the Chinese Economy*, Cambridge, UK: Cambridge University Press.

Lu, L. and McDonald, I. (2006) 'Does China save too much?', *Singapore Economic Review*, 51(3): 283–301.

Ma, G. and Yi, W. (2010) 'China's high saving rate: Myth and reality', BIS Working Papers 312.

Mankiw, N.G. (2012) *Macroeconomics*, New York: Worth Publishers.

Meng, X. (2003) 'Unemployment, consumption smoothing, and precautionary saving in urban China', *Journal of Comparative Economics*, 31: 465–85.

Miles, J. (2011) 'Rising power, anxious state. Special report. China', *The Economist*, June 25.

Modigliani, F. and Cao, S.L. (2004) 'The Chinese saving puzzle and the life-cycle hypothesis', *Journal of Economic Literature*, 42(1): 145–70.

Nabar, M. (2011) 'Targets, interest rates, and household saving in urban China', IMF Working Paper WP/11/223, September.

Naughton, B. (2007) *The Chinese Economy. Transition and Growth*, Cambridge, MA: The MIT Press.

OECD (2010) *OECD Economic Surveys: China 2010*, Paris: OECD.

OECD (2012) *China in Focus: Lessons and Challenges*, Paris: OECD, <http://www.oecd.org/China/50011051.pdf>.

Song, Z.M. and Yang, D.T. (2010) 'Life-cycle earnings and saving in a fast-growing economy', Working Paper, University of Hong Kong.

van Ark, B. (1996) 'Sectoral growth accounting and structural change in post-war Europe', in B. van Ark and N. Crafts (eds.), *Quantitative Aspects of Post-war European Economic Growth*, Cambridge, UK: Cambridge University Press.

Wang, X. and Wen, Y. (2012) 'Housing prices and the high saving rate puzzle', *China Economic Review*, 23: 265–83.

Wei, S.J. and Zhang, X. (2011) 'The competitive saving motive: Evidence from rising sex ratio and saving rate in China', *Journal of Political Economy*, 119(3): 511–64.

Yang, D.T., Zhang, J., and Zhou, S. (2011) 'Why are saving rates so high in China?', IZA Working Paper 5465.

Yu, E.S.H. and Ng, S. (2010) 'Balance or imbalance of China's economy versus the world', in D. Greenaway, C. Milner and S. Yao (eds.) *China and the World Economy*, Basingstoke, Hampshire: Palgrave Macmillan.

9

MACROECONOMIC MANAGEMENT OF THE CHINESE ECONOMY SINCE THE 1990s

Yu Yongding

This chapter aims to identify the pattern of China's macroeconomic management and explain how macroeconomic policy has been implemented for achieving non-inflationary growth in China.

The Chinese economy's performance has maintained a cyclical pattern: rapid investment growth, supported by expansionary policy, drives up the economic-growth rate. Inflation follows, so policy is tightened and growth slows. But inflation remains high or rising, so more tightening is imposed. Inflation falls at last, but growth slows more than desired, owing to the overcapacity that resulted from excessive investment in the earlier phase of the cycle. In response, policy becomes expansionary again, and the cycle begins anew: led by investment growth, the economy rebounds.

The chapter reviews briefly China's macroeconomic management since the early 1990s. Based on this review, the chapter goes on to discuss the question of how monetary policy, fiscal policy and exchange rate policy are used to achieve the objectives of growth and price stability in China, respectively. The chapter ends by concluding that while on the whole China's macroeconomic management over the past two decades is successful, how to strike a balance between short-run macroeconomic stability and long-run structural adjustment is still a big challenge facing China.

Introduction

Over the past three decades, China succeeded in achieving an average annual growth rate of slightly below 10 percent while having maintained an average annual inflation rate of less than 3 percent.

China's high growth potential is attributable to rapid capital accumulation supported by a very high savings rate, abundant supply of skilled workers and engineers, and sizable improvement in total factor productivity (TFP). China's economic reforms have played an important role in the rise of TFP (Perkins, 2005: 4).

However, China's growth over the past three decades was by no means smooth. The economy constantly suffers from overheating and sluggish growth in tandem. Given the scale of the growth potential, the government has to manage the demand side of the economy to achieve full utilization of the potential, iron out cyclical fluctuations, and offset the impact of external shocks.

China has become a market economy after a thirty-year transformation. However the transformation is not fully complete yet. State-owned enterprises and local governments remain key players in China's economic activities. State-owned commercial banks continue dominating the financial market. Financial liberalization is still in progress. As a result, while China's macroeconomic management shares the fundamental characteristics of a typical market economy, it has its own features.

This chapter aims to identify the pattern of China's macroeconomic management and explain how macroeconomic policy has been implemented for achieving non-inflationary growth in China. The chapter is organized as follows. The first section is a brief review of China's macroeconomic management since the early 1990s. The second section is devoted to discussing how monetary policy is used to achieve the objectives of growth and price stability. The third section is about China's fiscal policy. The fourth section discusses China's exchange rate policy. The final section presents concluding remarks.

1 A brief review of China's macroeconomic performance since the early 1990s

Starting from the early 1990s, China's macroeconomic development can be divided into five major periods: 1990–1997, 1998–2002, 2003–2008, 2008–2010, and 2010 to the present. The division above is not entirely based on economy cycles China has experienced; rather it is based on the occasions when difficult decisions were made to alter the direction of macroeconomic policy.

1.1 The period from 1990 to 1997

At the beginning of the 1990s, the Chinese economy was in a poor condition. Though the inflation rate had fallen as a result of China's anti-inflation campaign in the late 1980s, GDP growth was just 4.1 percent in 1990, the lowest rate since 1978.

Deng Xiaoping's call for speeding up reform and expansion of the "opening up" in his famous tour to southern China in the spring of 1992 dispelled any lingering doubt among the public about the future direction of the Chinese economy. Facilitated by a spurt in money supply and credit, investment surged at astonishingly high rates of 42.6 percent in 1992 and 58.6 percent in 1993. As a result, China's GDP growth rate shot up to 14.2 percent and 13.5 percent in 1992 and 1993, respectively. Following the strong growth, inflation in 1992 rose to 6.4 percent, and in 1993 it rocketed further to 14.7 percent.

The investment fever in this period in turn was attributable to the investment fever in real estate development, which grew at breath-taking speeds of 93.5 percent in 1992 and 124.9 percent in 1993. Being concerned with inflation and the dire consequences of a burst of real estate bubbles, in August 1993 Zhu Rongji, as Governor of the People's Bank and Vice Premier, took drastic action to clamp down on real estate investment by cutting credit growth, among other measures. He even went as far as sacking local officials who failed to rein in local bank lending.[1] The growth rate of money supply started to fall rapidly.

Though the growth rate of money supply fell, with a delayed effect inflation peaked at 24.1 percent in 1994, the worst on record since 1979. The causes of the continuous rise in inflation were multi-fold, and included the administrative adjustment of prices aimed at rationalizing the price structure, a very large increase in grain prices due to supply shortages, a temporary increase in transaction costs because of the restructuring of the grain circulation system, and an increase in foreign exchange reserves thanks to strong capital inflows. However, according to Zhu Rongji, the fundamental reason was still the investment fever in infrastructure and real estate development.[2]

Faced with worsening inflation, the government continued the tightening of money supply further in 1995.[3] In 1996, the excess supply of manufacturing goods became ubiquitous and inflation continued to fall precipitately from the 1994 peak. In 1996 the People's Bank of China (PBOC) cut interest rates on loans and deposits for the first time since 1993.

In 1997, the growth rate of real GDP as well as the inflation rate fell continuously. The rapid deterioration of the economic situation and the gloomy global economy prompted the government to cut the interest rate on loans and deposits in October again, sending a strong signal of policy change from tight to "accommodative." However, despite the intention of loosening by the PBOC, both the growth rates of money supply and credits fell precipitately in 1997. By the end of 1997, the growth rate of GDP and the inflation rate fell to 8.8 percent and 2.8 percent, respectively.

1.2 The period from 1998 to 2003

In 1998, due to the impact of the Asian crisis, China's export growth dropped drastically and then, with some lag, investment growth also dropped commensurately. Despite the further loosening of monetary policy, China's growth rates fell to below 7 percent in the first half of 1998. An important phenomenon in 1997–2001 was that despite the PBOC cutting the reserve requirement ratio from 13 percent to 8 percent and having lowered benchmark interest rates six times since, the growth rates of money supply and credit continued to fall and only bottomed out at 13 percent and 11 percent in the last quarter of 2001.

In response, and after some hesitation, the government turned to expansionary fiscal policy ("proactive fiscal policy") in the second half of 1998. Expansionary fiscal policy proved effective. China achieved a growth rate of 7.8 percent in 1998. But the inflation rate fell to −0.8 percent. It was the first time in history that the inflation rate over the course of a year became negative.

The PBOC's policy initiatives taken during the period of deflation to encourage the expansion of mortgage loans started bearing fruit in 2000. Investment growth in real estate development rebounded strongly from negative in 1997 to 13.7 percent in 1998 and rose further to 21.5 percent in 2000. These trends played a pivotal role in the improvement in the growth outlook that year.

The growth of the Chinese economy has accelerated since the second half of 2002. Again, this was led by strong investment growth, which was partially a response to the ubiquitous "bottlenecks" resulting from lack of investment in infrastructure and many key industries since 1997. By this time GDP growth returned to 9.1 percent.

1.3 The period from 2003 to 2008

Growth momentum, led by the investment boom since 2002, was maintained and became increasingly evident in 2003. Again, the strong growth of real estate investment was the single most important contributing factor to the growth of total investment and hence that of GDP.

In October 2003 the PBOC raised benchmark interest rates for the first time since 1997. It showed that macroeconomic policy had shifted from loosening to cautious tightening. Efforts were also made to shift fiscal policy towards a more neutral stance.

Despite the shift in monetary policy, investment fever continued unabated. In response, the government not only tightened macroeconomic policy further but also resorted to various administrative methods once more. Throughout 2004, growth of money supply and credit fell rapidly to 13.5 percent and 10.9 percent in October 2004, respectively.

In early 2005, due to the strong investment growth from 2002 to 2004, signs of overcapacity became prevalent and profitability of the enterprises fell significantly. It seemed that the rebound in the economy that began in 2002 had come to an end. Some economists started to advocate the shift of policy direction from "moderate tightening" to loosening. However, the expected slowdown of the economy failed to materialize in 2005. At the same time, the growth rates in the money supply and credit rebounded from relatively low levels of 2004. Overcapacity was absorbed temporarily by the creation of new capacity and rapid increase in exports. In fact, exports grew at an astonishing rate of 220 percent in 2005, which was attributable partially to the prevalent overcapacity in the domestic market. As a result, the PBOC was able to decide to de-peg the renminbi from the US dollar, and allowed the renminbi to appreciate by 2.1 percent in July 2005.

Despite prevalent overcapacity, growth momentum was unexpectedly strong in 2006. The growth rate of investment accelerated, while net export growth maintained a high rate of 41.4 percent.

The robustness of the economy in 2006 was commonly attributed to the fact that 2006 was the first year for the implementation of the eleventh Five-Year Plan and the last year before the leadership change in provincial governments. Local authorities and enterprises were very keen on putting up good performances and positioning themselves for future development by increasing investment in their respective localities as much as possible.

Because the central bank was reluctant to allow the renminbi to appreciate more speedily, the large current account and capital account surpluses created abundant liquidity. How to mop up the excess liquidity became a hot topic in 2006. A puzzling phenomenon in 2006 was that despite the abundance of liquidity, the inflation rate was very low until the second half of 2006. In hindsight, the low inflation rate can be explained by rising asset prices. Large amounts of money were attracted to the real estate market and hence reduced inflationary pressure on goods and services. In 2006 the economy grew at 12.7 percent, while inflation was just 1.5 percent.

After five consecutive years of high growth since 2003, red lights suddenly started to flash in the second quarter of 2007. Thanks to favorable internal and external conditions, China's share price index, which had been in the doldrums for years, began to increase gradually in 2006 and then exponentially. It took eighteen months for the Shanghai composite share price index to rise from 2,000 to 3,000 points and then just another thirty-one working days for it to rise from 3,000 to 4,000 points. After soaring to more than 6,200 in October 2007, it crashed. Until then China's share price index was still languishing at just under 2,500 points.

Since the fourth quarter of 2006, inflation was steadily worsening. Initially, the increase in CPI was caused almost exclusively by food prices, especially by pork prices. Therefore, many economists and government officials argued that, as soon as piglets matured, the supply of pork would increase and pork prices would fall, along with CPI. However, inflation continued to worsen unabated throughout 2007 and until February 2008, though the pork price had peaked in August 2007.

Despite the fact that the PBOC raised reserve requirements, increased benchmark interest rates five times, and even imposed quantitative limits on bank lending, the economy sustained strong growth and inflation continued to worsen. The high growth rate of GDP in 2007 was on par with the historical record registered in 1992.

In February 2008, the annualized growth rate of CPI reached 8.7 percent, the highest in eleven years, while signs of the weakening of the economy were becoming more evident.

Before the Chinese government was able to decide whether it should tighten monetary policy further or not, the US subprime crisis struck. The consequent dramatic slowdown of the global economy hit the Chinese economy very badly. Following the free fall in the global economy, Chinese economic growth fell to 6.8 percent in the fourth quarter of 2008, the lowest annualized quarterly growth rate in decades, because of dramatic falls in exports. In fact, the growth rate of exports fell from 20 percent in October to −2.2 percent in November, and extended further, because the share of exports in China's GDP was 36 percent in 2007. The impact of the fall in exports on growth of GDP was bound to be huge. Following the fall in GDP growth, inflationary pressure disappeared suddenly and became negative in February 2009; house prices in some major cities and share price indexes fell precipitously.

The Chinese government reacted very quickly. In September 2008, the PBOC loosened monetary policy and renminbi appreciation was stopped. Much more importantly, the government introduced a 4,000 billion yuan (US$580bn, €404bn, £354bn sterling) stimulus package for 2009 and 2010 in November 2008.

In response to extremely expansionary monetary and fiscal policy, the Chinese economy rebounded quickly to 7.9 percent in the second quarter of 2009. Fixed asset investment growth was 30.5 percent in 2009, and contributed 8 percentage points to the overall growth that year. Inflation returned to positive in November 2009.

Despite the success in achieving a V-shaped recovery, the rescue package and excessive expansionary monetary policy also produced serious negative side effects. To launch a large number of projects in a very short time span inevitably would lead to serious waste and deterioration of investment efficiency. Asset bubbles and inflation also reemerged.

1.4 From 2010 to the present

In the first quarter of 2010, China's growth rate peaked at 12.1 percent, while inflation continued to rise from a low level. To rein in housing bubbles and preempt the worsening of inflation, in January 2010, the PBOC raised the reserve requirement for the first time since the middle of 2008. This was subsequently repeated five times and benchmark interest rates on deposits and loans were hiked twice in 2010. At the same time, both the growth rates of credit and broad money fell significantly. The growth rate of GDP and the rate of inflation in 2010 were 10.3 percent and 3.3 percent, respectively. In the last quarter of 2010, the inflation rate rose to 4.6 percent.

It was expected that China's inflation situation would improve in early 2011, because of the changes in the direction of monetary and fiscal policy. However, inflation failed to fall, due to the rise in commodity prices in early 2011. The government tightened monetary policy further by raising reserve requirements and benchmark interest rates on deposits and loans in June. Inflation started to fall after having hit the three-year high of 6.5 percent in July 2011.

While the vigorous liquidity tightening eventually mitigated inflationary pressures, it put the brakes on economic growth. In fact, economic growth had been slowing continuously after it peaked in the first quarter of 2010. In the last quarter of 2011, the growth rate fell to 8.9 percent. More importantly, in the last month of 2011, growth rates of total investment, real estate investment, and manufacturing investment all fell. Home sales fell by 8 percent and housing starts fell by 18.3 percent. Due to the worsening of the global environment, China's exports also performed poorly.

Therefore, despite the fact that China's GDP growth rate for 2011 was still as high as 9.2 percent, concern about a hard landing for the Chinese economy was on the rise. The PBOC lowered the reserve ratio in November 2011 and signaled the change of policy direction from tightening to loosening.

Most economists in China expected that China's growth would rebound in 2012. But the performance of the Chinese economy in 2012 since the second quarter of the year has been disappointing.

This is attributable to three factors. First, the direct and indirect impact of the decline in growth of real estate investment on the economy was stronger than expected. Second, the European sovereign debt crisis had been worse than expected. A more fundamental cause is that in order to achieve sustainable development and shift priorities from growth to transforming the economic development patterns and restructuring the economy, the government refrained from ushering in new policies to stimulate the economy. By May 2012, however, the government changed its mind, with the National Development and Reform Commission approving 7 trillion renminbi (US$1.3 trillion) in new projects. That, together with one ensuing reserve ratio cut and two benchmark interest-rate cuts by the PBOC, guaranteed an end to the economic slowdown in the third quarter of 2012. However, because the pickup of the economy was once again led by investment growth, the recovery of the growth momentum perhaps will leave more problems to be resolved in the future.

2 China's monetary policy

2.1 The reform of China's financial system

Since 1979, the structure and functions of the Chinese banking system have been gradually reformed. In 1984, the PBOC was restructured as a central bank and its commercial banking functions were transferred to four specialized banks.

The PBOC established the first unified national interbank lending market in January 1996. A reserve system was established in March 1998, when the required reserves account and excess reserves account were merged by the PBOC. All reserves that banks deposited with the PBOC would be paid a unified interest rate. After the merger, the required reserve ratio was set at 8 percent, a fall of 5 percentage points from before the reforms. As of 2012, the ratio is 20 percent. In December 2003, the interest rate on required reserves and excess reserves was set at 1.89 percent and 1.62 percent, respectively. In March 2005, the latter rate was lowered to and remains at 0.99 percent.

China's money market consists of the interbank loan market, the bond repurchase market, and the bill discount market. Its capital market comprises the bond market and the stock market. The interest rate in the interbank loan market, the China Interbank Loan Offered Rate (CHIBOR), is calculated and reported according to interbank loan interest rates determined by the supply of and demand for loans by twelve commercial banks and fifteen financial centers on each working day. The PBOC's interest rate on bank reserves and that on relendings set the ceiling and floor respectively for the CHIBOR. The interest rate in the bond repurchase market, Repurchase Offered Rate (REPOR), is the market rate determined by the supply of and demand for government bonds. The Shanghai Interbank Offer Rate (SHIBOR) was introduced in January 2007, which is calculated as an arithmetic average of offered rates for interbank loans by sixteen participating banks, and fixed at 11:30 a.m. on each working day. SHIBOR is similar to LIBOR, with the aim of becoming China's benchmark interbank interest rate.

China's financial system is still dominated by banks. In 2011, bank loans accounted for 75 percent of total "social finance," while bond and equity issues accounted for 10.6 percent and 3.4 percent, respectively. In the same year, government bonds, financial bonds, enterprise bonds, and central bank bills accounted for 35.49 percent, 32.82 percent, 22.32 percent, and 9.36 percent of total bond issuance, respectively.

2.2 Final objectives of monetary policy

Since 1978, China's monetary policy has undergone various changes in terms of objectives, intermediate targets, and instruments.

According to the official version, the final objective of monetary policy is "to maintain the stability of currency value and thereby promote economic growth." The stability of currency value means that both price stability and the stability of the exchange rate of the renminbi should be maintained.[4] In fact there are at least three final objectives in China's monetary policy: growth, price stability, and exchange rate stability. To harmonize these three objectives is by no means an easy job. In practice, the number one final objective is to guarantee a minimum growth rate of 7 percent. The second final objective is an inflation rate of around 3 percent, which is defined as a medium-term average rather than as a rate (or band of rates) that must be held at all times. The final objective is to maintain the stability of the exchange rate of the renminbi that once was pegged to the US dollar and now enjoys some degree of volatility but still refers to a basket of currencies.

China's experience shows that the trade-off between growth and inflation exists. To raise growth, policy makers need to accept a higher rate of inflation; to lower inflation, the PBOC has to allow growth to fall. Normally, changes in inflation follow those of growth. The complication lies in the variation in the time lag between growth and inflation in each economic cycle. Hence to get the timing right is very difficult.

As for exchange rate stability, due to the PBOC's ability to carry out large-scale sterilization operations and the existence of capital controls, the PBOC is able to achieve growth and inflation objectives without being constrained too much by exchange rate considerations. However, in some circumstances, because of the difficulty in fully sterilizing excess liquidity, the maintenance of exchange rate stability is bound to weaken the dependence of monetary policy. On the other hand, when the PBOC is considering tightening monetary policy, it has to consider the impact on the exchange rate. In short, due to various constraints in the sense of Tinbergen's rule that the number of policy instruments must be equal to the number of available policy instruments, conflicts among these three objectives are inevitable.

2.3 Intermediate targets of monetary policy

In the third quarter of 1994, Chinese monetary authorities formally took the supply of broad money (M2) rather than its counterpart – total bank credit, as the intermediate target of monetary policy.

Although the growth rate of money supply is officially the intermediate target of monetary policy and the PBOC sets a target for the growth rate of money supply each year, it has never strictly adhered to such a target in practice. The target is just a policy manifestation, a reference target. More often than not, the PBOC fails to hit the target. First, whenever the inflation rate had surpassed certain thresholds, irrespective of the growth rate of money supply, it will tighten monetary policy. On the other hand, whenever the growth rate of the economy falls below certain thresholds, irrespective of the growth rate of money supply, it will loosen monetary policy. Fortunately, over the past thirty years, China has never come across a situation where inflation is very high and the growth rate is very low simultaneously. Second, when the economy suffers from serious overheating or deflation, the PBOC tends to return to credit controls via "moral persuasions." To put it more bluntly, the PBOC would ask commercial banks directly to reduce or increase credit to enterprises and households and without exception, commercial banks will duly comply with reluctance. In fact, each year in recent years, the PBOC will set a target for the increase in credit for the year. Third, in recent years, due to the burgeoning of financial innovations, various kinds of near-money are supplementing traditionally defined money to play the role of medium of exchange and store of value. Hence, the usefulness of keeping M2 as the intermediate target is becoming more and more questionable. The PBOC also used in recent years the so-called "total social finance" that includes all forms of finance as a reference target.

2.4 Monetary policy instruments

Open market operations

In developed countries, until recently changes in interbank interest rates create cascading effects on the interest rate structure of the entire financial system and eventually influence the real economy. In China, because of the fragmentation of the money market and control over interest rates on loans and deposits, changes in interbank interest rates cannot have the same effect. Hence, the PBOC's open market operations (OMOs) are aimed mainly at influencing money supply rather than the key short-term interbank interest rates such as CHIBOR, SHIBOR, and the repo rate.

The PBOC initiated OMOs in May 1996. The operational target of OMOs is the level of bank deposits with the PBOC. Trading between the PBOC and primary dealers consisting of forty commercial banks takes the form of the repurchase of government bonds or central bank bills (CBBs). The maturities of repurchases (reserve repurchases) are divided into three time spans: seven days, fourteen days, and twenty-one days. The prices of the traded bonds and bills are determined by offering and bidding. The transactions between the central bank and the commercial banks are conducted via a computerized trading network managed by the PBOC.

Because of the persistent increase in current account and capital account surpluses and the PBOC's reluctance to allow the renminbi to appreciate, increase in foreign exchange reserves became the single most important, if not the only, source of increase in the monetary base. To control the expansion of the monetary base, the PBOC sells its assets continuously to sterilize the increase in base money. In the beginning, cash bond trading was the most common means of adjusting the monetary base. It was replaced by government bond repo transactions later. The PBOC sold all government bonds with which repos had been conducted quickly. Since May 2003, it has conducted OMOs via CBB repo. In other words, the OMOs in China are basically sterilization operations. Changes in base money are equal to changes in the gap between the base money created by increase in foreign exchange reserves and the base money that has been sterilized through selling CBBs by the PBOC.

The adjustment of required reserve ratio

Besides OMOs, in its toolkit, another important instrument used by the central bank to change the money supply is the required reserve ratio. In quantitative terms, changes in multiplier rendered by changes in the reserve ratio have the same effect on the money supply as changes in the monetary base for a given multiplier. Hence, when the reserve ratio is increased by a certain number of basis points, it can be said that a corresponding amount of liquidity is frozen. In short, by changing the reserve ratio, the PBOC is able to control money supply through changing the money multiplier.

In a typical market economy, the central bank will refrain from changing the required reserve ratio as much as possible, because the measure is regarded as too drastic and clumsy. However, in China the adjustment of the reserve ratio is often regarded as a more powerful and cheaper monetary instrument than OMOs. Since 1998, the central bank has changed the required reserve ratio forty-two times in total. As of the end of 2012, the required reserve ratio stands at 20 percent.

Benchmark interest rates

Despite the progress in interest rate liberalization, due to the fragmentation of China's money market and the abundance of liquidity in the banking system, there is no benchmark interest rate in China equivalent to the Fed Funds rate in the US, the base rate in the US, and the overnight call rate in Japan.

The benchmark interest rates the PBOC administers are the one-year lending rate and the one-year deposit rate. Although changes in the benchmark lending and deposit rates cannot influence the entire interest rate structure of the economy in a cascading manner, changes in the benchmark interest rates can affect real GDP and inflation through its influence in the financial costs of enterprises and, to a certain degree, household saving behavior. Chinese enterprises have rather high leverage ratios, probably above 100 percent currently. The changes in the benchmark lending rate will influence the profitability of enterprises, and hence influence investment and production decisions. The interest rate spread between deposits and loans is an important source of revenues for commercial banks. Hence, changes in the benchmark interest rates will also influence the behavior of commercial banks and other financial institutions. Changes in the benchmark lending and deposit rates also influence real GDP and inflation via their influence in household investment and saving behavior. Furthermore, changes in the benchmark interest rate have important announcement effects.

While continuing to use the one-year deposit rate and lending rate as benchmark interest rates, the PBOC has been increasing the freedom of commercial banks in deciding their interest rates. Now only a ceiling on the deposit rate and a floor on the lending rates remain. In June 2012, the PBOC further announced that commercial banks could raise their deposit interest rates up to 110 percent of the benchmark deposit rate. Up until then commercial banks could lower their one-year lending rates to no more than 90 percent of the benchmark-lending rate.

Moral suasion

Despite financial liberalization, when the economy suffers from overheating, the PBOC often resorts to the annual bank-by-bank caps on credit growth, and uses official "window guidance" to influence the bank lending; when the economy suffers a serious slowdown, the same measures will be used to "persuade" commercial banks to increase their loans. Without exception, when moral persuasion is applied, commercial banks would obey, regardless of their business conditions. The reason is simple: all major banks are state owned and the governors of the major banks are officials with the rank of deputy minister.

2.5 The effectiveness of monetary policy

The majority of empirical studies show that there is a strong correlation between money supply, real GDP, and inflation in China. However, causalities among them are complicated. The complication is caused mainly by two problems.

The first problem is about the exogeneity of money supply, which is conditional on the exogeneity of the monetary base and stability of the multiplier. In China the two conditions for the exogeneity of money supply cannot be met entirely. The expansion of China's monetary base comes overwhelmingly from the increase in foreign exchange reserves. The PBOC sells CBBs to offset the influence of the increase in foreign exchange reserves on the monetary base. Due to all sorts of complications, it is difficult for the PBOC to control the size of the monetary base as it wishes. Furthermore, the monetary multiplier is unstable, because commercial banks can hold more or less the level of reserves than the PBOC deems satisfactory. When the economy is in deflation, the monetary multiplier tends to fall, because of banks' reluctance to lend and hence the resulting rise in banks' reserves. For example, during the 1998–2001 period of deflation, not only was base money released in 1998, but also the banks' reserve requirement was lowered in 1999, yet growth of money supply still declined continuously and credit growth similarly fell until the end of 2001.[5] Conversely, when the economy is overheating, the multiplier tends to increase. When the PBOC raises the reserve requirements, commercial banks can satisfy this increased reserve requirement simply by reducing its excess reserves, without cutting credit.

The second problem is the time lags between changes in the money supply and changes in real GDP growth and inflation. When the economy is below full employment, changes in the quantity of money alter the level of output rather than prices. Normally, the increase in money supply will lead immediately to the increase in investment, because state-owned enterprises, which still dominate the economy, have unsaturated appetite for investment; as long as credit is available, they will increase investment. The increase in investment and the resulting increase in the income level will create a second-round increase in growth via the increase in consumption demand. When the economy reaches full capacity, faced with an inflation rate higher than the implicit target, the monetary authority will tighten money supply. Mainly due to the unavailability of credit, investment demand will fall and so will growth. Overcapacity will put pressure on the price level and inflation will fall several quarters after monetary tightening. It is common in periods of monetary tightening that while growth has been falling, inflation is still high. To tighten or not to tighten is a difficult decision for the monetary authority to make. It is also common in periods of monetary loosening that while the economy is growing at a rate higher than the trend rate, inflation is still low.

It is worth noting that under certain circumstances, the transmission from the money supply to real GDP and inflation can fail to work. For example, during and in the wake of the Asian financial crisis, despite the fact that the growth rate of M2 is significantly higher than that of nominal GDP, both real GDP and inflation refused to budge. The growth rate of money supply was much higher than that of credit. This situation is attributable to the credit crunch as banks feared for the safety of their loans, as well as higher demand for the real balance by households and enterprises during a bad time.

The burgeoning of the capital market caused another important complication. The rise in asset prices will increase the demand for money. As a result, even though the growth rate of money supply is much higher than that of nominal GDP, inflation can be moderate. The low inflation rate makes the monetary authority complacent. As a result, asset bubbles will get worse and burst eventually with all their dire consequences.

Despite the fact that the growth in quantity of credit and that of broad money M2 is highly correlated, there is a great temptation for the PBOC to jump the gun to instruct or "persuade" state-owned commercial banks to increase or decrease credit extended to enterprises. China did not suffer a serious credit crunch and liquidity shortage, when the global financial crisis struck. The reason is simply that the PBOC instructed commercial banks to increase their credit to enterprises to accommodate the government's stimulus package, and commercial banks duly complied. However, the direct intervention by the PBOC on commercial banks' lending activities certainly will create serious distortions in the economy.

All in all, despite the complications, money matters in China. Changes in money supply will eventually lead to changes in real GDP and inflation, though with various lags that are difficult to predict. Some empirical studies have shown that there are stable econometric relations between money supply, prices and output. Since this chapter is devoted to historical and institutional description and analysis of macroeconomic policy, quantitative relations are not discussed here.

3 Fiscal policy

3.1 China's reform of the fiscal system

Before 1994, despite the high growth rate of the Chinese economy since reform and opening, the Chinese government's fiscal position was very weak. Both the share of total government revenues in GDP and that of central government revenues in total government revenues were very low. The extremely weak fiscal position seriously weakened the government's ability to exercise macro control over the economy (Wang and Hu, 2001). To strengthen the central government's fiscal position, China introduced fiscal reform in 1994. The aim of the reform was to establish a tax-assignment system, which was called the revenue-sharing system *(fenshui zhi)*. Under the new system, revenues were shared between the central and provincial governments. Taxes were divided into three categories: central, local, and shared. The central taxes included tariff, consumption tax, and value-added tax on imports, vehicle purchase tax, and cargo tax. These tax revenues would go into the central coffers. The local taxes that would go into local budgets included urban maintenance and development tax, tax on contracts, resource tax, tax on the use of arable land, urban land using tax, and agriculture tax. Shared tax included value-added tax, business tax, stamp duty on securities transactions, personal income tax, and enterprise income tax. Among all taxes, in terms of magnitude, the value-added tax was by far the single most important tax. The tax rate of value-added tax on most products was 17 percent. Among the value-added tax collected, 75 percent would go to the central government, and 25 percent to local government. Other important taxes included enterprise income tax and business tax. The tax rate on enterprise income was 33 percent, and among the tax collected 30 percent goes to the central government and 3 percent goes to local governments. Local administrations were responsible for the collection of the enterprise income taxes on local firms, while the State Administration of Tax was for the others.

There have been some more incremental reforms since 1994, including a conversion of the value-added tax to the standard sales tax; rationalization and consolidation of the corporate income tax; abolishment of agricultural tax, and moving the responsibility of collecting personal income tax to the State Administration of Tax; equalizing foreign enterprise income tax rate to 33 percent, and experimenting with property taxes in a few cities.

The 1994 reform eventually led to a significant improvement in the central government's fiscal position. In 2000, China's national fiscal revenues rose to 1339.5 billion yuan, a 17 percent increase over 1999. This trend continued thereafter. The tax revenues grew persistently by double digits. In 2007, before the global financial crisis struck, tax revenues increased by an astonishing 27.56 percent over the previous year. Because the national fiscal revenues had grown much faster than GDP every year over a decade, the share of the national fiscal revenues in GDP increased to 20.57 percent in 2011, compared with 10.83 percent in 1994. The rapid increase in tax revenues, which constitute the bulk of government revenues, was attributable mainly to the high growth rate of GDP under the new tax regime, and the vastly improved tax collection.[6]

3.2 China's government budget

China's national fiscal revenues consist of central government revenues and local government revenues. The most important sources of central government revenues are value-added tax, enterprise income tax, non-tax revenue, and business tax. It is worth noting that export tax rebate is one of the most important items that subtract the government revenues. Land value added tax and arable land use tax are two very important resources of local government revenues.

China's national expenditures consist of central government expenditures and local government expenditures. The top ten central government expenditures are central government revenue transfer to local governments, national defense, agriculture, forestry and water affairs, social security, communication and transportation, education, science and technology, interest payment on public debt, social housing, energy conservation and environment protection, and public security.

Local governments bear large shares of fiscal expenditures in government administration, social security, education, science and technology, agriculture, forestry and water affairs, medical care and sanitation, communication and transportation, social housing, and so on.

3.3 The implementation of fiscal policy

In developed countries, in the short run, the built-in stabilizers within fiscal systems can smooth the variations in demand in a counter-cyclical way in support of or supplement to monetary policy to achieve given growth and inflation targets. There are built-in stabilizers in China's fiscal system. However, because of the extremely low shares of personal and enterprise income tax revenues in GDP, which until 2011 were just 1.3 percent and 3.6 percent, respectively, the role of taxes in automatically stabilizing the economy is virtually non-existent. The same is true of government expenditures. The most important stabilizer in the spending side is government expenditure in social security and employment, which accounted for just for 2.36 percent of GDP in 2011.

The functions of the Chinese government's budget include:

- the maintenance of the smooth running of government administrations;
- the provision of public goods and services;
- narrowing the income distribution gap between regions and social strata;
- support of reform and economic transition by providing necessary financial support; and
- investment in capital construction.

Usually, the government would refrain from changing government revenues and expenditures as policy instruments to stimulate growth or contain inflation. In other words, China's fiscal policy has been neutral or moderately expansive for most of the time since the 1990s. The government adheres to the principle of "calculating how much revenues received before deciding how much to spend." Over the past decades, China's budget deficit-to-GDP ratio has mostly been kept below 3 percent, and hence, China's public debt-to-GDP ratio is still about 20 percent at this moment.

Only when the economy is in deflation or falling dramatically and monetary policy is impotent or would take too long to deliver results, will the government use very expansive fiscal policy to boost or stabilize conditions. Since the early 1990s, there have been only two occasions when China tried to spend its way out of trouble. One was in the second half of 1998 when the government under Zhu Rongji implemented expansionary fiscal policy during the Asian financial crisis; another was during the 2008–2009 global financial crisis when the government under Wen Jiaobao ushered in a very large stimulus package.

In the first episode, the Ministry of Finance sold 100 billion renminbi bonds to commercial banks to raise money to fund investment in infrastructures. At the same time, commercial banks were instructed to extend another 100 billion renminbi loans to supplement the government financing of infrastructure investment.

In the second, the government introduced a 4,000 billion yuan (US$580 billion, €404 billion, £354 billion sterling) stimulus package. The prescribed dosage of the stimulus was very large, at 14 percent of GDP in 2008. To support the fiscal expansion, with the PBOC's moral persuasion, commercial banks extended 9.6 trillion renminbi loans, an astronomical figure China had never seen before in history

China's experience shows that expansionary fiscal policy is very effective in stimulating economic growth when the economy is operating below capacity. When the economy is overheating or under the threat of asset bubbles, the government usually will rely on monetary tightening to rein in the economy; the fiscal measures such as raising stamp duty and property taxes are used scantly and only in a very modest manner.

One of the most important features of China's expansionary fiscal policy is that the Chinese government is very conscientious in using market mechanisms to ensure that public money will be used more efficiently. When the government has decided to support a certain project, it will finance it only partially. The contractors, whoever they are, have to find the bulk of the finance themselves in financial markets, and subject their projects to the scrutiny of market forces. During the 2008–2009 fiscal expansion, though the central government was responsible for approvals of all major investment projects, among the 4 trillion yuan stimulus package, only 1.2 trillion yuan came from the central government's coffers. To fill the funding gap, local governments were encouraged to create "local financing platforms," a sort of special purpose vehicles, to borrow from banks with future government revenues or land as collateral to finance the investment projects packaged in their localities. They were allowed to issue local government bonds, but the issuances were done by the central government on their behalf. With a very loose credit policy implemented by the PBOC and obedient commercial banks, local governments were able to raise 10.7 trillion yuan, of which 79.1 percent was in bank loans.

Because of the adoption of expansionary fiscal policy to fight deflation during the Asian financial crisis, China's budget deficit increased from a meager 0.78 percent of GDP in 1997 to 1.16 percent in 1998. Because of the increase in budget deficits, though moderate, the debt-to-GDP ratio increased from 10 percent in 1998 to 13.8 percent in 2000. The government shifted to a more neutral fiscal stance in 2003, and as a result budget deficit fell continuously. In 2008, China even ran a budget surplus of 0.58 percent. As a result, China's public debt-to-GDP ratio increased only slowly. In 2008, China's debt-to-GDP ratio was about 20 percent. In 2009, because of China's extremely large stimulus package, its budget turned to negative. In 2010, the budget deficit peaked at 2.8 percent of GDP. In 2012, the ratio is expected to fall back to less than 2 percent and China's public debt-to-GDP ratio will still be maintained at relatively low levels.

4 China's exchange rate policy

4.1 China's exchange rate system

Since April 1991, China's official exchange rate regime shifted from fixed exchange rates to a managed float. The official renminbi exchange rate fluctuated much more frequently, but devalued for the most of the time until 1994. At the beginning of 1994, the official and swap markets were merged. The official rate fell from 5.80 yuan per dollar to 8.70 yuan per dollar upon completion. Because a large proportion of foreign exchanges had already been traded in the swap market before the merger, the impact of the large devaluation of the official exchange rate in 1994 on China's trade was not very significant. Between 1994 and 1997, China's exchange rate regime was supposed to be "a unified, managed, floating exchange rate system." Under this system, the central parity was set solely against the US dollar with a small band, and the central parity was allowed to crawl. During this period of time, the renminbi nominal exchange rate appreciated by 4.5 percent, because of the increase in China's international balance-of-payments surplus. In 1996, the renminbi was made convertible for current account transactions.

After the outbreak of the Asian financial crisis in 1997, China shifted to a de facto peg to the US dollar. With the help of capital controls, the firm commitment of "no devaluation" enabled China to come out of the Asian financial crisis relatively unscathed.

Since 2003, the US government started to press China to appreciate the renminbi. In July 2005, China gave up the peg to the dollar and returned to managed floating. At the same time, the yuan's exchange rate against the dollar appreciated from 8.28 yuan per dollar to 8.11 yuan per dollar, an appreciation of 2.1 percent.

The new exchange rate regime is characterized by the so-called "referring to a basket of currencies." According to the PBOC, the yuan's closing rate against the dollar at the end of each business day was to become the central parity rate for a trading band on the following day. The yuan would be allowed to fluctuate up to 0.3 percent plus/minus the central rate against the dollar each day. It is worth noting that the renminbi exchange rate is not strictly pegged to a basket of currencies. The basket is just a reference: the yuan's central parity against the dollar still can be decided at PBOC's discretion. It seems that in the daily determination of the yuan's exchange rate, there are two important considerations: first, the renminbi exchange rate against the dollar determined by the given basket of currencies; second, the magnitude of renminbi appreciation that is desirable or affordable for China. Only after weighing the two considerations, will the central parity be announced each day. Hence, the central parity is not necessary based on the parity set on the previous business day. Primary dealers in the foreign exchange market will offer bid-and-ask prices, but it is hard to say that they can determine the central parity rate, because they will try their best to toe the line. Persistent outliers will lose their position as primary dealers in the foreign exchange market.

After the outbreak of the global financial crisis in 2008, the yuan re-pegged to the dollar temporarily, and de-pegged and resumed appreciation again in June 2010 after an eighteen-month hiatus.

In April 2012, the PBOC widened the yuan's daily trading band against the US dollar to 1 percent from 0.5 percent, as part of the effort by the central bank to allow market supply and demand to play a larger role in the determination of the renminbi exchange rate. The central bank pledged that it would maintain the "normal fluctuation" of the renminbi exchange rate, stabilize the rate at "reasonable and balanced levels," and keep the macro economy and financial markets stable.

4.2 China's current exchange rate policy

In the 1980s, China was still in the process of forming its growth strategy, and hesitated in choosing between import substitution and export promotion. In the 1990s, China's exchange rate policy was increasingly aimed at promoting exports, which in turn was driven by the desire for the accumulation of foreign exchange reserves.

After the reform of the exchange rate system in 1994, China achieved a comfortable position in international balance of payments. It seems that China was happy with the managed float and had no problem with allowing market demand and supply to determine the exchange rate. In fact, after the 1994 reform, the renminbi exchange rate was on the rise, driven by the international balance-of-payments surplus. However, the Asian financial crisis changed China's policy prospects abruptly.

During the Asian financial crisis, to adopt a de facto peg to the US dollar rather than to engage in competitive devaluation was absolutely the right decision. The question is why after the crisis, the Chinese government refused to de-peg from the US dollar. The causes behind China's insistence on pegging are multi-fold. First, in 2003 the Chinese government was still not sure whether the economy had recovered truly. It was widely believed that even a small appreciation of the renminbi would lead to widespread bankruptcy and millions of jobs would be lost. Second, it was believed by many that because of "irrational renminbi appreciation expectations," one small appreciation would invite more capital inflows betting on renminbi appreciation, which in turn would put more appreciation pressure on the renminbi. Hence, a de-peg would make appreciation uncontrollable and eventually cause excessive appreciation of the renminbi with dire consequences for the economy. Third, some US economists successfully persuaded many Chinese economists who have the ear of Chinese decision makers to believe that Japan's economic bubble was caused by the yen appreciation after the Plaza accord in 1985 and that if China allowed the renminbi to de-peg and appreciate, the Chinese economy would suffer in the same way as Japan has since 1985. Fourth, the US government's open campaign to press China to appreciate the renminbi created great public resentment. To give up the peg would be looked at as bowing to US pressure. Hence, renminbi appreciation, to a certain extent, became a political issue.

Having entered 2005, the economic situation had become more favorable for appreciation: China's exports jumped by 20 percent on the year; the economy grew at a more than 10 percent per annum; house prices were rising rapidly, and China's foreign exchange reserves were approaching US$700 billion. The fear of the deflationary effect of appreciation on the economy receded significantly. At the same time global imbalances were worsening rapidly and international pressure on renminbi appreciation was gathering momentum. The PBOC finally was able to adopt a more flexible exchange rate regime and allow the yuan to appreciate by 2 percent in July 2005.

Because China had been running huge twin surpluses (current account and capital account surpluses), the renminbi has been constantly under appreciation pressure. In order to guide the renminbi to appreciate in a gradual way, the PBOC intervenes in the foreign exchange market constantly. When the PBOC is considering the intensity of intervention, it will take into consideration mainly the following factors:

- macroeconomic situation, especially with regard to growth and inflation;
- long-term adjustment needs;
- trade balance; and
- sterilization ability.

According to the theory of "impossible trinity," it is possible to have only two of the following three things: a fixed exchange rate, free flow of capital, and independence of monetary policy. As a large economy, there is no doubt that China has to maintain the independence of monetary policy. Hence, when it decided to embark on a process of gradual currency appreciation, China had to treat capital account liberalization in a cautious way. Otherwise, cross-border capital flows would destabilize the economy. In fact, the much talked-about excess liquidity since 2006 is partially attributable to the slow appreciation in the face of large twin surpluses.

One of the most important reasons for China to adopt the exchange rate regime of referring to a basket is that a basket peg can create the possibility of two-way movement for the renminbi exchange rate, regardless of what happens to China's international balance-of-payments position. The two-way movement of the exchange rate in turn will create uncertainty for international speculators so as to deter speculative capital inflows. Unfortunately, until the global financial crisis broke out in 2008, the US dollar had been depreciating continuously against all other major currencies. Hence, the renminbi had been appreciating almost uninterruptedly. When the new exchange rate regime fails to deter capital inflows betting on renminbi appreciation, capital control has to play an important role in blocking the inflow of hot money as well as reducing the appreciation pressure on the renminbi.

By and large, China's exchange rate policy has succeeded in allowing the renminbi to appreciate so as to reduce China's external imbalances, while maintaining economic and financial stability. In fact, since 2005 the renminbi has appreciated by more than 30 percent in real terms.

However, the downside of the gradualist approach to renminbi appreciation is also obvious. Gradual appreciation means that the PBOC has to intervene in the foreign exchange market constantly. As a result, China piled up huge foreign exchange reserves. In 2003 when the discussion on the pros and cons of renminbi appreciation was just starting, the amount of China's foreign exchange reserves was some US$400 billion; now it is approaching US$4 trillion, well beyond any reasonable need for China. The bulk of China's foreign exchange reserves are invested in US government securities and other sovereign government bonds. While China is a net creditor to the rest of the world with some US$2 trillion net international investment position, because of its low investment returns vis-à-vis high returns of foreign investment in China, its investment income in 2011 was US$270 billion. This is a reflection of serious misallocation of resources. The situation will become even worse, if the US dollar devalues further in the future. Because China's foreign assets are denominated mostly in the US dollar while its foreign liabilities are denominated mostly in the renminbi, any devaluation of the dollar against the yuan will cause capital losses to China.

Since April 2009, the PBOC started to promote renminbi trade settlement, which is widely regarded as the beginning of renminbi internationalization. The process of renminbi internationalization essentially is a process of capital account liberalization. Thanks to the internationalization, China has de facto opened up short-term cross-border capital movements. Because the liberalization was launched before interest rate and exchange rate liberalization, opportunities for interest rate and foreign exchange rate arbitrage in China's financial markets are abundant. In the future, global capital flows via short-term cross-border capital movements will play an increasingly important role in the determination of the renminbi exchange rate. The PBOC will be left with no choice but to speed up reform of China's financial markets and the liberalization of exchange rate and interest rates. Otherwise, China's ability in macroeconomic management will be seriously weakened.

5 Concluding remarks

Based on the review of the experience of the past twenty years, some basic patterns of China's macroeconomic fluctuations and management can be identified.

First, China's growth in the past two decades is mainly driven by investment. The increase in the growth rate of investment normally will persist until serious overheating occurs. The overheating develops in two stages: GDP grows at a rate higher than potential growth rate first and then inflation worsens.

Second, the correlation between growth and inflation was high, but with unpredictable time lags. Whenever the growth rate of GDP surpasses the potential growth rate, inflation would rise at an accelerating pace several quarters later. Whenever GDP growth slows, inflation will fall with similar time lags. Hence, before prices spin out of control, some preemptive action has to be taken. Similarly, when growth is slowing down, inflation may still be high and even rise further. If the government fails to change policy direction in time, deflation may set in several quarters later.

Third, money does matter in China. Changes in money supply will eventually lead to changes in real GDP and inflation, though with various lags that are difficult to predict.

Fourth, in normal times, to manage the macro economy via changing money supply is superior to credit control. However, because the availability of credit is the most important prerequisite to investment growth and hence GDP growth, in some extreme circumstances, despite side effects, targeting credit and using "moral persuasion" to achieve the credit target is more effective than control through money supply.

Fifth, following the progress in financial liberalization and innovation, it is becoming increasingly difficult for the PBOC to control the broad money M2 with precision and through controlling M2 to influence real output and inflation. Hence, the PBOC needs to shift from targeting monetary aggregates to targeting a market-determined benchmark interest rate in a timely fashion.

Sixth, fiscal policy is very effective in boosting economic growth and overcoming deflation. However, the Chinese government was very cautious in using fiscal policy to stimulate the economy. As a result, it was able to maintain a strong fiscal position, which in turn provided the government with ample room to boost the economy in the face of adversity.

While GDP growth and inflation fluctuate around a long-term growth trend in a cyclical pattern, some fundamental changes have occurred over the past twenty years. First, the share of fixed asset investment in GDP has reached 50 percent. It has become more and more difficult to promote GDP growth by stimulating investment. The same is true of exports. Second, thanks to the frequent use of expansionary monetary policy, the growth rate of broad money has been significantly higher than that of nominal GDP growth for the best part of the past two decades. As a result, China's M2-to-GDP ratio has reached 180 percent, the highest among major economies in the world. This extremely high degree of monetization of the economy implies that it will become increasingly difficult for the PBOC to control the liquidity of the economy via changes in money supply. This is attributable to the fact that the largest component of M2 – household saving deposits – is endogenous. Furthermore, its inflationary implications are also worrying. Third, the strongest point of the Chinese economy in terms of macroeconomic management was – still is – its low public debt-to-GDP ratio. However, complacency is dangerous. China's contingent liabilities in the forms of local government debts and state-owned enterprise debts are high. In the near future, China's fiscal position can worsen quickly, because the room for improving tax collection has been narrowing, potential economic growth is slowing, which of course is a controversial issue at the moment, and public expenditures are likely to rise rapidly.

All in all, one of the most important problems with China's macroeconomic management is that the short-run macroeconomic stability on many occasions is achieved at the expense of the structural adjustment and the rational allocation of resources. China has run down its ammunition gradually. To achieve decent growth and economic stability for the next decade, how to strike a balance between short-run macroeconomic stability and long-run structural adjustment is a big challenge facing China. The recent changes in the supply side of the economy, such as the decrease in the working-age population, have made the challenge even more acute.

Notes

1   Zhao (1994).
2   Rongji Zhu, "Speech at Central Economic Work Conference" (1994).
3   A puzzling phenomenon in 1995 is that while the growth rate of money supply fell rapidly, the growth rate of credits rose precipitately, peaking at 44 percent in June 1996.
4   Genyou (2001).
5   Green (2005).
6   A minor contributing factor to the increase in tax revenues was a result of the expiry of some tax concessions.

Bibliography

Allen, F., Qian, J., and Qian, M. (2007) 'China's Financial System: Past, Present and Future, China's Economic Transition: Origins, Mechanism, and Consequences', edited by L. Brandt and T. Rawski, Cambridge: Cambridge University Press.

Allsopp, C. J. and Vines, D. (2000) 'The Assessment: Macroeconomic Policy', *Oxford Review of Economic Policy*, 16(4).

Blanchard, O. and Giovanni, F. (2005) 'Rebalancing Growth in China: A Three-Handed Approach', MIT Department of Economics, Research Paper Series, MIT Department of Economics Working Paper No. 05–32.

Corden, M. (2006) 'Those Current Account Imbalances: A Skeptical View', Melbourne Institute of Applied Economic and Social Research Working Paper No. 13/06, University of Melbourne.

Chow, G. (2007) *China's Economic Transformation*, 2nd edition, Malden, MA: Wiley-Blackwell.

Genyou, Dai (2001) 'China's Monetary Policy: Retrospect and Prospect', *World Economy and China*, 3: 15.

Green, S. (2005) 'Making Monetary Policy Work in China: A Report from the Money Market Front Line', Working Paper No. 245, July 2005, Stanford University, p. 6.

Humphrey, T. (1979) *Essays on Inflation*, Federal Reserve Bank of Richmond, Library of Congress Catalog Card Number: 79-600183.

Jackman, R., Mulvey, C., and Trevithick, J. (1981) *The Economics of Inflation*, 2nd edition, Oxford: Martin Robertson.

Kwan, C. (2012) 'The Business Cycle in China since the Lehman Crisis', paper prepared for the Macroeconomic Conference, Nomura Foundation November 13, <http://www.nomurafoundation.or.jp/data/20121113_C-H_Kwan.pdf>.

Lardy, N. R. (1998) *China's Unfinished Economic Revolution*, Washington, DC: Brookings Institute Press.

Lardy, N. R. (2012) *Sustaining China's Economic Growth after the Global Financial Crisis*, Washington, DC: Peterson Institute of International Economics.

Liu, P. and Tao, X. (2006) 'The Monetary Policy Transmission in China's "Credit Channel" and Its Limitations', Paper No. 22, February 2006, Working Papers of the Business Institute Berlin at the Berlin School of Economics (FHW-Berlin) Badensche Str. 50–51, D-10825.

Ma, G. and Wang, Y. (2010) 'China's High Saving Rate: Myth and Reality', BIS Working Paper No. 312, June 2010.

McKinnon, R. I. (1991) *The Order of Economic Liberalization: Financial Control in the Transition to a Market Economy*, Baltimore, MD: Johns Hopkins University Press.

McKinnon, R. I. (1998) 'Exchange Rate Coordination for Surmounting the East Asian Currency Crisis', *Asian Economic Journal*, 12(4).

McKinnon, R. I. (2000) 'After the Crisis, the East Asian Dollar Standard Resurrected: An Interpretation of High-Frequency Exchange Rate Pegging', Economic Department, Stanford University.

McKinnon, R. I. and Ohno, K. (1997) *Dollar and Yen*, Cambridge, MA: MIT Press.

Perkins, D. H. (2005) 'China's Recent Economic Performance and Future Prospects', paper prepared for the Inaugural Issue of *Asian Economic Policy Research*, presented at a Japan Economic Research Center Workshop in Tokyo, October 22.

Porter, N. and Xu, T. (2009) 'What Drives China's Interbank Market?', authorized for distribution by Nigel Chalk, September 2009, IMF Working Paper, 09/189.

Taylor, J. (1995) 'The Monetary Transmission Mechanism: An Empirical Framework', *Journal of Economic Perspectives*, 9(4): 11–2.

Wang, S. and Hu, A. (2001) *The Chinese Economy in Crisis: State Capacity and Tax Reform*, New York: M. E. Sharpe, pp. 201–2.

Xie, D. and Yu, D. (1998) 'The development of monetary policy and open market operations in China', unpublished thesis, commissioned by Hong Kong City Polytechnics.

Yi, G. (2008) 'The Monetary Policy Transmission Mechanism in China', *Transmission Mechanisms for Monetary Policy in Emerging Market Economies*, BIS Paper 35, pp.179–81.

Yi, G. and Zhang, L. (1999) *International Finance*, Shanghai: Shanghai People's Publishing House.

Yu, Y. (2000) 'An Analytical Framework for Analyzing China's Fiscal Stability', *World Economy*, June issue (Chinese), Institute of World Economics and Politics, Beijing.

Yu, Y. (2000) 'China's Deflation during the Asian Financial Crisis, and Reform of the International Financial System', *Asian Economic Bulletin*, 17(2): 163–74.

Yu, Y. (2001) 'China's Macroeconomic Outlook', *World Economy and China*, 9(1).

Yu, Y. (2001) 'China's Macroeconomic Management of the Open Economy and China's Accession to the WTO', in Lee, K., Lin. J., and Kim, S. (eds.), *China's Integration with the World Economy: Repercussions of China's Accession to the WTO*, Seoul: Korea Institute for International Economic Policy.

Yu, Y. (2003) 'Overcome the Fear of RMB appreciation', *Review of International Economics*, September–October issue (Chinese), Institute of World Economics and Politics, Beijing.

Yu, Y. (2007) 'Global Imbalances and China', *Australian Economic Review*, 40(1): 1–21.

Yu, Y. (2008) 'Chinese Macroeconomic Management: Issues and Prospect', in Eichengreen, B., Wyplosz, C., and Park, Y. (eds.) *China, Asia, and the New World Economy*, Oxford: Oxford University Press.

Yu, Y. (2009) 'China's Policy Responses to the Global Financial Crisis', Richard Snaper Lecture, 25 November 2000, Australian Government Productivity Commission, Melbourne, and in Shaw, J. and Liu, B. (eds.) (2011) *The Impact of the Economic Crisis on East Asia*, Northampton, MA: Edward Elgar.

Yu, Y. (2011) 'Rebalancing the Chinese Economy', *Economic and Political Weekly*, 46(35).

Yu, Y. D. (1996) 'Macroeconomic Management and Capital Inflows', *World Economy*, October issue (Chinese), Institute of World Economics and Politics, Beijing.

Yu, Y. D. (1997) 'Strategic Thinking on the Accumulation of Foreign Exchange Reserves', *World Economy*, October issue (Chinese), Institute of World Economics and Politics, Beijing.

Yu, Y. D. and Zhang, Y. (1999) 'An Analysis of Monetary Policy and Its Prospect', in Liu, G., Wang. L., and Li, J. (eds.), *Outlook of the Chinese Economy, Spring Blue Book, 2001*, Beijing: Publishing House of Documentation of Social Sciences, 40–62.

Yu, Y., Li, J., and Cong. L. (2001) 'China's Proactive Fiscal Policy', in Liu, G., Wang. L., and Li, J. (eds.), *Outlook of the Chinese Economy, Spring Blue Book, 2001*, Beijing: Publishing House of Documentation of Social Sciences, 15–41.

Zhao, Pieya (1994) 'Real Estate Investment Is Stabilizing', *China Investment*, 9.

10

TRENDS IN INCOME INEQUALITY IN CHINA SINCE THE 1950s

Carl Riskin

China's phenomenal economic growth since 1978 has been matched by an equally impressive increase in economic inequality. As one of the most equal societies in the world in the 1970s, China had become perhaps the most unequal country in Asia by 2010. The official Gini coefficient for 2012 was 0.474 but some unofficial estimates were much higher.

During the "collective era" (1950–78), economic inequality declined because of policies that eliminated private property and squeezed public sector wages into a narrow range. However, different dimensions of inequality behaved quite differently. For instance, policies of local self-sufficiency increased inequalities among localities and enterprises. Additionally, the urban–rural income disparity widened because of urban bias in development policy and the population registration (*hukou*) system.

Post-1978 reforms began in the countryside and reduced the urban–rural gap for several years. Then it widened again to high levels by international comparative standards. However, regional inequality, correctly measured, seems to have increased at first and then fallen back to levels below its starting point.

Since the early years of this century, China's development model has given rise to growing economic imbalances. These are closely linked with the problem of inequality. The central government has been committed to reducing both; it faces, however, resistance from their entrenched beneficiaries.

1 Introduction: how unequal is China?

The fame of the "Chinese miracle" – the very high economic growth rates achieved by China over a period of more than three decades, which have pulled China up from low income status to make it both a middle income country and an industrial powerhouse – is almost matched by the notoriety of its burgeoning inequality. A country that in 1980 was among the world's most equal in terms of income distribution changed to the point that by 2010 it was more unequal than most countries in Asia (Table 10.1).

How great is inequality in China? According to the National Bureau of Statistics, China's Gini coefficient rose to a peak of 0.491 in 2008 and then declined (Figure 10.1) until 2012. Some independent estimates of the Gini range quite a bit higher: the Chinese Household Finance Survey Center of Southwestern University (Chengdu, China) has put it as high as 0.61,

Table 10.1 Income inequality in Asia (2000–2011)

Country	Gini coefficient
Vietnam	0.376
India	0.368
Sri Lanka	0.403
Philippines	0.44
Bangladesh	0.31
Pakistan	0.327
China	0.474

Source: UNDP, *Human Development Report, 2011*
Notes: Except for China, the Gini coefficients are from the most recent year available (2000–11). China's is for 2012, and is taken from Table 10.2, below (see below also for a discussion of the Gini measure of inequality)

which is in a class with the highest Ginis anywhere, those for parts of South America and southern Africa.[1] On the other hand, the China Household Income Project, an ongoing international research project that periodically surveys household income in urban and rural China, has estimated the Gini for 2007 (its most recent survey round) as 0.483, almost identical to the official estimate for that year.[2]

High incomes are well hidden and thus under-sampled in China. If such concealed high incomes could be included, the estimated Gini might rise by as much as four percentage points (Li and Luo 2011). Thus, the "real" Gini for China is a matter of contention or, at least, uncertainty. However, while estimates of its absolute value vary widely, there is widespread agreement that the trend of inequality has been mostly upward since the mid-1980s.

The balance of this chapter discusses the changes in China's income distribution and the roots of these changes in China's development model. We treat economic inequality primarily in terms of income. This is not an inevitable choice: other worthy candidates for attention include, *inter alia*, consumption, education, access to health care and other keys to a better life, and political rights. In the 1950s, for instance, a highly egalitarian income distribution masked

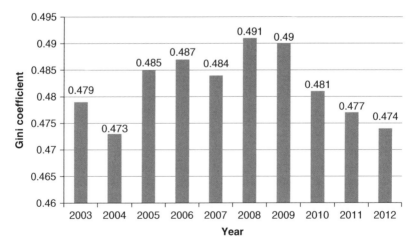

Figure 10.1 Official Gini coefficient estimates for China (2003–2012)

Source: *China Daily USA* (February 1, 2013)

substantial inequalities in political power that produced abusive treatment of ordinary people by government officials or Communist Party cadres. Such political inequality helps to explain the severity of China's 1959–61 famine, which left ordinary people – mainly rural residents – without recourse when misguided policies pushed their food supply below subsistence level. Despite substantial equality in income distribution, then, great inequality in the crucial dimension of political power could be said to have been responsible for millions of famine deaths.

Health care is another component of well-being not adequately represented by income. The World Health Report of the year 2000, the World Health Organization (WHO) focused critically on inequality of health care in China, ranking that country as low as 188 out of 191 countries in "fairness of financial contribution" (India is ranked 42). The report was critical of the fact that Chinese paid 75 percent of health care expenses privately out of pocket. China was also ranked 144 in overall health system performance, well below India's rank of 112. Yet China's rank for health *status* was 81 (India, 134) and for distribution of health, 101 (India, 153). How did China's unfair and low performing health system somehow manage to produce a much healthier population than that of other countries with fairer and better performing systems? There are undoubtedly inequities and inefficiencies in the Chinese health care system, but these may have been overstated in the World Health Report, at least in international comparative terms.

2 Measurement issues

The degree of inequality of income distribution is conventionally measured in several ways. The Gini coefficient is the most common measure. It is a single number summary of the Lorenz Curve, which maps the entire distribution of something over all individuals in the population that have it (if it's a stock) or receive it (if a flow). A chief virtue of the Gini coefficient is that it conveys an intuitive idea of the extent of inequality: the Gini ranges from zero (for total equality of distribution) to one (total inequality). A country with a Gini of 0.25 has relative income equality, while one whose Gini is 0.6 is quite unequal. Also, the Gini is a very widely used measure for China as well as other countries, which facilitates international comparisons. It has a few disadvantages as well: one such disadvantage is the potential for ambiguity, in that it is possible for different Lorenz curves to intersect and two different distributions could thus yield the same Gini coefficient. Moreover, the Gini for a population cannot be directly broken down into Ginis for its constituent parts (say, states or provinces), nor can those of its parts be aggregated to get that of the whole. However, it can be indirectly broken down because of its property that $G = \Sigma r_i\, C_i$, where G is the Gini coefficient of total income (for instance); r_i is the ratio of the ith source of income (e.g. wage income) to total income; and C_i is the concentration ratio, or "pseudo-Gini coefficient" of that income source. The concentration ratio measures the distribution of a particular income source over its recipients ranked by their *total* income, not by their income from only that source.[3]

Another common measure of inequality is the Theil indexes, instances of a general entropy (GE) index. "Entropy" here refers to the non-randomness of data. Inequality of something's distribution implies that it is not randomly distributed over a population but is concentrated in a non-random way. The general entropy index includes a parameter, α, which measures the sensitivity of the index to changes in income in different parts of the distribution. When $\alpha = 1$, the sensitivity is the same throughout the distribution, and this yields the Theil T index:

$$GE(\alpha) = \frac{1}{N} \sum_{i=1}^{N} \left[\frac{y_i}{\bar{y}} \ln\left(\frac{y_i}{\bar{y}} \right) \right], \qquad \text{for } \alpha = 1$$

Where N is the size of the population, y_i is per capita income, and $\bar{y}$ is mean per capita income. The Theil L index is the GE index when $\alpha = 0$, which is more sensitive to changes in the lower income region of the distribution.[4]

The Theil indexes have different advantages and disadvantages than the Gini coefficient. Their chief attraction is that they can be broken down directly, allowing one to distinguish how much of total inequality in a population derives from inequality between its sub-groups and how much derives from inequality within those sub-groups. On the other hand, it is not as intuitive as the Gini index: a Theil index value does not immediately signal a high, low or average degree of inequality in a particular population.

To gauge inter-regional income inequality, a good, common, and easily calculated measure is the coefficient of variation of the regional means of income per capita (CV, equal to the standard deviation of regional mean incomes divided by their mean). Of course, this measure ignores inequality within each region (which in China contributes the great bulk of total inequality), being concerned only with dispersion of the regional means. For China, special care must also be taken as to how income per capita is measured. That is because of China's household registration (*hukou*) system, which assigns every household a particular location. If people move to another place, their *hukou* usually does not move with them. Therefore, in an age of large-scale migration, the registered population of a place may differ considerably from the actual resident population. More about this below.

3 The collective era

If we divide the decades since 1949 into two segments – the collective era, 1950–78, and the reform era since 1979, then it is fair to say that the first segment was marked by falling income inequality and the second by rising inequality (although the second began with a burst of equalizing changes, see below). Rising equality in the first period followed from the drastic socioeconomic changes that were implemented by the government, led by the Communist Party. These changes leveled income inequalities by eliminating most forms of private property. In the countryside, private ownership of land and capital disappeared by the mid-to-late 1950s, as China went from small peasant farming to large agricultural collectives and then "communes" within a few short years, and the income inequality associated with the distribution of property ownership disappeared with it. In urban China, as well, private enterprise was eliminated by 1957, with former owners transformed into rentiers who received interest payments on their appropriated property for several years until these lapsed in 1966.

The majority of urban residents worked for wages whose structure was set by the state to embody only small differentials. Mao Zedong's view of socialism did not favor individualism but rather the constant promotion of collective effort and solidarity within farms and factories, a position that generally implied reduced differentials in individual incomes within work units. During the "Great Leap Forward" (1958–60) and "Cultural Revolution decade" (1966–76), when material incentives were distinctly out of favor, workers went for years with no increase in pay. Those at the top of the wage scale eventually retired, while those at the bottom were not promoted, causing the distribution of wages to be increasingly truncated. By the late 1970s, China had one of the world's most egalitarian income distributions. Yet the aversion to income inequality applied mainly to distribution within local institutions, such as production teams (consisting of neighborhoods within villages) or factories. Distribution among such units, however, was a different story. As Mao repeatedly weakened the central planning system with assaults on bureaucratism, urban hegemony and the "bourgeoisie" of educated intellectuals, China of necessity devolved into a relatively "self-reliant" structure of quasi-autonomous localities and enterprises.

Substantial differences in income could and did exist among these. Within the countryside, for instance, prosperous villages with fertile, irrigated land, and easy access to urban markets coexisted with poor, remote, and upland ones. Such differentials were based on what economists would consider "rents," i.e. arbitrary differences in locational characteristics that affect the returns to local resources without providing incentives to work hard, be efficient, acquire skills or exercise entrepreneurship. Such incentives were notably lacking at the end of the collective era.

Another glaring exception to the general egalitarianism of the time was China's urban–rural income disparity, which was even then quite large compared to that of other developing countries. This is because of two basic and closely related aspects of the Chinese Communist Party and government polices: first, socioeconomic institutions and national development plans were both biased toward urban areas and neglectful of the rural majority of the population. For instance, urban workers and their families enjoyed cradle-to-grave access to many social benefits, including guaranteed employment, subsidized housing, medical care, and education for their children, none of which was available to rural residents. The great bulk of investment spending under the Five-Year Plans was also aimed at urban industry, and very little went to agriculture. As a result, capital accumulation proceeded rapidly in industry, continuously raising labor productivity. By the late 1970s, the ratio of output per worker in industry to that in agriculture had grown to about 8:1, from only about 2.5:1 in the early 1950s. Such wide productivity differentials were bound to be reflected eventually in urban–rural differences in personal incomes.

Second, the imposition of the household registration (*hukou*) system in the 1950s built a wall separating urban and rural populations. Those with a rural *hukou* were prohibited from moving to urban areas. This sanction was reinforced by the rationing of food: even if a farmer evaded the prohibition and reached a city in search of a better job (s)he would have no means to acquire food. Without such a constraint, many rural–urban migrants would have taken marginal urban jobs that paid far more than their farming incomes, even if less than the wages of full-status urban residents, and this would have brought down average urban incomes. Moreover, the outflow of labor from agriculture would also have raised rural incomes (in areas with surplus labor, the marginal product of rural labor had fallen below the average product). With lower urban and higher rural incomes, the urban–rural gap – or at least its rate of growth – would have declined. The *hukou* system effectively blocked the labor mobility that would otherwise have countered the constant increase in urban–rural inequality.

Ironically, one of Mao Zedong's principal objectives was to reduce the "three great differences" – namely, those between mental and manual labor, worker and peasant, and town and countryside – two of which directly reflect the urban–rural income gap. This goal became a much repeated admonishment of Mao's last decade, and he took heroic measures to bring it about, most famously by uprooting urban health care facilities during the Cultural Revolution and moving them out to rural areas to serve the needs of peasants. Despite such measures, the urban–rural gap continued to grow. Official statistics for consumption per capita indicate that the relative advantage of the urban over the rural population increased by 27 percent from 1952 to 1975 (Table 10.2). Even during the Cultural Revolution decade – when efforts to reduce it were at their height – it increased by 7.6 percent. Thus, throughout the pre-reform collective era, the income advantage of being a city resident grew. As to the absolute size of the income differential between urban and rural residents, estimates for the late 1970s range from the World Bank's 2.2:1, excluding all subsidies, up to Thomas Rawski's 5.9:1, which includes the value of urban subsidies in urban income (World Bank 1983; Rawski 1982).

In sum, the "collective period" of China's recent economic history, ending in the late 1970s, was characterized by declining inequality of income distribution except for that between urban

Table 10.2 Index of the ratio of urban to rural consumption per capita

Year	Index
1952	100
1957	108
1965	118
1975	127

Source: Riskin (1987: 241)

and rural populations, which grew substantially despite vigorously expressed ideological objections to it by Mao Zedong, and equally vigorous efforts to reduce it. The reason for this is the structure of institutions and policies put in place in the 1950s, which privileged the nonagricultural economy and urban dwellers while walling off the rural population from the possibility of entering the privileged sectors through migration.

4 The reform era: the urban–rural gap

In late 1978 China began the process of economic reform and transition from a weak and decentralized form of central planning to a still evolving combination of market economy with substantial state involvement. The initial stage of this transformation was a basic agrarian reform: dissolution of the rural people's communes during the first few years of the 1980s and their replacement by family farming, abandonment of the previous insistence upon local self-sufficiency in grain production in favor of the encouragement of diversification and the division of labor; and sharp increases in the prices paid to farmers for grain, cotton, and subsidiary crops. Farm output responded with rapid growth and a shift of resources from low value crops into higher value products (poultry, eggs, fish, pork, fruits, and vegetables, etc.). Together, higher farm prices, increasing output, and higher value products produced a dramatic increase in farm incomes: average per capita real net income of the rural population more than doubled from 1978 to 1984 and, for the first and only time in the history of the People's Republic, rural per capita incomes grew faster than urban. The official household surveys found that rural income grew by 98 percent from 1978 to 1983, compared to a 47 percent increase in urban income (Riskin 1987: 292–3). Since the farmers were universally poor relative to the urban population, their faster income growth reduced the urban–rural disparity. Ironically, therefore, the era of reform and transition that was to greatly widen income disparities – began by doing the opposite.

By 1985, however, the boom in farm output and incomes had ended. The growth potential from redirecting resources into higher value production and from exploiting farmland capital construction done in the past had been exhausted. Moreover, farm prices stopped rising and various institutional changes reduced production incentives facing farmers (Sicular 1988). Agricultural output and incomes essentially stagnated through the second half of the 1980s (Table 10.3). Yet, real GDP grew by an average annual rate of 9.86 percent between 1984 and 1989, while industrial output increased by 134 percent over those five years. The urban–rural income gap may now have widened once again. The late 1980s were also marked by the Tiananmen crisis of 1989, which severely affected the urban economy. Official survey figures for urban disposable income and rural net income show the gap between them widening from

Table 10.3 Food grain production (1984–1989)

Year	Millions of metric tons
1984	407.3
1985	379.1
1986	391.5
1987	403.0
1988	394.1
1989	407.5

1.86 in 1985 to 2.2 in 1990.[5] But these figures are flawed in several respects, especially in leaving out urban subsidies, which biases the ratio downward, but also in not correcting for urban–rural price differences, which biases it upward.

From 1988 to 1995, the State Statistical Bureau (SSB, as China's National Bureau of Statistics was then called) showed the urban–rural gap increasing from 2.19 to 2.63 (in 1988 prices). However, independent estimates for those years tell a different story, namely, that the gap remained basically the same, measuring 2.42 in 1988 and 2.38 in 1995.[6]

From the mid 1990s, the urban–rural disparity was influenced by new forces, especially the reform of state-owned enterprises (SOEs), which resulted in a 30 percent reduction in public enterprise employment (SOEs and collective enterprises). Altogether, urban public enterprises shed about 50 million workers between 1993 and the end of the decade. These laid-off workers were treated in a variety of ways: some received modest maintenance stipends from their former enterprises or from reemployment centers established by local governments. Others were prematurely retired or found jobs in the informal sector. It is safe to say that few if any avoided a substantial cut in their former incomes. The negative impact of all this on the growth of average urban incomes restrained the increase in the urban–rural gap. Independent estimates of this gap, in constant prices corrected for urban–rural price differences, show the gap growing very little between 1995, when it was 2.24, and 2002, when it was 2.27 (Sicular *et al.* 2008). However, that slowdown was a temporary byproduct of the SOE reform, and the gap resumed its upward trend when the restructuring had largely concluded, widening more than 20 percent to 2.91 in 2007 (Li *et al.* 2011).[7] However one measures it, the urban–rural income gap in China remains unusually wide by international comparative standards (Knight *et al.* 2006).

Why is China's urban–rural income disparity so large in international comparative context? China is by no means the only developing country to have adopted strongly urban-biased policies favoring cities over countryside.[8] However, China went farther than other developing countries in adopting a system of population movement control – the *hukou* system – which placed a high wall between urban and rural China and kept the poorer rural residents from sharing in the benefits of fast economic growth. Still, the great variation in estimates of urban–rural disparity that comes from the choice of precise methods of measurement constitutes a warning: when making international comparisons of income inequality, the results are likely to reflect to some degree differences in measurement methods (e.g. whether regional living costs are taken into account and how rural–urban migrants are treated) rather than differences in inequality.

5 Regional inequality

In China, regional inequality refers to differences among the thirty-one provinces and province-level units (including four large municipalities and five autonomous regions – the two "special administrative regions' of Hong Kong and Macao are usually omitted because of their special circumstances). Like many large developing countries, China contains substantial regional differences in income and development level. In 2010, Shanghai's average urban disposable income of 31,838 renminbi was over twice as high as that of Guizhou (14,142 renminbi), while its average rural income exceeded Guizhou's by more than four times.[9] Similar differences occur in social indicators, such as infant mortality and literacy rates (Fan *et al.* 2011). The fact that industrial development after 1978 was centered in the already more industrialized eastern coastal regions constitutes a prima facie reason to believe that the regional distribution of income became more unequal over time, at least in the earlier stages of the reform period. There was evidence that, while the per capita incomes of all the provinces might have been converging somewhat, the eastern, western and central groups of provinces were growing apart.[10] The CHIP project found evidence of overall convergence of regional income per capita by 2002 (Gustafsson *et al.* 2008). For 2007, they divided their sample into four regional groups: (1) large, province-level metropolitan cities; (2) the eastern region; (3) the central region; and (4) the western region.[11] In calculating provincial per capita incomes, they also used prices that reflected differences in cost of living among the regions ("purchasing power parity" or PPP prices). Since cost of living is considerably higher in the richer regions, the use of PPP prices brought about a sharp decline in measured inequality among the regions.

As shown in Table 10.4, there were small increases in regional inequality between 2002 and 2007. A considerable part of regional inequality, however, is due to urban–rural inequality; in general, inequality within regions accounts for most national inequality, and that between regions for less than 12 percent of overall inequality (Li, Luo, and Sicular, 2011).

The significance of regional inequality is further reduced by considering the distorting effect of migration on the measures of regional distribution. We noted above that the regional distribution of actual resident population differs considerably from that of official, registered population, due to the population registration (*hukou*) system. Thus, the city of Shenzhen had a registered population in the year 2000 of one million but an actual population of seven million (Drysdale 2012), while the poor western province of Guizhou had a registered population of 41.9 million in 2010, a 20 percent overstatement of its actual resident population of only 34.8 million (Li and Gibson 2012). If regional inequality is measured using regional per capita income based on registered population, the figures for poor Guizhou will be underestimated while those for rich Shenzhen will be overestimated, thus greatly exaggerating the gap between them. The CHIP estimates discussed above are not prone to this error as they are based on income surveys, but a large number of studies of regional inequality have used GDP per capita as their main indicator.[12] This is sometimes a useful way of defining regional inequality, but if differences in individual well-being are the objective, then personal disposable income, rather than GDP per capita, is the better unit of analysis, especially in China, where household incomes are an uncommonly low fraction of GDP.

Using regional GDP per capita but correcting for the use of registered instead of resident population, Chan and Wang (2008) find that regional income disparities rose significantly in the

Table 10.4 Regional income gaps

	2002	2007
Large cities	2.34	2.44
Eastern	1.65	1.74
Central	1.12	1.16
Western	1	1

early 1990s but remained quite stable thereafter, as one indeed might expect from the increasing role of long distance migration. A more recent correction along the same lines, Li and Gibson (2012) cast light on the entire period since the beginning of the reform era in 1978 up until 2010. They find that, properly measured, regional inequality (in terms of GDP per capita) fell for a decade after the reforms began; rose in the early 1990s; and fluctuated thereafter, such that by 2010 it was back to the low levels of 1990 and below the starting point of 1978. By this measure, then, there has been no long-term upward trend of regional inequality. However, it needs to be remembered that GDP is not a good indicator of well-being (nor is it intended to be one), and that other studies, such as the CHIP project, that focus on household income, have indeed found significant increases in such inequality.

6 Conclusion: inequality and imbalance

There is a widespread consensus that China's economy became highly unbalanced after the turn of the century in a number of ways: excessive dependence on exports, a high savings rate, heavy manufacturing, large state enterprise monopolies, an under-valued currency, and financial repression (interest rates held below their market value); insufficient domestic consumption demand, services, and labor-intensive small and medium enterprises. Income inequality is closely linked with such imbalances, which have constrained household income relative to corporate and government income, labor incomes relative to those derived from profits, and disfavored poorer interior regions relative to richer coastal ones. The Chinese government, concerned about the potential impact of both imbalance and growing income disparities upon social stability, has tried since the early 2000s to reformulate its approach to development to make it more equitable and pro-poor, more focused on the rural interior and more sensitive to environmental protection, *inter alia*. Large quantities of central government funding have been spent on improving rural education and public health and providing a safety net for both urban and rural populations. Yet, despite real advances in the well-being of the population as a whole, the vested interests that have grown out of the unbalanced economy – coastal provinces, heavy manufacturing industries, export industries, the banking system, etc. – are powerful and, as of this writing, the central government has not been able, despite over a decade of dedicated effort, to alter China's unbalanced development model.

At the same time, over thirty years of hyper-growth has finally begun to use up the huge labor surplus with which China began the reform era in the late 1970s. A model in which growth brings upward pressure on wages is more consistent with rebalancing objectives than a surplus labor model giving labor no real bargaining power. A crucial question, moving through the second decade of the twenty-first century, is whether this change in objective conditions, together with the progressive inclinations of China's central leaders, is enough to bring about a more equitable development model in the face of the vast inequalities that mark Chinese society.

Notes

1 This figure, for the year 2010, was reported in <http://english.caixin.com/2012-12-10/100470648. html>.
2 CHIP's sample households are taken from the larger sample used by the National Bureau of Statistics, so it is perhaps not surprising that their results are similar. However, CHIP uses a definition of income that is closer to international standard practice than the official one. Also, as will be shown below, the CHIP Gini estimate declines considerably when regional price differences are accounted for.
3 The latter would produce the true Gini coefficient for that income source.

4 A good discussion of the different common measures of inequality can be found in the World Bank's *Poverty Manual*, ch. 6, available at <http://siteresources.worldbank.org/PGLP/Resources/PMch6.pdf>, accessed January 14, 2013.

5 See table for "Per Capita Annual Income and Expenditure Urban and Rural Household", All China Data Center, at <http://www.chinadataonline.com/member/macroy/macroytshow.asp?code=A0501>, accessed January 14, 2013.

6 See Azizur Rahman Khan and Riskin (2001: 44–5). This report on the China Household Income Survey (CHIP) project, which commissioned surveys of rural and urban incomes in 1988 and 1995 (and later for 2002 and 2007), finds that the SSB understated the urban–rural disparity in 1988 and overstated it in 1995. Many but not all subsidies were included in CHIP's definition of income, unlike in SSB's definition. Neither one completely corrected for urban–rural differences in cost of living, although the CHIP study corrected for *changes* in those costs between 1988 and 1995.

7 These estimates correct for differences in prices between urban and rural areas and among provinces, but not for the migrant population living in cities. Additional adjustment for this further reduces the urban–rural gap by a small amount. See Sicular *et al.* (2008) and Li *et al.* (2011).

8 See the classic treatment of this topic, Lipton (1977).

9 These data are from China's National Bureau of Statistics and are available to consortium members at <http://www.chinadataonline.com/>.

10 This implies that convergence within these groupings exceeded their divergence from each other.

11 CHIP sample sizes tend to be too small at the province level to make meaningful inferences, so grouping the provinces in this way has statistical benefits as well as reflecting a common classification in China.

12 For a list of some of these, see table 2 in Li and Gibson (2012). The CHIP data for 1988 and 1995 lack information about migrants, while the 2002 and 2007 rounds included migrant surveys.

Bibliography

Carter, C. A. (1997) 'The Urban–Rural Income Gap in China: Implications for Global Food Markets', *American Journal of Agricultural Economics*, 79(5): 1410–18.

Chan, K. W. and Wang, M. (2008) 'Remapping China's Regional Inequalities, 1990–2006: A New Assessment of de facto and de jure Population Data', *Eurasian Geography and Economics*, 49(1): 21–56.

Drysdale, P. (2012) 'Chinese Regional Income Inequality', *East Asia Forum*.

Eastwood, R. and Lipton, M. (2004) 'Rural and Urban Income Inequality and Poverty: Does Convergence between Sectors Offset Divergence within Them?', in *Inequality, Growth and Poverty in an Era of Liberalization and Globalization*, G. A. Cornia (ed.), Oxford: Oxford University Press.

Fan, S., Kanbur, R., and Zhang, X. (2011) 'China's Regional Disparities: Experience and Policy', *Review of Development Finance*, (1): 47–56.

Fang, X. and Yu, L. (2012) 'Government Refuses to Release Gini Coefficient', *Caixin* (China Economy and Finance) <http://english.caixin.com/2012-01-18/100349814.html>, accessed January 14, 2013.

Gustafsson, B., Li, S., and Sicular, T. (eds.) (2008) *Inequality and Public Policy in China*, New York: Cambridge University Press.

Khan, A. R. and Riskin, C. (2001) *Inequality and Poverty in China in the Age of Globalization*, Oxford: Oxford University Press.

Khan, A. R. and Riskin, C. (2005) 'China's Household Income and Its Distribution, 1995 and 2002', *China Quarterly*, June.

Knight, J., Li, S., and Song, L. (2006) 'The Rural–Urban Divide and the Evolution of Political Economy in China', in Boyce, J. K., Cullenberg, S., Pattanaik, P. K., and Pollin, S. (eds.), *Human Development in the Era of Globalization: Essays in Honor of Keith B. Griffin*, Cheltenham, UK: Edward Elgar.

Li, C. and Gibson, J. (2012) 'Rising Regional Income Inequality in China: Fact or Artefact?', University of Waikato Working Papers in Economics, September.

Li, S. and Luo, C. (2011) '*Zhongguo shouru chaju jiujing you duo da*? (How Unequal is China?)' *Jingji Yanjiu*, (4): 68–78.

Li, S., Luo, C., and Sicular, T. (2011) 'Overview: Income Inequality and Poverty in China, 2002–2007', CIBC Working Paper Series, University of Western Ontario (2011–10).

Lipton, M. (1977) *Why Poor People Stay Poor: Urban Bias in World Development*, London: Maurice Temple Smith.

Rawski, T. G. (1982) 'The Simple Arithmetic of Chinese Income Distribution', *Keizai Kenkyu*, 22, 1.

Riskin, C. (1987) *China's Political Economy: The Quest for Development since 1949*, Oxford: Oxford University Press.

Sicular, T. (1988) 'Agricultural Planning and Pricing in the Post-Mao Period', *China Quarterly*, (116): 671–705.

Sicular, T., Yue, X., and Gustafsson, B. (2008) 'The Urban–Rural Gap and Income Inequality', in G. Wan (ed.), *Understanding Inequality and Poverty in China: Methods and Applications*, Basingstoke, Hants.: Palgrave Macmillan.

UNDP (2011) *Human Development Report, 2011*, New York: Oxford University Press.

Wei, T. (2013) 'Index shows wealth gap at alarming level', *China Daily USA*, updated 01/19/2013, at <http://usa.chinadaily.com.cn/business/2013–01/19/content_16142627_2.htm>, accessed on February 1, 2013.

Whyte, M. K. (2009) *Myth of the Social Volcano: Perceptions of Inequality and Distributive Injustice in Contemporary China*, Stanford, CA: Stanford University Press.

Wong, C. (2010) 'Paying for the Harmonious Society', *China Economic Quarterly*, June.

World Bank (1983) *China: Socialist Economic Development*, Washington, DC: World Bank, Annex A, p. 275.

11

CHINA'S AGRICULTURE

Past failures, present successes and enabling policies

Jikun Huang and Scott Rozelle

Introduction

In the first part of this chapter we will document the performance of China's agricultural sector over the past five to six decades. Specifically, we will examine the rises in output, productivity and efficiency for both the Socialist era, 1950–78, and for the reform era, 1978 to the present. In the second part of the chapter, we intend to go beyond describing the successes and failures of China's agricultural economy. We also aim to identify the factors that have induced the performance that we observe. Specifically, we seek to point out both policies that have facilitated the performance of the agricultural sector and those that have constrained it.

1 Agriculture in China's pre-reform era: policy failure

The record on the performance of agriculture in producing food and other raw materials for industry during the Socialist period is mixed. Overall trends demonstrate that the agricultural sector was key in raising the supply of food, especially that of grains. Although total sown area increased by 6.3 percent, between 1952 and 1978 grain sown area remained constant. Yields, however, rose by 91 percent from 1952 to 1978. In the aggregate, grain output in China rose by more than 2.5 percent per year. The growth rate of grain production rose slightly faster than the growth rate of the population (1.9 percent). In this dimension China's agricultural sector increased the number of per capita calorie availability during the Socialist period.

While China's leaders were successful in maintaining the levels of food availability, the record of China during the Socialist period was not transformative. Between 1950 to 1980 the population remained on rationed diets. In most parts of the country, food was limited to staple grains. Other products were severely limited.

The food production systems also experienced catastrophic failure. The most notable episode was the famine of the late 1950s and early 1960s (Aston *et al.*, 1984). During these years, more than 30 million people starved to death. And, while there were different sources for the famine, crop failures and the absence of sufficient food supplies (due to other reasons such as poor incentives for producers and marketers) were in part to blame (Chang and Wen, 1997).

Other measures of performance almost all point to the failure of China's farming economy during the 1950s, 1960s and 1970s. For example, rural income per capita was stagnant. Rural income of the average family in the 1970s was almost the same as in the 1950s (Lardy, 1983). The absolute levels of consumption for most types of food commodities in 1978 were low – only 1.1 kilograms of oil and 6.4 kilograms of meat per year. There also was little increase in the quantity or quality of housing. The rates of poverty (measured as the share of the rural population living at less than US$1 per day) were nearly 40 percent.

There are also reasons to believe the productivity growth was almost non-existent. Using the data sources that are available, Stone and Rozelle (1995) and Wen (1993) come to the same conclusion. The authors show that the agricultural sector's total factor productivity (TFP) growth during the 1950s, 1960s and 1970s was close to zero.

The Socialist period also experienced many policy changes. After the conclusion of the civil war, in the late 1940s officials implemented a comprehensive land reform (Perkins, 1994). Taking land mostly from landlords and rich farmers – sometimes by violence and almost never with compensation – land was divided among all of China's rural households. With few exceptions every rural household in China was endowed with farmland.

While there is no real research linking changes in output in the early 1950s to the incentives that were embodied in the new land-holding arrangements, even if there had been, any effect would have quickly disappeared. By the mid-1950s the Socialist leadership was already taking actions that dampened the incentives embodied in private land ownership (Lardy, 1983). As early as 1953 and 1954 officials began to organize farmers into collectives. In the mid-1950s, collectives were merged into communes. Such actions largely eliminated the household farm in China.

Shortly after the shift to communes (actions that were accompanied by a number of other radical policies), China's agriculture suffered a huge negative shock (Lardy, 1983; Aston *et al.*, 1984). Output fell in almost all provinces. Famine broke out in many parts of the country.

While there is still debate about the relative importance of different factors which triggered the famine, there is mostly agreement that the communization movement and its absence of incentives is one of the main causes of the large falls in output during the late 1950s and early 1960s (Putterman, 1993). The basic problem was that individual families were not the residual claimant of production and decision-making was left to the collective leadership that was not doing all of the work. The failure to raise productivity during the Socialist era is almost certainly due to the poor incentives that were embodied in the collectivized farming institutions.

The Socialist leadership's food-pricing strategy also did not encourage efficient production or allocation of goods and services. Officials set prices by regulation (Sicular, 1988b). During the 1960s and 1970s, grain prices were almost unchanged. Input and output (grain) prices played mainly an accounting function; shortages were widespread.

There were also almost no markets of exchange during the 1950s, 1960s and 1970s. State marketing/procurement organizations did not encourage the sale of agricultural commodities for profit. In addition, there was little competition. Procurement officials did not have an incentive to search out low-cost or high-quality producers (Sicular, 1988a; Huang and David, 1995). The procurement and transport of agricultural products became monopolized by the state by the mid-1950s.

The absence of pricing signals and active marketing agents meant that the state was responsible for setting supply and demand targets. Specifically, output levels were not determined by agents that were responding to pricing signals. Instead, production volumes were being set by planners who determined target acreage and output volumes. To suppress the demand for agricultural products that were in short supply (and priced low), marketing/procurement policy officials also exercised tight control over food sales and distribution in urban areas. Coupons were distributed on a per capita basis and food was sold and rationed through urban grain stores.

In short, after three decades of Socialism, China's farm economy was rigid, in disarray and underperforming. On the one hand, production was up. The increase in output was in no small part due to state-led investment that was provided by taxing the labor of farmers (forcing farmers to provide labor without compensation). On the other hand, productivity was flat; rural incomes were not increasing. The organization of production, the nation's system of pricing and its marketing institutions provided no incentives. There was no structural transformation.

2 Agriculture in China's transition era

The underperformance of agriculture in the pre-reform period (1950–78) disappeared after the onset of the reforms (China's National Bureau of Statistics (CNBS)). Regardless of how success was measured, after 1978 agriculture finally began to contribute to the nation's economic development. During the first six years of reform (1978–84), the annual growth rate of agricultural production (as measured by GVAO – or the Gross Value of Agricultural Output) nearly tripled to 7.1 percent. Although during the later time periods the average annual growth rate fell to 3.8 percent in 1985–2000 and 4.4 percent in 2000–10, by international standards, these sustained rates of growth are high.

Growth was experienced in all sectors of China's farming economy (CNBS). Between 1978 and 1984, grain production, in general, increased by 4.7 percent per year. Production rose for each of the major grains. While sown area did not rise, grain yields more than doubled. Between 1978 and 1984, the growth of grain yields exceeded the growth of yields during the early and mid-1970s.

Far more fundamental than rises in the output and yields of the grain sector, during the reform era (1978 to the present) China's agricultural economy has been steadily remaking itself from a grain-first sector to one that is producing higher valued cash crops, horticultural goods and livestock/aquaculture products. Like the grain sector, cash crops, in general, and specific crops, such as cotton, edible oils and vegetables and fruit, also grew rapidly in the during the entire reform period when compared to the 1970s (CNBS).

China also moved rapidly away from a crop-first agriculture during the 1980s and 1990s (CNBS). The rise of livestock and fishery sectors outpaced the cropping sector, in general, and most of the subcategories of cropping. Livestock production rose 9.1 percent per year in the early reform period and has continued to grow at between 6.5 to 8.8 percent annually since 1985. The fisheries subsector has been the fastest growing component of agriculture, rising more than 10 percent per year during the reform era.

The reform era brought even more fundamental, transformative changes to the rural economy (when rural is defined more broadly than agriculture). While the annual growth of agriculture (as seen above) averaged nearly 5 percent throughout the entire reform period, the growth rate of the economy, as a whole, and the growth rates of industry and the service sector were even faster. In fact, since 1985, the growth of industry and the service sector has been two to three times faster than agriculture. Because of the differences in the sectoral growth rates, agriculture's share of GDP has fallen from 40 percent in 1970 to 15 percent in 2000. In 2012 agriculture's share of the economy fell to under 10 percent. These figures clearly show that one of the ironic features of successful agricultural development has appeared in China. The key role that agriculture has played in the transformation of the economy has meant that its importance has fallen.

2.1 Other changes

The nature of China's agriculture has been affected dramatically by the opening of the agricultural sector's external economy (Huang and Chen, 1999). As early as the 1980s and early 1990s,

China began turning itself from a hermit country into one of the world's great trading nations. This opening has also had an effect on agricultural trade. From 1980 to 2000, the total value of China's agricultural trade grew by about 6.0 percent on an annual basis (CNBS). Since 2000, it has more than doubled, making China one of the largest importers of agricultural commodities in the world. However, China is more than an importer. Until 2003, the level of agricultural exports exceeded that of imports (CNBS, 2010). Over the past decade, food exports have been growing faster than imports, but, in 2010 China still was largely self-sufficient (97 percent) in food (including processed food).

In addition to the rise of the overall volume of trade, China has experienced a sharp change in the composition of agricultural trade over the reform period. The net export of *land-intensive bulk commodities*, such as grains, oilseeds and sugar crops, has fallen (Anderson *et al.*, 2004). At the same time, the export of higher-valued, more *labor-intensive products*, such as horticultural and animal products (including aquaculture) has risen.

In today's China (after more than thirty years of reform) one of the most striking differences in the nature of agriculture is the role being played by central government officials and local leaders in the production and marketing process. In the years immediately after reform, there was some reduction in the role of the state. During those early years, however, perhaps more than anything, the government continued to be involved with farm production and marketing (Sicular, 1988b, 1995). Things changed, however, in the late 1980s and 1990s. The state gradually, but steadily, reduced its role and allowed markets and private agents to take over. By the 2000s the situation had changed dramatically. Indeed, one of the most notable features of China's agricultural economy today (with several exceptions) is the absence of government involvement in the day to day transactions that define agricultural investment, production, marketing and consumption.

Two of this open economy's most prominent features – even after thirty years of reform – are that farms are run by the household and that farms are still small. Between 1980 and 2000, the average size of land controlled by the household fell from 0.70 to 0.55 hectares. Although average farm size has gradually increased recently, the average farm in rural China was only about 0.75 of a hectare in 2010.

Moreover, there has been little movement in the effort to organize the small farms into larger cooperative organizations. While the rate of growth of production and marketing cooperatives (called Farmer's Professional Associations – FPAs) has risen in recent years, only about 20 percent of China's villages had FPAs in 2008 (Deng *et al.*, 2010). Only 10 percent of farmers belong to any FPA. Such a level of participation means that the prevalence of cooperatives in China is far below that of almost all other East Asian nations and many Western nations (where participation rates were almost 100 percent).

Because of this (and other policies – discussed below), China today may have one of the least distorted domestic agricultural economies in the world, made up of tens of millions of small farms. In a recent survey done by the Center for Chinese Agricultural Policy, in nearly 100 percent of the responses, farmers said that they made the planting decision and were not compelled in any way by local officials (Rozelle *et al.*, 2006). In another survey of randomly selected households in eight provinces, every farmer in the survey stated that they purchased all of their chemical fertilizer on their own and that local officials had no role in the transaction (Zhang *et al.*, 2005). All purchases were made from private vendors. On the procurement side, whereas it used to be that government state-run procurement agencies were responsible for purchasing the output of China's farms, today, a large majority of sales of grains and oilseeds and fiber crops and literally all purchases of horticulture and livestock products are to small, private traders (Wang *et al.*, 2009).

China's markets epitomize the laissez faire nature of the farm economy (Rozelle *et al.*, 2000). There are millions of small traders. In most markets they compete among each another with no regulation. This level of competition has produced agricultural commodity markets that have been shown to be highly integrated and efficient. Park *et al.* (2002), Huang *et al.* (2004) and Rozelle and Huang (2004, 2005) find that output prices are integrated across regional markets at rates that meet or exceed those of the United States. Fertilizer prices are also integrated across provinces (Qiao *et al.*, 2003).

2.2 Productivity trends and rural incomes

While it is possible that agricultural productivity trends during the reform era differ from those of output (as was the case during the pre-reform period), this is not the case in the past three decades. As discussed above, since the early 1980s output and output per unit of land (or yields) both rose sharply. In addition, for the entire reform period, trends in agricultural labor productivity, measured as output per farm worker, parallel those of yields.

So what is the record of China's reform-era agriculture with respect to more complete measures of productivity? Do these measures move in the same or opposite directions? In fact, researchers mostly find that total factor productivity (TFP) trends move largely in the same direction as the partial measures. There are many papers that measure China's TFP in agriculture (McMillan *et al.*, 1989; Fan, 1991; Lin, 1992; Wen, 1993; Huang and Rozelle, 1996; Fan, 1997; Jin *et al.*, 2002). Most empirical work shows that in the first years after reform (1978–84), comprehensive measures of productivity (either constructed TFP indices or their regression-based equivalents) rose by 5 to 10 percent per year. Fan (1997) and Jin *et al.* (2002, 2010) have papers in which they show that during the 1990s and 2000s, TFP continued to rise at a rate of more than 2 percent per year (a healthy rate in any country).

In part due to rising productivity, and perhaps even more due to the increasing efficiency associated with specialization (which resulted in farmers shifting their efforts to the production of more, higher value crops and livestock commodities as well as the expansion of off farm work), rural incomes during the reforms have steadily increased. Between 1978 and 2011, average rural per capita incomes have risen (in real terms) 10.6 times. Per capita incomes reached 6,977 yuan in 2011. This annual rise (7.5 percent per year for more than thirty years) is remarkable and is as high as the growth rates experienced in Japan and Korea during their takeoff years (though rural incomes have risen at a slower rate than urban per capita incomes).

3 Building the institutional base and policy strategy of reform: the enabling factors

In this section we review the policies that have been behind the performance and changes in China's farm/rural economy. In as many places as possible, we also try to provide empirical evidence of the impact of the policies on the performance of the agricultural sector.

3.1 Price policy changes

While in the first years of the reforms China's leaders did not plan to deregulate markets and turn them into the driving force of decision-making, leaders – even in the earlier years – did move to remake the incentives faced by producers. As early as 1979, leaders provided farmers with incentives by embodying them in the prices that farmers received from selling their crops (still to the state in the early years – Lardy, 1983; Sicular, 1988b). According to data from CNBS, the relative price of grain to fertilizer rose by more than 60 percent during the first three years after reform.

Close attention to the timing of events in the early reform period would suggest that pricing policies appear to have been effective – due to their timing and the nature of their implementation. The first increase in price occurred (in 1979) at almost the same time as when reformers were deciding to decollectivize. However, given the leadership's decision to gradually implement the Household Responsibility System, beginning first in the poorest areas of China, there is no reason to believe that there should have been an immediate impact on China's overall agricultural growth (since only a small share of farmers in some of the worst farming areas were initially affected). However, the price increases immediately affected all farmers/farming teams, both those in areas that had been decollectivized and those that had not. By 1981, the time of the second major price increase, according to Lin (1992), less than half of China's farmers had been allowed to dismantle their communes.

Empirical studies demonstrate that price changes had an impact on output during the first years of transition (Lin, 1992; Fan, 1991; Huang and Rozelle, 1996; Fan and Pardey, 1997). Lin (1992) finds that 15 percent of output growth during the first six years of reform came from the rise in relative prices. Huang and Rozelle's (1996) decomposition exercise for rice demonstrates that about 10 percent of the output between 1978 and 1984 came from price effects.

3.2 Institutional reforms

Beyond pricing policies, the household responsibility system (HRS) is often thought to have been at the heart of China's rural economic reforms (Lardy, 1983). The HRS reforms dismantled the communes and contracted agricultural land to households. Although land ownership rights remained with the collective (i.e., the village or the local state), control and income rights were given to individual households.

While HRS was initiated over thirty years ago, China's land rights have always been complicated (Brandt *et al.*, 2002). The first term of the land contract was stipulated to be for fifteen years. The effects of this initial decollectivization policy (at least for control and income rights) on the equitable distribution of land to farmers and its effect on food security and poverty alleviation have been obvious and well documented (Lin, 1992).

The reality of secure land tenure, however, is more complicated. Although local leaders were supposed to have given farmers land for fifteen years in the early 1980s and thirty years starting in the late 1990s, collective ownership of land in many areas has been less secure (Brandt *et al.*, 2002). Specifically, village leaders and local governments – especially in the 1980s and 1990s – often used their ownership rights to reallocate village land among households. These reallocations were done for a variety of reasons, including concerns for equity and concerns for efficiency as well as for reasons that are closer to corruption. Regardless of the reason for the reallocations, during the 1980s and 1990s (and since) observers and policy makers have been concerned that such moves could result in insecure tenure (from the viewpoint of households as agricultural producers) and have negative effects on investment and production. Despite these concerns, there have been a large number of authors (e.g., Jacoby *et al.*, 2003) who have conducted empirical studies that consistently have shown that there has been little effect on either short- or long-run land productivity.

Even with these findings, during the late 1990s and early 2000s a number of top leaders were concerned that collective ownership and weak alienation and transfer rights could have negative effects on migration and rural credit. As a result, in the early 2000s, China passed the Rural Land Contract Law (RLCL) which sought to increase security (Deininger and Jin, 2005). Among other things, the RLCL explicitly prohibited reallocation for almost all reasons.

Today the issue of land rights is revolving around a new set of issues. A number of leaders are now searching for mechanisms that permit those who stay in farming to be able to gain access to additional cultivated land in order to be able increase income from farming. In fact, even without complete legal protection, over the past decade researchers are finding that increasingly more land in China is being rented in and out (Deininger and Jin, 2005; Gao *et al.*, 2012). In order to accelerate this process, the RLCL further clarified the rights for transfer and exchange of contracted land. The new legislation also allowed family members to inherit the land during the contract period.

4 The effect of property rights reform on performance

Changes in incentives due to the HRS reforms unleashed increases in both agricultural production and productivity. In one of the first studies on the subject, Lin (1992) uses regression analysis to estimate that China's HRS accounted for 42 to 46 percent of the total rise in output during the early reform period (1978–84). Also using the results of regression analysis, Fan (1991) and Huang and Rozelle (1996) find that even after accounting for technological change, institutional change during the late 1970s and early 1980s contributed about 30 percent of output growth.

The effects of HRS go beyond increasing production. McMillan *et al.* (1989) use a TFP accounting approach to show that decollectivization increased total factor productivity (TFP). Better incentives accounted for nearly all of the increase in TFP (23 percent) between 1978 and 1984. Using regression analysis, Jin *et al.* (2002) also demonstrate that the HRS reforms contributed to 7 percent annual TFP growth in the early 1980s.

After the mid-1980s, however, the direct effects of decollectivization and the improved incentives diminished. DeBrauw *et al.* (2004) demonstrates that the end of the one-time property rights reforms accounts for much of the slowdown of grain (although growth rates were still positive) and other crop production in the 1990s.

4.1 Domestic output market liberalization policies

In addition to pricing changes and decollectivization, another major task of the reformers was to create more efficient institutions of exchange. Markets – whether classic competitive ones or some workable substitute – increase efficiency by facilitating transactions among agents to allow specialization and trade and by providing information through a pricing mechanism to producers and consumers about the relative scarcity of resources. But markets, in order to function efficiently, require supporting institutions to ensure competition, define and enforce property rights and contracts, ensure access to credit and finance and provide information (McMillan, 1997). These institutions were almost completely absent in China during the Socialist era. Instead, as discussed above, China's central and provincial planning agencies directed production and other economic transactions and their directives served to enforce contracts involving exchanges among various agents in the chain. Market liberalization requires the elimination of planning. However, to implement a market-driven system successfully requires the process to be executed in a way that will allow producers to continue to have access to inputs and marketing channels while the necessary market-supporting institutions are emerging.

An examination of policies and the extent of marketing activity in the early 1980s illustrates the limited extent of changes in the marketing environment of China's food economy before 1985. It is true that reformers did allow farmers increased discretion to produce and market crops in ten planning categories, such as vegetables, fruits, and coarse grains. Moreover, by 1984, the state only claimed control over twelve commodities, including rice, wheat, maize, soybeans, peanuts, rapeseed, and several other cash crops (Sicular, 1988b). However, while this may seem to represent a significant move towards liberalization – the crops that remained almost entirely under the planning authority of the government still accounted for more than 95 percent of sown area in 1984. Hence, by state policy and practice, the output and marketing of almost all the sown area was still directly influenced by China's planners.

Reforms proceeded with equal caution when reducing restrictions on free market trade. The decision to permit the reestablishment of free markets came in 1979, but only initially allowed farmers to trade vegetables and a limited number of other crops and livestock products within the boundaries of their own county. Reformers did gradually reduce restrictions on the distance over which trade could occur from 1980 to 1984, but as Sicular (1988b) and Skinner (1985) point out, the predominant marketing venue during the early 1980s was mainly local rural periodic markets. Farmers also did begin to sell their produce in urban settings, but free markets in the cities only began to appear in 1982 and 1983. In addition to being small and infrequent, traders could not engage in the marketing of China's monopolized commodities, which were still under strict control of the state procurement stations.

The record of the expansion of rural and urban markets confirms the hypothesis that market liberalization had not yet begun by the early 1980s. Although agricultural commodity markets were allowed to emerge during the 1980s, their number and size made them a small player in China's food economy. In 1984, the state procurement network still purchased more than 95 percent of marketed grain and more than 99 percent of the marketed cotton (Sicular, 1995). In all of China's urban areas, there were only 2,000 markets in 1980, a number that rose only to 6,000 by 1984 (deBrauw et al., 2004). In Beijing in the early 1980s, there were only about fifty markets transacting around 1 million yuan of commerce per market per year. Each market site would have had to serve, on average, about 200,000 Beijing residents, each transacting only 5 yuan of business for the entire year.

After 1985, however, market liberalization began in earnest. Changes to the procurement system, further reductions in restrictions to trading of commodities, moves to commercialize the state grain trading system, and calls for the expansion of market construction in rural and urban areas led to a surge in market-oriented activity (Sicular, 1995). For example, in 1980, there were only 241,000 private and semi-private trading enterprises registered with the State Markets Bureau; by 1990, there were more than 5.2 million (deBrauw et al., 2002). Between 1980 and 1990, the per capita volume of transactions of commerce in Beijing urban food markets rose almost 200 times. Private traders handled more than 30 percent of China's grain by 1990, and more than half of the rest was bought and sold by commercialized state grain trading companies, many of which had begun to behave as private traders (Rozelle et al., 1999, 2000).

Even after the start of liberalization in output in 1985, the process was still partial and executed in a start and stop manner (Sicular, 1995). For example, after the initial commercialization of the grain bureau, when grain prices rose in 1988, leaders halted the grain reforms and allowed provincial leaders to intervene in the flow of grain into and out of their provinces. The policies were relaxed again in the early 1990s and retightened in the mid-1990s. Another round of liberalization and retrenchment occurred in the late 1990s.

Despite its start and stop nature, as the right to private trading was extended to include surplus output of all categories of agricultural products after contractual obligations to the state were fulfilled, the foundations of the state marketing system began to be undermined (Rozelle et al., 2000; Huang and Rozelle, 2006). After a record growth in grain production in 1984 and 1985, a second stage of price and market reforms was announced in 1985 aimed at radically limiting the scope of government price and market interventions and further enlarging the role of market allocation. Other than for rice, wheat, maize and cotton, the intention was to gradually eliminate planned procurement of agricultural products; government commercial departments could only continue to buy and sell at the market. For grain, incentives were introduced through the reduction of the volume of the quota and increase in procurement prices. Even for grain, after the share of compulsory quota procurement in grain production reached 29 percent in 1984, it reduced to 18 percent in 1985 and 13 percent in 1990. The share of negotiated procurement at market price increased from 3 percent only in 1985 to 6 percent in 1985 and 12 percent in 1990.

4.2 Technology and water infrastructure development

Agricultural research and development (agricultural R&D) in China during the 1980s, 1990s and 2000s was still almost fully controlled by the state agricultural research system. Initially reflecting the need to provide urban residents with low cost food, a large share of the government's breeding programs focused on rice and wheat. Officials have also been focused on national food security. As such, high yields were the target of most research programs. Only after 2000 did research programs begin to consider quality. Although there have been several private domestic and joint venture investments into agricultural research and development (and this is increasing in recent years), policies still discriminate against them.

China's agricultural research system could not be considered an elite institution in the 1980s and 1990s, being staffed by personnel who were poorly trained. There was also a lot of duplication of research effort. Research, in short, was not being effectively managed. In response, in the 1980s, government officials began a comprehensive program to reform China's research and development system for agriculture. Science and technology funding agencies shifted funding from institutional support to competitive grants. Priorities were given and more development efforts were supported. The government also encouraged applied research institutes to generate their own revenue by taking their technologies to the market.

While not perfect, in the 2000s the record on research reform is considered mostly successful. Empirical studies have found that the move to competitive grant programs increased the effectiveness of China's agricultural research system (Jin *et al.*, 2002). Interestingly, the reliance on commercialization revenue to subsidize research created few gains. Scientists today have more funding and are better trained. At least through the 1990s and early 2000s, it is almost certain that imperfections in the seed industry partly contributed to the ineffectiveness of research reform measures in crop breeding. In recent years, investments in plant biotechnology have become one of China's major priorities (Huang *et al.*, 2005).

While the private sector has played an important role in agricultural R&D in many countries around the world, only a small share of agricultural R&D in China is performed by the private sector (although the share is rising in recent years). The reasons for the absence of an active private sector probably reflect a "crowding out" effect that is due to the importance that China's government attaches to national food security and the huge investments they have made into agricultural R&D.

Beyond agricultural R&D, investment by the state in water control – both irrigation and flood control – far overshadowed the amount invested into R&D. In the 1950s, 1960s and 1970s, water officials invested a majority of their funds into dams and surface irrigation networks. Much of this investment was in the form of forced unpaid labor that was extracted from farmers. In the early 1980s officials paid greater attention to the use of China's groundwater (Wang *et al.*, 2005a). By 2005, China had more tubewells than any country in the world. Although initially investment was put up by local governments, by the late 1990s, the government was encouraging investment into groundwater by the private sector (Wang *et al.*, 2005b). The main policy initiative after the mid-1990s in the surface water sector was management reform (with the goal of trying to make water use more efficient).

The empirical literature has clearly shown that investments by the state have been effective in raising the performance of agriculture. Huang and Rozelle (1996) and Fan (1991) demonstrate the impact of technology investment on agricultural output. Jin *et al.* (2002, 2010) show that the effect has been felt in TFP in the 1980s, 1990s and 2000s. Huang *et al.* (2002, 2004) show that biotechnology has benefited millions of farmers and boosted agricultural productivity. While there are few empirical studies on the impact of irrigation on agricultural productivity, China's irrigation area rose from 16 million hectares in 1950 to nearly 60 million hectares in 2010 (covering about 50 percent of cultivate land – CNBS, 2011).

4.3 Trade policy

Trade and other external policies have played a major role in the reform of China's farming economy during the reform era. Lower tariffs and policies allowing rising agricultural trade began to affect domestic terms of trade in the 1980s. In the initial years, most of the fall in protection came from depreciation of the exchange rate as well as a reduction in the number of commodities that were controlled by single-desk state traders. In addition, officials allowed the entrance of private firms to compete in the agricultural trade sector, both imports and exports (Martin, 2001). Such moves were shown to stimulate the level of exports in the case of a number of farm products. Policy makers also liberalized the rules on imports, allowing the state traders to increase the volume of imports in the 1980s and 1990s.

The efforts to increase competition were implemented in parallel with reductions in the levels of tariffs on imports. In the 1990s officials launched a new effort to decrease the level of protection. In the mid 1990s, the simple average agricultural import tariff fell from 42 to 24 percent (Rosen *et al.*, 2004). The rate fell further to 21 percent in 2001.

The trade policy efforts have yielded results in making China's farming economy less distorted (Huang *et al.*, 2004). Empirical work shows that a large share of the lower protection has come from allowing more competition in trade and reducing the rules on licensing procedures. Changes in foreign exchange rates also have played an important role (Rosen *et al.*, 2004). Officials not only have reduced tariff and relaxed quotas, they also sought to reduce the severity of non-tariff barriers (NTBs) during the 1990s (Huang and Chen, 1999).

Given the changes made prior to the nation's accession to the WTO, it is not surprising that, while accession was a major event in China (and it certainly had an effect on many sectors), the WTO accession process is best thought of as a continuation of previous trade liberalization policy efforts. Hence, the commitments embodied in China's WTO accession agreement in the agricultural sector – market access, domestic support and export subsidies – are essentially what China was doing in the 1990s.

4.4 Trade and poverty impacts

In the same way that the forces of development have generated progress and problems, the nation's efforts at pushing ambitious agricultural trade liberalization policies have had both positive and negative consequences (Anderson *et al.*, 2004). Research has shown that, on average, the nation's accession to the WTO will help rural residents and improve incomes. In fact, according to Anderson *et al.* (2004), China gained more than almost any other country in the world from more liberalized trade agreements.

In any trade agreement, however, there will be both winners and losers. The nature of China's agricultural economy – its competitiveness and extent of marketization – means that the effects of trade liberalization have been transmitted rapidly throughout the economy. Households that were producing competitive products generally gained from liberalization (as a more liberalized trade environment has increased exports and led to higher domestic prices) while those that were producing uncompetitive ones were hurt (as imports have risen and domestic prices have fallen).

Huang *et al.* (2007) recently have studied the effect of WTO and future trade liberalization on China's farmers. According to their analysis, the subset of all farmers who were hurt by trade liberalization was small (and quite specific). In particular, farmers in poor maize, cotton and wheat producing areas in the central and western parts of the nation are the ones who were hurt (due to rising imports and falling prices). Farmers in most of the rest of China gained (as rising exports helped support the domestic price of these goods).

In assessing the reasons for the negative effects, research shows that there are several determining factors. First, households in these poor areas – due to lower social capital – were less diversified into the off farm sector. Thus, while richer households were able to offset the loss from trade liberalization with the gains that came from their participation in the off farm sector, poorer households, in general, were less able to do so (although the rise in migration is making this less of an issue). Second, farmers in poor areas often were growing the crops that were internationally less competitive – maize, cotton and wheat. They were less likely to be growing crops in which China had a comparative advantage – horticulture crops and aquaculture products. Finally, because farmers in poorer areas had less physical and human capital than those in richer areas, they often had more difficulties in shifting from those crops that were hurt by trade liberalization into those that benefited from trade.

5 Summaries and conclusions

To summarize the findings of the chapter, whereas the pre-reform period experienced little change, during the reform era China's farming economy has changed fundamentally. Ironically, while the farming sector grew steadily in absolute terms during the reforms, the more rapid rise of industry and the service sector means that agriculture has fallen in terms of the importance in the overall economy. This fall has been experienced in both output value and employment. In this way China's agriculture has diminished in importance (a feature common to most all countries experiencing economic development and urbanization).

Although falling in importance, the farming sector was not stagnant. The structure of agriculture changed dramatically. The sector diversified out of coarse grains into fine grains. China's agriculture moved out of staple grains into higher valued crops. Cropping fell in relative terms and livestock and fisheries increased their share.

The rest of the greater agricultural economy has also changed. Trade increased. Trade patterns have changed more in line with the nation's comparative advantage. Most remarkably, China's trade changes have affected all households – mostly for the good. Dramatic changes have been experienced by both richer and poorer households.

The source of the changes in no small part has been shown to be the result of China's policy efforts during the reform era. Policy shifts were made in pricing, the organization of production and in marketing. China's officials invested large volumes of resources into in agricultural technology and water. Fundamental shifts were made in trade and the external economy.

One of the most important characteristics of agricultural reform in China is the pace of reform. Our analysis is consistent with that of Rozelle (1996) which shows that the sequencing of agricultural reform policies followed the gradualism strategy of China's more general, economy-wide reforms that McMillan and Naughton (1992) describe. In the initial stages of reform, leaders consciously restricted the promotion of market-based economic activity, allowing at most the exchange of minor products (e.g., minor fruits and vegetables) in sharply circumscribed regions. Not until 1985, after the completion of the HRS policies, did policy makers begin to encourage market activity for more important commodities (e.g., grain). Even the early marketing system changes occurred within the framework of China's two tier price system (Sicular, 1988b). Leaders did not commit themselves to more complete market liberalization until the early 1990s, more than a decade after the initiation of HRS. From this description, it is clear that China's reforms fall into two distinct stages: the incentive reforms that dominate the period from 1978 to 1984; and a period of gradual market liberalization that begins in 1985 and extends through the 1990s and early 2000s.

In addition, outside of agriculture many policies and other factors (that are discussed in other chapters in this volume) affected the sector. Other rural policies, for example, such as those that governed fiscal reform, township and village enterprise emergence and privatization and rural governance almost certainly had a large, albeit indirect, effect on agriculture. Urban employment policies, residency restrictions, exchange rate management and many other policy initiatives also affected agriculture by affecting relative prices in the economy, the access to jobs off the farm and the overall attractiveness of staying on the farm.

When taken together, these policies have been shown to have a dramatic effect on China's agricultural sector. They have increased output of food, driven prices down and improved supplies of non-grain food and raw materials for industry. The mix of policies – pricing; improved property rights; market liberalization; investment; trade – also have made producers more efficient, freed up labor and resources that helped trigger the structural transformation in the agricultural/rural economy. One of the most convincing indicators showing that agriculture in China is beginning to play effective roles in the nation's development is that the importance of grain is shrinking inside the cropping sector; the importance of the cropping sector is shrinking inside the overall agricultural sector; and the importance of agriculture is shrinking in the general economy. Rural incomes are up; productivity is up.

Bibliography

Anderson, K., Huang, J. and Ianchovichina, E. (2004) 'Will China's WTO Accession Worsen Farm Household Income?', *China Economic Review*, 15: 443–56.

Aston, B., Hill, K., Piazza, A. and Zeitz, R. (1984) 'Famine in China, 1958–1961', *Population and Development Review*, 10 (4 December): 613–45.

Brandt, L. (1989) *Commercialization and Agricultural Development: Central and Eastern China*, New York: Cambridge University Press.

Brandt, L., Huang, J., Li, G. and Rozelle, S. (2002) 'Land Rights in China: Facts, Fictions, and Issues', *China Journal*, 47: 67–97.

Chang, G. and Wen, G. (1997) 'Communal Dining and the Chinese Famine of 1958–61', *Economic Development and Cultural Change*, 15: 1–15.

CNBS (National Statistical Bureau of China) *Statistical Yearbook of China*, various issues from 1981–2012. Beijing: China Statistical Press.

deBrauw, A., Huang, J., Rozelle, S., Zhang, L. and Zhang, Y. (2002) 'The Evolution of China's Rural Labor Markets during the Reforms', *Journal of Comparative Economics*, 30(2) (June): 329–53.

deBrauw, A., Huang, J. and Rozelle, S. (2004) 'The Sequencing of Reforms in China's Agricultural Transition', *Economics of Transition*, 12(3): 427–66.

Deininger, K. and Jin, S. (2005) 'The Potential of Land Rental Markets in the Process of Economic Development: Evidence from China', *Journal of Development Economics*, 78 (October 2005): 241–70.

Deng, H., Huang, J., Xu, Z. and Rozelle, S. (2010) 'Policy Support and Emerging Farmer Professional Cooperatives in Rural China', *China Economic Review*, 21(2010): 495–507.

Fan, S. (1991) 'Effects of Technological Change and Institutional Reform on Production Growth in Chinese Agriculture', *American Journal of Agricultural Economics*, 73: 266–75.

Fan, S. (1997) 'Production and Productivity Growth in Chinese Agriculture: New Measurement and Evidence', *Food Policy*, 22 (3 June): 213–28.

Fan, S. and Pardey, P. (1997) 'Research Productivity and Output Growth in Chinese Agriculture', *Journal of Development Economics*, 53 (June): 115–37.

Gao, L., Huang, J. and Rozelle, S. (2012) 'Rental Markets for Cultivated Land and Agricultural Investments in China', *Agricultural Economics*, 43(2012): 391–403.

Huang, J. and Chen, C. (1999) *Effects of Trade Liberalization on Agriculture in China: Commodity and Local Agricultural Studies*, United Nations, ESCAP CGPRT Centre, Bogor, Indonesia.

Huang, J. and David, C. (1995) 'Policy Reform and Agricultural Incentives in China', Working Paper, Center for Chinese Agricultural Policy, Institute of Geographical Sciences and Natural Resource Research, Chinese Academy of Sciences, Beijing, China.

Huang, J., Hu, R., Rozelle, S. and Pray, C. (2005) 'Insect-Resistant GM Rice in Farmer Fields: Assessing Productivity and Health Effects in China', *Science*, 308 (29 April): 688–90.

Huang, J., Hu, R., van Meijl, H. and van Tongeren, F. (2004) 'Biotechnology Boosts to Crop Productivity in China: Trade and Welfare Implications', *Journal of Development Economics*, 75(2004): 27–54.

Huang, J., Jun, Y., Xu, Z., Rozelle, S. and Li, N. (2007) 'Agricultural Trade Liberalization and Poverty in China', *China Economic Review*, 18: 244–65.

Huang, J., Pray, C., Rozelle, S. and Wang, Q. (2002) 'Plant Biotechnology in China', *Science*, 295 (25 January): 674–77.

Huang, J. and Rozelle, S. (1996) 'Technological Change: Rediscovering the Engine of Productivity Growth in China's Agricultural Economy', *Journal of Development Economics*, 49: 337–69.

Huang, J. and Rozelle, S. (2006) 'The Emergence of Agricultural Commodity Markets in China', *China Economic Review*, 17(3): 260–80.

Huang, J., Rozelle, S. and Chang, M. (2004) 'The Nature of Distortions to Agricultural Incentives in China and Implications of WTO Accession', *World Bank Economic Review*, 18(1): 59–84.

Jacoby, H., Li, G. and Rozelle, S. (2003) 'Hazards of Expropriation: Tenure Insecurity and Investment in Rural China', *American Economic Review*, 92(5) (January 2003): 1420–47.

Jin, S., Huang, J., Hu, R. and Rozelle, S. (2002) 'The Creation and Spread of Technology and Total Factor Productivity in China's Agriculture', *American Journal of Agricultural Economics*, 84(4) (November): 916–39.

Jin, S., Ma, H., Huang, J., Hu, R. and Rozelle, S. (2010) 'Productivity, Efficiency and Technical Change: Measuring the Performance of China's Transforming Agriculture', *Journal of Productivity Analysis*, 33: 191–207.

Johnston, B. (1970) 'Agriculture and Structural Transformation in Developing Countries: A Survey of Research', *Journal of Economic Literature*, 8: 101–45.

Johnston, B. and Mellor, J. W. (1961) 'The Role of Agriculture in Economic Development', *American Economic Review*, 15(4): 566–93.

Lardy, N. R. (1983) *Agriculture in China's Modern Economic Development*, Cambridge: Cambridge University Press.

Lin, J. (1992) 'Rural Reforms and Agricultural Growth in China', *American Economic Review*, 82: 34–51.

McMillan, J. (1997) 'Markets in Transition', in Kreps, David and Wallis, K. F. (eds.), *Advances in Economics and Econometrics: Theory and Applications, vol. 2*, Cambridge: Cambridge University Press, pp. 210–39.

McMillan, J. and Naughton, B. (1992) 'How to Reform a Planned Economy: Lessons from China', *Oxford Review of Economic Policy*, 8: 130–43.

McMillan, J., Walley, J. and Zhu, L. (1989) 'The Impact of China's Economic Reforms on Agricultural Productivity Growth', *Journal of Political Economy*, 97: 781–807.

Martin, W. (2001) 'Implications of reform and WTO accession for China's Agricultural Policies', *Economics of Transition*, 9(3): 717–42.

Park, A., Jin, H., Rozelle, S. and Huang, J. (2002) 'Market Emergence and Transition: Arbitrage, Transition Costs, and Autarky in China's Grain Market', *American Journal of Agricultural Economics*, 84(1) (February): 67–82.

Perkins, D. (1994) 'Completing China's Move to the Market', *Journal of Economic Perspectives*, 8(2) (spring): 23–46.

Putterman, L. (1993) *Continuity and Change in China's Rural Development*, New York: Oxford University Press.

Qiao, F., Lohmar, B., Huang J., Rozelle, S. and Zhang, L. (2003) 'Producer Benefits from Input Market and Trade Liberalization: The Case of Fertilizer in China', *American Journal of Agricultural Economic*, 85(5) (December): 1223–7.

Rosen, D., Huang, J. and Rozelle, S. (2004) 'Roots of Competitiveness: China's Evolving Agriculture Interests', *Policy Analysis in International Economics*, vol. 72. Washington, DC: Institute for International Economics.

Rozelle, S. (1996) 'Stagnation without Equity: Changing Patterns of Income and Inequality in China's Post-Reform Rural Economy', *China Journal*, 35 (January): 63–96.

Rozelle, S. and Huang, J. (2004) 'China's Maize Economy: Supply, Demand and Trade', report for the US Grains Council, Beijing, China.

Rozelle, S. and Huang, J. (2005) 'China's Soybean Economy: Supply, Demand and Trade', report for the American Soybean Association, Beijing, China.

Rozelle, S., Huang, J. and Sumner, D. (2006) 'China's Horticulture Economy: Supply, Demand and Trade', report for the Western Growers American Soybean Association, Beijing, China.

Rozelle, S., Li, G., Shen, M., Hughart, A. and Giles, J. (1999) 'Leaving China's Farms: Survey Results of new Paths and Remaining Hurdles to Rural Migration', *China Quarterly*, 158 (June): 367–93.

Rozelle, S., Park, A., Huang, J. and Jin, H. (2000) 'Bureaucrat to Entrepreneur: The Changing Role of the State in China's Transitional Commodity Economy', *Economic Development and Cultural Change*, 48(2): 227–52.

Sicular, T. (1988a) 'Plan and Market in China's Agricultural Commerce', *Journal of Political Economy*, 96(2): 283–307.

Sicular, T. (1988b) 'Agricultural Planning and Pricing in the Post-Mao Period', *China Quarterly*, 116: 671–703.

Sicular, T. (1995) 'Redefining State, Plan, and Market: China's Reforms in Agricultural Commerce', *China Quarterly*, 144: 1020–46.

Skinner, W. (1985) 'Rural Marketing in China: Repression and Revival', *China Quarterly*, 103: 393–413.

Stone, B. and Rozelle, S. (1995) 'Foodcrop Production Variability in China, 1931–1985', in *The School for Oriental and African Studies, Research and Notes Monograph Series*, vol. 9, London, August.

Wang, H., Dong, X., Rozelle, S., Huang, J. and Reardon, T. (2009) 'Producing and Procuring Horticultural Crops with Chinese Characteristics: The Case of Northern China', *World Development*, 37(11): 1791–1801.

Wang, J., Huang, J. and Rozelle, S. (2005a) 'Evolution of Tubewell Ownership and Production in the North China Plain', *Australian Journal of Agricultural and Resource Economics*, 49 (June): 177–95.

Wang, J., Xu, Z., Huang, J. and Rozelle, S. (2005b) 'Incentives to Water Management Reform: Assessing the Effect on Water Use, Productivity and Poverty in the Yellow River Basin', *Environment and Development Economics*, 10: 769–99.

Wen, G. (1993) 'Total Factor Productivity Change in China's Farming Sector: 1952–1989', *Economic Development and Cultural Change*, 42: 1–41.

Zhang, L., Li, Q. and Rozelle, S. (2005) 'Fertilizer demand in China: What Is Causing Farmers to Use So Much Fertilizer?' Working Paper, Center for Chinese Agricultural Policy, Chinese Academy of Sciences, Beijing, China.

12

STATE AND NON-STATE ENTERPRISES IN CHINA'S ECONOMIC TRANSITION

Ligang Song[1]

Introduction

China's enterprise system reform constitutes a key part of its economic transition from a centrally planned to a market-based economy. The reform process began in 1978 and has continued right through the first decade of the twenty-first century and beyond. The key elements in enterprise system reform consist of the ownership reform of the state-owned enterprises (SOEs) and the development of the non-state enterprises including both foreign-funded firms and indigenous private firms. The ownership reform in the state sector has unleashed strong productive forces through improved incentives that, together with the rising private sector, have formed the micro-foundation for the rapid economic growth in China over the past thirty years. The reform has nurtured rising entrepreneurship which has in turn injected further dynamics into the system powering the strong growth of the Chinese economy. These reforms have led to the changes in the relative importance of the state versus the non-state sector, with an increasing share of the non-state sector in the total economy. To accommodate these fundamental changes taking place in its enterprise system China has been reforming its institutions, such as the financial and banking system, labor market system, local government system and the legal system. The significance of the enterprise system reform in China is that the private sector has now contributed more than 60 percent of China's GDP, more than 80 percent of the total industrial value added, and more than 97 percent of its total workforce employed.

There are, however, some key unfinished tasks in reforming both the state and the non-state sector such as the state–enterprise relationship, state monopoly and competition, corporate governance, business finance and the regulatory system governing the enterprise system. There is also a need to both nurture entrepreneurship through improving the way that the market functions and to further develop China's legal system and the enforcement of court decisions. The difficulties in accomplishing those tasks lie in the existing institutions that, despite the progress made to change them in the past, have still not been entirely compatible with what a market system requires. Overcoming these difficulties by deepening institutional reform holds the key for China to complete its tasks of enterprise system reform and through that to sustain long-term growth and development. Failure to do so will see rising distortions and inefficiency in resource allocations which are inconsistent with the ultimate objective of an economic transformation that is designed to achieve an improved standard of living for the Chinese people in the most efficient and equitable way.

This chapter reviews the progress made so far in reforming China's enterprise system by dividing the reform into three stages, highlighting the key issues involved in each stage and their impact on China's economic performance. The chapter then identifies the unfinished tasks in reforming the system and points the way forward.

1 Enterprise reform in China: a review

Before reform, almost all enterprises in China were SOEs or collectively owned enterprises which were wholly or mainly owned and directly or indirectly controlled and managed by either the central or local governments. In particular, the governments set the SOEs' production targets, as well as all inputs of factors of production (such as labor and raw materials used in production) according to the state plan. Managers of SOEs had no role in deciding what to produce or at what prices their inputs of factors of production should be purchased and their final products be sold. Planning mechanisms replaced market mechanisms in the operation of Chinese enterprises. The consequences of such a system were low efficiency of SOEs resulting from the lack of incentive on the part of managers as well as workers, the stagnation of industrial production because of the misallocation of resources, and the shortage of manufacturing products for consumption due to the distortions in its price system. Economic studies have concluded that there was stagnant or even declining total factor productivity (TFP) in the SOE sector in the pre-reform period (World Bank 1995; Chow 2002; Zhu 2012).

Since China officially adopted the reform policy in 1978, the Chinese government has taken a gradual, experimental and pragmatic approach to reforming SOEs and letting the private economy exist, develop and flourish. The industrial system reform centering on SOEs was carried out following the successful reform in rural areas which aimed to provide incentives to farmers by granting them production responsibility and by partially liberalizing the planned prices for agricultural products (Lin 1992). Similarly, the core elements in industrial reform involved the granting of autonomy to enterprises through various kinds of enterprise system reform. These included ownership reform, liberalizing the prices for industrial products, and handling the rising social tension resulting from the massive retrenchment in the state sector (Garnaut *et al.* 2006).

This gradual and ongoing reform process can be divided into three stages. At each stage, the relative performance of both SOEs and non-SOEs is discussed, and more importantly each stage of reform reveals how the development of the non-state sector has been influenced by the progress in reforming the SOE sector.

1.1 Stage 1 (1978–92): exploring ways of reforming SOEs

Granting SOEs more autonomy and financial incentives

In December 1978, the Third Plenary Session of the Eleventh Central Committee of the Communist Party of China (hereafter "the Party") declared that: "a serious shortcoming in the economic management system in China is that the power is too centralized, thus bold decentralization should be carried out under the leadership, so that local industrial and agricultural enterprises can obtain more autonomy in their business management under the guidance of national planning." Under this guideline, in May 1979, the State Economic and Trade Commission and six ministries selected eight enterprises in Beijing, Tianjin and Shanghai to start a pilot program on granting autonomy of management to enterprises. In July 1979, the State Council issued a series of documents on the expansion of the autonomy of operation and management and the profit retention requirements of SOEs. In 1980, the number of pilot enterprises increased to 6,000, accounting for about 16 percent of the national budget, 60 percent of the gross industrial output value, and 70 percent of the total industrial profits (Chen 2008).

The implementation of the managerial system reform and profit retention under the program of decentralization stimulated enterprises to increase production. However, since the pilot program of decentralization lacked clear responsibilities for managers and sufficient macroeconomic institutions to regulate the process, China encountered a huge budget deficit for two consecutive years in 1979 and 1980. To solve this problem, in 1981, the central government launched the "economic responsibility system," under which managers were given an incentive to keep part of the profits above what was set in their contract with the government. In May 1984, the State Council issued the Regulation on Further Expanding Autonomy of State-owned Enterprises, which granted SOEs more autonomy in making a production plan and for profit retention. The government also realized that for the decentralization program to work, the centrally controlled pricing system had to be changed, which led to price liberalization, a crucial element in economic reform and transformation.

In January 1987, the government started promoting the "contract responsibility system" and the "dual-track price system," which allowed SOEs to sell their products that exceeded the planned quotas at market prices. This measure gave SOE managers financial incentives to produce more. This market-oriented reform measure set in train a series of crucial developments within the enterprise system, as well as China's nascent market system. By the end of 1987, about 80 percent of the large and medium-sized SOEs had adopted the "contract responsibility system," and by 1989 almost all SOEs adopted this system (Chen 2008). Under the "dual-track price system," the market started playing its role of allocating resources alongside the planning mechanism. This is what Naughton (1992) called "China is growing out of the plan" (without radically shifting its ownership structure). In July 1992, the State Council issued the Regulation on Transforming the Management Mechanism of State-owned Industrial Enterprises, granting SOEs more rights in setting their own prices and wages, hiring and firing labor, determining investment of fixed capital, and engaging in foreign trade. The Regulation gave SOEs more bargaining power to negotiate with governments and even to resist government interferences. After the Regulation was issued, many SOEs began laying off workers in order to cut their burdens and improve their business performance. These reform measures started changing the relationship between the governments and enterprises with the latter becoming more and more independent in decision-making at the enterprise level. At the same time, the governments began facing the issues of rising unemployment and started working on compensation schemes for those who were losing jobs in the enterprise restructuring. This task became more and more necessary as the ownership reform deepened at later stages of the reform.

Consequences of the first-stage enterprise system reform

The first stage of reform produced some positive outcomes. In 1978, SOEs still played a predominant role in the economy, accounting for about 80 percent of the total industrial output and employing the majority of the urban labor force (Figures 12.1 and 12.2). However, their importance in the economy declined gradually and steadily over time. Figure 12.1 shows that the share of SOEs in gross industrial output value declined from 78 percent in 1978 to 48 percent in 1992, when for the first time the non-state sector (mainly comprising collectively owned private and other types of enterprises) surpassed the state sector. This is a significant change as it is consistent

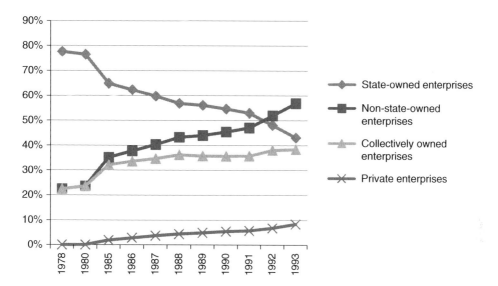

Figure 12.1 Share of gross industrial output value by ownership (1978–1993)

Source: Calculated using data from *China Statistics Yearbook* in various issues

with the goal of economic transition, namely to increase the share of the non-state sector in the total economy in order to establish a market system.

The majority of the non-state sector was made up of collectively owned enterprises, mainly involving those urban enterprises that were not state-owned, as well as township and village enterprises (TVEs) located in rural areas. Collectively owned enterprises are usually legally owned by their workers and other economic entities, but in practice local governments often play a controlling role in their management (OECD 2000). The State Council first used the term

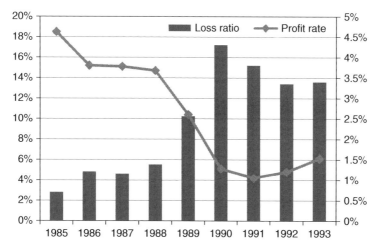

Figure 12.2 Profits and losses of SOEs (1985–1993)

Source: Calculated using data from *China Statistics Yearbook* in various issues

Notes: Profit rate (left axis): total profits divided by net value of fixed assets. Loss ratio (right axis): total losses of loss-making firms divided by net value of fixed assets

"TVE" (*xiangzhen qiye*) in 1984. These enterprises were previously known as "Commune and Brigade Enterprises" dating from the "Great Leap Forward" period from 1958 to 1961. During that time, TVEs had a limited role and were restricted to the production of iron, steel, cement, chemical fertilizer, hydroelectric power, and farm tools. Starting from the early 1980s, TVEs were largely detached from central planning requirements and their growth was promoted by local authorities, in order to encourage rural employment and to provide revenues to local governments (OECD 2000).

Figure 12.1 also shows that the share of private enterprises in total gross output value was still relatively small although steadily increasing at this stage of reform. Private enterprises remained marginal or supplementary in China's national economy for a relatively long time after reform began, even after their legitimate status was clearly established in the Constitution in 1999. Private ownership itself made these firms vulnerable to a variety of discriminating treatments partly due to the legacies of central planning which favored the state sector. The governmental agencies especially at local levels, such as those dealing with taxation, industrial and commercial administration and registration, technology and quality control, and hygiene, would scrutinize private firms more carefully or frequently but would be relatively more lenient to state-owned and collectively owned enterprises when violations occurred in these firms. Among the emerging private firms, there was still a profound distrust of the stability of and consistency in the state policies toward private economy during the first stage of reform. In what was known as "wearing a red hat," many private firms disguised themselves as either state-owned or collectively owned so as to have easier access to bank loans or land, have the privilege of engaging in imports and exports, using public resources and facilities, and escaping from harassment by local officials. Local officials could in turn obtain considerable funds from private firms, not only through formal means such as taxation, but also by collecting various kinds of fees which were in many cases at the discretion of the local officials, thus increasing their local revenues and employment. The main problem with such disguised relations became prominent when disputes between governments and enterprises appeared due to the ambiguities of their relations in terms of their respective ownership over assets and their shares of profits (Garnaut *et al.* 2001).

The first stage of reform granted more autonomy and financial incentives to SOE managers. However, the SOEs' financial performance did not improve very much and in fact they even declined after the mid-1980s. By this standard, the SOE reform was far from being satisfactory. Figure 12.2 shows that the profit rates of SOEs had been declining from 1985 to 1993. The SOE profit rate (total profits divided by net value of fixed assets) was about 18 percent in 1985 but had fallen to below 6 percent during the early 1990s. This declining trend was substantially attributable to increasing competition caused by the entry of non-SOEs, but also to the incompleteness of the SOE reform itself which affected their performance. Other indicators of SOE performance had also deteriorated over time. Total losses of loss-making SOEs rose sharply during the latter half of the 1980s and reached their peak in relation to output in 1990 (Figure 12.2). The number of SOEs running at losses was also rising, and the amount of total losses was increasing. Due to the wide scope and huge amount of losses in the state sector, the government's subsidy to SOEs also swelled, taking a 37 percent jump from 1986 to 1992 (Chen 2008). As expected, the SOEs' contribution to the government's revenue was also declining during that period. The loss-making by SOEs and the loss of revenues on the part of the governments worsened the governments' budgetary positions. Therefore, further reform that could protect the state's interests and rights while increasing SOE managers' incentives was desired.

Key issues related to the first stage of SOE reform

SEPARATION OF OWNERSHIP AND CONTROL

To find a solution for deepening SOEs' reform, it is important to understand what the problems associated with the first stage of SOE reform were. The SOEs were owned by the state but run by managers and workers. The separation of ownership and management control led to at least three common problems that may arise in any enterprise with the separation of ownership and management control (Lin 1998; Chen 2008).

First, "incentive incompatibility": the owner and the manager of the enterprise had different goals and interests. The owner always intended to obtain the largest possible return from his investment, while the manager wanted to maximize his personal income and welfare. Because of the incentive incompatibility, the manager had the incentive to engage in opportunistic behavior that benefited the manager, possibly at the expense of the owner.

Second, "information asymmetry": the owner was not involved in the production process and did not have direct information about the material requirements, actual expenditures, revenues, and so on. Because of the information asymmetry, the potential opportunistic behavior could become a reality. In the case of SOEs, the managers might have required more inventories, used more inputs, and reduced the profits submitted to the state by overstating costs and/or under-reporting revenues. When initial reforms were taking place involving decentralization and price liberalization, there were ample opportunities for the managers to take advantage of this partially reformed system to make profits for themselves.

Third, "disproportional liability": the punishment that the owner could impose on a manager of a failed enterprise was disproportionate to the value of the enterprise. Therefore, the manager might engage in investing in overly risky projects. If the projects succeeded, the manager might gain very high rewards. If the projects failed, the enterprise might be bankrupt in which case the manager's loss might be proportional to the owner's loss.

POLICY BURDENS ON SOEs AND COMPETITION FROM THE NON-STATE SECTOR

Moreover, the first stage of economic reform provided an opportunity for the rise of TVEs, private firms, joint ventures with foreign firms, and other non-SOEs whose development before the reform was suppressed because of their lack of access to both inputs and output markets. Market competition appeared as a result. Without state subsidies and protection, the non-SOEs' survival depended on their own strength in market competition. Non-SOEs were more adaptive to market and flexible in management. With the enlargement of the non-state sector and the shrinkage of the state sector in terms of output share, SOEs were under growing competitive pressure.

Nevertheless, SOEs still had to bear many policy-determined burdens that went well beyond the levels that enterprises typically provide in other market economies, including redundant labor that enterprises were not free to shed, disproportionately high tax burdens, and expenses for social benefits such as medical care, pensions, housing, and education. The large SOE policy burdens were a major reason for their profitability to remain relatively low (Lin *et al.* 1998). Policy burdens were mostly a legacy of prior central planning mechanisms but their persistence is substantially attributable to structural problems such as the lack of national social security systems and social supporting programs and the scarcity of government revenues for providing public goods. For the reasons mentioned above, SOEs were in a disadvantageous position in competing with non-SOEs. The existence of such causes made it harder to distinguish the SOEs' losses between those arising from policy legacies and those from mismanagement. The profit level of an SOE could not serve as sufficient information or criteria in measuring its managerial competency and efficiency. The costs for the state to monitor the manager of an SOE were extremely high because, under the price-distorted economic environment in China, the profits or losses of an SOE would not reflect its managerial performance and there existed no other simple, sufficient indicator of the manager's efficiency in performance under this circumstance. Since the information asymmetry problem was not overcome, managerial decentralization increased the possibility of manager's opportunistic behavior. Especially with the existence of a dual-track price system, it was very easy for SOEs to under-report revenue and over-report costs without being detected. As a result, the SOEs' taxes that were paid to the state and the SOEs' profits that were shared by the state were both declining, even though managerial decentralization improved the SOEs' productivity.

1.2 Stage 2 (1993–2002): innovating SOEs' reform

Ownership transformation (Gaizhi)

The earlier reform of SOEs was successful in improving the incentives of managers and freeing the government from direct involvement in the management of SOEs. Because the "contract of responsibility" of managers needed to be renegotiated every three years and the insiders had more control over the terms of the contract, it promoted short-term behavior by the managers. In fact, despite the reform, SOE performance deteriorated further from 1993 to 1997 (Figure 12.4). Policy makers and many researchers in China believed that the major problems of SOEs were unclearly defined property rights, continued government interference in enterprise management, and so on. In the subsequent SOE reform, a major focus was given to clarify property rights through ownership transformation (*Gaizhi*), such as privatization of small and medium-sized SOEs, and the separation of government ownership and regulatory functions from the direct interference and management of large SOEs.

In November 1993, the Third Plenum of the Fourteenth Party Congress adopted the Decision on Issues Concerning the Establishment of a Socialist Market Economic Structure, which provided a package of reform measures to carry out the vision of a "socialist market system" set forth by the Fourteenth Congress. The Decision set forth the task of transforming SOEs into "modern enterprises" with "clarified property rights, clearly defined responsibility and authority, separation of enterprises from the government, and scientific internal management." It also allowed for the privatization of small and medium-sized SOEs to take place. "As for the small state-owned enterprises, the management of some can be contracted out or leased; others can be shifted to the partnership system in the form of stock sharing, or sold to collectives and individuals."

Privatization started in earnest after a visit by Deng Xiaoping to southern China in 1992, while privatization of small SOEs occurred on a large scale in 1995. By the end of 1996, over half of the small SOEs were privatized. Over this period, over ten million workers were laid off as a result of SOEs ownership reform and restructuring. In September 1997, the Fifteenth Party Congress issued the Decisions on Issues Related to State-Owned Enterprise Reforms and Development, officially recognizing that "China is a mixed economy in which a variety of ownership forms, including private ownership, co-exist."

The Fifteenth Party Congress further promoted the privatization of small SOEs by putting forward the slogan: "grasping the large (SOEs), letting go the small (SOEs)" (*Zhua Da Fang Xiao*). This was an important measure because most of China's SOEs fell in the category of "small or medium size," and only about 1,000 SOEs were considered "large scale" with a need to remain state owned. The large SOEs were encouraged to form business groups through various kinds of internal restructuring aimed at increasing their efficiency in management and operation. The status of the private sector was further strengthened in March 1999 by the Ninth National People's Congress, which approved a constitutional provision upgrading the non-state sector from an "important complement" to a state-dominated economy to an "essential component" of a mixed economy.

Since 2000, the reform of China's SOEs has accelerated and acquired some qualitatively new features. First, the scale of change has expanded to affect almost every kind of SOE – small, medium, and large ones who are under both the central and local government control. Second, ownership diversification has been so extensive that the wholly state-owned nonfinancial enterprise has become rare. Third, the range of restructuring mechanism being used has expanded dramatically to include bankruptcies, liquidations, listings, sales to private firms, auctioning of state-owned firms and their assets or liabilities, and so on. By the end of 2001, about 86 percent of SOEs went through *Gaizhi* and about 70 percent were partially or fully privatized (Garnaut *et al.* 2005).

Consequences of the second stage of reform

Through the second stage of reform, the number of SOEs declined from 104,700 in 1993 to 29,449 in 2002.[2] According to Garnaut *et al.* (2005), about two-thirds of the decline was due to privatization. Privatization in China was not limited to small enterprises only: the average size of privatized SOEs was about 600 employees. The process had been socially painful: more than thirty million SOE workers had been laid off from 1998 to 2002. Meanwhile, a dynamic *de novo* private sector has been able to absorb most of the laid-off workers, thus alleviating the social cost of restructuring. The governments have also done their part in easing the social tension by establishing the re-employment centers that accommodated those who lost their jobs through restructuring.

As the reform progressed, the significance of SOEs in the economy in terms of total gross output value continued to decline, giving way to the rapidly growing TVEs during the 1980s (Figure 12.1) and to the even more explosive growth of foreign-funded and privately owned enterprises during the 1990s (Figure 12.3). The importance of collectively owned enterprises declined dramatically after 1999 because the central government issued a policy in November 1998 to encourage firms registered as collectives but in reality privately run to take off the "red hats." By the end of 1999, more than 80 percent of state and collective firms at the local level had gone through *Gaizhi*, which involved direct privatization in most cases (Garnaut *et al.* 2006). The private firms and foreign-funded firms increased rapidly during the 1990s, and eventually replaced the collectives to become the major type of non-SOEs in China.

Figure 12.4 shows the change of the profit rates of SOEs during the second stage of reform from 1993 to 2002. The annual SOE profit rate (total profits divided by net value of fixed assets) continued its declining trend until 1997, when it reached the lowest point, at only about 1.7 percent, and then rebounded rapidly back to 6 percent in 2000, keeping this level steady for the next two years. This significant change was substantially attributable to the progress made in reducing SOEs' overhead burdens and more substantially through ownership reform during the second stage of reform.

SOEs were not alone in experiencing weak financial performances in the 1990s. According to the estimates made by the OECD, profit rates for collectively owned and private enterprises as a whole were also relatively low by international standards. A high proportion of collectively

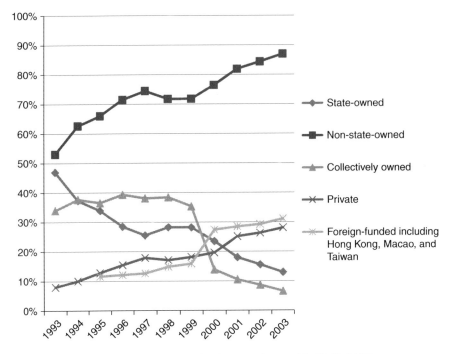

Figure 12.3   Share of gross industrial output value by type of ownership (1993–2003)

Source: Calculated using the data from *China Statistics Yearbook* in various issues

Notes: The share of private enterprises in gross industrial output value 2000–03 are estimates as the China Statistics Bureau only included private enterprises above a designated size into their statistics since 2000

owned firms were also experiencing losses, although the fraction was only about half that of SOEs (OECD 2000). Furthermore, the profitability of foreign-funded enterprises, while it had been substantially higher than that of the other segments in the economy, had fallen markedly from 15 percent of assets in 1995 to 4 percent in 1996–97 (World Bank 1999) but back to 15 percent in 2002 according to the *China Statistics Yearbook* from 2000. These low profit rates of SOEs and non-SOEs before 1997 suggested there might be serious structural problems in terms of both supply and demand in the Chinese economy at that time.

The Chinese government had further pushed forward the economic transformation of SOEs (*Gaizhi*) during its second stage of economic reform from 1993 to 2002. Over this decade or so, the Chinese economy had made the transition from being completely reliant on state-owned and collectively owned enterprises to a mixed economy where private enterprises played a leading role. According to the estimates made by Garnaut *et al.* (2005), the private sector became the largest sector of the Chinese economy, accounting for about 37 percent of gross domestic product in 2003. Overall, the non-state sector accounted for about two-thirds of China's GDP in 2003.

Key issues related to the second stage reform

OWNERSHIP TRANSFORMATION (*GAIZHI*)

The use of the term "*Gaizhi*," instead of "privatization," during the second-stage reform illustrated the cautious approach taken by the central government. The central government's main

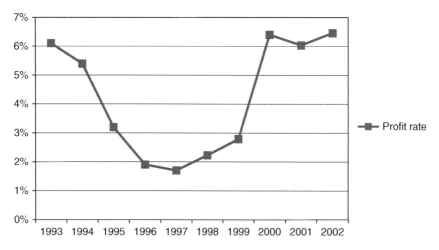

Figure 12.4   Annual profit rates of SOEs (1993–2002)

Source: Calculated using the data from *China Statistics Yearbook* in various issues

concerns were that *Gaizhi* might lead to the loss of state assets and bank loans owed and unpaid to the state banks, and possible social unrest trigged by massive unemployment resulting from large-scale privatization. The Chinese public was concerned that private companies and SOE managers might enrich themselves at the expense of the state and society at large. The policy response has been to introduce regulations on the restructuring SOE process and to strengthen their enforcement. There was a need to build an effective and transparent asset valuation system to achieve a fair and smooth transfer of state assets. However, the administrative capability to handle state assets, both within the government and within firms, was often inadequate and needed to be strengthened. Nonetheless, a properly managed transfer of assets from the state to private owners was a crucial part of the *Gaizhi* process, with strong implications for preventing losses of state assets and maintaining social stability in the transition.

During the process of *Gaizhi*, a large number of SOE employees were laid off. Between 1995 and 2003, the number of SOEs fell from 118,000 to around 34,000, and total employment in the SOE sector fell by around 44 million. The number of lost state-sector jobs totaled 17 percent of urban employment in 2003 (Garnaut *et al.* 2005). The Chinese central government pressured local governments to adopt every possible means to maintain employment, and thus social stability, during *Gaizhi*. This created a conflict of interest between the central and local governments over the responsibility for the costs of *Gaizhi*. Some local governments did not have the resources to compensate all SOE employees and so offered discounts on state assets to potential buyers of state firms in order to avoid resistance to the process of *Gaizhi*.

Two economic factors emerged as being critically important in alleviating the social cost of *Gaizhi*: the development of the national social security system and the promotion of the growth of new private enterprises to absorb laid-off workers from the state sector. There was a significant increase in central budget expenditures on social security from 1993 to 2002: from less than 1 percent in 1993 to 6.3 percent in 2002. Significant progress was made in reducing enterprise overhead burdens during the second-stage reform, but not sufficient alone to ensure a lasting improvement in enterprise competitiveness.

Domestic private enterprises became one of the major players in the Chinese economy during the second stage of reform (Figure 12.3). At the beginning of the second stage of reform, private enterprises were supporting SOE restructuring, largely indirectly, by creating the jobs needed to absorb laid-off workers. While this indirect role continued to be important, domestic private enterprises emerged as significant players in the privatization process. A growing number of private enterprises began to look at acquisitions of SOEs as their main growth strategy. These private firms injected capital and dynamism into moribund SOEs thus helping to preserve jobs.

The second stage of reform characterized by SOEs' ownership transformation (*Gaizhi*) brought about efficiency-enhancing changes in China's state enterprise sector (Garnaut *et al.* 2005). While the successes of *Gaizhi* were significant, the potential harmful social impact associated with restructuring on such a massive scale also attracted public attention. The efforts at enterprise restructuring still had a further way to go and the financial gains to enterprises depended on progress in capabilities to generate profits. Measures to upgrade technology and product quality and to improve industry organization have been the keys to lasting improvements in enterprise efficiency. Reforms in these areas were in some respects more difficult and subject to greater constraints than reforms to reduce overhead burdens.

Impact of China's accession to the World Trade Organization

During the second stage of economic reform from 1993 to 2002, China was preparing for and finally joined the World Trade Organization (WTO) in 2001. WTO membership was generally perceived as beneficial by China, given the welfare gains from a more open economy as predicted by economic theory (Drysdale and Song 2000). However, some sectors of the economy, especially SOEs which remained rather inefficient and relied heavily on government subsidies, were concerned about the negative impact caused by the increased competition derived from membership in the WTO. Nonetheless, by the late 1990s, almost the entire SOE sector was in debt and the state banks were on the verge of insolvency burdened with non-performing loans resulting from the lending to SOE firms. In view of this situation, China had to further implement deeper reforms that included further privatization and deregulation (Bajona and Chu 2004).

The WTO is a multilateral trading system, which lays out the legal ground rules for international commerce. By gaining access to the WTO, China was forced to be in line with the international standard in many aspects of a market-based economy and to provide a relatively level playing field for all market participants including both foreign and domestic firms. The latter includes both the state and non-state enterprises. A series of domestic laws, regulations and market rules had to be changed and adjusted for the accession to the WTO. Particularly, upon accession China committed to partially eliminate state subsidies to SOEs and to eventually let all SOEs operate on a commercial basis, making them responsible for their own profits and losses. Hai (2000) explicitly pointed out that one important implication of China's WTO accession was to accelerate the reform of the SOEs and to help develop private enterprises in the Chinese economy.

China's WTO accession played an important role in supporting domestic reforms even before its formal accession in December 2001, as the Chinese government had decided to allow private ownership to take place throughout all sectors in order to become a member of the WTO. In this way, the WTO accession easily solved issues related to the status of domestic private firms: if national treatment was to be granted to foreign companies there was no excuse not to grant national treatment to domestic private enterprises (Bajona and Chu 2004). Through WTO accession, domestic private sectors, despite their weak political voices, were further promoted to become a growing part of the Chinese economy.

The Chinese government has used WTO membership as an instrument to lay down a framework for economic reform and to bring external forces toward the implementation of domestic reforms, including the difficult SOE reform. For example, the WTO agreement makes direct subsidies to SOEs more difficult to implement. Moreover, by requiring a more open financial sector, WTO membership forces banks to be more profit-oriented and to reduce lending to non-performing SOEs. Both factors combined to promote the restructuring of the SOE sector and the closing of inefficient SOEs (Bajona and Chu 2004). At the time of accession, SOEs still represented 60 percent of the total fiscal revenues and were deeply vested in various government agencies. The reform was expected to encounter strong resistance if it confronted all these vested interests directly. However, by tying the domestic reforms together with the accession to the WTO, the SOE reforms became an obligation to fulfill and an international commitment.

1.3 Stage 3 (2003 to present): deepening SOE reform

Establishing the modern enterprise system

During this latest stage of reform, deepening ownership reform and improving corporate governance became the main targets of SOE reform. For the management of remaining large SOEs, the government established the State-Owned Asset Supervision and Administration Commission (SASAC) in March 2003, representing the state in performing its duty and exercising its rights as the owner through its management of assets, personnel, and operations. Local SASACs were set up at provincial level in 2004 to manage local-level SOEs.

In October 2003, the Third Plenum of the Sixteenth Party Congress issued the Decision on Issues of Perfecting Socialist Market Economy System, which made a few ideological breakthroughs that were to have a profound impact on the further development of China's corporate governance system. For the first time, the Party acknowledged property rights as the "core issue" of ownership reform and made building a "modern system of property rights" an important task of future reform. Second, the Party redefined public ownership in a socialist economy and made "shareholding companies" the main organizational form of public ownership. The Party further made promotion of "mixed economy" its main task in establishing a market system in China. Last but not least, private enterprises were promoted and allowed to operate on an equal footing in terms of business financing and taxation with SOEs.

Corporatization of SOEs has become an important reform measure taken by the government since the mid-1990s with the goal of building China's own modern enterprises in a market system. After undergoing ownership reform, some SOEs went public. With the new ideological breakthroughs in 2003, more SOEs have turned into shareholding companies. In October 2007, in the report of the Seventeenth Party Congress, SOE reform was mentioned ten times. Deepening the SOE reform has been a top priority for China's economic reform in recent years. By the end of 2010, the number of SOEs under the direct control of the central government was limited to 121, among which only twenty-two were corporatized according to the Corporation Law.

Consequences of the third stage of reform

The non-state sector in China has experienced the developing process from virtual non-existence to existence and from weak to strong in the last three decades. SOEs contributed about 80 percent of the total industrial output in 1978, but the SOEs' share of industry output has declined steadily to less than 30 percent since 2007. On the other hand, the non-state sector of the economy has become the most important engine of economic growth in China, as the non-state sector accounted for more than 73.8 percent of the total economic output value in 2011 (Figure 12.5). Non-SOEs have surpassed SOEs in many aspects of economic activity such as total employment, taxation, and industrial profits (Figures 12.6–12.8). Chinese domestic private

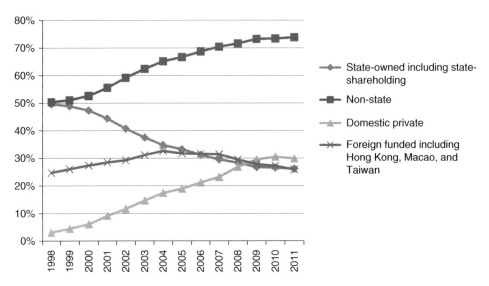

Figure 12.5   Share of gross industrial output value by types of ownership above designated size (1998–2011)

Source: Calculated using the data from *China Statistics Yearbook* in various issues

Notes: Comparing Figure 12.5 with Figure 12.3, we find that there is an inconsistency in the share of gross industrial output value by types of ownership. It is because before 1998 all enterprises were included in the statistics, but since 1998, especially since 2000, only enterprises above designated size, whose annual sales revenue was over 5 million Yuan, were surveyed and reported. Moreover, in Figure 12.5, SOEs also includes state-shareholding ones, which also increases the share of SOEs in the total. For the statistics in year 1998 and 1999, both enterprises above and below designated size were reported (the same note applies to Figures 12.6–12.9)

enterprises have also become the major market force in the Chinese economy, surpassing the foreign-funded and SOEs in output (Figure 12.5). Nonetheless, the development of the non-state economy is still facing many problems, such as difficulties for small and medium-sized private businesses to get loans from the formal banking sector, inadequate human capital and technical investment of private enterprises, as well as unfair competition conditions caused by

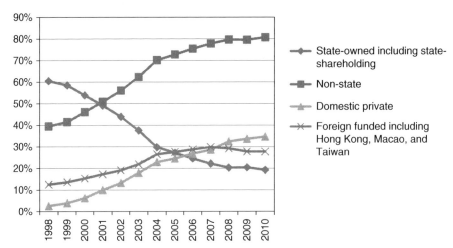

Figure 12.6   Annual average employment ratio by types of ownership above designated size (1998–2011)

Source: Calculated using the data from *China Statistics Yearbook* in various issues

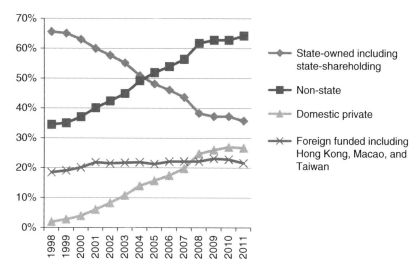

Figure 12.7 Annual ratio of value-added tax payable by types of ownership above designated size (1998–2011)

Source: Calculated using the data from *China Statistics Yearbook* in various issues

existing government regulations toward private and state operated enterprises such as market entry to certain industrial sectors and state monopolies.

SOEs' deteriorating financial performance turned better as the second stage of economic reform progressed. Profit rates had been declining from 1985 to 1997, but started to increase after 1997 (Figures 12.2, 12.4, and 12.9). Nevertheless, Li *et al.* (2012) largely attributed the rising profitability of SOEs in the first decade of this century to their enhanced monopolized market power. They showed that the upstream SOEs extracted rents from the liberalized downstream sectors in the process of industrialization and globalization. They implied that the relatively high profit rate in the past decade could be merely a growth-undermining symptom of the incompleteness of market-oriented reforms rather than proof of their efficiency dominance over non-SOEs.

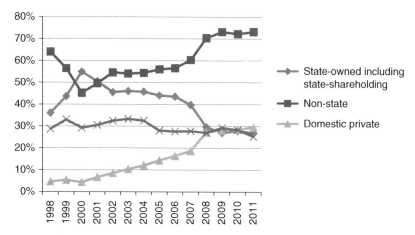

Figure 12.8 Annual ratio of total profit by types of ownership above designated size (1998–2011)

Source: Calculated using the data from *China Statistics Yearbook* in various issues

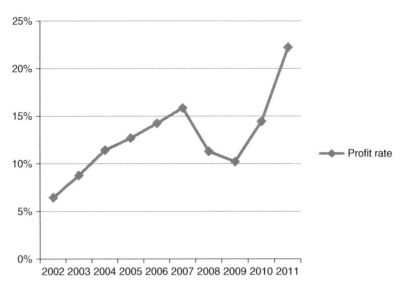

Figure 12.9   Profit rates of SOEs (2002–2011)

Source: Calculated using the data from *China Statistics Yearbook* in various issues

Key issues related to the third stage of enterprise reform

CORPORATE GOVERNANCE

Establishing an effective corporate governance system has become a key priority of China's current enterprise reform, with an objective to establish and develop a "modern enterprise system." Effective corporate governance ensures that the behavior of the managers is transparent, accountable and competitive, and firms can adapt to the changing demands of the market more efficiently. The Chinese government has tried to develop modern governance systems by pushing SOEs to restructure and reorient managerial incentives in order to engage in profit-oriented, value-augmenting activities, in line with social or public interests. Moreover, to cope with the increased competition from both domestic and international sources, China's enterprises need to improve their decision-making mechanisms to compete successfully in domestic and international markets. Adoption of corporate governance mechanisms in line with international practice is also essential to the ability of China's enterprises to attract foreign capital in increasingly competitive global capital markets. The development of China's equity markets contributes to the improvement of corporate governance practice for those listed firms. However, further changes are much needed to improve the practice (Tenev and Zhang, 2002).

As domestic private enterprises have developed quickly and started to become a dominating force in China's economy, how to improve their internal governance turns out to be a key issue for their success and sustainable development. Most private firms in China are owned by an individual or a family and also managed by the owners, or their relatives. However, as many private firms grow larger, the old family-type management style may not be suitable for their business development. Compared to the corporate governance of advanced economies, there is still a large gap for the Chinese domestic private companies to catch up. In recent years, there have been many examples of Chinese domestic private companies failing due to mismanagement.

Mature corporate governance goes beyond the simple purpose of making profit for companies. A modern company should have its corporate social responsibility combining both the interests of developing the company and caring for society. Morris Chang, Chairman and CEO of Taiwan Semiconductor Manufacturing Company (TSMC), indicated on its website that TSMC tries to improve its performance in the following seven dimensions of "morals, business ethics, economy, rule of law, work/life balance, caring for the earth and the next generation, and philanthropy" in order to act as a good corporate citizen, inspire others to follow, and make society better.[3] SOEs in China also increased corporate responsibility reports from five in 2006 to seventy-six in 2011.[4] However, the number of Chinese enterprises demonstrating their corporate social responsibility is still very small.

Governance reform in China has involved a series of institutional and organizational transformations, such as establishment of a multi-tiered state asset management system, the introduction of boards of directors and other modern governance mechanisms into corporatized firms, and the promotion of corporate social responsibility. The success of the reforms in improving enterprise governance has been uneven: governance has improved most for SOEs in competitive sectors and much less, if at all, for those in protected industries (World Bank 2012). To improve corporate governance, the state shareholder and regulatory functions should be sufficiently separated in practice. It is also important to effectively protect the rights and obligations entailed in modern corporate governance mechanisms in China through strengthened institutional and regulatory enforcement.

TECHNOLOGY AND INNOVATION

Sustaining high growth poses a considerable challenge for China. In the past three decades, high levels of investment have been a major driving force of growth in China, but with population growth slowing rapidly and investment rates also declining, China's future growth will be more dependent on gains in total factor productivity (TFP), as has been argued by the World Bank (2012) among others.

According to the estimates made by Zhu (2012), the average annual TFP growth rate for the Chinese state sector is 1.68 percent, while that for non-state sector is 3.91 from 1978 to 2007 (see Table 12.1). Zhu (2012) also separated the time-frame into three stages, which are roughly consistent with the three stages described in this chapter. As we can see from Table 12.1, from 1978 to 1988, the average annual TFP growth rate for the state sector was negative, indicating that the first stage of SOE growth was mainly due to the increases of capital and labor. Even up to 1998, the state sector still had very low productivity growth rates, reflecting the deteriorating performance of SOEs during that period. From 1988 to 1998, the productivity growth in the non-state sector also dropped to 2.17 percent from 5.87 percent during the period between 1978 and 1988, indicating there was a structural problem in China's economy. After 1998, TFP in the state sector grew rapidly, averaging 5.5 percent annually and exceeding the average growth rate in the non-state sector, which is 3.67 percent. Zhu (2012) attributed the increase in TFP

Table 12.1 Total factor productivity growth by sector

Period	Average annual total factor productivity growth (%)		
	Non-state	*State*	*Aggregate*
1978–2007	3.91	1.68	3.61
1978–1988	5.87	−0.36	3.83
1988–1998	2.17	0.27	2.45
1998–2007	3.67	5.5	4.68

Source: Zhu (2012)

growth in state and non-state sectors after 1998 to the combined effects of privatization and trade liberalization.

To maintain relatively high TFP growth, China needs to further accelerate its industrial structural upgrading, speed up technological innovation, and create a more competitive and open economy. China's President Hu Jintao first proposed to build an "innovative nation" in October 2005. In 2006, the Chinese government laid out a strategy for enterprise-led indigenous innovation (Zhang *et al.* 2009). As Zhang *et al.* (2009) pointed out, in implementing this strategy, China faces great challenges from its current development stage and economic transitional nature. First, Chinese enterprises must derive their competitiveness from innovation while continuing to create jobs for the huge Chinese labor force. Second, the major performers of R&D activities in China are SOEs and government-run research institutes, while private enterprises only accounted for 3.5 percent of total R&D expenditure in 2006. Third, the supporting market institutions, such as weak intellectual property protection, barriers to entry, exit, and fair competition, and an underdeveloped venture capital system, are not functioning well enough to promote innovation in China.

To overcome the above problems, Zhang *et al.* (2009) suggest pursuing a balanced strategy, creating the right incentives, building the capacity of private enterprises and strengthening the supporting market institutions including the venture capital system. Similar to their suggestions, a key reform recommendation given by the World Bank (2012) on China's innovation policy is to redefine the government's role in the national innovation system, "shifting away from targeted attempts at developing specific new technologies and moving toward institutional development and an enabling environment that supports economy-wide innovation efforts within a competitive market system."

2 Unfinished tasks

After three decades of economic reform, China has been moving toward establishing a market-based economy. Competition is strong in many though not all industries. The economic behavior of enterprises has become increasingly responsive to market forces as a result of competition, the growth of non-state enterprises, and management reforms within SOEs. The main tasks remaining are to develop legal, financial, and other institutions including the functions of the government necessary to the working of a market-based economy; convert SOEs including those with monopolies into modern commercial entities; improve corporate governance; and upgrade China's economic structure where more innovative firms can flourish.

In a mature market economy, there exist a number of institutions that facilitate its functioning. The crucial factors are as follows: institutions which protect private property rights; a fair, level playing field for competition in both product and factor markets; fewer barriers to entry or exit. The essential step in China's SOE reform is to create a market environment in which enterprises with all kinds of ownership arrangements can compete with each other under a fair environment and in which "the fittest survives." To do so, a few questions need to be further addressed.

2.1 State, market, and entrepreneurship

The ongoing economic reform has introduced and allowed free-market forces to function in China albeit on a gradual and trial basis. However, as development economics indicates, the market alone cannot solve all the problems; market and state are both necessary factors for coordinating economic activity and promoting a country's development (Hayami 2001; Otsuka and

Kalirajan 2006). Market failures in the supply of public goods can also occur in the case of private goods. The key question for a country's development is how to arrive at an optimal combination of the roles of market and state in promoting a country's welfare (Otsuka and Kalirajan 2006). The contribution of markets toward improving economic welfare will gradually be increased in response to the new opportunities opened up by the introduction of new technologies. The key process in technological change is described by Schumpeter as the introduction of innovation through the process of "creative destruction." What drives entrepreneurs to undertake innovation is nothing but profit motives shaped by free-market forces (Schumpeter 1975).

In the case of China, the ongoing economic reform has been a process of interactions between the market and state, plus the fostering of entrepreneurship in China. The Chinese government has been trying to progress in this direction by promoting market economy in China while adjusting the role of government in the process of economic development. However, in many aspects, state interventions or personal disposition instead of market forces still play a major role in China's economy, causing inefficient allocation of resources. Wu and Fan noticed that corruption is holding China back (see Chapter 4 in this volume) and some "special interest groups" in China are resistant to reform.[5]

The past experience of reform shows that the development of the Chinese economy has been to some extent accompanied by a process of "creative destruction," as Joseph Schumpeter long ago labeled it. The improved environment since the economic reform in 1978 has nurtured private entrepreneurship in China. Entrepreneurial opportunities emerged from market development as well as from changing institutional rules in China. During the first stage of reform, a popular but transient behavior of entrepreneurs was the practice of taking advantage of gaps in both markets and institutional structures. As a result, informal processes that could lead to corruption are still rampant in China.

Ahmad and Hoffman (2008) suggested a framework for addressing and measuring entrepreneurship, in which six themes (regulatory framework, market conditions, access to capital, access to R&D and technology, entrepreneurial capabilities, and culture) were described as the major determinants affecting entrepreneurial performance. These determinant indicators are all important for the development of entrepreneurship in a country. It implies that if China wants to further promote its economic development it must hold onto the market-oriented economy with an adaptable regulatory framework, provide fair access for both SOEs and non-SOEs to capital and technology, and enhance a social culture to respect entrepreneurship and to increase entrepreneurial capabilities.

2.2 The state vs. the non-state (and breaking up the state monopoly)

Since 2002, there has been a hot debate on whether China's state-owned economy expands while its private economy shrinks. Some Chinese economists call this phenomenon "the advancement of the state and the retreat of the non-state," and believe it has led to unintended but foreseeable social consequences that have weakened the momentum of the growing economy. If we look at the Figures 12.5–12.8, however, we find that in general the importance of the state sector in China has been shrinking but the non-state sector has been growing over time. For example, the proportion of state-owned industrial output was about 40 percent in 2002, but dropped to 26.2 percent in 2011, indicating that overall economic development is moving toward privatization. However, if we look more closely at the data in the *China Statistics Yearbook*, we find that the proportions of state-owned economy in oil and natural gas, tobacco, and non-ferrous metals industries have been increasing over recent years. A survey done by the Chinese Entrepreneurs indicates that the top industries with high domination of state-owned economy are oil, petrochemicals, aviation, steel, coal, finance, telecommunications, and railways. These industries are highly related to people's livelihood and they are profitable monopoly industries in China. *The Australian* reported that "the 150,000 Chinese SOEs receive more than three-quarters of all formal bank loans, with the 4.5 million domestic firms receiving less than 10 percent. In 2009, the three largest Chinese SOEs earned more revenue than the largest 500 domestic private sector firms combined."[6]

Experiences of many countries strongly suggest that the contribution of SOEs to overall economic performance is likely to be greatest when they are confined to natural monopolies or other industries where extensive public ownership is clearly needed on economic or compelling social grounds (OECD 2000). Although China is still a developing economy, defining the strategic industries where SOEs will dominate fairly narrowly is likely to be most conducive to economic growth and development. In particular, the economic gains from SOE reorganization could be greater if the current policies were directed at a more rapid and broader withdrawal of SOE monopolies from competitive industries, including its service sectors, and a wider and deeper participation of private capital in the restructuring of the SOE sector. With the high concentration of social resources and funds, SOE monopolies are getting larger and larger and becoming less and less energetic due to a long-term monopoly operation. Large SOE monopolies have created a drag on the economy through price distortion and vast opportunity for corruption and waste, leading to higher cost for consumers and a more unequal distribution of income.

In 2005 and 2010, the State Council respectively issued policies to encourage the non-state economy and to guide private investment flowing into these monopolized industries. However, in reality, there are still many visible and invisible barriers for private investment to flow into monopolized industries in China. Earlier in 2012, China's Premier, Wen Jiabao, promised to push forward the reform of state monopolies: "We must move ahead with reform of the railway, power and other monopolized industries, complete and implement policies and measures aimed at promoting the development of the non-state economy, break monopolies and lower industry thresholds for new entrants."[7] In order to give a more important role to private investment by breaking up the monopolized industries, private business should be promoted with more accessible bank loans and other financial resources, such as equity markets, and should be allowed to invest in more high-end areas, such as finance and telecommunications.

2.3 Business financing

The banking system reform

Since the economic reform in 1978, the Chinese banking system has gradually evolved from a government-owned and centrally planned loan provider toward an increasingly competitive market in which different types of banks compete to provide a variety of financial services. One of the main purposes of the Chinese banking system reform has been to create incentives for its banks to behave more like competitive and commercial entities. Nonetheless, China's banks have not been granted full autonomy, and are still heavily controlled and influenced by the government. Since banking reform is dealt with in Chapter 15 is this volume, the discussion here will deal only briefly with the relationship of banking reform to state enterprise reform.

There are two distinctive features of China's banking system, which have important implications for the development of the enterprise sectors in China. First, China's banking sector itself is still highly dominated by state-owned and state share-holding banks, although entry of new private institutions is encouraged in principle. The second distinctive feature is the concentration of financing on SOEs. SOEs have been traditionally favored by banks for loans, as SOEs are perceived to be lower risk or at least backed by the government in the event of loan forfeiture. Although the share has declined somewhat in recent years, SOEs still dominate the majority of bank loans in China, accounting for about 75 percent of total bank loans.[8] Since the Chinese government initiated its economic stimulus policy after the global financial crisis in late 2008, there have been some signs showing that more shares of bank loans go to the state-owned or state-dominated sector. In 2009 alone, 85 percent of the newly added bank loans were granted to SOEs.[9] The World Bank (2012) reported that the majority of the economic stimulus plan issued by the Chinese government went to the construction and infrastructure sector, which were still dominated by SOEs. SOEs also enjoy lower interest rates and preferential access to equity and bond market financing (Martin 2012). In contrast, non-state enterprises receive only a small fraction of commercial bank lending (World Bank 2012). Not surprisingly, non-state enterprises, with the exception of foreign-funded businesses, rely noticeably more on internal funds to finance their investment than do the SOEs.

Development of China's banking system is therefore essential to the success of reforms to the enterprise sector. A key challenge to the current banking system that now disproportionately focuses on SOEs is to better serve the needs of the growing non-state sectors. Non-state enterprises are in general more efficient than SOEs in terms of total gross output value, employment, taxation and profits and more importantly productivity. Nonetheless, they are in a disadvantageous position to obtain financial support from banks. Therefore, the government needs to take steps to standardize the treatment of private capital in the banking sector, and banks need to make their lending process more transparent and fair so that small and medium-sized private enterprises have an equal means to finance their business and compete with SOEs. However, efforts to improve their financing are focused on adapting existing facilities but have met with limited success so far.

With more than twenty years' development of equity markets in China since the 1990s, China's stock markets have played an important role in the development of the Chinese economy and its market system. The stock markets have not only helped Chinese companies to raise the much-needed financial capital, but also helped to improve the corporate governance of listed companies. On the two national stock exchanges there were 2,342 firms listed by the end of 2011 and the overall stock market capitalization reached about two-thirds of China's GDP.[10] However, nearly all the listed firms are large SOEs, and the development of China's equity markets is far from satisfactory.

The development of China's stock markets has been hampered by excessive government control, segmented market structure, insufficient liquidity, lack of transparency, and an underdeveloped legal and regulatory framework. The inefficient performance of equity markets in China is due to the absence of a trading platform based on fairness and transparency, effective price-setting mechanisms driven by market forces, and a compensation mechanism designed to protect investors' interests and especially the interests of small investors. With regard to financing in equity markets, there is tremendous bias in favor of SOEs over non-SOEs (Zhang 2005). This is in contrast with the increasing importance of non-state-owned firms in the Chinese economy since the 1990s. One may question to what extent China's stock market performance is due to the fact that some listed companies sold junk shares at high prices; the interests of the investors were not duly protected and the market lacked credibility. In 2011, 252 companies raised IPO, but 55 of them, or 21.8 percent, had a decreased net profit in their first three-quarters. More recently, however, the authorities have been accelerating efforts to develop and better regulate the stock markets. The major motivation behind these efforts is twofold: to broaden and augment financing sources for SOEs; and to strengthen external financial discipline and the corporate governance of large SOEs.

2.4 *Evolving legal institutions and China's enterprise reform*

Enterprise reform in China has been accompanied by the reform of China's legal system because economic growth requires legal institutions put in place to offer stable and predictable rights of property and contract (North 1990; Hall and Jones 1999; and Clarke 2003). In the transition from "planned economy" to "a market economy," China's SOEs need to operate independently of the government and deal with other legal entities through market transactions. For private sector development, an independent, transparent, and enforceable legal system can offer guarantees to private property rights, facilitate business transactions, and build confidence among the entrepreneurs for reinvestment. With the ongoing and deepening economic reform, it is necessary for China to improve its legal system to meet the needs of further economic development and enterprise reform. Because Chapter 16 in this volume deals with legal reform, the discussion here will only summarize briefly the relevance of legal reform to enterprise reform.

To create a legal environment in which all enterprises – including both SOEs and non-SOEs – participate as independent market players, namely free of government interventions, reform is needed in the following legal areas: first, enterprise and labor contract laws need to be further strengthened, which define enterprises' rights and obligations, regulate enterprises' establishment and operation, and protect the legal rights of labor; second, contract law needs to be further improved to protect the legal rights of contracting parties and allow economic transactions between parties to replace administrative controls; third, bankruptcy and competition laws (anti-monopoly) need to be fully implemented to promote fair and effective competition among all kinds of enterprises and to ensure the continued protection of the public interest even without direct state management of enterprises; finally, China needs to strengthen its financial laws, including securities laws and regulations, to allow enterprise financing activities to take place in a market-driven environment rather than through a planning mechanism or being influenced by the governments. Through more than three decades' efforts, China has made great improvements in its legal framework. Various laws and regulations mentioned above have been promulgated, implemented, and revised according to the needs of economic development. However, much more work needs to be done to improve the legal system and practice.

Among all these laws and regulations, the Corporate Law and the Labor Contract Law have played a significant role in enterprise reform and attracted a great deal of attention from the public. The Corporate Law of 1993 was important in protecting the interests of both corporations and shareholders by clearly defining the formation of corporations, corporate governance structure, corporate finance, shareholders' rights, and so on. However, the majority of the existing SOEs were still essentially governed by the State Enterprise Act of 1988 and its subordinate regulations of 1992. To a great extent, the State Enterprise Act of 1988 was still influenced by the planned economy, while the Corporate Law of 1993 was the product of adopting a market economy in China. The Corporate Law of 1993 provided the solid legal foundations for the SOEs to be transformed into corporations and shareholding corporations. Meanwhile, through the economic and legal reforms, many relevant laws, including bankruptcy law, securities law and competition law, have also been promulgated and updated. The legal regime governing business organization was substantially revised in the middle of the first decade of the twenty-first century, so as to further support economic reform in China.

Another important legal update is the formation and development of the Labor Contract Law, aiming at the protection of labor rights. With the ongoing economic reform, industrial relationships have inevitably experienced fundamental changes, and labor legislation became necessary in the process of reform. The labor contract system was first experimented with in joint ventures in the Special Economic Zones (SEZs) in the 1980s and later extended to applying in SOEs. The Labor Law of 1995 was the first national law to introduce a labor contract system to break the "iron rice bowl" (permanent employment) in China. However, the Labor Law of 1995 did not provide adequate protection for employees. Employee abuse was rampant in China and labor–employer relations were precarious without the legal protection of labor rights. Labor disputes in China increased more than thirteen-fold between 1995 and 2006 (Ngok 2008). The continued privatization of SOEs has led to an increasing unemployment rate, especially among the poorly paid migrant workers since the late 1990s. The Labor Contract Law was passed in 2007 and came into effect in 2008 with the hope of filling some gaps left open by the Labor Law of 1995. It was designed to give employees greater rights and easier enforcement of their rights so as to achieve the ultimate social policy of creating and sustaining a "harmonious society."

2.5 New challenges faced by Chinese enterprises

The rising wage rate resulting from demographic, statutory, and economic developments has put increasing pressures on enterprises in China, including both domestic and foreign-funded ones. China now is facing "the Lewis turning point" with reduced supply of surplus labor from rural to urban areas (Cai and Wang 2009). It has a significant impact on the structural changes in the Chinese economy as it will be more and more difficult for China to achieve extraordinary productivity growth while keeping inflation under control under the influence of this demographic change (Garnaut 2010). China's enterprises will be compelled to grow based more on the improvement of productivity rather than the input of labor. To manage the change, the labor force needs to be provided with more training in service sectors and high-end manufacturing.

The global financial and economic crisis has reduced the demand for Chinese exports substantially. Many Chinese export-oriented enterprises went bankrupt, and millions of jobs were lost during the crisis period of 2008–9. To mitigate the negative impact caused by the international financial crisis, the Chinese government used various measures to promote its economy, such as increasing government investment, expanding domestic demand, encouraging indigenous innovation, and upgrading its economic structure. However, some of these measures may take a long time to be effective. The key is that China could still have room for further growth created by deepening its institutional reform. China should promote employment by opening up and developing the service sector. The service sector has a great potential to absorb the workers released from the export sector. To boost investments in the service sector, the Chinese government should first break up the monopolies of SOEs in such fields as finance, insurance, education, medical care, telecommunications, and transport – and open up these activities to private investment.

Further development of Chinese enterprises and their ambitions to become multinational companies have motivated them to invest overseas. The relatively limited domestic natural resource supplies and the fear of resource constraints on growth have motivated the Chinese government to encourage its SOEs and domestic private firms to invest overseas. China's outward direct investment (ODI) has increased rapidly in recent years. By the end of 2009, China's 108 central government-owned SOEs had invested in 5,901 foreign firms (SOASAC 2010). The total overseas assets belonging to central government-owned SOEs exceeded renminbi 4,000 billion (equivalent to US$ 597 billion using the 2009 exchange rate). In 2009, the profits received from overseas operations accounted for 37.7 percent of the total profits of central government-owned SOEs. According to the Ministry of Commerce, ODI from China's SOEs accounted for 69.2 percent of total ODI stock by the end of 2009, whereas that from private firms only accounted for 1 percent of total ODI stock.[11] All the top thirty firms ranked by size of overseas assets and firm size are SOEs.

Song *et al.* (2011) linked the participation of SOEs in overseas markets with domestic structural reform and firm development, as they are forced to navigate a new business and political or institutional environment in which privileges enjoyed in China are no longer available. The heightened competition abroad forces SOEs to increase their competitiveness through efficiency-enhancing measures. Therefore, for them, changes must occur in three fundamental areas of reform: competition, ownership, and regulation. The changes in these areas are crucial for the success of SOEs' investment abroad and will have some impact on China's reform agenda for the state sector in the future.

3 Conclusions

There has been a remarkable transformation in China's enterprise sectors over the past three decades (1980–2010). In 1978, there were no Chinese mainland companies in the Fortune Global 500 list – in 2012 there were seventy, among which sixty-five were SOEs; China has made great achievements in enterprise reform and economic development. The non-SOE sector, especially domestic private enterprises, has become the largest share of output. Enterprise reform in China is shaped by several distinctive characteristics, reflecting policy-imposed constraints and other special characteristics of the economy, that need to be taken into account in drawing conclusions about the process.

Measures to be taken in the future should help boost enterprise financial performance and provide a further impetus to real growth in the economy as a whole. In many areas, reforms undertaken so far provide necessary institutional frameworks and mechanisms for improving enterprise performances, but the conditions required for their effective functioning are often lacking. Lack of adequate progress in some areas, such as the end of policy lending by commercial banks, is limiting or preventing progress in other areas. Nonetheless, several conclusions seem reasonable based on the evidence cited in this chapter.

First, non-state enterprises have become the main contributors to overall growth in output and employment in the economy in the past three decades and they are likely to remain the key player in determining the economy's performance in the future. Reforming the SOE sector is essential to improving its efficiency and to releasing more resources for use in those more productive areas involving private businesses. But the extent to which these reforms result in improved performance of the economy as a whole depends on the degree to which the problems of the non-state sectors are alleviated, and their operational environments are improved.

Second, measures to reduce unfavorable conditions in financing the private sector have the potential to significantly improve financial performances of the commercial banks and other lending institutions as well as boosting the development of non-state enterprises. Further development of money and capital markets is important to ensure that financial discipline becomes firmly rooted. These markets are also needed to provide mechanisms for market-based enterprise restructuring, which is much required in China. In that process of enterprise restructuring, those inefficient enterprises whether SOEs or non-SOEs should be allowed to go bankrupt in order to free up the resources to be directed to those enterprises that are more efficient and productive. This is the only effective way for China to move toward optimizing its industrial structure and through this, its welfare improvement.

Third, the success of SOE reform depends on the creation of an egalitarian competitive environment, supported by more transparent and well-functioning institutions including China's legal system. There need to be fundamental improvements in corporate governance of SOEs, in parallel with direct efforts to bolster the financial performance of enterprise. Many of the current financial problems of enterprises reflect past mistakes in investment and other business decisions arising from weaknesses in management and in financial discipline. Enterprises will need to respond more effectively to market forces than they often have in the past. The reforms need to make substantial progress in the above key areas in order for China's enterprises to contribute more positively to future growth. This urgency partly reflects the fact that reforms have become increasingly interdependent, as well as the need for rapid and effective adjustments by enterprises to the changes in both the internal and external business environments that will come with growing domestic as well as international competition.

Finally, China is facing enormous challenges in the next phase of its growth and development. Deepening its enterprise system reform involving both the state and the non-state sector is an important part of China's overall strategy. The success will depend on how China tackles the problems associated with the existing institutions and policies in relation to the future development of its state and non-state enterprises.

Notes

1 Able research assistance provided by Haiyang Zhang is gratefully acknowledged. All remaining possible errors are mine.
2 See *China Statistics Yearbook* in 1996 and 2003.
3 See "Message from Chairman and CEO" at <http://www.tsmc.com/english/csr/message_from_chairman.htm>, accessed on 18 December 2012.
4 See "Corporate Social Responsibility in China: Outlook and Challenges" at <http://www.triplepundit.com/2012/09/corporate-social-responsibility-in-china/>, accessed on 18 December 2012.
5 See "Special groups obtaining vested interests through power are reluctant to reform" by Jinglian Wu at <http://business.sohu.com/20121218/n360730175.shtml>, accessed on 20 December 2012 (in Chinese).
6 See "Retreat of private sector a millstone for Beijing's next leaders", by John Lee, *The Australian*, at <http://www.theaustralian.com.au/opinion/world-commentary/retreat-of-private-sector-a-millstone-for-beijings-next-leaders/story-e6frg6ux-1226509440039>, accessed on 27 November 2012.
7 See "Special Report: China's other power struggle", by Reuters, at <http://www.reuters.com/article/2012/10/16/us-china-soe-idUSBRE89F1MP20121016>, accessed on 27 November 2012.
8 See "Economy of the People's Republic of China", *Wikipedia*, <http://en.wikipedia.org/wiki/Economy_of_the_People's_Republic_of_China>, accessed on 15 January 2013.
9 See "SOEs Are Important, But Let's Not Exaggerate", *China Economic Watch*, <http://www.piie.com/blogs/china/?p=776>, accessed on 15 January 2013.
10 See "Listed Domestic Companies Total in China", at Trading Economics <http://www.tradingeconomics.com/china/listed-domestic-companies-total-wb-data.html>, accessed on 15 January. 2013.
11 See *Statistics Bulletin of China's Outward Foreign Direct Investment* published by the Ministry of Commerce of China, 2009.

Bibliography

Ahmad, N. and Hoffman, A. (2008) 'A Framework for Addressing and Measuring Entrepreneurship', OECD Statistics Working Papers 2008/02, OECD Publishing http://dx.doi.org/10.1787/243160627270.

Arrow, K. (2001) 'The Role of Time', chapter 6 in L. R. Klein and M. Pomer (eds.), *The New Russia: Transition Gone Awry*, Stanford, CA: Stanford University Press, 85–91.

Ayyagari, M., Kunt, A. D., and Maksimovic, V. (2010) 'Formal versus Informal Finance: Evidence from China', published by Oxford University Press on behalf of the Society for Financial Studies.

Bajona, C. and Chu, T. (2004) 'China's WTO Accession and Its Effect on State-Owned Enterprises', EAST–WEST Center Working paper, online version downloaded from http://www.eastwestcenter.org/sites/default/files/private/ECONwp070.pdf.

Cai, F. and Wang, M. (2009) 'China's Process of Ageing before Getting Rich', chapter 3 in C. Fang and D. Yang (eds.), *The China Population and Labor Yearbook, Volume 1: The Approaching Lewis Turning Point and Its Policy Implications*, Leiden and Boston, MA: Brill, 49–64.

Chan, A. and Unger, J. (2009) 'A Chinese State Enterprise under the Reforms: What Model of Capitalism?', *China Journal*, 62.

Chen, J. (ed.) (2008) *Zhong Guo Qi Ye Gai Ge Fa Zhan San Shi Nian*, Beijing: China Financial, Political and Economic Publishing House.

Chow, G. C. (2002) *China's Economic Transformation*, Malden, MA: Blackwell.

Clarke, D. (2003) 'Economic Development and the Rights Hypothesis: The China Problem', *American Journal of Comparative Law*, 51: 89–111.

Deer, L. and Song, L. (2012) 'China's Approach to Rebalancing: A Conceptual and Policy Framework', *China and World Economy*, 2(1): 1–26.

Drysdale, P. and Song, L. (eds.) (2000) *China's Entry to the WTO: Strategic Issues and Quantitative Assessment*, London: Routledge.

Garnaut, R., Song, L., Yao, Y., and Wang, X. (2001) *Private Enterprise in China*, Canberra: Asia Pacific Press at the Australian National University.

Garnaut, R., Song, L., Tenev, S. and Yao, Y. (2005) *China's Ownership Transformation: Process, Outcomes, Prospects*, Washington, DC: International Finance Corporation, and the World Bank.

Garnaut, R., Song, L. and Yao, Y. (2006) 'Impact and Significance of State-Owned Enterprise Restructuring in China', *China Journal*, 55: 35–63.

Garnaut, R. (2010) 'Macroeconomic Implications of the Turning Point', *China Economic Journal*, 3(2): 181–90.

Hai, W. (2000) 'China's WTO Membership: Significance and Implications', China Center for Economic Research Working Paper Series, Peking University, No. E2000007.

Hall, R. and Jones, C. (1999) 'Why Do Some Countries Produce So Much More Output per Worker than Others?', *Quarterly Journal of Economics*, 114(1): 83–116.

Hayami, Y. (2001) *Development Economics: From the Poverty to the Wealth of Nations*, 2nd edition, Oxford: Oxford University Press.

Hayami, Y. (2009) 'Social Capital, Human Capital and the Community Mechanism: Toward a Conceptual Framework for Economists', *Journal of Development Studies*, 45(1): 96–123.

Jefferson, G. H. and Singh, I. (eds.) (1999) *Enterprise Reform in China: Ownership, Transition, and Performance*, Oxford: Oxford University Press.

Li, H., Meng, L., Wang, Q., and Zhou, L. (2008) 'Political Connections, Financing and Firm Performance: Evidence from Chinese Private Firms', *Journal of Development Economics*, 87: 283–99.

Li, X., Liu, X. W., and Wang, Y. (2012) 'A Model of China's State Capitalism', draft online version downloaded from http://igov.berkeley.edu/sites/default/files/55.Wang_Yong.pdf.

Lin, J. Y. (1992) 'Rural Reforms and Agricultural Growth in China', *American Economic Review*, 82(1): 34–51.

Lin, J. Y. (1998) 'State Intervention, Ownership and State Enterprise Reform in China', chapter 4 in Wu, Rong-I and Chu, Yun-Peng (eds.), *Business, Markets and Government in the Asia-Pacific Competition Policy, Convergence and Pluralism*, London: Routledge.

Lin, J. Y., Cai, F., and Li, Z. (1998) 'Competition, Policy Burdens, and State Owned Enterprise Reform', *American Economic Review Papers and Proceedings*, 88(2).

McKay, H. and Song, L. (2010) 'China as a Global Manufacturing Powerhouse: Strategic Considerations and Structural Adjustment', *China and World Economy*, 18(1): 1–32.

McMillan, J. and Naughton, B. (1992) 'How to Reform a Planned Economy: Lessons from China', *Oxford Review of Economic Policy*, 8: 130–43.

Martin, M. F. (2012) 'China's Banking System: Issues for Congress', Congressional Research Service Report, downloaded from http://www.fas.org/sgp/crs/row/R42380.pdf.

Naughton, B. (1992) 'Growing out of the Plan: Chinese Economic Reform, 1978–90', mimeo.

Nga, N. T. (2013), 'Ownership bias and economic transition: evidence from manufacturing sector in Vietnam', Ph.D. dissertation, Crawford School of Public Policy, Australian National University, Canberra.

Ngok, K. (2008) 'The Changes of Chinese Labor Policy and Labor Legislation in Context of Market Transition', *International Labor and Working-Class History*, 73: 45–64.

North, D. (1990) *Institutions, Institutional Change and Economic Performance*, Cambridge: Cambridge University Press.

OECD (2000) *Reforming China's Enterprises*, Paris: OECD.

Otsuka, K. and Kalirajan, K. (2006) 'Rice Green Revolution in Asia and Its Transferability to Africa: An Introduction', *Developing Economies*, 44(2): 1–10.

Schumpeter, J. (1975) *Capitalism, Socialism and Democracy*, New York: Harper.

SOASAC (State-owned Assets Supervision and Administration Commission of the State Council) (2010) *Report on China's Central SOEs' Overall Performance in 2009* (online; cited 13 August 2011). Available from: http://news.xinhuanet.com/fortune/2010–08/13/c_12444135.htm.

Song, L. and Zhang, Y. (2010) 'Will Chinese Growth Slow after the Lewis Turning Point?', *China Economic Journal*, 3(2): 211–21.

Song, L., Yang, J., and Zhang, Y. (2011) 'State-owned Enterprises' Outward Investment and the Structural Reform in China', *China & World Economy*, 19(4): 38–53.

Tenev, S. and Zhang, C. with Loup, B. (2002) *Corporate Governance and Enterprise Reform in China*, Washington, DC: World Bank and the International Finance Corporation.

World Bank (1995) 'Policy Options for Reform of Chinese State-Owned Enterprises', World Bank Discussion Paper No. 335.

World Bank (1996) 'China: Reform of State-Owned Enterprises', World Bank Report No. 14924–CHA, China and Mongolia Department.

World Bank (1997) *China 2020*, Washington, DC.

World Bank (1999) 'China: Weathering the Storm, Learning the Lessons', Country Economic Memorandum, Report No. 18678 CHA.

World Bank and Development Research Center of the State Council, the People's Republic of China (2012) *China 2030*, Washington, DC.

Zhang, C., Zeng, D. Z., Mako, W. P., and Seward, J. (2009) *Promoting Enterprise-Led Innovation in China*, Washington, DC: World Bank.

Zhang, W. (2005) 'The Role of China's Securities Market in SOE Reform and Private Sector Development', chapter 5 in D. Vandenbrink and D. Hew (eds.), *Capital Markets In Asia: Changing Roles for Economic Development*, Tokyo Club Foundation for Global Studies.

Zhu, X. (2012) 'Understanding China's Growth: Past, Present, and Future', *Journal of Economic Perspectives*, 26(4): 103–24.

13

FOREIGN TRADE OF CHINA

K. C. Fung and Sarah Y. Tong

Introduction

Trade expansion has been important to China's growth in recent decades. With an annual growth rate of 17 percent since 1978, trade has consistently outstripped the already staggering 10 percent a year growth of the overall economy (Tong 2013). In 1978, when China first adopted its "open door" policy, China's merchandise exports amounted to US$9.8 billion while its merchandise imports were US$10.9 billion (Fung 1998; Fung *et al.* 2004). China's exports and imports stood at US$1.90 trillion and US$1.74 trillion, respectively in 2011. Indeed, during the last three decades, trade liberalization and expansion served as an essential force underlying China's remarkable development and transformation.

Since 2001, when China joined the World Trade Organization (WTO), China's trade expansion had further accelerated (Tong and Zheng 2008). Between 2001 and 2008, when the global economic crisis hit, China's trade still grew by a staggering 26 percent a year in nominal terms. Overall, annual growth in total trade was over 20 percent in the 2000s, up from 12 percent in the 1980s and 15 percent in the 1990s. As a result, China has become a leading trading nation, ranking number one in export and number two in imports in 2009, accounting for 9.6 percent and 7.9 percent of the world total, respectively.

As such, China's foreign trade now has a significant global impact. While the European Union (EU) and the United States are its largest export markets, it is among the most important trading partners for many other countries around the world. Some of the economies affected and the extent they are affected may seem a bit surprising to those who do not work in this area. For example, in 2010, China had become the largest export market for Brazil and it was Brazil's second largest source of imports. This is up from a rank of number twelve and number eleven in 2000, respectively. For Mexico, China in 2010 was the third largest export market and its second largest source of imports. This is up from number nineteen and number six in 2000 (Aminian *et al.* 2009; Fung and Garcia-Herrero 2012).

In Asia and the Pacific Region, China has been among the largest trading partners for many economies, perhaps unsurprisingly (Tong and Chong 2010). In 2011, China was the largest export market and source of imports for Australia, Japan, and South Korea. It was also the largest trading partner and the number one source of imports for Taiwan and the ten members of the Association of Southeast Asian Nations (ASEAN).

In this chapter, we will discuss various important aspects of China's trade. In the next section, we will focus on the general characteristics of China's trade. In section 3, we focus on China's participation in the regional and global supply chains. In section 4, we examine how China's trade may have been facilitated by foreign direct investment, focusing particularly on China's involvement in various production networks. In the last section, we conclude.

1 General characteristics of China's trade

China's foreign trade has several interesting characteristics (Fung *et al.* 2004; Fung 2004), in addition to its impressive expansion. First, a substantial amount of Chinese trade is conducted by foreign-invested enterprises (FIEs). In the mid-2000s, nearly 60 percent of China's exports were carried out by FIEs, up from around 30 percent in 1995 (Tong 2013). The figure has since come down gradually, but still sat at over half in 2011 (see Figure 13.1).

Second, a large amount of China's trade consists of processing trade. This phenomenon is closely related to Chinese trade in parts and components and its deep participation in regional and global value chains. In other words, China imports materials, inputs, and parts and components, assembles them together and then exports them. Processing trade was most significant in the years between 1996 and 2005, when its share in total export and import was around 55 percent and 45 percent, respectively. Although the figures have since come down considerably to 44 percent and 27 percent in 2011, the prevalence of processing trade continues to be a distinctive feature of China's trade. The most famous recent case study is of course the study on i-Phone (Xing and Detert 2010). In the i-Phone study, the authors use disaggregated company-level data and estimate the value added originated in different countries, including that from China.

There is also some evidence that this feature of trade is facilitated by foreign direct investment (Fung *et al.* 2009). For example, of all exports conducted by FIEs, a major portion is through processing trade, ranging from 80 percent in the early 2000s to 70 percent in recent years (Tong 2013). We will go into further details of the link between foreign direct investment and China's supply chains in section 4.

Third, China's trade is highly unbalanced (Tong 2012). Since 1990, China has consistently run a trade surplus, with the exception of 1993. The ratio of trade surplus to total trade ranges between a modest 2 percent in 2004 to over 10 percent in the late 1990s and in the years before

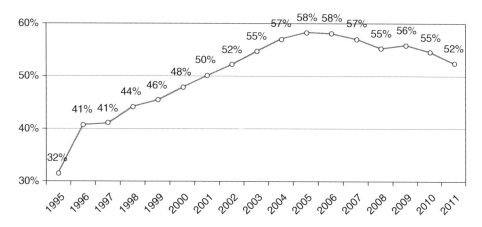

Figure 13.1 Share of FIEs in China's total exports (1995–2011)

Source: China Customs Statistics, various issues, Economic Information and Agency, Hong Kong

the outbreak of the current global economic crisis (Figure 13.2). Before 2005, although the surplus in China's merchandise trade rose considerably, from less than US$1 billion in 1994 to US$33 billion in 2004, its ratio to the country's GDP remained at below 5 percent. For four consecutive years after that, trade surpluses rose sharply to reach nearly US$260 billion and US$300 billion in 2007 and 2008, nearly 9 percent and 8 percent of China's GDP for the respective years.

Such large and rising imbalances are also closely tied to the role played by FIEs and by processing trade. As the main participant of China's export activities, FIEs are also the main source of China's trade surplus. In 2005, the trade surplus due to activities by FIEs was around US$57 billion, or around 55 percent of China's total trade surplus. The significance of FIEs in driving up trade imbalances is most obvious in China's trade with the United States. Between 2004 and 2006, over 70 percent of the Sino–US trade surplus was contributed by FIEs (Tong and Zheng 2009). In recent years, although FIEs' share in total export was declining, their contribution to China's trade surplus had reached new highs, to over 60 percent of the total in 2009 and further to over 80 percent of the total in 2011.

Even more significant to China's trade imbalance is the country's heavy reliance on processing trade. By definition, processing trade generates surpluses, thus the more processing trade, the higher the trade surplus. In the case of China, not only is processing trade pretty much the sole generator of surpluses, it actually more than compensates for the deficits created by non-processed or ordinary/normal trade, so that as a whole China is left with a huge surplus. This is particularly obvious in recent years (see Figure 13.3). In 2011, for example, the surplus in processing trade amounted to more than twice that of China's total trade surplus.

Fourth, as an important link in the global supply chain, China has a distinct pattern of trade relations with its key trading partners. To a substantial extent, China imports from its neighbors in East Asia, especially Taiwan, Korea, and Japan, and exports to the world's major consumer markets in the United States and in the EU. Again, this is related to the role of FIEs and processing trade in China's total trade. By importing inputs, parts, and components, domestic firms and especially FIEs located in China process and assemble these parts before shipping the finished products to consumers in the advanced countries. In fact, products that appear "Made in China" are really "Made in Asia" (Wong and Tong 2012).

Consequently, China has trade deficits with most of its trading partners in Asia while running large surpluses with the United States and the EU. In 2011, China's trade surpluses with the

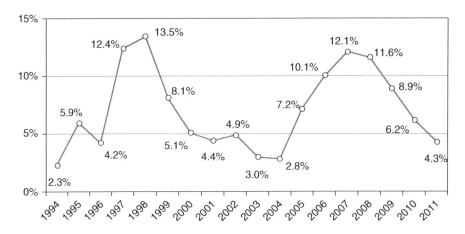

Figure 13.2 Ratio of China's trade surplus to total trade (1994–2011)

Source: China Customs Statistics, various issues, Economic Information and Agency, Hong Kong

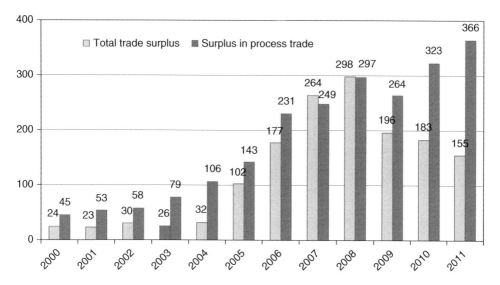

Figure 13.3　China's trade imbalance (2000–2011)

Source: China Customs Statistics, various issues, Economic Information and Agency, Hong Kong

United States and EU amounted to US$202 billion and US$145 billion, respectively. At the same time, China incurred large trade deficits with Taiwan, Korea, and Japan that amounted to US$90 billion, US$80 billion, and US$46 billion, respectively. China also had deficits of around US$50 billion each with Australia and with four major ASEAN members – Indonesia, Malaysia, the Philippines, and Thailand (see Figure 13.4).

It should be noted that mainland China also runs a huge trade surplus with Hong Kong (Figure 13.4), a special administrative region of China. In 2011, the figure was US$253 billion, a quarter more than that with the United States. This is due to the large volume of re-exports through Hong Kong. Although such re-exports have been increasingly less relevant, it complicates Chinese trade data in a substantial way (Fung and Lau 2006; Tong 2005). One major implication of the importance of re-exports in China's trade is on the different reports and estimations of China's bilateral trade balances. We will go into further details of this issue in the next section.

Finally, despite growing efforts by the central government to diversify China's trade and investment activities, China's trade remains geographically concentrated along the coastal regions. Indeed, the two coastal regions of Pearl River Delta and Lower Yangtze River Delta, that together include Shanghai, Zhejiang, Jiangsu, and Guangdong, jointly conduct around 70 percent of China's national exports and one-third of its imports. There are emerging signs that FIEs and associated trade activities have started moving to inland regions, especially since 2009. The changes, however, are still very limited. For example, with over a quarter of the total population, the six central provinces, including Shanxi, Anhui, Jiangxi, Henan, Hubei, and Hunan, accounted for respectively 4.9 percent and 4.2 percent of China's total exports and imports in 2011, less than one percentage point from the figures a decade ago.

2　Re-exports through Hong Kong and their implications

During China's three decades of reform and economic opening up, Hong Kong has played a unique and significant role, particularly in trade. Many features in China's trade are directly or

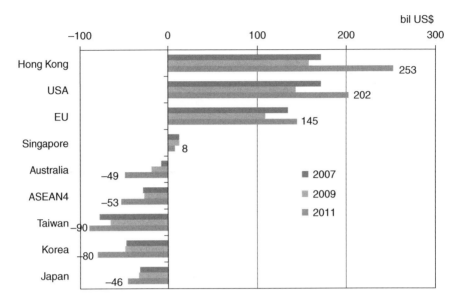

Figure 13.4 China's trade balances with selected economies (2007–2011)

Source: China Customs Statistics, various issues, Economic Information and Agency, Hong Kong

indirectly related to Hong Kong, as an investor, an entrepôt, and a financial center in Asia. In other words, Hong Kong served as a window and a platform as China was expanding its interaction with the rest of the world, especially in the earlier years of China's economic opening up.

In the mid-1990s, Hong Kong took roughly a quarter of China's total exports, when the United States and the EU each accounted for a much lower 18 percent and 13 percent of the total. There are good reasons to believe that a large portion of China's exports to Hong Kong has been in fact re-exported to a third market. In 1995, for example, Hong Kong's re-exports originating from mainland China amounted to HK$636 billion, equivalent to over US$80 billion. With transport and other related costs, as well as mark-ups, this could be adjusted to about US$60 billion Chinese exports to Hong Kong, more than the total amount reported by the Chinese Customs. This leads us to believe that, in the 1990s, China's exports to Hong Kong were primarily for the purpose of re-exporting.

A direct implication of the importance of re-exports is that it complicates China's trade figures with major trading partners, especially with the United States. In the 1990s, over two-thirds of Hong Kong's re-exports originating from mainland China were shipped to the United States. Another quarter was destined for Europe. Japan also accounted for around 10 percent of these re-exports. Generally speaking, re-exports through Hong Kong lead the importing countries of these exports to over-estimate the amount from the original exporting country. Since the Chinese mainland has been the main source of imports for Hong Kong's re-exports, bilateral trade figures between China and the United States and the EU are the most affected. Similarly, China also receives a considerable amount of re-exports from Hong Kong, but these largely originated from neighboring Japan and Taiwan.

As a result, large discrepancies in trade figures have been reported by China and its trading partners. In the late 1990s and early 2000s, Sino-US trade deficits reported by the United States government were typically two to three times those reported by the Chinese government. A major portion of the gap can indeed be accounted for by re-exports through Hong Kong.

In the latest decade, while re-exports have become more significant in Hong Kong's exports, the territory's share in China's overall trade declined. Since the mid-1990s, Hong Kong's share in China's total exports decreased gradually to 18 percent in 2000 and further to about 14 percent in recent years. Moreover, Hong Kong's exports are increasingly concentrated on re-exports, which accounted for over 95 percent of the total in recent years.

As shown in Table 13.1, although the share of re-exports in world trade was less than 5 percent in value, they remain an essential part of world trade today, especially in East Asia and also in the trade of parts and components. In 2010, 9 percent of East Asia's exports are of re-exports, within which 49 percent are in parts and components. Although re-export figures from China are not available, the mainland's strong and deep participation in East Asia's supply chains has made it clear that re-exports remain important to China. In recent years, over half of Hong Kong's re-exports were to the Chinese mainland, up from around one-third in the late 1990s. Among all re-exports to China, from Hong Kong and elsewhere, more than two-thirds were parts and components (Table 13.1). In the next section, China's participation in the regional and global supply chains is further examined.

3 China's participation in the regional and global supply chains

Early attempts to empirically measure production sharing or vertical specialization (VS) include work by Ng and Yeats (2001) of the World Bank and work by Hummels, Ishii, and Yi (2001). Ng and Yeats used only COMTRADE data. Hummels *et al.* (2001) used trade data and input–output tables but did not work on China and did not differentiate between processing and non-processing trade. Subsequent to these pioneering works, we have work by Chen *et al.* (2013); Ping (2005); Dean, Fung, and Wang (2008); Lau *et al.* (2007) – together with other papers they add to a growing literature.

For organizational purposes, one may say there are *four* different approaches in the economic literature used to measure supply or value chains. Ng and Yeats (the trade data approach) use internationally compatible trade data only. Their method has the merit of simplicity and it avoids the heavy data demand of using input–output tables. But this way of classifying trade in parts and components may be subject to the criticism of ignoring the iterated use of imported intermediate goods in China's exports.

In contrast, Dean *et al.* (2008), as well as Koopman, Wang, and Wei (2012) all use the Hummels, Ishii, and Yi (2001) method (HIY approach) as a starting point but develop new ways to generate estimates of input–output coefficients associated with processing and ordinary/normal trade as well as new ways of identifying imported intermediates. This is often called the Split input–output approach or the KWW approach. Measurements conducted without differentiating the input–output coefficients associated with processing trade and non-processing trade are called the Non-Split results. More detailed explanations of the difference between the Split and the Non-Split approaches can be found in Dean *et al.* (2008). Essentially the Split approach combines input–output data and trade statistics to separate China's input–output matrix into four sub-matrices, using a quadratic programming model. The estimation uses a quadratic penalty function, with the optimization model solving for the four unobserved sub-matrices, with minimum deviations from both the officially published input–output data, and the officially published normal and processing trade statistics. But the Split approach still has some assumptions that others may question, e.g. it assumes that sectors use imported inputs in the same proportion for normal exports and for domestic sales. If the imported input intensity of normal exports is actually higher than that of domestic sales, then the foreign content (or vertical specialization VS) share should be a weighted sum of three components, and the Split

Table 13.1 Re-export values of Greater China in various major markets (2010)

Partner	Exporter					
	China	Hong Kong	Taiwan	HKG+TWN	E. Asia (12)	World
Re-export value of parts and components ($ million)						
China	—	127,949	3,015	130,964	130,964	131,117
Hong Kong	—	—	2,131	2,131	2,131	3,020
Taiwan	—	4,294	—	4,294	4,294	6,012
Greater China (3)	—	132,243	5,146	137,389	137,389	140,150
East Asia (9)	—	21,748	1,089	22,837	22,837	27,823
East Asia (12)	—	149,697	6,235	155,932	160,227	161,961
EU (27)	—	11,990	168	12,157	12,157	18,959
NAFTA (3)	—	12,393	328	12,720	12,722	45,858
World	—	189,941	6,836	196,777	196,779	265,326
Re-exports of parts and components as % of total re-exports (%)						
China	—	62.3	68.6	62.4	62.4	61.7
Hong Kong	—	—	62.5	62.5	62.5	34.1
Taiwan	—	50.6	—	50.6	50.6	46.5
Greater China (3)	—	61.8	66.0	62.0	62.0	59.8
East Asia (9)	—	47.1	35.9	46.4	46.4	45.3
East Asia (12)	—	59.5	57.5	59.4	59.1	57.3
EU (27)	—	28.0	31.9	28.1	28.1	26.4
NAFTA (3)	—	26.7	27.6	26.7	26.7	31.9
World	—	49.2	52.6	49.3	49.3	41.1
Re-export value of all goods ($ million)						
China	—	205,450	4,394	209,844	209,844	212,584
Hong Kong	—	—	3,408	3,408	3,408	8,847
Taiwan	—	8,492	—	8,492	8,493	12,944
Greater China (3)	—	213,942	7,803	221,745	221,745	234,375
East Asia (9)	—	46,138	3,036	49,173	49,174	61,371
East Asia (12)	—	251,588	10,838	262,426	270,919	282,801
EU (27)	—	42,815	526	43,340	43,341	71,854
NAFTA (3)	—	46,409	1,188	47,597	47,599	143,547
World	—	385,894	12,996	398,890	398,894	644,826
Re-exports of all goods as % of total exports (%)						
China	—	97.7	5.7	73.1	31.9	20.3
Hong Kong	—	—	9.0	1.3	0.9	1.9
Taiwan	—	91.2	—	21.8	6.3	2.7
Greater China (3)	—	97.4	6.8	38.1	18.7	11.9
East Asia (9)	—	94.1	4.3	11.1	4.7	3.8
East Asia (12)	—	97.0	5.9	26.6	12.1	9.1
EU (27)	—	93.8	1.9	11.3	6.9	1.4
NAFTA (3)	—	97.4	3.4	11.7	6.8	6.2
World	—	96.3	4.7	17.7	9.0	4.5

Source: Based on UN COMTRADE Statistics

Notes: Due to the missing data of China's re-export values, Greater China's figures included Hong Kong and Taiwan only. East Asia (9) = Indonesia, Japan, Korea Rep., Malaysia, Mongolia, Philippines, Singapore, Thailand, and Vietnam. East Asia (12) = East Asia (9) plus Greater China (3)

Table 13.2 The split and non-split approaches

Method	Exports	VS share	1997	2002
Non-split	All	Direct	9.0	15.0
	All	Total	17.9	25.4
Split	All	Direct	46.1	42.4
	Processing	Direct	81.7	72.5
	Ordinary	Direct	1.9	4.5
	All	Total	47.7	46.1
	Processing	Total	81.9	74.3
	Ordinary	Total	5.3	10.8

Note: The data in this table are value-added contributed by entities outside of China as a percent of the gross value of exports

method would underestimate the foreign content of Chinese exports. In addition, it is not certain how robust the estimates will be to alternative minimization criteria. We summarize in Table 13.2 results from Dean *et al.* (2008) and in Table 13.3 from Koopman *et al.* (2012).

In contrast, Chen *et al.* (2008), Lau *et al.* (2007), and Chen *et al.* (2013) use the extended input–output literature approach. Basically this method uses unpublished data (the raw data behind the published input–output tables) to create two input–output tables – one for China's processing exports and one for China's non-processing exports. We summarize results from these papers as set out in Table 13.4.

In general, results obtained by Chen *et al.* using the extended input–output approach are broadly consistent with those obtained by the Split input–output approach or the KWW approach. In terms of sectors, higher-technology industries typically have higher foreign content. It seems that the perceived sophistication of Chinese exports may partly reflect a higher degree

Table 13.3 Foreign merchandise and domestic merchandise

	HIY method			KWW method		
	1997	2002	2007	1997	2002	2007
All merchandise						
Total foreign value-added	17.6	25.1	28.7	46.0	46.1	39.4
Direct foreign value-added	*8.9*	*14.7*	*13.7*	*44.4*	*42.5*	*31.6*
Total domestic value-added	82.4	74.9	71.3	54.0	53.9	60.6
Direct domestic value-added	*29.4*	*26.0*	*20.3*	*22.2*	*19.7*	*17.1*
	Normal exports			Processing exports		
	1997	2002	2007	1997	2002	2007
All merchandise						
Total foreign value-added	5.2	10.4	16.0	79.0	74.6	62.7
Direct foreign value-added	*2.0*	*4.2*	*5.0*	*78.6*	*73.0*	*58.0*
Total domestic value-added	94.8	89.6	84.0	21.0	25.4	37.3
Direct domestic value-added	*35.1*	*31.9*	*23.4*	*11.7*	*10.1*	*10.9*

Note: The data in this table are foreign content or domestic content as a percentage of the total value added of Chinese exports

Table 13.4 Value-added and employment generated by China's processing and non-processing exports

Year	Types of exports	Domestic value-added per US$1,000 exports			Employment (man-year) per US$1,000 exports		
		Direct	Indirect	Total	Direct	Indirect	Total
2002	Aggregate	204	262	466	0.095	0.147	0.242
	Processing	166	121	287	0.045	0.066	0.111
	Non-processing	240	393	633	0.142	0.221	0.363
2007	Aggregate	226	365	591	0.031	0.067	0.098
	Processing	174	193	367	0.022	0.029	0.051
	Non-processing	270	510	780	0.038	0.100	0.138

Effects of US$1,000 of Chinese exports to the world, FOB, on total Chinese domestic value-added by sector, 2007 (US$)

Sector	Processing exports	Non-processing exports	Aggregate exports
1. Agriculture	204	929	933
2. Coal mining, washing, and processing	158	844	845
3. Crude petroleum and natural gas products	159	878	881
4. Metal ore mining	474	855	788
5. Non-ferrous mineral mining	441	873	636
6. Manufacture of food products and tobacco processing	533	830	753
7. Textile goods	598	877	834
8. Wearing apparel, leather, furs, down, and related products	589	891	797
9. Sawmills and furniture	733	840	815
10. Paper and products, printing, and record medium reproduction	632	794	696
11. Petroleum processing, coking, and nuclear fuel processing	268	447	381
12. Chemicals	320	690	556
13. Nonmetal mineral products	488	860	814
14. Metals smelting and pressing	300	659	619
15. Metal products	520	840	738
16. Common and special equipment	391	786	657
17. Transport equipment	424	793	639
18. Electrical equipment and machinery	411	782	565
19. Telecommunication equipment, computer, and other electronic equipment	524	703	541
20. Instruments, meters, cultural, and office machinery	451	814	517
21. Other manufacturing products	376	873	702
22. Scrap and waste	872	960	954
23. Electricity and heating power production and supply	565	875	747
Weighted average	367	780	591

of imported inputs (or higher vertical specialization VS). This main result is however in contrast to those obtained by Rodrik (2006) and by Schott (2008).

The starting point of both the Split input–output approach and the extended input–output method is the use of official Chinese input–output tables. Using input–output tables has its inherent drawbacks since the tables assume fixed input–output coefficients. Consequently, results on domestic value added (in some other papers, results on domestic employment) obtained from the input–output tables of any given year to forecast results in future years may be prone to errors. One way to overcome this difficulty is to estimate changes in the input–output coefficients across years based on changes in factor prices and composition of products, etc., as done in Feenstra and Hong (2007). Another way is to use input–output tables from different years to directly estimate the changes of domestic value added.

Furthermore, the extended input–output approach uses unpublished official data instead of estimates to directly measure domestic value added and employment generated by Chinese exports. But it is difficult to judge the quality of the data that are unpublished. Also the results may be difficult to replicate. Both of these approaches have some merits and their results seem reasonable.

Erumban, Stehrer, Timmer, and de Vries (2011) use a different approach, one we can call the world input–output approach. They attempt to construct an input–output table with imported intermediates for the world to measure foreign value-added shares and they also use the world input–output table to estimate the value-added shares contained in Chinese exports. In some sense, this study is the most ambitious and it is comparable to efforts of ongoing research by the OECD and other international organizations. One drawback of this approach is that the data requirements can be even more challenging, and when the method is applied to China, this approach cannot distinguish between the intensities of imported intermediates of processing vs. non-processing trade. This approach still needs to use COMTRADE data and the UN BEC (United Nations Broad Economic Category Classifications) to link the different tables. Revisions to classifications of industries to match different data can be substantial. The consistency of various time-series data may also be an issue. Overall the various approaches in the literature have merits as well as some drawbacks, particularly in terms of data quality or even a severe lack of data.

Some of the results from the world input–output approach seem to indicate that the share of foreign value added of China increased between 1995 and 2006. Just to recap, foreign value-added share refers to the following: if China exports 1 dollar worth of a computer, how much of

Table 13.5 Top ten exports of parts and components from China to Japan (2010)

SITC	Parts and components	Exports (US$ million)	% of parts and components
764	Parts of telecommunication equipment	6,663	24
65	Textile yarn, fabrics, and made-up materials	4,098	15
776	Parts of electronic components	2,601	10
759	Parts of office and adding machinery	2,580	9
772	Parts of switchgear	2,420	9
784	Parts and accessories for motor vehicles	1,795	7
82122	Furniture	884	3
691	Parts of structure in iron and steel	687	3
82119	Parts of chairs and seats	407	1
7239	Parts of construction machinery	403	1

Source: Computations based on UN COMTRADE Statistics

Table 13.6 Top ten imports of parts and components by China from Japan (2010)

SITC	Parts and components	Imports (US$ million)	% of parts and components
776	Parts of electronic components	18,545	32
784	Parts and accessories for motor vehicles	7,790	13
772	Parts of switchgear	7,638	13
759	Parts of office and adding machinery	3,813	7
764	Parts of telecommunication equipment	3,758	6
65	Textile yarn, fabrics, and made-up materials	3,146	5
88411	Parts of unmounted optical elements	1,980	3
7139	Parts of internal combustion engines	1,364	2
7239	Parts of construction machinery	1,296	2
8749	Parts of instruments and accessories	934	2

Source: Based on UN COMTRADE Statistics

this 1 dollar is accounted for by value added contributed by firms or entities outside of China? For manufacturing, the share went from 14 percent in 1995 to 21 percent in 2006 with the trend being true for most industries. For electrical machinery, almost one-third of the output value is generated by labor and capital outside of China. There are also some inconsistent results across various studies. For example, using the world input–output tables, China's foreign value-added shares in Chinese exports are rising. But using the Split method (or the KWW method) or the extended input–output approach of Chen *et al.* (2008), the foreign value-added shares seem to be falling over time. The difference may be due to the fact that the world input–output table approach lumps processing exports and non-processing exports together. Indeed, in Dean *et al.* (2008), if we use the non-Split method, foreign value added of Chinese exports seem to be rising as well. In sum, there have been a variety of attempts to correctly measure the domestic value added (or conversely the foreign content) contained in Chinese exports. Generally, if we take into account the differences between processing and non-processing trade, the domestic content of Chinese exports seems to be rising over time. But in electronics and computer-related exports, foreign content seems to be substantial, with the extreme example provided by the case study of the i-Phone.

4 China's supply chains and foreign direct investment

It is well known that China's participation in the Asian production network is deep and substantial. China trades extensively with its Asian neighbors, particularly in parts and components. For an illustration, suppose we use the approach pioneered by Francis Ng (2003) to pick out trade items that match the standard notions of parts and components and examine such trade between China and Japan. The top ten items are set out in Table 13.5.

It is generally true that the top parts and components traded between China and other East Asian countries (such as Japan) tend to be electronic products and telecommunication products. Automobile parts also play an important role. Both China and Japan play an important role in maintaining and expanding the production network in East and Southeast Asia. In the literature, one important question has been whether China's participation in the supply chains has to do with the large amount of foreign direct investment in China and in other economies in Asia. In other words, is the trading and combining of various parts and components to produce the final goods facilitated by non-local factories (foreign affiliates) or are they mainly produced by local suppliers? Aminian *et al.* (2007) and Fung *et al.* (2010) ran regressions trying to identify whether foreign direct investment in East and Southeast Asia can partly explain the bilateral trade in parts and components in East and Southeast Asia. The results seem to show that indeed, after controlling for standard gravity-type determinants, foreign direct investment is an additional important explanatory variable. Furthermore, among various sources of foreign direct investments (Japanese, US, and Korean), Japanese direct investment seems to be most important in facilitating China's and other Asian countries' supply chains in the region. Partly because of the role that foreign direct investment plays in the Asian production network, foreign direct investment flowing into China is actually positively related to foreign direct investment flowing into other East and Southeast Asian economies (Chantasasawat *et al.* 2009). Because supply chain networks are not nearly as deep in Latin America and in Eastern and Central Europe, foreign direct investment flowing into China and into Latin America as well as into Eastern and Central Europe is not systematically related to one another (Chantasasawat *et al.* 2010; Fung *et al.* 2009).

5 Conclusion: future perspective

China has made great strides over the last three decades in modernizing its economy. Trade liberalization and subsequent expansion have underscored this remarkable transformation. However, as China emerged to become a leading trading nation and its participation in regional and global supply chains became increasingly entrenched, imbalances have grown and accumulated.

The global financial and economic crisis that broke out in 2008 exposed the weakness of China's export-oriented development strategies, forcing the country to adjust its overall policy priorities. In the most export-dependent regions and industries, sharp declines in export demand caused massive problems of bankruptcy and unemployment in China. It also has led to a deceleration in growth and the Chinese government had to take drastic fiscal measures to restore confidence and growth.

Since then, modest restructuring in trade has taken place, due in part to continuing weak external demand from advanced countries. The overall trade surplus declined. At the same time, the shares of FIEs and processing trade were reduced moderately. Inland regions are also gaining gradually in importance in conducting trade.

Nonetheless, policy-driven structural changes are yet to take place. Such restructuring is facing several challenges. First of all, China's export-oriented production capacities are the results of years of investment, which will take time to adjust. Second, moving away from mostly low-end processing trade and trying to move up the value chain into high-technology industries is dependent on the upgrading of the overall economy, as well as significantly improving the quality of its labor force. Third, a reorientation toward a domestic consumption-driven economy needs to be built upon a large and more equal consumer society that China currently still lacks. More radical reforms in both economic and social spheres are required.

Given the dire situation in the global economy, China may have to implement policies to encourage structural changes in trade. Even when the global economy finally improves, China cannot expect its trade to grow as rapidly as it did in the pre-crisis era. Countries around the world are expected to introduce policies that will likely constrain imports from China. Nonetheless, as a large continental economy, China has sufficient potential to sustain a healthy growth rate even if external demand remains depressed.

Bibliography

Aminian, N., Fung, K. C., and Iizaka, H. (2007) 'Foreign Direct Investment, Intra-Regional Trade and Production Sharing in East Asia', Research Institute of Economy, Trade and Industry (RIETI) Discussion Paper 07-E-064, Government of Japan, Tokyo, December.

Aminian, N., Fung, K. C., and Ng, F. (2009) 'A Comparative Analysis of Trade and Economic Integration in East Asia and Latin America', *Economic Change and Restructuring*, 42: 105–37.

Aminian, N., Fung, K. C., Iizaka, H., and Siu, A. (2008) 'Trade in Components and Parts and Foreign Direct Investment in East Asia', *Emerging Trade Issues for Developing Countries in the Asia-Pacific Region*, United Nations Economic and Social Commission (UNESCAP), Studies in Trade and Investment 64, United Nations Publication, Chapter III, 45–74.

Chantasasawat, B., Fung, K. C., Iizaka, H., and Siu, A. (2005) 'The Giant Sucking Sound: Is China Diverting Foreign Direct Investment from Other Asian Economies?', *Asian Economic Papers*, 3 (3): 122–40, Cambridge, MA: MIT Press.

Chantasasawat, B., Fung, K. C., Iizaka, H., and Siu, A. (2010) 'FDI Flows to Latin America, East and Southeast Asia and China: Substitutes or Complements?', *Review of Development Economics*, 14 (3): 533–46.

Chen, X., Cheng, L. K., Fung, K. C., and Lau, L. J. (2008) 'The Estimation of Domestic Value-Added and Employment Induced by Exports: An Application to Chinese Exports to the US', in Y. Cheung and K. Wong (eds.), *China and Asia: Economic and Financial Interactions*, Abingdon, UK: Routledge.

Chen, X., Cheng, L., Fung, K. C., Lau, L. J., Sung, Y., Zhu, K., Yang, C., Pei, J., and Duan, Y. (2013) 'Domestic Value Added and Employment Generated by Chinese Exports: A Quantitative Analysis', *China Economic Review*, forthcoming.

Dean, J., Fung, K. C., and Wang, Z. (2008) 'How Vertically Specialized Is Chinese Trade?', United States International Trade Commission (USITC) Working Paper EC2008-09-D, US Government, Washington, DC, September.

Dean J., Fung, K. C., and Wang, Z. (2011) 'Measuring Vertical Specialization: The Case of China', *Review of International Economics*, 19 (4): 609–25.

Erumban, A. A., Los, B., Stehrer, R., Timmer, M., and deVries, G. (2011) 'Slicing Up Global Value Chains', paper presented at World Bank Workshop, Fragmentation of Global Production and Trade in Value Added, June 9–10, Washington, DC.

Feenstra, Robert C. and Hong, Chang (2007) 'China's Exports and Employment', National Bureau of Economic Research Working Paper 13552.

Fung, K. C. (1998) 'Accounting for Chinese Trade: Some National and Regional Considerations', in R. Baldwin, R. Lipsey, and J. D. Richardson (eds.), *Geography and Ownership as a Basis for Economic Accounting*, NBER Conference Volume, Chicago, IL: University of Chicago Press.

Fung, K.C. (2004) 'Trade and Investment: China, the United States and the Asian-Pacific Economies', in *China as an Emerging Regional and Technological Power*, Hearing before the US–China Economic and Security Review Commission, One Hundred Eighth Congress, Second Session, Congress of the United States, Washington, DC: US Government Printing Office.

Fung, K. C. and Garcia-Herrero, A. (eds.) (2012) *Sino-Latin American Economic Relations*, Abingdon, UK: Routledge.

Fung, K. C., Iizaka, H., and Tong, S. (2004) 'FDI in China: Policy, Recent Trend and Impact', *Global Economic Review*, 32 (2): 99–130.

Fung, K. C., Korhonen, I., Li, K., and Ng, F. (2009) 'China and Central and Eastern European Countries: Regional Networks, Global Supply Chain or International Competitors?', *Journal of Economic Integration*, 24 (3): 476–504.

Fung, K. C., Lau, L. J., and Xiong, Y. (2006) 'Adjusted Estimates of United States–China Bilateral Trade Balances – An Update', *Pacific Economic Review*, 11 (3): 299–314.

Hummels, D., Ishii, J., and Yi, K. (2001) 'The Nature and Growth of Vertical Specialization in World Trade', *Journal of International Economics*, 54: 75–96.

Koopman, Robert, Wang Z., and Wei, Shang-Jin (2012) 'The value added structure of gross exports and global production network', unpublished preliminary draft, 43 pages.

Lau, L. J., Chen, X., Cheng, L. K., Fung, K. C., Pei, J., Sung, Y., Tang, Z., Xiong, Y., Yang, C., and Zhu, K. (2006) 'Estimates of US–China Trade Balances in Terms of Domestic Value-Added', Working Paper No. 295, Stanford Center for International Development, Stanford University.

Lau, L. J., Chen, X., Cheng, L., Sung, Y., Yang, C., Zhu, K., Pei, J., and Tang, Z. (2007) 'A New Type of Input–Holding–Output Model of the Non-Competitive Imports Type Capturing China's Processing Exports', *Chinese Social Science* (in Chinese), 2 (5): 91–103.

Ng, F. (2003) 'Major Trade Trends in Asia – What are the Implications for Regional Cooperation and Growth', World Bank Policy Research Working Paper 3084.

Ng, F. and Yeats, A. (2001) 'Production Sharing in East Asia: Who Does What for Whom, and Why?', in L. K. Cheng and H. Kierzkowski (eds.), *Global Production and Trade in East Asia*, Boston, MA: Kluwer.

Ping, X. (2005) 'Vertical Specialization, Intra-Industry Trade and Sino-US Trade Relationship', CCER Peking University Working Paper No. C2005005.

Rodrik, D. (2006) 'What's So Special about China's Exports?', *China and the World Economy*, 14: 1–19.

Schott, P. (2008) 'The Relative Sophistication of Chinese Exports', *Economic Policy*, 53: 5–40.

Tong, S.Y. (2005) 'The US–China Trade Balance: How Big Is It Really?', *China: An International Journal*, 3 (1).

Tong, S.Y. (2012) 'Global Crisis and China's Trade Adjustment', in D. L. Yang (ed.), *The Global Recession and China's Political Economy*, New York: Palgrave Macmillan.

Tong, S. Y. (2013) 'China's Economy Remains Highly Export-Oriented', in Wang Gunwu and Zheng Yongnian (eds.), *China: Development and Governance*, Singapore: World Scientific.

Tong, S.Y. and Siew Keng Chong (2010) 'China's Trade Prospects and China–ASEAN Trade Relations', in Y. Zheng and S.Y. Tong (eds.), *China and the Global Economic Crisis*, Singapore: World Scientific.

Tong, S. Y. and Yi Zheng (2008) 'China's Trade Acceleration and the Deepening of an East Asian Regional Production Network', *China & World Economy*, 16(1).

Tong, S. Y. and Yi Zheng (2009) 'China's Mounting External Imbalances: Trade, Foreign Investment and Regional Production Sharing', in D. Yang and L. Zhao (eds.), *China's Reforms at 30*, Singapore: World Scientific.

Wong, J. and Tong, S. Y. (2012) 'China's New Patterns of Relationship with East Asia', in S. T. Devare, S. Singh, and R. Marwah (eds.), *Emerging China: Prospects for Partnership in Asia*, New Delhi: Routledge.

Xing, Y. and Detert, N. (2010) 'How the iPhone Widens the United States Trade Deficit with the People's Republic of China', Asian Development Bank Paper No. 257, Tokyo, December.

14

CHINA'S INBOUND AND OUTBOUND FOREIGN DIRECT INVESTMENT

Yasheng Huang[1]

China now is one of the largest recipients and exporters of foreign direct investment (FDI) in the world. From 1979 to 2011, on a cumulative basis, China absorbed a total of US$1,177 billion in FDI, as shown in Figure 14.1. (Figure 14.2 presents the flow figures.)[2] In 2010, the FDI into China stood at US$116 billion, about half of the FDI the United States received in the same year. But arguably the Chinese FDI has a bigger impact on the Chinese economy than the FDI that has gone to the United States. As will be explained later in this chapter, much of the FDI inflows into developed economies are really merger and acquisition deals, whereas almost all of the FDI into China consists of greenfield investments.

On the exporting side, China is a newcomer but the speed of its increase as an exporter of FDI (commonly referred to as outbound FDI, or OFDI) is extremely fast. As of 2010, the stock of China's OFDI stood at US$317.2 billion. This is still small in terms of the share of the world's OFDI stock, given that China only began to export OFDI very recently. China now accounts for 1.5 percent of the world's OFDI stock and slightly under 10 percent of the OFDI going to developing countries. But in 1990, the Chinese OFDI stock was only US$4 billion and only US$28 billion in 2000. Today China is already a bigger holder of OFDI stock than Singapore or Brazil.

This chapter presents some basic facts about China's inbound FDI (IFDI) and its OFDI. The main argument is two-fold. First, there are complex issues both about how the IFDI and OFDI are measured and about their relationships with each other. Second, both China's IFDI and OFDI are driven, not exclusively but substantially, by the institutional features of the Chinese economy, in addition to firm-specific characteristics (i.e., those factors that FDI economists tend to emphasize).

1 Inbound FDI

First it is important to define FDI precisely. Foreign investment is defined as "*direct*" when the investment gives rise to "*foreign control*" of domestic assets. Thus, according to the International Monetary Fund (IMF), FDI is made to acquire a lasting interest in an enterprise operating in an economy, other than that of the investor, the investor's purpose being to have an effective voice in the management of the enterprise.

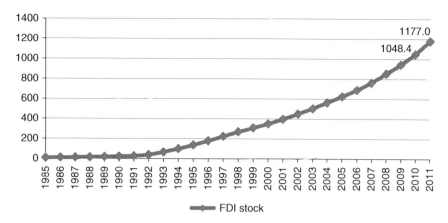

Figure 14.1 Stock of Chinese inbound FDI (US$ billion)

Source: National Bureau of Statistics of China (2012)

How to set the threshold at which a foreign firm has "an effective voice" is a matter of judgment. It is a convention among developed countries to set that threshold at 10 percent. This is the prevailing definition among countries in the Organisation of Economic Co-operation and Development (OECD) and is laid out in the fifth edition of the IMF's *Balance of Payment Manual*. This means that the most standard sources of data on FDI implicitly accept 10 percent as the threshold. The other definitional issue is what constitutes "direct." Often in the popular press and even among scholars, there is a view that FDI refers to investments that lead to the building of real assets such as factories. This is not quite true. FDI can occur through acquisitions and through public capital markets, such as stock exchanges. The defining characteristic of FDI is the equity threshold, not the form or the venue of the investments or asset transactions. Under this definition, if a *single* foreign firm acquires a stake of more than 10 percent in a US concern on the New York Stock Exchange, this capital inflow is credited to the FDI account in the balance-of-payments statistics, not to the portfolio account.[3]

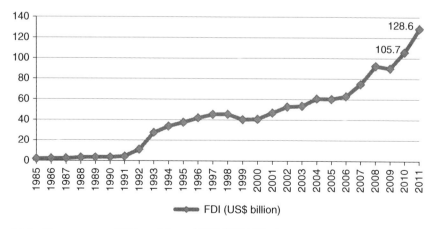

Figure 14.2 Flow measure of Chinese inbound FDI (US$ billion)

Source: National Bureau of Statistics of China (2012)

In this regard it is important to note one key difference between China and other countries in terms of how FDI is defined. In China, foreign equity capital inflows are classified as FDI only if they lead to a foreign equity stake at or above 25 percent. In the 1990s when China opened up its B-share market to foreign investments, none of the foreign investments in China's B shares were counted as FDI as they were all under 10 percent of the equity of the issuing companies. In 1993, Ford purchased 20 percent of Jiangling Motors on the B-share market. Under the US definition this transaction would have been counted as FDI but not under the Chinese definition.

The Chinese set a more stringent threshold for FDI and for corporate controls. The different statistical thresholds for FDI may impose some problems in comparing the specific dollar amount of FDI between China and other countries because the Chinese definition precludes those foreign investments that establish an equity stake of between 10 and 25 percent in a Chinese firm. Thus, the Chinese classification scheme understates China's inward FDI. But conceptually, the higher FDI threshold in China in fact helps the analyst get to the heart of the FDI concept – that FDI is about *foreign control* of a domestic firm, not about the specific dollar amount of foreign capital. As Graham and Wada (2001) have noted, much of the inward FDI in the United States has financed acquisition of existing enterprises listed on the stock market, while the majority of China's inward FDI has financed the establishment of new enterprises. (The UK is also a large recipient of FDI but most likely almost all of the UK's IFDI consists of equity acquisitions on the UK stock exchange.) Because the ownership of the Chinese assets is far more concentrated than firms listed on the stock exchanges in the West, foreigners have to acquire a greater equity stake to establish *an effective voice in the management of the enterprise*.

Another issue important to clarify is the definition of "foreign." Much of the Chinese FDI inflow consists of capital from ethnically Chinese economies (ECEs), i.e., Hong Kong, Taiwan, and Macao. FDI from these three ECEs accounted for 48.8 percent of China's total FDI inflows between 2000 and 2011.[4] The FDI from Hong Kong alone accounted for 43.3 percent of China's total FDI inflows between 2000 and 2011. Because these three ECEs are tied to mainland China politically, albeit to varying degrees and in complicated ways, the question arises as to how "foreign" their capital actually is. If the FDI originating from these three ECEs is reclassified as intra-country capital flows, then China would be an underachiever in terms of FDI relative to its economic potential, not an overachiever. Wei (1995) argues that China is an underachiever if only FDI from the OECD countries is included. He excludes FDI from the ECEs not on the grounds that the ECEs and China are politically integrated but on the grounds that FDI from the ECEs is not a traditional form of FDI.

Classifying direct investments from ECEs as FDI is not wrong. Note that the IMF defines FDI as an investment activity across two different economies, not across two different countries. In some cases different economies may nevertheless belong to the same political sovereign entity (country). That Hong Kong and Macao are now sovereign territories of China does not change the fact that their firms are subject to a completely different economic and regulatory regime from firms based in mainland China. Hong Kong and Macao maintain their own currencies, economic institutions, and court systems. In addition, they are separate members of the World Trade Organization (WTO). Their governments pursue autonomous monetary, taxation, and tariff policies. All of the above is even truer of Taiwan.[5]

However, the existence of ECEs – especially Hong Kong – does introduce some distortions into the FDI data and phenomenon and these distortions tend to overstate the size of China's true FDI inflows as well as the true size of China's FDI outflows. This is due to the existence of "round-trip" FDI – the capital that is first exported as OFDI and then imported back into China as IFDI. As such, round-trip FDI has no effect on China's total capital inflows as the capital that is imported is canceled out by the capital that is first exported.

Almost all of the round-trip FDI uses Hong Kong as the transactional conduit. One indirect piece of evidence is the huge IFDI from Hong Kong and regions such as the British Virgin Islands and the huge OFDI to them. Between 2005 and 2011, China's FDI share from Hong Kong and the British Virgin Islands was 44.6 percent and 14.7 percent, respectively, while the proportion of Japan was only 5.8 percent.[6] On the exporting side, in 2010, China's OFDI to Hong Kong, Cayman, and the British Virgin Islands accounted for about 70 percent of China's total OFDI.

It is difficult to know the exact magnitude of round-trip FDI. The World Bank estimated round-trip FDI to be around 25 percent of total FDI inflows in 1992.[7] There are lower estimates as well. One study estimates that 15 percent of foreign investments in Shanghai between 1980 and 1992 originated from Chinese subsidiaries in Hong Kong (Naughton 1996: 316). Tseng and Zebregs (2002) report an estimate that puts round-trip FDI in 1996 at 7 percent of China's FDI inflows. It is safe to assume that China's round-trip FDI has led to overstatements of China's true IFDI.

The following paragraphs will present some data on Chinese IFDI that are more disaggregated. The importance of IFDI to an economy is not measured in absolute terms but relative to the size of its GDP and its level of capital investments. There are some interesting trends in terms of the relative measures of Chinese IFDI. (See Figures 14.3 and 14.4.)

Before 1992, the FDI:GDP ratio was very low, below 1 percent. But this ratio rose sharply from 1992 and peaked in 1994 when the ratio stood at 6 percent, which is a six-fold increase compared with 1991. By 2004, this ratio settled down at 3 percent. China was most dependent on FDI during this period. Whether at 3 percent or at 6 percent, the Chinese FDI:GDP ratio is among the highest in the world. The prevailing ratios among developed countries are around 3 percent; for some developing countries this ratio is higher, around 3 to 4 percent. However, no other continental economy the size of China has a ratio as high as 3 or 6 percent. After 2005, the FDI:GDP ratio declined rather sharply. By 2011, this ratio declined to 1.7 percent, which puts China in the normal range of countries in terms of its dependency on FDI. In 2010 world's average FDI:GDP ratio was 1.8 percent, comparable to China's ratio. The trend of FDI stock as a ratio of GDP is presented in Figures 14.4. As expected, that ratio peaks later than the FDI flow ratio to GDP.

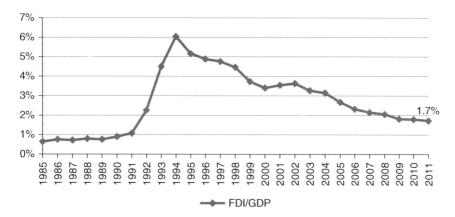

Figure 14.3 FDI flows:GDP ratios (1985–2011)

Source: National Bureau of Statistics of China (2012)

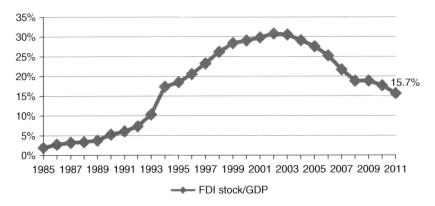

Figure 14.4 FDI stock:GDP ratios (1985–2011)

Source: National Bureau of Statistics of China (2012)

In terms of industry distribution of Chinese IFDI, the two largest recipient industries are manufacturing (47 percent) and real estate (23 percent). There is some evidence that over time Chinese IFDI has become more even in terms of its industry distribution, with the share of the top two industries declining over time. There is also some evidence that Chinese IFDI has become more dispersed geographically. Traditionally, FDI has been clustered around a few coastal provinces but this has been changing rather rapidly in recent years. Interior regions are gaining in their FDI share. The year 2003 seems to be a turning point. Before 2003, the coastal/interior shares of FDI largely held very steadily. The coastal share varied within a narrow band around 84 percent between 1995 and 2003 and the interior share accounted for the rest. But, since 2003, the coastal share declined rather precipitously, from 84 percent in 2003 to only 69 percent in 2010.

It is not clear why the year 2003 was the turning point but it is possible that this development is related to the real estate boom China experienced since 2003. The real estate boom may have had a number of effects. One is that it pushed up the production costs in the coastal regions, forcing manufacturing investments to move inland. The second effect is that the rapid appreciation of property prices in the first-tier cities such as Beijing and Shanghai – all in the coastal regions – pushed the second wave of real estate investments inward, to the second- and third-tier cities many of which are located in the inland provinces.

It is also possible that this industry compositional change explains the rising FDI share of the Yangtze River Delta and the declining share of the Pearl River Delta. This regional shift also coincided with the regional shift of FDI toward inland provinces in 2003. Before 2003, the Pearl River Delta accounted for over 30 percent of Chinese IFDI, compared with 25 percent for the Yangtze River Delta. By 2010, the two regions nearly reversed their relative shares. The Yangtze River now accounted for about 28 percent of Chinese IFDI, compared with only 10 percent for the Pearl River Delta.

Why does China attract so much FDI? Economic theory suggests that firms invest abroad because they possess some firm-specific advantages as compared with firms in the home economy. This is the so-called industrial organization theory of FDI.[8] Applying this theory to Chinese IFDI would lead to a number of puzzles. Much of the Chinese IFDI is low-tech, simple manufacturing, and export oriented. This does not mean that this type of IFDI is not beneficial to China but that the usual economic theory of IFDI that emphasizes the importance of technology probably does not quite apply here. One possible reason is the presence of round-trip FDI. The reasoning underpinning the industrial organization theory of FDI is that FDI is costly and only those investors endowed with special competitive advantages are able to undertake FDI and to overcome the intrinsic disadvantages of operating in unfamiliar foreign economic, political, and cultural environments. But since round-trip FDI investors do not face these intrinsic disadvantages, they can operate successful businesses in China even if their operations are not high-tech.

Similarly, this reasoning explains the predominance of overseas Chinese investments in China. Since the early 1990s, of China's huge FDI inflows, overseas Chinese – from Hong Kong, Taiwan, Macao, and Southeast Asia – delivered the lion's share. Between 1978 and 1999, Hong Kong, Macao, and Taiwan accounted for 59 percent of stock FDI in China, and between 2000 and 2011, Hong Kong, Taiwan, and Singapore accounted for 54.5 percent of total stock FDI in China. The scale of overseas Chinese FDI is substantial. Take the example of Macao, a small island economy with a population of 550,000 mainly known for its gambling and money laundering, which has invested a vast sum of money in China. In 1994, IFDI from Macao amounted to US$509 million, as much as 70 percent of Korean investments, 197 percent of German investments, 74 percent of British investments, or 236 percent of Canadian investments.

In 2011, the top nine source economies of Chinese IFDI were Hong Kong, the British Virgin Islands, Cayman Islands, Japan, Germany, USA, Singapore, Korea, and Taiwan. The prominence of the British Virgin Islands and Cayman Islands on this list is especially interesting and it is related to their roles facilitating capital flight, tax evasion, and round-trip FDI, a topic I will return to when discussing China's outbound FDI. China's FDI sources are relatively dispersed. Other than Hong Kong and the British Virgin Islands, no other source economy has supplied more than 10 percent of China's total FDI inflows. And the FDI share from overseas Chinese has increased over time.

After China's admission to the WTO, IFDI from non-overseas Chinese source countries initially increased but beginning in 2005 its share of total IFDI began to decline and since 2008 its absolute level declined as well. In 2005, the share of overseas Chinese IFDI was below 40 percent but that share went up to 70 percent in 2011. In 2011, overseas Chinese IFDI stood at US$80 billion, twice the level of IFDI from other source countries. (See Figures 14.5 and 14.6.)

That China has received so much capital from its overseas expatriates is often admired by outside analysts. For example, many in India bemoan the fact that overseas Indians do not invest nearly as much in India as overseas Chinese in China. This perspective merits closer scrutiny. First, it is important to know whether IFDI from overseas Chinese sources are a complement to

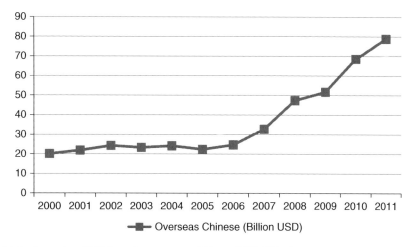

Figure 14.5   Increasing IFDI flows from overseas Chinese (US$ billion)

Source: National Bureau of Statistics of China (2012)

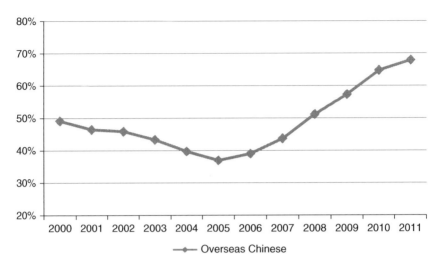

Figure 14.6　Rising share of overseas Chinese IFDI

Source: National Bureau of Statistics of China (2012)

or a substitute for IFDI from non-overseas Chinese sources. Available evidence suggests that increasingly they are substitutes for each other. As pointed out before, since 2005 overseas Chinese FDI has risen sharply but non-overseas Chinese FDI has declined relatively and even absolutely in recent years. For some Western countries, the falling level of their FDI into China is quite substantial. For example, German firms invested US$2 billion in 2006 but only US$1.1 billion in 2011. For the US, the FDI went from US$5.4 billion in 2002 to only US$2.4 billion in 2011. Japan's FDI declined from US$6.5 billion in 2005 to US$5.3 billion in 2011. Is the overseas Chinese FDI crowding out Western FDI? The answer seems to be yes, at least during the recent period.

It is important to distinguish between the demand and the supply sides of this development. One could argue that it was the 2008 financial crisis that reduced the level of IFDI from Western developed economies. The financial crisis had some effect but not a big effect. The IFDI from the United States, Japan and Korea peaked before 2008 rather than in 2008 and the rising share of overseas Chinese IFDI preceded 2008 by many years. The year 2008 was not a turning point and it is more likely that it is the changing composition of the Chinese economy – more real estate driven – that led to this change in the country mix of Chinese IFDI. Real estate is an area in which overseas Chinese firms excel and have a strong competitive edge.

This substitution effect can be a problem for the Chinese economy. It turns out that the overseas Chinese IFDI is increasingly concentrated in the real estate sector. About 20 percent of Chinese massive IFDI in 2011 – about US$116 billion in total – is in the real estate sector and IFDI in real estate is completely dominated by overseas Chinese investors.[9] The Chinese real estate sector is known for its highly speculative nature and potentially high volatility. In addition, the Chinese real estate sector is also an important source of China's macroeconomic imbalances, social instabilities, and corruption. It is not clear that these huge investments in a sector of the Chinese economy plagued with so many problems are a welcome development.

Analysis based on micro data shows that overseas Chinese firms tend to perform poorly as compared with non-overseas foreign firms in China. Many hold the view that overseas Chinese firms should have a superior performance record in China. They are supposed to possess superior cultural knowledge about China and they are more familiar with the Chinese market and business environment. They may also have better political connections in China. Based on a large dataset of firms – over 50,000 firms per year and over a period of eight years – Huang *et al.* (2013) show that these assumptions are false. They find that overseas Chinese firms in China do not outperform non-overseas Chinese firms by a set of conventional profitability measures, such as returns on assets and returns on equity, and that their performance further deteriorates over time.

The authors then conducted a detailed analysis to understand why this supposed advantage of overseas Chinese firms does not exist. They find that overseas Chinese firms tend to under-invest in those firm attributes that may enhance their long-term performance, such as human capital and technology. They hold fewer intangible assets as compared with non-overseas Chinese firms in China. All of these findings are generated after detailed controls over firm-level characteristics, such as firm size, industries, number of years of operations in China, etc. In brief, the class of overseas Chinese firms that has invested in China is inferior in quality and perfor-mance to the class of non-overseas Chinese firms that has increasingly invested less in China. To the extent there is a substitution effect between the two, the increasing share of overseas Chinese firms making investments in China at the expense of non-overseas Chinese firms is an alarming development.

As of 2010, foreign-invested enterprises (FIEs) – those firms funded by IFDI – employed over 10 million workers. FIEs also produce a very high share of Chinese exports. Several studies also show that FIEs are among the most productive firms in the Chinese economy. The contri-butions of FIEs to China's economic growth are substantial. However, assessing the economic contributions of FIEs more accurately requires not only listing the gross contributions of FIEs but ascertaining their net contributions. Until 2007, the Chinese government provided huge tax exemptions and breaks to the FIEs and taxed domestic enterprises, especially domestic private enterprises, to fund those tax benefits.

The favorable policy benefits granted to FIEs are wide ranging and substantial (Huang 2003). There have been recent systematic attempts to document and analyze the effects of these policy benefits. Huang and Tang (2010) use value-added tax data and show that the tax policy benefits granted to FIEs not only exist in tax legislation but also in tax collection enforcement. Guariglia and Poncet (2008) show the interaction effects between financial discrimination against the pri-vate sector and the ability of FIEs to compete effectively in the Chinese economy. I together with others in 2012 examined an industry characterized by technological homogeneity and estimated that financial discrimination against the domestic private sector has led to about a 30 percent loss in the equity share of the joint ventures between foreign investors and domestic entrepreneurs.

Given the massive policy benefits granted to FIEs (funded either explicitly or implicitly by private firms or Chinese households), it is necessary to impose a higher standard to evaluate the contributions of FIEs than simply listing their employment and export shares. The most relevant contribution here is the productivity spillovers from FIEs to the rest of the Chinese economy and this is the standard method to assess contributions of FDI (Haddad and Harrison 1993). There have been numerous studies estimating the productivity spillovers of Chinese FIEs and the best characterization of these studies is that the results are either mixed or negative (i.e., there is no spillover effect). The most comprehensive study is by Hale and Long (2011). Hale and Long review the previous empirical literature on FDI in China and conduct their own empirical analysis. The finding is that the positive findings on the FDI spillovers are generated either by aggregation errors or by the failure to control for the endogeneity effects of FDI. Their paper concludes: "Attempting over 6000 specifications that take into account forward and backward linkages, we fail to find evidence of systematic positive productivity spillovers from FDI in China."

2 China's outbound FDI

Compared with Chinese IFDI, Chinese OFDI has a shorter history and there have not been an equal number of academic studies on it. This section of the chapter will be relatively brief.

Figure 14.7 presents dollar amounts of Chinese OFDI between 1991 and 2010. The pattern is striking. Before 2004, Chinese firms invested only a modest amount abroad, averaging between US$1 and US$4 billion a year. Beginning in 2004, Chinese OFDI shot up sharply. In 2005 it was US$12 billion and within just five years it reached US$68.8 in 2010. China is a significant source of OFDI to the rest of the world, accounting for about 4 percent of the world total with about 18 percent of OFDI going to developing countries in 2010.

The theoretical expectations are that a country gains firm-level competitiveness gradually over time. The fact that Chinese OFDI increased over ten-fold within a short five-year span (2005–10) is prima facie evidence that the Chinese OFDI flows are driven or at least induced by policies or policy changes. Policies, rather than firm-level characteristics, are a more important determinant of Chinese OFDI flows. One important policy development during this period was the appreciation of Chinese yuan. Since 2005, the Chinese currency has appreciated by more than 20 percent, thereby reducing the prices of foreign acquisitions calculated in yuan terms by 20 percent. But the ten-fold increase is substantially more than 20 percent currency appreciation so there must be developments other than the currency appreciation that explain this substantial rise of Chinese OFDI.

China's OFDI pattern does not fit well with theoretical expectations in another sense. Traditional economic theory holds that a country exports FDI in those industries in which it holds an absolute advantage. Thus Japanese firms have typically invested in the automobile and electronics industries; US firms in high-tech industries, and German firms in precision machinery. Our priors dictate that a lot of Chinese OFDI should originate from China's manufacturing sector. China is known for its competitiveness in manufacturing and as the "factory of the world." But data contradict this expectation. As of 2010, China's OFDI stock in manufacturing was only US$17.8 billion or 5.6 percent of China's total OFDI stock. This is actually down from 10 percent as of 2004. Clearly, the massive increase in China's OFDI

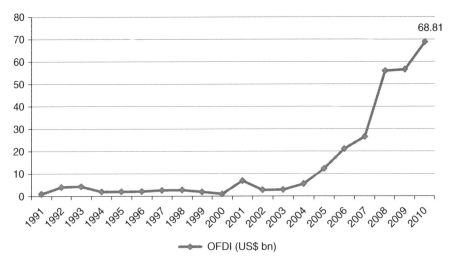

Figure 14.7 China's OFDI (1991–2010)

Source: National Bureau of Statistics of China (2012)

is not driven by one industry widely viewed as the most competitive – its manufacturing sector.

By far, China's OFDI is dominated by the service sector: leasing, business services, financial services, retail and wholesale, etc. For example, Huawei Technologies, a telecommunications giant based in Shenzhen, is one of the most active investors abroad. Huawei first excelled in equipment manufacturing but the firm has now branched out to providing critical services to its clients. In 2004, service sector OFDI accounted for 74.8 percent of the OFDI stock and it was 79.4 percent of the OFDI stock in 2010. One reason could be that Chinese firms are using OFDI as a way to acquire know-how and distribution channels. The idea here is that Chinese firms are traditionally strong in manufacturing but they lack direct interfacing with customers, branding, and distribution channels. Service OFDI thus is a way for Chinese firms to integrate forward and to acquire the know-how and the necessary assets. This is a plausible hypothesis but the data are too scant to test it directly.

Another explanation for the dominance of the service sector OFDI is China's real estate boom. Most of China's service OFDI flows have gone to regions that can be described as "the special purpose designations" (SPDs), such as Hong Kong, Cayman, and the British Virgin Islands. The functions of the SPDs are to facilitate tax evasions, capital flight, round-trip FDI, etc. OFDI is classified as service OFDI, i.e., service operations in Hong Kong and financial service operations in Cayman and the British Virgin Islands. The prominent role of SPDs is one reason why service OFDI is so substantial.

This analysis also suggests that there is a connection between the rising IFDI from ethnic Chinese source economies and the rapid rise of China's OFDI. A portion of China's rising OFDI is to fund round-trip FDI. A good test of this hypothesis is to see what happened to China's OFDI to SPDs after a policy change that affected the incentive to engage in round-trip FDI. In 2007 China unified the income tax rates for FIEs and for domestic enterprises, eliminating one source of policy advantages for FIEs. As seen in Figure 14.8, China's OFDI to Cayman Islands declined, apparently in anticipation of this policy change in 2006, whereas that to Hong Kong declined in the aftermath of the policy change in 2008.

Of course, a substantial portion of China's OFDI is genuine and it is likely to be related to China's rising appetite for commodities and energy resources. According to the *Statistical Review of World Energy* by BP (2012), global oil trade in 2011 grew by 2 percent and China alone accounted for roughly two-thirds of the growth in trade in 2011, with net imports of oil at six million barrels per day rising by 13 percent annually. At the same time, US net imports of oil

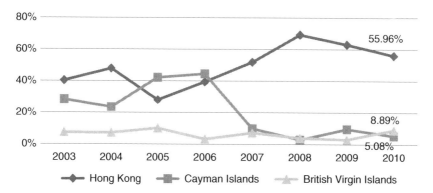

Figure 14.8   Share of OFDI to Hong Kong, Cayman Islands, British Virgin Islands

Source: National Bureau of Statistics of China (various publications)

were 29 percent below their 2005 peak. In terms of broad energy consumption, China alone accounted for 71 percent of global energy consumption growth in 2011.

China's rising OFDI coincided closely in timing with this rise of its energy consumption. According to the data from National Bureau of Statistics of China, China turned from a net energy exporter to a net energy importer between 2003 and 2006 and, as pointed out before, this was also the period when China's OFDI began to rise. What is surprising is that the mining share of China's OFDI stock has not increased substantially. In 2004 it was 13.4 percent of China's total OFDI stock and in 2010 it was only 14.1 percent.

One possibility is that China's energy explorations only partially take the form of equity transactions but China's loan programs and policy grants are probably far more important than OFDI. For example, China Development Bank provides massive loan programs to finance energy explorations in Latin America and in Africa. According to a report published by the Brookings Institution, in 2009 and 2010, China Development Bank extended lines of credit to energy companies and government entities in Latin America and Central Asia totaling some US$65 billion.[10] This is almost equivalent to China's entire OFDI in 2010 (US$68 billion). Another Chinese policy bank, Export–Import Bank of China, extended US$67.2 billion to projects in Africa between 2001 and 2010, more than the US$54.7 billion by the World Bank during the same period.[11]

The regional distribution of China's OFDI also does not suggest a paramount role of energy in China's OFDI. Asia by far is the largest recipient of China's OFDI. In flow terms, Asia accounted for 65.3 percent and 63 percent in stock terms. The proportion of Latin America is stable, which is 13.9 percent in 2004 and 13.8 percent in 2010; the proportion of Africa has nearly tripled from 1.5 percent in 2004 to 4.1 percent in 2010; the proportion of Australia doubled, from 1.2 percent in 2004 to 2.5 percent in 2010.

Even though the share of energy-related OFDI is small, energy is an intensely political area and it receives more press scrutiny than manufacturing investments. This may be one reason why there is now so much attention focused on China's OFDI. Even though Africa's share of China's OFDI was only 3.1 percent of the total Chinese OFDI flow in 2010, the poor political governance, poverty, and human rights violations in the continent have made China's involvement in Africa controversial. There are also criticisms that Chinese investments in Africa are purely extractive and do not generate many employment opportunities.

The energy–politics nexus is two-fold. One part is that energy explorations are viewed in many countries as a foreign policy and security issue. The other is that government plays a more important role in energy explorations. Both of these considerations are relevant to China's OFDI to the United States. From 2000 to Q2 2012, the stock of China's OFDI in the United State rose to US$20.9 billion. Of this amount the proportion in fossil fuels and chemicals is about 39.7 percent ($8.3 billion) and one estimate puts the proportion involving government actions as high as 69 percent.[12]

The most controversial case in China's OFDI to the United States concerned the China National Offshore Oil Corporation (CNOOC), which bid for Unocal Oil Company in 2005. This was the largest takeover attempt ever made in the United States by a Chinese company till then. The bid met considerable political opposition from media and politicians in the United States. The United States House of Representatives took a vote in opposing the deal. In the end, CNOOC withdrew its acquisition offer which was valued at US$18.5 billion and Unocal instead accepted a lower offer by Chevron worth US$17.5 billion.

While many Chinese commentators believed that the controversy was rooted in a "containment strategy" of the United States against China, a far simpler explanation is the state ownership of CNOOC. There were concerns that the state-owned CNOOC might act as a proxy for the Chinese government, and thus jeopardize the security of US energy assets. It should be noted that in 2004 the takeover bid of the manufacturing division of IBM by Lenovo – widely viewed as less state owned – went through without any controversy. There is nothing China-specific about controversies over takeover bids in certain industries. Japanese acquisition activities in the 1980s were also widely challenged by objections from the US government for national security concerns. The most famous case of Japanese failed acquisitions in the 1980s was Fujitsu's attempted acquisition of Fairchild Semiconductor in 1986. Fujitsu also ended by withdrawing its bid.

3 Conclusion

There are several aspects to China's IFDI and OFDI that warrant some special considerations. For a country that still has a very strong role of government in economic management and asset ownership, China's openness to IFDI is probably unusual. In fact, until 2007 China's tax codes favored FIEs more than domestic private enterprises. The share of IFDI in China's export production and investments is substantial. It is in part because of these policy and institutional features of the Chinese economy that the patterns of China's IFDI – for example, in terms of industry distribution – vary considerably from what one might expect from economic theory.

The most important issue of China's OFDI is the degree of involvement of the state. China's OFDI is overwhelmingly from the state sector. In 2010 the SOE share of OFDI was 66.6 percent and SOEs directly managed by the central government funded some 70 percent of China's OFDI. This degree of state ownership in FDI activities is potentially unprecedented. Hong Kong, Taiwanese, Japanese, Korean, and Indian OFDI firms are all private sector actors and the substantial size of China's OFDI means that the current international system, which was designed on the basis of the private sector as the main source of investments, will have difficulties in integrating China. Either the international system or China has to make the adjustments – otherwise there will be more political turbulence lying ahead.

Notes

1 The writing of this chapter benefited from excellent research done by Rui Kong, Hong Gao, and Lin Fu. The usual caveat applies.
2 In this chapter, unless otherwise noted, all the data on China's inbound and outbound FDI is from *The Statistical Yearbook of China* compiled by National Bureau of Statistics (2012).
3 A more detailed discussion of issues related to the standard definition of FDI can be found in Graham and Krugman (1994).
4 The data presented in this section refer to utilized FDI and are from National Bureau of Statistics of China (2011).
5 Taiwan became a separate member of the WTO after China's accession.
6 The proportions of Hong Kong, the British Virgin Islands, and Japan are 40.4 percent, 13.0 percent, and 7.0 percent, respectively, from 2000 to 2011.
7 See World Bank (1996) and also Tseng and Zebregs (2002). In an earlier study, I arrive at a similar estimate by correlating China's capital outflows with its FDI inflows, using data from the 1980s to the mid-1990s. According to this methodology, round-trip FDI accounted for about 23 percent of China's FDI inflows. See Huang (1998), especially chapter 3.
8 The classic work is Hymer (1976), restated by Caves (1996).
9 The figure is from a report published by the Overseas Chinese Affairs Office of the State Council (August, 2012).
10 From http://www.brookings.edu/research/papers/2011/03/21-china-energy-downs, downloaded on December 24, 2012.

11 From http://www.theafricareport.com/north-africa/chinas-exim-bank-africas-largest-financier-looks-for-an-even-bigger-role.html, downloaded on December 24, 2012.
12 Data source: China Investment Monitor, http://rhgroup.net/interactive/china-investment-monitor

Bibliography

Caves, R. E. (1996) *Multinational Enterprise and Economic Analysis*, Cambridge, MA: Cambridge University Press.

Graham, E. M. and Krugman, P. R. (1994) *Foreign Direct Investment in the United States*, Washington, DC: Institute for International Economics.

Graham, E. M. and Wada, E. (2001) *Foreign Direct Investment in China: Effects on Growth and Economic Performance*, Canberra: Australia National University. Paper (post-conference draft) (September 6–7).

Guariglia, A. and Poncet, S. (2008) 'Could Financial Distortions Be No Impediment to Economic Growth after All? Evidence from China', *Journal of Comparative Economics*, 36(4): 633–57.

Haddad, M. and Harrison, A. (1993) 'Are There Positive Spillovers from Direct Foreign Investment? Evidence from Panel Data for Morocco', *Journal of Development Economics*, 42(1): 51–74.

Hale, G. and Long, C. (2011) 'Are There Productivity Spillovers from Foreign Direct Investment in China?', *Pacific Economic Review*, 1(2): 135–53.

Huang, Y. (1998) *FDI in China: An Asian Perspective*, Singapore: Institute of Southeast Asian Studies.

Huang, Y. (2003) *Selling China: Foreign Direct Investment during the Reform Era*, New York: Cambridge University Press.

Huang, Y. and Heiwai Tang (2010) 'Ownership Biases in China: A Firm-level Analysis of Value Added Tax Rates', mimeo, MIT Sloan School of Management.

Huang, Y., Jin Li, and Yi Qian (2013) 'Does Ethnicity Pay? Evidence from Overseas Chinese FDI in China', forthcoming, from *Review of Economics and Statistics*.

Huang, Y., Yue Ma, Zhi Yang, and Yifan Zhang (2008) 'A Fire Sale without Fire: An Explanation of Labor-Intensive FDI in China', MIT Sloan Research Paper No. 4713-08.

Hymer, S. H. (1976) *The International Operations of National Firms*, Cambridge, MA: MIT Press.

National Bureau of Statistics of China (2012) *Chinas Statistical Yearbook*, Beijing: Chinese Statistics Press.

Naughton, Barry (1996) 'Distinctive Features of Economic Reform in China and Vietnam', in John McMillan and Barry Naughton (eds.), *Reforming Asian Socialism: The Growth of Market Institutions*, Ann Arbor, MI: University of Michigan Press.

Tseng, W. and Zebregs, H. (2002) 'Foreign Direct Investment in China: Some Lessons for Other Countries', IMF Policy Discussion Paper (February).

Wei, S. (1995) 'Attracting Foreign Direct Investment: Has China Reached Its Potential?', *China Economic Review*, 6(2): 187–99.

World Bank (1996) *Managing Capital Flows in East Asia*, Washington, DC: World Bank.

15

BANKING AND FINANCIAL INSTITUTIONS

Gang Yi and Kai Guo

This chapter gives an overview of China's large, growing, and continuously evolving financial sector, with a focus on the reforms that shaped the transformation of the sector since 1978. The first section starts with a snapshot of the pre-reform financial sector to provide some historical context. It then goes through the key reforms of banks, security firms, insurance companies, and non-bank financial institutions since 1978 and ends with a snapshot of China's financial sector in 2011 to depict the enormous transformation of the financial sector. The reform of the financial sector and progressive changes in the policy framework are mutually reinforcing processes and section 2 describes the major reforms of financial policies, including interest rate liberalization, exchange rate regime reform, monetary policy, and bank supervision. Section 3 provides the logic behind the reforms described in the previous sections to offer a bird's-eye view of the complex reforms that were undertaken. It follows with critical assessments on financial institutions as well as the financial sector as a whole to demonstrate what has been achieved and more importantly what remains to be done. The chapter concludes with the medium-term financial reform agenda set out in the twelfth Five-Year Plan.

Introduction

China's financial sector, like the Chinese economy, underwent enormous transformations in the last three decades – from a handful of institutions with extremely limited functions before the start of market-oriented reform in 1978 to a sector that is home to some of the worlds largest banks, security firms, and insurance companies today. There are continuing developments in the sector – some are planned but more are driven by market forces, as of this writing. To understand China's financial sector, it has to be viewed in the broad context of the overall economic reform, which transformed China from a closed, stagnant, central-planned, agrarian economy to an open, dynamic, market-oriented, industrial economy. The financial sector, which was largely sidelined or even eliminated and played no role other than as cashier and accountant in the central-planning machinery before the reform, has gradually emerged to greater prominence, as more resources started being allocated by the market. It must also be kept in mind that China's financial sector today is shaped by both reforms and legacies, reforms that brought about the changes and legacies that remained to be addressed. This chapter provides an overview of

China's financial sector, with emphasis on key reforms and developments that shaped the current financial industry in China. As it is not feasible to cover all important reforms and every aspect of China's financial industry in one single chapter, we chose, therefore, to focus more on recent reforms and on banks, which continue to be dominant in the financial sector.

1 Reforms and evolution of banking and financial institutions in China since 1978

1.1 The pre-reform financial sector in China

The pre-reform Chinese economy was a centrally planned economy, where resource allocation was largely dictated by the government (see Chapter 3 in this volume). In order to support the development of certain priority industries, financial resources had to be directed in a way that would not have occurred in a market economy (e.g. developing capital-intensive industries in a capital-scarce country like China) and key prices, such as wage, interest rate and exchange rate, were heavily regulated and distorted (Lin *et al.* 2003).

In such an environment, there were neither the conditions nor the needs for a real financial sector, that priced and allocated resources based on demand and supply, to exist and grow. The People's Bank of China (PBOC), now the central bank, was essentially the only bank in China before the reform. Other than serving as a cashier and an accountant for the government, PBOC's main function was to take deposits from households and provide short-term loans and working capital that did not fall within the domain of fiscal appropriation to various businesses (mostly SOEs). Long-term investments and working capital within the central plan were financed in the budget. In 1978, only 23.4 percent of all funds allocated were in the form of bank credit and the rest were through fiscal appropriations.

Understandably, the size of the banking sector was not large. At the end of 1978, total deposits and total loans amounted to RMB 114 billion and RMB 185 billion, about 31 percent and 51 percent of GDP at the time, respectively (Shang 2000). Other financial products, markets, and services were essentially non-existent before the reform. The only insurance company had long suspended its domestic business by 1978. There were no markets for issuing and trading securities, or any financial products for that matter.

1.2 Banking sector and reform

Major state-owned commercial banks

The year 1978 marked the start of China's market-oriented reform, of which reforming China's banking system and developing the financial sector in general were an integral part.

The Agricultural Bank of China (ABC), China Construction Bank (CCB), and Bank of China (BOC) were rehabilitated in 1979 to serve as specialized banks for agriculture loans, infrastructure, and construction loans and foreign exchange business, respectively. In 1984, Industrial and Commercial Bank of China (ICBC) was separated from PBOC to become a specialized bank for business loans and PBOC became China's central bank. The rehabilitation and creation of specialized banks was the first step toward establishing a commercial banking system.

At the same time, a pilot program was started to replace appropriations with bank loans as a means to allocate funds to enterprises in 1979. Instead of getting funds from fiscal appropriations at no cost, enterprises had to borrow from banks for financing needs, paying interest, and repaying principal under the new scheme. By 1984, fiscal appropriations to enterprises were completely replaced by bank loans. A seemingly small step initially and nothing out of the ordinary from today's perspective, this practice set into motion that resources would be channeled through and eventually allocated by the financial sector and at a price. This reform established an environment where the financial sector could develop and prices would become relevant over time. It also created preconditions to alleviate and solve the "soft-budget constraint" problem (Kornai 1980) that was prevalent among SOEs.

Despite these efforts, a large number of bank loans in the 1980s and early 1990s continued to be provided to SOEs, many of which were loss-making, and for various policy objectives, such as employment, social stability, transfers, and subsidies (Lin and Tan 1999). Policy loans, as such loans were called, created "soft-budget constraint" problems for both firms and banks, as firms could continue to have access to bank financing even if they were not financially viable and banks could not be held accountable for their NPLs and poor performance. While policy loans helped ensure social and economic stability during the transition, they prevented banks from becoming truly commercial. To address this problem, three policy banks, the China Development Bank, the Export–Import Bank of China, and the Agriculture Development Bank were established in 1994 with a mandate to provide policy loans. Commercial banks, on the other hand, were supposed to provide commercial loans only. While this reform was a step in the right direction, the boundary between policy loans and commercial loans was extremely murky in an economy dominated by SOEs, many of which were not operated on a commercial basis. As a result, banks continued to extend and roll over loans that were destined to become nonperforming through the late 1990s.

The Asian financial crisis in 1997 made the urgency of overhauling major state-owned commercial banks apparent. On the one hand, the crisis showed how devastating a financial crisis could be and banks with problematic balance sheets were a key vulnerability. On the other hand, the official NPL ratio in the four major state-owned banks was already 24.75 percent at the time (Dai 2010)[1] and was set to rise even more as economic growth slowed and corporate profits fell in the wake of the crisis.

In 1998, RMB 270 billion special bonds were issued by the ministry of finance to recapitalize the four major state-owned commercial banks – ABC, CCB, BOC, and ICBC (hereafter, the Big Four). Even after the recapitalization, it was estimated that the Big Four would have had negative capital, i.e. were so-called "technically bankrupted," under stricter prudential standards (Tang 2005). In 1999, following the "good bank-bad bank" model of bank resolution, four asset management companies (AMCs) were established to assume and dispose of RMB 1,400 billion bad loans from the Big Four and China Development Bank. These steps, while significant, focused mostly on clearing up banks' balance sheets and did not address more fundamental problems such as corporate governance, property rights, and market discipline.

In 2003, the second round of major state-owned bank reform started in the context of China's accession to the WTO, for which China was committed to opening up fully to foreign banks after a five-year transition period. The fear at the time was that Chinese banks could not survive the competition with global banks after they were allowed to operate freely in China. This time, the central bank balance sheet was involved to further recapitalize the Big Four. More specifically, Central Huijin, a government investment company, was established at the end of 2003 with US$45 billion foreign reserves as capital. Central Huijin injected US$ 22.5 billion to CCB and BOC each in 2003, US$15 billion to ICBC in 2005 and RMB130 billion equivalent of US$ to ABC in 2008.[2] At the same time, CCB, BOC, ICBC, and BoComm auctioned off roughly RMB 1 trillion bad loans, at market-determined prices, to AMCs for disposal.[3] After this round of balance sheet clean-up, major commercial banks were on a much more solid financial footing than before.

More importantly and different from the first-round reform, considerable efforts were made in strengthening corporate governance, clarifying property rights, and introducing market discipline during this round of reform so that the Big Four would be fundamentally transformed. The measures taken included introducing strategic investors,[4] revamping the corporate governance framework, strengthening internal control, adopting prudential accounting standards, and increasing transparency.

Finally, all of the Big Four were successfully listed on the Shanghai and Hong Kong stock exchanges. The listing of the Big Four helped raise needed capital, but more crucially it cemented the commercial orientation of the Big Four and imposed stricter market discipline, supervision, and information disclosure requirements on these banks. As of 2011, all Big Four had CARs comfortably above the regulatory requirement, NPL ratios around 1 percent, and were very profitable. Although there were concerns about the health of the banks' balance sheets due to exposures to the real estate sector and local government financing vehicles, stress tests showed that the major banks' capital buffer was strong enough to withstand significant shocks (IMF 2011).

Rural credit cooperatives

Rural credit cooperatives (RCCs) are on the opposite end of the size spectrum compared to the Big Four. RCC reform was less publicized but by no means less important than the reform of major banks.

RCCs were started in the early 1950s as part of the collectivization movement to provide financial services in the rural areas (Shang 2000). The importance of RCCs should be understood in the context of the importance of agriculture and rural areas to the Chinese economy and society. Despite rapid urbanization in the past thirty years, about half of China's population still lives in the rural areas. Agriculture continues to underpin food security, provide employment, and hence is crucial to the stability of the economy and society in general. RCCs were and remain the primary form of the formal financial sector in the rural areas and operate an extensive network of branches in townships and remote areas. A functioning RCC network is crucial for providing financial services to the rural population and to ensure the overall health of the rural economy (Yi 2009).

Although RCCs were in theory independent accounting units, they were de facto grass-root units of the ABC before 1996. In 1996, RCCs became independent from the ABC and were directly supervised by the PBOC. By 2003, RCCs were in even worse shape than the major commercial banks. In 2001, 44 percent of RCCs' loans were non-performing, 46 percent of RCCs were loss-making, and 58 percent of RCCs had negative capital (Zhang and Gao 2006). The problems of RCCs were similar to major banks in certain aspects including weak balance sheets and corporate governance, property rights, and internal control issues, but were more severe and complex in other aspects as RCCs were numerous (there were more than 30,000 independent RCCs in 2003), typically small, extremely diverse and operated in areas that often did not have competition from other financial institutions.

In 2003, a progress-based asset swap and capital injection program, using PBOC's balance sheet through central bank bill issuance,[5] was launched to clean up RCCs' balance sheets, inject capital, clarify property rights, and improve corporate governance, internal control, and management. Central bank bills were issued to swap for bad assets from RCCs and fill in capital shortages. However, certain progress had to be made before central bank bills were committed, issued, and cashed. The progress and conditions, somewhat like structural benchmarks and performance criteria in IMF lending programs, included numerical targets such as capital adequacy ratio as well as critical reforms that clarify ownership structure, improve corporate governance, and strengthen internal control and management. The design of the program followed the "incentive compatibility" principle, which leveraged central bank resources to provide clear incentives to individual RCCs to carry out difficult reforms by themselves (Zhou 2004; Yi 2009).

By 2010, more than RMB 171 billion was injected into RCCs through the central bank bill program. As a result, balance sheets and capital positions of RCCs were significantly improved. More importantly, considerable progress was made in transforming RCCs into profitable rural financial institutions with clear shareholding structures, better corporate governance, and stricter internal control. Some RCCs later became rural commercial banks or rural cooperative banks.

Other commercial banks

The reforms of the major state-owned commercial banks and RCCs were accompanied by the development and reform of other commercial banks, including joint-stock banks and city commercial banks. Bank of Communications, the first joint-stock bank, was established in 1987, followed by more than ten national or regional joint-stock banks in the next decade. The purpose of establishing joint-stock banks was two-fold: introducing more competition into the banking industry, which was dominated by the major state-owned banks and gaining experiences in improving the commercial orientation of Chinese banks. The rapid expansion of Urban Credit Cooperatives (UCCs) in the 1980s and early 1990s exposed the inherent weakness of UCCs, such as weak internal control and problematic governance structure, prompting the government to consolidate UCCs into city commercial banks in the mid 1990s. The first city commercial bank – Shenzhen city commercial bank – was launched in 1995 and by the end of 2011 there were more than 140 city commercial banks country wide. Similar to the reform of the major state-owned commercial banks and RCCs, many joint-stock banks and city commercial banks in the past ten years also went through a series of steps to clean up balance sheets, strengthen internal control and risk management, introduce strategic investors, and eventually get listed.

Security, insurance, and other non-bank financial institutions

China's first security firm was established in Shenzhen in 1985. In 1990, the Shanghai and Shenzhen stock exchanges were launched and CSRC was established in 1992 to regulate and supervise the security sector. In the 1990s, significant efforts were made to establish relevant regulations and rules to ensure the proper functioning of a nascent market, which exposed many irregularities, speculations, and risks.

In the 2000s, the security sector reform focused on two key areas: first, clarifying property rights. This included not only defining clearer ownership structure in security firms, but also the shareholding structure and associated corporate governance in listed companies. One signature reform was the so-called "split share structure" (*gu quan fen zhi*) reform. Before the reform, considerable amounts of shares of listed companies were non-tradable and ultimately owned by the government. This unique feature of China's equity market hampered its proper functioning as well as the governance and management of listed companies. This was due to the very fact that not all shares are equal (stock prices could be distorted as a result) and the dominance of government as the main stakeholder. The split share structure reform helped mitigate, if not fully resolve, these problems by merging non-tradable shares with tradable shares on a company-by-company basis and reducing state-held shares during the process. Second, risk control was strengthened. There were significant loopholes in the regulations and practices of security firms and the payment system during the development of China's security market. One example was that security firms also served as custodians of their own clients' funds, which led to illegal use of clients' funds by security firms. Reforms were carried out to close these identified loopholes to minimize risks. Third-party custody was introduced and strictly enforced to successfully close the particular loophole regarding client funds. Other than these two main areas of reform, a few security firms with severely impaired balance sheets were bailed out and restructured. Considerable efforts were also made to enhance transparency and build a retail investor base in the equity market.

The insurance business in China was restored in 1979. In the following years, a number of insurance companies were established. The insurance law, which mandated the separation of life insurance and property insurance, was passed in 1995 and the CIRC was established in 1998. After 2000, a number of major insurance companies were listed on domestic or international markets. Correspondingly, management, governance, and services in the insurance sector have improved markedly. Other non-bank financial institutions, including trust, leasing, finance companies, pawn shops, auto loan companies, consumer financing companies, also experienced considerable development in the last thirty years, particularly since 2000, complementing the function of the banking sector, particularly in SME financing, although there are growing concerns over the risks in many of these so-called "shadow banking" institutions at the time of this writing.

1.3 Opening up and international cooperation

The opening up of China's financial sector, which was an essential part of financial reform, followed a gradual and prudent approach initially and was greatly accelerated after the WTO accession. The opening of the representative office of the Export–Import Bank of Japan in 1980 marked the start of foreign bank presence in China (PBOC 2012). In the next twenty years, China and foreign banks cautiously embraced each other and the process was occasionally disrupted by events like the Asian financial crisis. By the end of 2002, there were 160 foreign bank entities, including subsidiaries, joint ventures, and branches, operating in China, with RMB 288.1 billion in assets, about 1.3 percent of total banking sector assets. Following accession to the WTO in 2001, China committed to fully opening RMB business to foreign banks after a five-year transition period and has since fulfilled this commitment. At the end of 2011, there were 318 foreign bank entities in China with assets of RMB 2.15 trillion, about 1.9 percent of total banking sector assets, down from 2.4 percent in 2007, as foreign banks slowed their expansion in China following the global financial crisis.

The opening up of the security and insurance sectors also accelerated after the accession to the WTO and all relevant WTO commitments have been met. However, certain restrictions on foreign institutions in the security sector remain, including the 49 percent cap on foreign shares in security firms. As a result, China continues to be one of the few emerging economies that impose significant restrictions on foreign security firms and the overall openness of the security sector remains limited. On the other hand, almost all restrictions on foreign insurance companies have been eliminated following the WTO accession except that foreign shares cannot exceed 50 percent in life insurance companies, and foreign property insurance companies are not allowed to offer bodily injury and property damage liability coverage in auto insurance.

Participation in and cooperation with international financial organizations (IFOs), such as the IMF and the World Bank Group, is instrumental in facilitating China's reform and opening up, particularly the financial sector reform. China restored its membership at the IMF and the World Bank Group in 1980. Over the years, the IMF and World Bank, among other IFOs, contributed to China's reform process by providing financial support, policy advice, technical assistance, training, and knowledge transfer. In 2011, the IMF and World Bank jointly conducted the first Financial Sector Assessment Program (FSAP) in China, making an overall assessment of the entire financial sector and related policy framework, taking stock of China's financial reform and providing policy recommendations for future policy actions and the financial reform agenda.

1.4 China's financial sector in 2011

After more than thirty years of reform and opening up (see Table 15.1 for a summary of major financial reforms), the Chinese economy has become the second largest economy in the world, with a large and fairly sophisticated financial sector (Table 15.2). The total size of the financial sector, measured by total assets, is about RMB 122 trillion (about US$19 trillion) in 2011, some 260 percent of China's GDP and among the largest in the world. The banking sector remains the predominant player in the financial sector, accounting for close to 90 percent of overall financial sector assets, although other financial institutions have also been growing very rapidly. The bond

Table 15.1 Major financial reforms (1978–2012)

Year	Events
1978	Start of China's economic reform and opening up
1979	Agriculture Bank of China, China Construction Bank, and Bank of China
1980	Membership restored at IMF and World Bank Group
1984	Industrial and Commercial Bank separated from the PBOC and PBOC became the central bank
1990	Shanghai and Shenzhen Stock Exchanges launched
1992	China Security Regulatory Commission established
1994	Policy Banks established, unified exchange rate regime established
1998	China Insurance Regulatory Commission established, lending interest rate liberalization started, Rmb 270 billion capital injection to major banks
1999	Four AMCs established to dispose NPLs from major commercial banks
2001	Accession to the WTO
2003	Capital injection in BOC and CCB by central Huijin, China Banking Regulatory Commission established
2004	Deposit rate floor and lending rate ceiling eliminated, Basel I capital requirement for commercial banks issued
2005	Capital injection in ICBC by central Huijin, CCB IPO, start of exchange rate regime reform
2006	BOC and ICBC IPOs, RMB business fully opened to foreign banks
2008	Capital injection in ABC by central Huijin
2010	ABC IPO
2012	Basel III capital requirement for commercial banks issued

Sources: Shang (2000), People's Bank of China (2012), IMF (2011), and Yi (2009)

Table 15.2 Size and structure of China's financial sector[*]

	2010		2011	
	Assets (rmb billion)	*Share (%)*	*Assets (rmb billion)*	*Share (%)*
Banking institutions	*93216*	*88.2*	*110681*	*89.3*
Policy banks	7652	7.2	9313	7.5
Major commercial banks	46894	44.4	53634	43.3
Joint stock banks	14904	14.1	18379	14.8
City commercial banks	7853	7.4	9985	8.1
Rural commercial banks	2767	2.6	4253	3.4
Rural cooperative banks	1500	1.4	1403	1.1
Urban credit cooperatives	2	0.0	3	0.0
Rural credit cooperatives	6391	6.0	7205	5.8
Foreign banks	1742	1.6	2154	1.7
New-type rural financial institutions and postal savings bank	3510	3.3	4354	3.5
Non-bank financial institutions	*12484*	*11.8*	*13250*	*10.7*
Insurance companies	5048	4.8	6014	4.9
Security firms	1969	1.9	1572	1.3
Fund management companies	2521	2.4	2188	1.8
National social security fund	857	0.8	869	0.7
Other non-bank financial institutions	2090	2.0	2607	2.1
Total	*105700*	*100.0*	*123930*	*100.0*

Sources: CEIC, CSRC, Almanac of China's Finance and Banking (2011 and 2012), and authors' calculations

Note: [*]See Almanac of China's Finance and Banking for the coverage and classifications of financial institutions

and stock markets are also relatively small despite significant growth (Table 15.3). Consistent with these developments, bank loans, including both RMB loans and foreign currency loans, continue to be the major form of financing, while other types of financing grew increasingly important over the years (Table 15.4). Within the banking sector, major commercial banks play a significant but gradually diminishing role, accounting for about half of total banking sector assets in 2011 (Figure 15.1), down from more than 60 percent in 2003.

Table 15.3 Snapshot of China's bond and stock markets (2011) (in RMB bn)

Bond market		Stock market	
Market capitalization	21357.6	Market capitalization	21475.8
Government bond	7383.9	Shanghai stock exchange	14837.6
Financial bond	7456.3	Shenzhen stock exchange	6638.2
Central bank bill	2129.0	Main board	3151.9
Corporate bond	1679.9	SME board	2742.9
Medium-term note	1974.3	Chinex	743.4
Other	734.2		

Sources: China Bond, Shanghai stock exchange, and Shenzhen stock exchange

Table 15.4 Structure of social financing

Year	Bank loans	Entrusted loans and trust loans	Bank acceptance bill	Corporate bond	Equity	Other
2006	77.2	8.2	3.5	5.4	3.6	2.0
2007	67.4	8.5	11.2	3.8	7.3	1.8
2008	73.0	10.6	1.5	7.9	4.8	2.1
2009	75.6	8.0	3.3	8.9	2.4	1.7
2010	60.1	9.0	16.7	7.9	4.1	2.2
2011	62.7	11.7	8.0	10.6	3.4	3.6

Sources: People's Bank of China and authors' calculations

As the financial sector grew, financial markets also developed in tandem. A full range of financial markets were established, including the money market, bond market, stock market, foreign exchange market, gold market, futures market, and derivatives market; a wide range of financial products, such as currency swaps, stock index futures, and interest rate swaps, have become available and new financial products are continually being introduced.

2 Reform and evolution of financial sector policies

The reform and development of banking and financial institutions in China did not happen in a vacuum. It happened when the macro policy framework was also undergoing profound changes. In fact, the gradual approach of reform meant that the reform of financial institutions and the overhaul of the macro policy framework were mutually reinforcing processes. The

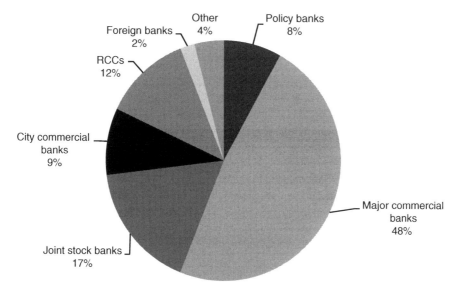

Figure 15.1 Asset distribution in China's banking sector (2011)

Sources: Almanac of China's Finance and Banking (2012) and authors' calculations

Note: Includes RCCs, rural commercial banks, and rural cooperative banks reform of the financial sector could not have happened without progressive changes in the policy framework. On the other hand, without the micro foundations laid down by the financial sector reform, it would also be impossible to push forward policy initiatives such as interest rate liberalization and exchange rate regime reform.

2.1 Interest rate liberalization

Although interest rate liberalization was conceived as a future goal of market-oriented reform as early as in 1993, it was not until 2003 that interest liberalization (which meant the interest rate would be market determined and the central bank would adjust interest rates through indirect market-based measures) was formally set as such a goal.

Interest rate liberalization in China took a dual-track approach: the first track was to gradually liberalize regulated interest rates, particularly the lending and deposit rates, and the other track was to develop a market-based interest rate system, represented by, for example, SHIBOR and interest rates on government bonds (Yi 2009).

The way China liberalized regulated interest rates was to gradually allow more flexibility in setting first lending rates and then deposit rates, around benchmark rates which are set by the central bank. As early as in 1983, PBOC was allowed to set lending rates at a ±20 percent band around the benchmark rates. However, when financing costs grew and pressures from enterprises mounted in the early 1990s, interest rate liberalization regressed with the upward band narrowed to 10 percent and only applied to working capital loans. After the Asian financial crisis, the tension between regulated interest rates and financing difficulties faced by SMEs became more acute, since banks had no incentive to lend to SMEs under the same benchmark rates. Over a period of seven years, PBOC progressively loosened the upper limit on lending rates while maintaining the floors on these rates. By October of 2004, all upper limits on lending rates were eliminated except RCC and UCC loans, whose rates could not exceed 230 percent of the benchmark rates.

The PBOC took a more cautious approach in liberalizing deposit rates, as there were concerns that banks with soft-budget constraint problems might compete for deposits by outbidding each other on deposit rates, which would create financial stability problems. In 1999, PBOC allowed insurance companies to negotiate deposit rates on large long-term institutional agreement deposits with banks and gradually expanded the list of institutions. Although flexibility of setting deposit rates increased somewhat over the years, concerns over financial stability prompted the PBOC to continue to set ceilings on retail deposit rates.

While maintaining ceilings on deposit rates and floors on lending rates creates distortions, it is not necessarily without merit under China's specific circumstances. The interest margin created by these regulations prevented excessive competition among banks, whose behavior has not been entirely profit-maximizing as commercial bank reform is still ongoing. Profits from a reasonable interest margin also help banks to rebuild their balance sheets, which were a key obstacle in the process of commercial bank reform. Interest rate margin management also provided incentives for banks to extend loans at the same time that they were cleaning up their balance sheets and strengthening their capital base, which helped avoid the deleveraging problem seen during the Euro area debt crisis and were crucial in supporting China's economic growth (Zhou 2012b). There are also concerns that interest margin management allowed banks to have excessive profits. While legitimate, such concerns failed to recognize the cyclicality of the banks' profits. If both past and prospective losses are appropriately taken into account, banks' profits in recent years may not be excessive after all.[6] In fact, all pre-tax profits of the Big Four between 2001 and 2012 added up to slightly more than RMB 4 trillion in 2011 prices (using the one-year deposit rate as a discount factor), while all capital injections into and bad assets removal from the Big Four since 1997 may ultimately cost the government RMB 3.8–4.2 trillion, depending on the recovery ratio of bad loans. The Big Four barely broke even over the last decade if the cost of their restructuring is taken into account.

On the second track of interest rate liberalization, PBOC made efforts to introduce market-based interest rates other than deposit and lending rates, such as interbank rates, bond rates, and SHIBOR. Unlike the deregulation of deposit and lending rates, this track of reform allowed more efficient resource allocation at the margin, resulting in Pareto improvement. Moreover, as the wholesale funding market does not directly affect the financing cost of enterprises, whose borrowing cost is more related to benchmark lending rates, this track of reform ran into little resistance. In 1996, interbank borrowing rates were fully liberalized, followed by repurchase and outright purchase of bonds in the interbank market in 1997. In 1999, yields on Chinese government bonds were determined by auction for the first time. In 2007, SHIBOR was launched with the aim of becoming a benchmark for short-term rates. Since then, SHIBOR has made considerable progress toward this goal. The pricing of a significant portion of corporate bonds, financing bills, and derivatives is now based on SHIBOR. SHIBOR is also widely used as the internal transfer price within and across banks (Yi 2009). As the international use of RMB grew, SHIBOR started to gradually become a benchmark in offshore RMB markets as well (Li 2012). Having a credible benchmarked rate, which SHIBOR has the potential to become, will be a critical step toward full interest rate liberalization. The central bank can only relinquish direct control over interest rates when there is a benchmark rate that the central bank recognizes and can influence. A market-based benchmark rate such as SHIBOR would also be instrumental to enhancing banks' competitiveness and balancing the interests of various parties; as such a benchmark would allow banks to price risks more competitively and make interest rate setting more objective as well as more market based (Yi 2008).

Moving in small steps, China has made great strides toward interest rate liberalization. At the time of this writing, most interest rates in China have been liberalized and PBOC only controls the ceiling on deposit rates, which can be 10 percent above the benchmark rates, and the floors on lending rates, which can be 30 percent below the benchmark rates, plus interest rates on certain short-term foreign currency deposits. However, it has to be emphasized that excessive competition and moral hazard, which may jeopardize interest rate liberalization, cannot be fully ruled out if there are no clear property rights, free competition, and credible exit mechanisms for financial institutions. Therefore, full interest rate liberalization would not be compatible with state-controlled banks, implicit deposit insurance and financial bail-outs during crisis. To this end, clear property rights, diversified ownership, orderly exit mechanisms, and hard budget constraints would be the necessary conditions for full interest rate liberalization.

2.2 Exchange rate regime reform

Like the interest rate, the exchange rate is another key price that has critical macro importance and global implications. Before 1994, China maintained multiple exchange rate arrangements, including the official exchange rate, the official internal settlement rate (which ceased to exist after 1984) and the market rate. Multiple arrangements were in part a result of the persistent overvaluation of the official exchange rate, but they also reflected the dual-track approach China took to reform the exchange rate regime, where the planned, heavily regulated official exchange rate coexisted with the increasingly important market rate. In 1994, the Chinese government decided to merge the official exchange rate (about 5.7 RMB/US$) and the market rate (about 9 RMB/US$) to form a single official exchange rate, which was set to be

8.7 RMB/US$. This reform marked the establishment of a unified exchange rate regime. While the nominal depreciation of the official exchange rate appeared to be very large (about 33 percent), the actual depreciation was much smaller (somewhere close to 4 percent), as about 80 percent of foreign exchange transactions were conducted at the much weaker market rate at the time of the reform (Yi 2009). Between 1994 and 1996, the RMB appreciated about 5 percent against the US$, reflecting, to a large extent, market demand and supply conditions. During the Asian financial crisis, China resisted the pressure to devalue and maintained a stable exchange rate against the US dollar. Between 1997 and 2005, the RMB exchange rate was maintained at RMB 8.27/US$ and the effective exchange rate of the RMB tracked that of the US$ closely as a result. Such an arrangement was initially a responsible move to avoid competitive devaluation during the Asian financial crisis and contributed to the restoration of regional financial stability. Following the WTO accession in 2001, China experienced rapid economic and export growth, which, to a large extent, reflected the underlying productivity improvement. China's current account surpluses surged and foreign reserve accumulation accelerated, both of which were usually associated with a stronger currency. However, the nominal and real effective exchange rates (NEER and REER) of the RMB depreciated following the gradual devaluation of the US$ after 2002 (see Figure 15.2). These developments called for a more flexible RMB exchange rate regime. On July 21, 2005, the PBOC announced that RMB would move toward a managed floating exchange rate regime with reference to a basket of currencies based on market demand and supply. The announcement was accompanied by a step appreciation of the RMB from RMB 8.27/US$ to RMB 8.11/US$, followed by gradual and accelerating appreciation afterwards. During the process, China also made efforts to further develop the foreign exchange market and products, increased the daily band around the central parity from ±0.3 percent to ±0.5 percent, and improved foreign exchange management. By August 2008, the RMB had appreciated 16 percent against the US$, 9 percent in nominal effective terms and

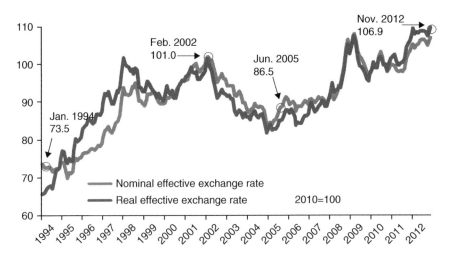

Figure 15.2   Evolution of RMB effective exchange rates*

Source: Bank for International Settlements

Notes: *Nominal effective exchange rate is calculated as the geometric weighted average of bilateral exchange rates between RMB and a basket of partner currencies. Real effective exchange rate is the same weighted average of bilateral exchange rates adjusted by relative consumer prices. The weighting pattern is time-varying and the most recent weights are based on trade in 2008–10

14 percent in real effective terms (as consumer price inflation was higher in China than in partner countries) since July 2005. The reform was, however, temporarily interrupted and put on hold by the outbreak of the global financial crisis in 2008 and the ensuing financial turmoil. The RMB exchange rate stabilized at RMB 6.83/US$ for about two years, before the reform of the RMB exchange rate regime restarted in June 2010. At the time of this writing, the NEER of RMB reached its highest level since 1994, about 45.4 percent higher than the level in 1994 and 21.4 percent more appreciated compared to the July 2005 level (Figure 15.2). The consumer-price-based REER of RMB followed a similar pattern to that of NEER, and the real appreciation of the RMB in recent years could be more pronounced if asset price inflation and rapid wage growth were considered. Overall, the RMB exchange rate has become more flexible with a daily band of ± 1 percent, more determined by market forces, as reflected by a much slower pace of reserve accumulation, and closer to the level where it would be possible to have genuine two-way fluctuations, rather than one-way appreciation pressure.

A related but different reform is the convertibility of RMB. China accepted the obligations under Article VIII of the IMF in 1996, namely, RMB became convertible under the current account. However, China took a very cautious approach toward capital account convertibility. While China took important steps to remove unnecessary capital controls over the years and introduced schemes like QFII, QDII, and RQFII to allow for limited inward and outward portfolio investment, considerable capital controls remain, particularly toward equity, debt, and bank flows.

2.3 Monetary policy

China's monetary policy framework has also undergone substantial changes during the reform process. Consistent with a central-planned economy, the monetary policy framework at the start of the reform was largely a command-and-control system, where monetary policy was conducted through allocating loan quotas and making cash management plans. Starting from 1994, the role of loan quotas began to diminish and was eventually phased out in 1998 and money supply formally became an intermediate target in 1996. More market-based indirect monetary policy tools, including reserve requirements, central bank loans, the discount window, open market operations, foreign exchange operations, and interest rates, are being increasingly used. To contain financial risks, the PBOC was also an early proponent of macro-prudential tools, including loan-to-value ratio for the real estate sector and more recently dynamic differentiated reserve requirements.[7] China's current monetary policy framework also has distinct features, reflecting the fact that China is still a transition economy, the degree of market sophistication remains to be strengthened, and the transmission mechanism of monetary policy is constrained by ongoing financial sector reform, interest rate liberalization, and exchange rate regime reform. To name a few special features, rather than focusing exclusively on inflation, as many inflation targeting central banks do, China's monetary policy has four objectives: inflation, growth, full employment, and balanced external position, with inflation given the highest priority; quantity tools continued to be extensively used to control monetary conditions; moreover, the central bank balance sheet and the conduct of monetary policy are occasionally used for the purpose of maintaining financial stability and financial sector reform, such as the reforms of the major state-owned commercial banks and RCCs discussed earlier.

2.4 Bank supervision

China started to formally adopt Basel I capital requirement in 2004, requiring all banks to reach the minimal capital adequacy by 2007. This was a landmark development in the following two senses: first, China's banks were finally subject to internationally accepted supervision standards, which were more transparent and stricter than the earlier prudential standards. This move also signaled that the health of China's banking sector, after the reforms discussed earlier, would become broadly satisfactory. Second, Basel I requirement also transformed banks' behavior and risk management, as it provided a good benchmark as well as a hard constraint on how banks would manage their balance sheet and more broadly their business. Originally, Basel II capital requirement was planned to be introduced over 2011–13 for six banks on a mandatory basis and some other banks on a voluntary basis. With the advent of Basel III framework, the CBRC issued new capital requirement based on Basel III, which would be implemented starting from 2013, ahead of many advanced economies. Other Basel III requirements, such as liquidity ratio and countercyclical capital buffer, are also being actively studied and designed by regulatory authorities and the PBOC, with a view to implementing them in due course.

3 The logic of financial reform and assessment

3.1 The logic of financial reform

The reform and evolution of China's financial institutions are both complex and still ongoing. Yet, there is clear logic behind the gradual reforms that took place in the last thirty years and this will continue to guide reforms in the future.

Clarifying and strengthening property rights. Property rights are the foundation of market transactions. Only under clearly defined property rights can there be meaningful market exchanges and prices, appropriately assigned responsibilities, and associated consequences. Clarifying and strengthening property rights has been a consistent goal during the entire financial reform process. For instance, the separation of commercial banks and the central bank, the creation of policy banks and the IPOs of commercial banks all shared the same purpose of better defining financial institutions' property rights and, by implication, their responsibilities.

More market and less government. The hallmark of China's economic reform is to have more market and less government, which also applies to the financial sector reform. Major prices, such as the interest rate and exchange rate, are greatly liberalized and increasingly determined by market forces. Direct intervention was gradually replaced by market-based indirect tools when conducting macro-management. Significant efforts were spent to enhance the commercial orientation of financial institutions, including phasing out policy loans, imposing stricter market discipline, strengthening internal control and risk management, and establishing a proper corporate governance structure, which all aimed at making financial institutions more market oriented.

Better incentive and supervision. One of the key reasons that a market economy outperforms a central-planned economy is that a market economy provides the right incentives, with rewards and profits aligned with efforts. The design and objectives of China's financial sector reform, therefore, have always aimed at getting incentives right. The RCC reform, as described earlier, was carefully designed to make sure that the incentives were compatible with the objectives. Interest rate liberalization, exchange rate regime reform, and the use of more market-oriented monetary policy tools all created an environment where prices could be more determined by the market and provide the right signals and incentives. At the micro-level, stricter supervision, accounting standards and disclosure requirements, as well as improved corporate governance, internal control, risk management, and remuneration schemes are all elements providing the right incentives in financial institutions.

Gradualism. China's financial sector reform took a gradual approach and sometimes not necessarily the most direct route. This was, first of all, dictated by the overall gradual economic reform itself. It is impossible to establish a modern, market-oriented financial system on a largely central-planned economy with highly regulated prices and widespread government interventions. Therefore, the progress of financial reform was constrained by reforms elsewhere. More importantly, a gradual financial reform supported the smooth transition from a planned economy to a market economy. Economic transition is not without cost and the fiscal resources of the government were limited. As a result, some of the cost incurred by the reform was borne by the financial sector, manifested as delayed financial reforms, NPLs, and interest margin management, which was sometimes considered as financial repression by some observers, e.g. Lardy (2012). For example, many of the NPLs removed from the major commercial banks before their reform were loans extended to SOEs, which supported SOE reform and helped maintain social stability. Had the bank reform proceeded before the SOE reform, banks could have avoided these NPLs, but many SOEs could be forced into bankruptcy for lack of financing and there could be widespread disruptions to the overall Chinese economy. Later, interest rate margin management helped improve the financial health of the banking industry and ultimately facilitated the banking reform. China's banking reform may appear too slow and interest rate management may resemble financial repression if viewed only from the narrow perspective of the financial sector, but these may well be the second best options under the overall constraint of an economy in transition.

Learning from international best practices. The reform process of China's financial system is also a learning process, particularly at the technical level. Many Chinese financial institutions are able to take advantage of state-of-the-art technologies, such as IT systems, as they develop and grow. One objective of introducing strategic investors during bank reforms was to allow strategic investors to transform these banks by bringing in international best practices, including corporate governance structure as well as internal control and risk management systems, which would take much longer to develop without outside expertise. The IMF and World Bank also helped bring in technical assistance to help modernize China's policy making. Learning allowed China to quickly bridge the gaps in management, technology, and product innovation as well as policy making in the financial sector. These, ultimately, catalyzed and accelerated China's financial reform.

3.2 Assessment of China's financial institutions

After three decades of financial reform, financial institutions in China undoubtedly made enormous transformation and progress. The fact that China is home to four out of ten of the world's largest banks in terms of market capitalization in 2011 was hardly conceivable, even just a decade ago, when all these four banks were thought by some as "technically bankrupted."[8] But one must also bear in mind that China's financial institutions have relatively short histories, carry many legacy problems, and operate in a transition economy where market discipline and principles are still being built. Notwithstanding the great distance traveled, there are still many problems remaining in China's financial institutions to be addressed in the future.

Clear property rights? The property rights of many Chinese financial institutions are clear on paper but not necessarily so in reality, although recent reforms of financial institutions have made significant progress in clarifying them. One key problem is that the government is usually the largest shareholder and effectively controls financial institutions. The agency problem under such a setting is very difficult to overcome, as the government is not the most natural owner to run financial institutions. Additionally, the interest of minority owners is very difficult to protect if government has such a dominant role in financial institutions. Moreover, the government still has direct or indirect influence over financial institutions other than the simple shareholding relationship, as government interventions are not yet fully market based. The implicit government guarantee or insurance on financial institutions, in which government is presumed to bail out financial institutions when in trouble, further complicates the relationship between government and financial institutions. Therefore, the key reform to improve the clarity on property rights in financial institutions is to have the government play a significantly lesser role in financial institutions, including becoming a minority stakeholder and a passive financial investor. Clearer property rights also hinge on more market-based government policies and schemes, such as an explicit deposit insurance system.

International standards? China's banking sector is quite open, competitive, large, and diverse. Large banks, particularly those listed globally or domestically, have gone through substantial reforms and are subject to both official supervision as well as market scrutiny. To the extent that China's regulatory, legal, and accounting standards are comparable with international standards, which is by and large the case according to the FSAP assessment (IMF 2011), these banks should technically be able to meet international standards in terms of regulatory, accounting, and legal requirements (although this does not necessarily mean these banks are internationally competitive, which requires much more than just being able to meet international standards). However, there are large numbers of banking institutions, for example, city commercial banks and RCCs that are still in need of further improvement before they can meet international standards. China's security firms continue to operate in a protected environment where opening to foreign security firms and competition is only partial. There are also a few gaps in the regulatory framework as documented by the FSAP assessment. While the insurance sector is more open, the sector itself is relatively new and the regulatory framework also needs further improvements. Understandably, the security and insurance sectors in general are less advanced in terms of meeting international standards.

Global competitiveness? China's financial institutions, particularly banks, grew very fast, are quite profitable and after their reform in the 2000s usually show healthy numbers, such as adequate capital, abundant liquidity, and good profitability. In fact, major Chinese banks are in much better financial shape than many of the world's prominent banks after the global financial crisis. There is also emerging evidence that efficiency of banks has improved after the reform (e.g. Berger *et al.* 2009). But in our view, it is too early to conclude that Chinese banks have become globally competitive. First of all, Chinese banks, to a large extent, are not competing directly with global banks. Foreign bank presence in China remains very small, partly due to interest rate regulation and capital control, which put foreign banks in a disadvantageous position, as their room for financial innovation is limited and their balance sheet is constrained by the lack of a domestic deposit base. The presence of Chinese banks in global markets, despite recent expansions, also remains very limited. The good financial shape of Chinese banks after the global financial crisis has less to do with banks' risk management and competitiveness and more to do with China's relatively closed capital account and robust economic fundamentals. Second, Chinese banks continue to rely very much on loans and deposits, as their main sources of income and financial innovations are limited. One piece of evidence is that interest income accounts for some 80 percent of the banking sector's overall income, while this ratio is around 50 percent or even lower for many global banks. Third, the good financial indicators of banks are partially a result of financial regulation. Loan and deposit rates continue to be regulated, which provides banks with a comfortable interest margin without the need to take on risks. Alternative sources of financing and investment, particularly the bond market, are underdeveloped and the capital account is controlled. Consequently, savings naturally flow to banks, not because of high returns or good services, but rather the lack of other means to invest. Taking all this together, the apparent strength of China's banks is not necessarily a result of global competitiveness and there is no clear evidence that China's banks have become globally competitive.

In summation, assessing China's financial institutions: property rights need to be further clarified, global competitiveness remains to be established, and there is still some distance to go before many financial institutions meet international standards.

3.3 Assessment of China's financial sector

While individual institutions are building blocks of the entire financial sector, the functioning of the financial sector also depends on the structure of the sector, the policy framework, and the legal environment, among many other factors. Efficiency at the institutional level does not automatically translate into efficiency at the sector level. To assess the overall financial sector, one has to take a view on whether the sector, as a whole, fulfills its functions, including resource allocation, price discovery, and financial services.

Efficient resource allocation? There is ample evidence that China's resource allocation is far from being efficient. At the macro level, China has an exceptionally high investment rate (nearly 50 percent of GDP) and very low private consumption (less than 40 percent of GDP). The very fact that nearly 50 percent of GDP is investment raises the question about the efficiency and quality of investment at such a large scale. Compared with countries with similar income per capita, China's service sector appears to be underdeveloped (Guo and N'Diaye 2009), reflecting the bias of resource allocation toward export and investment rather than consumption. Consistent with this pattern, overcapacity in some industrial sectors, such as steel, cement, and shipbuilding in addition to bottlenecks in other sectors, such as education and healthcare, coexist. Access to credit is uneven, with large SOEs having easy access to formal financing and private SMEs facing credit constraints and sometimes having to resort to informal financing (Song *et al.* 2011). This meant that resources did not always go to the most productive firms. As documented in Hsieh and Klenow (2009), if inter-firm resource allocation in China were as efficient as in the US, China's TFP would have been 30–50 percent higher. Of course, the inefficiency in resource allocation is a symptom of many structural problems in China, many of which do not rest in the financial sector. Rather, it is a manifestation of the incompleteness of China's market-oriented reform. However, a more efficient financial sector, more market-based interest rate, exchange rate and other factor prices, better financial intermediation and more use of market-based policy tools, would all certainly be part of the solution to improve the efficiency of resource allocation.

Price discovery? As discussed earlier, China has made significant progress in liberalizing interest rates and reforming the exchange rate regime. Nevertheless, the incomplete nature of these reforms necessarily leads to insufficient price discovery by the market. While only the ceiling on deposit rates and the floor on lending rates are now being regulated and other interest rates are by and large liberalized, the liberalized rates continue to be heavily influenced by the regulated rates both in theory (He and Wang 2011) and in reality (Porter and Xu 2009). Given the high marginal return to capital (Bai *et al.* 2006) and fast economic growth, the regulated interest rates could be structurally too low (Lardy 2012; He and Wang 2011). The underdeveloped bond and equity markets plus regulated interest rates also make the pricing of risks less effective, if at all. The large current account surplus, strong capital inflows, unabated appreciation expectations on the RMB and domestic inflation pressure on both goods and asset prices during much of the time between 2002 and 2011 all pointed to a stronger and, more importantly, a more flexible RMB. Notwithstanding significant progress on the reform of the exchange rate regime, there remains significant scope to make the RMB exchange rate more flexible.

Good financial services? The growth of the financial sector, development of financial markets, and competition among financial institutions in recent years have significantly increased the quality and scope of financial services available to households and businesses. Taking bank cards for example, the total number of bank cards issued increased from 277.4 million in 2000 to 2.95 billion in 2011, and transactions through bank cards grew from RMB 4529.9 billion to RMB 323.8 trillion annually during the same period. However, provision of financial services remains inadequate at a more fundamental level. From the demand side for financial resources, about one third of all fixed asset investments in 2011 were financed by so-called self-raised funds, much of which were the firms' own cash. On the supply side of financial resources, households held 71 percent of their financial assets in the form of cash or deposits and less than 1 percent in bonds in 2010. The recourse to self-raised funds for financing needs and the dominance of cash and deposits on households' balance sheet reflected the fundamental inadequacy of China's financial services' ability to adequately serve both demand and supply sides of financial resources and provide efficient financial intermediation.

Monopoly and oligopoly? It is difficult to characterize China's financial sector, particularly the banking sector, as monopoly or oligopoly. Banks are numerous in China – there are four major commercial banks, twelve joint-stock banks, more than 140 city commercial banks, and thousands of RCCs. The Big Four account for less than 50 percent of all banking assets and even less in terms of new loans. However, it should be acknowledged that China's banking sector is highly concentrated and the cause of concentration is not that large banks enjoy economies of scale. In fact, it is widely documented that large commercial banks are less efficient compared to joint-stock banks (e.g. Zhang and Wang 2009). The concentration is partly due to legacy reasons, as the major commercial banks were even more dominant ten or twenty years ago, but also partly due to policy distortions, including, for example, interest rate regulation and implicit deposit insurance, which help protect large banks more.

Excessive growth? The growth rate of China's financial sector in terms of its balance sheet is very high, not only in comparison to international peers but also to China's own economic growth. Using broad money to approximate the size of China's financial sector (note that banks still dominate China's financial sector), M2 grew about seven-fold from RMB 13.84 trillion at the end of 2000 to 94.48 trillion at the end of November in 2012, or from 140 percent of GDP in 2000 to around 180 percent in 2012. While faster M2 growth in the past was mainly a result of the monetization process and financial deepening (Yi 1994 and 2003), the extraordinary M2 growth more recently was a result of a confluence of domestic and international factors. Domestically, fast economic growth and the strong impetus to invest, coupled with loose monetary policy in the wake of the global financial crisis, led to fast credit expansion. Internationally, quantitative easing adopted by major central banks created ample global liquidity, part of which found its way into China. The persistent balance of payment surpluses and large foreign reserve build-up, symptoms of both domestic and global imbalances, also resulted in money creation under incomplete sterilization by the central bank. The fast M2 growth is increasingly associated with growing leverage, asset price inflation, and overcapacity in many manufacturing sectors, all of which point to potential risks to the financial sector. These potential risks must be given due consideration when carrying out future financial reforms. Improper pace and sequencing of reforms without recognizing these risks could jeopardize the financial stability in China. For example, fast interest rate liberalization before the commercial orientation of financial institutions is fully established, may narrow the interest rate margin too much too quickly, which will leave little room for banks to absorb losses from potential bad loans that are a likely result of recent balance sheet expansion.

Overall, despite rapid growth and its size, the functioning of China's financial sector continues to be hampered by the remaining problems in the financial sector as well as the structural problems in the overall economy. To a large extent, this is a natural outcome of the gradual reform from a central-planned economy to a market economy. Persistent, determined, and coordinated reform would be needed to have a more efficient, well-functioning, and market-oriented financial sector. Moreover, reform must be carefully paced and sequenced to address the potential risks associated with the fast balance sheet expansion of China's financial sector in recent years.

4 Concluding observations

Looking back on the evolution of China's banking and financial institutions, much has been achieved since the launch of China's economic reform. However, like the overall reform itself, more remains to be done in the financial sector. The twelfth Five-Year Plan (FYP) laid out a blueprint for China's financial reform in the medium term. The key objectives envisaged in the FYP include further advancing reforms of banks, security firms, and insurance companies, developing financial markets and products, prudent liberalization of interest rates, a more flexible exchange rate, gradually achieving capital account convertibility, and establishing a countercyclical macro-prudential management system, as well as strengthening financial supervision. There is perhaps nothing revolutionary in the twelfth FYP, reflecting the continued gradual approach of financial reform. But the market orientation of the plan is also evident. Ultimately, China is aiming to have a financial sector that is fully market based, a policy framework that uses market-friendly tools, key prices that are market determined and financial markets and products that fulfill the demand of the market – the financial sector will continue to evolve as reforms are being carried out.

Notes

1   The actual NPL ratio could be much higher than 24.75 percent if NPLs were classified more properly.
2   Bank of Communications (BoComm) also received a capital injection from Central Huijin.
3   RMB 815.7 billion bad loans were removed from ABC's balance sheet in 2008, of which RMB 150.6 billion were swapped for interest rate free central bank loans and 665.1 billion were put into a co-managed account by ABC and the ministry of finance. See ABC's 2009 annual report for more details.
4   For example, Royal Bank of Scotland, Temasek Holdings, UBS, and Asian Development Bank in BOC, Bank of America and Fullerton Financial Holdings in CCB and Goldman Sachs, Allianz and American Express in ICBC.
5   There was also a parallel central bank lending program, in which central bank loans were disbursed in tranches to RCCs and conditions had to be met for each disbursement. But very few RCCs opted for the central bank lending program.
6   See the press conference held by Zhou Xiaochuan, Hu Xiaolian, Liu Shiyu, and Yi Gang during the 2012 National People's Congress.
7   Dynamic differentiated reserve requirement links credit expansion with capital requirement for macro-prudential purpose, and takes into account systemic importance and the soundness of individual financial institutions as well as business cycles (Zhou 2012a).
8   The ranking of banks is based on FT Global 500, which ranks the world's largest companies. The 2011 rankings of ICBC, CCB, BOC, and ABC were, respectively, 1, 2, 6, and 7.

Bibliography

Bai, C. E., Hsieh, C. T., and Qian, Y. Y. (2006) 'The Return to Capital in China', *Brookings Papers on Economic Activity*, 37(2): 61–102.

Berger, A. N., Hasan, I., and Zhou, M. (2009) 'Bank Ownership and Efficiency in China: What Will Happen in the World's Largest Nation?', *Journal of Banking and Finance*, 33: 113–30.

Dai, X. L. (2010) 'Recollections on the 1997 National Finance Work Conference', *China Finance*, 2010(Z1): 28–31.

Guo, K. and N'Diaye, P. (2009) 'Employment Effects of Growth Rebalancing in China', *IMF Working Papers* 09/169.

He, D. and Wang, H.L. (2011) 'Dual-Track Interest Rates and the Conduct of Monetary Policy in China', *Hong Kong Institute for Monetary Research Working Paper* No. 21/2011.

Hsieh, C. T. and Klenow, P. (2009) 'Misallocation and Manufacturing TFP in China and India', *Quarterly Journal of Economics*, 2009(4): 1403–48.

IMF (2011) 'People's Republic of China: Financial System Stability Assessment', *IMF Country Report* No. 11/321.

Kornai, J. (1980) *Economics of Shortage*, Amsterdam: North-Holland.

Lardy, N. (2012) *Sustaining China's Economic Growth after the Global Financial Crisis*, Peterson Institute for International Economics.

Li, D. R. (2012) *Remarks at 2012 SHIBOR Work Conference*, http://www.pbc.gov.cn/publish/hanglingdao/917/2012/20121012150921081738404_.html (accessed December 4, 2012).

Lin, J. Y. and Tan, G. F. (1999) 'Policy Burdens, Accountability, and the Soft Budget Constraint', *American Economic Review*, 89(2): 426–31.

Lin, J. Y., Cai, F., and Li, Z. (2003) *The China Miracle: Development Strategy and Economic Reform*, Hong Kong: Chinese University Press.

People's Bank of China (2012) *A Brief History of Financial Development under the Leadership of the Chinese Communist Party*, Beijing: China Financial Publishing House.

Porter, N. and Xu, T. T. (2009) 'What Drives China's Interbank Market?', *IMF Working Paper* 09/189.

Reinhart, C. and Rogoff, K. (2004) 'The Modern History of Exchange Rate Arrangements: A Reinterpretation', *Quarterly Journal of Economics*, 119(1): 1–48.

Shang, M. (ed.) (2000) *50 Years of Finance in New China*, Beijing: China Financial and Economic Publishing House.

Song, Z., Storesletten, K., and Zilibotti, F. (2011) 'Growing Like China', *American Economic Review*, 101(1): 196–233.

Tang, S. N. (2005) 'On Several Problems Regarding State-owned Bank Reform', speech at the 2005 Annual Meeting of China Society for Finance and Banking.

Wu, X. L., Xie, P., Shen, B. X., Hu, Z. Y., Wang, Z. X., Wang, Z. J., and Mao, H. J. (1997) 'Tracking China's Financial Reform (part 2)', *Reform*, 1997(4): 83–98.

Yi, G. (1994) *Money, Banking and Financial Markets in China*, Boulder, CO: West View Press.

Yi, G. (2003) *The Monetization Process in China*, Beijing: Commercial Press.

Yi, G. (2008) *Remarks at 2008 SHIBOR Work Conference*, http://www.pbc.gov.cn/publish/hanglingdao/60/1156/11566/11566_.html (accessed on December 4, 2012).

Yi, G. (2009) *On the Financial Reform of China*, Beijing: Commercial Press.

Zhang, J. and Gao, X. H. (2006) 'Game in Capital Injection and Reform of Rural Credit Union System', *Journal of Financial Research*, 3: 48–56.

Zhang, J. H. and Wang, P. (2009) 'Frontier Efficiency of China's Banking Sector and its Determinants', *Journal of Financial Research*, 12: 1–18.

Zhou, X. C. (2004) 'A Few Thoughts on Rural Financial Reform', *Economic Perspectives*, 2004(8): 10–15.

Zhou, X. C. (2012a) 'China's Monetary Policy since 2000', per Jacobsson Lecture.

Zhou, X. C. (2012b) *The Global Financial Crisis: Observations, Analysis and Countermeasures*, Beijing: China Financial Publishing House.

16

LAW AND THE ECONOMY IN CHINA

Jacques deLisle

Analyses of reform-era China's economic development often emphasize policies that have made China's economy much more market oriented and internationally open than it had been from the founding of the People's Republic through the succession to Mao Zedong. Such assessments rarely describe law as playing much of a role (Naughton 1996; Lin *et al.* 2003; Chow 2007: 366–84; Huang 2008). Yet, since the beginning of Deng Xiaoping's tenure as China's top leader, commitments to building law, ruling through law and establishing a (socialist) rule of law have been prominent in official ideology, policy statements, and even constitutional amendments. In many measurable respects, China's laws and legal system have followed an upward trajectory rivaling that of the Chinese economy. In terms of the number of laws, lawyers, court personnel and lawsuits, popular awareness of law, and other such metrics, China's legal order has expanded dramatically.

While these patterns and trends are clear, assessments of China's legal development are strikingly varied and often middling. Conclusions about the quality or efficacy of law (except perhaps for those that find it very feeble) do not lead ineluctably to any judgment about law's importance – or lack of importance – to China's economy and economic development. Appraisals of the first decades of China's reform era that discern a weak connection between law and development, or that find China to have achieved impressive economic gains without much law, do not tell us whether that configuration will persist as China's economy becomes more advanced and diversified and Chinese society and politics continue to change. Overall assessments of whether China has relatively much or relatively little law, or rule by law, or rule of law do not answer more fine-grained questions about what roles law plays, how it functions, or how its strength varies across economic (and other) contexts.

There are, thus, good reasons to be somewhat agnostic and not to expect simple, definitive answers to questions about aspects of China's legal order relevant to China's economy. Nonetheless, a few broad features are evident. The resources devoted to law – and especially law for the economy – have increased greatly during the reform era. Formal law, legal institutions, and reliance on law have grown substantially. Economic policies, and economy-related policies more broadly, have been put in legal form to a great and, for China, unprecedented extent. Regime agendas have assigned roles to law, in promoting and sustaining economic development, that much exceed prior Chinese practice; law's place remains small, however, when compared to its position in market economies in the developed world with a robust rule of law.

Chinese law's efficacy and impact have differed markedly across time, region and subject matter. China faces growing pressures for greater legality although their ultimate effect remains unknown, partly because they confront formidable counter-forces.

1 Law and the economy under planning

Law – or, at least, law as the term is understood in developed market economies – had only marginal roles in the economy of the People's Republic of China during its first three decades. Soviet-style economies of the sort that the early PRC moved to create have little need for many functions law performs in market-oriented economies. Economic planning – with state-issued rights to acquire inputs and obligations to produce outputs at state-set prices – displaced myriad voluntary, bargained-for, horizontal economic arrangements and the need they create for contract law in market economies. State or collective ownership or socialization of the means of production left little room for property law, in contrast to its central place in economies based on private ownership. An industrial and commercial economy dominated by state-owned firms under the direct control of government "departments in charge" and collective enterprises that were, functionally, local state-owned firms meant there was no call for the elaborate structure of company law, securities law, and other business laws that are important features of market economies. With capital allocated according to the state's financial plan (partly through state-owned, non-commercial banks), banking laws and securities market laws were unnecessary. Because Chinese enterprises faced "soft budget constraints" (Kornai: 1992: 140–5) – including no consistent expectation of profitability or requirement to repay capital to state providers, and few economic performance-based threats of closure – the system could do without bankruptcy law and its functions of protecting creditors and disciplining debtor firms. International economic policies of near autarky and state trading companies that were monopolies in their fields meant there was minimal scope for foreign trade law. The Chinese economy under planning could largely dispense with competition law, tort law, tax law and various other economics-related laws that are ubiquitous and essential in market-based economies.

This does not mean that law played no role in China's economy during the pre-reform era. In part, law was a tool of planning. In part, China's incomplete adoption and limited institutional capacity to pursue Soviet-style planning left room, and created demand, for law to play roles at the periphery of China's limited plan (Naughton 1996: 26–55). Contract law provides the most abundant examples.

The label "contract" sometimes attached to what were, in substance, state administrative orders. Sometimes, nominally "contractual" arrangements specified "vertical" obligations of component units to higher-level superiors in China's multi-tiered state and collective economic structure. More horizontal contracts filled in the details of coarse and aggregated planning targets. Contracts matched particular suppliers and users or buyers and sellers, and adapted general or poorly differentiated plan directives to widely varying and often-shifting local circumstances. Once a contract was in place, it provided a means to monitor parties' performance of duties rooted in the plan but specified in contracts between enterprises that, notwithstanding their state or collective ownership, had independent legal personality and capacity to bear legal rights and obligations. Contracts also were meant to serve as mobilizational and motivational devices, giving grassroots actors nominal participation in the process of creating obligations, clearer pictures of their roles in larger projects of economic construction, and perhaps a sense that obligations set forth in a contract were, at least in some small part, quasi-voluntary choices rather than purely orders from the state. Contracts linked the planned economy to individuals, entities and economic activities that were, to varying degrees, outside the plan. These included, for example: a residual private sector that was tolerated during the PRC's early years but that was eventually socialized, in part through contracts with state entities that imposed lopsided terms and steered private firms toward state policy goals; and agricultural producers which sold above-quota or non-plan-covered output to state purchasers (Lubman 1970; Pfeffer 1963a, 1963b, 1966).

The existence of contracts also meant contract disputes and problems of non-performance. Oversight by Chinese Communist Party and government organs and state-owned banks were principal means for promoting compliance. A party's failure to perform was commonly addressed by an order for specific performance, penalties in amounts set by administrative regulations, administrative sanctions, or state-directed adjustments to obligations. Disputes were often handled through informal negotiation or appeals to state authorities, including a common administrative superior of the parties. There was little role for adjudication or arbitration producing awards enforcing contractual rights.

Law had at least one other significant economy-related function during the planning era: punishing and deterring behavior deemed harmful to the economy or the socialist economic order. Thus, China's laws specified economic crimes, including theft or destruction of state property. Technically non-criminal administrative punishments and less formal sanctions targeted relatively minor offenses, for example, stealing grain ration coupons. The category of sanction employed and its severity depended on the authorities' discretionary decisions and several factors that varied in importance over time. Relevant considerations included the magnitude of economic consequences of the offender's act, the offender's record of criminal or antisocial behavior, the offender's class background and degree of repentance, and whether a campaign against economic crime or other relevant behavior was underway (Cohen 1968; Fu 2005).

2 Law and legal institutions for the reform-era economy[1]

2.1 Investing in law

Developing, and relying on, law has been a major and enduring theme in the regime's ideology since the late 1970s. In 1978, the reform era's founding charter (the Communiqué of the Third Plenum of the Eleventh Central Committee) included a directive that there must be laws, that the laws must be followed and strictly enforced, and that violations of law must be corrected. A key slogan of the Jiang Zemin years – partly reflected in constitutional amendments – called for "ruling the country by law" and "building a socialist rule of law state." On coming to power in 2002, Hu Jintao called the constitution the country's fundamental and inviolable law and insisted all public and private entities were to follow and implement it. Hu referred to law a record number of times in his 2007 political report to the 17th Party Congress. In 2011, Wu Bangguo, then chairman of the National People's Congress, declared that construction of China's socialist legal system was basically complete. With Xi Jinping's ascension to China's top leadership posts came renewed official insistence on law's importance. In 2012, the 18th Party Congress political work report ordered the party to operate "within the limits of the constitution and the law" and to uphold their authority. In remarks celebrating the thirtieth anniversary of the 1982 constitution, Xi proclaimed "we must firmly establish, throughout society, the authority of the constitution and the law." The key reform document issued by the 18th Central Committee's Third Plenum in 2013 reiterated calls for a "rule of law government" and pledge to build a commercial environment under the rule of law.

China's accession to the World Trade Organization in 2000 prompted many official statements emphasizing the importance of law – particularly laws affecting the economy, which China had revised extensively to secure entry into the global trading body and which fellow

WTO members would press China to implement. Throughout the reform era, and especially in recent years, many State Council-issued "white papers" and other formal documents have pledged, and touted, progress toward a more robust and effective legal order.

Rhetoric about law, of course, does not translate reliably into reality. The commitment to law has been thinner than the pursuit of economic modernization although it has been less hollow than the embrace of political democracy. Still, investment of material and political resources has been substantial and undertakings to build law and a legal system have been extensive. A compendium of the "complete" laws of the PRC from 1949 through 1985 fit within a single, several hundred-page volume, with most of the content from the final few years. Two decades later, a less comprehensive collection of a single year's output of legislation and major regulations dwarfed the 1949–85 volume. Since the reform era began, the NPC and its Standing Committee have passed hundreds of major laws and more numerous lesser ones. The State Council and its subordinate organs and local legislatures and governments have issued tens of thousands of regulations and lesser rules (Zhu and Han 2013). Many laws, regulations, and rules have been amended repeatedly, to adjust to changing circumstances in China or to adapt to international norms or international legal requirements. Compared to pre-reform era baselines, a vastly larger share of Chinese law focuses on economic affairs.

After closing law schools during part of the Cultural Revolution decade, China now has more than 600 law faculties that have educated many lawyers (who now number around 200,000), judges (who are as numerous as lawyers and staff more than 10,000 courts), and a larger group of law degree holders who have taken legal training into jobs in government and the private sector. Economics-related fields of law, including business law and international economic law, have been especially popular subfields.

People's congresses and state administrative organs have strengthened their lawmaking and law-interpreting capacity by adding legal staff and employing legal scholars as advisers. Both the NPC, in its Legislative Affairs Commission, and the State Council, in its Legislative Affairs Office, include specialized bodies focusing on law and legal affairs. Large-scale, long-lasting public education efforts have promoted popular knowledge of law and legal rights.

Business enterprises and citizens regularly turn to law firms (which number roughly 17,000), legal assistance offices (which serve the poor) and individual lawyers for legal services. In recent years, Chinese courts annually handle around ten million complaints from parties who seek redress on matters ranging from business dealings to property and intellectual property, to accidentally and intentionally inflicted harms, to employment disputes, to defamation, to divorce. During the last few years, courts each year have accepted and adjudicated over three million contract cases, about 1.5 million property, torts and other civil law cases, and 30–50,000 intellectual property cases. Courts execute over two million civil judgments per year. They annually handle over 100,000 suits against the state, with the vast majority focusing on state actions affecting economic interests such as property rights, government benefits, application of industrial and commercial regulations, and intellectual property. Convictions for crimes of disrupting the socialist market economy and financial crimes have reached over 60,000 per year (China Law Yearbook 2009–11; Supreme People's Court 2013).

2.2 *Law for a market-oriented, internationally integrated economy*

A principal role for law in reform-era China has been to set forth rules to support economic development – specifically, development of an economy that has turned from plan to market and from international isolation to integration. Economic policies that advance and reflect this reorientation have been written into laws and relied on legal means for implementation.

The Economic Contract Law of 1981, a 1993 revised version, a unified Contract Law in 1999 and related legislation and regulations have defined a framework for economic actors to undertake more freely chosen, diversely structured, market-based transactions with a widened array of partners. These laws grant economic actors much freedom to make (and not make) contracts, choose suppliers and customers, negotiate terms, and operate without significant constraint from the state plan. More recently, a labor contract law has promised employees greater protection of rights and interests in employment.

Contract law and related laws offer parties increased discretion in choosing procedures for resolving disputes and, in some international contracts, to select which nation's law governs their contracts. Remedies have shifted from a preference for specific performance (which was reminiscent of planning-era, state-mandated obligations and which had stronger economic justification early in the reform era when it was often difficult to find substitutes in the market for a defaulting party's non-performance) toward money damages (which are the principal legal remedy in market economies for making the victim of a breach whole without sacrificing economic efficiency) and even liquidated damages (which reflect rising principles of party autonomy, allowing parties to set by advance agreement damages for breach) (Jiang 1996; Hsu 2007).

Laws governing business enterprises have undergone rapid development and transformation. For firms still owned or controlled by state organs, legal reforms have mandated greater insulation from intervention in management decisions by government overlords and increased autonomy in hiring and firing staff, acquiring and selling assets, and making many ordinary and strategic business decisions. More fundamentally, many laws have affirmed the legitimacy and defined the structures and powers of new business organizations that have had relatively market-oriented environments – and relatively little state control or state subsidization – from their inception. These entities, which have proliferated and now comprise most of the industrial and service economy, include some types of township and village enterprises (which have ranged, functionally, from local government-run enterprises to disguised private enterprises), new types of collective enterprises, and many forms of private and foreign-invested firms (including proprietorships, partnerships, corporations, joint ventures, and holding companies) (Clarke 1991, 2005; Simon 1996; McDonnell 2004).

The Company Law and Securities Law of the 1990s, their mid-2000s revised versions, and related laws and regulations have been among the major moves redefining legal rights and roles of ownership and management (and other stakeholders) in terms that converge with similar laws in market economies. These laws also are key elements in a structure that increasingly has authorized and encouraged more varied and complex forms of ownership and modes for transferring ownership of firms. They have created legal templates for corporations that issue shares, including shares traded on stock exchanges that China first established in the 1990s. Such reforms – through directly creating legal rights and responsibilities in corporate governance rules and through indirectly encouraging pressures from product, factor, and capital markets – undertook to drive owners and managers to exercise their powers to advance firms' economic interests (Art and Gu 1995; Zhang 1999; Schipani and Liu 2002; Wei 2005; Dickinson 2007).

Laws governing fiscal relations between enterprises and the state have become less market-distorting and more arm's-length. For firms owned or controlled by the state, income tax and other rule-based taxes displaced arrangements of complete, arbitrary or ad hoc negotiated payments by enterprises to the state. For private, privatized, or partly privatized entities, fiscal laws applied more straightforwardly, making rule-governed taxation a principal form of legitimate state revenue extraction (Shirk 1993: 245–79; Ho 2001). Although such reforms have been especially important because investment in China often relies on retained profits, other laws have addressed other important sources of capital, including securities and futures markets, security interests and guarantees, and commercial banking. These laws have mandated more market-based (and less political or policy-based) standards for allocating capital and authorized more numerous, diverse, and market-oriented providers of capital and credit (in contrast to the prior systems of state allocation or "policy lending" by a handful of large state-owned banks) (Lardy 1998; Wu 2009). Bankruptcy law has been another component of this trend. The idea that enterprises, their managers and staff would bear significant consequences for unprofitability and inability to repay credit was largely absent from Chinese law until a rudimentary law for state-owned enterprise bankruptcy came into effect in 1987. Compared to its predecessor, the 2007 Bankruptcy Law offered more power to creditors, less discretion to the state as gatekeeper to bankruptcy, and weaker protection for employees' "iron rice bowls" – the term for permanent employment and benefits that workers in state-owned enterprises once enjoyed (Peng 1987; Rapisardi and Zhao 2010).

Many of these legal reforms entwined with another major element of market-oriented law: property rights. Building on earlier changes to the 1982 constitution, a 2004 amendment raised private property nearly to formal equality with state and collective property, and pledged that takings of private property required a public purpose and compensation. After long delays and criticism that it undermined socialism, a Property Rights Law passed in 2007, giving clearer content and higher status to rights in property, especially land (Zhang 2008; Rehm and Julius 2009). Such reform has been limited, even in the law on the books, notably for land. Urban real estate remains owned by the state and rural land by the collective. But legal reforms have provided for broad "usufruct" rights that include rights to use and derive profits from land and, to some extent, transfer or mortgage land rights. A somewhat similar less-than-ownership legal regime has applied to the shrinking share of state-owned enterprises' capital assets that are formally state-owned assets assigned or entrusted to enterprises. Driven by the terms of China's WTO accession and reflecting policies to promote more knowledge-intensive sectors, China has repeatedly revised and expanded intellectual property laws – which date to the early reform era – so that the law on the books now conforms to international, largely treaty-based standards for copyright, patents, trademarks, and trade secrets (Zhang 2003).

Law has also taken on new roles in addressing economic behavior that causes broader social or public harms. For example, after a decade-long drafting process, China enacted an Anti-Monopoly Law in 2008 to target threats to market competition (and competitors and consumers) from firms that have acquired or, with planned acquisitions could acquire, dominant market positions and engage in collusive practices or impose competition-undermining discriminatory or unfair terms. Tort law has developed from near-zero pre-reform era baselines. Developments in this economically important area have included expanded liability for producers and sellers of defective products, which has evolved from sparse provisions in the General Principles of Civil Law (1987), through a Product Quality Law (1993, 2000) and a Consumer Rights and Interests Protection Law (1993), to a scandal-expedited Food Safety Law (2009) and a full-fledged Tort Liability Law (2010). The Tort Liability Law, like the General Principles' torts provisions, operates in conjunction with more specialized law to address economically significant harms, including those due to faulty products, medical malpractice, environmental pollution, poor construction, infringement of intellectual property rights, traffic accidents, and defamation (Zhang 2011; deLisle 2012).

The PRC's first full-fledged Criminal Law was adopted in 1979 and several rounds of amendments since then have adopted provisions targeting economic misbehavior that, if sufficiently widespread, could undermine China's market-oriented economic development strategy. Examples include prohibitions of embezzlement, money-laundering, tax evasion, securities, and other financial offenses, kidnapping for ransom, environmental harms, and intellectual property infringement, as well as more traditional property crimes such as theft and destruction. Among offenses that have roots in the planning era but that have new market-era justifications are destruction of state property or violent disruption of public order in ways that cause significant economic damage. Tellingly, official justifications for emergency powers laws and other exceptional uses of state power have routinely pointed to economic – and not just social order or political control – rationales (Dobinson 2002; deLisle 2010a).

Chinese law addressing international economic integration has paralleled and supported these trends in domestic economic legal reform. China has adopted increasingly and, by developing country standards, strikingly liberal trade and investment laws. New laws dismantled restrictions on enterprises' foreign trading rights, lowered barriers to imports and exports and pursued conformity with WTO requirements as China sought to join, and after its accession, to implement WTO obligations. Laws, and revisions to laws, on Chinese–foreign equity joint ventures, contractual joint ventures, wholly foreign-owned enterprises, foreign ownership of shares in – and full acquisition of – PRC companies, foreign institutional investors and foreign exchange regulation have become much more flexible and foreigner-friendly since "opening to the world" began in 1979. Legal reforms have designated more regions open to foreign investment on favorable terms, from the original four Special Economic Zones in the southeast, to many coastal cities and adjacent regions, to economically less developed border areas and the struggling inland West. Legal changes have opened more economic sectors to foreign investment, moving from a narrow emphasis on foreign exchange-generating and technology-transferring projects to a system that does the following: encourages foreign investment in many fields, allows it in other sectors and restricts or prohibits it in a few areas (primarily still-emerging, or vulnerable and declining, or national security-sensitive sectors) (Potter 1995; Lardy 2002; Wang 2006; Huang 2009).

In all of these areas, the impact of laws in promoting market-oriented development has been limited, and assessment of their effects is complicated and controversial. Laws continued formally to require that contracts be consistent with the state plan and vaguely defined public interests. Some contracts and projects, including many large-scale ones, still need legal approval from China's vast, fragmented and often unaccountable bureaucracy. Still, changes toward more market-oriented and internationally open economic laws have coincided with changes in practice that have partly tracked what the laws envisioned. Some studies have found that, especially in China's most developed areas, businesses engage in more transactions with strangers and rely less on connections (*guanxi*) or corruption, in part because of pressures from market competition and the law. Other assessments, however, have found that economic reform has permitted or encouraged *guanxi* to endure in economic transactions and that law has made only modest headway in creating reliably enforceable, neutral rules that allow parties to make business decisions solely on economic grounds (Cheng and Rosett 1991; Guthrie 1999; Gold *et al.* 2002). Although the labor contract law has expanded employment protections for covered workers, it has drawn criticism – not only from employers – for making some employees too difficult to fire, even as it has done little to create job security for many of China's workers. Labor law and workplace regulation more generally have not alleviated problems of non-payment of wages and dangerous work conditions (as reflected in large-scale industrial and mining accidents) (Gallagher 2005).

Many large enterprises have remained wholly state-owned or effectively state-controlled, often through complex corporate structures. By the latter part of the Hu era, analysts noted the phenomenon of *guojin mintui* –the resurgence of large, state-linked enterprises at the expense of smaller firms with private ownership. Despite corporate governance law reform, the state as owner and state-selected managers face opportunities and pressures to steer firms to ends – often politically defined ones – other than maximizing profits or shareholder value (Clarke 2010). For small and non-state-linked enterprises, access to capital from banks, stock markets or any legally authorized channels other than retained earnings has remained limited, relegating them to sources outside the reach of reformed laws (Yu and Zhang 2008). Despite the growth of legal regulation, equities markets remain flawed – plagued by volatility in share prices and much fraud in the books of listed firms – and limited as means for raising capital and disciplining listed firms. Although bankruptcies have risen sharply, the law still has not subjected many state-linked firms to hard budget constraints.

Contract-based property rights were instrumental in the productivity-enhancing return from collectivized agriculture to household farming and the promotion of urban residential and commercial development during the reform era. Still, formal legal rights to use the land (but not full ownership) have proved a weak defense against authorities' collaboration with, and appropriation and transfers of land to, developers for urban redevelopment or conversion of rural land to urban use. The law's "public interest" requirement for state taking of land use rights is vague and has not imposed effective constraints. The law's "compensation" requirement does not formally require full, market-rate compensation and has not prevented meager payments that often fall short of low state-set standards. Much recent housing construction has depended on extralegal mechanisms such as the "minor property rights" that have been the vehicle for developing land still legally limited to agricultural and rural uses (Pils 2005, 2010a; Zhang 2008). The gap between legal promise and practice in protection of intellectual property rights has been the subject of sustained and strident criticism from foreign rights holders and a growing concern for domestic rights holders as well (Yu 2005; USTR 2012: 96–107).

The Anti-Monopoly Law is in its infancy, but some of its most famous early uses have drawn criticism for stymieing foreign acquirers' bids in order to protect Chinese target companies or assist rival Chinese bidders (Zhang 2009; USTR 2012: 70–1). The growth of tort law has been limited by its newness and incompleteness, ongoing restrictions on class action lawsuits that have been key drivers of tort law in other systems, and larger legal and institutional structures that assign much of the task of addressing socially harmful activities – especially in cases involving significant social harm, such as those caused by mass consumer products or environmental pollution – to administrative oversight, state sanctions and government-brokered compensation plans (deLisle 2012).

Prosecution and punishment for economic crimes have produced complicated reactions and assessments. Official media tout convictions, often of well-known rich business people and more ordinary defendants involved in notorious cases or swept up in campaigns against particular types of economic crime. Many cases are relatively uncontroversial on the merits and in public perception. Still, such laws are not seen as being very effective, as is reflected, for example, in opinion polls that identify corruption in business as a top public concern or in the common view that tycoons who face prosecution are selected partly for political reasons while some of their peers escape similar fates thanks to political connections. The legitimacy with audiences at home and abroad of charges of economic crime (and lesser, administratively sanctionable actions) suffers from laws' political or politicized uses: to repress social unrest (principally in the form of allegations of destruction of property or disruption of economic order against Tibetans and Uyghurs), or to harass political dissidents (for example, in the form of charges of tax evasion or engaging in various business activities without the required legal authorization) (deLisle 2010b; Wong 2011; Pew 2012).

China's trade and investment laws have been adequate for China to rise to the top ranks in inbound foreign investment, exports and overall trade. Still, China has faced sharp and growing criticism – and a rising number of formal quasi-judicial proceedings in the WTO's dispute resolution mechanism – for laws, policies and practices that the US and others claim breach WTO obligations on market access, intellectual property rights, unfair support for exports, and other matters. Foreign investors complain of legal and regulatory playing fields that are tilted – in many accounts increasingly so – against them and in favor of Chinese competitors (American Chamber of Commerce 2012).

Assessments of economic dispute resolution are mixed. Adjudication has drawn the most attention. Some studies find that parties in ordinary commercial disputes often believe that the result in their cases comported with law. One study found that ordinary citizens were more likely to litigate if someone they knew had done so – a result suggesting relatively positive experiences with the legal system. On the other hand, some assessments conclude that many Chinese – especially the less well-off and less educated – turn to court not because they expect a just or satisfactory result but because bringing suit offers hope of a moral victory and a limited sense of empowerment. Some research discerns deep – and growing – popular disillusionment with the legal system. But this appears to be partly due to highly optimistic ex ante views about legal processes and low respect for outcomes that are procedurally proper but appear substantively unjust (O'Brien and Li 2005; Landry 2008; Pei *et al.* 2010; Gallagher and Wang 2011; Michelson and Read 2011).

Progress has been made in building a more educated, professional and capable judiciary and increasing judicial autonomy, especially in relatively ordinary economic cases. Nonetheless, assessments of courts point to persisting, significant shortcomings. One issue is lack of resources, both human and material, allocated to courts in some areas. Another is judicial corruption, whether in the form of bribery or trading on connections. Perhaps most significant is "local protectionism": courts favor local parties, especially large or state-linked firms, because courts depend on the local state for budgets (and judges depend on the local party for advancement), and the local party–state protects local companies as sources of taxes, profits (for the local state as owner), growth and jobs (which are key components for evaluating cadres), or political support (given the entanglement of local business elites and officials and the importance of jobs and growth for local social stability) (Lubman 1999: 250–97; Peerenboom 2000: 280–342; Li 2010a).

2.3 Law to address market economy-undermining party–state behavior

Another principal function for law has been to check dysfunctional state behavior that could undermine the development strategy that China's economic law seeks to promote. Laws provide a possible means to address corruption, *guanxi*, parochialism (including local protectionism), abuses of power or abdication of responsibility by those wielding power, and the problems that come from failure to avoid or redress badly designed or poorly executed economic policies. Such concerns have become serious. Public opinion polls and top leaders identify China's most serious challenges as including official corruption and, increasingly, threats to public health and safety allowed by lax regulation of pollution, food and products (Pew 2012; Xinhua 2013). Well over 100,000 "mass incidents" of social unrest occur annually, with many focusing on issues related to official abuse of, or failure to protect, citizens' economic rights and interests.

Law's roles in pursuing these public governance goals have included much that is formally part of private law addressing economic activity. Beginning in the 1980s, contract cases involved peasants and entrepreneurs who profitably managed assets leased from collective or state owners and faced efforts from lessors to extract larger payments or nullify agreements, for motivations ranging from suspicions about insider deals in making contracts, to views that contracts unfairly distributed the fruits of public assets, to simple rent-seeking (Zweig *et al.* 1987). Commercial litigation by industrial and commercial enterprises also has addressed problems rooted in official disregard for law. For example, state owners or overseers have diverted enterprise revenues or issued orders preventing enterprises from fulfilling obligations. Enterprises have engaged in opportunistic, unlawful behavior because they could expect their state patrons to insulate them from legal accountability. In handling these kinds of cases, courts have played not only the conventional market-supporting role of upholding parties' legal rights, but also policy-implementing and official-abuse-checking roles through criticizing and sanctioning state-related behavior that violates policies embodied in laws.

Beginning early in the reform era, local governments and state-linked parent companies sometimes were held liable for acts of sham enterprises that they had created. In more recent times, corporatized formerly state-owned enterprises that sell shares increasingly have been foci of corporate law and litigation. For example, state-linked majority shareholders' abuse of private, minority shareholders' rights helped prompt reforms, especially in the mid-2000s, to the Company Law and Securities Law that authorized new types of shareholder suits, articulated fiduciary duties of controlling shareholders and managers, and authorized "piercing the corporate veil" and other means to hold an enterprise's owners or controllers liable for unlawful actions (Howson 2010; Huang 2012).

Much of China's new property law regime has focused on restraining problematic state behavior. Constitutional amendments that addressed the relative status of state, collective, and private property, and imposed public interest and compensation requirements for taking private property, regulations on land registration, tenure, expropriation, and reclassification of land from rural to urban, rules on court jurisdiction over land disputes, and litigation (sometimes in the form of administrative litigation challenges to state eviction orders) and protests (sometimes invoking property law) by citizens ousted from their homes and farms all have addressed state agents' behavior. Often this has been in the form of local authorities' collusion with developers to obtain land without adequate compensation and beyond legal and policy authorization. Law-invoking challenges to such state or state-linked acts have received extraordinary government and public attention. One famous and unusually successful example is the "nailhouse" in Chongqing where two residents clung to a home and business perched atop a spike of land in a vast construction site, brought a legal challenge to the local government's order to leave, waged a mediagenic campaign invoking the principles of still-emerging property law, and ultimately received much-increased compensation. Another example is the challenge prominent legal scholars brought against State Council regulations on housing demolition and relocation. They argued – with some effect, given changes to the rules that soon followed – that the permissive rules were too vague and inconsistent with higher laws (Zhang 2008; Wang 2009; Hess 2010).

In China's emerging tort law, many provisions address regulators' roles and responsibilities. Other provisions, concerning specific torts, read like an inventory of areas of perceived government regulatory failure leading to social harm and economic loss, including product liability, pollution, medical malpractice, and internet-based harms. Especially in cases of mass torts such as melamine-tainted milk products, offshore oil spills, or deaths due to shoddy and inadequately inspected construction in earthquake zones, Chinese authorities have displaced the private civil remedies that tort law seemed to offer with state-managed compensation funds and criminal and administrative penalties for responsible private actors and neglectful officials. Such phenomena may reflect the regime's perception that leaving such incidents to civil litigation, or leaving them unredressed and uncompensated, would invite unwanted rights assertiveness, political activism, or anger toward a state that, through its pervasive reach, has created public expectations that it is responsible for any public safety failure. Whatever the reason, they show concern with the state's actions or omissions that is a principal feature of Chinese tort law and related practice (deLisle 2012).

The limits to private law's effectiveness in protecting citizens' and enterprises' economic legal rights also undermine its capacity to check abuse and underuse of state power. Litigation provides some of the most discussed illustrations. Criticisms of courts' delivery of justice in economic cases are strikingly "statist," focusing on structural bias toward state-linked or party-linked litigants, or influence by party or state actors, or other problems of local protectionism, or the relatively low status accorded to courts in the Chinese party–state hierarchy. Continuing impediments to class action lawsuits limit potential for civil litigation to tackle systemic issues, including economically deleterious patterns of behavior that ultimately have roots in state acts and omissions.

Public law has been a principal legal means to address official behavior that threatens to undermine market-oriented economic policies and laws. Administrative law has been the most prominent component. Under the Administrative Litigation Law, citizens bring challenges in court to state decisions that affect economic interests, ranging from land rights to government benefits and fines to enforcement of business regulations. The Administrative Reconsideration Law provides a mechanism to request a government agency, or its superiors, to reverse specific decisions (including ones that might be addressed in administrative litigation), or change underlying rules (which cannot be challenged in administrative lawsuits). The State Compensation Law offers victims a legal right to seek damages when harmed by unlawful government actions (Potter 1994; Wang 2003; Ohnesorge 2006). The Administrative Licensing Law, the Administrative Enforcement Law and lower-level rules paralleling a long-pending Administrative Procedure Law address processes by which state organs allocate benefits and burdens, including ones affecting economic interests. Specific economic regulatory laws also address official overreaching and shirking. Examples include the Anti-Monopoly Law's prohibition of improper use of government power to restrain competition and product safety law's and banking law's sanctions for officials' failure to perform oversight duties.

Other developments in public law have provided for some popular input into lawmaking and thereby for citizens to seek protection for their economic interests, to challenge what they see as ill-advised state laws, policies or behavior, and to provide "crowd sourced" wisdom to lawmakers and policymakers. Laws for direct elections at the village level and the lowest level people's congresses formally promise democratic input and accountability. A law on legislation and rules on administrative procedure provide for hearings, comments, and other public input on proposed laws and rules – the contents of which are increasingly available due to open government information and "e-government" reforms. Experiments with consultative democracy, especially on budget and fiscal issues, at the local government level are another emergent source of public input (Wang 1998, 2000; Paler 2005; Horsley 2007).

Criminal and administrative punishments for law-violating officials range up to capital punishment. They have been most aggressively used in recurring drives against official corruption that began under Deng, accelerated under Jiang, continued under Hu and received new emphasis under Xi. Those prosecuted for corruption have included a handful of high ranking and high profile officials, including former Beijing Mayor Chen Xitong in the 1990s, Shanghai Party chief Chen Liangyu in 2008, Railway Minister Liu Zhijun in 2013, and former Chongqing Party Secretary, Minister of Commerce and aspiring Politburo Standing Committee member Bo Xilai in 2013.

Despite these numerous and diverse developments, Chinese public law has not resolved problems of unlawful actions and potentially economic development-undermining behavior by the party–state's agents. How far practice has fallen short of promise is an uncertain and contentious question. Examples from administrative litigation suggest the broader problem. In administrative lawsuits, plaintiffs have prevailed 20 to 40 percent of the time – a respectable to high rate of success for citizens suing their government by international standards. But the small number of administrative law cases (around 100,000, in contrast to millions of civil cases each year) invites skepticism about the law's actual or perceived utility. It also compounds the already difficult task of assessing the proportion of filed claims that are meritorious (and how that rate compares to rates in other jurisdictions).

Some studies, especially those focusing on developed regions, find relatively high competence and perceptions of fairness of administrative litigation (Pei 1997; Hung 2005). Some accounts indicate that threatening to sue can drive officials to reverse unlawful decisions, out of fear of losing or fear that being sued counts against them in performance evaluations. But this also can lead to perverse results in terms of the rule of law: in recent years, there have been growing complaints about what in the US are called "strike suits" – meritless litigation (or, more broadly, false assertions of unlawful behavior) to pressure authorities to pay off complainants. Some other analyses, especially those looking at poorer, often rural areas, find futility and frustration in administrative litigation, with local authorities wielding influence over unskilled or pliable courts, using coercion to deter potential litigants, and retaliating against victorious ones. Suing the state is often an act of desperation by those who have little hope (O'Brien and Li 2005; He 2011a). Even in principle, much economically harmful behavior by the regime's agents lies beyond this law's reach. Administrative lawsuits can review only specific state acts and decisions – not underlying laws, regulations or rules, or normative documents that are not law but have de facto law-like effect. Administrative law does not provide a means to challenge party actions or policies.

Legally promised means for quasi-democratic input have been weak in practice (deLisle 2008). Hearings on proposed legislation and opportunities to comment on proposed regulations have given actors outside the state – and, notably, business and industry groups (Pearson 1994; Kennedy 2005) – opportunities to weigh in, but mechanisms for public input fall well short of a legal right to be heard or answered, much less to influence outcomes. Increasingly, lawmakers and regulators are deluged with public comments that they do not, and sometimes as a practical matter cannot, take into account. Although it has provided means to oust some bad officials and glimmers of hope for greater democracy, the village elections law has been unevenly implemented, vulnerable to authorities' manipulation, often failed to fulfill its mandate for open and contested elections, and reaches only very low-level posts (O'Brien and Li 2000; Fewsmith 2012). The electoral law for local people's congresses has led to only a few heterodox candidates, fewer victories for them, and still fewer wins that survive authorities' efforts to overturn them or prevent their recurrence (Nathan 1985; deLisle 2010c).

Legal measures targeting official corruption have had limited impact and often provoked skeptical or cynical assessments. Although corruption is hard to measure, the prevalent perception is that it is pervasive and costly, that it has become more organized and large scale, and that it is more harmful now that China has moved beyond the early reform phase when violations of legal rules by state actors could overcome inefficiencies in a system in transition from planning. Criminal punishment reaches only a small fraction of reported instances and a still smaller share of corrupt behavior. The Party's Central Commission for Discipline Inspection, not state prosecutors, is the dominant institution for addressing corruption among officials, who are overwhelmingly party members and thus subject to party discipline. The Commission acts as gatekeeper for the small share of cases criminally prosecuted. Far more common than prosecution is the extra-legal – and, Chinese law scholars argue, often illegal – party discipline, including the *shuanggui* form of detention and investigation (Manion 2004; Fu 2013). Recent reform agendas have called, with limited effect, for more reliance on criminal law to address corruption and for measures requiring officials to disclose assets and thereby facilitate monitoring for corruption.

To the extent that economically harmful state behavior in China involves official shirking in following central laws and directives, rather than overreach and abuse, law is generally a relatively weak mechanism. Bureaucratic discipline and ideological motivation are the more common and perhaps the more potent tools for addressing such problems – all the more so in the Chinese Communist tradition (Selznick 1952; Schurmann 1968; Weber 2009).

3 Assessing the rule of law and economic development in China

3.1 The "level" of rule of law

Evaluating China's – or any country's – "level" of rule of law is problematic and controversial, given issues of definition, measurement, weighting, and aggregation of diverse components of legality, dynamism in laws and practices, and comparison across radically different systems. Nonetheless, broad comparative assessments can be instructive, particularly when they place a controversial case such as China along a cross-national spectrum that tracks widely held views in ranking less contested cases. In one of the most prominent metrics, China receives comparatively high marks on the World Bank's "Rule of Law" index. China scores around the fortieth percentile globally and near median for countries in its "upper middle income" group. China's standing is stronger than this implies, given that its per capita income is near the bottom of the wide income-category range, that rule of law rankings correlate strongly with wealth, and that China had to rebuild its legal system after the devastation wrought during the Cultural Revolution. This global ranking puts China on par with or ahead of much of Latin America and the former Soviet areas, above the median for the ten ASEAN states, third among the four BRIC countries, and far behind China's wealthier East Asian neighbors (World Bank 2012). More qualitative scholarly assessments of China's level of "rule of law" or "rule by law" range widely, from some that are relatively positive and suggest China is following the trajectory of some of today's more economically developed rule-of-law states to others that find a strikingly low or eroding level of legality (Peerenboom 2000: 450–7; 2007; Pei 2006; Minzner 2011).

A principal basis for more critical assessments is the implementation problem – the difference between what laws on the books promise and what law in practice delivers. As the discussion in the preceding sections and nearly every account of Chinese law indicates, this is a significant problem. But simply stressing the implementation gap risks oversimplification and adopting an unduly narrow view of Chinese law and its roles, including in economic development. The "implementation gap" arguably reflects more than a shortage of will, capacity or competence. It may also reflect other features that are prominent in China's legal system, although not unique to it, and that point less uniformly to a low level of rule of law (deLisle 2007).

First, the gap stems partly from laws being based on overly ambitious or literal adoptions of foreign models – reprising China's late nineteenth-century quest to import legal structures that seemed to account for the West's success, and perhaps reflecting contemporary pressures from foreign investors, the WTO and others to adopt laws that conform to international standards. Economics-related laws, which have become similar to those of developed capitalist and Anglo-American models, are among the more significant examples. Such "legal transplants" face daunting challenges, not least because China does not yet have complementary legal and economic institutions, such as a rich body of judicial opinions, autonomous and experienced courts, expert and professional enforcement agencies, a robust and specialized bar, institutional investors, non-state-linked controlling shareholders, a strong financial and business press, a pool of experienced managers to serve as independent directors, and so on, to give laws the efficacy and impact they have had in their systems of origin (deLisle 1999; Potter 2003; Pistor *et al.* 2003; Clarke 2010).

Second, much of law's effect – and even aim – in China has been in signaling policy.[2] Laws' impact often comes through the invocation of legal norms in extralegal or informal contexts. Economic development-promoting laws have communicated political commitments and invited rights-holders to seek enforcement by informal, often political means. Pressing legal rights often occurs through the *xinfang* system of petitions to officials (which outnumber civil court cases) or mass protests (which are roughly as numerous as administrative lawsuits). Those facing law-violating officials beseech higher authorities to secure the promises of policy commitments embodied in laws, bringing bureaucratic or party discipline to bear on lower-level officials. Or they turn to journalists, social media or legal and other pro-reform intellectuals to press their case publicly (Pils 2005; Hand 2006; Minzner 2006; van Rooij 2012). Distrustful of Chinese courts, frustrated in enforcing judicial and arbitral awards, or confident in their ability to address problems through political channels, foreign investors also sometimes pursue informal means to resolve business and regulatory conflicts.

Sometimes, Chinese laws provide little alternative to informal enforcement. They set forth rights without clear remedies. Laws authorized state-owned enterprise managers to reject improper exactions or redirection of funds by government departments-in-charge or ordered government functionaries not to engage in market-infringing activities long before administrative law provided any judicial method for challenging state actions. Legal prohibitions of opportunistic acts by directors and officers came long before key civil law means for shareholders to enforce those duties were in place. The Supreme People's Court for a while banned most "collective" securities suits, and clear legislative endorsement of shareholders' derivative actions came more than a decade after substantive company and securities laws.

Third, and conversely, formal law often lags practice, ratifying or codifying behavior that lacked legal foundation and that ordinarily would seem to be evidence of a lack of rule of law. Among areas relevant to the economy, law governing property and ownership provides especially significant examples. At the dawn of the reform era, decollectivization and the return to household farming preceded legal authorization for its contract-based framework. A few years later, secondary markets that had sprung up in contracted rural land use rights were retroactively legalized. Sale of controlling ownership of firms began through transfer of shares in amounts and across categories of owners long before reforms created clear legal permission. Land-use rights-holders resisting expropriation (including the owners of the famous Chongqing "nail-house") appealed to technically inapplicable legal norms, such as the 2004 constitutional amendments (which, like the constitution generally, lacked effect absent implementing legislation) and the Property Law (which evictees invoked before the law had gone into effect). The "small/minor property rights" that became the basis for suburban residential construction on unreclassified rural land lacked a legal basis. The apparent expectation was that the authorities would tolerate the behavior and again allow law to catch up with an economically fruitful practice rather than impose economic losses and provoke public anger by enforcing existing law. The same calculus, ultimately misplaced, likely motivated foreign investors' efforts a few years earlier to circumvent rules requiring domestic majority ownership of telecommunications firms by creating a Sino-foreign joint venture as a Chinese legal person to be the "domestic" majority owner of a firm with a foreign minority co-owner. In recent years, investors have used a different, contract-based vehicle with questionable legal foundation – the "variable interest entity" – as a means for foreign parties to establish control, without formal ownership, of Chinese companies that operate in restricted sectors.

3.2 An uneven rule of law[3]

However one assesses China's overall rule of law, one of its most striking features is its unevenness. First, China's rule of law has been uneven across the country. Law and legal institutions are generally seen as more robust and effective in more developed and cosmopolitan regions, especially urbanized areas along the coast. This view is nearly universally accepted among observers in China and abroad. It draws support from studies of civil and administrative litigation which typically find relatively high levels of satisfaction and perceptions of fairness and relatively great reliance on law when they focus on places such as Shanghai, Beijing or urban Guangdong, and much lower levels when they look at poorer, more rural and inland areas (Guthrie 1999; Hung 2005; O'Brien and Li 2005; Woo and Wang 2005; Zhu 2007; Pei *et al.* 2010; Michelson and Read 2011; He 2012).

Several factors may account for this pattern. The large, diversified economies of the major coastal cities reduce entanglements between local officials and a dominant local enterprise (or small group of them) that underpin local protectionism. In more fully marketized economies of the more advanced regions, firms face pressure to compete on price and quality, and this may reduce opportunities for law-disregarding behavior, including predation or rent-seeking by local officials. In more open and prosperous areas, potentially wayward officials and enterprise officers may face greater scrutiny and demands for lawful behavior from anti-corruption watchdogs, lawsuits by sophisticated and well-funded enterprises, new and old media, foreign investors who hew to their home-country views of law, and, increasingly, Chinese who can withdraw capital or lobby higher officials. Legal and judicial talent – and an accompanying legal culture – are in thicker supply in the most economically advanced areas. For example, the five provincial units with the highest density of lawyers (Beijing, Shanghai, Tianjin, Guangdong, and Chongqing) have nearly seven times as many lawyers per capita as the provincial units with the lowest density of lawyers (Tibet, Guizhou, Jiangxi, Gansu, and Qinghai). Average income for lawyers follows similar patterns, with the five top provincial-level units (Beijing, Shanghai, Zhejiang, Guangdong, Jiangsu) at nearly twenty times that of the bottom five (Henan, Heilongjiang, Tibet, Gansu, Inner Mongolia) (Zhu 2013). As the income data suggests, quantitative gaps are compounded by qualitative ones. For example, almost all judges in Shanghai have college degrees and many at the high and intermediate court levels have graduate law degrees. Their counterparts in less-developed areas lag far behind in terms of such credentials. Lawyers and law firms – especially elite and internationalized ones – are similarly unevenly distributed. Similar regional variations in educational and professional levels characterize officials in law-related roles in the party and state.

Second, China's legal development has been uneven across subject matter. Qualitative accounts commonly find that rule of law or the role of law in China is significantly greater on economic and economic-regulatory issues than political or government-under-law-related ones. Singapore and Hong Kong – generally seen as having market economies and strong rule of law in economic affairs alongside relatively undemocratic politics and somewhat (Hong Kong) or significantly (Singapore) weaker rule of law in political affairs – reportedly and apparently have held much appeal for China's reform-era leadership (Peerenboom 2007; deLisle 2009). Quantitative cross-national comparisons point to similar conclusions. Among the components of the World Bank's composite "rule of law" score, China fares notably better on those concerning economic and commercial law than those addressing political rights or civil liberties. China's mid-range aggregate score on "rule of law" (38.9th percentile) falls between its higher rank on governance indicators relatively closely related to economic law (43.5th percentile for "regulatory quality" and 56th for "government effectiveness") and much lower marks for the governance indicator most associated with "political" law (4.7th for "voice and accountability") (World Bank 2012). A similar pattern characterizes assessments of China's record on the law-related issue of human rights: China fares comparatively well on economic and social rights and very poorly on civil and political rights (Peerenboom 2005; deLisle 2013; US State Department 2013).

3.3 Law and development in China, in comparative perspective

Whether law, or rule of law, is necessary or important for China's economic development is a question that cross-national comparative inquiry could help to answer. The relationship between law and economic development globally and regionally, and the relationship of the Chinese case to any general patterns, however, are sharply contested.

The idea that development depends on some level of legality – and increasingly so at higher levels of development – is long-standing and recurring. It was a core tenet of the "law and development" school that was prevalent in the 1960s and 1970s (Galanter 1966; Trubek 1972). It was a motivating idea of legal assistance and development programs that were supported by the US and other Western states and nongovernmental organizations during the Cold War and again in the aftermath of the collapse of the Soviet Union and that often saw markets, democracy and the rule of law as going hand in hand (deLisle 1999, 2009). It was also a key strand in the Washington Consensus which, although focused on economic policy, includes legal elements (such as strong protection of property rights) and seemingly assumes reliance on law and a capable legal system (in its emphasis on tax reform, foreign investment, and privatization of ownership) (Williamson 1990). Comparative rule of law rankings show strong correlations at the extremes, with the most affluent countries showing the highest levels of rule of law and the poorest economies the lowest. A substantial body of research continues to support the view that some level of infrastructure of legality, at least for the economy, is necessary for economic development (North 1990; Posner 1998; Dam 2007; World Bank 2013).

On the other hand, the law and development school and governments' and foundations' rule of law promotion programs have drawn criticism for being misguided or ineffective (Trubek and Galanter 1974; Carrothers 2003; Haggard *et al.* 2008; Tamanaha 2011). The Beijing Consensus emerged as a self-conscious if very thin and empirically questionable paradigm – alongside a more substantive but inchoate and dissensus-provoking China Model of development – to challenge the much-criticized Washington Consensus (Ramo 2004; Rodrik 2006; Hsu *et al.* 2011). Cross-national correlations between levels of rule of law and levels of wealth are relatively weak for many countries between the polar extremes in comparative rule of law rankings (World Bank 2012). Even a strong correlation, of course, does not establish the existence or direction of causation.

The debate over the Beijing Consensus and a China Model echoed a longer-running discourse over an East Asian Model.[4] Accounts of that model – which in most assessments and many respects China has followed – typically accords law little role (Johnson 1982; Berger and Hsiao 1988; Vogel 1991). In the East Asian Model, economic regulation through negotiation between state and industry, or informal administrative guidance to bureaucrat-entrepreneurs or state-appointed managers or state-collaborating oligopolistic large enterprises, marginalizes legal rules and often leaves little scope for administrative law challenges to state actions taken under broad, discretion-conferring laws. Such features are in tension with rule-of-law ideals of general, neutral rules that bind rulers and ruled and are applied effectively, predictably and relatively uniformly to all, with some form of review by independent, often judicial institutions. The model's purported cultural norms reject an emphasis on legal rights and litigiousness. During the East Asian Model exemplars' high-growth phases (and in some cases beyond), undemocratic or single-party dominant politics, executive-dominated technocratic governments and other political and structural features differed from the competitive democratic politics and strong separation of powers among relatively equal branches that are often associated with, if not necessary for, robust rule of law.

But the relative lack of law in the East Asian Model is not so clear. There is, at minimum, much internal diversity. Two of the model's five paradigmatic cases, Hong Kong and Singapore, have had strong rule-of-law regimes, particularly in economic affairs. Although the rhetoric of the model often elides the point, the two city-states' ability to attract foreign investment and climb the ladder to high-value added sectors depended, on many accounts, on laws and legal institutions that met international standards for predictability, neutrality, and efficacy. Whether seen as a benevolent British colonial legacy or a sensible or necessary response to Hong Kong's and Singapore's international economic situations and development strategies, the rule of law figures prominently in analyses of the economic success of the East Asian Model's two smallest examples.

As studies of law and legal development in other East Asian Model countries suggest, law argu-ably has played significantly greater (if sometimes distinctive) roles in the economic success of Japan – and other regional states – than the more "anti-legal" depictions of the East Asian Model admit (Young 1984; Milhaupt 1996; Haley 2002). Some studies of economic development in East Asia as a whole have found law (or at least economic law) to have played a significant role in the region's remarkable success (Asian Development Bank 1998).

To grant that some significant level of legality or rule of law is generally important or necessary for economic development would not fully resolve questions about the Chinese case. To some observers, China appears as a great exception, its success a counterexample of impressive devel-opment despite weak protections for legal rights in property, contracts, financial markets, and so on. On this view, China may have succeeded because of weak law. Weak legal rights may have boosted development, with, for example, vulnerable property rights removing impediments to transferring land to more productive uses (often by recipients who have means for protecting their own interests that do not rely on legal processes and institutions) (Clarke 2003; Allen *et al.* 2005; Upham 2009; Wang *et al.* 2011).

Even if China's economic development during the first third of a century since the reform era began has not depended on law, continued success might still mean more robust legality and legal institutions. Analyses that emphasize poor legal protection for property rights, for example, note that legal reform to provide greater security for such interests may become necessary (Upham 2009; Pils 2010b). Otherwise conflicting assessments of China's likely future some-times have a common view on future needs for law, with pessimistic accounts linking expected economic (and political) troubles to inadequate legal institutions and respect for law and more optimistic assessments foreseeing a China that will more closely resemble today's developed, rule-of-law-governed states, both economically and legally (Pei 2006; Peerenboom 2007; deLisle 2009; Nocera 2013). Expectations that China can achieve very high levels of economic devel-opment with much lower levels of legality require claiming that China is a rare, perhaps unique, exception to a pattern of cross-national correlation of upper-tier scores on rule of law with high per capita income.

There are plausible functionalist explanations of why China may need more law as it achieves more development. Law may be more necessary to sustain economic growth as: China's market economy becomes more mature and complex; economic integration with the international economy and its legal norms deepens; China's international cost advantage dissipates and erodes China's capacity to pay the risk premium that is a cost of weak legality; growth becomes more dependent on domestic demand and thus on the internal legal order's capacity to perform con-ventional tasks of enforcing contracts, securing property, protecting consumers and so on; the economy tilts more toward intellectual property-intensive activities (ranging from technology to valuable brands) that may be more law dependent; or the costs of low respect for legality among officials and economic actors reach critical levels, perhaps triggering serious social unrest, or collapsing demand for Chinese products at home and abroad. On the other hand, continued success in economic development means more wealth, which provides more resources to invest in stronger laws and legal institutions – a first turn in a virtuous circle that may challenge simple theses of development's dependence on law but that nonetheless portends more legality and more development if China's economy continues to advance.

3.4 The prospects and politics of law in contemporary China[5]

Whether China maintains or establishes whatever degree of legal development might be neces-sary to sustain economic development and, less dramatically, what path China might follow within the range of levels and types of legal development that are likely compatible with avoiding economic failure will be partly determined by China's politics of law, broadly defined.

Several factors indicate pressure toward greater legality or rule of law. China now has a small but expanding and increasingly influential cohort of judges, lawyers, and others with legal education who have professional interests, intellectual habits, and normative preferences that support stronger, more autonomous law and legal institutions (Liebman 2007; Michelson and Liu 2010; He 2010). Their agendas surface in proposals for greater judicial independence and professionalism, reduction of burdensome regulation and intrusive oversight of law firms, and expansion of "access to justice" initiatives. They also have emerged as opinion leaders and key constituencies for rising public criticism of official corruption, abuse of power, disregard for law, and failure to enforce laws and regulations concerning public health and safety and the rights of ordinary citizens. Some among China's growing group of lawyers are "rights protection" lawyers who have pushed the boundaries of what law can do – in individual cases, in attempted impact litigation and in political activism. Their clients and causes are often political, but their efforts emphasize legal rights, including rights of citizens facing expropriation of property rights (Pils 2005; Hand 2006; Fu and Cullen 2008).

At least some members of the Chinese leadership appear to support – if only in limited ways and on conditional terms – a greater turn toward law. Reform-minded legal intellectuals have increasingly gained the attention (if not the requisite policy commitment) of top leaders. These thinkers are advisers to key officials, participants in briefings for leaders, and members of the emerging cluster of public intellectuals whose comments become known to China's rulers. Legally trained people have come to hold key posts in the party and state. After the 18th Party Congress, China had its first legally educated Premier (Li Keqiang) and leaders with strong legal backgrounds at the head of the two principal legal institutions (Cao Jianming at the Supreme People's Procuracy and Zhou Qiang at Supreme People's Court). To the considerable extent that China's rulers see law and legal institutions as serving fundamental goals of promoting economic development – as well as effective governance and social stability – they are likely to continue at least contingent support for law. Backsliding on legality may face constraints of the regime's own making. After decades of official endorsement of law, moves to reverse legal development or commitments to law can pose serious risks to the regime's credibility. In China's softened authoritarian system, elites also must, to some extent, respond to social demands for law.

There are indications of rising social demand for law within the political space created by official policies formally favoring law. Although such trends are hard to measure, "rights consciousness" (awareness of legal rights and belief that they should be protected) or, at least, "rules consciousness" (knowledge of the legal rules that the state has promulgated and belief that the state should follow and enforce them) appears to have risen markedly among the Chinese public (Perry 2009; Li 2010b). Social expectations of law seem to have increased – as indicated by the millions of claimants who pursue litigation, arbitration, and mediation each year; millions more who invoke legal norms in their petitions and informal appeals to party and state organs; and the social anger that erupts around incidents of perceived lawlessness by officials or failures by the state to enforce laws to protect citizens' health, safety, or livelihoods. If cross-national comparative patterns, long-standing social science theories, and preliminary evidence from contemporary China hold true, the rising social and economic status of China's expanding middle class means higher demand for law and legal protection of interests. Growing demand for law also comes from lower reaches of society, where people turn to legal institutions or invoke legal norms when some unlawful act threatens their precarious well-being, whether through land expropriation, environmental pollution, dangerous goods, non-payment of wages, or detention (in institutions ranging from formal prisons to the illegal "black jails" created to suppress petitioners).

Forces favoring stronger law and a larger role for law face formidable counter-pressures, however. Policy proposals for moderate and incremental legal reform have failed to make headway during most of the Hu Jintao era and beyond. Blueprints for more transformative change, such as the liberal–democratic constitutionalism set forth in Charter 08, in 2008, elicited a long jail term for its principal author, Nobel Prize-winner Liu Xiaobo (Beja *et al.* 2012). Rights protection lawyers faced a harsh crackdown at the beginning of the 2010s (Fu and Cullen 2011; Pils 2013). In the early months of Xi Jinping's tenure, no major reorientation appeared to be at hand. Rule-of-law-related ideals were among seven topics reportedly banned from classroom and media discussion, and one of the most prominent rights protection lawyers and co-founder of the pro-rule-of-law Open Constitution Initiative (*gongmeng*) was arrested.

Law reform-supporting intellectuals' access to China's leaders has not brought a turn to law that reflects their beliefs and preferences. The top elite – including those especially responsible for law – have not consistently and effectively pressed agendas of legal reform and development. From 2002 to 2008, the Supreme People's Court was headed by law graduate and former justice minister Xiao Yang, who pressed for judicial autonomy and professionalism and a larger role for the formal legal system. But his successor, Wang Shengjun, had no formal legal education, had worked primarily in the party bureaucracy and public security system, and pressed the "three supremes" – a policy initially set forth by Hu Jintao that called on courts to decide cases according to policy and public opinion as well as law. Under Hu, policy on law included a renewed emphasis on mediation and harmony over litigation and legal rights-enforcement, and members of the Politburo Standing Committee assigned to legal–political affairs – Luo Gan and his successor Zhou Yongkang – took a skeptical view of rule-of-law agendas. Before Bo Xilai fell in 2012 after a disruptive and ill-fated bid for a place among the top leadership, his "Chongqing Model" had become anathema to legal intellectuals (and many others), including for the persecution of lawyer Li Zhuang, who had defended a target of Bo's anti-mafia crackdown in Chongqing (He 2011b; Liu 2011). Early signals under Xi have been mixed, with the reported ban on media and academic discussions of some law-related topics and the ongoing persecution of activist lawyers coexisting with a resurgence of pro-law rhetoric from Xi and others, the appointment of the legally trained and reputedly more pro-law reform Zhou Qiang as China's top judge, and a departure from the Hu-era practice (thanks to a reduction in the size of the Politburo Standing Committee) of assigning the law and courts portfolio to the most unsympathetic member of China's most powerful body.

More broadly and in the longer term, the enduring, if slow and uneven, trend toward convergence with Western or international or developed-country models of legality may continue in China. Elite choices, functional requirements, constituency demands, public pressure, foreign influences, and other factors may exert effective pressure toward more robust law, especially in economic affairs. It also remains possible, however, that China will reject "Western" or "capitalist" forms of legality as intolerable threats to the regime's ability to maintain power and, in turn, political order and, in turn, economic advancement. What approach China will follow remains unknown, as does the impact of whatever legal path China chooses on its prospects for ongoing success in the quest for economic development that has been the regime's principal priority since the beginning of the reform era and for much of the nearly two centuries since China's encounter with the wealthy, powerful, and law-governed states of the more developed world began.

Notes

1 This section draws upon portions of deLisle (2003, 2009, 2011). A discussion of the issues addressed in this section and later sections of this chapter, but emphasizing political rather than economic issues in contemporary Chinese law, appears as deLisle (2014).

2 This remainder of this subsection draws on deLisle (2011: 153–5).
3 This subsection draws on deLisle (2007).
4 The remainder of this subsection draws on deLisle (2009, 2011).
5 This section draws on and updates deLisle (2008).

Bibliography

Allen, Franklin, Qian, Jun and Qian, Meijun (2005) 'Law, Finance and Economic Growth in China', *Journal of Financial Economics*, 77: 57–116.

American Chamber of Commerce in the People's Republic of China (2012) *China Business Climate Survey* <www.amchamchina.org/businessclimate2011>.

Art, Robert C. and Gu, Minkang (1995) 'China Incorporated: The First Corporation Law of the People's Republic of China', *Yale Journal of International Law*, 20: 273–308.

Asian Development Bank (1998) *The Role of Law and Legal Institutions in Asian Economic Development, 1960–1995*, Manila: ADB.

Beja, Jean-Philippe, Fu, Hualing and Pils, Eva (eds.) (2012) *Liu Xiaobo, Charter 08 and the Challenges of Political Reform in China*, Hong Kong: Hong Kong University Press.

Berger, Peter L. and Hsiao, Michael (eds.) (1988) *In Search of an East Asian Development Model*, New Brunswick, NJ: Transaction Books.

Carrothers, Thomas (2003) 'Promoting the Rule of Law Abroad: The Problem of Knowledge', Washington, DC: Carnegie Endowment <carnegieendowment.org/files/wp34.pdf>.

Cheng, Lucie and Rosett, Arthur (1991) 'Contract with a Chinese Face: Socially Embedded Factors in the Transition from Hierarchy to Market, 1978–1989', *Journal of Chinese Law*, 5: 143–244.

China Law Yearbook 中国法律年鉴 (2009–11) Beijing: Law Press.

Chow, Gregory C. (2007) *China's Economic Transformation*, Malden, MA: Blackwell.

Clarke, Donald C. (1991) 'What's Law Got to Do with It? Legal Institutions and Economic Reform in China', *UCLA Pacific Basin Law Journal*, 10: 1–76.

Clarke, Donald C. (2003) 'Economic Development and the Rights Hypothesis: The China Problem', *American Journal of Comparative Law*, 51: 89–111.

Clarke, Donald C. (2005) 'How Do We Know When a Chinese Enterprise Exists?', *Columbia Journal of Asian Law*, 19: 50–71.

Clarke, Donald C. (2010) 'Law without Order in Chinese Corporate Governance Institutions', *Northwestern Journal of International Law and Business*, 30: 131–98.

Cohen, Jerome A. (1968) *The Criminal Process in the People's Republic of China, 1949–1963*, Cambridge, MA: Cambridge University Press.

Dam, Kenneth W. (2007) *The Law–Growth Nexus: The Rule of Law and Economic Development*, Washington, DC: Brookings.

deLisle, Jacques (1999) 'Lex Americana?: United States Legal Assistance, American Legal Models, and Legal Change in the Post-Communist World and Beyond', *University of Pennsylvania Journal of International Economic Law*, 20: 179–308.

deLisle, Jacques (2003) 'Chasing the God of Wealth while Evading the Goddess of Democracy: Development, Democracy and Law in Reform-Era China', in Sunder Ramaswamy and Jeffrey W. Cason (eds.), *Development and Democracy: New Perspectives on an Old Debate*, Middlebury, VT: Middlebury Press.

deLisle, Jacques (2007) 'Traps, Gaps and Law: Prospects and Challenges for China's Reforms', in *Is China Trapped in Transition? Implications for Future Reforms*, Oxford: Oxford Foundation for Law, Justice and Society.

deLisle, Jacques (2008) 'Legalization without Democratization in China Under Hu Jintao', in Cheng Li (ed.), *China's Changing Political Landscape: Prospects for Democracy*, Washington, DC: Brookings.

deLisle, Jacques (2009) 'Development without Democratization? China, Law and the East Asian Model', in Jose V. Ciprut (ed.), *Democratizations: Comparisons, Confrontations and Contrasts*, Cambridge, MA: MIT Press.

deLisle, Jacques (2010a) 'Exceptional Powers in an Exceptional State: Emergency Powers Law in China', in Victor V. Ramraj and Arun K. Thiruvengadam (eds.), *Emergency Powers Law in Asia*, Cambridge, UK: Cambridge University Press.

deLisle, Jacques (2010b) 'Security First?: Patterns and Lessons from China's Use of Law to Address National Security Threats', *Journal of National Security Law & Policy*, 4: 397–436.

deLisle, Jacques (2010c) 'What's Happened to Democracy in China?: Elections, Law and Political Reform', *Foreign Policy Research Institute E-Note* <www.fpri.org/enotes/201004.delisle.democracyinchina.html>.

deLisle, Jacques (2011) 'Law and the China Development Model', in Philip Hsu, Yushan Wu and Suisheng Zhao (eds.), *In Search of China's Development Model: Beyond the Beijing Consensus*, New York: Routledge.

deLisle, Jacques (2012) 'A Common Law-like Civil Law and a Public Face for Private Law: China's Tort Law in Comparative Perspective', in Chen Lei and C. H. (Remco) van Rhee (eds.), *Towards a Chinese Civil Code*, Leiden, Netherlands: Brill.

deLisle, Jacques (2013) 'From Economic Development to What – and Why? China's Evolving Legal and Political Engagement with International Human Rights Norms', in Yu Guanghua (ed.), *Rethinking Law and Development: The Chinese Experience*, New York: Routledge.

deLisle, Jacques (2014) 'China's Legal System', in William A. Joseph (ed.), *Politics in China*, 2nd edition, New York: Oxford University Press.

Dickinson, Steven M. (2007) 'An Introduction to the New Company Law of the People's Republic of China', *Pacific Rim Law and Policy Journal*, 16: 1–11.

Dobinson, Ian (2002) 'The Criminal Law of the People's Republic of China (1997)', *Pacific Rim Law and Policy Journal*, 11: 1–62.

Fewsmith, Joseph (2012) 'Guangdong Leads Call to Break up "Vested Interests" and Revive Reform', *China Leadership Monitor*, No. 37.

Fu, Hualing (2005) 'Re-education through Labour in Historical Perspective', *China Quarterly*, 184: 811–30.

Fu, Hualing (2013) 'The Upward and Downward Spirals in China's Anti-corruption Enforcement', in Mike McConville and Eva Pils (eds.), *Comparative Perspectives on Criminal Justice in China*, Cheltenham, UK: Edward Elgar.

Fu, Hualing and Cullen, Richard (2008) 'Weiquan (Rights Protection) Lawyering in an Authoritarian State', *China Journal*, 59: 111–27.

Fu, Hualing and Cullen, Richard (2011) 'Climbing the Weiquan Ladder: A Radicalizing Process for Rights-Protection Lawyers', *China Quarterly*, 205: 40–59.

Galanter, Mark (1966) 'The Modernization of Law', in Myron Weiner (ed.), *Modernization*, New York: Basic Books.

Gallagher, Mary E. (2005) '"Use the Law as Your Weapon": Institutional Change and Legal Mobilization in China', in Neil J. Diamant, Stanley B. Lubman, and Kevin J. O'Brien (eds.), *Engaging the Law in China*, Stanford, CA: Stanford University Press.

Gallagher, Mary E. and Wang, Yuhua (2011) 'Users and Non-Users: Legal Experience and its Effect on Legal Consciousness', in Margaret Y. K. Woo and Mary E. Gallagher (eds.), *Chinese Justice: Civil Dispute Resolution in Contemporary China*, New York: Cambridge University Press.

Gold, Thomas, Guthrie, Doug, and Wank, David (eds.) (2002) *Social Connections in China: Institutions, Culture, and the Changing Nature of Guanxi*, Cambridge, UK: Cambridge University Press, 2002.

Guthrie, Doug (1999) *Dragon in a Three Piece Suit*, Princeton, NJ: Princeton University Press.

Haggard, Stephan, MacIntyre, Andrew, and Tiede, Lydia (2008) 'The Rule of Law and Economic Development', *Annual Review of Political Science*, 11: 205–34.

Haley, John O. (2002) 'Litigation in Japan: A New Look at Old Problems', *Willamette Journal of International Law and Dispute Resolution*, 10: 121–42.

Hand, Keith J. (2006) 'Using Law for a Righteous Purpose: The Sun Zhigang Incident', *Columbia Journal of Transnational Law*, 45: 114–95.

He, Haibo (2011a) 'Litigations Without a Ruling: The Predicament of Administrative Law in China', *Tsinghua China Law Review*, 23: 257–81.

He, Weifang (2011b) 'A Letter to Chongqing Colleagues', (Apr. 12, 2011), <http://cmp.hku.hk/2011/04/12/11481>.

He, Xin (2010) 'The Judiciary Pushes Back: Law, Power and Politics in Chinese Courts', in Randall Peerenboom (ed.), *Judicial Independence in China*, New York: Cambridge University Press.

He, Xin (2012) 'A Tale of Two Chinese Courts: Economic Development and Contract Enforcement', *Journal of Law and Society*, 39: 384–409.

Hess, Steve (2010) 'Nail Houses, Land Rights, and Frames of Injustice on China's Protest Landscape', *Asian Survey*, 50: 908–26.

Ho, Daniel H.K. (2001) 'Tax Law in Modern China: Evolution, Framework and Administration', *Hong Kong Law Journal*, 31: 141–59.

Horsley, Jamie P. (2007) 'Toward a More Open China', in Ann Florini (ed.), *The Right to Know: Transparency for an Open World*, New York: Columbia University Press.

Howson, Nicholas C. (2010) 'Corporate Law in the Shanghai People's Courts, 1992–2008: Judicial Autonomy in a Contemporary Authoritarian State', *University of Pennsylvania East Asia Law Review*, 5: 303–442.

Hsu, Philip, Wu, Yushan, and Zhao, Suisheng (eds.) (2011) *In Search of China's Development Model: Beyond the Beijing Consensus*, New York: Routledge.

Hsu, Stephen C. (Xu Chuanxi) (2007) 'Contract Law of the People's Republic of China', *Minnesota Journal of International Law*, 16: 115–62.

Huang, Hui (2009) 'The Regulation of Foreign Investment in Post-WTO China', *Columbia Journal of Asian Law*, 23: 185–215.

Huang, Hui (2012) 'Piercing the Corporate Veil in China', *American Journal of Comparative Law*, 60: 763–74.

Huang, Yasheng (2008) *Capitalism with Chinese Characteristics*, Cambridge, UK: Cambridge University Press.

Hung, Veron Mei-Ying (2005) 'Judicial Reform in China: Lessons from Shanghai', Washington, DC: Carnegie Endowment for International Peace <www.carnegieendowment.org/files/CP58.Hung.FINAL.pdf>.

Jiang, Ping (1996) 'Drafting the Uniform Contract Law in China', *Columbia Journal of Asian Law*, 10: 245–58.

Johnson, Chalmers H. (1982) *MITI and the Japanese Miracle*, Stanford, CA: Stanford University Press.

Kennedy, Scott (2005) *The Business of Lobbying in China*, Cambridge, MA: Harvard University Press.

Kornai, Janos (1992) *The Socialist System*, Princeton, NJ: Princeton University Press.

Landry, Pierre (2008) 'The Institutional Diffusion of Courts in China: Evidence from Survey Data', in Tom Ginsburg and Tamir Moustafa (eds.), *Rule by Law: The Politics of Courts in Authoritarian Regimes*, Princeton, NJ: Princeton University Press.

Lardy, Nicholas R. (1998) *China's Unfinished Economic Revolution*, Washington, DC: Brookings.

Lardy, Nicholas R. (2002) *Integrating China into the Global Economy*, Washington, DC: Brookings.

Li, Lianjiang (2010b) 'Rights Consciousness and Rules Consciousness in Contemporary China', *China Journal*, 64: 47–68.

Li, Ling (2010a) 'Corruption in China's Courts', in Randall Peerenboom (ed.), *Judicial Independence in China*, New York: Cambridge University Press.

Liebman, Benjamin L. (2007) 'China's Courts: Restricted Reform', *China Quarterly*, 191: 620–38.

Lin, Justin Yifu, Cai, Fang and Li, Zhou (2003) *The China Miracle*, Hong Kong: Chinese University of Hong Kong Press.

Liu, Yawei (2011) 'Bo Xilai's Campaign for the Politburo Standing Committee and the Future of Chinese Politicking', *China Brief*, 11(21), Washington, DC: Jamestown Foundation.

Lubman, Stanley (1970) 'Methodological Problems in Studying Chinese Communist "Civil Law"', in Jerome A. Cohen (ed.), *Contemporary Chinese Law*, Cambridge, MA: Harvard University Press.

Lubman, Stanley (1999) *Bird in a Cage: Legal Reform in China after Mao*, Stanford, CA: Stanford University Press.

McDonnell, Brett H. (2004) 'Lessons from the Rise and (Possible) Fall of Chinese Township-Village Enterprises', *William and Mary Law Review*, 45: 953–1009.

Manion, Melanie (2004) *Corruption by Design: Building Clean Government in Mainland China and Hong Kong*, Cambridge, MA: Harvard University Press.

Michelson, Ethan and Liu, Sida (2010) 'What do Chinese Lawyers Want?', in Cheng Li (ed.), *China's Emerging Middle Class*, Washington, DC: Brookings.

Michelson, Ethan and Read, Benjamin L. (2011) 'Public Attitudes toward Official Justice in Beijing and Rural China', in Margaret Y. K. Woo and Mary E. Gallagher (eds.), *Chinese Justice: Civil Dispute Resolution in Contemporary China*, New York: Cambridge University Press.

Milhaupt, Curtis J. (1996) 'A Relational Theory of Japanese Corporate Governance: Contract, Culture and the Rule of Law', *Harvard International Law Journal*, 37: 3–64.

Minzner, Carl F. (2006) 'Xinfang: An Alternative to Formal Chinese Legal Institutions', *Stanford Journal of International Law*, 42: 103–79.

Minzner, Carl F. (2011) 'China's Turn against Law', *American Journal of Comparative Law*, 59: 935–84.

Nathan, Andrew J. (1985) *Chinese Democracy*, Berkeley, CA: University of California Press.

Naughton, Barry (1996) *Growing out of the Plan*, Cambridge: Cambridge University Press.

Nocera, Joe (2013) 'The Baby Formula Barometer', *New York Times*, July 26, 2013.

North, Douglass C. (1990) *Institutions, Institutional Change and Economic Performance*, Cambridge, UK: Cambridge University Press.

O'Brien, Kevin J. and Li, Lianjiang (2000) 'Accommodating "Democracy", in a One-Party State: Introducing Village Elections in China', *China Quarterly*, 162: 465–89.

O'Brien, Kevin J. and Li, Lianjiang (2005) 'Suing the State: Administrative Litigation in Rural China', in Neil J. Diamant, Stanley B. Lubman, and Kevin J. O'Brien (eds.), *Engaging the Law in China*, Stanford, CA: Stanford University Press.

Ohnesorge, John (2006) 'Chinese Administrative Law in the Northeast Asian Mirror', *Transnational Law and Contemporary Problems*, 16: 103–64.

Paler, Laura (2005) 'China's Legislation Law and the Making of a More Orderly and Representative Legislative System', *China Quarterly*, 182: 301–18.

Pearson, Margaret M. (1994) 'The Janus Face of Business Associations in China', *Australian Journal of Chinese Affairs*, 31: 25–46.

Peerenboom, Randall (2000) *China's Long March toward the Rule of Law*, Cambridge, UK: Cambridge University Press.

Peerenboom, Randall (2007) *China Modernizes: Threat to the West or Model for the Rest*, New York: Oxford University Press.

Pei, Minxin (1997) 'Citizens *v.* Mandarins: Administrative Litigation in China', *China Quarterly*, 152: 832–62.

Pei, Minxin (2006) *China's Trapped Transition: The Limits of Developmental Autocracy*, Cambridge, MA: Harvard University Press.

Pei, Minxin, Zhang, Guoyan, Pei, Fei and Chen, Lixin (2010) 'A Survey of Commercial Litigation in Shanghai Courts', in Randall Peerenboom (ed.), *Judicial Independence in China*, New York: Cambridge University Press.

Peng, Xiaohua (1987) 'Characteristics of China's First Bankruptcy Law', *Harvard International Law Journal*, 28: 373–84.

Perenboom, Randall (2000) 'Assessing Human Rights in China: Why the Double Standard?', *Cornell International Law Journal*, 38: 71–172.

Perry, Elizabeth (2009) 'A New Rights *Consciousness*?', *Journal of Democracy*, 20: 17–20.

Pew Global Attitudes Project (2012) 'Growing Concerns in China about Inequality, Corruption', <www.pewglobal.org/files/2012/10/Pew-Global-Attitudes-China-Report-FINAL-October-10-2012.pdf>.

Pfeffer, Richard M. (1963a) 'The Institution of Contracts in the Chinese People's Republic (Part 1)', *China Quarterly*, 14: 153–77.

Pfeffer, Richard M. (1963b) 'The Institution of Contracts in the Chinese People's Republic (Part 2)', *China Quarterly*, 15: 115–39.

Pfeffer, Richard M. (1966) 'Contracts in China Revisited, with a Focus on Agriculture, 1949–63', *China Quarterly*, 28: 106–29.

Pils, Eva (2005) 'Land Disputes, Rights Assertion and Social Unrest in China', *Columbia Journal of Asian Law*, 19: 235–92.

Pils, Eva (2010a) 'Peasants' Struggle for Land in China', in Yash Ghai and Jill Cottrell (eds.), *Marginalized Communities and Access to Justice*, Abingdon, UK: Routledge.

Pils, Eva (2010b) 'Waste No Land: Property, Dignity and Growth in Urbanizing China', *Asian-Pacific Law and Policy Journal*, 11: 1–48.

Pils, Eva (2013) '"Disappearing" China's Human Rights Lawyers', in Mike McConville and Eva Pils (eds.), *Comparative Perspectives on Criminal Justice in China*, Northampton, MA: Edward Elgar.

Pistor, Katharina, Berkowitz, Daniel, and Richard, Jean-François (2003) 'The Transplant Effect', *American Journal of Comparative Law*, 51: 163–203.

Potter, Pitman B. (1994) 'The Administrative Litigation Law of the PRC', in Pitman B. Potter (ed.), *Domestic Law Reforms in Post-Mao China*, Armonk, NY: M.E. Sharpe.

Potter, Pitman B. (1995) 'Foreign Investment Law in the People's Republic of China: The Dilemma of State Control', *China Quarterly*, 141: 155–85.

Potter, Pitman B. (2003) 'Globalization and Economic Regulation in China: Selective Adaptation of Globalized Norms and Practices', *Washington University Global Studies Law Review*, 2: 119–50.

Posner, Richard A. (1998) 'Creating a Legal Framework for Economic Development', *World Bank Research Observer*, 13: 1–11.

Ramo, Joshua Cooper (2004) *The Beijing Consensus*, London: Foreign Policy Centre.

Rapisardi John J. and Zhao, Binghao (2010) 'A Legal Analysis and Practical Application of the PRC Enterprise Bankruptcy Law', *Business Law International*, 10: 49–62.

Rehm, Gebhard M. and Julius, Hinrich (2009) 'The New Chinese Property Rights Law', *Columbia Journal of Asian Law*, 22: 177–234.

Rodrik, Dani (2006) 'Goodbye Washington Consensus, Hello Washington Confusion?', *Journal of Economic Literature*, 44: 973–85.

Schipani, Cindy A. and Liu, Junhai (2002) 'Corporate Governance in China: Then and Now', *Columbia Business Review*, 2002: 1–69.

Schurmann, Franz (1968) *Ideology and Organization in Communist China*, Berkeley, CA: University of California Press.

Selznick, Philip (1952) *The Organizational Weapon*, Santa Monica, CA: Rand.

Shirk, Susan (1993) *The Political Logic of Economic Reform in China*, Berkeley, CA: University of California Press.

Simon, William H. (1996) 'The Legal Structure of the Chinese "Socialist Market" Enterprise', *Journal of Corporation Law*, 21: 267–306.

Supreme People's Court, Work Report (2013) 最高人民法院工作报告(第十一届全国人民代表大会第五次会议) <www.court.gov.cn/qwfb/gzbg/201204/t20120413_175925.htm>.

Tamanaha, Brian Z. (2011) 'The Primacy of Society and the Failures of Law and Development', *Cornell International Law Journal*, 44: 209–47.

Trubek, David M. (1972) 'Toward a Social Theory of Law: An Essay on the Study of Law and Development', *Yale Law Journal*, 82: 1–50.

Trubek, David M. and Galanter, Marc (1974) 'Scholars in Self-Estrangement', *Wisconsin Law Review*, 1974: 1062–103.

US Department of State (2013) *Country Reports on Human Rights: China 2012*, <www.state.gov/documents/organization/204405.pdf>.

US Trade Representative (2012) '2012 Report to Congress on China's WTO Compliance', <www.ustr.gov/webfm_send/3620>.

Upham, Frank (2009) 'From Demsetz to Deng: Speculations on the Implications of Chinese Growth for Law and Development Theory', *New York University Journal of International Law and Politics*, 41: 551–602.

van Rooij, Benjamin (2012) 'The People's Regulation: Citizens and Enforcement of Law in China', *Columbia Journal of Asian Law*, 25: 116–79.

Vogel, Ezra F. (1991) *The Four Little Dragons: The Spread of Industrialization in East Asia*, Cambridge, MA: Harvard University Press.

Wang, Heng (2006) 'Chinese Views on Modern Marco Polos: New Foreign Trade Amendments after WTO Accession', *Cornell International Law Journal*, 39: 329–69.

Wang, Jingqiong (2009) 'Scholars Bid Government to Abolish Housing Law', *China Daily*, Dec. 9, 2009

Wang, Xiaozu, Xu, Lixin Colin, and Zhu, Tian (2011) 'Foreign Direct Investment under Weak Rule of Law: Theory and Evidence from China', *Policy Research Working Paper* 4790, Washington, DC: World Bank.

Wang, Xixin (1998) 'Administrative Procedure Reforms in China's Rule of Law Context', *Columbia Journal of Asian Law*, 12: 251–77.

Wang, Xixin (2000) 'Rule of Rules: An Inquiry into Administrative Rules in China's Rule of Law Context', in *The Rule of Law: Perspectives from the Pacific*, Washington, DC: Mansfield Center for Pacific Affairs.

Wang, Xixin (2003) 'Suing the Sovereign Observed from the Chinese Perspective', *George Washington International Law Review*, 35: 681–9.

Weber, Max (2009) 'Bureaucracy', in H. H. Gerth and C. W. Mills (eds. and trans.), *From Max Weber: Essays in Sociology*, New York: Routledge.

Wei, Yuwa (2005) 'The Development of the Securities Market and Regulation in China', *Loyola Los Angeles International and Comparative Law Review*, 27: 479–514.

Williamson, John (1990) 'What Washington Means by Policy Reform', in John Williamson (ed.), *Latin American Adjustment: How Much Has Happened?*, Washington, DC: Peterson Institute.

Wong, Edward (2011) 'Chinese Defend Detention of Artist on Grounds of "Economic Crimes"', *New York Times*, Apr. 7, 2011.

Woo, Margaret Y. K. and Wang, Yaxin (2005) 'Civil Justice in China: An Empirical Study of Courts in Three Provinces', *American Journal of Comparative Law*, 53: 911–40.

World Bank (2012) *Worldwide Governance Indicators*, <http://info.worldbank.org/governance/wgi>.

World Bank (2013) *Economic Development and the Quality of Legal Institutions*, <http://web.worldbank.org/WBSITE/EXTERNAL/TOPICS/EXTLAWJUSTINST/0,,contentMDK:23103355~menuPK:1989584~pagePK:210058~piPK:210062~theSitePK:1974062~isCURL:Y,00.html>.

Wu, Richard (2009) 'The Changing Regime for Regulating State-Owned Banks in China', *UCLA Pacific Basin Law Journal*, 26: 107–41.

Xinhua (2013) 'Xi Jinping Vows Unswerving Fight against Corruption', January 22.

Young, Michael K. (1984) 'Judicial Review of Administrative Guidance: Governmentally Encouraged Dispute Resolution in Japan', *Columbia Law Review*, 84: 923–83.

Yu, Guanghua and Zhang, Hao (2008) 'Adaptive Efficiency and Financial Development in China: The Role of Contracts and Contractual Enforcement', *Journal of International Economic Law*, 11: 459–94.

Yu, Peter K. (2005) 'Still Dissatisfied After All these Years: Intellectual Property, Post-WTO China, and the Avoidable Cycle of Futility', *Georgia Journal of International and Comparative Law*, 34: 143–58.

Zhang, Mo (2000) 'Freedom of Contract with Chinese Legal Characteristics', *Temple International and Comparative Law Journal*, 14: 237–62.

Zhang, Mo (2008) 'From Public to Private: The Newly Enacted Chinese Property Law and the Protection of Property Rights in China', *Berkeley Business Law Journal*, 5: 317–62.

Zhang, Mo (2011) 'Tort Liabilities and Torts Law', *Richmond Journal of Global Law and Business*, 10: 415–95.

Zhang, Naigen (2003) 'China's Intellectual Property Regime and the WTO', *Journal of Chinese and Comparative Law*, 6: 189.

Zhang, Xian Chu (1999) 'The Old Problems, the New Law, and the Developing Market – A Preliminary Examination of the First Securities Law of the People's Republic of China', *International Lawyer*, 33: 983–1014.

Zhang, Xian-chu (2009) 'An Anti-Monopoly Legal Regime in the Making in China as a Socialist Market Economy', *International Lawyer*, 43: 1469–93.

Zhu, Jingwen (ed.) (2013) *China Law Development Report 2012: China Legal Workers' Professionalization*, (朱景文中国法律发展报告2012：中国法律工作者的职业化), Beijing: Renmin University.

Zhu, Jingwen and Han, Dayuan (eds.) (2013) *Research Report on the Socialist Legal System with Chinese Characteristics*, vol. 1, Singapore: Enrich.

Zhu, Suli (2007) 'Political Parties in China's Judiciary', *Duke Journal of Comparative and International Law*, 17: 533–60.

Zweig, David, Hartford, Kathy, Feinerman, James and Deng, Jianxu (1987) 'Law, Contracts and Economic Modernization: Lessons from the Recent Chinese Rural Reforms', *Stanford International Law Journal* 23: 319.

17

POLITICAL MECHANISMS AND CORRUPTION

Lynn T. White

Political leadership, national and especially *local*, has been the major factor of Chinese economic development or non-growth in various eras since 1949. The late 1960s saw "green revolution" (triple cropping, walking tractors, pumps) in rich rural/suburban areas. This led to quick industrial growth there after 1971 (not just 1978), the substantive beginning of "reforms." Deng Xiaoping was vice-premier in 1973–74 and said honestly that farmers started this industrialization. Rural factories destroyed most planning by 1984–87, outbidding SOEs for inputs and manufacturing profits. Unenforceable contracts replaced unenforceable plans. Inflation led to Zhu Rongji's recentralization and tax reforms of the 1990s. In all decades, reformers (Zhu, Deng) have conflicted with Party conservatives (oddly called "leftists," Li Peng, Bo Xilai) – in local institutions too. Profits from leading the exploitation of labor decreased, because of demographic aging and the decline of subsistence-wage workers. Protests against overhasty development rose.

"Corruption" occurs when a larger group perceives that benefits went unfairly to a smaller group (in the state or not). Public and private corruption grow together. Corruption hinders growth by scaring ethnically foreign investors – but this effect is minor in China. Leaders note corruption is China's biggest threat; so they should establish an "ICAC," though it would thwart Leninist appointments. "Strike hard" campaigns are counter-effective. Family relationships, often reflected within the Party, hinder China's economic modernization.

Politics has been the most important factor of economic growth (and non-growth) in China since 1949 – but most of this politics has been local or medial, not central. Especially since the early 1970s, when the substance of reforms began, most Chinese growth has been led by the heads of enterprises, family-like communities, and kin groups.

Think of China in a new way. The country is often conceived as if it were a homogeneous lump, with all consequential decisions taken in Beijing. Economists and political scientists alike over-concentrate on famous personages, as if behavioral power were solely national.

Yet "power" is defined by evidence that followers do what leaders want when the followers would otherwise act differently (Dahl 1961). Behavioral power occurs in non-state polities and small or medium-sized units, even firms and families, as surely as in the national state.

"All politics is local," as US Speaker of the House Tip O'Neill famously said. Even politics among state elites is local from their viewpoint. Some politics is vertical/hierarchal; some is horizontal, as in markets that involve bargaining between equals. China now has a mixed "bureaucratic market economy" (Chow 2007), involving official commands mainly for very large firms but markets for most sectors. Each hierarchal network of any size has leaders, who maintain their power with classic Weberian means like charisma, coercion, and money (Bendix 1960).

The title of this chapter was assigned, and the author likes it because vertical politics can always imply force, which is sometimes perceived as unclean or corrupt (see Machiavelli (1532/1952) or Weber (1919/1962)). Just as important in a modern economy, politics shapes regulations that create or preserve markets by preventing markets from commodifying people, environment, and rightful earnings (Polanyi 1944/1957). Politics is implicitly coercive as well as normative, and it is the mechanism that can join humane sustainability to allocative efficiency.

So this chapter deals first with political mechanisms. It stresses the role of local powers that were not fully under state control, and it shows how they weakened socialist planning in the 1971–89 era, after which the national and medial sizes of government came to terms with markets they could partially regulate but could not wholly control. The second half of the essay deals with corruption, which is the greatest threat to the Communist Party of China (CCP) according to its own leaders.

1 Political mechanisms of economic leadership

China is now generally a "decentralized" market economy; but previously, it was socialist. Political centralism is an ancient Chinese value, and commands from Beijing still rule some economic sectors. Government is naturally the main mover in developing military industries, for example. In banking, and in activities that require heavy capitalization or materials from large point sources such as oilfields, central "politics is in command" (*zhengzhi gua shuai*, was a Maoist slogan). But fifty years ago, a far greater portion of China's resources were allocated by socialist plans. The government fixed practically all prices. What caused the reform change?

The usual (wrong or incomplete, but still official) answer is that top leaders, notably Deng Xiaoping, ordered the shift in 1978. A more accurate answer is that the first reform chiefs were heads of very local economic polities such as production teams and brigades, from about 1971 (not 1978). Data to show this are below. They indicate that many local leaders, rather than a few national ones, initiated China's reforms.

The economic history of the late 1960s and early 1970s, in rich rural parts of China such as the Yangzi or Pearl River deltas, is background to the start of the general (though fluctuating) move from central to local economic leadership. The roots of industrial reform lie in farmers' fields: triple cropping and agricultural mechanization rose very sharply in the late 1960s. That era is famous as the Cultural Revolution; but a "green revolution" in agriculture was just as important. It gradually affected as many people as did the urban chaos of that era, although it has been omitted from practically all historical accounts. It began in traditionally wealthy rural areas. In 1965, for example, the percentage of suburban Shanghai's then-extensive cultivated area that was tilled by machine was only 17 percent; but by 1972, 76 percent; and by 1974, 89 percent (Kojima 1978: 293–99). The wattage used by agricultural machinery in these fields rose 19 percent annually, compounded, between 1965 and 1978 (Xie 1991: 104). Such changes were quickest on rich delta farmlands along the eastern coast and then on the Chengdu plain, but even in the nation as a whole (which included many destitute regions) the number of these machines in 1978 stood at the following percentages of those in 1970: large and middle-size tractors, 355 percent; walking tractors, 631 percent; and agricultural pick-up trucks, 914 percent (Wu 1991: 53). Repair shops for these became factories, proliferating into many lines of production.

Processing raw materials is almost always more profitable than extracting or growing them. Farmer-entrepreneurs, even in the era of communes, did not miss this point (Zhou 1996).

As conservative rural leaders became more aware of the popularity among their peasant-clients of this new source of prosperity, rural reformism became contagious (Gallagher 2005). Human capital for economic development has been evident in the form of rural entrepreneurship, not just tertiary education.

On the Yangzi Delta, reformer Xu Jiatun was a province-level administrator in Jiangsu during the early 1970s. He later wrote, "I tell you, we took a different road from the rest of the country". "The planned economy was crucial, and the market economy was a supplement." We had openly to support this, but in fact we had gone beyond it" (Xu 1993/5/6). Actually, Xu needed to do nothing but blink at what more local leaders were doing. The main province-level leader in Shanghai then, Zhang Chunqiao (1975), was by contrast a socialist-conservative desperate to preserve the Party's planning power. He was not willing to blink at "sprouts of capitalism in the countryside." Fei Xiaotong (1988: 5) plainly says that many rural factories in the early 1970s were "illegal" and "underground." Radicals dominated the central administration for much of this period – although Deng Xiaoping was First Vice-Premier in 1974–75.

Political splits between reformists and conservatives have persisted at *all* sizes of China's polity from that period to the present. Local leaders replaced central authorities in running most of China's economy, especially as regards employment or the production of consumer items that socialist planners had neglected. Deng Xiaoping, unlike practically all officials or academics (either now or then), saw this change and was totally frank about it. As Deng said:

> Generally speaking, our rural reforms have proceeded very fast, and farmers have been enthusiastic. *What took us by surprise completely was the development of township and village industries ... This was not the achievement of our central government.* Every year, township and village industries achieved 20 percent growth ... This was not something I had thought about. Nor had the other comrades. This surprised us.
>
> *(RMRB 1987/6/13, emphasis added)*

Deng reached for an ancient phrase to describe his astonishment: *yijun tujing* ("a strange army suddenly appeared from nowhere"). A few academics also recorded this early rural industrialization (Perkins 1977) – but it was largely forgotten in post-Mao analyses even by academics. Practically everyone still writes as if economic reforms began in 1978. Yet if the term "reforms" has any substantive meaning outside official rhetoric, evidence of quick growth of rural industrial output in earlier years of the 1970s, naturally starting in rich areas of China, shows the usual discourse to be inaccurate.

By the mid-1980s, Deng's "army" of rural factory managers was taking most raw materials and markets that had earlier been under state command. They oversaw nimble, exploitative, profitable firms that could afford to buy inputs at prices the budgets of state companies could not afford. So the government in effect had to legalize a black market; it let state factories sell items at 20 percent above the planned prices (*jihua jia*) after those firms claimed to have fulfilled their production quotas. This marked-up rate was euphemized as a "state-guided price" (*guojia zhidao jia*). But the two-price policy was, at first, unintended and unwanted by planners. It was praised as wise not just by governments, but also by many economists – who ordinarily say that a commodity of standard quality at a single time in a single-place market has just one price.

In 1985 alone, rural industries spent so much money buying raw materials and energy from state enterprises, the national companies gained at least 10.7 billion yuan – equal to at least 6 percent of total government revenues at all levels – as pure profit from speculative exchanges (Wang *et al.* 1992: 30). The Shanghai market price of coal in 1988 was 220 percent of the "fixed" state price; for electricity, 176 percent; for steel, 160 percent; for aluminum, 250 percent; and for timber, over 550 percent (Hu 1989: 10–15). This situation was politically *led*, but not by central leaders.

State clothing and cigarette factories ran short of wool and tobacco (Wu 1990: 6). The government issued a document as early as on May 4, 1981, ordering the closure of many rural enterprises that produced textiles, cigarettes, and salt (*RMRB* 1981/5/4). But Beijing's decrees could not reverse local entrepreneurs' reforms. Rural enterprises won the "tobacco war," the "wool war," and others.

The "unified purchasing policy," which for decades had extracted huge coerced rents from peasants to urbanites, collapsed. Commercial small and medium enterprises, SMEs, flourished along with industrial ones. Willy Kraus (1991: 63) estimates that in the 1980s "a non-licensed 'individual economy' existed which was just as large as the licensed." The portion by value of all Shanghai factory inputs allocated by plan plummeted from about 70 percent to about 20 percent in the mid-1980s (*JFRB* 1988/5/15). National planners did not wish this – it meant the end of socialism in most sectors – but they could not enforce deliveries of inputs.

The number of products from Shanghai state factories under mandatory production quotas dropped in the mid-1980s, from 150 in 1984 to 37 in 1987 (*SHJJNJ* 1988: 90). Even then, not all the mandated deliveries were fulfilled. As a sardonic pair of local journalists observed, "Developing the commodity economy without commodities is a major vexation for many enterprises in Shanghai" (*Foreign Broadcast Information Service* 1986/11/26: 3).

"Contracts replace plans" thus became a mid-1980s slogan. More rule-of-contract-law surely sounds modern. But contracts at this time were no more enforceable than plans. The Leninist appointment system, under which all important posts are filled by officials chosen by Party personnel departments at a higher administrative level, did not effectively put central (or even provincial or county) managers over local managers for most economic decisions. If a rural unit failed to deliver to an urban factory a contracted amount of raw materials at the contracted price, the factory could sue. Even if the factory won in an urban court, the judge there was not appointed by the same CCP personnel department as were police in the rural jurisdiction – which might, or might not, enforce the decision.

Of all economic litigations filed in Shanghai courts during October 1988, the judges classified more than half as "unresolvable" within three months of the filing (*HDXXB* 1989/1/28). Some rural firms claimed to have closed, or managers absconded. Judges lacked time to spend on trials when they guessed the plaintiffs had meritorious cases but knew their decisions would remain unenforced. They responsibly defended their courts.

Centralists in 1980 pushed to have all cadre appointments approved by Party personnel departments "two levels up" (rather than having them approved just one level up, the previous norm). But this experiment failed and was abandoned in 1983, because the appointers two levels up lacked enough reliable information to make sensitive choices or to sanction their appointees (Landry 2008). This span-of-control problem stymies centralizers in such a big country.

Despite very high Chinese regard for government and for ideals of centralist hierarchy, many rural industrialists consciously competed with rival state firms – to make money for their local polities, not to undermine the Party. A mid-1980s survey of 5,600 rural enterprises suggests the managers were keenly aware of the state enterprises in their fields. Fully 48 percent responded they were in "competition" with state factories that produced the same products (and another 19 percent said they were in a mixed mode of "cooperation and competition" (*NMRB* 1988/9/8)). They were surely proud to be state cadres, even as their behavior was derogating power from the state to themselves.

Politics still controlled the economy, as SMEs flourished in rich parts of the mainland, but these were increasingly local non-state politics. Markets or any other means of making social decisions do not thrive without political constituencies – and in China, markets became extremely popular among both patrons and their clients in the rural places where most Chinese people lived. Markets allowed not just more prosperity and jobs, but also more freedom for local leaders to build their small polities, supporting their families and their own self-identifications (compare Shieh 1992, on local "bosses" and Taiwan's boom).

Savvy Xi Jinping, now China's President, when he was just 30 in 1983, resigned a cushy military adviser's job and volunteered to work in rural Zhengding, Hebei. He emerged as a reformer in village politics. "Mr. Xi formed a clever alliance with Maoists and used his family ties in Beijing to cut Zhengding's grain quota by one-quarter. That freed up farmers to use their land more lucratively, such as for raising fish, geese, or cattle" (Johnson 2012/9/30). New local institutions were also required, especially illegal local banks that still provide finance for dynamic SMEs (Tsai 2002).

Premier Zhu Rongji in the 1990s did his best to overcome Beijing's 1980s loss of authority. He partially succeeded in reversing the earlier decade's trend (Yang 2005). The point is not that free markets defeated central planners in the 1980s, but that local leaders using markets did so. Party hierarchs had been duly scared by the 1989 Tiananmen public reactions to myriad social problems, of which the main economic example was rampant inflation. Socialist conservatives, having tried to control more than they could, had forced efficiency-promoting local entrepreneurs underground. Premier Zhu Rongji could not centralize China, but he might be said to have "medialized" economic administration by urging more independence for high-medial sizes of polity such as sub-provincial cities and prefecture-level cities, whose boundaries were extended to take in more of the new suburban economic activity.

Zhu led a reform of China's tax code, which raised central revenues. He persuaded his comrades to admit, in effect, that small firms had already been "released" into the market sea and that the state should only try to run some big corporations (*zhuada fangxiao*). Product quality became subject to somewhat better monitoring. Risky loans from large state banks became subject to more screening. Some bureaucrats were fired. Military entrepreneurs, who had been running many enterprises, were ordered out of the economy. Continuations of similar policies, after the start of the new millennium, changed fees to taxes and then abolished the main agricultural tax altogether.

Premier Zhu and other high-placed reformers persuaded at least some of their comrades in a nervous, control-freak-like Party that markets, which can never be fully controlled, had already brought benefits to the Chinese people that the CCP in its own interest had to preserve. He could not restore socialism, but he could adapt it to new demands of efficiency.

Zhu's reforms penetrated to medial sizes of government organization within China's political economy, including large state corporations and large collectives, but not to low or local sizes that remained very important for employment, exports, and income. Much later in 2012, an economist with IHS Global Insight in 2012, Ren Xianfang, claimed that unregistered "lending and investing networks" in China manage US$1.3 trillion. "Shadow banks" still provide immense amounts of credit to the nonstate economy. Premier Wen Jiabao explains that, "Chinese companies, especially small ones, need access to funds. Banks [official ones] have yet to be able to meet these companies" needs, and there is a massive amount of private capital. We need to bring private finance out into the open" (Bloomberg 2012/11/4).

Exploitation of labor in factories has supported both external and domestic trade. Even while PRC manufactures declined, exports still generated 31 percent of GDP in 2011. Exports supported 200 million jobs (*SCMP*/Reuters 2012/9/30). A riot followed a strike in a Taiyuan Foxconn electronics factory, which closed (Barboza 2012/9/24). Nonpayment of salaries to migrant workers in export factories has caused "mass incidents," e.g. in the denim-manufacturing town of Zengcheng, Guangdong. In June 2011, Zengcheng suffered major riots in which government offices and police cars were burned. A year later, the same thing happened at Longshan, Shaxi, Zhongshan, Guangdong, where local villagers stabbed a Sichuan immigrant teenager. So "several thousand Sichuan people working in Guangdong engaged in a bloody clash with police" (Lau 2012/6/27).

By 2012, 60 percent of all villages in the export manufacturing county Dongguan, Guangdong, were running deficits. A Ministry of Finance researcher claimed that, throughout China, village debts were one-tenth of GDP – "but there is no official data … Village chiefs he interviewed had no idea how much debt they had." In Dongguan, the CCP secretary told village heads "to stop raising money to pay dividends … Few took heed." Townships, which are formally responsible for fire and police departments, failed to finance these services fully, and "in some counties, police would refuse to investigate a crime unless it involved more than 20,000 yuan" (So 2012/9/28). Many coastal boom towns had extracted rents from migrant workers who lacked household registrations. These workers returned inland when export factories closed. So the towns had budget shortfalls.

Environmental problems related to development have also brought large protests by citizens, e.g., in Haimen, Guangdong, 2011, where residents rioted against the air pollution that the proposed expansion of a coal-powered electric plant would have created. In Qidong, Jiangsu, 2012, fishermen opposed water pollution that a Japanese-invested paper mill would have fed into the Yangzi; so they took over the local government offices.

Large mass demonstrations erupted in all the cases listed above and many others that received less press. Police often used violence and tear gas. Afterwards, local governments and developers occasionally backed down, cancelling their previous plans.

At least 40 to 50 million peasants since 1980 have lost land to developers who had business ties to cadres or were themselves still cadres. Fully 94 percent of entrepreneurs in the CCP at the turn of the millennium went into business *after* joining the Party (Pei 2006: 93). The PRC Constitution gives ownership of practically all rural land to collectives, managed by town or village committees, but under a 2004 amendment, land can be switched from collective to state ownership either through "temporary" land acquisition (*zhengyong*) or through expropriation (*zhengshou*). "Expropriation" requires high-level approvals and compensation to peasants. So, local cadres have instead used "acquisition," which becomes permanent and can in effect privatize land for their own use (Kochhar 2012/1/23).

Wukan, a village in Guangdong, erupted in protests after such a "land grab." Peasants forced all the local officials and police to flee, and they set up an "Autonomous Body of Village Residents." They marched to the county (Lufeng) and elected a representative, Xue Jinbo, to negotiate with the government. Xue was arrested and died in custody. Much larger demonstrations followed. The prefecture (Shanwei) then called a press conference to announce that the villagers' demands had been mostly agreed and that their "provisional" council officially replaced the cadres who had fled. Province party secretary Wang Yang said the handling of the Wukan unrest should be an example of the right way to manage other cases (Lau 2012/5/1). But, a year later, peasants said, "We still haven't got our land back." The expelled officials had signed contracts granting land to developers, and these could not easily be reversed (Reuters 2012/9/22).

Migrant workers' complaints were directed against medial rather than high levels of government. Local cadres and landlords or businesspeople were often lineage kin, providing space for factories from which they could collect rents. In July 2012, province-level authorities in Guangzhou had planned to ease registration requirements of NGOs supporting migrant workers. But these NGOs (e.g. the Shenzhen Spring Breeze Labor Dispute Service Center, Shenzhen Migrant Worker Center, Green Grass Worker Service Center, Times Female Worker Service Center) were instead shut down because of powerful opposition by "sub"-provincial local cadres. Such NGOs had trouble finding office space. One of them "moved to a new location in the outskirts of Baoan district … The landlord demolished our signboard and suspended our water and power supply" (Tam 2012/7/27). These complaints were not against "the government" in any general sense. They reflected conflict between two types of very local polities, one run by rentiers and investors, the other by migrant workers.

Arthur Lewis (1954) suggests that the supply of labor at subsistence wages may dry up after a take-off boom in any country. This is starting to happen in China. But Peking University economics professor Fan Gang (2010/8/30) is not worried that China's rising wages will hurt its competitive advantage soon, even though he admits China's market efficiency and innovative capacity need further development. "Wage efficiency" in other low-compensation countries such as Bangladesh or Mozambique remains less than in China. Also, one-third of China's workforce is still in agriculture, but because older farmers seldom migrate to cities so that urban wages tend to rise.

Worker politics are thus livelier than before. Sociologist Anita Chan once condemned quasi-military discipline in export factories – but recently, she describes less of such repression (Chan 1996, 2005). Proletarian dissident Han Dongfang, founder of the Beijing Autonomous Workers' Federation in 1989, by 2011 wrote, "Some ACFTU [Party union] officials are trying to make a positive impact … Even the Party, which in the past only had its own interests to consider, now has to listen to the voice of the workers and respond to their increasingly clear and angry calls for change" (Han 2011). He notes a few recent decent pay packages, as well as strikes and worker riots.

China has become a pluralized country as it has developed economically. Political initiatives now start from more nodes. This pluralization is "the emergence of polities other than the state, where polity stands for any form of social organization within which (among other things) politics takes place" (Wissenburg 2009: 2). A Leninist machine for centralist control does not work as well as local mechanisms, in a country that is increasingly diversified, educated, well informed, and rich.

Five partial heresies can sum up this treatment of the political mechanisms of China's economic development. First, powerful leadership and policy are local, not just national. Second, late 1960s China saw "green" revolution, not just "Cultural" Revolution. Third, behavioral reforms began in rich rural areas about 1971, not 1978. Fourth, the thoughts, deaths, and lives of top leaders have been deemed too exclusively influential (though Deng Xiaoping deserves credit for outstanding honesty in admitting what he had not done). Fifth, social scientists – notably economists – failed to predict China's economic rise before it happened (as they also failed to explain Taiwan's, or Thailand's, or the perennial Philippine stagnancy before those events) largely because they ignored causal factors in local politics. Zooming in, to find more detail, can help us all see long-term trajectories more clearly.

China's main economic recessions and successes alike have been mainly political, coming from many sizes of polity. The reform period's major success is that local SMEs have flourished under little dictators. Nationally, the government's stimulus package of 2009 was, in Nicholas Lardy's words, "early, large, and well-designed." Such benefits have been welcomed. Other politics have been less successful economically, implying major costs: the government's low-interest-rates policy meant that Chinese families put less of their savings into banks, buying real estate and threatening a house-price bubble. Nationally, PRC civilian aircraft use twice as much fuel as do such planes in other countries, because the military makes them fly at low altitudes (Johnson 2012/9/27). So in major and minor ways alike, politics in various sizes of Chinese communities have been the most obvious crucial factors of economic development and non-development. The segue into this chapter's next major topic is that China's increasing wealth gap, as the country booms economically, demoralizes rather than incentivizes workers when they think political corruption causes it.

2 Corruption and economic leadership

Corruption is risky behavior, and so is entrepreneurship that drives "dynamic efficiency" (Schumpeter 1911/1934, 1942). Because corruption is difficult for those not directly involved to observe directly, it is generally sought through attitude surveys. Unsurprisingly, it is correlated with the extent of "black" or "grey" economies in which business activities are not officially registered (Johnson *et al.* 1998). Corruption and non-registration are both common in fast-growing economies. Chinese planners may rue the rambunctiousness of firms that sell "fake" and irregularly branded goods. Yet such entrepreneurship has helped China boom.

Political scientists have tried harder to define corruption than to show how it evolves. They have reached some consensus on a definition, albeit a debatable one. Scott relies on Nye's words, and Nye relies on Banfield's. In this view, corruption is

> behavior which deviates from the formal duties of a public role because of private-regarding (personal, close family, private clique) pecuniary or status gains, or violates rules against the exercise of certain types of private-regarding influence.
>
> *(Scott 1972: 4)*

This definition salves the professional itch that social scientists have for numbers; it helps calculate costs or benefits of governmental corruption, and it implies a procedure for research. Public laws can be documented; normative duties can be imputed from attitude surveys that generate statistics. Once rules are thus set, a researcher can try to show the results of violations – and to assess the effects on political stability or economic growth.

This method mainly tells what *official* corruption does, but not how it *changes* or how it relates to corruption in private. Realism is lost in two ways: first, the focus is on public politics, as if proper authority were exercised only in government organizations and only by formally higher administrative offices over lower ones. The scope of corruption, however, is broader. Much malfeasance is secret, so that in practice corruption is almost always measured by surveying perceptions of it, not by observing behavior. Public and private infractions of norms are in practice linked. The government elites of some countries thoroughly dominate sources of data about public norms, which might more realistically be induced from all social networks. Especially in China, where many organizations become ideally governmental, any premise that public and private politics are easy to separate is far-fetched.

Second, this usual definition of corruption refers to duties that are assumed to be stable over time. This may fulfill one purpose of the definition, which is to judge the efficiency of corruption in a political economy, but it involves another loss of realism because it ignores that concepts of corruption can change, sometimes rather quickly. The standard definition has no dynamic aspect. It cannot tell why particular acts (usury is the classic case; Nelson 1953) are deemed corrupt in some periods and places, but not in others.

Corruption changes. During the first half of the 1950s in China, for example, campaigns (e.g., in the "*sanfan wufan*" era) were launched to alter norms of cleanliness in many fields together: in business, in cadres' loyalty, in demands for patriotic purity among all citizens, in physical cleanliness on streets, against insect pests and schistosomiasis snails, against diseases such as smallpox (which was ended by a mandatory inoculation campaign then), against religions the

Communists judged unmodern, and against foreign enemies. In the first half of the 1980s, norms in each of these fields documentably moved, again together, in exactly opposite directions to their trends in the early 1950s (White 1988).

Corruption always implies two identifiable groups. It is a claim that benefits went to one (usually the smaller network of people) that should instead have gone to the other (usually the larger network). Such networks are political; they are led. This is a definition of corruption that allows research on the full practical scope of the topic. Subjective assessments must determine whether network leaders are regarded as corrupt or clean. If the heads of enterprises or states are perceived to be successful and kind, most people think their authority is uncorrupt. Mencius said that rulers must be benign to their subjects – and if they are not, they cannot properly be called rulers. Mencius even condoned assassination of a "despised creature" whose behavior meant he could no longer be called a king (deBary 1960: 92–7).

Julia Kwong (1997) used data about ideology and institutions to argue that corruption in China had a "parabolic" trajectory: it decreased in Mao's time because of egalitarian anti-materialistic campaigns, but during reforms it increased again as individuals and small groups concentrated on making money and the Party tried to rectify governance. Sun Yan (2004) shows that cadres and citizens obey market incentives now, though formerly they attended more to the norms of a puritan party-state.

Lü Xiaobo (2002) takes a type-of-organizational-solidarity view of corruption, seeing it as an unintended consequence of "organizational involution" during attempts to consolidate socialism. The Party did not hold together well, because its functionaries neither fully prioritized its policies (bonding the CCP through common "gung-ho" consciousness or "human organization," to use others' phrases) nor because their behavior together created success through legal–rational bureaucracy and markets (integration through complementarity and "technical organization"; see Schurmann 1966). Corrupt groups took rents from the Party-state that was disorganized rather than integrated.

Many social variables that are easier to observe than corruption link in a nonlinear fashion to development, especially to early modern development. For example, Charles Jones (2002: 60) offers a scatter diagram relating many countries' GDP growth rates over four decades to the wealth index of GDP per worker. Despite a nearly random scatter of growth rates among poor countries, the averaged growth rises sharply until a middling wealth level is reached (US$7,000 by Jones's measure *c*.1990). Then, for richer countries, the growth rate goes down as GDP/per capita increases, with fewer points far from it as economies "converge" into modernity. China (with India slightly behind it) is not far from the soft spot for high growth on this scatter diagram.

Pell-mell growth usually sharpens differences between rich and poor, who may perceive themselves as two groups. Arthur Lewis (1954) truly earned his Nobel Prize for pointing out that managers of capital enjoy windfall profits during a time window when they can combine modern technology and markets with labor that is still willing to work for near subsistence wages. A small group (capitalists or high cadres) can temporarily take most of the value of work by a large group (a majority who are workers). The gap can make perceptions of corruption rise.

The famous Kuznets curve suggests that income stratification usually increases during the heydays of expansion in many countries, before economies converge to lower growth at higher per-capita incomes. For example in the United States, the long sprint of growth from the late nineteenth century until 1929 was also a period of labor–capital clashes, criminal gangs, and reputed corruption (especially in the 1920s) – as well as prosperity. The Teapot Dome scandal of 1922–23 saw a secretary of the interior jailed, along with an oil company executive who had given him a multimillion dollar bribe. In Japan during an early boom time, when the Hokkaidô Colonial Office was sold on soft terms to the Kansai Trading Company, public reaction was such that "even those who had never heard the term "rights" or "popular rights" before" took notice and demanded more transparent government (Kim 2007: 288–328). Corruption has often accompanied booms.

Local "land grabs" by developers may be the most reported form of corruption in China now, but arguably, the most pervasive form comes from discrimination by established urbanites against people they disdain as unwashed peasants. Many of the latter now live in cities, although most are still in the countryside. The household registration system officially enforces this discrimination. The urban group is large, and the mainly rural group of ex-peasants is much larger, though politically unorganized across most of the nation. Use of state power to inhibit migration into cities may have positive effects on planning (fewer slums, more industrial jobs in rural areas), but it perpetuates resentments between peasants and city elites such as have contributed to rebellions in China for decades and longer. When ex-farmers are able to live in cities, their children (if education is available) are segregated into schools that established urban families do not want their offspring to attend. Wages, access to medical help, and services are worse for rural people or recently rural people than for city dwellers with permanent household registrations. Official attempts to limit migration into cities maintain income gaps. Further economic development may reduce this inequality, but change would be quicker if the state made migration easier.

Yu Jianrong and Li Renqing (2012), both in the Rural Development Institute of the Chinese Academy of Social Sciences, suggest reforms to reduce these gaps. They suggest that peasants should have rights to own land they use, that more low-income housing should be built in cities, that rural and urban social security systems be linked, that ex-peasants' children in cities receive better schooling, and that peasants and ex-peasants should receive more government support. Hirschman (1973) speculates that growth, when it produces resentments, is likely to do so with some delay. China may currently be in such a hiatus.

Corruption (measured as a perceived variable) usually correlates with fast growth, but the situation is complex. There are plausible arguments that on purely domestic grounds corruption hinders economic growth (Chow 2006); more empirical research on this link is needed. Corruption sometimes hinders growth, and hardheaded research shows that a reason in most developing countries is the desire of *foreign* investors to avoid paying bribes (Rose-Ackerman 1999: 3). Low corruption, as perceived, can be linked statistically with capital inflows (in many countries), and this relationship is robust when controlled for per-capita income, domestic savings rates, and raw materials exports. The scatter diagram relating inflows to perceived corruption in many countries is revealing. When perceptions of corruption are graphed against productivity (the ratio of GDP to capital stock), there is even more scatter than in a diagram relating corruption to inflows (Lambsdorff 2004: 311–12). Corrupt rake-offs discourage influxes of foreign capital, lowering that factor of growth. Bribes act like a tax on FDI.

Foreign investor-entrepreneurs, however, may discount this cost if they expect an economic "rise" to continue and want to establish themselves early in a national market, notably China's. Yet on domestic grounds alone, it remains unclear whether corruption hinders growth. Also, China has been fortunate in recent decades because large portions of its external capital have come from ethnically Chinese places (Hong Kong, Taiwan, Singapore – and startlingly large amounts from the Cayman Islands and the British Virgin Islands, much of which is probably recycled from the mainland). So would Chinese "foreign" investors, who can more easily develop "social capital" with PRC entrepreneurs, be less deterred than other foreigners if they get more benefit for the bribes they pay? Are Chinese domestic investors less deterred from corruption too? Reliable research on these questions is difficult to conduct. Sociopolitical trust aids growth, and it also abets corruption.

As a businessman said, "There are two kinds of corruption. The first one is where you pay the regular corrupt price and you get what you want. The second is where you pay what you have agreed to pay, and you go home and lie awake every night worrying whether you will get it or if somebody is going to blackmail you instead" (see Lambsdorff 1998: 83). Predictable corruption of the first kind probably does not impede investment and entrepreneurship, but dangers of blackmail impede growth.

When is a bribe a bribe, and when is it a gift or tip? The World Bank tries to estimate amounts of corruption, defining it by "perceptions of the extent to which public power is exercised for private gain, including both petty and grand forms of corruption, as well as "capture" of the state by elites and private interests." (Such a definition suggests that corruption always involves the government; unrealistic premises are rife in studies of this subject.) The Bank surveyed various respondents, ranking all countries from corrupt (0) to clean (100). In 1996, the Bank's number-crunchers put China on this scale at 43 (e.g., as compared to 97 for Canada, 39 for India, or 10 for the Republic of Congo). By 2010, China's perceived rank was down to 33 (still 97 in Canada, 36 in India, and 11 in Congo; World Bank 2012). Definitions, sources, and methods vary and are debatable; so changes in such indicators may be almost as meaningful as their levels. High Chinese growth correlated with rising corruption.

Corruption also varies within countries. Ideological democrats, e.g. in the US, sometimes fail to stress that elected officials can be corrupt; some analysts suggest stringent rules are appropriate for appointees, but lax ones for politicians who win votes and make laws. This approach is faulty. Thailand has laws allowing police to investigate officials who are "unusually rich" – but corruption still flourishes there, in part because private citizens are generally exempt from prosecution. Pasuk and Sungsidh (1997) attempted an econometrics of Thailand's corruption, and they found that leakage by their definition was between 3 and 5 percent of total government spending during a period of quick Thai growth under six premiers (ending with Chattichai) before 1991. This estimate did not include all types of bribes. The Philippines almost surely has higher rates of corruption, both public and private, although that country has not enjoyed fast growth (Florintino-Hofileña 1998; Chua 1999; Coronel 2000; Hutchcroft 2000).

Corruption is a behavioral, not national, phenomenon. "Cultural" norms are causal in this, though not determinative; and the "culture" word despite its proper uses irritates so many allergies among so many social scientists, it may be unnecessary to cite. Corruption is a moral phenomenon too; but when an elite has lost most of its charisma (as the CCP has), corruption's remedy is likely to be institutional.

An exemplar institution for China is not hard to find. Hong Kong once had flagrant corruption (Elliott/Tu 1971). But the city is now famous for its Independent Commission Against Corruption (ICAC), established in 1974 when the British colonial government responded to extensive malfeasance in its own police force (led by an Englishman, aided by Chinese). *The ICAC has staff and authority to arrest anyone – officials (including police) or non-officials (including businesspeople) – to face corruption charges in regular courts.* Secret societies' violence and bribery to private businesses have been rightly perceived as corrupt, with or without any involvement of officials.

The ICAC reports to the head of government but is not part of the civil service; its sole role is to fight corruption. So it is unlike Party discipline committees, procurators, or police on the mainland. Such an organization would be incompatible with Leninist appointment institutions that still prevail in China. Equal enforcement of serious laws in politically independent courts is also crucial for ICAC effectiveness. Hong Kong's 1971 Prevention of Bribery Ordinance allows courts to consider "unexplained income or property." As Manion (2004: 2) says, "Hong Kong has sustained a consistent ranking as one of the "cleanest" countries of the world since 1980, on a par with established liberal democracies. Mainland China, by contrast, experienced an explosion of corruption in the early 1980s." Both societies are now thoroughly Chinese.

The corruption sore continues to bleed so severely in China that Hu Jintao, opening his last Party Congress, said it could become fatal to the CCP. Yet as Academy of Social Sciences historian Zhang Lifan moaned, "They could punish their men, such as Bo [Xilai] or [Railways ex-minister] Liu, but they don't want any supervision from outside the Party" (Zhai 2012/11/8). As long as the CCP handles most cases of corruption internally or controls non-Party judges tightly, Leninist appointment norms prevent effective corruption control.

Judges and procurators who deal with major corruption cases in China have potentially dangerous jobs. In 2003, thirteen heads or deputy heads at the very high province/ministry level were convicted of corruption. So was the former chairman of the Kiyang enterprise group in Shenyang, who was sentenced to death for giving big bribes and owning weapons for criminal gangs. Then, surprisingly, an intermediate court overturned his sentence. It was reinstated only by China's supreme court. As two Chinese researchers write, "The general public was not informed about what motivated the vacillations over his sentence" (Transparency International 2005: 132).

Development requires contracts, for which officials often demand kickbacks. In 2000, China passed a Tendering and Bidding Law, and many cities have established "tangible construction markets" where contracts are supposed to be auctioned. But Transparency International claimed these remained "under-resourced and under-utilised." In 2005, five provinces (Jiangsu, Zhejiang, Sichuan, Chongqing, and Guangxi) established blacklists of contractors who had been convicted of bribery (Transparency International 2005: 131). Companies on the blacklists might, however, change their names. Kickbacks on contracts were especially common in the Railway Ministry. A Guangzhou terminus that had been budgeted for US$316,000,000 finally cost seven times as much (Osnos 2012/22/10: 50). Large agencies had large contracts; so public scandal about totals of rake-offs (when discovered) was great. Yet corruption on millions of medium and smaller contracts may well have been cumulatively greater.

Privatization could sometimes give new owners market incentives to use resources more efficiently than the state does. When local authorities are given a great deal of regulatory power that they can use in ways they can hide from the public, corruption can grow. As Gregory Chow (2006: 265) writes, "Reducing the size of the government sector is a basic solution to the corruption problem in China, while attention should be paid to the privatization process." It is hard to assure transparency in that process. Transferring ownership is fraught with opportunities for corruption.

Reformers have tried to adapt from agriculture a "responsibility system," which gives industrial and commercial managers full responsibility for running firms. Yet when the managers abuse this power, they can create a corrupt irresponsibility system, stealing public or collective property. In semi-state and nonstate polities, especially companies and local business networks, Chinese hierarchal traditions often trump the lively Chinese traditions of transparent bargaining.

"Private" and "collective" are often hard to distinguish behaviorally. Management can be more important than legalities, not all corruption involves officials, private firms can be as anti-competitive as local or large "state" firms, and the variety of sizes of companies in an immense nation creates myriad sorts of semi-private management (compare Burnham 1944).

Corrupt officials have been a top concern of Chinese people surveyed during recent reforms, second only to inflation. (Food safety concerns were third on the worry list – up three times during the 2008–12 period; Pew Research 2012.) Despite the high priority that surveyed citizens give for fighting corruption, they are legally inhibited from being whistleblowers. PRC laws against publicizing state secrets are broadly written. If anyone senses that a listed corporation in China has committed an accounting fraud, no agent may file a lawsuit until after the China Securities Regulatory Commission has already punished the company (Opper 2005: 210). So the Party group in this Commission, rather than any court, has first authority to penalize fraud; other actors are not supposed to act.

Campaigns to "strike hard" (*yanda*) against corruption, such as Bo Xilai led in Chongqing – or former Premier Thaksin Shinawatra in Thailand – have been suspect as factional struggles. They can catch criminals while also purging local rivals of apparently puritanical populist demagogues, who themselves are later found to have been very corrupt. Use of a campaign (*yundong*) suggests that regular, reliable legal punishments must be ineffective. During these temporary movements, courts become clogged with many cases – so much that Manion claims (2004: 207), "Campaigns were effectively peaks of leniency, not punishment."

Corruption in the military is particularly difficult to subdue. Liu Yuan, a deputy head of the Army's Logistics Department (and as son of Liu Shaoqi, a high princeling), gave a 2012 Chinese New Year speech favoring a "do or die" fight against corruption in the PLA. Shortly thereafter, one of his fellow deputy heads in the same department was indicted for selling Army property illegally and was jailed. There are detailed "Regulations on the Performance of Official Duties with Integrity by Leading Cadres with Party Membership in the Armed Forces" – but it is difficult to enforce rules on powerful soldiers (Mulvenon and Ragland 2012).

"Zero tolerance" rhetoric against corruption may be somewhat useful, but the optimal level of corruption is arguably not zero. Manion (2004: 4) quotes Anechirico and Jacobs, who write that, "not only is corruption control costly, but the "pursuit of absolute integrity' is quite dysfunctional. . . " (Mulvenon and Ragland 2012).

Measures that seem aimed to reduce corruption can have the opposite result. For example, when Wenzhou's city government in 2012 suffered decreased revenues because of the global economic slowdown, it sold 215 fancy cars and planned to sell or auction another 1,300 vehicles by the end of the year. This may have seemed a sensible, even puritanical, measure to reduce cadre luxury. (One in every five German Audis in China is government owned, some police cars are Porsches, and a Maserati has been spied with PLA plates; Rabinovitch 2012/1/25.) But it is unclear who *buys* cars that abstemious local governments sell, at what prices, and with what funds.

A whole state may undertake arguably corrupt acts that it can legalize. A massive example in China was investment in the "Great Third Front" (*da san xian*), when two-thirds of the entire 1964–71 state construction budget was squandered on non-productive inland factories (Naughton 1991). This was and is not clearly perceived as corruption; the aims of economic Maoists at that time may have seemed patriotic, and the egregious waste might be considered just a mistake. But this extravagance, following the whims ("preferences") of a small ideological group, objectively and severely hurt a very large group, the population of China. It was at least comparable to corruption, even though it was also an act of state. This gargantuan waste of capital delayed China's economic rise and prolonged poverty for many, because the money did not regenerate itself. (Earlier, the PRC's worst economic depression followed the 1958 "Great Leap Forward." The accompanying famine caused so many deaths, this event is better conceived as a tragedy than a corruption; money is less important than people. Two groups, i.e., Maoist zealots and the general population, are nonetheless identifiable – and Chinese have recently begun to allow exploration of what they did to themselves – see Yang 2012; Dikötter 2010.)

Liberal economist Wu Jinglian, formerly an adviser to Deng Xiaoping, in 2012 said that corruption is holding China back. Wu described China's stock market as a "casino." "When you play cards, you should not know what cards are in your rival's hand, but in China's stock market information asymmetry is a very big and serious problem." He said many top leaders agree with him, although some princelings and "special interest groups" did not. Wu protested that "ridiculous" amounts of government money go into huge infrastructure projects – and into SOEs that "decide to expand aggressively, even outside their own industries. They pour a lot of money into the real estate sector, and then you see ordinary Chinese complaining about rising property prices" (Chen and Chen 2012/26/3).

"Rebalancing" consumption and investment, i.e., promoting consumption, was by 2012 a major economic policy of China's reformers. Many actors resist this, however, because their budgets would suffer from it. Cross-national research suggests that portions of public investment in GDP can be correlated with a perceived-corruption index that is restricted to state (rather than nonstate) abuses. This public investment portion can also be linked to low-quality investment: paved roads in bad condition, electricity losses as a proportion of total power output, faulty telecommunications, and low proportions of railway engines in working order (Tanzi and Daavodi 1997). In China, the increased independence of many collective and private market actors could reduce corruption, even though the PRC government still calls itself socialist. And this same independence allows them to engage more easily in corrupt acts.

The 2011 Wenzhou train crash became iconic for those who felt China was running too fast. Computers at Sinaweibo soon counted 26 million tweets, especially about bureaucrats' hasty efforts to bury a railcar that had fallen from a high viaduct (Wines and LaFraniere 2011/7/29). A state TV newscaster broke from his script: "Can we drink a glass of milk that is safe? Can we stay in an apartment that will not fall apart? Can we travel roads that will not collapse?" The reformist journal *Caixin* called the Railway Ministry "a broken system" and paraphrased Lord Acton: "since absolute power corrupts absolutely, the key to curbing graft is curbing power" (Osnos 2012/22/10: 47).

The Party is still largely a family affair, and old elites enjoy their power whether they are corrupt or not. Mao Xinyu, the sole surviving grandson of Mao Zedong and the youngest general in PLA history, publicly admits that his lineage helped his career. He is not known to be very rich. Other princelings are so, however. Yang Jisheng, a CCP journalist, probably overstates when he claims that

> The corruption in China is more severe than at any time in history, and what we have today is a market economy ruled by power – every business activity needs assistance or approval from people with power. Say your father is the provincial governor, one word from you means government approval for a real estate deal, followed by several hundred million [renminbi]. What's the big deal if I give you renminbi 100 million [US$15.7 million] back?

This report adds that

> It doesn't matter if an official's son is well-behaved or not. Even if you sit tight at home, people will knock on your door and give you money, and businesses will offer you a sinecure. Your name is the shortcut to getting bank loans, land, and other resources. This is caused by the bad system, not necessarily by princelings themselves.
>
> *(FT 2012/7/10)*

Influence-peddling cannot always be kept secret. Firms needing political relationships (*guanxi*) retain princelings as "consultants." A Hong Kong court case arose because of a dispute about the "consulting fee" that Tian Chengang, son of former Politburo Standing Committee leader Tian Jiyun, wanted from Beijing Henderson Properties (or from its parent company in HK) to "build a bridge" to the State Administration of Foreign Exchange. The HK judge wrote that Tian "tried to project an air of superiority … His attitude was contemptuous and disrespectful" when he was asked to explain his demand for a fee of US$5.5 million (Higgins 2012/24/4).

From 2007 to 2011, Chongqing among China's cities had the fastest growth of multimillionaire residents (*Guardian* 2012/10/5). Bo Xilai was Chongqing Party chief from 2007 until 2012, when the central government sent a team to investigate "the Bo family's connections and the alleged huge amount of assets held by the family in Hong Kong." Bo's elder brother used an assumed name (Li Xueming) when serving as executive director of HK's China Everbright International Corp. Bo's sister-in-law held directorships in at least nine HK companies over more than two decades. Xu Ming, a billionaire in Dalian, the city that Bo governed before moving to Chongqing, helped Bo's wife to transfer assets overseas (*SCMP* Staff 2012/23/4). Understandably, the HK government made no comment on the work of this investigation team from the mainland. Strong circumstantial evidence suggests that HK and Dalian actors helped Bo in corrupt activities.

Bo's family also bought apartments in London's classy South Kensington district, with ownership technically vested in a shell company called Golden Map, Ltd. No bank loan was needed. Michael Marks, son of Lord Marks of Broughton and descendant of the "Marks & Spencer" company founder, arranged the sale. The Chinese and British aristocracies thus cooperated (Gainsbury 2012/6/27).

Shortly after Bo's downfall, the party's official Xinhua News Agency, together with the *People's Daily* and *China Youth Daily*, all published commentaries calling for the political system to be "restructured," albeit not in a "Western" way. Government news organs called for efforts to "deepen political reform, ensuring that the people are the masters" – and they implied consensus among top leaders at that time (Huang 2012/4/24). But China has many scopes and types of polity, and conservative resistance to such change was strong in medial administrative layers and perhaps among some soldiers. Bo Xilai's demise was not mainly caused by his corruption. He was purged because his populist policies threatened liberal policy groups and other sixth-generation leaders. Political and economic reform might be somewhat helped by the fall of Bo Xilai (Hu 2012/10/11). Yet his populism (like Thaksin's) struck some observers as quasi-democratic, despite his anti-liberalism. Other high leaders united against Bo quickly.

Bo wanted power, and he caused a reset of elite politics without determining future policy trends. As Cheng Li (2012/11/4) writes:

> All of Bo's earlier activities were really directed at acquiring a seat on the Politburo Standing Committee or even higher because he sensed – perhaps earlier than others – that the old promotion game was over. [The Bo case] also served as a wake-up call for the party: more systematic institutional mechanisms are needed to deal with corruption, introduce intra-party democracy and demonstrate a real commitment to the rule of law. The leadership also needs to eventually allow for an open and independent media.

These personnel and policy questions go beyond one person's corruption, even though it was egregious and (except for his wife's conviction on murder charges) typical of other cases. Hong Kong analyst Willy Lam claimed that, "Compared to other families in the Party, the corruption problem of Bo's family is not necessarily very serious… And they face the risk of expanding the problem to other Party members" (Richburg 2012/6/15).

Government officials have found myriad ways to take abroad some of the money they have received as bribes in China. In 2004, the former head of the Bank of China in Kaiping, Guangdong, was extradited from the US back to China, after having embezzled US$485 million. Transparency International guessed that "cases such as this one may well be just the tip of the iceberg: research indicates that there may be as many as 4,000 others suspected of corruption or bribery who are still abroad [in 2005]. The total sum of money stolen may amount to 5 billion yuan (US$600 million), according to official sources" (Transparency International 2005: 132).

That was an estimate for just one year, by one NGO. Another NGO called Global Financial Integrity ventured in a report that, over the first decade of the millennium, Chinese took US$3.8 trillion in money out of their country. Presumably the main mechanism for such transfers would be various accounting devices that the Beijing government could not easily trace. That NGO's director claimed that "The magnitude of illicit money flowing out of China is astonishing." According to this report, "the outflow – much of it from corruption, crime or tax evasion – is accelerating: China lost 472 billion US dollars in 2011, equivalent to 8.3 percent of its gross domestic product, up from 204.7 billion in 2000" (Dawson 2012/10/25). It is hard to be sure whether these immense figures are correct. It is not at all hard to observe essentially anecdotal confirmations of financial outflows.

VIP rooms in Macao casinos, including those run by Americans Steve Wynn and Sheldon Adelson, attract rich Chinese, many of whom are apparently cadres or cadre-associated entrepreneurs. The origins of the gamblers' opulence are unclear. It is only clear that their number is considerable, and their purses are full.

Hong Kong's "Cyberport" was originally billed as South China's answer to Silicon Valley's research parks. The local government gave the son of the territory's richest tycoon (Li Ka-shing) scarce reclaimed land for Cyberport, on which high-rise luxury apartment buildings with a fancy French name ('Residence Bel-Air') are now more obvious than research labs. Many of the apartments have reportedly been bought by rich mainlanders. Similar money is flowing into flats and office spaces in the "West Kowloon Cultural District," still under construction, where an art museum is planned – but the main business there is clearly real estate. Both corrupt and non-corrupt wealth from the mainland has affected Hong Kong and Macao, which are magnets for money flowing into the mainland and out of it.

Some rich PRC citizens move their residences abroad. Three-quarters of applicants for US green cards, under the investor-immigrant program (EB5 visas) in 2011 came from China. Green cards can be had for investments of US$1 million, if they lead to ten full-time jobs in the US within two years (or for half as much, if the jobs are in high-unemployment areas). Canada on July 1, 2011, announced a tranche of 700 available investor applications for the next fiscal year – but the quota was filled within a week. Of the 700 applicants, 697 were Chinese (Chow and Loten 2012/11/5). The sources of the investment money were undoubtedly various.

PRC reformers worked in a structure they could not fully control. Premier Wen Jiabao, for example, was the highest official of his era to speak often of a need for liberal reforms. He had a good reputation for hard work and public sympathy, popularly called "Grandpa Wen," not deemed personally corrupt. But his son, mother, daughter, younger brother, and brother-in-law reportedly "controlled assets worth at least 2.7 billion US dollars," accumulated during his period in China's top leadership. A US State Department 2010 confidential cable, released by WikiLeaks, "suggested Mr. Wen was aware of his relatives' business dealings and unhappy about them" (Barboza 2012/10/25). But many wealthy Chinese so revered the state – and the even more important political unit of the family – they intuitively entrusted money to a premier's relatives. Wen was unable or unwilling to stop them, because family norms (which are sources of power) trumped state norms. This documented corruption was in a collective network that apparently did not include the most famous member. It is rumored by some in China that other leaders' relatives have stashed away larger amounts of corrupt money more artfully, so that news reporters cannot file stories about them.

Xi Jinping earned a reputation for anti-graft work in China's most entrepreneurial province, Zhejiang, in 2002. Xi spoke against graft in a 2004 conference call: "Rein in your spouses, children, relatives, friends and staff, and vow not to use power for personal gain." By 2007, Xi was promoted to Shanghai party chief, after a scandal under his predecessor Chen Liangyu, whose administration had misappropriated US$582 million in Shanghai pension funds.

Bloomberg reporters found public documents showing that Xi's extended family (but not he or his immediate family) had acquired interests including

> minerals, real estate, and mobile phone equipment, [and] investments in companies with total assets of 376 million US dollars; an 18 percent indirect stake in a rare-earths company with 1.73 billion US dollars in assets; and a 20.2 million US dollars holding in a publicly traded technology company. These figures don't account for liabilities and thus don't reflect the family's net worth. No assets were traced to Xi... his wife Peng Liyuan, 49, a famous People's Liberation Army singer, or their daughter... There is no indication Xi intervened to advance his relatives' business transactions, or of any wrongdoing by Xi.
> *(Forsythe 2012/6/29)*

The reporters wrote that, "While the investments are obscured from public view by multiple holding companies, government restrictions on access to company documents, and in some cases online censorship, they are identified in thousands of pages of regulatory filings." They also claimed the extended family (not Xi's immediate family) owned US$55.6 million in Hong Kong real estate. His elder sister Qi Qiaoqiao (a.k.a. Chai Lin-hing), her husband, her daughter, and a brother-in-law were mostly responsible. Their relationship is not just to Xi Jinping, but also to his father the revolutionary general Xi Zhongxun (1913–2002). Many other old leaders' family trees became bases for economic trust relationships that were very profitable.

"Princeling" sons and daughters form social groups, often riven between reformers and conservatives. Sometimes they dine with each other at fancy hotels. A Chinese magazine editor rephrased Mao: "Right now, revolution is precisely a dinner party." These post-revolutionary elites recognize their shared status but do not all agree with each other (Wines 2012/7/17). As Pareto explained long ago, any elite such as the CCP has functional reasons to circulate, balancing its need for adaptive reform with its need to know who in each locality is legitimate to sit at a decision table (Pareto 1901/1979; or Shirk 1993: 116–28). Corruption in China will be reduced when elite reformers trump elite conservatives not just at the top of the polity, but in many smaller political units.

This analysis has attempted new approaches to the study of corruption, which can be summarized as "partial heresies" like the ones posited near the end of the earlier subsection about political mechanisms. First, corruption and quick economic growth have a complex relationship. In many countries, as in China today, high corruption and quick growth have been concurrent. Both involve entrepreneurial willingness to take risks for which social trust is the collateral. But truly "foreign" involvements, e.g. by non-Chinese (or perhaps by puritanical Singaporeans), involves less "social capital" and militates against corruption at least in international commerce and investment, where many of the fastest-growing firms have been exporters. Corruption correlates with some sources of growth, and corruption hinders other sources of growth.

Second, corruption can best be defined as always involving two identifiable groups, one of which receives benefits that many people believe should have gone to the other. Corruption is inherently a subjective, perceived variable – not just because an attitude survey is usually the sole practical way to measure it. As Kuznets noted and Lewis explained, periods of quickest growth (as in China recently) tend to stratify income, creating rich groups that may be seen as corrupt if they are not also seen as virtuously led.

Third, perceived corruption changes over time in terms of the many sorts of uncleanness (usury, embezzlement, lax patriotism, religious heresy, dirty streets) that tend to vary together. Criminologists' "broken windows theory," which asserts that obvious minor vandalisms create conditions in which major infractions arise, applies to corruption as well as to neighborhoods.

Fourth, and relatedly, corruption by officials is by no means the only kind. Corruption by cadres of "the state" and many "local states" flourishes during blooms of corruption by unofficial citizens among themselves (and with cadres). Temporary campaigns against corruption are counter-effective. Permanent institutions to combat corruption should have powers to arrest any officials or non-officials on whom they have evidence about violations of impartial laws. They should be independent of all other governmental functions in their regions. Such an institution, the ICAC, already exists in Hong Kong. If it existed in other parts of China, Leninist mechanisms for choosing all state and nonstate leaders on the mainland would be threatened.

3 Conclusion: what to do about politics and corruption?

A key to cleaning politics is transparency, spreading information. An optimal (not maximal) amount of struggle between interests can achieve this goal. An ICAC on the mainland, more legitimacy for independent lawyers and reporters, well-monitored privatization of companies that remain accountable and transparent to large publics, and similar institutional reforms would regulate China's boom – and would be resisted by many Party conservatives.

Hu Jintao constantly repeated a mantra about stability (*wending*) as his main policy. Transparent information about power abuses and corruption can indeed threaten instability, which under some conditions can harm a regime (Huntington 1968). While the CCP in its present form would eventually suffer from further liberal reform and democracy, China would benefit. China is the most populous nation on earth, and it is in no danger of collapse, even though some of its leaders have an interest in speaking as if the apocalypse were coming. Conservatives may dominate the Politburo Standing Committee even as Xi has replaced Hu (Shi 2012/11/5). It is unclear they can solve China's many economic problems: the needs to promote consumption and imports, to obtain enough energy and water, to pay for clean-ups of pollution, to continue growth while the portion of the population in the work force declines, to reverse trend of income inequality, and to fight corruption.

Party diehards often beat gongs of paranoia, but long ago a reactionary Italian count advised his fellow conservatives:

> In a country in which the parties are strong and well-organized, there is a chance that, since each guards itself against the others ... scrutinizers who are morally sound and absolutely independent will be obtained; but it is clear that these guarantees would disappear were a single party so organized and constituted above the rest as never to need worry about them ... What do you want to keep, in a world which is being transformed and changed? Do you believe that only you will be allowed to remain immobile? Only you will be allowed to violate with impunity the eternal principles that support creation?
>
> *(Pareto 1872/1980: 16–17)*

CCP conservatives would serve both their and China's interests by heeding reformers in their midst, who see dangers in excessive control and fewer dangers in lively enterprise.

Bibliography

Ades, A. and Di Tella, R. (1996) 'Causes and Consequences of Corruption: A Review of Recent Empirical Contributions', in *Liberalization and New Corruption*, E. H. White and G. White (eds.), *Institute of Development Studies Bulletin*, 27(2): 6–11.

Anechiarico, F. and Jacobs, J. (1996) *The Pursuit of Absolute Integrity: How Corruption Control Makes Government Ineffective*, Chicago, IL: University of Chicago Press.

Barboza, D. (2012/10/25) 'Billions in hidden riches for family of Chinese leader', <http://www.nytimes. com/2012/10/26/business/global/family-of-wen-jiabao-holds-a-hidden-fortune-in-china.html?ref= world&pagewanted=all>. All <http://…> notes in this chapter bibliography were accessible on 2012/11/13 by entering article titles in Google from a US computer – but this 2012/10/25 note was reported non-accessible from China.

Barboza, D. (2012/9/24) 'Foxconn factory in China is closed after worker riot', <http://www.nytimes. com/2012/0/technology/foxconn-factory-in-china-is-closed-after-worker-riot.html>.

Bendix, R. (1960) *Max Weber: An Intellectual Portrait*, New York: Doubleday.

Bloomberg (2012/11/4) 'China's war against the informal economy or the shadow banks', <http://pru-dentinvestornewsletters.blogspot.hk/2012/04/China's-war-against-the-informal-economy-or.html>.

Burnham, J. (1944) *The Managerial Revolution*, London: Putnam.

Chan, A. (1996) 'Boot camp at the shoe factory', *Washington Post*, 1996/11/3: C1.

Chan, A. (2005) 'Recent Trends in Chinese Labour Issues', *China Perspectives*, 57: 23–31.

Chen, G. and Chen, L. (2012/26/3) 'Deng Xiaoping's Former Advisor Says Beijing Should not Fear Change but Embrace it, and Warns Rampant Corruption is Holding the Country Back', *South China Morning Post*.

Chow, G. C. (2006) 'Corruption and China's Economic Reform in the Early 21st Century', *International Journal of Business*, 11(3): 265–82.

Chow, G. C. (2007) *China's Economic Transformation*, 2nd edition, Oxford: Blackwell.

Chow, J. and Loten, A. (2012/11/5) 'More Wealthy Chinese Said to Prepare Exits', *Wall Street Journal*.

Chua, Y. T. (1999) *Robbed: An Investigation of Corruption in Philippine Education*, Quezon City: Philippine Center for Investigative Journalism.

Coronel, S. S. (ed.) (2000) *Betrayals of the Public Trust: Investigative Reports on Corruption*, Quezon City: Philippine Center for Investigative Journalism.

Dahl, R. (1961) *Who Governs: Democracy and Power in an American City*, New Haven, CT: Yale University Press.

Dawson, S. (2012/10/25) 'Dirty money cost China $3.8 trillion 2000–2011', <http://www.reuters.com/ article/2012/10/25/us-china-dirtymoney-idUSBRE89O1RW20121025>.

deBary, W. T. (1960) *Sources of Chinese Tradition*, vol. 1, New York: Columbia University Press.

Dikötter, F. (2010) *Mao's Great Famine*, London: Bloomsbury and Walker.

Ding, X. (2000) 'The Illicit Asset Stripping in Chinese Firms', *China Journal*, 43 (January): 1–28.

Dorfman, R., Samuelson, P. A., and Solow, R. (1958) *Linear Programming and Economic Analysis*, New York: McGraw-Hill.

Economist blog (2012/10/20) 'China's Consumer-Led Growth', <http://www.economist.com/blogs/ freeexchange/2012/10/rebalancing-China?fsrc=rss>.

Elliott, E. (1971) now Elsie Tu, *The Avarice, Bureaucracy and Corruption of Hong Kong, Vol. 1* (vol. 2 was just threatened, not intended), Hong Kong: Friends Commercial.

Fan, G. (2010/8/30) 'Is Low-Wage China Disappearing?', <http://www.project-syndicate.org/commen-tary/is-low-wage-china-disappearing>.

Fei, X. with Luo, Y. (1988) *Xiangzhen jingji bijiao moshi* (Comparative Models of Village and Town Economy), Chongqing: Chongqing Chuban She.

Florintino-Hofileña, C. (1998) *News for Sale: The Corruption of the Philippine Media*, Quezon City: Philippine Center for Investigative Journalism and Center for Media Freedom and Responsibility.

Foreign Broadcast Information Service (1986/11/26): 3.

Forsythe, M. (2012/6/29) 'Xi Jinping millionaire relations reveal fortunes of elite', <http://www.bloom-berg.com/news/2012-06-29/xi-jinping-millionaire-relations-reveal-fortunes-of-elite.html>.

FT reporters (2012/7/10) 'The Family Fortunes of Beijing's New Few', *Financial Times*.

Gainsbury, S. (2012/6/27) 'Bo Family Bought Luxury London Flats', *Financial Times*.

Gallagher, M. E. (2005) *Contagious Capitalism: Globalization and the Politics of Labor in China*, Princeton, NJ: Princeton University Press.

Gerring, J. and Thacker, S. C. (2005) 'Do Neoliberal Policies Deter Political Corruption?', *International Organization*, 59 (winter): 233–54.

Gong, T. (1994) *The Politics of Corruption in Contemporary China: An Analysis of Policy Outcomes*, New York: Praeger.

Guardian anon. (2012/10/5) <http://www.guardian.co.uk/news/datablog/interaactive/2012/oct/05>.

Han, D. (2011) 'China's main union is yet to earn its job: strikes and riots are now pushing China's official trade union into properly defending workers' rights', <www.guardian.co.uk/news/2011/jun/26>.

Higgins, A. (2012/24/4) 'In China Relatives of Party Officials Build Lucrative Businesses on Family Contacts', *Washington Post*.

Hirschman, A. (1973) 'Changing Tolerance for Income Inequality in the Course of Economic Development', *World Development*, 1(12): 24–36.

Hu, H. (1989) '1988 nian woguo zujin jiazhi de gusuan' (Estimation of Chinese Rent-Seeking in 1988), *Jingji shehui tizhi bijiao*, 5: 10–15.

Hu, S. (2012/10/11) 'Bo Xilai as a catalyst for political reform', <http://english.caixin.com/2012/10/11/100445969.html>.

Huadong xinxi bao (East China News) (1989/1/28).

Huang, C. (2012/4/24) 'State-run press issues rare call for political overhaul', <http://www.scmp.com/article/999066/state-run-press-issues-rare-call-political-overhaul>.

Huntington, S. P. (1970) 'Modernization and Corruption', in *Political Corruption: Readings in Comparative Analysis*, A. J. Heidenheimer (ed.), New York: Holt, 479–86.

Hutchcroft, P. D. (2000) 'Obstructive Corruption: The Politics of Privilege in the Philippines', in *Rents, Rent-seeking, and Economic Development: Theory and Evidence in Asia*, M. H. Kahn and K. S. Jomo (eds.), New York: Cambridge University Press, 207–47.

Jiefang ribao (Liberation Daily) (1988/5/15).

Johnson, I. (2012/9/27) 'China's lost decade', <http://www.nybooks.com/articles/archives/2012/sep/27/chinas-lost-decade>.

Johnson, I. (2012/9/30) 'Elite and Deft Xi aimed high early in China', <http://www.nytimes.com/2012/09/30/world/asia/aiming-for-top-Xi-Jinping-forged-ties-early-in-China.html>.

Johnson, S., Kaufman, D., and Zoido-Lobaton, P. (1998) 'Regulatory Discretion and the Unofficial Economy', *American Economic Review*, 88: 387–92.

Johnston, M. (1999) 'A Brief History of Anticorruption Agencies', in *The Self-Restraining State: Power and Accountability in New Democracies*, A. Schedler, L. Diamond, and M. F. Plattner (eds.), Boulder, CO: Lynne Rienner, 217–26.

Jones, C. I. (2002) *Introduction to Economic Growth*, New York: Norton.

Kim, K. H. (2007) *The Age of Visions and Arguments: Parliamentarianism and the National Public Sphere in Early Meiji Japan*, Cambridge, MA: Harvard University Press.

Klitgaard, R. (1988) *Controlling Corruption*, Berkeley, CA: University of California Press.

Kochhar, G. (2012/1/23) 'Land acquisition in China: Wukan protests', *IIT Madras China Studies* <http://www.csciitm.ac.in/sites/default/files/home_featured/geeta10.pdf>.

Kojima, R. (1978) *Chûgoku no toshika to nôson kensetsu* (Chinese Urbanization and Rural Construction), Tokyo: Ryûkei Shosha.

Kraus, W. (1991) *Private Business in China: Revival between Ideology and Pragmatism*, trans. E. Holz, Honolulu: University of Hawai'i Press.

Krugman, P. (2012) 'An issue whose time has passed', <http://krugman.blogs.nytimes.com/2012/10/22/an-issue-whose-time-has-passed>.

Kwong, J. (1997) *The Political Economy of Corruption in China*, Armonk, NY: M.E. Sharpe.

Lambsdorff, J. G. (1998) 'Corruption in Comparative Perception [sic]', in *Economics of Corruption*, A. K. Jain (ed.), Boston, MA: Kluwer, 80–93.

Lambsdorff, J. G. (2004) 'How Corruption Affects Economic Development', in Transparency International, *Global Corruption Report 2004*, London: Pluto.

Landry, P. (2008) *Decentralized Authoritarianism in China: The Communist Party's Control of Local Elites in the Post-Mao Era*, New York: Cambridge University Press.

Lau, M. (2012/6/27) 'Zhongshan Township Sealed off After Riot', *South China Morning Post*.

Lau, M. (2012/5/1) 'Base Reforms on Wukan Way, Party Boss Says', *South China Morning Post*: 21.

Lee, P. N. S. (1990) 'Bureaucratic Corruption during the Deng Xiaoping Era', *Corruption and Reform*, 5: 29–47.

Lewis, W. A. (1954) 'Economic Development with Unlimited Supplies of Labour', *Manchester School of Economic and Social Studies*, 22: 139–91.

Leys, C. (1965) 'What is the Problem about Corruption?', *Journal of Modern African Studies*, 3: 215–30.

Li, C. (2012/11/4) 'The Trial of Bo Xilai and What It Means for the Rule of Law in China', <http://www.eastasiaforum.org/2012/11/04>.

Li, E. X. (2012/26/4) 'Most of China's Communist Party princelings aren't like Bo Xilai', <http://www.csmonitor.com>.

Li, R. (2012/10/18) 'Top mainland press official Jiao Li dismissed amid corruption claims: former close aide to propaganda chief may also face discipline in rumoured link to sex scandals', *South China Morning Post*, <http://www.scmp.com/news/china/article/1063495>.

Liu, A. P. L. (1983) 'The Politics of Corruption in the People's Republic of China', *American Political Science Review*, 77 (September): 602–23.

Lü, X. (2000) 'Booty Socialism, Bureau-preneurs, and the State in Transition: Organizational Corruption in China', *Comparative Politics*, 32(3): 273–95.

Lü, X. (2002) *Cadres and Corruption: The Organizational Involution of the Chinese Communist Party*, Stanford, CA: Stanford University Press.

Machiavelli, N. (1532/1952) *The Prince*, New York: Mentor Classic.

Manion, M. (2004) *Corruption by Design: Building Clean Government in Hong Kong and Mainland China*, Cambridge, MA: Harvard University Press.

Moran, J. (2001) 'Democratic Transitions and Forms of Corruption', *Crime, Law, and Social Change*, 36(4) (December): 379–93.

Mulvenon, James and Ragland, Leigh Ann (2012) 'Liu Yuan: Archetype of a "Xi Jinping Man" in the PLA', *China Leadership Monitor*, 36.

Naughton, B. (1991) 'Industrial Policy During the Cultural Revolution', in *New Perspectives on the Cultural Revolution*, W. Joseph and C. Wong (eds.), Cambridge, MA: Harvard University Press, 153–81.

Nelson, B. (1953) *The Idea of Usury: From Tribal Brotherhood to Universal Otherhood*, No. 3, 'History of Ideas' Series, Princeton, NJ: Princeton University Press.

Nongmin Ribao (Farmer's Daily) (1988/9/8).

Nye, J. S. (1967) 'Corruption and Political Development: A Cost–Benefit Analysis', *American Political Science Review*, 61(2): 417–27.

Opper, S. (2005) 'Inefficient Property Rights and Corruption: The Case of Accounting Fraud in China', in *The New Institutional Economics of Corruption*, J. G. Lambsdorff, M. Taube, and M. Schramm (eds.), London: Routledge.

Osnos, E. (2012/22/10) 'Boss Rail: The Disaster that Exposed the Underside of the Boom', *New Yorker*. 44–53.

Ostergaard, C. and Petersen, C. (1991) 'Official Profiteering and the Tiananmen Square Demonstrations in China', *Corruption and Reform*, 6(2): 87–107.

Pasuk, P. and Sungsidh, P. (1996) *Corruption and Democracy in Thailand*, Chang Mai, Thailand: Silkworm Books.

Pareto, V. (1872/1980) *The Other Pareto*, P. and G. Bucolo (trans. and eds.), New York: St. Martin's Press.

Pareto, V. (1901/1979) *The Rise and Fall of the Elites: An Application of Theoretical Sociology*, New York: Arno Press.

Pei, M. (2006) *China's Trapped Transition*, Cambridge, MA: Harvard University Press.

Perkins, D. (1977) with eleven co-authors, *Rural Small-Scale Industry in the People's Republic of China*, Berkeley, CA: University of California Press.

Pew Research (2012) 'Growing concerns in China about inequality, corruption', <http://www.pewglobal.org/2012/10/16/growing-concerns-in-China-about-inequality-corruption>.

Philippine Centre for Investigative Journalism and Institute for Popular Democracy (1998) *Pork and Other Perks: Corruption and Governance in the Philippines*, Pasig City: Philippine Center for Investigative Journalism.

Phongpaichit, P. and Piriyarangsan, S. (1997) *Corruption and Democracy in Thailand*, Chang Mai, Thailand: Silkworm.

Polanyi, K. (1944/1957) *The Great Transformation: The Political and Economic Origins of our Time*, New York: Beacon.

Rabinovitch, S. (2012/1/25) 'China's Officials Forced to Sell Luxury Cars', *Financial Times*.

Renmin Ribao (People's Daily) (1987/6/13).

Renmin Ribao (People's Daily) (1981/5/4).

Reuters (2012/9/22) 'Wukan's democracy bid faltering; no hope: the village shot to fame last year when locals rebelled against land grab, but one year on, many still don't have their land and warned of another uprising', <http://www.taipeitimes.com/news/world/archives/2012/09/22/2003543401>.

Richburg, K. B. (2012/6/15) 'Risks Over Bo Xilai Case Could Prompt China to Seek Low-profile Resolution', *Washington Post*; also www.washingtonpost.com.

Rocca, J. L. (1992) 'Corruption and Its Shadow: An Anthropological View of Corruption in China', *China Quarterly*, 130 (June): 402–16.

Rose-Ackerman, S. (1999) *Corruption in Government: Causes, Consequences, and Reform*, Cambridge: Cambridge University Press.

Sands, B. N. (1990) 'Decentralizing and Economy: The Role of Bureaucratic Corruption in China's Economic Reforms', *Public Choice*, 65(1): 85–91.

Schumpeter, J. A. (1911/1934) *The Theory of Economic Development*, New York: Oxford University Press.

Schumpeter, J. A. (1942) *Capitalism, Socialism, and Democracy*, New York: Harper.

Schurmann, F. (1966) *Ideology and Organization in Communist China*, Berkeley, CA: University of California Press.

SCMP/Reuters (2012/9/30) 'Drop in factory activity puts pressure on China growth: HSBC PMI Shows', <http://www.scmp.com/news/china/article/1050448>.

SCMP Staff (2012/23/4) 'Probe into Bo family's HK links', <http://www.scmp.com/article/998980/probe-bo-familys-hk-links>.

Scott, J. C. (1969) 'Corruption, Machine Politics, and Political Development', *American Political Science Review*, 63(4) (December): 1142–58.

Scott, J. C. (1972) *Comparative Political Corruption*, Englewood Cliffs, NJ: Prentice-Hall.

Shanghai jingji nianjian (Shanghai Statistical Yearbook) (1988) Xiao Jun *et al.* (eds.), Shanghai: Shanghai Renmin Chuban She.

Shi, J. (2012/11/5) 'Conservatives dominate the latest line-up for new Communist Party leadership', <http://www.scmp.com/news/china/article/1074459>.

Shieh, G. S. (1992) *"Boss" Island: The Subcontracting Network and Micro-entrepreneurship in Taiwan's Development*, New York: P. Lang.

Shirk, S. L. (1993) *The Political Logic of Economic Reform in China*, Berkeley, CA: University of California Press.

So, C. (2012/9/28) 'Boom city Dongguan faces bankruptcy as village debts soar', <http://www.scmp.com/news/china/article/1048977/boom-city-dongguan-faces-bankruptcy>.

Sun, Y. (2004) *Corruption and Market in Contemporary China since Economic Reform*, Ithaca, NY: Cornell University Press.

Tam, F. (2012/7/27) 'Provincial Authorities Evict from their Offices Groups that Advocate for the Rights of Migrant Workers, Despite Pledge to Ease Registration Requirements', *South China Morning Post*.

Tanzi, V. and Daavodi, H. R. (1997) 'Corruption, Public Investment, and Growth', IMF Working Paper WP/97/139.

Transparency International (2005) *Global Corruption Report 2005*, London: Pluto.

Treisman, D. (2000) 'The Causes of Corruption: A Cross-National Study', *Journal of Public Economics*, 76 (June): 399–457.

Tsai, K. (2002) *Back-Alley Banking: Private Entrepreneurs in China*, Ithaca, NY: Cornell University Press.

Twitter (2012/10/25) <http://twitter.yfrog.com/z/ocoipuyj>.

Varese, F. (1997) 'Transition to the Market and Corruption in Post-socialist Russia', *Political Studies*, 45(3): 579–96.

Walecki, M. (2006) 'Political Corruption: Democracy's Hidden Disease', *Democracy at Large*, 2(4): 16–19.

Wang, S., Li, X., and Yang, S. (1992) *Zhongguo gaige daquan* (Encyclopedia of China's Reforms), Dalian: Dalian Renmin Chubanshe.

Wantchinatimes (2012/10/03) Taipei, 'Corruption is PLA's greatest enemy: academic' <http://www.wantchinatimes.com/news-subclass/cnt.aspx?id=20121003000073&cid=1101>.

Weber, M. (1919/1962) 'Politics as a Vocation', in *From Max Weber: Essays in Sociology*, H. Gerth and C. W. Mills (eds.), New York: Galaxy, 77–128.

White, L. (1988) 'Changing Concepts of Corruption in Communist China: Early 1950s vs. Early 1980s', in *Changes and Continuities in Chinese Communism*, Yu-ming Shaw (ed.), Boulder, CO: Westview Press, 316–53.

White, L. (2004) 'Future Fortunes vs. Present People in China's Richest Cities', in *Social Policy Reform in Hong Kong and Shanghai: A Tale of Two Cities*, L. Wong, L. White, and S. Gui (eds.), Armonk, NY: M.E. Sharpe, 239–56.

Wines, M. (2012/7/17) 'As China Talks of Change, Fear Rises on the Risks', *New York Times*.

Wines, M. and LaFraniere, S. (2011/7/29) 'Baring facts of train crash, blogs erode China's censorship', <http://www.nytimes.com/2011/07/29/world/china/29html?>.

Wissenburg, M. (2009) *Political Pluralism and the State: Beyond Sovereignty*, Abingdon, UK: Routledge.

World Bank (2012) 'Worldwide governance indicators', <http://info.worldbank.org/governance/wgi/index.asp>.

Wu J. (1990) "Guomin jingji de kunjing he chulu" (Difficulties and Solutions in the Civil Economy) *Jingji shehui tizhi bijiao* (Comparative Economic and Social Systems), 6.

Wu, S. (1991) *Dangdai Zhongguo de nongye jixie hua* (Agricultural Mechanization in Contemporary China), Beijing: Zhongguo Shehui Kexue Yuan.

Xie, Z. (1991) *Shanghai shi nongye jixie hua fazhan zhanlue yanjiu* (Studies on Strategy for Developing Agricultural Mechanization in Shanghai Municipality), Shanghai: Shanghai Kexue Puji Chuban She.

Xu, J. (1993/5/6) 'Xu Jiatun's Reminiscences', *Shijie ribao* (World Daily).

Yang, D. L. (2005) *Remaking the Chinese Leviathan: Market Transition and the Politics of Governance in China*, Stanford, CA: Stanford University Press.

Yang, J. (2012) *The Great Chinese Famine, 1958–1962*, New York: Farrar Straus Giroux.

Yao, S. (2002) 'Privilege and Corruption: The Problem of China's Socialist Market Economy', *American Journal of Economics and Sociology*, 61(1) (January): 279–99.

YouTube (2012/10/25) <http://www.youtube.com/watch?v=kbtMjJQ-b9E&feature=player_embedded>.

Yu, J. and Li, R. (2012) 'Reform Practice and Policy Proposals of the Rural and Urban Household Registration Systems', <http://chinaelectionsblog.net/?p=18400>, from *Strategy and Management*, 1(2).

Yu Jianrong and Li Renqing (2012) 'Practice and Policy Recommendation for Reform of the Huji System' (in Chinese), *Strategy and Management*, 1(2).

Zhai, K. (2012/11/8) 'Corruption crackdown as Party tells of "profound lessons" of Bo Xilai Scandal', <http://www.scmp.com/news/china/article/107770>.

Zhang, C. (1975) *On Exercising All-Round Dictatorship over the Bourgeoisie*, Peking: Foreign Languages Press.

Zhou, K. X. (1996) *How the Farmers Changed China: Power of the People*, Boulder, CO: Westview Press.

18

ENERGY AND ENVIRONMENTAL ISSUES AND POLICY IN CHINA

ZhongXiang Zhang

China's rampant environmental pollution problems and rising greenhouse gas emissions and the resulting climate change are undermining its long-term economic growth. China, from its own perspective cannot afford to and, from an international perspective, is not meant to continue on the conventional path of encouraging economic growth at the expense of the environment. Instead, concerns about a range of environmental stresses from burning fossil fuels, energy security as a result of steeply rising oil imports and international pressure on it to exhibiting greater ambition in fighting global climate change have sparked China's determination to improve energy efficiency and cut pollutants, and to increase the use of clean energy in order to help its transition to a low-carbon economy. This chapter focuses on China's efforts toward energy conservation, nuclear power and the use of renewable energy. The chapter examines a number of market-based instruments, economic and industrial policies and measures targeted for energy saving, pollution cutting, energy greening. To actually achieve the desired outcomes, however, requires strict implementation and coordination of these policies and measures. The chapter discusses a variety of implementation/compliance/reliability issues. The chapter ends with some concluding remarks and recommendations.

Introduction

Since launching its open-door policy and economic reforms in late 1978, China has experienced spectacular economic growth, and hundreds of millions of the Chinese people have been raised out of poverty. In this course, China has been heavily dependent on dirty-burning coal to fuel its rapidly growing economy. Moreover, until recently, China had valued economic growth above environmental protection. A combination of these factors has given rise to unprecedented environmental pollution and health risks across the country (World Bank, 2007; CAEP, 2013).

As a result, until 2009 urban air quality across the country still did not meet the air quality standards for more than one-third of a year (MEP, 2010a, 2010b), and one-third of China's land is affected by acid rain. The deterioration of the environment has led to frequent pollution disputes across the country. In 2009, serious environmental risks resulted in one sudden environmental incident every other day (MEP, 2010c). Together with corruption, income inequalities and soaring house prices, the environment is considered to be one of the leading causes of social unrest within the Chinese society.

The rising environmental degradation associated with China's rapid economic growth has led to significant economic costs. Existing estimates for such costs vary, depending on the comprehensiveness of the assessments. China's first official estimate for the economic costs of environmental pollution in 2004 put the figure at US$64 billion, or 3.05 percent of gross domestic product (GDP) (SEPA and NBS, 2006). This cost estimate was raised to about US$250 billion in 2010, or 3.5 percent of GDP (CAEP, 2013). This is a very conservative estimate; other estimates put the figure much higher. The World Bank (2007), for example, has estimated that the total cost of air and water pollution in China is about 5.8 percent of GDP.

While being confronted with rampant conventional environmental pollution problems, China became the world's largest carbon emitter in 2007 (IEA, 2007). The number one position put China in the spotlight, just at the time when the world's community started negotiating a post-Kyoto climate regime under the Bali roadmap. There were renewed interests and debates on China's role in combating global climate change. Given the fact that China's emissions are projected to rise rapidly in line with its industrialization and urbanization on the one hand, and the fact that China overtook Japan as the world's second largest economy on the other hand, China is seen to have greater capacity, capability and responsibility for taking on climate commitments. Clearly, China's rampant environmental pollution problems, rising greenhouse gas emissions and the resulting climate change are undermining its long-term economic growth. China, from its own perspective cannot afford to and, from an international perspective, is not meant to continue on the conventional path of encouraging economic growth at the expense of the environment. Instead, concerns about a range of environmental stresses and energy security, as a result of steeply rising oil imports, have sparked China's determination to green its economy.

To that end, China has incorporated for the first time in its five-year economic plan an input indicator as a constraint – requiring that energy use per unit of GDP be cut by 20 percent during the 11th five-year period running from 2006 to 2010. This Five-Year Plan also incorporated the goal of reducing SO_2 emissions and chemical oxygen demand (COD) discharge by 10 percent by 2010, relative to their 2005 levels. Just prior to the Copenhagen Climate Change Summit, China further pledged to cut its carbon intensity by 40–45 percent by 2020 relative to its 2005 levels, and reaffirmed its plan to have alternative energy sources to meet 15 percent of the nation's energy requirements by 2020.

This chapter focuses on China's efforts toward energy conservation, nuclear power and the use of renewable energy. The chapter examines a number of economic policies and measures targeted for energy saving and pollution cutting. To actually achieve the desired outcomes, however, requires strict implementation and coordination of these policies and measures. This chapter discusses a variety of implementation/compliance/reliability issues and concludes with remarks and recommendations.

1 China's efforts toward energy conservation

Given the inevitable trend that China's energy demand continues to rise over the next two decades and beyond, the key issue is how China can drive its future energy use and carbon emissions below the projected baseline levels to the extent possible. In this regard, improving energy efficiency is considered the cheapest, fastest and most effective way to keep energy growth under control and address environmental concerns. Indeed, China has taken considerable efforts to control the growth of its demand for energy.

Given that industry accounts for about 70 percent of the country's total energy consumption (Zhang, 2003), this sector is crucial for China to meet its own set goal. So the Chinese government has taken great efforts toward changing the current energy-inefficient and environmentally unfriendly pattern of industrial growth. To that end, China is exploring industrial policies to encourage technical progress, strengthen pollution control, and to promote industrial upgrading and energy conservation. On the specific energy-saving front, China established the "Top 1000 Enterprises Energy Conservation Action Program" in April 2006. This program covered 1,008 enterprises in nine key energy supply and consuming industrial subsectors. These enterprises each consumed at least 0.18 million tons of coal equivalent (tce) in 2004, and all together consumed 47 percent of industrial energy consumption in 2004. The program aims to save 100 million tce cumulatively during the period 2006–10 (NDRC, 2006). While there are areas that need further improvements, this program has gone very much as planned as far as the energy-saving goal is concerned. In September 2011, NDRC reported that the Top-1,000 Program had estimated achieving total energy savings of 150 million tce during the 11th Five-Year Plan period (NDRC, 2011c).

To help to meet the goals of energy-saving and carbon intensity reduction for the 12th Five-Year Plan, NDRC and eleven other central government organizations in December 2011 announced the expansion of the Top-1,000 Program to the 10,000 Program. This enlarged program covered about 17,000 enterprises. These enterprises include those industrial and transportation enterprises consuming energy of 0.10 million tce or more and other entities consuming energy of 0.05 million tce in 2010. Altogether these enterprises consumed at least 60 percent of the national total in 2010. The program aims to save 250 million tce cumulatively during the period 2011–15 (NDRC, 2012).

For power generation, coal-fired power plants dominate total electricity generation in China, accounting for about 75 percent of total capacity and more than 80 percent of total power generation. China's total installed capacity of coal-fired power plants is more than the current total of the US, the United Kingdom and India combined. As the largest coal consumer, power and heat generation is consuming over half of the total coal use. This share is expected to rise to well above 60 percent in 2020, given the rapid development of coal-fired power generation. Thus, efficient coal combustion and power generation is of paramount importance to China's endeavor of energy-saving and pollution-cutting. To that end, China has adopted the policy of accelerating the closure of thousands of small, inefficient coal-fired and oil-fired power plants. The total combined capacity that needs to be decommissioned is set at 50 gigawatts (GW) during the period 2006–10.

In addition to mandatory closures at many small power plants, NDRC instituted a series of incentives for small, less-efficient power plants to shut down. Feed-in tariffs for small plants were lowered, power companies were given the option to build new capacity to replace retired capacity, and plants designated for closure were given electricity generation quotas which could be used to continue operation for a limited time or sold to larger plants (Williams and Kahrl, 2008; Schreifels *et al.*, 2012). These incentive-based policies helped the government surpass the goal of closing 50 GW of small thermal power plants. By the end of the first half year of 2009, the total capacity of decommissioned smaller and older units amounted to 54 GW, having met the 2010 target one and half years ahead of schedule (Wang and Ye, 2009). By the end of 2010, the total capacity of decommissioned smaller and older units had increased to 76.8 GW (*China News Net*, 2011), almost ten times the total capacity decommissioned during the period 2001–05.

The Chinese government's policy has concurrently focused on encouraging the construction of larger, more efficient and cleaner units. By the end of 2010, 72.7 percent of fossil fuel-fired units comprised units with the capacities of 300 MW and more, relative to 42.7 percent in 2000 (Zhu, 2010; CEC, 2011). The combined effect of shutting down small, less-efficient power plants and building larger, more efficient plants led the average coal consumed per unit of electricity generated to decline by 12.8 percent by 2012 relative to its 2005 levels (CEC, 2011; CEC and EDF, 2012).

Due to higher thermal efficiency and relatively low unit investment costs, China's power industry has listed supercritical (SC) power generation technology as a key development focus. To date, this generation technology is the only advanced, well established and commercialized clean power generation technology in the world. As a result, an increasing number of newly built plants are more efficient supercritical or ultra-supercritical (USC) plants. With cost comparative advantages over other cleaner coal technologies, such as integrated gasification combined cycle and polygeneration technologies, SC and USC technologies will be developed and deployed in China.

With China dependent on coal to meet the bulk of its energy needs over the next decades, the commercialization and widespread deployment of carbon capture and storage technology is a crucial option for reducing both China's and global CO_2 emissions when meeting the country's energy needs. As a critical first step, IEA (2009b) recommends twenty large-scale CCS demonstration projects by 2020. This is of strategic importance to establishing CCS as a viable major carbon mitigation option. To that end, cooperation among countries will reduce both the costs and risks of CCS research and demonstration projects. To take advantage of the high level of manufacturing and low costs of manufacturing, labor and other factors in China, the US, the EU – Japan, and other key players should cooperate with China to build more joint demonstration CCS projects in China, based on their currently proven technologies, to achieve economies of scale enough to bring down the cost. In the meantime, these countries should initiate a major new initiative to jointly develop more advanced and innovative CCS technologies with shared intellectual property rights. Until CCS projects are developed to the point of achieving economies of scale and bringing down the costs, China will not feel confident about committing to absolute greenhouse gas emissions caps. Given current trends, it is unlikely that this technology will find large-scale application either in China or elsewhere before 2030. This is one of the six reasons why expecting China to cap its greenhouse gas emissions well before 2030 is unlikely (Zhang, 2011b, 2011c).

For residential buildings, China has tightened building efficiency standards over time. In 1986, the Chinese government issued the energy-saving design standard for heating in new residential buildings, requiring a 30 percent cut in energy use relative to typical Chinese residential buildings designed in 1980–81. This standard was revised in December 1995, requiring that new buildings be 50 percent more efficient by 2010 and 65 percent by 2020 (Zhang, 2008). In recent years, China has been enforcing the energy efficiency design standard more strictly, requiring that in the very cold area all buildings be renewed in large and middle cities before 2001, in small cities before 2003 and nationwide from 2006 onwards, complying with the energy efficiency standard of 50 percent (MOHURD, 2002, 2005). In northern and coastal developed areas, and in large cities, all the newly built buildings should meet the requirements of 65 percent of the local building energy efficiency standard (MOHURD, 2005).

In the transport sector, the excise tax for vehicles has been adjusted over time to incentivize the purchases of energy-efficient cars. The excise tax levied at the time of purchase was first introduced in 1994 when China reformed its taxing system, and the rate increases with the size of engines, set at 3 percent for cars with engines of 1.0 liter or less, 8 percent for cars with engines of more than 4 liters, and 5 percent for cars with engines in between. To further rein in the production and use of gas-guzzling cars and promote the production and use of energy-efficient small cars, from September 1, 2008, the rate for small cars with engines of

1.0 liter or less further decreased to 1 percent, whereas the rate for cars with engines of no less than 3 liters but no larger than 4 liters was set at 25 percent. Cars with engines of larger than 4 liters were taxed at the highest rate of 40 percent (Zhang, 2010a). China has set even more stringent fuel economy standards for its rapidly growing passenger vehicle fleet than those in Australia, Canada, the US, and the more stringent standards of the state of California, although they are less stringent than those in Japan and the EU. In the meantime, expanding Chinese cities are prioritizing public transport and are promoting efficient public transport systems (Zhang, 2010).

2 Nuclear power

The expansion of nuclear power is inevitable in China to cope with its daunting energy security and environmental challenges. China has established a very ambitious plan for the development of nuclear power, and leads the world in the construction of nuclear power plants (CEC, 2011; Li, 2011; World Nuclear Association, 2011). The Fukushima accident will have no effect on China's stance on nuclear power, but will slightly affect the pace of its development. The likely target of 60–70 GW by 2020, instead of the more ambitious one of 86 GW planned prior to the Fukushima Daiichi nuclear power plant accident, still sets a pace that is unprecedented elsewhere. This, combined with great need for standardization of design, operational safety, and ease of maintenance, suggests that China should give careful consideration to the suitability of a foreign nuclear power technology for use in the country and avoid importing multiple examples of similar foreign nuclear technologies as it is currently doing. That will enhance China's ability to assimilate any particular nuclear technology, reduce the high cost, and see it through to widespread deployment. This is the lesson that China should learn from importing coal gasification technologies from abroad. Chinese companies have imported more than twenty variants of such technologies. This has impaired China's ability to assimilate any particular technology (IEA, 2009a).

Moreover, given that nuclear power capacity is expected to increase significantly, securing the supply of uranium resources is seen as crucial for achieving its upward revised nuclear goal. China needs to enhance cooperation with uranium-rich countries and establish its strategic reserves for uranium resources. Processing and storing nuclear wastes will become an issue as well. Thus, China also requires making parallel progress in the area of processing and storing nuclear waste to match the significantly scaled-up development of nuclear power.

Furthermore, the Fukushima accident has raised safety concerns to an unprecedented level. No doubt, more advanced reactor designs and improved operation standards help to reduce the likelihood of risks for serious accidents. However, as the nuclear power construction program scales up, the probability of something going wrong increases. As illustrated in the radioactive leak, which occurred at the Daya Bay plant on May 23, 2010, an increased transparency and better communication to the public is of paramount importance for China to ensure the safe development of nuclear power. In a national business culture where quality and safety sometimes take a back seat, China particularly needs to keep a close eye on nuclear safeguards to ensure construction quality and operation safety of nuclear power plants. This will have a bearing on public acceptance. The public's acceptance exacerbates the already serious concerns about reactor safety, radioactive waste management and disposal, and the potential proliferation of nuclear weapons, as well as the locating of related fuel cycle facilities in the US, Japan, and the EU, even prior to the Fukushima accident. While such concerns and opposition are not publicly expressed in China, this situation may change in the future as the development of nuclear power accelerates there.

3 The use of renewable energy

China has targeted alternative energy sources to meet 15 percent of its energy requirements by 2020. The Chinese government has also identified the development of the renewable energy industry as one of the seven strategic emerging industries.

On the specific front, China launched the so-called "Golden Sun" program to boost the solar sector. Through this program, the Chinese government will subsidize 50 percent of investment costs for more than 500 MW of solar power capacity up to 2011, with a maximum subsidy rate of 70 percent for independent solar power projects in remote areas. After years of simply taking advantage of overseas orders to drive down the cost of manufacturing solar panels, NDRC (2011a) enacted feed-in tariffs for solar power in July 2011 to form its own solar power market. As a result, project developers can sell electricity generated from solar power to utilities at the tariffs of 1 renminbi per kilo-hour from August 1, 2011. With this first nationwide feed-in tariffs scheme for solar power, the government plans to have 50 GW of solar power by 2020 from 3 GW in 2011 (Guo, 2012; State Council, 2012). To be more effective and to work to the full potential, the feed-in tariffs should be differentiated across regions according to the quality of solar energy resources and the conditions of engineering construction. With the economically exploitable hydropower potential estimated at 400 GW, the largest in the world, China has sped up the development of hydropower in recent years, planning to have the total capacity installed of 300 GW (including 75 GW small hydropower) in 2020. This target amounts to three-quarters of its economically exploitable potential. If the target is fulfilled, the economically exploitable potential of hydropower with favorable exploitation conditions will be fully developed by 2020 in China. Even so, China is still several percentage points away from its commitment to have alternative energy sources to meet 15 percent of its energy requirements by 2020. (See Figure 18.1.)

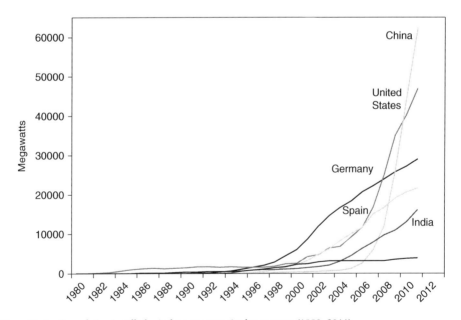

Figure 18.1 Cumulative installed wind power capacity by country (1980–2011)

Sources: Based on data from Global Wind Energy Council (2010 and 2012) and Earth Policy Institute (2008)

To fill this gap, China aims to increase its total installed capacity of wind power to 200 GW by 2020 (State Council, 2012), almost seven times the 30 GW target as set as late as September 2007. Along with this, NDRC enacted feed-in tariffs for wind power, which took effect on August 1, 2009. According to the quality of wind energy resources and the conditions of engineering construction, four wind energy areas are classified throughout China, and on-grid tariffs are set accordingly as benchmarks for wind power projects across the nation, respectively (NDRC, 2009a). By letting investors know the expected rate of return on their projects through announcing on-grid tariffs upfront, the Chinese government aims to encourage the development of wind energy resources of good quality, thus supporting the development of wind power in proper order, furthermore promoting the healthy development of the whole wind industry in China. Moreover, given the significantly scaled-up wind power capacity planned for 2020, China should now place more emphasis on companies ensuring the actual flow of power to the grid rather than just meeting capacity. In this regard, improving the quality of increasingly used, domestically made turbines is seen as crucial for this endeavor (Zhang, 2010a, 2011b). While being less costly, domestic wind turbines in China break down more often, even collapse in the worst cases (China Environment News, 2010) and have overall capacity factors of several percentage points lower than foreign models. These few percentage points' difference might not seem significant, but could well make a difference between a wind farm that is economically viable and one that is not.

4 Economic policies and engagement of the private sector

Having the right economic policies is crucial because it sends clear signals to these energy consumers, helping polluting enterprises to be held accountable for their environmental behavior as well as their profits and costs. Given the widespread use of fossil fuel subsidies in the developing Asian region, removing these subsidies is essential to provide incentives for efficient fuel use and the adoption of clean technologies that reduce emissions at sources. By definition, a subsidy lowers the cost of production, increases the price received by producers or lowers the price paid by consumers. By lowering the prices of fossil fuels, such fossil fuel subsidies not only are widely considered to distort international trade, but also increase the amount of such fuels consumed and moreover the amount of harmful emissions (Zhang and Assunção, 2004). China, Indonesia, and Malaysia are among the developing Asian countries that have since 2005 raised domestic energy prices to bring them more into line with international prices. This has led to a sharp fall in overall energy subsidies in these countries despite rising international prices. For example, China cut its total energy subsidies to around US$11 billion in 2006. This corresponds to a reduction of 58 percent compared to its 2005 level of around US$26 billion (IEA, 2006, 2007). China has since raised its producer prices of gasoline and diesel several times. On June 1, 2010, China increased the domestic producer price of natural gas by 25 percent (Wan, 2010). Since July 1, 2012 China has implemented tier-tariffs for household electricity use. The levels of such tier-tariffs are differentiated across provinces, and are set significantly higher for non-basic electricity use. Despite these long-awaited actions, removing such subsidies is but a first step in getting the energy prices right. Further steps to be taken include incorporating the costs of resources themselves to reflect their scarcity and internalizing the costs of externalities.

4.1 Market-based instruments

Market-based instruments, such as pollution charges, green taxes, traceable permits, and penalties for the infringement of environmental regulations, are common ways to internalize externality costs into the market prices. With one-third of China's territory widely reported to be affected by acid rain, China has since 1996 started levying the charges for SO_2 emissions in the so-called Two Control Zones based on the total quantity of emissions and at the rate of 0.20 renminbi per kilo of pollution equivalent (Yu, 2006). Since July 1, 2003, this charge was applied nationwide and the level of this charge was raised step by step. From July 1, 2005 onwards, the charge was applied at the level of 0.60 renminbi per kilo of pollution equivalent. The pollutants that are subject to pollution charges are broadened to include NO_x as well, which is charged at the rate of 0.60 renminbi per kilo of pollution equivalent since July 1, 2004 (SDPC *et al.*, 2003). To help to meet the energy saving and environmental control goals set for the 11th five-year economic plan, the Chinese government planned three steps to double the charges for SO_2 emissions from the existing level to 1.2 renminbi per kilo of pollutant equivalent within the next three years (State Council, 2007). Local governments are allowed to raise pollution charges above the national levels. Jiangsu province raised charges for SO_2 emissions from the existing level of 0.6 to 1.2 renminbi per kilo of pollution equivalent from July 1, 2007 onwards, three years ahead of the national schedule (Sina Net, 2007). China's Ministry of Finance, the State Administration of Taxation and the MEP have proposed levying environmental taxes to replace current charges for SO_2 emissions and COD. This proposal is subject to the approval of the State Council. While their exact implementation date has not been set yet, it is generally expected to be introduced during the 12th Five-Year Plan period. As experienced in environmental taxes in other countries (Zhang and Baranzini, 2004), such taxes will initially be levied with low rates and limited scope, but their levels will increase over time. Once implemented, the long-awaited environmental taxes will have far-reaching effects on technology upgrading, industrial restructuring, and sustainable development in China.

To shut down inefficient and highly polluting plants, NDRC ordered provincial governments to implement the differentiated tariffs that charge more for companies classified as "eliminated types" or "restrained types" in eight energy-guzzling industries from October 1, 2006 onwards. While provinces like Shanxi charged even higher differentiated tariffs than the levels required by the central government (Zhang *et al.*, 2011), some provinces and regions have been offering preferential power tariffs to struggling, local energy-intensive industries. The reason for this repeated violation is the lack of incentive for local governments to implement this policy, because all the revenue collected from these additional charges went to the central government. To provide incentives for local governments, this revenue should be assigned to local governments in the first place, but the central government requires local governments to use the revenue specifically for industrial upgrading, energy saving, and emissions cutting (Zhang, 2007b, 2010). In recognition of this flaw, the policy was adjusted in 2007 to allow local provincial authorities to retain revenue collected through the differentiated tariffs (Zhou *et al.*, 2010).

To avoid wasteful extraction and use of resources while alleviating the financial burden of local governments, China needs to reform its current coverage of resource taxation and to significantly increase the levied level.

In 1984, China started levying resource taxes for coal and oil. While the prices of coal and oil have since significantly increased, the levels of their resource taxes have remained unchanged over the past twenty-five years (Zhang, 2011b). As a result, the resource taxes raised amounted to only 33.8 billion renminbi, accounting for about 0.57 percent of China's total tax revenues and about 17.5 percent of the national government expenditure for environmental protection in 2009 (NBS, 2010). Therefore, to avoid wasteful extraction and use of resources while alleviating the financial burden of local governments, the way of levying taxes on resources in China should be changed. Such taxation should be levied based on revenues. In addition, current resource taxes are only levied on seven types of resources including coal, oil, and natural gas. This coverage is too narrow, falling far short of the purposes of both preserving resources and protecting the environment. Thus, overhauling resource taxes also includes broadening their coverage so that more resources will be subject to resource taxation.

The Chinese central government started a pilot reform on resource taxation in Xinjiang after June 1, 2010. It is estimated that the new resource tax levied at a rate of 5 percent will generate additional annual revenues of 4–5 billion renminbi for Xinjiang (Dai, 2010). This is a significant increase, in comparison with the total resource tax revenues of 1.23 billion renminbi in 2009, inclusive of those from resources other than crude oil and natural gas (NBS, 2010). This will contribute 17–21 percent of the total tax revenues for Xinjiang, in comparison with the contribution level of about 4.1 percent in 2009.

China has been experimenting with SO_2 emissions trading in Hubei, Hunan, Jiangsu, Zhejiang provinces, and Tianjin metropolitan city. Zhejiang province has implemented provincial wide trial SO_2 emissions quotas that can be purchased and traded since 2009. It as well as Jiangsu is experimenting with trading COD permits in Taihu Basin. In its Jinxing city, 890 enterprises were reported to participate in the paid use and trade of pollution quotas by mid-November 2009, representing rising trends of both volumes and prices of quotas transacted (CAEP, 2009). Even in Shanxi province, China's coal and power base, power-generating plants sold SO_2 emissions quotas to the State Grid. The traceable permits scheme thus entered the essentially operational stage in the province after years of preparation. China is experimenting with low-carbon provinces and low-carbon cities in five provinces and eight cities. Aligned with such an experiment, pilot carbon trading schemes are expected to be established in 2013. Based on these piloted schemes, China aims to establish a national carbon trading scheme by 2016.

However, these economic instruments do not work to their full potential, because the charges and fines are often set too low. The average charge for urban sewage treatment was reported to be 0.7 renminbi per ton for 36 large and medium cities in China by the end of 2008, whereas the corresponding treatment cost is 1.1 renminbi per ton (NDRC, 2009b; CAEP, 2009). Even for the aforementioned case of Jiangsu province, where the charges for SO_2 emissions at 1.2 renminbi per kilo of pollution equivalent were levied from July 1, 2007 onwards, three years ahead of China's national schedule, this charge was still less than half of the real abatement cost, which was reported to be 3 renminbi per kilo of pollution equivalent for abating SO_2 emissions from coal-fired power plants (Sina Net, 2007). As a result, many polluting companies see their compliance costs higher than the fines, and accordingly choose to pay the fines rather than to reduce their pollution. To change this situation, pollution charges should be raised to reflect the cost of abating pollution, and the fines for offenders should be set higher than the abatement cost.

4.2 Supportive economic policies

The central government is also providing supportive economic policies to encourage technical progress and strengthen pollution control to meet the energy-saving and environmental control goals. To support the Ten Energy-Saving Projects, China's Ministry of Finance and the NDRC (2007) award 200 renminbi to enterprises in East China and they award 250 renminbi to enterprises in the Central and Western part of the country for every tce saved per year since August 2007. Such payments are made to enterprises that have energy metering and measuring systems in place that can document proved energy savings of at least 10,000 tce from energy-saving technical transformation projects. China is also introducing energy management companies (EMCs) to promote energy saving. China had only three EMCs in 1998 (*China News Net*, 2008). This number increased to over 80 by 2005 and further increased to over 800 in 2010

(NDRC, 2011b). NDRC and the Ministry of Finance of China award 240 renminbi to EMCs for every tce saved, with another compensation of no fewer than 60 renminbi for every tce saved from local governments (State Council, 2010). As a result of an increasing number of EMCs and the resulting awards, the total annual energy saving by EMCs increased to 13 million tce in 2010 from 0.6 million tce in 2005 (NDRC, 2011b).

With burning coal contributing 90 percent of the national total SO_2 emissions and coal-fired power generation accounting for half of the national total, the Chinese central government has mandated that new coal-fired units must be synchronously equipped with a flue gas desulphurization (FGD) facility and that plants built after 1997 must have begun to be retrofitted with a FGD facility before 2010. Furthermore, policies favorable to FGD-equipped power plants are being implemented, e.g. on-grid tariff incorporating desulphurization cost, priority being given to connect to grids, and permission for longer operation time than those plants that do not install desulphurization capacity. Some provincial governments provide even more favorable policies, leading to priority dispatching of power from units with FGD in Shandong and Shanxi provinces. Moreover, the capital cost of FGD has fallen from 800 renminbi/kilowatt in the 1990s to the level of about 200 renminbi/kilowatt (Yu, 2006), thus making it less costly to install FGD facility. As a result, newly installed desulphurization capacity in 2006 was greater than the combined total over the previous ten years, accounting for 30 percent of the total installed thermal (mostly coal-fired) capacity. By 2011, the coal-fired units installed with FGD increased to 630 GW from 53 GW in 2005. Accordingly, the portion of coal-fired units with FGD rose to 90 percent in 2011 of the total installed thermal capacity from 13.5 percent in 2005 (Sina Net, 2009; CEC and EDF, 2012). As a result, by the end of 2009, China had reduced its SO_2 emissions by 13.14 percent relative to its 2005 levels (Xinhua Net, 2010), having met the 2010 target of a 10 percent cut one year ahead of schedule.

4.3 Industrial policies

In addition to supportive economic policies and market-based environmental instruments, governments are exploring industrial policies to promote industrial upgrading and energy conservation. With the surge in energy use in heavy industry, China's Ministry of Finance and the State Administration of Taxation started levying export taxes from November 2006 on a variety of energy and resource intensive products to discourage export of those products that rely heavily on energy and resources. From July 1, 2007, China's Ministry of Finance and the State Administration of Taxation (2007) eliminated or cut export tax rebates for 2,831 exported items. This is considered as the boldest move to rein in exports since China joined the World Trade Organization. Among the affected items, which account for 37 percent of all traded products, are 553 "highly energy-consuming, highly-polluting and resource-intensive products," such as cement, fertilizer, and non-ferrous metals, whose export tax rebates were completely eliminated. From the point of view of leveling the carbon cost playing field, such export taxes increase the price at which energy-intensive products made in China, such as steel and aluminum, are traded in world markets. For the EU and US producers, such export taxes imposed by their major trading partner on these products take out at least part, if not all, of the competitive pressure that is at the heart of the carbon leakage debates. Being converted into the implicit carbon costs, the estimated levels of CO_2 price embedded in the Chinese export taxes on steel and aluminum are very much in the same range as the average price of the EU allowances over the same period. Zhang (2009, 2010) has argued that there is a clear need within a climate regime to define comparable efforts toward climate change mitigation and adaptation to discipline the use of unilateral trade measures at the international level. As exemplified by export tariffs that China applied on its own during 2006–08, defining the comparability of climate efforts can be to China's advantage (Zhang, 2010).

China's Ministry of Commerce and the SEPA (2007) in October 2007 were in an unusual collaboration to jointly issue the antipollution circular. Targeted at its booming export industry, this new regulation would suspend the rights of those enterprises that do not meet their environmental obligations to engage in foreign trade for a period of more than one year and fewer than three years. A significant portion of China's air pollution can be traced directly to the production of goods that are exported. In the city of Shenzhen alone, the regional leader in industrial development and trade in the Pearl River delta, Streets *et al.* (2006) found that 75 percent of VOCs, 71 percent of PM, 91 percent of NO_x, and 89 percent of SO_2 emissions from the industrial sector were released through the manufacture of exported goods.

4.4 *Environmental performance ratings and disclosure*

The central government is also exploring other ways to enhance the efficacy of environmental monitoring and compliance. Naming and shaming polluters is one vehicle. In April 2010, China's MEP for the first time unveiled offending polluters and blacklisted state-owned enterprises. Out of 7,043 major polluting enterprises under the national environmental monitoring system, about 40 percent were found to have discharged substandard waste water or exhaust emissions in 2009. The offending polluters included the state-owned China Power Investment Corp., China Huaneng Group, and China Guodian Corp., the three major national power-generating groups. This fact will help change the general public's perception that it is the small, private enterprises that are the country's main sources of pollution. The listing of some sewage treatment plants was another remarkable sign in the report as 47 percent of 1,587 monitored waste water facilities were found guilty of substandard discharges (Deng, 2010).

Governments can go beyond simply naming and shaming polluters by implementing environmental performance ratings and disclosure (PRD). The PRD relies on non-regulatory forces to create incentives for (mainly industrial) facilities to improve environmental performance. Such programs will motivate polluters to reduce emissions, even in developing countries where regulatory infrastructures are insufficiently developed, subject to corruption, or even absent but where enough information can be reliably obtained to provide credible performance ratings (World Bank, 2000; Dasgupta *et al.*, 2006). Modeled on Indonesia's successful Program for Pollution Control, Evaluation and Rating (PROPER), China introduced the Green Watch program in Zhengjiang, a relatively well-off city in Jiangsu province in June 1999, and Hohhot city, Inner Mongolia. This program developed color-coded systems to rate corporate environmental performance. The first Green Watch ratings were disclosed through the media in 1999. The program was extended from Zhenjiang city to all of Jiangsu province in 2001, and to eight other provinces in China during 2003–05. Nationwide implementation of the Green Watch program has been promoted since 2005. The companies under the Green Watch programs have dramatically changed their corporate environmental behavior. The Green Watch program in Jiangsu province indicates both increasing participation by firms and improvement in their compliance rates, with the number of rated firms increasing more than tenfold, from 1,059 in 2001 to 11,215 in 2006; and the percentage of firms with positive ratings (green, blue, and yellow) increasing from 83 percent in 2001 to 90 percent in 2006. Moreover, the Jiangsu case suggests that Green Watch ratings have stronger effects on firms with red ratings (moderate noncompliance) than those with black ratings (extreme noncompliance) (Legislative Affairs Office of the State Council, 2007; Jin *et al.*, 2010).

4.5 Cooperation with financial institutions

The support of financial institutions is another avenue through which to promote improved corporate environmental performance. From April 1, 2007, China's SEPA has worked with the People's Bank of China on a new credit-evaluation system under which companies' environmental compliance records are incorporated into the bank's credit-evaluation system. This information will serve as a reference for commercial banks' consideration of whether or not to provide loans. The bank could turn down requests for loans from firms with poor environmental records (Zhang, 2007a). In mid-July 2007, SEPA announced the "green credit" policy jointly with the People's Bank of China and the China Banking Regulation Commission. They will work together to enforce it, with the financial bodies denying loans to firms that SEPA identifies as failing to meet environmental standards. SEPA later posted on its website and notified China's central bank and top banking regulatory commission of thirty offending companies that would be barred from receiving credits (Xinhua Net, 2007). Some bank branches go further. Jiangyin Branch of the People's Bank of China in Jiangsu province issued the color-coded lending guidance, favoring those companies with superior environmental performance. For those green-rated companies, banks will enhance their lending scale and give priority to their financial needs. By contrast, the lending scale for those red-rated ones at best remains at its current level unless lending is requested for environment-improving equipment and technical transformation. Particularly strict lending conditions are attached to those black-rated companies. They cannot receive any new borrowing, and if they still fail to comply with the environmental regulations within a given period, banks will cut their borrowing and in the worst cases can even ask them to return all their previous loans (Legislative Affairs Office of the State Council, 2007). Clearly, this concerted action by the central bank and SEPA is expected not only to reduce the risks borne by commercial banks, but also to encourage companies to think more about the environmental effect of their operation and self-discipline their environmental behavior. Aided by the International Finance Corporation, the finance arm of the World Bank Group, China is experimenting with the green credit policy in the steel industry in Sichuan province (CAEP, 2009). In August 2007, SEPA (2007) also clearly stipulated that highly polluting enterprises are subject to auditing of their environmental records in case these enterprises want to list shares in the Chinese stock markets or get refinanced. China Securities Regulation Commission will incorporate information on their environmental auditing into its decision on whether or not to allow these enterprises to be listed or get refinanced. Moreover, investors in capital markets can be an important ally, reacting to the disclosure of environmental performance related to the companies that they invest in. The Shanghai Stock Exchange has disclosed environmental information since late 2009, in line with the rules of the exchange to disclose corporate information (Ban, 2008). The reports from companies like PetroChina and Sinopec for example are still incomplete, because they have just released discharge data, but have not mentioned their records of violations and the subsequent penalties (Chung, 2010). With the so-called H-shares from companies incorporated in Mainland China traded on the Hong Kong Exchanges and Clearing, the Hong Kong exchange could amend its listing rules to require all those listed companies to disclose environmental information.

5 Implementation/compliance/reliability

5.1 Implementation/compliance holds the key

To actually achieve the desired outcomes, however, requires strict implementation and coordination of these policies and measures. It has been stipulated that leaders of local governments and heads of key state-owned enterprises are held accountable for energy saving and pollution cutting in their regions, and that achieving the goals of energy efficiency improvements and pollution reductions has become a key component of their job performance evaluations. But no senior officials have ever been reported for failing to take responsibility for meeting the energy-saving and pollution-cutting targets to date, not to mention having been asked to step down from their positions on these grounds.

Another example is the enforcement of FGD operation to ensure that those generation units with FGD facility always use it. The government offered a 0.015 renminbi per kilowatt-hour premium for electricity generated by power plants with FGD facility installed to encourage the installation and operation of FGD facility at large coal-fired power plants. The premium was equivalent to the average estimated cost of operating the technology. However, this price premium was provided for FGD-equipped power plants regardless of FGD performance. This created an incentive for power plants to install low-cost, poor-quality FGDs in order to obtain the price premium, but not to operate the FGD (Schreifels *et al.*, 2012). When NDRC conducted field inspections in July 2006, it found that "up to 40 percent of those generation units with FGD facility did not use it" (Liu, 2006). Given that FGD costs are estimated to account for about 10 percent of the power generation cost, combined with lack of trained staff in operating and maintaining the installed FGD facility, notwithstanding the lack of government enforcement, this should not come as a surprise, unless there is adequate enforcement. Even if the installed FGD facilities were running, they do not run continuously and reliably. MEP field inspections in early 2007 found that less than 40 percent of the installed FGD were running continuously and reliably (Xu *et al.*, 2009). With the portion of coal-fired generation capacity with FGD increasing, the government desulphurization policy should thus switch from mandating the installation of FGD to focusing on enforcing units with FGD to operate through on-line monitoring and control.

Clearly, implementation holds the key. This will be a decisive factor in determining the prospects for whether China will clean up its development act. There are encouraging signs that the Chinese government is taking steps in this direction: for example, given that the said price premium for FGD-equipped power plants was based on the installation of FGD facility, not its operation or performance. When requiring continuous emission monitoring systems (CEMS) at coal-fired power plants in May 2007, NDRC and MEP modified the price premium to address FGD performance, basing the electricity price premium on FGD operation and performance. The revised policy continued to provide a price premium of 0.015 renminbi per kilowatt-hour for power plants operating FGDs, but a penalty of 0.015 renminbi per kilowatt-hour is imposed for plants operating FGDs between 80 percent and 90 percent of total generation, and a penalty of 0.075 renminbi per kilowatt-hour for plants operating FGDs less than 80 percent of the time. Regardless of the duration of FGD operation, all plants were ordered to return the compensation for their desulphurization costs in proportion to the time when their FGD facilities were not in operation (NDRC and MEP, 2007; Xu, 2011). In its 2008 assessment of the total volume reduction of major pollutants, MEP found that FGD facilities of five coal-fired power plants were either in improper operation or their on-line monitoring and control data were false. These plants were ordered to return the compensation for their desulphurization costs in proportion to the time when their FGD facilities were not in operation and to make necessary adjustments in the specified period (K. Zhang, 2009).

The efficacy of basing policies on performance not process, suggests that the accuracy of SO_2 data is critical. Nowadays emission reports are verified by the central government. Prior to that, they were undertaken by the local environmental protection bureaus (EPBs), as MEP and NDRC mandated the installation of CEMS and the transfer of real-time data to EPBs in May 2007.

This had led to nationwide underreporting of emission levels. While in the 11th Five-Year Plan, MEP and EPBs collected SO_2 data from CEMS at most power plants, data quality concerns limited the use of the data (Zhang *et al.*, 2011). To ensure the reliability of emissions data, MEP instituted an inspection program for provinces, fuel suppliers, and major emitters. Based on the analyses of MEP inspectors, MEP rejected 30–50 percent of SO_2 reductions claimed by some provinces. This inspection system raised the level of accountability for plant owners and operators, but MEP's investment in the inspections in terms of both staff and financial resources was large. Staff at regional supervision centers spent up to 60 percent of their time conducting these inspections (Schreifels *et al.*, 2012).

5.2 Reliability issues

Take China's commitments to cut its carbon intensity by 40–45 percent by 2020 relative to its 2005 level as a case in point. China is not known for the reliability of its statistics (e.g., Rawski, 2001). As long as China's pledges are in the form of carbon intensity, the reliability of both emissions and GDP data matters.

Assuming the fixed CO_2 emissions coefficients that convert consumption of fossil fuels into CO_2 emissions, the reliability of emissions data depends very much on energy consumption data. Unlike the energy data in the industrial product tables in the *China Statistical Yearbook*, the statistics on primary energy production and consumption are usually revised in the year after their first appearance. The adjustments made to production statistics are far smaller than those made to consumption statistics, because it is easier to collect information on the relatively small number of energy producers than on the large number of energy consumers. Figures 18.2 and 18.3 show the preliminary and final values for total primary energy consumption and coal consumption in China between 1990 and 2008, measured in million tons of coal equivalent (Mtce). Until 1996 revisions of total energy use figures were several times smaller than in the late 1990s

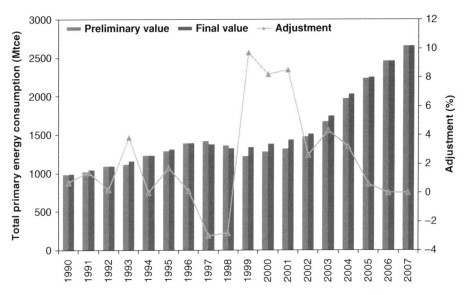

Figure 18.2 Preliminary and final values for total primary energy consumption in China (1990–2008)

Source: Based on *China Statistical Yearbook* (various years)

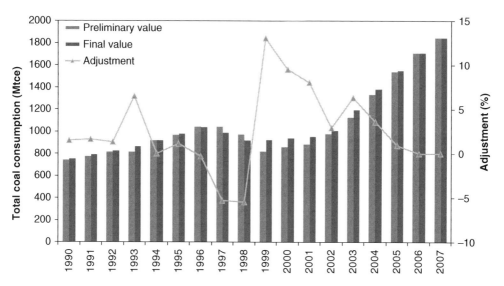

Figure 18.3 Preliminary and final values for coal consumption in China (1990–2008)

Source: Based on *China Statistical Yearbook* (various years)

and early 2000s. The preliminary figures for total energy use in 1999–2001 were revised upwards by 8–10 percent (shown in the right y-axis in Figure 18.2). In all three years, these adjustments were driven by upward revisions of 8–13 percent made to the coal consumption figures (shown in the right y-axis in Figure 18.3) to reflect the unreported coal production mainly from small, inefficient and highly polluting coal mines. These coal mines were ordered to shut down through a widely publicized nationwide campaign beginning in 1998, although many had reopened because in many cases local governments had pushed back to preserve local jobs and generate tax revenues as well as personal payoffs. In recent years, preliminary figures for energy use are close to the final reported ones.

Similarly, China first releases its preliminary GDP figures and then revises them. These revised GDP figures for the years 2005–08 are further verified based on the second agricultural census released in February 2008 and the second nationwide economic census released in December 2009. With upward revisions of both GDP and the share of services, there is a big variation between the preliminary value for China's energy intensity and the final reported one. As shown in Table 18.1, such revisions lead to a differential between preliminary and final values as large as 123 percent for the energy intensity in 2006. With the government's continuing efforts to improve the quality of China's statistics, there is a downward trend of such a differential as a result of the revisions.

From the preceding discussion, it follows that GDP figures are even more crucial to the impacts on the energy or carbon intensity than are energy consumption and emissions data. As long as China's commitments are in the form of carbon intensity, establishing a robust and transparent emissions and performance accounting framework is helpful, but not enough to remove international concern about the reliability of China's commitments. The aforementioned revisions of China's GDP figures reflect part of the government's continuing efforts to improve the accuracy and reliability of China's statistics on economic activity. Such revisions have huge implications for meeting China's energy-saving goal in 2010 and its proposed carbon intensity target in 2020.

Table 18.1 Reduction in China's energy intensity: preliminary value versus final value

Year	Preliminary value (%)	Revised value (%)	Re-revised value (%)	Final value (%)	Differential between preliminary and final values (%)
2006	1.23 (March 2007)	1.33 (12 July 2007)	1.79 (14 July 2008)	2.74 (15 July 2010)	*122.8*
2007	3.27 (March 2008)	3.66 (14 July 2008)	4.04 (30 June 2009)	5.04 (15 July 2010)	*54.1*
2008	4.59 (30 June 2009)	5.20 (25 Dec. 2009)		5.20 (15 July 2010)	*13.3*
2009	3.98 (March 2010)	3.23 (15 July 2010)	3.61 (15 July 2010)		

Source: Zhang (2011a)
Note: The dates when the corresponding data were released are in parentheses

6 Concluding remarks

China has gradually recognized that the conventional path of encouraging economic growth at the expense of the environment cannot be sustained. It has to be changed. To that end, China has strengthened existing policies and measures toward energy saving, pollution cutting, and the use of clean energy. This will aim: first, to address concerns about a range of environmental stresses and health risks from burning fossil fuels and steeply rising oil imports; second, to honor its carbon intensity pledge in 2020; and, third, to drive its future energy use and carbon emissions below the projected baseline levels to the extent possible.

In this course, the country has faced great difficulty ensuring that local governments act in accordance with centrally directed policies, since the past three decades of economic reforms have witnessed a shift in the control over resources and decision making to local governments. This not only has led China to miss its energy-saving goal in 2010, but also has huge implications for meeting its proposed carbon intensity target in 2020 and whatever climate commitments beyond 2020 that China may make. Clearly, the central government needs to set appropriate incentives to get local governments' cooperation.

One way to ensure that local officials are held accountable for energy saving and pollution cutting in their regions is developing criteria that incorporate energy conservation and environmental performance into the overall evaluation of local officials' performances and applying those criteria consistently to ensure energy saving and pollution cutting are carried out in a rational way and to avoid last-minute shutdown operations of factories across the country for meeting the energy-saving goals. Alleviating the financial burden of local governments is another avenue through which to incentivize them not to focus on economic growth alone. The central government really needs to cultivate steady and sizeable sources of revenues for local governments. Enacting property taxes or real estate taxes for local governments is urgently needed. Broadening the current coverage of resource taxation and significantly increasing the levied level also helps to increase local governments' revenues while conserving resources and preserving the environment. The resource tax levied on crude oil and natural gas by revenues rather than by existing extracted volume, which was applied nationwide since November 1, 2011, is the first step in the right direction. However, the current coverage of resource taxes is too narrow, falling far short of the purposes of both preserving resources and protecting the environment. Thus, overhauling resource taxes includes broadening their coverage so that more resources will be subject to resource taxation.

Moreover, China mostly relied on administrative means to achieve its energy-saving goal for 2010. The country has had limited success in meeting that goal, and continues to face rising energy demand and increasing difficulty in further cutting energy and carbon intensities. It is becoming increasingly crucial for China to harness market forces to reduce its energy consumption and cut carbon and other conventional pollutants. To that end, China is experimenting with low-carbon provinces and low-carbon cities, aiming to establish a national carbon trading scheme by 2016. However, in terms of timing, given that China has not levied environmental taxes yet, it is better to introduce environmental taxes first, not least because such a distinction will enable China to disentangle additional efforts toward carbon abatement from those broad energy-saving and pollution-cutting ones.

Also China needs to significantly scale up its efforts toward strengthening industrial restructuring to keep the frenzied expansion of highly energy-consuming, highly polluting, and resource-intensive industries under control, and further transform the industrial structure and the development model toward a more energy-efficient, serviced-oriented economic structure. The decline in real energy intensity was the overwhelming contributor to the decline in China's industrial energy use over the past three decades and is expected to continue to play a major role, but structural change will become a crucial factor to determine whether China will meet its future energy-saving and carbon intensity goals (Zhang, 2003, 2011b).

The Chinese government has also identified the development of the renewable energy industry as one of the seven strategic emerging industries. Now China aims to increase its total installed capacity of wind power to 200 GW by 2020. However, wind turbines often have to wait a few months before they are hooked up to the power grid. Therefore, China needs to significantly improve its power grids and to coordinate the development of wind power with the planning and construction of power grids, including smart grids. New transmission lines will have to be constructed simultaneously as more wind power farms are built.

The expansion of nuclear power is inevitable in China to cope with its daunting energy security and environmental challenges. The Fukushima accident will have no effect on China's stance on nuclear power. However, China should give careful consideration to the suitability of using a foreign nuclear power technology and avoid importing multiple examples of foreign nuclear technology. Moreover, securing the supply of uranium resources is seen as crucial for achieving its upward revised nuclear goal. China also requires making parallel progress in the area of processing and storing nuclear waste to match the significantly scaled-up development of nuclear power. Furthermore, China particularly needs to keep a close eye on nuclear safeguards to ensure construction quality and operation safety of nuclear power plants.

Given continuous coal dominance in China's energy and power generation mix over the next two decades and beyond, China has adopted the policy of accelerating the closure of small, inefficient coal-fired and oil-fired power plants. Currently, China is set to decommission small, inefficient coal-fired power plants with a unit capacity of 50 MW or less. To benefit energy saving and the environment, China should consider doubling or even quadrupling that unit capacity to 100 MW or 200 MW below which inefficient coal-fired plants need to be decommissioned. The Chinese government's policy has concurrently focused on encouraging the construction of larger, more efficient and cleaner units. In the meantime, the country needs to accelerate the construction of large, more efficient, supercritical or ultra-supercritical coal-fired units. With China dependent on coal to meet the bulk of its energy needs over the next decades, the commercialization and widespread deployment of carbon capture and storage technology is a crucial option for reducing both China's and total global CO_2 emissions when meeting the country's energy needs. Until CCS projects are developed to the point of achieving economies of scale and bringing down the costs, China will not feel confident about committing to absolute greenhouse gas emissions caps. Given current trends, it is unlikely that this technology will find large-scale application either in China or elsewhere before 2030. This suggests that expecting China to cap its greenhouse gas emissions well before 2030 is unlikely.

Bibliography

Ban, J. (2008) 'Shanghai Stock Exchange requires listed companies to timely disclose environmental information, penalties being imposed on those violators', *China Environmental Daily*, May 16, available at: <http://www.csfee.org.cn/ReadNews.asp?NewsID=149>.

China Electricity Council (CEC) (2011) *Annual Development Report of China's Power Industry 2011*, Beijing.

China Electricity Council (CEC) and Environmental Defense Fund (EDF) (2012) *Studies on Pollution Cutting in China's Power Industry*, Beijing.

China Environment News (2010) 'National Energy Administration initiates a thorough investigation into the equipment quality reacting to frequent collapses of domestic wind turbines', Sina Net, December 6, available at: <http://finance.sina.com.cn/chanjing/cyxw/20101206/09319059835.shtml>.

China News Net (2008) 'The World Bank: a significant energy saving with the rapid development of China's energy management industry over the past decade', January 6, available at: <http://news.sohu.com/20080116/n254683016.shtml>.

China News Net (2011) 'China decommissioned 76.825 GW of smaller and older coal-fired units during the 11th five-year period', September 28, available at: <http://www.chinanews.com/ny/2011/09-28/3358876.shtml>.

Chinese Academy for Environmental Planning (CAEP) (2009) 'National research and pilot project on environmental economics and policy: 2009 report', Beijing, December 30.

Chinese Academy for Environmental Planning (CAEP) (2013) *China Green National Accounting Study Report 2010*, public version, Beijing.

Chung, O. (2010) 'China's listed polluters made public', *Asia Times*, April 17, available at: <http://www.atimes.com/atimes/China_Business/LD17Cb01.html>.

Dai, L. (2010) 'Oil and gas-producing areas in Xinjiang call for the adjustment for the distribution of resource tax revenues', *People Net*, November 29, available at: <http://finance.sina.com.cn/china/dfjj/20101129/07149023055.shtml>.

Deng, L. (2010) 'MEP unveiled offending polluters: Huaneng group and other state-owned enterprises blacklisted', *21st Century Business Herald*, April 3, available at: <http://finance.sina.com.cn/g/20100403/05257687753.shtml>.

Dasgupta, S., Wang, H., and Wheeler, D. (2006) 'Disclosure strategies for pollution control', in T. Tietenberg and H. Folmer (eds.), *The International Yearbook of Environmental and Resource Economics 2006/2007: A Survey of Current Issues*, Cheltenham, UK: Edward Elgar, pp. 93–119.

Earth Policy Institute (2008) 'Global wind power capacity reaches 100,000 Megawatts', Washington, DC, March 4.

Global Wind Energy Council (2010) *Global Wind 2009 Report*, Brussels, March.

Global Wind Energy Council (2012) *Global Wind Report: Annual Market Update 2011*, Brussels, March.

Guo, L. (2012) 'PV projects may be subject to national approval, the capacity in the first phase set at 3 GW', *China Securities Journal*, January 13, available at: <http://finance.chinanews.com/ny/2012/01-13/3603897.shtml>.

International Energy Agency (IEA) (2006) *World Energy Outlook 2006*, Paris: International Energy Agency.

International Energy Agency (IEA) (2007) *World Energy Outlook 2007*, Paris: International Energy Agency.

International Energy Agency (IEA) (2009a) *Cleaner Coal in China*, Paris: International Energy Agency.

International Energy Agency (IEA) (2009b) *Technology Roadmap: Carbon Capture and Storage*, Paris: International Energy Agency.

Jin, Y., Wang, H., and Wheeler, D. (2010) 'Environmental performance rating and disclosure: an empirical investigation of China's Green Watch program', Policy Research Working Paper 5420, Washington, DC: World Bank.

Legislative Affairs Office of the State Council of China (2007) 'Work report on pilot corporate environmental performance disclosure in Jiangsu province', June, available at: <http://www.chinalaw.gov.cn/article/dfxx/dffzxx/js/200706/20070600021431.shtml>.

Li, Y. Q. (2011) 'NDRC: China's overall target of nuclear power unchanged, but improvement of its plan expected after an assessment of safety', *Oriental Morning Post*, March 31, available at: <http://finance.eastmoney.com/news/1355,20110331127693240.html>.

Liu, S. X. (2006) 'Why did 40% of generation units with FGD facility not use it?', *China Youth Daily*, August 8, available at: <http://zqb.cyol.com/content/2006-08/08/content_1471561.htm>, accessed September 11, 2012.

Ministry of Environmental Protection of China (MEP) (2010a) '2009 evaluation report on cities' environmental quality', November 8, Beijing, available at: <http://www.gov.cn/gzdt/att/att/site1/20101105/001aa04b79580e3d8a6301.pdf>.

Ministry of Environmental Protection of China (MEP) (2010b) 'MEP released the 2009 evaluation results on cities' environmental quality', November 8, Beijing, available at: <http://www.mep.gov.cn/gkml/hbb/qt/201011/t20101108_197235.htm>.

Ministry of Environmental Protection of China (MEP) (2010c) '2009 environment in China', May 31, available at: <http://www.gov.cn/gzdt/2010-06/04/content_1620569_14.htm>.

Ministry of Finance of China and National Development and Reform Commission (NDRC) (2007) 'A circular on interim measures for fund management of financial incentives for energy-saving technical transformation', August 10, Beijing, available at: <http://www.mof.gov.cn/zhengwuxinxi/caizhengwengao/caizhengbuwengao2007/caizhengbuwengao200711/200805/t20080519_27902.html>.

Ministry of Housing and Urban–Rural Development of China (MOHURD) (2002) 'A circular on the 10th five-year outline of energy-saving plan for the building sector', June 20, Beijing, available at: <http://www.cin.gov.cn/zcfg/jswj/jskj/200611/t20061101_158478.htm>.

Ministry of Housing and Urban–Rural Development of China (MOHURD) (2005) 'A circular on requiring new residential buildings to comply with energy-saving design standard', April 15, Beijing, available at: <http://www.cin.gov.cn/zcfg/jswj/jskj/200611/t20061101_158471.htm>.

National Bureau of Statistics of China (NBS) (2010) *China Statistical Yearbook 2010*, Beijing: China Statistics Press.

National Development and Reform Commission (NDRC) (2006) 'The top 1000 enterprises energy conservation action program', April 7, Beijing, available at: <http://hzs.ndrc.gov.cn/newzwxx/t20060414_66220.htm>.

National Development and Reform Commission (NDRC) (2009a) 'A circular on improving on grid feed-in tariffs for wind power', July 22, Beijing, available at: <http://www.fenglifadian.com/zhengce/512169872.html>.

National Development and Reform Commission (NDRC) (2009b) 'Updates on recent reform on energy and resource prices', August 3, Beijing, available at: <http://www.sdpc.gov.cn/xwfb/t20090803_294551.htm>.

National Development and Reform Commission (NDRC) (2011a) 'A circular on improving on grid feed-in tariffs for solar PV', July 24, Beijing, available at: <http://www.ndrc.gov.cn/zcfb/zcfbtz/2011tz/t20110801_426501.htm>.

National Development and Reform Commission (NDRC) (2011b) 'A rapid development of energy service industry: energy saving and pollution cutting during the 11th five-year period in retrospect', October 8, Beijing, available at: <http://zys.ndrc.gov.cn/xwfb/t20111008_437224.htm>.

National Development and Reform Commission (NDRC) (2011c) 'The thousand enterprises exceeded the energy-saving target during the 11th Five Year Plan period', available at: <http://zys.ndrc.gov.cn/xwfb/t20110314_399361.htm>, accessed October 28, 2012.

National Development and Reform Commission (NDRC) (2012) 'List and energy-saving targets of the ten thousand enterprises committed to energy-saving and low-carbon activities', May 12, Beijing, available at: <http://www.ndrc.gov.cn/zcfb/zcfbgg/2012gg/t20120521_480769.htm>, accessed November 26, 2012.

National Development and Reform Commission (NDRC) and Ministry of Environmental Protection (MEP) (2007) 'A circular on the interim administrative measures for price premium for coal-fired power plants equipped with FGD facility and FGD operation', Beijing, May 29, available at: <http://www.ndrc.gov.cn/zcfb/zcfbtz/2007tongzhi/t20070612_140883.htm>, accessed December 3, 2012.

National Development and Reform Commission (NDRC) and Eleven Other Central Government Organizations (2011) 'A circular on implementation option for the ten thousand enterprises committed to energy-saving and low-carbon activities', December 7, Beijing, available at: <http://www.ndrc.gov.cn/zcfb/zcfbtz/2011tz/t20111229_453569.htm>, accessed November 26, 2012.

Rawski, T. G. (2001) 'What is happening to China's GDP statistics?', *China Economic Review*, 12(4): 347–54.

Schreifels, J., Fu, Y., and Wilson, E. J. (2012) 'Sulfur dioxide control in China: policy evolution during the 10th and 11th Five-Year Plans and lessons for the future', *Energy Policy*, 48: 779–89.

Sina Net (2007) 'Jiangsu will double the charges for atmospheric pollutants from 1 July', June 11, available at: <http://news.sina.com.cn/c/2007-06-11/012711994856s.shtml>.

State Council (2010) 'A circular of the National Development and Reform Commission and other departments to speed up the implementation of energy management contract to promote the energy service industry', April 2, available at: <http://www.gov.cn/zwgk/2010–04/06/content_1573706.htm>.

State Council (2012) 'The national 12th Five-year development plan for strategic emerging industries', July 20, available at: <http://www.gov.cn/zwgk/2012-07/20/content_2187770.htm>.

State Development and Planning Commission (SDPC), Ministry of Finance, State Environmental Protection Agency and State Economic and Trade Commission (2003) 'Administrative measures on the levying levels of pollution charges', Beijing, February 28, available at: <http://www.sepa.gov.cn/epi-sepa/zcfg/w3/ling2003-31.htm>.

State Environmental Protection Agency of China (SEPA) and the National Bureau of Statistics (NBS) (2006) 'China green national accounting study report 2004', public version, Beijing.

State Environmental Protection Agency of China (SEPA) (2007) 'SEPA clearly stipulates highly polluting enterprises listed subject to auditing', Beijing, August 19, available at: <http://www.gov.cn/banshi/2007-08/20/content_721678.htm>.

Streets, D. G., Yu, C., Bergin, M. H., Wang, X., and Carmichael, G. R. (2006) 'Modeling study of air pollution due to the manufacture of export goods in China's Pearl River Delta', *Environmental Science and Technology*, 40(7): 2099–107.

Wan, X. (2010) 'Reform of natural gas price broke ground: a one-time 25% hike', *Daily Economic News*, June 1, available at: <http://finance.sina.com.cn/roll/20100601/03408034884.shtml>.

Wang, P. and Ye, Q. (2009) 'China about to release new energy development plan by the end of 2009', *Xinhua Net*, August 9, available at: <http://news.sina.com.cn/c/2009-08-09/140918397192.shtml>.

Williams, J. H. and Kahrl, F. (2008) 'Electricity reform and sustainable development in China', *Environmental Research Letters*, 3(4): 1–14.

World Bank (2000) *Greening Industry: New Roles for Communities, Markets, and Governments*, New York: Oxford University Press.

World Bank (2007) *Cost of Pollution in China: Economic Estimates of Physical Damages*, Washington, DC: World Bank.

World Nuclear Association (2011) 'Nuclear power in China', updated September 22, London, available at: <http://www.world-nuclear.org/info/inf63.html>.

Xinhua Net (2007) 'SEPA together with the People's Bank of China and the Banking Regulatory Commission restrict lending to highly energy-consuming and heavily polluting companies', July 30, available at: <http://news.xinhuanet.com/newscenter/2007-07/30/content_6451563.htm>.

Xu, Y. (2011) 'Improvements in the operation of SO_2 scrubbers in China's coal power plants', *Environmental Science & Technology*, 45(2): 380–5.

Xu, Y., Williams, R. H., and Socolow, R. H. (2009) 'China's rapid deployment of SO_2 scrubbers', *Energy & Environmental Science*, 2(5): 459–65.

Yu, Z. F. (2006) 'Development and application of clean coal technology in Mainland China', in Zhang, Z. X. and Bor, Y. (eds.), *Energy Economics and Policy in Mainland China and Taiwan*, Beijing: China Environmental Science Press, pp. 67–88.

Zhang, D., Aunan, K., Seip, H. M., and Vennemo, H. (2011) 'The energy intensity target in China's 11th Five-Year Plan period – Local implementation and achievements in Shanxi Province', *Energy Policy*, 39(7): 4115–24.

Zhang, K. (2009) 'Ministry of Environmental Protection penalizes 8 cities and 5 power plants based on the assessment of pollutant-cutting', *China Business News*, July 24, available at: <http://finance.sina.com.cn/roll/20090724/04006522664.shtml>.

Zhang, X. and Schreifels, J. (2011) 'Continuous emission monitoring systems at power plants in China: Improving SO_2 emission measurement', *Energy Policy*, 39(11): 7432–8.

Zhang, Z. X. (2003) 'Why did the energy intensity fall in China's industrial sector in the 1990s?: the relative importance of structural change and intensity change', *Energy Economics*, 25(6): 625–38.

Zhang, Z. X. (2007a) 'China's reds embrace green', *Far Eastern Economic Review*, 170(5): 33–7.

Zhang, Z. X. (2007b) 'Greening China: can Hu and Wen turn a test of their leadership into a legacy?', Plenary Address at the first-ever Harvard College China–India Development and Relations Symposium, March 30–April 2, New York City.

Zhang, Z. X. (2008) 'Asian energy and environmental policy: promoting growth while preserving the environment', *Energy Policy*, 36: 3905–24.

Zhang, Z. X. (2010) 'China in the transition to a low-carbon economy', *Energy Policy*, 38: 6638–53.

Zhang, Z. X. (2011a) 'Assessing China's carbon intensity pledge for 2020: Stringency and credibility issues and their implications', *Environmental Economics and Policy Studies*, 13(3): 219–35.

Zhang, Z. X. (2011b) 'Energy and environmental policy in China: Toward a low-carbon economy', *New Horizons in Environmental Economics Series*, Cheltenham, UK: Edward Elgar.

Zhang, Z. X. (2011c) 'In what format and under what timeframe would China take on climate commitments? A roadmap to 2050', *International Environmental Agreements: Politics, Law and Economics*, 11(3): 245–59.

Zhang, Z. X. (2012) 'Who should bear the cost of China's carbon emissions embodied in goods for exports?', *Mineral Economics*, 24(2–3): 103–17.

Zhang, Z. X. and Assunção, L. (2004) 'Domestic climate policy and the WTO', *World Economy*, 27(3): 359–86.

Zhang, Z. X. and Baranzini, A. (2004) 'What do we know about carbon taxes? An inquiry into their impacts on competitiveness and distribution of income', *Energy Policy*, 32(4): 507–18.

Zhou, N., Levine, M. D., and Price, L. (2010) 'Overview of current energy-efficiency policies in China', *Energy Policy*, 38: 6439–52.

Zhu, X. R. (2010) 'China Electricity Council released data on fossil fuel-fired power plants in 2009', *China Energy News*, July 19, available at: <http://paper.people.com.cn/zgnyb/html/2010–07/19/content_572802.htm>.

19

THE FUTURE OF THE CHINESE ECONOMY[1]

David Daokui Li

In order to form some educated guess at the future of the Chinese economy, the chapter first summarizes the most salient features of today's Chinese economy and then the fundamental challenges facing new Chinese leadership as of late 2012. Based on this, I venture to offer a picture of the Chinese economy of the coming decades. It is argued that the Chinese economy is likely to continue growing at a reasonably fast pace for the coming decade. Together with rapid growth, there will be far-reaching structural changes, which are mainly driven by the relative shortage of labor and ensuing higher wage rates. Meanwhile, China's social–economic institutions will continue evolving. The direction of the institutional evolution is unlikely to be the Anglo-American model of modern market economy. Rather a unique model similar to the German–Singaporean one might be closer to the future of the Chinese economy.

In this chapter, I will discuss the future of the Chinese economy, a very broad topic commanding wide interests. However, it is also a very difficult subject to work on. Of all issues, economists know the least about the future. In order to form some educated guess at the future of the Chinese economy, I will first summarize the most salient features of today's Chinese economy and then the fundamental challenges facing new Chinese leadership as of late 2012. Based on this, I venture to offer a picture of the Chinese economy of the coming decades. There are three aspects of my picture of the future, including continued and relatively fast growth, structural changes caused by increasing labor cost, and continued institutional changes.

1 The landscape of the Chinese economy after 33 years of reform

The landscape of the Chinese economy has changed beyond the expectations most people in the world held thirty-three years ago. This is by no means an overstatement. Three related perspectives will be considered.

1.1 The Chinese economy is now the world's second largest economy and biggest contributor to world economic growth

As of the end of 2011, the size of China's mainland GDP was about 50 percent that of the US, accounting for 10 percent of the world GDP, and contributing to 20 percent of the growth of the world GDP. Note that this calculation is based on the nominal exchange rate of the Chinese

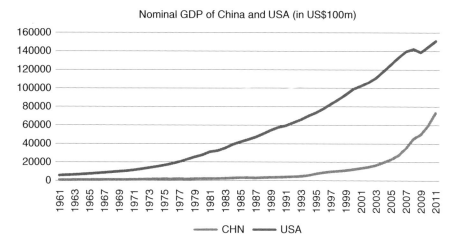

Figure 19.1 Chinese GDP relative to US GDP

Source: WDI (2012)

currency RMB. If we use the purchasing power parity (PPP) exchange rate, then the relative size of the Chinese economy as of 2011 will double relative to that of the US. That is, the size of the Chinese economy was almost as big as the US by 2011 and accounted for almost 20 percent of the world economy. (See Figures 19.1 and 19.2.)

Interestingly, GDP-based statistics may very well understate the size and global impact of the Chinese economy. The reason is that the market exchange rate of the RBM (roughly 1/6.2 of US$ as of November 2012) under-reports the actual purchasing power of the RBM in China. In other words, 6.2 RMB can buy (or represents) more economic activities in China than US$1 in the US or other parts of the world. The World Bank in 2007 stated that 2.3 RMB to US$1 would equate the purchasing power of the two currencies in their respective economies.

Rather than disputing the purchasing power equating exchange rate between the RMB and the US$, i.e. the PPP exchange rate, let us look at a few types of products in order to appreciate the real size of the Chinese economy (see Table 19.1.)

It is also worthwhile to keep in mind that the past three decades of Chinese growth have not only been rapid but also relatively smooth. It is a situation comparable to the economic emergence of Japan after the Meiji Restoration and the economic emergence of the US at the beginning of the twentieth century. (See Figures 19.3–19.5.)

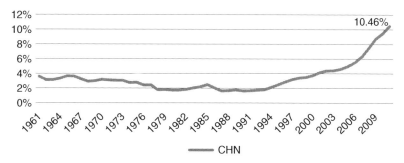

Figure 19.2 Global share of Chinese GDP using RMB market exchange rate

Source: WDI (2012)

Table 19.1 Share of output of Chinese products in the world economy (2011)

Products	Production capacity	Share in the world (%)	Ranking in the world
Iron and steel	700 million tons	33	1st
Cement	2.94 billion tons	65	1st
Machine tools	4 million tons (mining machinery)	50	1st
Automobile	18.40 million	23	1st
Home appliances	150 million (air conditioners)		1st

Source: Ministry of Commerce of the PRC

Despite the surprisingly rapid pace of growth of the Chinese economy during the past decade, it is important to keep in mind that the Chinese economy as of 2012 is still a "poor" economy. (See Figure 19.6.)

1.2 Tremendous economic disparities

Despite the legacy of the centrally planned economy, today's Chinese economy features one of the world's highest degrees of disparities both among the population and across regions. (See Figures 19.7 and 19.8.)

What is the reason for the tremendous disparities? The fundamental reason is very simple: the lack of free flow of populations. That is, due to policy restrictions, the population cannot easily migrate from low income regions to high income ones. Population flow in a mature market economy makes sure that population flows from lower per capita income areas to higher per capita income areas, adjusting for climate and other non-economic factors. This is an equalizing force for per capita income. In China, although population flow across regions has increased in

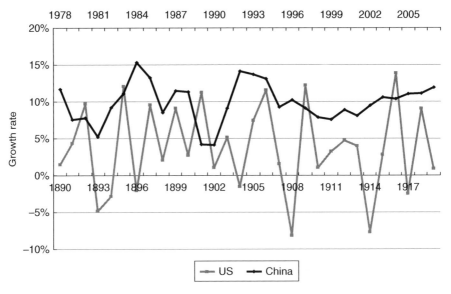

Figure 19.3 Chinese and US economic emergence compared

Source: *Palgrave World Historical Statistics*

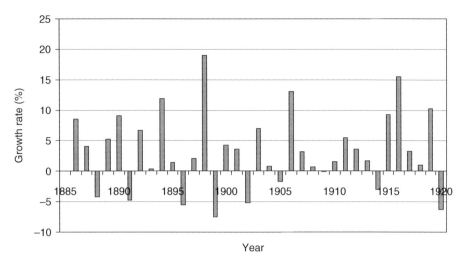

Figure 19.4 Japanese economic emergence after Meiji Restoration

Source: *Palgrave World Historical Statistics*

the reform era, especially since the 1990s, the government has greatly relaxed policies that forced capital to flow into relatively underdeveloped regions. For example, since the late 1990s, the central bank had basically eliminated policies forcing banks to lend to poor regions. Before then banks had loan quotas independent of the amount of deposits so that banks in rich regions such as Guangdong had surplus funds which had to flow into poor regions.

Another reason for the huge interregional income disparity is the fact that the economy no longer has a powerful social welfare system. Many basic social welfare provisions are lacking.

The consequence of the large economic disparity is social anxiety and social discontent. Many in the population are worried about the high cost of health care, living expenses in post-retirement life, etc.

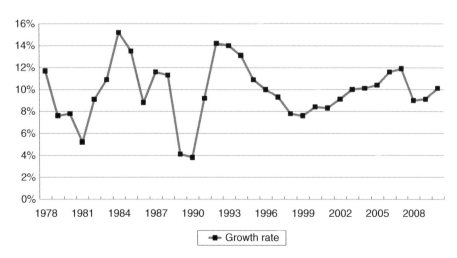

Figure 19.5 China's GDP growth rate (1978–2010)

Source: National Bureau of Statistics of China

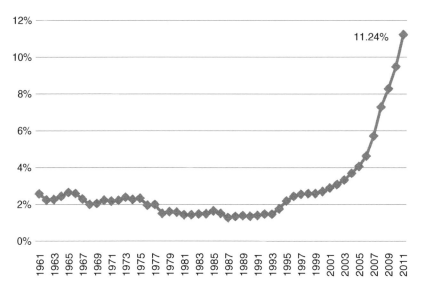

Figure 19.6   China's per capita income as a percentage of US per capita income (1961–2011)

Source: WDI (2012)

1.3 Unique economic institutions

China still has a system of unique economic institutions. The main feature is strong government intervention in economic decisions, although the intervention is often pro-business and pro-investment, and therefore pro-growth.

The political system can still be characterized as that of a Party State (Kornai, 1992), which means that major political decisions, the most important of which are (government?) personnel decisions, are discussed and decided within the Party before being implemented in the state hierarchies. Therefore, the Party and the state hierarchies, to a large extent, overlap. Thus, one can

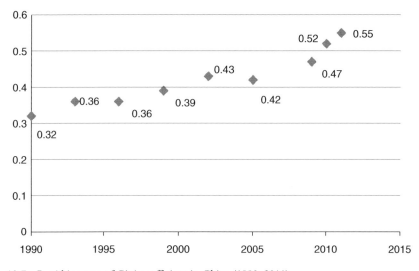

Figure 19.7   Rapid increase of Gini coefficient in China (1990–2011)

Source: IMF and World Bank

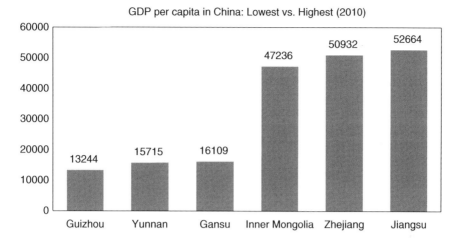

Figure 19.8　Regional disparities among Chinese provinces

Source: National Bureau of Statistics of China

conclude that the political system is rather centralized in that local governments are accountable to higher-level government agencies.

But in terms of economic decisions within the government, the Chinese institutions are very much decentralized. Decentralization is the key for economic development in China. Local government officials behave like board members of the holding company of local enterprises, state owned or non-state owned. Local government officials continue to push for more invest-ments and faster economic growth.

2　Challenges facing the Chinese economy and its institutions

Despite the surprising success of China's economic performance over the past three decades, China is facing a long list of challenges in its efforts to sustain its economic growth. I will discuss three of the most significant ones.

2.1　A new model of development

The first and most imminent challenge facing the new Chinese political leadership is the search for a new model of economic development. This new model should differ from the current one in three very important ways. First, the new growth model must be less dependent upon exter-nal demand than the current growth pattern. This is not only because of the anemic state of the world economy, which is unlikely to improve soon and therefore unlikely to support China's continued rapid growth, but also because surging global protectionism will make it increasingly difficult for China to maintain its high trade surplus with the rest of the world. (See Figures 19.9–19.10.)

The second dimension of the new growth model is that the model has to rely more upon domestic consumption, especially household consumption, and less upon investment. Investment as measured by capital formation has been increasing in its share of GDP. This is unlikely to be sustainable, since this implies that more and more of national savings will be poured into investments and both the commercial and social rate of return of investment will decline, which

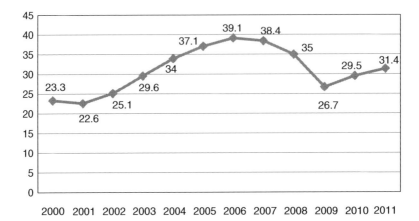

Figure 19.9   Ratio of export to GDP

Source: National Bureau of Statistics of China

implies there will be increased pressure upon the financial and fiscal systems in China. (See Figure 19.11.)

The third dimension of the new growth model is that the model will need to be less dependent upon consumption of resources and energy. As the world's largest consumer and importer of many types of resources and energy, China is spending an increasing proportion of its international diplomatic capital to secure the supply of these commodities. More importantly, perhaps, is that the huge consumption of such commodities leads to pollution and rapid increase in the emission of global warming gas. In fact, China is already the world's largest emitter of CO_2, making it the target of international negotiations regarding climate change. (See Figures 19.12 and 19.13.)

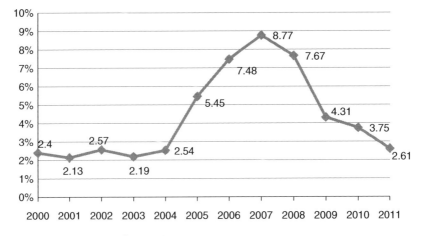

Figure 19.10   China's trade surplus to GDP

Source: National Bureau of Statistics of China

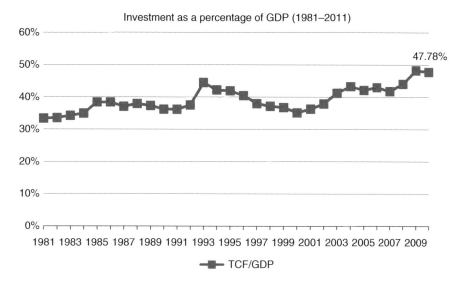

Figure 19.11   Capital formation as a share of GDP

Source: National Bureau of Statistics of China

2.2 *Mitigating social and political tensions*

The second challenge is how to mitigate the mounting social discontent, especially among the young and educated population. Inequality generates anxiety and discontent among young people. A major contributing factor is that Chinese college enrollment has more than quadrupled since 1999 and today's youth are much more aware of social and political issues. Meanwhile, economic inequality has been expanding, often at the expense of the young; examples include

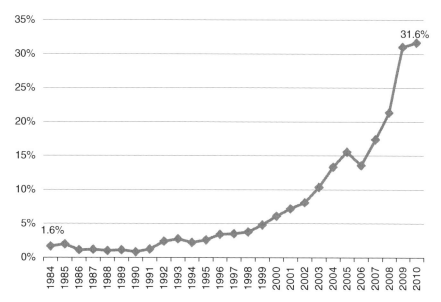

Figure 19.12   China's share of iron and other ore imports

Source: WDI (2012)

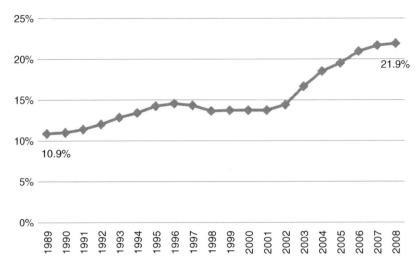

Figure 19.13   China's share of CO_2 emissions

Source: WDI (2012)

the rapid surge in housing prices favoring members of the older generation who bought housing units before or during the rapid increases of price. To make matters worse, in many cases, children of the rich and powerful receive head starts and advantages over their peers. That is, opportunities are visibly unequal among the younger generation. The internet, with its rapid flow of information around the global and quick interaction of social opinions, only intensifies social sentiments. (See Figure 19.14.)

Even though a major source of the social discontent originates in the economic area and can be mitigated by better economic policies and institutions, social discontent easily migrates to

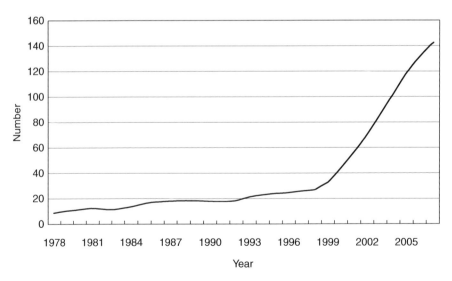

Figure 19.14   University and college enrollments (per 10,000 pop.)

Source: Ministry of Education of the PRC

politics. For example, in recent years, during the annual March sessions of the National People's Congress and the Chinese People's Political Consultative Conference (CPPCC), some young people have gone beyond merely criticizing government policies by challenging the qualifications of the delegates of the NPC and members of the CPPCC.

2.3 Easing international anxiety about China's economic emergence

The third challenge emanates from China's external economic and political relations. It is very clear that today's China faces a much trickier international environment than a decade ago. China in 2001 had just been accepted into the WTO; subsequently, China's trade and inflow of investment took off. Today, China has become the largest target of trade disputes. The exchange rate of the Chinese currency has become an issue of dispute. Protectionist policies against Chinese products and Chinese investment are increasing.

Ten years ago, China was able to avoid direct pressures from global warming negotiations, citing the Kyoto Protocol as an international principle. Today, China has become the world's largest emitter of global warming gas. China faces huge pressure to commit to some form of decreasing its global warming gas emission.

Ten years ago, China faced questions from the international community as to whether its economy would collapse, following in the footsteps of other economies during the Asian financial crisis. Today, because of its economy's huge size and rapid growth, China is again facing questions about its geopolitical strategic intentions. Often, China is perceived as a threat to its neighboring countries, and makes economic collaborations much more difficult to come by.

Most people in China who have a reasonable amount of knowledge of the world (including myself) believe that the world is misreading China. Indeed, China is growing extremely quickly in many dimensions. However, the fundamental socio-political institutions of the country are not capable of implementing an expansionist strategy. The mentality of the population is too middle-kingdom-centric to be adventurous in the world. The history of the country is about making peace and achieving unity among the population; this attitude does not create a desire to expand beyond our borders. Certainly, disputes with neighbors over territory and ocean rights will continue to emerge, but these are historical legacy issues and conflicts of old claims and are relatively very small issues if put it in the global context.

In order to ease the world's anxiety over China's economic emergence, Chinese leaders will definitely have to do a better job of explaining China's long-term intentions. Moreover, through pragmatic negotiations, they also have to demonstrate their willingness and ability to resolve thorny issues.

3 The future of the Chinese economy

The topic of the future of the Chinese economy is in itself very subjective, since we obviously have no observations of the future and therefore a lot of subjective judgments have to be made in tackling such a topic. Surely, there is a large range of opinions on this. Many analysts in the West are pessimistic about the future of the Chinese economy, arguing that a slowdown is near in sight. Perkins (2012) carefully presents factors behind this view but would not give specific predictions as to when the slowdown will happen. Chow (2012) argues almost the opposite, that is, a growth rate around 8 percent will persist in the coming ten to fifteen years. He is sophisticated in assessing China's political economy institutions, predicting that the institutions will evolve but are unlikely to become similar to those in Western Europe or the US. The picture I will paint in the following tends to be close to that of Chow (2012) but many arguments are different. The readers are of course encouraged to form their own opinions.

3.1 The potential and prospects for economic growth

Despite the rapid growth of the past three decades, China still possesses a large potential for continued growth. The main reason is that China is still very poor; China's per capita income is still 18 percent that of the US. When a country is still so far behind the technology and institutional frontier and has embarked on the path of rapid growth, the potential for growth will remain huge. Figure 19.5 is a graph of economies that took off while beginning with such a low level of per capita income.

The second reason for China's potential for rapid growth is that the Chinese economy is a large country economy; that is to say, a large population with a large stretch of land. A large country economy, like that of the US but unlike that of Korea and Japan, has, in principle, the potential to develop a large domestic market rather than rely upon international trade and trade surplus. For example, the inland provinces like Sichuan and coastal provinces like Jiangsu can trade with each other in a manner similar to the international trade between Malaysia and Japan. China is currently a great underachiever in this regard. Once the potential of intra-country trade is unlocked, China's dependence upon foreign markets can be reduced drastically.

Needless to say, one can never write off the danger of China running into the so-called middle-income trap. That is, many economies in the world simply stopped rapid development once they reached the mid-income level with per capita GDP between US$8,000–17,000. Today's Chinese per capita income is around US$5,000. The often-cited examples include countries such as Argentina, whose per capita income is around US$10,000. For the sake of argument, assume China runs into that trap and becomes another Argentina. The per capita income of such trapped middle income countries is around 35 percent that of the US. Therefore, China still has room to double its per capita income before getting caught in the trap.

More importantly, today's China is still bursting with reform energy at the grass-roots level, which is very differently from Japan in the late 1990s or many middle-income-trapped countries. Market-oriented economic reforms proved to be the most important engine of efficiency improvement and therefore fast economic growth during the past decades of the Chinese

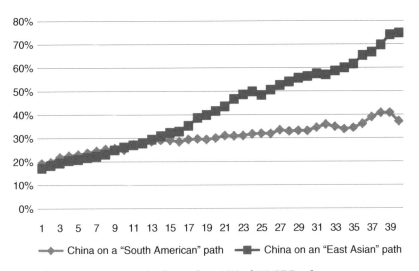

Figure 19.15 China's economic growth after reaching 18% of US GDP: a forecast

Note: Horizontal axis = number of years after 2012; vertical axis = percentage of China's per capita GDP relative to that of the US

economy. The young and educated Chinese are not content with current economic and political institutions. They are calling for further reforms. No leaders in China are openly supporting inhibiting reform. On the contrary, all the leaders favor reform, although different camps have different visions of what reform actually is. In any case, the appetite for reform is still high in China.

It should be the noted that there is also a good possibility that China's rapid growth may end relatively soon. Perkins (2012) provides a careful analysis of this possibility. He argues that recent world economic history shows that no country was able to have very rapid growth like today's China longer than thirty years, which China already had. Also, the lack of very fast productivity growth and China's heavy reliance on capital investment and export are factors pointing at an overall economic slowdown before too long.

3.2 Structural change of the economy

Together with economic growth, the structure of the Chinese economy will undergo fundamental changes, and some of the early signs of the structural changes are already in sight.

Blanchard and Giavazzi (2006) raise the rebalancing issues of Chinese economy. In their paper, they presented a so-called "Three-handed approach" as the solution based on China's economic situation: action on the fiscal and budgetary front, accompanied by currency revaluation. Lardy (2007) suggests that China should promote consumption-driven growth as the engine for the whole economy, and at the same time try to reduce household saving rates. Prasad (2009) enlarges the field of vision to all of Asia, and also recommended that the transformation of the economic development mode should be implemented. In Naughton's book (2007), he talks about the unsustainability of economic growth driven by investment.

As a matter of fact, China's economic structure improvement has already begun, and we can see signs of some important changes. The most fundamental change is demographics. The aging of China's population implies that savings rates will gradually decline. The growth of labor supply will gradually decrease. Most relevant for the coming decade will be the disappearance of surplus labor in rural areas. This is now beginning to cause wage rates for manual labor to increase faster than nominal GDP and in many cases labor productivity (Fang Cai, 2011). (See Figure 19.16.)

The increase in wage rates will cause Chinese firms to be less competitive in the international marketplace. Therefore, China will no longer be a major trade surplus economy. Indeed, China's

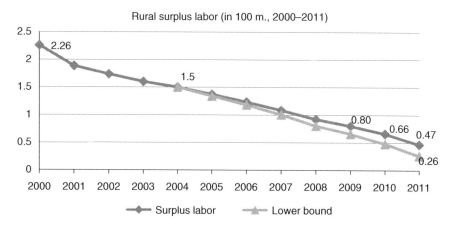

Figure 19.16 Estimates of surplus labor

Source: Li and Xu (2012)

trade surplus has been declining since 2007. By 2012, trade surplus dropped to just above 2 percent of GDP, a number that is significantly below the 4 percent target of the G20 Summit of 2010.

Will the trend of China's continued wage rate increase reduce China's international competitiveness so that China will experience a long period of significant trade deficits? I would argue that this is unlikely. Increases in labor productivity will partially or completely compensate for the impact of wage rate increases on trade competitiveness. More importantly, Chinese policy makers are usually very cautious about trade deficits so that when there is a trend of significant trade deficits, policy makers are most likely to implement policy changes or reforms to mitigate the problem, such as more flexible exchange rates, and the lowering or elimination of VAT on exporting firms (a WTO-compatible policy).

Consumption will almost surely increase and increase faster than GDP, having the implication that China will be one of the largest consumption markets in the world. That is, consumption as a share of GDP will increase. This is a consequence of higher wage rates. Indeed there are early signs of this. In a recent study (Li and Xu, 2012), we found that consumption, carefully measured, actually has been increasing as a share of GDP ever since 2007. By 2012, it reached over 41 percent, improving by almost 1 percent a year. Moreover, the increase is found to be driven by the trend of diminishing surplus labor and increasing wage rates.

The increasing share of consumption in GDP is not contradictory to traditional theories of consumption that are familiar to well-trained economists in Western countries. One leading theory is Milton Friedman's permanent income hypothesis, which argues that consumption is proportional to permanent rather than transitory income. In the Chinese context, the rapid pace of change of the economy has been driving up household permanent income, which in turn drives up consumption. However, before 2007, according to Li and Xu (2012), the increase in permanent income has been slower than GDP, and, after 2007, it is faster. This explains the rising share of consumption to GDP after the global financial crisis.

Consistent with the structural change, China's service sector is increasing disproportionately with respect to GDP. Figure 19.17 illustrates this. The reason is that when consumption rises

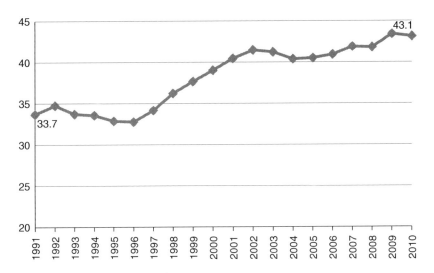

Figure 19.17　Service sector as a share of GDP

Source: National Bureau of Statistics of China

quickly and many consumers upgrade from basic consumption needs, service as a component of the consumption bundle will assume more weight than before. (See Figure 19.17.)

Finally, urbanization almost surely will accelerate. China's urbanization ratio, defined as the ratio of urban residence relative to the population, is just over 50 percent. In a study (Feng and Li, 2006), we found that the Chinese ratio of urbanization is 11 percent below the level of a country at a comparable degree of development. More importantly, the 50 percent urbanization ratio includes those migrant workers, who work in cities on a long-term basis but do not have resident permits and therefore cannot bring their family with them from rural areas and thus are semi-urban residents at most. These semi-urban residents typically do not identify themselves with the city in which they live and therefore do not consume as much as a normal urban resident. That is, the 50 percent urbanization ratio in China overstates China's progress in urbanization.

Chinese policy makers have already identified urbanization as the engine of future growth. Many policy initiatives are implemented to facilitate urbanization. Most importantly, economic forces such as the growth of the service sector will lead to faster urbanization in China. (See Figure 19.18.)

In summary, China's economic structure will undergo fundamental changes, and there are already signs of these changes. Market forces will be the most important factor driving these changes.

3.3 Institutional reforms

There should be no doubt that the Chinese economic, social, and political institutions will undergo further changes. A fundamental reason is that Chinese society is currently unstable and energized for change. The grass-roots population is not happy with many aspects of the economy

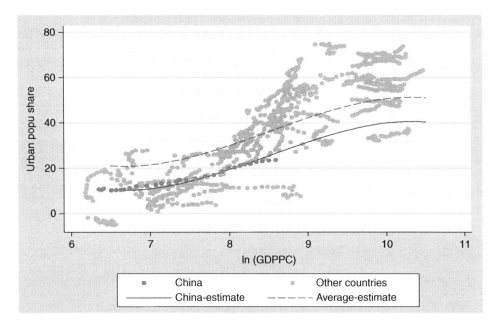

Figure 19.18 Estimates of urban population share in China

Source: Feng and Li (2006)

and societal management, ranging from high and ever-increasing prices in housing, medical care, and education. Meanwhile, the elites are asking and pressing for more individual liberty.

Another extremely important but often neglected reason for continued reform is the Communist Party itself. The Chinese Communist Party is an indigenous political party deeply rooted in the Chinese political tradition, very much different from its counterparts in Eastern Europe. Mao Zedong repeatedly reminded his colleagues of this and he himself often drew political ideas from Chinese history books. Moreover, it is a party that had to wage twenty-two years of brutal military fights before assuming national power, in which there was not the luxury of relying upon ideological and strategic dogmas. Both facts imply that the Party is pragmatic and adaptive, and holds a deep belief that the only way to survive is to continue to innovate and reform.

Will Chinese social, political, and economic institutions eventually evolve into ones similar to those in the US, UK, or continental Europe? This is a critically important question that not surprisingly elicits a wide spectrum of answers.

At one end of the spectrum is the view that China will eventually emulate the institutions in present-day US and Europe. For simplicity, we call this the convergence school. Many elites inside China hold this view. Most observers in the West argue that despite China's economic success, China's institutions are not duplicable in other developing countries and eventually will converge to the Western practice themselves. See, for example, Williamson (2012). Very interestingly, legal scholars and economists tend to be among the most vocal elites inside China who argue for this point, while the political scientists and sociologists are more diversified in their views. A plausible explanation is that the disciplines of legal studies and economics in China possess many more Western influences than other disciplines.

Two often implicit arguments are behind the belief that China will evolve to Western-style institutions. First, there is a set of universal values that all human society holds to be true, including individual liberty, equal rights for all, etc., and Western institutions are sanctuaries of such values. Second, today's China is filled with fundamental social, economic, and political tensions, which can only be resolved by embracing the universal values through reforms of establishing Western-style institutions. Thus, those arguing for China's evolution toward Western institutions are sometimes labeled as believers in universal values. Not surprisingly, many people who hold this view are highly educated social elites. In addition, this camp also includes many government officials who have extensive educational backgrounds and deal with sophisticated and often international affairs. However, the official party ideology apparatus openly denounces these views. Universal values is a topic of discussion that is banned in public forums.

At the other end of the spectrum is what one may call the divergence school. This group believes that China will gradually adopt a social, economic, and political system that is very different from the West and possibly similar to contemporary Singapore. The reason behind this is the belief in Chinese values instead of universal values. The fundamental argument of the divergence school is based on Chinese history and the population's preference for current-day China. The main theme of China's history is basically one of a unified empire. By far the dominant political philosophy is Confucianism, which assigns tremendous weight to social order relative to individual liberty and is almost the opposite of US political ideology. To the divergence school, one can never underestimate the power of history, especially for a country like China. Education is the medium of continuity. As a result, the political tradition as embodied in history gives rise to the Chinese population's preference, which differs from that of the West.

Therefore, according to the divergence school, the future of Chinese social, political, and economic institutions will most likely not only be different from those of the US, but a polar opposite. The Chinese institutional landscape may well be similar to that of today's Singapore.

In the following, I will delineate the vision of the future of Chinese institutions according to the divergence school, excluding the perceptions of the convergence school. The reason is obvious: our readers are already very familiar with the institutions in the West, which, according to the convergence school, represents the future China.

The Party

The official ideology of the Party has gone through tremendous evolution: from achieving communist revolution, to representing the interests of most of the population, to scientific development. The evolution will continue as every generation of the Party's leadership tends to create a new version of the ideology as their most important legacy.

Democracy within the Party has been widely discussed and gradually incorporated. The consensus in this regard is to push democracy from top down. Starting at the level of the Standing Committee of the Politburo, instead of mostly following the views of the General Secretary, the committee now acts collectively in decision making. The meetings of the Politburo and the Central Committee are also widely covered and members are conscious of following formal procedures. It is very likely that in the coming decade, there will be more changes, including open voting and open questioning of the work of the Politburo by members of the Central Committee.

According to the divergence school, the nature of the party state will definitely change. The key change will be that more non-communist party members will increasingly occupy key positions in the government. More non-party individuals will be in the People's Congress (PC) and the CPPCC. The Party will be less dominant in the decision making of the government, a trend Deng Xiaoping pressed for in the mid-1980s but later slowed down. The delegates of the PC and members of the CPPCC have become more and more vocal, opinionated, and critical of the government.

The rule of law

Pressures are mounting for the country to follow the spirit and practice of the rule of law. The pressure is not only to encourage better functioning of the market economy, including proper functioning of the financial system and technological innovation, but also to encourage proper ruling and better disciplining of the Party itself. There are almost daily reports of misbehavior among party members and government agencies that is detrimental to the overall political regime.

Therefore, the independence and sanctity of the legal system will gradually be enhanced. In the past decade, this has not been the case. Court and legal affairs were put under stricter control of the party committees, which caused tremendous social discontent among the elites and the even party members. The case of Bo Xilai highlighted the damage that can occur when the Party dominates law, and will serve as a reminder that even in regard to the Party's own interests, the rule of law is important.

According to the divergence school, the future legal system in China is unlikely to be a copy of the US or UK institutions. It is unlikely that the Chinese legal system will be as independent as that of the US. On critical issues, the courts will closely coordinate with the government, protecting fundamental interests of the government and the Party. The government and the Party will still have an important say in some of the most critical decisions of the courts, similar to the situation in Singapore. Instead of arguing that this system is superior or inferior in supporting economic prosperity and social welfare, I would only like to say that it is a big stride toward improving the current state of affairs.

Democracy

Democracy is the trend. This is very obvious, since the population is increasingly better educated, more open, more diversified, and the economy is ever more complicated with increasing intensity of conflicts concerning economic interests and rights. According to the divergence school it is unlikely that the future evolution toward democracy will lead China to a US or even European-style system. Rather, a Singaporean-style system may be a better reference. Specifically, there will be (higher-level) government or party-nominated candidates for election to the People's Congress. There might be seats reserved for professional society, e.g. accountants, professional managers, etc.

In the view of the divergence school, the elites will have more voice and influence. It is possible that some seats in the legislative council will be voted on by the elites. CPPCC will very likely remain a political institution similar to the House of Lords in the UK but without lifetime tenure. But the procedure to choose its membership will evolve to become more transparent and the function of the CPPCC will surely become even more active than it is today.

Regulations

In the eyes of the divergence school, while direct government intervention in economic decisions such as investment project approval will likely be greatly reduced, regulations of those critical areas of economic transactions will likely be greatly enhanced. Examples include safety standards for food and other products, environmental protection standards, financial market transactions, and health care products and services. In this dimension, the Chinese government will be more powerful than it is today and perhaps more so than in the US and other Western governments.

The state ownership of assets

The divergence school argues that, unlike the US and most European economies, the Chinese governments, central and local, will most likely continue to hold large amounts of production assets. However, the production assets may not be in the form of majority shares of SOEs. Instead, the Chinese governments may divest their current holdings of SOEs and use the proceeds to establish a sequence of investments funds, which in turn will invest in a large cross-section of enterprise shares. This is the Temask model of Singapore. The reason is that it is unlikely that Chinese governments will completely retreat from involvement in the economy. Meanwhile, it is very attractive to follow the Temask model since it not only provides a solid foundation for public finance but also enables the government to intervene in the economy without causing too much distortion.

Social welfare

Almost surely, there will be systemically more provisions for social welfare in the Chinese economy. The Chinese economy needs to reestablish a system of social welfare. The current situation of limited state provisions for social welfare is not socially sustainable. Again, according to the divergence school, the Chinese social welfare system will most likely be very different from the US and European model. Given the strong aversion to excessive social welfare as an aftermath to the pre-reform era, the future system in China will not be comprehensive. Second, given the desire of the government to intervene in the economy, the system is likely to be based on benefits in kind, rather than monetary transfers.

Which vision is more likely to be the future of Chinese institutions, the convergence school or the divergence school? As is often the case, the reality lies between the two extremes. Future Chinese institutions are unlikely to be exact copies of the US or other Western countries. Neither will they be completely different from those of the West. Many fundamental principles underlying the configurations of the institutions, such as separation of powers and checks and balances, will be the same.

Corruption

Corruption has become a major social and political issue rather than an economic concern in China. It is not a drag on economic growth, since corruption in China, unlike that in other developing countries, mostly happen when business deals are facilitated. However, corruption has caused mounting social discontent.

There are two views on the future of corruption in China. One view is that corruption in China cannot be eradicated since this is incompatible with one-party control. The implicit logic is that senior party officials benefit from corruption and therefore it is unrealistic to expect them to eliminate corruption. In other words, it takes credible and external forces to get rid of corruption, which are lacking. The other view is that corruption is a passing phenomenon. The ruling party has the political will to clean it up since the Party is fully aware of the fatal consequences of continued corruption and rapid economic growth provides the Party with good economic means to do so. For example, the Party can pay explicitly high monetary amounts to government officials in order to set up a system of meritocracy. The example is Singapore, where a cabinet minister's compensation is set to be comparable to that of the CEO of a multinational corporation. The Chinese Communist Party has not been able to do it. Part of the reason is that doing so contradicts its traditional ideology, which states that party officials should be diligent servants of the people, while average income of the people is still very low and the average income of the elite is much higher. Arguably, it takes time to change the officials' ideology.

Which view is more relevant to the future of corruption in China? It is hard to judge. The reality again may lie in between. After the 18th Party Congress in November of 2012, the new leadership of the Communist Party has repeatedly pushed for reforms to control corruption arguing that this is the life and death issue of the ruling party. The second view seems to be gaining currency.

4 Concluding remarks

Nothing excites analysts more than predicting the future but predicting the future is the most challenging task. The past three and half decades of the Chinese economy have consistently proved many predictions wrong. Indeed, China is not only fundamentally different from the US and Western Europe but also far apart from those former Western colonies such as India and Latin America. In my effort to predict the future of the Chinese economy, I base my analysis upon the fact that it is still a poor economy with a fundamental drive for continued institutional change under the control of an indigenous, nationalistic, and dominant political party. Therefore, I argue that most likely the Chinese economy will continue growing at a reasonably fast pace with far-reaching structure changes, which are mainly driven by the relative shortage of labor and ensuing ever-higher wage rates. More importantly, China's social–economic institutions will continue evolving. The direction of the institutional evolution is unlikely to be the Anglo-American model of modern market economy. Rather a model similar to the German–Singaporean one might be closer to the future of the Chinese economy.

Note

1   The author would like to thank Neil Schwartz, Sean X. Xu, and Lin Fu for their excellent research
    assistance. Gregory Chow and Dwight Perkins provided insightful comments on an early draft of the
    chapter, which were instrumental in making the chapter much more informative and readable.
    Research support from the Social Science Impact Enhancement program of Tsinghua University is
    gratefully acknowledged.

References

Blanchard, O. and J. Giavazzi (2006) 'Rebalancing Growth in China: A Three-Handed Approach', *China and World Economy*, 14(4): 1–20.

Chow, G. (2012) 'What is the future of the economy and political system in China?', manuscript, Department of Economics, Princeton University, NJ.

Fang Cai (2011) 'The Hukou Reform and Unification of Rural–Urban Social Welfare', *China and World Economy*, 19(3): 33–48.

Feng, J. and D. Li (2006) 'Stages of Urbanization: Is China's Urbanization Poised to Take Off?', Working Paper, Center for China in the world Economy, Tsinghua University, Beijing.

Kornai, J. (1992) *The Socialist System: The Political Economy of Communism*, Oxford: Oxford University Press.

Lardy, N. (2007) 'China: Rebalancing Economic Growth', in *The China Balance Sheet in 2007 and Beyond* (Center for Strategic and International Studies and the Peterson Institute of International Economics), ch. 1, 1–24.

Li, D. and X. Xu (2012) 'The Structural Change of the Chinese Economy', Working Paper, Center for China in the world Economy, Tsinghua University, Beijing.

Naughton, B. (2007) *The Chinese Economy: Transitions and Growth*, Cambridge, MA: MIT Press.

Perkins, Dwight, H. (2012), 'China's GDP and Investment Growth Boom: When and How Will It End?', in Masahiko Aoki and Jinglian Wu (eds.), *The Chinese Economy: A New Transition*, Basingstoke, UK: Palgrave Macmillan.

Prasad, E. (2009) 'Rebalancing Growth in Asia', NBER Working Paper, No. 15169.

Williamson, J. (2012) 'Is the "Beijing Consensus" Now Dominant?', *Asia Policy*, 13 (January): 1–16.

INDEX

Note: Page numbers in bold refer to tables; those in italic refer to tables and *n* attached to a page number denotes an endnote, with appropriate number.

For Product Safety Concerns and Information please contact our EU
representative GPSR@taylorandfrancis.com Taylor & Francis Verlag GmbH,
Kaufingerstraße 24, 80331 München, Germany

Printed and bound by CPI Group (UK) Ltd, Croydon, CR0 4YY

11/05/2025

01866597-0001